W9-BXG-683

Theodore Lownik Library
Illinois Benedictine College
Lisle, Illinois 60532

Handbook of Cross-Cultural Psychology

# DEVELOPMENTAL PSYCHOLOGY

## VOLUME 4

EDITED BY

*Harry C. Triandis*
*University of Illinois at Urbana-Champaign, USA*

*Alastair Heron*
*University of Sheffield, England*

WITHDRAWN

## ALLYN AND BACON, INC.

Boston    London    Sydney    Toronto

155.8
H 236
v. 4

Copyright © 1981 by Allyn and Bacon, Inc., 470 Atlantic Avenue, Boston, Massachusetts 02210. All rights reserved. No part of the material protected by this copyright notice may be reproduced or utilized in any form or by any means, electronic or mechanical, including photocopying, recording, or by any information storage and retrieval system, without written permission from the copyright owner.

Library of Congress Cataloging in Publication Data
Main entry under title:

Handbook of cross-cultural psychology.

   Includes bibliographies and index.
   Contents: v. 1. Triandis, H. C. and Lambert,
W. W., editor. Perspectives. — v. 2. Triandis,
H. C. and Berry, J. W., editors. Method-
ology. — (etc.) — v. 4. Developmental psychol-
ogy / by H. C. Triandis, A. Heron.
   1. Ethnopsychology—Collected works.
I. Triandis, Harry Charalambos, 1926-
GN502.H36        155.8        79-15905
ISBN 0-205-06500-7   (v.4)

Printed in the United States of America.

# Contents

## Volume 3.  BASIC PROCESSES

## Volume 4.  DEVELOPMENTAL PSYCHOLOGY

## Volume 5.   SOCIAL PSYCHOLOGY

## Volume 6.    PSYCHOPATHOLOGY

# Preface

Cross-cultural psychology has been expanding in the past twenty years[1] to the point that there is now a need for a source book more advanced than a textbook and more focused than the periodical literature. This is the first handbook of cross-cultural psychology. It is an attempt to assemble in one place the key findings of cross-cultural psychologists. In addition to serving the needs of graduate instruction, the *Handbook* will be useful to advanced undergraduates and to professional social and behavioral scientists.

This *Handbook* will do more than summarize the state of cross-cultural psychology in the 1970s. It should provide a bridge that will allow more traffic in the direction of a new kind of psychology. One of the key facts about psychology is that most of the psychologists who have ever lived and who are now living can be found in the United States. About 50,000 psychologists live in the United States and several thousand more graduate each year. The rest of the world has only about 20 percent of the psychologists that are now or have ever been alive. Moreover, psychology as a science is so overwhelmingly the product of German, French, British, Russian, and North American efforts that it is fair to consider it an entirely European-based enterprise (with American culture considered the child of European culture). Yet, science aspires to be universal. Cross-cultural psychologists try to discover laws that will be stable over time and across cultures, but the data base excludes the great majority of mankind who live in Asia and the Southern Hemisphere. Are so-called "psychological laws" really universal? Are theories merely parochial generalizations, based on ethnocentric constructions of reality? This *Handbook* assembles reports of the methods, procedures, and findings that ultimately will give definitive answers to such questions, answers that are crucial for the development of psychology. If psychology must be changed to understand the behavior and experience of the majority of mankind, then this is a fact of profound importance. If not, it is still good to know that no changes are needed. The reality probably lies between these two extremes, and different psychological laws can be held as "true" with varying degrees of confidence.

We engage in cross-cultural psychology for many reasons, which are enumerated in the Introduction to Volume 1. Volume 1 examines the field in broad perspective and examines how it relates to some other fields. Volume 2 focuses on methodology, since the cross-cultural enterprise poses formidable methodological difficulties. The remaining volumes concentrate on basic psychological processes such as learning, motivation, and perception (Volume 3); developmental processes (Volume 4); social psychological (Volume 5); and psychopathological (Volume 6) phenomena.

One key policy decision for a handbook is whether to cover the material exhaustively, saying a word or two about every study, or in depth, saying rather more about a few key studies. Our decision for greater depth resulted in incomplete coverage. However, much of the work in cross-cultural psychology is methodologically weak. Rather than attacking such studies, we decided to de-emphasize them in favor of those studies that are methodologically defensible. However, this was not a decision that was applicable to all the methodologically weak areas. In some areas of cross-cultural psychology, there has been so *much* weak work that any student starting to work on related problems is likely to find dozens of studies and hence get the impression that this is a respectable area of inquiry. In such cases we could not ignore the weak studies. But while we had to quote them and criticize them, we could not sacrifice much space in this effort. For instance, most of the work using versions of the prisoner dilemma game in different cultures results in uninterpretable findings. In Volume 5 Leon Mann and Gergen, Morse, and Gergen discuss this work and show why it is weak.

Some work was left out simply because space limitations did not allow complete coverage. Other work was omitted on the grounds that it really is not cross-cultural psychology, and may more appropriately be included in comparative sociology, cultural anthropology, or some other field. Some of these decisions are inevitably arbitrary. Obviously, a *Handbook* like this one is likely to *define* the field, both by what it includes and by what it excludes. We are distinctly uncomfortable about some of the exclusions. For instance, our coverage of Freudian, neopsychoanalytic, and related cross-cultural studies is extremely limited. However, other theoretical systems, such as a "liberated cognitive behaviorism" (Triandis, 1977) will encompass the insights derived from this tradition. We have very little discussion of ethnoscience, ethnomusicology, and ethnolinguistics; we believe these materials now belong to other neighboring disciplines. It is of course obvious that this judgment may be wrong. A revision of this *Handbook,* which may be necessary in a decade or two, could well give a central position to one of these topics.

In writing this *Handbook* we have been very much aware of the probability that psychologists from non-European-derived cultures will find it among the most useful books that they may obtain from European-derived cultures. Much of what psychologists teach in their own cultures is based on studies done with subjects from European-derived cultures. They cannot be sure that such information is culture-general. This *Handbook* faces this question and could become a companion volume of any European-derived psychology book. Since many psychologists do not have English as their first language, we have tried to keep the language as concise as possible. If the style appears telegraphic at times, it is intentional.

We allowed the authors of the chapters considerable freedom in expressing themselves. We felt that an international enterprise such as this *Handbook* should not impose narrow, possibly ethnocentric standards. Thus, authors have been allowed to use the style and spelling that is more appropriate in their own country. English now exists in many versions; the language of Scotland is not identical to Indian English. Rather than obliterate such differences with a heavy editorial hand, we have preserved them.

Volume 1 includes background material that any serious student of cross-cultural psychology would want to know. It examines the history, the major theoretical frameworks, and the relationship between cross-cultural psychology and some other closely related disciplines.

Volume 2 concentrates on methodological problems. Cross-cultural psychology has all the methodological problems of research done by psychologists in a homogeneous culture, plus additional ones that arise because it is cross-cultural. The authors describe the particular techniques and emphasize the special difficulties—the particular methodological dilemmas that one faces in cross-cultural work—stressing those strategies developed to deal with those dilemmas. For example, since the reader is assumed to know about experimental methods, the chapters on experiments deal only with special concerns of cross-cultural psychologists doing experiments.

Volume 3 focuses on basic psychological processes—perception, learning, motivation, and so on. Here we tried to give the experimental psychologists who investigate such processes a chance to expand their perspective. We focused on what appears to be universal, but also emphasized ways in which cultural factors may intrude and change some of the processes.

Volume 4 examines developmental perspectives. Some of the key areas discussed are the development of language, personality, and cognition. Since the major effort in the past twenty years in cross-cultural developmental psychology has been on testing aspects of Piaget's theoretical system, a major focus is on this topic.

Volume 5 deals with cross-cultural social psychology. It examines the major traditional topics—attitudes, values, groups, social change—and some of the newer topics—environmental psychology and organizational psychology.

Volume 6, the last one, is of greatest interest to clinical psychologists or psychiatrists. The focus is on variations of psychopathology, on methods of clinical work, as well as on the cultural and family antecedents of psychopathology.

Our expectation is that the committed student of cross-cultural psychology will want to own all six volumes. However, in this age of specialization and high costs we know that many will buy only Volume 1 plus one other. Finally, certain specialists will want a single volume to enlarge their perspective on their own discipline, by examining the related cross-cultural work. These different patterns of acquisition produce a serious policy problem concerning coverage. A key theory or key cross-cultural finding may have to be mentioned in each volume for those who purchase only one volume, which may create considerable overlap across volumes. However, the authors have cross-referenced chapters in other volumes. Also, we have allowed minimum coverage of a particular topic that has been covered extensively in another volume, so that purchasers of only one volume will acquire some superficial familiarity with that topic.

In some cases, the topics are sufficiently large and diffuse that coverage by two different authors does not result in redundancy. When this was the case, I simply sent copies of the relevant sections of other chapters to these authors and asked them, when revising, to be fully aware of coverage in other chapters.

The idea to publish a *Handbook of Cross-Cultural Psychology* originated with Jack Peters of Allyn and Bacon, Inc. He asked me at the 1972 meetings of the American Psychological Association, in Hawaii, whether I would be interested in editing such a handbook. The idea appealed to me, but I was not sure of the need. We wrote to a sample of distinguished psychologists for their opinions. They were almost unanimous in thinking that such a handbook would be worth publishing. At the conference on "The Interface between Culture and Learning," held by the East-West Center, in Hawaii, in January 1973 we asked a distinguished, international sample of cross-cultural psychologists for their opinion. They were also supportive. By the summer of 1973 a first outline of a handbook was available, but it also became very clear that I alone could not handle the editing. The handbook should reflect all of psychology; I was not competent to deal with such a vast subject. Hence the idea emerged of having several Associate Editors, who would cover different aspects of the topic.

The Society for Cross-Cultural Research, at its 1975 Chicago meetings, heard a symposium in which G. Kelly, G. Guthrie, W. Lambert, J. Tapp, W. Goodenough, H. Barry, R. Naroll, and I presented our ideas about the shape of the *Handbook* and we heard criticism from both anthropologists and psychologists in the audience about our plans.

In January 1976 we were fortunate to be able to hold a conference sponsored by the East-West Center, Hawaii, in which about two-thirds of the chapters were thoroughly discussed. We are most grateful to the Center for this support. The East-West Center held a course for post-doctoral level, young social scientists from Asia, the Pacific, and the United States, using the drafts of the *Handbook* chapters as a textbook. Richard Brislin, Stephen Bochner, and George Guthrie were the faculty. Fifteen outstanding young social scientists[2] were thus able to give us feedback from the point of view of the consumer, but even more important, they pointed out statements that may have been ethnocentric, incorrect, confusing, and outdated.

From the very beginning, we were committed to producing a handbook with authors from every continent. This was not possible. However, the *Handbook* includes chapters by authors from nine countries. To avoid as much ethnocentrism as possible, I appointed a board of twenty Regional Editors. These editors were asked to supply abstracts of publications not generally available in European and North American libraries. These abstracts were sent to those chapter authors who might find them useful. Thus, we increased the chapter authors' exposure to the non-English international literature. By summer 1975, fourteen of these twenty Regional Editors had supplied abstracts listed by cultural region. They were:

*Africa*

R. Ogbonna Ohuche (University of Liberia, Monrovia, Liberia)
The late M. O. Okonji (University of Lagos, Nigeria)
Christopher Orpen (University of Cape Town, South Africa)
Robert Serpell (University of Zambia, Lusaka, Zambia)

*Circum-Mediterranean*

Yehuda Amir (Bar-Ilan University, Israel)
Terry Prothro (American University, Beirut, Lebanon)

*East-Eurasia*

S. Anandalakshmy (Lady Irwin College, New Delhi, India)
John L. M. Dawson (University of Hong Kong)
Wong Fong Tong (Jamaah Nazir Sekolah, Kuala Lumpur, Malaysia)
S. M. Hafeez Zaidi (University of Karachi, Pakistan)

*Insular Pacific*

Subhas Chandra (University of South Pacific, Fiji)

*South America*

Eduardo Almeida (Mexico City)
Gerardo Marin (Universidad de los Andes, Bogotá, Colombia)
Jose Miguel Salazar (Universidad Central de Venezuela, Caracas, Venezuela)

It should be mentioned that with such an international group of authors, chapters required particularly skillful editing of the style so that all chapters would be excellent not only in content but in language. My wife, Pola, and Doris S. Bartle supplied this expertise and were among those who contributed to the realization of a truly international undertaking.

A number of colleagues functioned as special reviewers for individual chapters. Thanks are due to S. M. Berger, Charles Eriksen, Lucia French, Lloyd Humphreys, and Fred Lehman for their critical comments. In addition, the final version of each volume was read by a scholar, and I would also like to acknowledge their valuable suggestions and comments: Volume 1, Daniel Katz; Volume 2, Uriel Foa; Volume 3, Lee Sechrest; Volume 4, Barbara Lloyd and Sylvia Scribner; Volume 5, Albert Pepitone; and Volume 6, Ihsan Al-Issa.

Harry C. Triandis

## NOTES

1. Documentation of this point would include noting that several journals (the *International Journal of Psychology*, the *Journal of Social Psychology* and the *Journal of Cross-Cultural Psychology*) publish almost exclusively cross-cultural papers; there is a *Newsletter*, first published in 1967, that is largely concerned with this area; there are *Directories* of the membership of cross-cultural psychologists, first published by Berry in the *International Journal of Psychology* in 1969, then revised and extended and published as a booklet by Berry and Lonner (1970) and Berry, Lonner, and Leroux (1973); and finally, there is the International Association for Cross-Cultural Psychology, which has held meetings in Hong Kong (1972), Kingston, Canada (1974), Tilburg, Holland (1976), and Munich, West Germany (1978), which now has a membership of about 350 active researchers from about fifty countries. Psychology has been an international enterprise for almost a century, and the Union of Scientific Psychology, and the International Association of Applied Psychology have been meeting every two or so years, since the turn of the century. But the emphasis on collecting *comparable* data in several cultures is relatively new, and has expanded particularly after the mid 1960s. A number of regional international organizations, such as the Interamerican Society of Psychology, and the Mediterranean Society of Psychology, have become active in the last twenty years.

2. Listed by country the participants were:
   *Australia:* Brian Bishop (Perth, Institute of Technology), Margaret M. Brandl (Darwin, Department of Education), Betty A. Drinkwater (Townsville, James Cook University), Michael P. O'Driscoll (Adelaide, Flinders University).
   *Fiji:* Lavenia Kaurasi (Suva, Malhala High School)
   *Indonesia:* Suwarsih Warnaen (Jakarta, University of Indonesia)
   *Japan:* Yuriko Oshimo (University of Tokyo) and Toshio Osako (Tokyo, Sophia University)

*Pakistan:* Sabeeha Hafeez (Karachi University), Abdul Haque (Hyderabad, University of Sind)
*Philippines:* Liwayway N. Angeles (Rizal, Teacher Education)
*Thailand:* Jirawat Wongswadiwat (Chaingmai University)
*United States:* Angela B. Ginorio (New York, Fordham University), Howard Higginbotham (University of Hawaii), Caroline F. Keating (Syracuse University), and James M. Orvik (Fairbanks, University of Alaska)

At the conference, the following authors and editors, in addition to Brislin, Bochner, and Guthrie, were also present: Altman, Barry, Berry, Ciborowski, Davidson, Deregowski, Draguns, Heron, Holtzman, Hsu, Jahoda, Klineberg, Lambert, Longabaugh, Lonner, R. and R. Munroe, Michik, Pareek, Price-Williams, Prince, Sanua, Sutton-Smith, E. Thompson, Tseng, Triandis, Warwick, Zavalloni.

# Biographical Statements

HARRY C. TRIANDIS, the General Editor, was born in Greece, in 1926. During childhood he received several cross-cultural influences: German and French governesses, French and Italian high school years. After three years of engineering studies at the Polytechnic Institute of Athens, he attended McGill University in Montreal, Canada, where he graduated in engineering. He worked in industry for three years, during which he obtained a master's degree from the University of Toronto. But engineering was not as interesting to him as studying people. He returned to McGill to learn basic psychology, and studied with Wallace E. Lambert and Don Hebb. From there he went to Cornell University, where he studied with W. W. Lambert, W. F. Whyte, T. A. Ryan, Alexander Leighton, and others. From Cornell in 1958 he went to the University of Illinois, where he is now Professor of Psychology. He conducted cross-cultural studies in Greece, Germany, Japan, and India, and worked in collaboration with black psychologists on the perceptions of the social environment among blacks and whites. His books include *Attitude and Attitude Change* (1971), *The Analysis of Subjective Culture* (1972), *Variations in Black and White Perceptions of the Social Environment* (1975), and *Interpersonal Behavior* (1977). He was Chairman of the Society of Experimental Social Psychology (1973–74), President of the International Association of Cross-Cultural Psychology (1974–76), President of the Society for the Psychological Study of Social Issues (1975–76), President of the Society of Personality and Social Psychology (1976–77), and Vice-President of the Interamerican Society of Psychology (1975–77).

ALASTAIR HERON spent more than five years in Zambia, where he set up the national psychological services and helped plan the University, of which he was the first full professor. Cross-cultural studies commenced there in 1967 and were continued at the University of Melbourne, in Australia, where he was head of the psychology department from 1970 to 1974. That year he went to Paris, France, to conduct a seven-country policy study for OECD on early childhood care and education. Since 1975 he has directed an evaluation of the health, education, and social services for the mentally handicapped of all ages in Sheffield, England. The most recent (1979) of his many publications is the UNESCO International Institute for Educational Planning's official contribution to the International Year of the Child: *Planning Early Childhood Care and Education for Developing Countries.*

ELKE KROEGER is currently completing her doctoral dissertation at the Institute of Education, University of London, England. She has lived in Germany, England, and France, and obtained an M.A. in literature, but became interested in the problems of Third World countries. She participated in the literacy program of Kenya and there developed an interest in cross-cultural psychology. At the first conference of the International Association of Cross-Cultural Psychology, in Hong Kong, in 1972, she started a collaboration with Alastair Heron on a project that studied Yugoslav children in Berlin. She has also studied the learning abilities of West-Indian, Indian, and British primary school boys. Her publications have appeared in J. Berry's and W. Lonner's *Applied Cross-Cultural Psychology*, and in the *International Journal of Applied Psychology*.

CHARLES M. SUPER received his Ph.D. in developmental psychology from Harvard University in 1972, for research on the growth of memory in infancy. Subsequently, he lived for three years in rural Kenya, where he investigated several aspects of family life and child development among the Kipsigis and other cultural groups. He has also been involved in research in Guatemala, Zambia, Colombia, and the United States. Among his current projects is preparation of a field manual for use in comparative infant studies. Dr. Super has been affiliated with the University of Zambia, the University of Nairobi, and Clark University. He is currently Research Associate at the School of Education and the School of Public Health at Harvard University and is also affiliated with the Judge Baker Guidance Center in Boston.

NORMAN SEGALOWITZ was born in Canada in 1946 and grew up in Montréal. He received degrees from McGill University and Oxford University. In 1966, he spent one year as an exchange scholar at Moscow State University studying with Professor A. R. Luria. In 1975, he spent some time in the Philippines teaching and conducting research on language development. Currently, he is an Associate Professor at Concordia University in Montréal. His research work has included studies in bilingualism, speech perception, and adult and child language development.

MELISSA BOWERMAN was born in Syracuse, New York, in 1942. The daughter of an anthropologist, she spent three childhood years in Mexico and Spain. She received further exposure to life in other cultures when, as an undergraduate, she studied for a period in Italy and spent a summer working in west Africa. After graduating from Stanford University with a B.A. in psychology, she studied anthropology and social psychology at Harvard. Her primary interest was in the structure and psychology of language and, increasingly, in how language is acquired. Her dissertation research, conducted under Roger Brown, was a comparative study of early language development designed to disentangle universal acquisitional processes from processes specific to children learning languages with certain structural characteristics. She recieved a Ph.D. in social psychology from Harvard in 1971. Since 1970, she has been at the University of Kansas where she is now Associate Professor of Linguistics and Senior Research associate in the Bureau of Child Research. Her publications include *Early syntactic development: A cross-linguistic study with special reference to Finnish* (1973) and numerous articles on language acquisition.

DANIEL A. WAGNER received a B.S. (1968) in operations research at Cornell University, and a Ph.D. in psychology at the University of Michigan (1976). He is currently a postdoctoral fellow in the Laboratory of Comparative Human Development at Harvard University, while he is on leave from his regular position as Assistant Professor and Director of the Program in Human Learning and Development in the Graduate School of Education at the University of Pennsylvania. He has been a Peace Corps volunteer in Morocco, a Foreign Area Fellow for Africa (Social Science Research Council), a summer fellow at the East-West Population Research Institute in Hawaii, and a Fulbright-Hays lecturer in the Department of Philosophy and Education at Université Mohamed V (Rabat, Morocco). His main research interests have involved the impact of culture and society on cognitive development. Dr. Wagner is the editor of a forthcoming volume entitled *The Social and Cultural Origins of Memory* and is co-editor (with Harold Stevenson) of *Cultural Perspectives in Child Development.*

BARBARA ROGOFF is Assistant Professor of Psychology at the University of Utah in Salt Lake City, in the Developmental Psychology Program, and Coordinator of the Cross-Cultural Psychology Program. She received her doctorate in 1977 from Harvard University, where she was an NSF Fellow. She was a Rotary International Fellow to study psychology and genetic epistemology at the University of Geneva, Switzerland. Her research, investigating the teaching of cognitive skills in and out of school, was done with Highland Mayan children and has focused on the cognitive consequences of schooling and on the character of verbal instruction and demonstration outside of school.

PIERRE R. DASEN, born in 1942 in Geneva, Switzerland, completed his undergraduate studies in psychology at the University of Geneva, where he worked as a research assistant to the late Jean Piaget. He studied cognitive development in Australian Aborigines, obtained a Ph.D. from the Australian National University in 1971, and spent one year as postdoctoral fellow at the Université de Montréal, carrying out field work in the Arctic.

Subsequently based at the University of Geneva, where he works with B. Inhelder, he directed a research project in the Ivory Coast, West Africa, and recently spent two years as Senior Research Fellow at the University of Nairobi, Kenya. He is co-editor with J. Berry of *Culture and Cognition* (1974), editor of *Piagetian Psychology: Cross-Cultural Contributions* (1977) and co-author of *Naissance de l'intelligence chez l'enfant baoulé de Côte d'Ivoire* (1978), as well as co-editor of the yearly *Cross-Cultural Piagetian Research Newsletter*.

JUNE LOUIN TAPP is Professor of Child Psychology and Criminal Justice Studies and Adjunct Professor of Law at the University of Minnesota in Minneapolis. She has previously been at St. Lawrence University, Harvey Mudd College and the Claremount Graduate School, the University of Chicago, the Albert Schweitzer College (Switzerland), the University of Poona (India), and from 1976 to 1978 she was Professor of Psychology and Provost of Revelle College, University of California at San Diego. Her Ph.D. is from the Maxwell Graduate School of Citizenship and Public Affairs, Syracuse University, in 1963, with a dissertation that compared Swiss and United States religious leaders on a number of personality dimensions. She then studied coping mechanisms of competent youths in India and the relationship of parenting styles to beliefs about law and justice among children of various ages in Denmark, Greece, Italy, Japan, and the United States. Her books include *Ambivalent America: A Psycho-Political Dialogue* (1971), and *Law, Justice and the Individual and Society: Psychological and Legal Issues* (1971). She co-authored two volumes of *Authority, Rules and Aggression*, the first subtitled *A Cross-National Study of the Socialization of Children into Compliance Systems* (1969) and the second subtitled *A Cross-National Study of Children's Judgments of the Justice of Aggressive Confrontations* (1970). She was president of the Society for the Psychological Study of Social Issues and the American Psychology-Law Society.

BRIAN SUTTON-SMITH was born in New Zealand and became a United States citizen in 1962. He and his wife, Shirley, also a New Zealander, have five children. They have also co-authored one book, *How to Play with Children* (1974). Dr. Sutton-Smith received his Ph.D. in Educational and Developmental Psychology from the University of New Zealand in 1954. He has been a school teacher in New Zealand and a professor at Bowling Green State University, Ohio, and Teachers College, Columbia University, and is now Professor of Education as well as Professor of Folklore at the University of Pennsylvania. He has authored, co-authored, or edited, three children's novels, eleven books on play and games, and four on other aspects of child development. Books currently in preparation are on child development through narrative, through film making, and through play with toys. His major interests are in children's social and expressive development. He and John M. Roberts have done extensive work on the cross-cultural study of games.

JOHN M. ROBERTS is the Andrew W. Mellon Professor of Anthropology at the University of Pittsburgh. For more than a decade he was Professor of Anthropology at Cornell University. He has also taught at the University of Minnesota, Harvard University, the University of Nebraska, and the University of California at San Diego, and he was a fellow at the Center for Advanced Studies in the Behavioral Sciences, at Stanford. His doctorate is from Yale, where he first worked on the Cross-Cultural Survey. He has published many hologeistic studies in the area of expressive culture, including papers on games, the evil eye, privacy, riddles, oaths, and ordeals. He has been president of the American Ethnological Society, the Northeastern Anthropological Association, the Society for Cross-Cultural Research, and the Association for the Anthropological Study of Play.

# 1

# Introduction to Developmental Psychology

*Alastair Heron*
*Elke Kroeger*

## Introduction

This volume of the *Handbook* addresses itself to what we believe to be the most basic of all aspects of cross-cultural psychology. Such an affirmation is not, as might appear at first glance, a preempting of importance for a chosen field of special endeavour. On the contrary, it represents a sober recognition of the fact that any serious and systematic attempt to study human behaviour and experience must, in the very nature of things, be both developmental in depth and cross-cultural in breadth. In other words, general human psychology may not validly be approached as a branch of scientific inquiry in any other way—though it may prove to be both valid and necessary to approach particular systems within the constraints both of a limited range of chronological ages and of a particular culture.

Having staked such a claim, one is at once embarrassed by the necessity to select foci for the kind of special attention expected in a comprehensive handbook aimed at a heterogeneous readership. This problem has been compounded for the editors of this volume by the need for "basic" chapters elsewhere in the *Handbook* in which the authors quite properly address themselves to some of the same areas and issues with which we must be concerned in this volume. (See particularly the chapters by Pick, and Kornadt et al. in Volume 3.) An additional difficulty has been to find authors for the volume who have reasonably wide knowledge and first-hand experience of cross-cultural—not just cross-national—work in the principal fields of developmental psychology. Some of this small group

1

have not been in a position to make their contributions when it was sought, while others were already committed to the preparation of their material for publication elsewhere.

The aim of this introductory chapter is to draw together, as far as possible, the main points of generality and of difference provided by the authors of eight specialized chapters, noting where the gaps remain to be filled and endeavouring to provide some perspectives for future work in this area of cross-cultural research. Our approach is integrative rather than critical, since all our authors have drawn attention to the methodological and theoretical limitations evident in the work they have been reviewing (including their own). The simplest rubric for such an integrative approach is provided by the paradoxical statement, used on countless occasions at the beginning of introductory lectures on psychology: the two most obvious things about the human species are that its members (a) have a great deal in common and (b) are all unique. So we shall start here by reviewing the evidence provided in this volume for "universals" and then go on to consider what may (in our present state of inadequate knowledge based on imperfect methodology) appear to be some of the "differences," which are deep rather than superficial. With this in mind, let us consider how far it is reasonable to contemplate a general psychology that is *not* essentially developmental in character.

During recent years, our own research activity has focused on the cognitive performance of children born in parts of the world where the expression "rapid social change" is quite inadequate to describe what is happening. The children concerned were born into situations where the psychomotor, linguistic, intellectual, and social skills of parents and other adults had all been highly developed to serve patterns of behaviour now destined for obsolescence, or at the very least a high degree of inappropriateness. Such situations, in countries like Zambia or Papua New Guinea, perhaps can be seen to represent an extreme form of the same problem faced already in strata of our own heterogeneous cultures that are now described as "underprivileged," "deprived," or "disadvantaged." It is the same problem because of the primacy in both timing and importance of the preschool experience of the child; it is an extreme form because both the rate of cultural change and the baseline from which one starts are in sharp contrast with those characterizing the urban scene in Europe or North America. Intermediate between these lie the problems faced by the children of migrant workers in Europe or elsewhere and those of permanent immigrants into an unfamiliar culture.

By the expression, "the preschool experience of the child," we mean to indicate every input and interaction from birth onward that could reasonably have relevance for cognitive development before a first experience of organized schooling. From the aspect of cultural (or subcultural or "social class") value systems, that experience will be an amalgam of the intentional with the implicit. The "intentional" probably constitutes the greater part of what are usually called "child-rearing practices"; the "implicit" is perhaps what people had in mind when using the expression "taken in with his mother's milk"—but extended well beyond even the most delayed of weaning ages. Elsewhere this has been called "ambience," by which is meant

> the values with cognitive relevance that are implicit in the total pattern of adult and older sibling behaviour within which (early) development takes place . . . the vital feature . . . is the unintentionality, the day-by-day usualness, the taken-for-granted assumptions about what is and what is not important in life. (Heron, 1974 p. 97)

Without fairly detailed knowledge of this ambience surrounding children in various milieux, we do not see how we can advance beyond the stage of speculation in our endeavors to account for the observed differences in cognitive behaviour at 7, 12, or 18 years of age.

From this it is but a step to add "or at 25 or 30 years of age." And why stop there? The problem of the investigator is the same if, at *any* point in the lifespan, one is faced with the fact of observed differences in cognitive behaviour for which other variables (measured contemporaneously, or involving broadly based antecedent criteria or classifications) fail to account adequately. For example, it is easy to demonstrate "social class" or "socio-educational level" differences at 15 or 50 years of age, but quite another matter to identify the specific correlates of "class" or "level" that are the relevant causal variables for the cognitive behaviour being studied.

Such considerations militate against the scientific aims of psychologists (and others) who seek evidence for a general theory of adult human behaviour, i.e., one that holds for all human subjects at any age beyond physiological maturity and across all cultures and classes. One has only to state such aims thus baldly to risk a response of ridicule or of denial—except from Skinner and his more enthusiastic disciples. Most psychologists working toward general statements do so within narrowly defined areas of behaviour—sensation, perception, memory, learning—and by implication (though rarely explicitly) are generalizing about young adults in the age bracket 18–25 years. These psychologists understandably do not wish their difficulties to be multiplied unnecessarily—the amount of variance already encountered has considerable nuisance value—and so focus their efforts on what they hope is a flat section of whatever may be the lifespan curve for the specific function with which they are concerned. Even if this intention is realized successfully, their conclusions may still be limited by the problem of contingency variation: if the process characteristics of the function under study are contingent on other functions that are *not* similarly asymptotic, then variation in these must be taken into account when stating the limits within which any generalization is to apply.

In all that has been said so far, we have of course been treating the fact of *change* as salient for the human behaviour concerning which we seek to make general statements. This change is not constant in rate, nor is its variation similar across the range of identifiable functions with which we are faced. For some functions the genetic programming may be largely resistant to the impact of experience from conception onwards, but for others the experience may be an important factor. At any point in the life-span, we are obliged to use as subjects of our investigations a number of organisms, each of which represents a purely temporary product of the interactions between an active individual and an active environment. The extent to which that "temporary product" is significantly different from what we might have encountered five years earlier or five years later will depend on the behaviour we are studying, the extent to which its present characteristics depend on genetic programming not affected by environmental inputs, and the capacity of other variable behavioural functions to inhibit or facilitate the one under study.

In thus considering how far it is reasonable to contemplate a general psychology that is *not* essentially developmental in character, our purpose has been antithetical to that which would sustain support for the creation of a "special interest group," such as a division of developmental psychology, in a professional organization or learned society. Nor are we advocating a point of view such as seemed thirty years ago to generate the trite slogan "all psychology is social psychology." We identify ourselves instead with Zigler (1963, p. 344), when he said:

> The developmentalist is interested in change, not as a function of time, but rather as a group of organismic processes which take place over time. . . . Stated in this way developmental psychology becomes an extremely arbitrary subdivision of psychology. For if the concept of process is divorced from any particular theory, *all of psychology is concerned with change in behavior as a function of process* . . . when defined in terms of an interest in change, developmental theory is reducible to general behavior theory, since such theory, regardless of its orientation, must deal with the problem of change in behavior regardless of when in the life-cycle such change occurs. [Our emphasis]

Six years earlier, Werner (1957, p. 128) had observed that:

> a comprehensive comparative psychology of development cannot be achieved without the aid of a general experimental psychology broadened through the inclusion of developmental methodology and developmental constructs.

He went on to welcome:

> on the scene of general psychology [the] beginnings of an extremely significant trend toward the studying of perception, learning and thinking, not as

final products but as developing processes . . . [introducing] the dimension of time as an intrinsic property into all experimental data.

Our present thesis accords with these views but makes the *broadening of general experimental psychology* the primary aim.

An alternative way of approaching such an aim is put forward by Baltes and Goulet (1970) in the report of a conference on "life-span developmental psychology":

> A major task in categorising the universe of attributes into a set of behavioral categories will consist in examining the extent to which the structure of attributes can be assumed to be developmentally invariant, both with regard to ontogenesis and phylogenesis. In other words, the question is whether observed life-span changes in a fixed set of attributes consist of differences in level only (quantitative change) or whether the structure of attributes itself is undergoing developmental transformations (number of attributes, relationship among attributes) in the sense of structural change, as inherent for example in Piaget's theory of cognitive development. (p. 9)

Applying this to the characteristics of a developmental approach, noting first the emphasis on change taking place over time, and then such change being of most significance when structural rather than merely quantitative, it may be well to inquire what insights are available from the "traditional" developmental fields of childhood and aging. One way of answering this inquiry is to say that studies of the former emphasize process concepts such as Piaget's "assimilation" and "accommodation"—subserving the evolution for use of a series of "structures"—while the latter emphasizes the same process concepts, but without a maturational base for hypothesizing the appearance of new structures. Both are obviously concerned with biological adaptation, and in both this adaptation is to changes that are taking place within the organism and also within the total environment, with which it must interact. But whereas during the maturational phase the internal changes are characteristically positive—in the sense of "additive" or "more efficient"—during the adult phase, subsequent to the asymptote, wherever it may occur for a specific function (Heron & Chown, 1967) they are characteristically negative—in the sense of "less efficient." We must therefore ask ourselves whether the developmental concept of "structure"—or, perhaps, more appropriate, of "restructuring"—is applicable when adult behaviour is under investigation.

Langer (1969, p. 179) does not consider possible intermediate phases between progressive and regressive developmental change, but with respect to the latter he makes the important comment that although the developmental direction of aging is backward, it is "always backward to the forms of functional structures and actions that are present . . . never . . . to earlier, childhood forms of operation." For the purposes of the present chapter we wish to add that a total absence of restructuring is improbable during the assumed phase of stability in adult life: what seems to be likely is a process involving both progressive and regressive features, the biological objective of which is the maintenance of dynamic equilibrium at optimal efficiency. Almost by definition, such a process must involve restructuring of attributes in various overlapping domains.

Unfortunately for the seeker after a general theory of behaviour, common observation suggests a considerable interindividual variance during this phase: one extreme is represented by those individuals whose maximal capacity for adaptive restructuring seems to be coterminous with the achievement of physiological maturity. Such individuals appear to await passively—though not always to accept impassively at certain points—the onset of regressive change within and of environmental change without. Examples of the opposite extreme are also available, probably in the middle life of those individuals concerning whom at the age of 80 other people exclaim, "How incredibly *young* he seems!"

Between such extremes there is variation around some central tendency, and this latter is unlikely to be independent of systematic cultural influences, both geographical and historical and usually in combination. From this it is evident that a developmental approach to general psychology must insist on a sophisticated simultaneous use of the longitudinal and cross-sectional methods. As Wohlwill (1970, p. 191) put it:

> If *change* is to be made the object of study, it follows that our measures must have direct reference to relevant aspects of change—whence the emphasis on the analysis of developmental functions. A further consequence of this focus on change is the insistence on longitudinal data, not only to take account of individual variations in rate and patterning of development, but to provide direct measures of the parameters of developmental functions stipulated as the units of analysis, and of their relationship to other relevant variables.

The "lifespan" approach emphasized so far in this chapter was first drafted in late 1975 by Heron, and it has since been developed independently and more fully by Tapp in this volume (Chapter 8).

If against the background of such an orientation, as we have outlined in these pages, one turns to consider the cross-cultural field, it is obvious that the task is as formidable as the need is demonstrable. Despite the efforts of anthropologists, psychologists, and sociologists during the past fifty years or so, our knowledge about "change" as a central process of human living remains pathetically slight. This is patently the case even within a single (though highly complex) pattern of culture, such as that which characterizes much of the North American continent. This limited area has generated by far the largest part of our available research literature to date.

The need for the impact that this *Handbook* may provide is nowhere better evidenced than in the chapters on "developmental psychology" and on "adult development and aging" in the 1975 volume of the *Annual Review of Psychology:* almost all of the 639 references cited by the authors of these two chapters related to work carried out in North America. There is not so much as a nod in the direction of intercultural factors in development, and coverage of intracultural aspects is confined to "race" and "social class," essentially within the United States. And this is despite the fact that the "master plan" for the *Annual Review of Psychology* provides for only the occasional appearance of a chapter on cross-cultural psychology, let alone regular specialist treatment of the topic. Yet since World War II, and increasingly since the decolonizing process accelerated in the late 1950s, the unconscious ethnocentrism of social scientists has increasingly been disturbed. The 1970s was the decade in which cross-cultural work proliferated. So far as the traditional "developmental" approach is concerned, it opened with the chapter by LeVine (1970) in Mussen's revision of Carmichael's *Manual of Child Psychology,* and drew to a close with the publication of a handbook by Munroe, Munroe, and Whiting (1979) and of the present volume, both reflecting the rapid growth in quality and quantity of field research and of fresh theoretical orientations. During this same decade not only have the two specialist journals flourished (the *International Journal of Psychology* and the *Journal of Cross-Cultural Psychology*), but one can also note the accelerating growth of cross-cultural content in many well-established and familiar psychological journals all over the world. It is therefore not perhaps unduly sanguine to hope that the 1980s will see the demise of ethnocentric developmental psychology.

## Similarities Across Cultures

When concluding his chapter on infancy, Super feels able to say that "the literature as it stands already makes a substantial beginning towards sketching out the commonalities of our species' early ontogeny and the ways in which diversity is created around this core. The essential motor and mental competencies may become expressed in any particular behavior at slightly varying times, but they are strongly 'built-in' in that they seem to develop similarly in all children in the diverse niches humankind has created for its infant young" (p. 42). He bases this statement on his material which, *inter alia,* provides evidence for similarities in the structure of play activity; in attention; and in mental development. Concerning the latter two, he says (p. 27) that "tools from the three major approaches . . . the traditional psychometric 'baby tests,' scales derived from Piaget's theory, and measures of infants' visual attention to particular stimuli . . . all . . . indicate that normal infants in culturally normative care (not institutionalized) display the critical developments at about the same time, the world over."

Dasen and Heron (p. 302) ask: "How far is the universalist position justified by the available cross-cultural data?" And then they state "observe immediately that the vast majority of empirical cross-cultural Piagetian studies have been concerned with a single stage—that of concrete operations—and that until recently this has involved a concentration of attention on the conservations." Nevertheless, they are able to add some of the very recent data on the sensori-motor stage, which provides results supportive of Super's position, and to conclude (p. 306) "there are strong indications that universality predominates over differences." Moving up to the concrete operations stage, where the data resources are richer and the discussion on possible intercultural differences become complex and controversial, they are still able to stress (p. 308) that "the most important finding of almost all studies may be overlooked, namely that the same sequence of substages has been found everywhere, and for every concept in the concrete operational stage studied so far. There again we have a commonality which supports strongly the universalist position of Piaget's theory."

Turning to language development, Bowerman (p. 115) cites Lenneberg's "evidence that there is a 'critical period' for language acquisition from birth to puberty, and that the ages at which children reach certain basic 'milestones' of language development are consistent from one culture to the next, despite great differences in environmental conditions."

She also (p. 131) elaborates her summary statement that "despite the existence of gross disparities in the elaboration and complexity of the inflectional systems of different languages, the process of acquiring inflectional morphology is remarkably similar everywhere" by citing Slobin's 'four stages of inflectional marking of a semantic notion.' These are (1) no marking; (2) appropriate marking in limited cases; (3) overgeneralization of marking; and (4) full adult system.

Wagner is, in our view, understandably cautious about universality in his view of cross-cultural studies of development in various aspects of memory function. But he does observe (p. 204) that one of his own reports concluded with the words "stated in its strongest form, the present study supports the hypothesis that the structure of memory is a *universal* in cognition, while control processes seem to be more culture-specific, or a function of the particular experiences that surround each growing child. While the pattern of results appears to support this hypothesis, it is obviously difficult to claim a completely universal structure of memory, because: (1) only certain structural features of memory were studied; and (2) behavioral universals—like behavioral theories—are impossible to prove." (We ourselves note sympathetically that this is of course the classical problem of induction in scientific endeavour since Bacon). Quite properly, Rogoff, in her chapter on schooling and cognitive development, emphasizes that little or no basis exists for assumptions about possible generality across cultural settings. To her, it seems rather that schooling has specific effects on cognitive skills, and therefore she suggests that the overall impact be considered in the light of the uses to which skills learned in school are to be put.

We find it a little surprising that Sutton-Smith and Roberts, the authors of our chapter on play, games, and sports (Chapter 9), do not appear to address themselves directly to the "universality" question. This perhaps arises from the fact, which their data and review material attests, that these three activities are *as such* reported from all over the world and throughout recorded history. Consequently, the focus of attention in this domain of anthropologists, psychologists, and others has been on the differences between cultures and over time in the nature and social utility of intraindividual, interindividual, and group behaviours, which are already accepted as being universally characteristic of humankind as a whole.

Reviewing this (and some of the earlier topics considered here) from the ethological approach, Tapp (p. 396) draws attention to the judgment of Smith (1975) who "presented data on the rough-and-tumble play of children, noting the strategic importance of the few cross-cultural ethologically oriented studies on infant or child behavior. To Smith, there was sufficient data on the culture-invariant aspects of certain characteristics such as nonverbal communication (gestures, facial expressions), social development (attachment and aggression, exploration and play), and social organization (incest taboos) to describe certain species-specific personality phenomena."

Given the fact that cultural diversity impinges powerfully on the perceptions of the contemporary world-traveler, lay or professional, the amount of evidence for some degree of universality in human development provided in the chapters that follow is perhaps surprising and certainly encouraging. The other side of the coin—which we now examine briefly—will certainly be unsurprising but perhaps both encouraging and challenging.

## Cultural Differences—Real or Apparent

Starting again with infancy, Super devotes considerable space to reviewing the scattered evidence for and against "precocious development" of motor behaviour. He concludes (p. 22) that "there is no ready explanation for the pattern of specific differences and similarities in [newborn] motor performance found in these [African] studies," and "outside Africa, there are only scattered reports. . . . In general they find no group differences, lack meaningful data to support a claim of differences, or have failed to replicate" (p. 23). In contrast he presents substantial evidence to support (and to explain why) it is now well established that African babies who are reared in relatively traditional ways achieve a variety of motor milestones, especially in the first year, before their European and American peers. The explanation lies in the simple fact that they get more practice, and in some cultures they are actively taught.

Within the general area of "mental development," Super is at pains to emphasize that uncertainties stemming from apparent "differences" may in fact arise from lack of "detailed attention to the items which account for the differences and the environmental conditions which might relate to them." Turning to early social development, he notes cross-cultural agreement about the *appearance* of smiling at 4 months of age, but also considerable divergence at that age in the *natural rate* reported, with an observed range from "once or more in 5 percent of waking minutes . . . to 20 percent" (p. 36). Similarly "the range of spontaneous vocalization rates at 3 or 4 months appears to be between 27 percent (in a Kenyan tribe) and 59 percent (in urban America)" (p. 37). Finally Super emphasizes that there is evidence for substantial variation in the overt character, at least, of early (mother-infant) interaction.

For memory, Wagner suggests—on the basis of his own studies, a limited amount of other cross-cultural research, and a large body of relevant laboratory work, primarily in the United States—that control processes, such as acquisition and retrieval strategies, may be highly culture-dependent. But he stresses how little is known about how far the use of particular strategies is culture-specific or situation-specific.

Dasen and Heron show that in terms of Piagetian theory there are certainly both qualitative and quantitative differences between cultural groups within the concrete operations stage. However, they are careful to stress not only the methodological problems, but also the need to recognize (for example) the likelihood that "two concepts that develop congruently in the average Genevan child may develop at very different rates in another culture, if one of them is more highly valued (i.e., is more relevant or adaptive) in that other culture" (p. 327). They also cite examples of a new application of the "training" procedure—previously used exclusively in attempts to accelerate the transition to the next stage—as a means of "triggering" latent competence.

Bowerman notes that (one of the very few) important cross-cultural differences in language use is "the way in which directives are handled," while Sutton-Smith and Roberts—supposing "that play transformations are at least as universal as language"—go on to observe that "we do not therefore have to hold that children everywhere play the same way or even the same games," cite the Whitings' *Six Culture Study* as source support, and go on to say "there is no one language of play or games" (p. 443).

For reasons obviously intrinsic to the content of their chapters, our other authors do not highlight intercultural differences in such specific ways. This is particularly the case in respect of schooling, while Segalowitz has faced the daunting task of reviewing an area (bilingualism) in which the number and variety of well-established examples, which have received systematic attention, is so limited as to preclude strong emphasis on both "similarities" and "differences." The approach of Tapp to the vast field of "personality" development was clearly not intended in itself to be focused in such a way, but rather to be accepted by the reader as a systematic and encyclopedic overview, intended as the basis for an organizational model on which future interdisciplinary research might be based.

## A Consensus on Method

We do not see it appropriate for the authors of an introductory chapter to arrive at a prescription for the cure—or even the substantial alleviation—of the endemic "illness" of method in cross-cultural developmental research. But we cannot fail to note the high degree of consensus among several of our chapter authors concerning this question, and also that the obvious lack of cross-cultural material hampering the efforts of the other authors arises in large part from the same source. Here, we do not regard it as merely coincidental that the fieldwork and subsequent writings of Cole and his co-workers should so frequently be mentioned; it now matters little whether one refers to "experimental anthropology," "psychological anthropology," or "anthropological psychology." What has become clear is the necessity to integrate the accumulated experience, methods, and skills of two complementary disciplines.

In his chapter, Super notes the importance of subtle particulars of the testing situation, with examples drawn from work in both Africa and India. These examples implicate both the formal requirements of the task—the baby is repeatedly frustrated (during object-permanence testing) by having the object taken away for use in the next test item, just after he has succeeded in retrieving it—and of the intervention of caretakers—in New Delhi they were more likely to offer comfort to a frustrated baby during the hidden objects procedure, while the American mothers were more likely to redirect the child's attention to the unsolved problem. Later (p. 41) he draws attention to earlier speculations by LeVine, supported by more recent work as yet unpublished, concerning the variation among tribal groups in different parts of Africa in the "direct expression of intense affect" and "levels of face-to-face interaction" between mothers and infants. Elsewhere, Super (1979, p. 159) has welcomed the very recent trends towards "more emphasis on theoretically directed quantitative studies for the exploration of hypotheses, carried out with increased sensitivity to the social and cultural content of development." The former of course characterizes the methods favoured by the experimental developmental psychologist, the latter the concern of the field anthropologist and the social psychologist.

From within the framework of the Piagetian approach, Dasen and Heron do not hesitate to declare themselves (p. 319) profoundly dissatisfied with the quality of the empirical basis on which most cross-cultural fieldwork data has been resting. They discuss in particular two important issues raised by Kamara and Easley (1977): "the quality of the communication between experimenter and subject, and the necessity of using Piaget's 'method of critical exploration.' " This leads them to stress in their subsequent discussion "the more basic source of dissatisfaction . . . the responses of subjects in various cultural settings to stimuli devised in another culture . . . brought to a focus in an article by Cole and Bruner (1971)."

Bowerman explicitly draws attention to the two types of methodological bias identified by Ervin-Tripp—"linguistic" and "sociolinguistic"—regarding the latter as the "more serious problem" in the cross-cultural study of language development. Earlier (p. 98) Bowerman has described clearly how sociolinguistic rules for language use govern the communicative situation between speaker and hearer. It is in this context that Segalowitz provides an example of the way in which the *lack* of cross-cultural material is hampering our efforts to appreciate and understand such key relationships as those between language and thought: he is obliged to stress that almost all findings on the impact of bilingual development have been obtained primarily from European and North American sources. Yet a moment's reflection is enough to remind us how numerous are the situations in the new nations of the Third World in which such bilingual development is the rule rather than the exception. Bowerman's emphasis on the importance of rule-learning in language—and the appreciation of this importance by those seeking to identify the "culture-specific" from the "universal"—finds a parallel in the point made by Sutton-Smith and Roberts that the socialization of individual aggression through play, games, and sports involves learning (from parents and/or other children) "a system of rule-governed behaviors which control one's own egoistic behavior as well as permitting it expression." We do not know yet—for lack of appropriate developmental cross-cultural data—whether or not this hypothesized process is itself a universal, leaving the observed outcome differences to be properly regarded as the result of variety in the cultural values transmitted.

Returning to the cognitive domain, we find Wagner (p. 221) concerned about the presently available data to illumine the question of "spontaneity" in mnemonic behaviour in the context of what has come to be known generically as the "production deficiency" hypothesis—"the individual has no structural problem, but often needs some guidance or change in task context for good mnemonic behavior to be evidenced." He notes—correctly, in our view—that "the problem here is that it is seldom clear whether the *spontaneous* production of a given mnemonic behavior is in some important sense distinguishable from an induced (with ease? with difficulty?) behavior." This leads him (via a useful discussion of the "surface-deep" distinction borrowed from linguistics) to question the adequacy of cross-cultural data so far available, and to express a need for more in-depth ethnographic studies of "memory in naturalistic contexts."

Although Rogoff specifically addresses the relationship between schooling and cognitive development, she provides a very useful contribution to our overview of methodological problems. In addition to coverage of the child's familiarity (more accurately, lack of familiarity) with materials, with language (including dialect), and with situational and task demands, she also draws attention to a possibly important source of bias in comparative studies, which may arise from community and family-based selective processes deciding which children get the schooling. This is a neglected point in much cross-cultural work, surprising in view of the well-known intracultural effects to be found in such so-called "developed" parts of the world as the United Kingdom. On the general question of situational bias, we find especially engaging her remark (p. 270) that "schooled children are likely to have had more practice figuring out what an adult is really asking, when the adult does not reveal all aspects of performance that will be evaluated."

## The Near Future

It will by now be evident that we have no quarrel with any of our authors over their individual and shared—frequently congruent—views about the deficiencies of our present firm knowledge. But we do not feel easy about ending this chapter with the familiar urgent call for more and better research, however justified that call may be. It seems to us that attention should be drawn to the framework of assumptions within which future studies might be thought necessary, designed, executed, and evaluated.

Central to this concern is the very term "development." Its use in relation to the individual human being is less biased in the direction of purely biological maturation than it was a generation ago, but there is still a tendency toward an implicit rather than explicit assumption that there is some universal, "natural" process which an "ideal" environment and pattern of stimulation and response should subserve. This implicit assumption runs in double harness with another, which relates to the use of the terms "developed" and "developing" when applied to the new nations of the so-called Third World. Once again, there is the "ideal" towards which these countries are supposed to be moving as they—with or without various forms of external assistance or intervention—"make progress."

Here it is probably necessary to state categorically that we are *not* espousing a Rousseau-like emphasis on the natural, the simple, and the unsophisticated. But neither do we accept that "nasty, brutish and short" was a wholly accurate description of most people's lives before the social, political, religious, and occupational changes in Western Europe since the seventeenth century. We prefer to stress that ideas about "the quality of life" change over time as well as differ from place to place: value systems are once again being reexamined, this time in the light of a slowly growing awareness of the many alternative cultural sources on which to draw. Such trends are clearly of great potential significance for future work in the area of lifespan developmental psychology. Once liberated—or even beginning to be—from the built-in assumptions about the "optimal" development of the individual in the direction of targets, which are the product of value-systems derived primarily from the European model, developmental psychologists (and their colleagues in such closely related disciplines as anthropology and linguistics) will shake themselves free from culture-bound preoccupations, which determine their fields of systematic enquiry, as well as the methods they employ.

The ideal target of pure rationality, so well represented by the pinnacle of Piaget's system in formal operational thinking, is increasingly called in question; concentration on relatively trivial topics that are susceptible to wholly objective investigation at the expense of more significant issues that are "difficult" is becoming a legitimate object of criticism. The long-held notion that all truly scientific endeavour must by definition be "value-free" has been exposed as a myth by an imposing array of internationally recognized leaders of that endeavour. The essential feature is now increasingly seen to be its inherently self-correcting characteristics.

What we *are* concerned to emphasize may be epitomized by noting the recent general recognition among psychologists that there can never be any such thing as a wholly "culture-free" test of reasoning ability. Such a recognition is, however, only a useful point of departure; there is a very long way to go yet, as may be evidenced by some of the topics and contents not only of this volume, but also of the other volumes of this *Handbook*—and by the very absence of some at least of what is missing. The outlook is however more hopeful than it was even a few years ago. It will remain important to identify and to detail the biologically based universals on which a wide variety of value-determined cultural practices can and do operate to produce such a spectrum of difference in the outcome. This task will become progressively easier to the extent that the confounding effects of maternal, neonatal, and perinatal malnutrition and disease are reduced and eliminated in the very cultures about which information and understanding are most needed.

It will continue to be essential that nurturant, child-rearing, and both informal and formal educational practices be studied systematically and in detail, both cross-sectionally and longitudinally through the lifespan, by trained investigators who are members of the cultural group that is being observed. The absence of contributions to this volume of such authors— wholly contrary to editorial hopes five years ago—should signal the end of a "colonial" era in scholarship at exactly the point to be expected: one generation after the end of the colonial era in terms of political and cultural identity. There is at long last something new and exciting to look forward to: a wholly new kind of *Handbook* in which the contributors, the collaboration, and the contents will *all* be truly cross-cultural as well as interdisciplinary.

# References

BALTES, P. B., & GOULET, L. R. Status and issues of a life-span developmental psychology. In L. R. Goulet & P. B. Baltes (Eds.), *Life-span developmental psychology.* New York: Academic Press, 1970.

COLE, M. & BRUNER, J. S. Cultural differences and inferences about psychological processes. *American Psychologist,* 1971, *26* (10), 867–876.

HERON, A. Cultural determinants of concrete operational behaviour. In J. L. M. Dawson & W. J. Lonner (Eds.), *Readings in cross-cultural psychology.* Hong Kong: University Press, 1974.

HERON, A., & CHOWN, S. M. *Age and function.* Boston: Little, Brown, 1967.

KAMARA, A. I., & EASLEY, J. A., JR. Is the rate of cognitive development uniform across cultures?—A methodological critique with new evidence from Temne children. In P. R. Dasen (Ed.), *Piagetian psychology.* New York: Gardner Press, 1977.

LANGER, J. *Theories of development.* New York: Holt, 1969.

LEVINE, R. A. Cross-cultural study in child psychology. In P. H. Mussen (Ed.), *Carmichael's manual of child psychology* (Vol. 2). New York: Wiley, 1970.

MUNROE, R. H., MUNROE, R. L., & WHITING, J. W. M. *The handbook of cross-cultural human development.* New York: Garland Press, 1979.

WERNER, H. The concept of development from a comparative and organismic point of view. In D. B. Harris (Ed.), *The concept of development.* Minneapolis: University of Minnesota Press, 1957.

WOHLWILL, J. F. Methodological research strategy in the study of developmental change. In L. R. Goulet & P. B. Baltes (Eds.), *Life-span developmental psychology.* New York: Academic Press, 1970.

ZIGLER, E. F. Metatheoretical issues in developmental psychology. In M. H. Marx (Ed.), *Theories in contemporary psychology.* New York: Macmillan, 1963.

# 2

# Cross-Cultural Research on Infancy

*Charles M. Super*[1]

## Contents

## Abstract

Research reports on the motor, mental, and social development of infants in non-Western cultures are reviewed. Despite frequent methodological problems due to the interdisciplinary complexity of cross-cultural research on infancy, the literature describes both important commonalities in our species' early ontogeny and also ways in which diversity is created around this core. The essential motor and mental competencies may be expressed in any particular behavior at slightly varying ages, from society to society, but they nevertheless develop similarly in all normal children in the diverse niches humankind has created for its infant young. The use of these abilities in infancy to join in the social fabric becomes patterned in ways inadequately understood at present. It is argued that a variety of research perspectives and methodologies are needed for pan-human understanding of early human development, and that the structuring and integrating aspects of culture must become a central element in this emerging field.

## Introduction

The concept of infancy and the behavioral growth that characterizes it both have a strong central core in all cultures; at the same time, they are differentially sculpted in different contexts. Around the world, newborn babies enter life as the intense but relatively private focus of attention of a small number of people. They come equipped with essentially the same biological and social skills. In the succeeding months, they exhibit the same profound developments in their ability to attend to, understand, predict, engage, and manipulate their physical and social environment. They move, metaphorically, from organ to organism, from animal to human; along the way they pass markers apparently recognized by most societies. Around 3 or 4 months, for example, they "become a real person" to the American mother, and in Western Kenya the Kipsigis mother stops calling her baby a "monkey."

Nevertheless, children emerge from infancy as distinctly Irish, Egyptian, Rajput, Korean, Fijian, Yanamamo, Iroquois, or Azande, in their sounds and actions, their needs and skills. The concept of infancy is culturally divergent also. The English word "infant" is derived from Latin roots meaning without speech, and in their minds and textbooks most Europeans (including those transplanted to North America and other former colonies) think of infancy as lasting about two years. After this period, infantile behavior, such as wetting clothes, becomes a social embarrassment for the parents. Among the Kipsigis, however, infancy ends at about one year, roughly the time when the motor behaviors of particular parental interest are in operation. The child is safe from jealous witchcraft. The mother is no longer *saloita*, a "new mother," and she is freed from various prescriptions and proscriptions. A ritual traditionally marks the period of change.

This chapter is a brief review of the research literature on infant motor, mental, and social development outside of European, or Western, culture. Despite technical shortcomings in much of the work, we can sketch the major contours of initials status at birth, the emergence of important milestones, and variations in style, content, and use that appear around the universally developing abilities. Before applying the psychologist's microscope to particular behaviors, however, it is worthwhile taking a step backward to use the anthropologist's telescope. Infancy, when one inspects the obvious, does not exist in isolation. It is necessarily and profoundly enmeshed with other aspects of the culture, synchronically with the niche that is structured by daily life, and diachronically with events in the life cycle.

## The Integration of Infancy with the
## Larger Culture

Infancy has been of interest to anthropologists for two reasons. Historically their basic task has been the comprehensive description of life in other cultures, and classical ethnographies usually provide some information on infancy. Material artifacts such as cradleboards, or rituals such as those surrounding childbirth or kinship alignment provided common anchor points. As anthropological theory came to focus on individuals as the carriers of culture, however, the field of culture and personality emerged (Harris, 1968). The pioneering work of Mead (1930, Bateson & Mead, 1942) reflected the growing concern with the early acquisition of culture. During the formative years of psychological anthropology, as "culture and personality" has become, psychoanalytic theory was the most promising approach to understanding the effects of early experience. A number of studies attempted to link the typical child's socialization in a culture to the modal adult personality (e.g., Kardiner, 1944). The multicultural comparisons by Whiting and Child (1953) were seminal, both for their incorporation of learning theory and for their statistical method in which each culture provides a data point.

The integrative power of culture, connecting and structuring all aspects of human behavior, is the theoretical cornerstone of social anthropology; in the subdiscipline of psychological anthropology, John and Beatrice Whiting have drawn a developmental model for psychocultural studies that includes this perspective (e.g., J. Whiting, 1977). The physical environment and historical circumstances are seen in this theory to determine a society's maintenance systems, which include the social structure, economy, and household type. These maintenance systems, in conjunction with historically shaped value systems (Whiting et al., 1966), influence the number and identity of caretakers, feeding schedules, children's tasks, techniques of discipline, and other aspects of the child's environment (see, for example, Barry & Paxson, 1971). LeVine (1969, 1974b, 1977) has elaborated the role of cultural values of the adults as both expressive and adaptive mediators of child care, and many variations can be found in the literature. Some groups, for example the Kwoma of New Guinea (Whiting, 1971) and Zinacantecans of Mexico (Brazelton et al., 1969), have conceptions of the dangers of witchcraft that influence the way they keep their infants close and private. Cultures differ in their typical view of the fragility of the newborn (deVries & Super, 1979), the "naturalness" of crying (Rebelsky, 1973), and the value of encouraging babies in particular skills (Blount, 1972; Harkness & Super, 1977; Super, 1976).

The Whitings' theory, in agreement with most psychological views, postulates that the transaction between the environment, as previously described, and the universal, innate nature of human growth and development produces the personality and skills of the adult. Finally, adult personality is seen in psychological anthropology to contribute to the culture's projective-expressive systems, including religious and magical beliefs, rituals, art, recreation, and elements of folk theories of child development (LeVine, 1980).

The issue of long-term consequences of variations in child care lies at the heart of traditional theory in both psychology and anthropology. Ethnographic studies of single societies often draw qualitative connections that are consonant with the long-standing Western belief in the unique importance of early experience. Spiro (1953), for example, draws a series of parallels between Ifaluk beliefs about ghosts who can both cause and cure sickness, on one hand, and on the other the Ifaluk infant's experience of generally warm and permissive care during infancy, traumatically punctuated by morning baths in the very cold lagoon, and ended by severe rejection at the arrival of a new sibling.

Cross-cultural studies, in the narrow sense, have elaborated this line of inquiry by searching for statistically reliable relationships between a culture's typical infant care and adult projective-expressive systems. The Whiting and Child work (1953) on personality defenses has been mentioned. In addition, infant socialization has been related to the perceived nature of the gods (Lambert, Triandis, & Wolf, 1959; Spiro & D'Andrade, 1958); common games (Barry & Roberts, 1972); musical rhythms (Ayres, 1973); physical violence (Prescott, 1975); and several aspects of adult mental functioning (Munroe, Munroe, & Whiting, 1973; Zern, 1970, 1972).

It remains to integrate this tradition in anthropology with more recent advances in lifespan psychology and the continuing debate about the long-term effects of early experience in humans (e.g., Clarke & Clarke, 1976). After all, a substantial amount of development intervenes between infancy and adulthood, and a variety of conditions can lead to continuity or discontinuity. These conditions could in theory include innate and stable neonatal dispositions that covary with mating group, for example genetic differences (Freedman, 1974); persistence of learned dispositions (e.g., Du Bois, 1944); lasting, environmentally induced effects on biological systems, such as hormones (e.g., Landauer & Whiting, 1964); sensitization to relearning (Campbell & Spear, 1972); stability in the environmental circumstances that elicit or structure particular behaviors (e.g., Super & Harkness, in press b); maturationally controlled behavioral transformations (e.g., changes at adolescence); arbitrary but socially patterned behavioral standards (e.g., Kagan & Moss, 1962); and institutionally imposed efforts to affect the course of development, such as schooling or initiation rites (e.g., Super & Harkness, in press a).

Even though several of these possibilities have been used to explain patterns of cultural variation in development, there is to date no concerted attempt to reevaluate the anthropological literature with regard to long-term mechanisms in developmental continuity and change. Anthropological theory, in short, has not caught up with the past two decades of developmental psychology. The particular advantage of an anthropological perspective applied to the study of infancy, on the other hand, highlights integrative and systematic aspects of the physical, social, and cultural environment that are often difficult to see from a monocultural position (Harkness, 1980). Recent publications by Chisholm (1980), Landau (1976), and Super and Harkness (in press b) present divergent uses of this larger perspective. As American psychology more generally awakens to the outside world, and as anthropology increasingly recognizes the advances in other disciplines, one can expect a greater frequency of transdisciplinary studies of infancy and infant development.

## Motor Development

A substantial portion of cross-cultural research on infancy is concerned with motor development; that is, with the attainment of motor milestones such as rolling over, the finger-thumb pincer grip, sitting, and walking. This reflects, in part, the early development in Western psychology of formal tests for these skills, and perhaps also their high visibility to the itinerant researcher who may fail to see more subtle aspects of behavior. A strong and recurring theme in this literature is the "precocity" of babies from traditional, nonindustrial societies: they may sit or stand, on the average, two, four, or more weeks before European and American norms. Particularly in the African case, this has been linked at times to reports of precocity at birth. A review of the current literature, however, indicates that, in fact, only some behaviors are advanced and they constitute a variable cluster that depends, at least primarily, on environmental factors.

### Motor Behavior at Birth

Shortly after Geber's initial studies of advanced motor behaviors by Ugandan infants, reviewed in the following, she and Dean reported that the typical newborn in a Kampala hospital was comparable in level of maturity to a European infant of 4 to 6 weeks (Geber & Dean, 1957a). The frequent absence of primitive reflex activity was particularly significant, since the startle, Babinski, grasping, and several other reflexes are thought to disappear from the European infant's behavioral repertoire through inhibition by the rapidly maturing, higher cortical areas of the brain. These results fit smoothly enough with the picture of development initially described for the following months, and with other theories and preconceptions, that they were quickly accepted by many psychologists.

In retrospect, the Geber and Dean report is so flawed with regard to choice and administration of examination procedures, use of comparison groups, and data analysis and reporting that it is no longer convincing (see Super, 1980; Warren, 1972). More importantly, several later studies have found no difference in neurological maturity between African groups and Euro-American norms or comparison samples. Warren and Parkin's study (1974), also carried out in Kampala, is the most thorough and it challenges both the facts and logic of the original report. The normal presence of neonatal reflexes has also been found by Griffiths (1969), Konner (1972), Freedman (1974), Vouilloux (1959a), Brazelton, Koslowski, and Tronick (1976), Keefer, Dixon, Tronick, and Brazelton (1978), and Super (unpublished data), using samples from South Africa, Botswana, Nigeria, Cameroon, Zambia, and Kenya. The very few reports that do not clearly support this view lack sufficient detail for adequate interpretation (e.g., Vincent & Hugon, 1962).

Some debate remains about possible qualitative differences in motor behavior between African and Caucasian newborns. Although the reports are not fully consistent, several researchers have characterized African infants as having greater muscular or postural strength, coordination, or control. The clearest report is by Keefer, Dixon, Tronick, and Brazelton (1978), who used the Brazelton Neonatal Assessment Scale (NBAS) to study Gusii newborns in a modernizing rural district in Western Kenya. They found superior muscle tone and control, as indicated by relatively smooth arcs of arm movements and strong, but not hypertonic tone in response to the examination. This characterization bears some similarity to Geber and Dean's (1957a) report of lesser flexion and less hypertonicity in Ugandan neonates, a finding that Warren and Parkin (1974) did not replicate. Coll, Sepkoski, and Lester (1978) found higher scores for a sample of American blacks on a summary scale that includes amount of hand-to-mouth activity and defensive movements to a cloth being put over the face. An earlier report, using different procedures, found no black-white differences in muscular tension, but did yield higher black scores on a summary that included motor reflexes (e.g., grasp, head turn), defensive reactions, and perceptual orienting items (Graham, Matarazzo, & Caldwell, 1956). In London, Hopkins (1978) reports black West Indian infants to be superior to a white English sample in general muscular tone and postural control.

There is no ready explanation for the pattern of specific differences and similarities in motor performance found in these studies. Given the methodological complexities of newborn testing, especially in non-Western settings, it has not been established what characteristics, if any, are particular to the "motoric style" of African babies. Since so many prenatal and perinatal factors can influence behavior in the first days of life, such as birth order, maternal anxiety, and routines of early care, and since few studies involve the same mating groups, the complexity of interpreting any result is formidable (see Lester & Brazelton, in press; Super, 1980).

Outside Africa, there are only scattered reports of newborn motor behavior. In general, they find no group differences, lack meaningful data to support a claim of differences, or have failed to replicate. One possible exception is a set of studies from Latin America. In rural Guatemala, Ladino newborns were found to be lacking vigor and were disorganized in their motor behavior, which the authors attributed to the mothers' poor nutritional state. This interpretation is supported by a correlation within the sample between the socioeconomic background and level of motor organization (Brazelton, Tronick, Lechtig, Lasky, & Klein, 1977; see also Lasky, Lechtig, Delgado, Klein, Engle, Yarbrough, & Martorell, 1975). However, Coll, Sepkoski, and Lester (1977, 1978) tested infants of normal medical, and presumably nutritional, status in Puerto Rico and Florida, and also found the Puerto Rican newborns to be relatively low in motor maturity and muscle tone. Brazelton, Robey, and Collier (1969; also Brazelton, 1972, 1977) examined five Zinacantecan neonates in the southern highlands of Mexico. They were similar to Caucasian-American infants in motor behaviors elicited by the examiner, such as being pulled up to a sitting position, but their spontaneous activity seemed more "fluid" and subdued in quality. Even though some writers have related this latter finding, as a population trait, to later motor development (see next section), it is also consistent with the picture presented by deVries and Super (1979) as a probable outcome of testing in dark, quiet homes instead of in the standard hospital nursery context.

*Motor Development After Birth*

As indicated earlier, there is significant variation in the achievement of motor milestones among, as there is within, human groups. In accord with tradition, motor scores on the standard tests have usually been summed into Developmental Quotients, and scores over 100 were naturally given the traditional interpretation of precocity in the rate of motor development. More recent work has related the pattern of item attainment to specific environmental conditions, in a sense indicating the cultural bias of Developmental Quotients as a general measure of rate of growth. The majority of this work has been done in Africa, where enough environmental information is available to make the argument most clearly.

Despite serious methodological flaws in many of the studies (see

Super, 1980; Warren, 1972), it is now well established that African babies reared in relatively traditional ways achieve a variety of motor milestones, especially in the first year, before their European and American peers. The initial studies were by Geber and Dean in Uganda (Geber, 1956, 1958a, 1958b, 1958c, 1960, 1962, 1973, 1974; Geber & Dean, 1957b, 1958, 1964). At least partially similar results have been found in other Ugandan samples, as well as in Kenya, Tanzania, Zambia, Madagascar, Botswana, South Africa, Cameroon, Guinea, Nigeria, the Ivory Coast, and Senegal (Ainsworth, 1967; Kilbride, Robbins, & Kilbride, 1970; Kilbride, 1976; Leiderman, Babu, Kagia, Kraemer, & Leiderman, 1973; Leiderman & Leiderman, 1974a, 1974b, 1977; Ssengoba, 1978; Super, 1973, 1976; Varkevisser, 1973; Goldberg, 1972, 1977; Konner, 1976, 1977; Ramarasaona, 1959; Liddicoat, 1969; Liddicoat & Griesel, 1971; Vouilloux, 1959a, 1959b; Naidr, 1975; Durojaiye, personal communication; Mundy-Castle & Okonji, 1978; Poole, 1969; Dasen, Inhelder, Lavallée, & Retschitzki, 1978; Bardet, Massé, Moreigne, & Senecal, 1960; Faladé, 1955, 1960; Lusk & Lewis, 1972; Moreigne, 1970; Valantin, 1970).

The skills on which African infants are most advanced, it appears, are the ones in which they have considerably more practice than American infants. There are qualitative reports of deliberate "teaching" of walking and sitting in a variety of African groups; for example, the Baganda of Uganda (Kilbride & Kilbride, 1975), the Wolof of Senegal (Faladé, 1955), and the Yoruba of Nigeria (Mundy-Castle & Okonji, 1978). Quantitative measures from individual interviews and observations in several East African groups indicate that a great majority of mothers think such teaching is important, and that the mothers or sibling caretakers are likely actually to carry out the practice every day in the few months before the particular skill is expected (Super, 1976). The training procedure, which may or may not have a unique name, consists of structured practice for the baby, such as providing cloth props while sitting or holding the baby's hands while standing. In addition to deliberate training, a number of traditional child care routines unintentionally provide practice. Among the Kipsigis of Kenya, for example, infants spend over 60 percent of their waking time sitting, often in someone's lap. This is considerably more often than a sample from metropolitan Boston (Super, 1976). Riding on the caretaker's back, another common position, likewise develops trunk, buttock, and thigh muscles more than does reclining in an American infant seat.

Less frequently, it seems, is there traditional support for prone behaviors. It is less often specifically taught, and since African babies are rarely lying down while awake (e.g., 10 percent Kipsigis vs. 30 percent Boston), they have less opportunity for incidental practice. Correspondingly, African infants are less often precocious in crawling, turning over, and other prone behaviors. This has been reported for the Baganda (Kilbride, 1976), the !Kung San (Konner, in Chang, 1976), the Kipsigis (Super, 1976), and the Kikuyu (Leiderman, personal communication).

A causal interpretation of this patterning is supported by two kinds of reports. The logically weaker studies are correlational, in which the average age at crawling, for example, in a sample of societies is correlated with quantitative estimates of deliberate and incidental support. Super (1976) reports high cultural correlations of this sort, when there is adequate variation among groups. The more rigorous studies are experimental and indicate that specific training procedures, well within the species' normal range of experience, can significantly lower the age of walking and crawling in European and American samples, in some cases with a carry-over effect to other skills (Lagerspetz, Nygard, & Strandvik, 1971; Zelazo, Zelazo, & Kolb, 1972).

Attention to the patterning of item attainment in conjunction with the specifically relevant, environmentally orchestrated experiences contributes to the resolution of contradictory reports concerning the effects of culture change. Some studies have noted that infants from "modern," "elite," "urban," or "educated" families may not show advancement in the rate of motor development (Geber, 1956, 1958a; Super, 1976; Varkevisser, 1973; Vouilloux, 1959a, 1959b). This would be understandable if the daily care and training of infants in these families resembled the Euro-American pattern. Super (1976) provides evidence that this can be so. A few investigators (e.g., Poole, 1969) find no relationship between gross indicators of Westernization and motor development, and others (e.g., Janes, 1975; Leiderman et al., 1973) report higher scores in the less traditional families. Lacking specific information about the relevant environmental variables, it is not possible to re-evaluate each case, but there is no reason to think that conditions promoting early motor skills necessarily co-occur with economic or educational indices, especially under the variety of conditions that exists today in changing Africa. Super (1976) illustrates this with data from the village in which Leiderman et al. (1973) found infants from less affluent families to have lower motor scores: these families said they were less likely to give their babies special practice in walking and sitting.

For reasons that are not clear, standard psychometric tests of motor development usually contain more items sampling skills in which African babies are likely to receive practice than ones that are not particularly promoted. For progress in sitting and walking, for example, each skill has six items on the Bayley Motor Scale in the first year, compared to one for crawling. Consequently, these tests yield high Developmental Quotients in Africa, in the first 12 to 18 months. Changes in the content of motor tests accounts for a subsequent decline, and the cultural bias becomes more obvious. Walking items now include such skills as walking backwards, which is not particularly valued in traditional Africa; the rural child who has never seen a cup before may be less likely initially to drink from one. After weaning, nutrition, infectious disease, and parasites may become serious problems in some samples (e.g., Bardet et al., 1960; Ssengoba, 1978). Although the evidence is not as thorough on this point, it appears that healthy infants from urban, educated families show little decline after two years, with respect to Euro-American norms, as well as little precocity before age two (e.g., Geber, 1956).

Studies of motor development in Asia and the Americas indicate a similar picture of relatively rapid attainment of motor milestones in early infancy, accompanied by physically stimulating care, and followed by a relative decline. Within this generalization, however, significant variations in the timing and patterning of precocity and delay are reported. The level of documentation is not as complete as for Africa, especially with regard to the environmental factors that are implicated by the African work.

Babies from a range of social and economic levels in India have been shown to have developmental quotients well above 100 in the first year or two (Das & Sharma, 1973; Patel & Kaul, 1971; Phatak, 1969, 1970a, 1970b). There are some differences among subgroups (rural/urban; economic level) in the timing of decline in scores relative to American norms, and in the patterning of particular skills. Qualitative comments on infant care, in these groups and elsewhere in India, suggest the presence of both inadvertent support (e.g., back-carrying) and deliberate stimulation, by massage, of some aspects of motor development (Hopkins, 1976; Leboyer, 1976). There are, however, no quantitative figures that can be related to the modest discrepancies among Indian reports or to their common contrast with other groups.

Shorter periods of high Developmental Quotients occur in groups that appear to receive less stimulation. In Mysore, India, Venkatachar (cited in Phatak, 1970a) found advancement in only two early motor areas, lasting six months, among infants from families who were economically advantaged and who, one can thus speculate, may have modified their care routines toward more Western models. In Guatemala (Wug de Leon, De Licardie, & Cravioto, 1964), sitting and prehension were found to be advanced in the early months, while later locomotion was delayed. Solomons and Solomons (1975) report a similar pattern in three Mexican samples and related the patterning to their observations on frequency of mothers' carrying the infants and discouraging independent activity on the cold or dirty floors. Low levels of stimulation and maternal emphasis on keeping infants calm and quiet have been related to relatively slow motor development in Southern Mexico, Guatemala, and Japan (Brazelton, Robey, & Collier, 1969; Arai, Ishikawa, & Toshima, 1958; Kagan & Klein, 1973). Other variations among ethnic groups have been reported for groups living in Hawaii, also attributed to child-rearing practices (Werner, Bierman, & French, 1971; Werner, Simonian, & Smith, 1968),

and in Israel, where generational differences, corresponding to acculturation, support a similar interpretation (Ivanans, 1975; Palti, Gitlin, & Zloto,
1977).

Does the patterning of environmental stimulation account for all the
variation among samples, or could the patterning be imposed on a more
general advancement in some cases? One line of evidence suggests that a
general advance in motor development may be possible. Experimental
work with both laboratory animals and human beings demonstrates that
"handling," mild stresses, and particular kinds of physical stimulation can
substantially contribute to development. The most dramatic demonstration with human beings was made by Clark, Kreutzberg, and Chee (1977).
They gave infants spinning rides in an office swivel chair, at a moderate
speed, for a total of 80 minutes over a period of four weeks; the subjects
subsequently showed advanced reflexive and gross motor behavior in
comparison with a control group. Vigorous passive exercise such as
stretching and massaging is given to infants in a number of African and
Asian groups (Hopkins, 1976), and their daily life of being handled and
carried probably constitutes a long-term analogue. Some comparative data
are available on physical contact, presumably a rough index of tactile,
vestibular, and muscular stimulation, and they indicate significantly
higher levels in preindustrial samples. In the last half of the first year, for
example, American infants are in body contact with another person about
30 percent of their waking hours, while comparable figures for Kipsigis
(Kenya), !Kung (Botswana), Fijian, and Mayan (Guatemala) infants are
about 60, 65, 57, and 64 percent (Super, 1980; Konner, 1973; Katz, personal communication; Rogoff, personal communication).

## Mental Development

Tools from the three major approaches to mental development in infancy
have been applied in cross-cultural studies: (a) the traditional psychometric "baby tests," (b) scales derived from Piaget's theory, and (c) measures
of infants' visual attention to particular stimuli. For historical as well as
theoretical reasons, studies using the baby tests emphasize individual differences, and their cross-cultural extension often focuses, therefore, on
group differences. For analogous reasons, research in the other two traditions emphasizes the universal aspects of early mental growth. Nevertheless, studies of all theoretical persuasions indicate that normal infants in
culturally normative care (e.g., not institutionalized) display the critical
cognitive development at about the same time, the world over. This regularity can be seen as rather tight regulation or "canalization" of mental
growth in a variety of circumstances (Scarr-Salapatek, 1976). On the other

hand, group differences of a few months in average attainment are occasionally found, and this variation around the species' mean can seem impressive. Which aspect—commonality or diversity—is emphasized by a particular writer depends in part on the theoretical purpose of the moment. Both are true and both need explaining.

### Mental Status at Birth

Many developmental psychologists think that the neonatal period may be too early to derive any good measure of mental status within the normal range. The detection of abnormal mental functioning in the opening weeks of life currently rests on neurological and more general behavioral items, essentially to assess the integrity of the central nervous system. Orientation and habituation to repeated stimuli sample behavior that can be acknowledged as fundamentally cognitive, and they can be elicited in newborns under carefully specified conditions that take into account the state of arousal, intensity and suddenness of stimulation, perinatal medication, ambient stimulation, hunger, and a number of other factors. It is doubtful, however, that individual differences on such measures indicate stable differences in mental development or potential.

Using the rather gross measures of neurological integrity and some indications of attentional behavior, cross-cultural studies find equivalence of mental functioning at birth in unstressed samples (with the exception, previously refuted, of Geber and Dean's claim regarding Ugandan newborns). The scattered group differences on particular items are probably best accounted for by medical and nutritional measures, conditions of testing, or chance variation. Of far greater interest in the comparative research are qualitative reports of early care that provide different opportunities and support for the use of the existing cognitive apparatus. The quiet, dark homes in which many infants are born in nonindustrial communities, with the constant companionship of the mother, stand out in this respect, although there are no substantial observations of early "cognitive" behavior in these settings.

### Psychometric Baby Tests

Many of the items on the traditional baby tests form scales relevant to cognitive growth, such as the Bayley Scale of Mental Development and the Adaptive and Language schedules on the Gesell. The rationale of these scales appeals to face content and their coverage of the common "mental" accomplishments of infancy. Unlike the motor portions, however, the mental items are valued primarily not in their own right, but for what they are thought to index about some abstract quality of the infant's mental functioning. An item analysis of the mental index is therefore more difficult than one of the motor summary score, where general competence is directly expressed in a weighted average of competence in walking, sitting, and so on. In addition, we lack a taxonomy of functional equivalencies in environmental events to match with the equally unclear functional requirements of mental development, so it is more difficult to search for the connection between the test performance and the typical experiences of infants in a culture.

In fact, at some ages the various subscales of the traditional baby tests are highly correlated: for example, the correlation between the Bayley motor and mental scales ranges from .24 to .78 within the first two years. It is not surprising, therefore, that in cross-cultural application the subscales yield similar results. In general, children from disparate cultures master the test items at about the same time, but there are significant variations depending on the experiential supports provided by any particular culture. More obviously than for the motor test items, substantial lack of relevant experience can constitute overt inappropriateness or cultural bias of the test.

The most revealing analysis of experience and item performance does not directly involve cultural comparison but examines individual variation within a sample of Ugandan infants (Kilbride, 1976). A number of significant correlations, however, also correspond to sample differences. For example, performance on grasping and manipulative items was correlated with observed frequency in the supine position. At a more general level, the Kilbrides (1975) have related Baganda and American values toward social graces to the relative advances by the African infants in achieving the later smiling items on the Bayley Scale of Mental Development. In a similar but somewhat less theoretical vein, the Leidermans and their associates have related overall Bayley mental quotients to measures of "modernization" and plurality of caretakers (Leiderman et al., 1973; Leiderman & Leiderman, 1974a). Babies with richer and more educated parents, and those cared for by more than one caretaker (e.g., mother and older sister) tended to score higher.

It should be evident at this point that group comparisons of overall mental scores have rather limited meaning without detailed attention to the items that account for the differences and the environmental conditions that might relate to them. There is no shortage of evidence that performance on nonmotor scales of the baby tests can vary in both the pattern of timing of item attainment and in the overall score. Many of the reports previously cited concerning motor development in Africa include findings on mental scales. Faladé (1955), Geber (1958b), Ainsworth (1967), Liddicoat and Koza (1963), Lusk and Lewis (1972), Leiderman et al. (1973), and Kilbride (1976) all report high average scores for their African samples. This advance in mental scores is usually less than the motor precocity. Performance that does not average above American norms (although individual items may vary widely) has been found in other African samples by Massé (1969), Ramarasaona (1959), Theunissen (1948), Vouilloux (1959a, 1959b), and Falmagne (1962). It appears that in the first two years the verbal-vocal domain is most often found to develop at or below American norms.

Studies in India tend to show relatively high performance by upper class groups on the Gesell and Bayley mental scales, with infants from lower SES and seriously deprived families, respectively, scoring at and below American norms (Athavale, Kandoth, & Sonnad, 1971; Kandoth, Sonnad, & Athavale, 1971; Patel & Kaul, 1971; Phatak, 1969, 1970a, 1970b; Uklonskaya, Puri, Choudhuri, Dang, & Kumari, 1960). Israeli studies reveal both kibbutz- and home-reared infants to average over 100 on the Bayley mental scale, and to be essentially similar to each other (Kohen-Raz, 1967, 1968). The acculturation, education, and ethnicity comparisons on adaptive, social, and language scales (Gesell) generally parallel the results for motor development: infants from educated families or those from North Africa tend to excel, at least in the first 18 months or so (Ivanans, 1975; Smilansky, Shephatia, & Frenkel, 1976). Arai et al. (1958) found Japanese babies to fall behind American norms for vocal and verbal behavior at about 4 months, although a large middle class sample was shown by Koga (1967) to generally excel on the Cattell Infant Intelligence Scale after the first year.

Class comparisons in Europe and the Americas produce a complex pattern of results, with higher SES samples usually scoring higher in the second year, but sometimes relatively poorly in the first year (e.g., Brown & Halpern, 1971; Curti, Marshall, & Steggerda, 1935; Grantham-McGregor & Hawke, 1971). Specifically ethnic comparisons, however, usually find no overall differences (Walters, 1967; Knobloch & Pasamanick, 1958; Bayley, 1965), although Rebelsky (1972) found large "deficits" in performance by Dutch infants on the Cattell scale. She attributes this fact to infants' adaptation to Dutch child-rearing techniques and goals.

*Studies Using Piaget's Theory*

Several studies of infant mental development in non-Western cultures use tests derived from Piaget's seminal observations on the emergence of intelligence in the opening years of life. From the Ivory Coast, Dasen and associates have recently reported on infants of 5 to 31 months from a rural agricultural village of the Baoulé people (Bovet, Dasen, Inhelder, & Othenin-Girard, 1972; Dasen, 1973; Dasen, Inhelder, Lavallée, & Retschitzki, 1978; Dasen, Lavallée, Retschitzki, & Reinhardt, 1977). These babies proceeded through a series of behaviors indicating intellectual growth re-

markably similar to that originally described for Swiss children and replicated in detail in France by Lézine, Stambak, and Casati (1969), including,
for example, the exploratory manipulations of a matchbox. There were
some sample differences in the average age of passing particular test
items: the Baoulé infants were a month or two early in the use of intermediary instruments and combining objects, and they were slightly delayed
in one or two unrelated items. The French and Baoulé infants were equivalent in most other tasks concerning prehension, exploration, and object
permanence. (See also the chapter by Dasen and Heron in this volume.)

Other studies generally project a similar picture of consonance in the
sequence of early development, with some small sample differences in
timing. Konner used the Einstein scales (Corman & Escalona, 1969) to examine infants of the !Kung San hunter-gatherers of Botswana. They pro-
gressed through initial prehension items apace with Corman and Escalona's American sample, but were advanced by a couple of weeks in the
more complex visually guided reaching. In Lusaka, Zambia, Goldberg
(1972, 1977) found a similar result for babies from lower income families,
but no difference on the space or object permanence scales. All these authors interpret their findings as supportive of Piaget's general description
of early mental accomplishment, and attribute the instances of advancement to differences in experience.

Goldberg (1972) and Dasen et al. (1978) point out, in addition, that the
testing situation can be a very different experience for children reared in
the traditional African manner. This is most obvious during the object
permanence testing, when the baby is repeatedly frustrated by having the
object taken away for use in the next test item, just after succeeding in retrieving it in the last item. The Ivory Coast group took particular efforts to
avoid underestimating competence due to this problem (which raises the
question of whether any of their relative advances might be artifactual),
while Goldberg speculates that this testing problem accounts for the fact
that her Zambian infants tended to perform better on the space scale than
on object permanence, the reverse of the American pattern.

Subtle particulars of the testing situation were also thought by Kopp,
Khoka, and Sigman (1977) to account for two small differences between
their American and Indian samples. In New Delhi, the caretakers were
more likely to offer comfort to a frustrated baby during the hidden objects
procedure, whereas the American mothers were more likely to redirect
the child's attention to the unsolved problem. Second, the Indian babies
had slightly less success in using intermediary tools in the horizontal
plane, which the authors attribute to their lesser experience in the prone
position.

On all other tests there were no significant differences associated with
nationality or, within samples, with socioeconomic status or modernization. A single report from Japan suggests no differences from American

results on object permanence at 9 months (Takahashi & Hatano, 1976).

There are three reported instances of substantial delay in attaining object permanence. Hunt, Paraskevopoulos, Schickendanz, and Užgiris (1975) used a home-reared sample in Athens as one comparison group for an orphanage sample. The infants at home appeared to lag behind American babies by as much as six months on some of the more complex test items; but, as the authors point out, so many environmental and cultural differences overlap with the test results that it is difficult to draw a firm interpretation. In Guatemala, infants in a remote Mayan village achieved object permanence about three months later than expected, and a number of related measures showed similar delays (Kagan & Klein, 1973; Kagan, Kearsley, & Zelazo, 1978; Kagan, Klein, Finley, Rogoff, & Nolan, 1979). The delays were attributed to low levels of stimulation and little experience of variety in the first year. In a separate study, Lester, Kotelchuck, Spelke, Sellers, and Klein (1974) reported findings from a group of lower class Ladino infants who appear to lag substantially behind Corman and Escalona's (1969) New York sample. The lack of discussion about potential problems in testing, as well as lack of details on environmental supports for cognitive development, make it difficult to interpret these reported delays. Nevertheless, these studies warn that a simple maturational view of early development may not be adequate.

### Studies of Infant Attention

The seminal work of Fantz (e.g., Fantz, 1958), on infants' distribution of attention to visual stimuli of varying complexity, introduced a new methodology to the study of infant cognition. From laboratory experiments in this tradition, developmental psychologists have made substantial gains in understanding the powers and limits of infants' abilities to notice, process, and store various kinds of information. A number of discrete findings have been replicated in other societies (e.g., Lasky, Klein, & Martinez, 1974; Yamada, 1978). The major generalization from the infant attention literature that has been subjected to cross-cultural replication is the developmental pattern of interest in models of human faces. A number of American studies indicate that babies around 4 months of age will show great interest in human masks, but this interest declines to a nadir in the last quarter of the first year. Attention to the same stimuli then increases for the next year or two, especially to masks that are distorted by having the major features (eyes, nose, mouth) rearranged. The theory used to account for these phenomena, drawn in part from the constructionist views emerging from the American discovery of Piaget, is that, in the early months, the infant is attracted by slight discrepancies between the stimulus and his or her still developing schema for what a face should look like.

As the infant becomes more skilled in assimilating faces, the masks become less compelling. Late in the first year, however, the infant grows in ability to try to "understand" the discrepancies between the masks and real faces, and the distortions of the mask with scrambled features are particularly interesting (Kagan, 1970, 1971; Kagan, Kearsley, & Zelazo, 1978).

Figure 1 shows the results of similar studies with Ladino infants in Guatemala (Sellers, Klein, Kagan, & Minton, 1972), rural Mexicans (Finley, Kagan, & Layne, 1972), the !Kung San of Botswana (Konner, 1973), and Japanese subjects (Takahashi, 1973, and personal communication); the American results are also included (Kagan, 1970). Because of differences in procedures and detail of reporting, the comparisons are problematic: some plots are for the average first visual fixation over multiple presentations, others are for total fixation. The best available score was scaled to an arbitrary, common range of variation in constructing this figure. It is

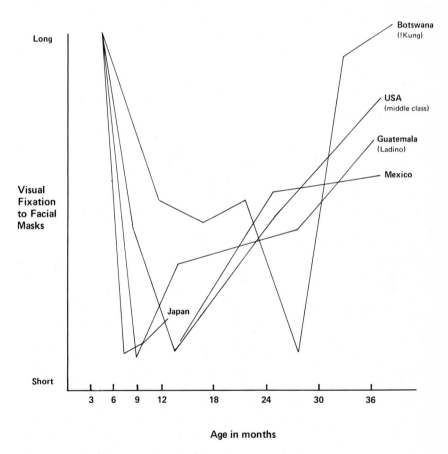

Figure 1. Infants' attention to facial masks.

immediately evident that the curvilinear relationship of age and attention to human masks is replicated in these widely diverse settings. In the American, Mexican, and Guatemalan samples the increase in attention after the trough is greatest to the scrambled face. In the Japanese case, where the upturn is barely caught, a different distortion (a face with no features) attracted the greatest increase. Konner does not report this detail for the !Kung.

A close examination of Figure 1 raises some interesting questions about the exact low point. Although the variations in procedures, measures, age of assessment, and context of testing render fragile any conclusion, it would appear that the trough of interest appears earlier in the Japanese and possibly the Guatemalan samples than in the American and !Kung ones. Kagan and associates have argued, from a large battery of measures used in more isolated Guatemalan (Mayan) samples, that low levels of variety and stimulation can result in a few months' delay in the ability to activate hypotheses about discrepancy; this should be reflected in the placement of the trough, but we lack an adequate combination of measures on the diverse samples used here to evaluate such an explanation for Figure 1 (if, in fact, the differences exist). The unusual dip at 27 months in the !Kung infants' attention might be an artifact of the small number of subjects, or as Konner argues, a reflection of heightened fear of strange events at that age.

## Social Development

The study of social development in cultural context involves a level of complexity not encountered in the motor and mental domains, for the goal is understanding not only performance, and not only competence, but also meaning. The path from observed behavior to theoretical construct is more treacherous, and there is less consensus than in the other two domains on the correct theoretical paradigms to chart this path in cultural studies. Nonetheless, the existing literature speaks to three major issues: (a) group differences in social disposition at birth; (b) universal emergence of the major components of social behavior; and (c) shaping of these components into culturally specific styles of interaction and affect.

### Social Behavior at Birth

Neonatal studies relating to social behavior are of particular importance for two reasons. First, early behavior is thought to influence the specific responses of parents and caretakers, and group differences at birth (from whatever cause) might therefore result in different patterns of care, development, and ultimately adult personality and culture. Second, new-born studies raise the possibility that some early differences among mating groups in behavioral disposition or temperament might be genetic in origin.

A number of reports from various parts of the world illustrate how early environmental factors can influence behavior in the newborn period, thus at least implicitly raising the question of differential consequences. Maternal health and nutrition unquestionably influence the level of activity and organization shown by a newborn, possibly rendering the baby less appealing to the mother. Geber (1973) and Brazelton, Koslowski, and Tronick (1976), using quite different methods, both report Zambian infants from lower income parents to be relatively quiet, inattentive, and irritable; recovery in this case appeared quite good over the first ten days. Studies in Guatemala, Greece, and Mexico also implicate economic, and particularly nutritional factors (Brazelton, Tronick, Lechtig, Lasky, & Klein, 1977; Brazelton, Tryphonopoulou, & Lester, in press; Cravioto, Birch, De Licardie, Rosales, & Vega, 1969). Several other studies find small but significant group differences in alertness and orientation that might quickly lead to divergent patterns of social interaction, but evidence is not available concerning either the cause or consequence (e.g. Coll, Sepkoski, & Lester, 1978; Horowitz, Ashton, Culp, Gaddis, Levin, & Reichmann, 1977).

Freedman appeals to a theory of gene pool differences to explain his findings of relatively low irritability in newborns of Oriental background (Freedman, 1971, 1974; Freedman & Freedman, 1969). He and his associates report Chinese-Americans and Japanese-Americans, compared to Caucasian-Americans, to have more stable states of arousal and excitement during a neonatal exam, to become less upset in response to several perturbing stimuli, and to be relatively easy to console when they do become upset. A similar picture is presented for the typical Navajo newborn, and Freedman argues that this reflects their genetic closeness to the Oriental samples. Some of Freedman's results have been confirmed by Chisholm (1978) and Kuchner (1978). Kagan, Kearsley, and Zelazo (1978) report a possibly related difference, that at older ages Chinese-American babies show more stable heartrates and more even dispositions during laboratory testing. Freedman (1974) theorizes that cultural diversity of innate disposition plays a role in the diversity of child care (e.g., the Navajo infants more readily accept the restrictive cradleboard) and the diversity of adult norms and behavior.

Even though the breadth of such a view may be appealing, the genetic theory of cultural differences in infant behavior is open to challenge on several levels. Chisholm (1978) and Rosenblith (1978; Rosenblith & Anderson-Huntington, 1975) do not replicate some of the item differences, such as defensive reactions to interference with easy breathing. Rosenblith's Hawaiian-born sample, predominantly Japanese in background, was not less irritable during testing. In addition, several observations of unusual irritability in older Japanese infants raise concern with the broad conceptualization of the differences as temperament (e.g., Field & Baber, 1973, p. 103; Freedman, 1974, p. 163f). Cardiovascular studies with adults raise a similar problem (Wolff, 1977). Finally, given the large set of factors that can influence group comparison of newborn behavior (Super, 1980, lists eleven), replication of the mating group difference in behavior is not, by itself, sufficient evidence of genetic cause. Chisholm (1978), for example, found maternal blood pressure to be strongly related to newborn irritability among his Navajo subjects, and Woodson replicated this relationship among three groups in Malaysia (Chisholm, Woodson, & DaCosta-Woodson, 1978). Even though there may be genetic influences on blood pressure, or on systemic reactions to stress, the finding serves to remind the reader of a number of pre- and perinatal conditions that have not been controlled in all these newborn studies.

*The Emergence of Social Behaviors*

The major components of social interaction emerge remarkably alike in the cases in which they have been studied. Smiling, for example, is relatively rare and arguable in its form in the first month or two of life, but it then grows dramatically in frequency to a peak around 4 months, in American (Wolff, 1963) and !Kung San babies (Konner, personal communication), as well as kibbutz, middle class, lower class, and Bedouin infants in Israel (Gewirtz, 1965; Landau, 1977). Kilbride and Kilbride (1974) found no difference in the emergence of smiling between their Baganda sample and Bayley's American norms.

By the time of the peak at 4 months, however, considerable divergence of the natural rates of smiling can be seen, as Gewirtz (1965) and Landau (1977) illustrate with their diverse Israeli samples. Estimating from different methodologies and reporting procedures, the frequency of smiling at 4 months appears to range from once or more in 5 percent of waking minutes (Navajo: Chisholm, 1978) to 20 percent (Kipsigis: Super, unpublished data), with rural Senegal (Lusk & Lewis, 1972), Yugoslavia (Lewis & Ban, 1977), urban Zambia (Goldberg, 1977), and urban America (Moss, 1967) falling in between these extremes.

There are fewer relevant studies on the emergence of vocalization as a channel of communication, largely because of difficulties of theory and method. Greenbaum and Landau (1977) present relevant data from several Israeli samples, indicating some similarities in the early growth of vocalizations. The range of spontaneous vocalization rates at 3 or 4 months appears to be between about 27 percent of waking minutes (Kipsigis: Super, unpublished data) and 59 percent (urban America: Moss, 1967). By 10 months the cultural divergence seems greater, and there is some reason to believe that rates are substantially higher in urban samples.

Regularity of emergence can be demonstrated for behaviors considerably more complex than smiling, to wit, the propensity to cry at seeing one's mother depart ("separation anxiety"). Figure 2 presents this measure for five groups: working class American (Kagan, 1976), !Kung San (Konner, 1973), Ladino Guatemalan (Lester, Kotelchuck, Spelke, Sellers, & Klein, 1974; Kagan, 1976) kibbutz-reared Israeli (Fox, 1975, 1977), and Mayan Guatemalan (Kagan et al., 1978). As always with data collected under different circumstances, there are some problems with this comparison, but it is nevertheless striking that very few infants in any sample cried to maternal departure until the middle of the first year, at which point distress becomes rapidly more common until a peak during the first half of the next year.

## Development of Social Relations

Understanding how social experience shapes the social relations and the personal growth of individuals was at the core of early interdisciplinary work on infancy, but applying objective techniques to this level of analysis has proven more difficult than merely counting the frequency of discrete behaviors (Lewis & Ban, 1977). At present, three foci can be identified in the literature on early social relations. The first concerns the theory of attachment, that is, growth of the infant's affective and behavioral ties to the caretaker. The other two aim at characterizing and explaining the divergence of typical development among culture groups: quiet, passive dependence among Japanese and Chinese infants, and low affect in interaction with infants in some traditional African societies.

*Attachment.* Attachment theory, as first put forward by Bowlby (1969), grew out of concern with the psychological disturbance that was often observed to result from enforced separation of young children from their usual caretakers (i.e., their mothers), for reasons of war, hospitalization, or family crisis. Taking a broad, evolutionary perspective, Bowlby's theory noted the adaptive value of an emotional system that promotes physical proximity between infant and mother, thus preventing accidents, predation, and abandonment of the helpless young. The theory relates the secure establishment of this affective, behavioral bond to successful functioning later as the young human begins to explore the physical and social environment more independently (see also the chapter by Kornadt et al., in Volume 3 of this *Handbook*.)

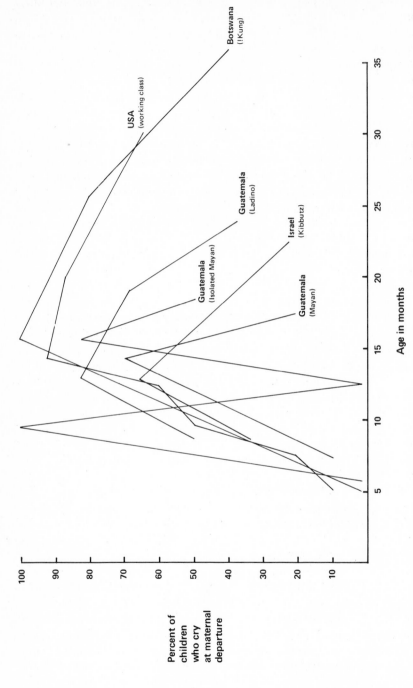

Figure 2. Infants' protest to maternal departure.

38

Attachment theory provides a framework for asking a number of important questions about social development in cultural context (Ainsworth, 1977a, 1977b), and at the same time those questions point to the strengths and weaknesses of the theory. The apparent universality of attachment behaviors is illustrated by numerous qualitative accounts of infancy, as well as by more formal methods, such as the data presented in Figure 2. Several kinds of evidence support the particular role of physical contact in forming the infant-caretaker bond. In a Hausa sample from northern Nigeria, for example, where most infants had several regular caretakers, the central attachment was strongly related to the relative frequency of physical contact, not to feeding (Marvin, VanDevender, Iwanaga, LeVine, & LeVine, 1977). This is in agreement with Bowlby's theory and the classic experiments with monkeys (Harlow & Harlow, 1965; Mason, 1968) which contributed to it.

The role of contact as an "instinct" in search of expression, rather than a learned behavior reinforced by "spoiling," is supported by two studies showing greater frequency of attachment to "cuddly blankets" and cloth animals in samples where breast feeding, carrying, and sleeping with the mother were relatively rare. Gaddini (1970) demonstrated this relationship in rural and urban Italy; Hong and Townes (1976) used children of Korean and American medical students. Comparative evidence also supports the postulated relationship between secure attachment in the first year and later independence. Konner's (1976) study of !Kung San and English children is the clearest example. The social and geographic niches in which the toddlers try out independence from the mother are quite different, however, leaving open the question of causality.

The cultural diversity of development either conflicts with or seriously complicates attachment theory in several instances. Bowlby's initial emphasis on the singularity of the infant's bond ("monotropy") is not in accord with the several reports of multiple attachments. Rabin's (1958) work on the success of group care in an Israeli kibbutz is widely known, and Fox (1977, 1978) has recently demonstrated that mother and *metapelet* (the group caretaker) can usually provide equivalent comfort.

More generally, the number of available caretakers reflects the household type and the larger maintenance system, and there is diverse evidence that the responsiveness of caretakers is related to their density, both between and within societies (Minturn & Lambert, 1964; Munroe & Munroe, 1971; Whiting, 1961, 1971). Older siblings, especially sisters between 6 and 10 years, are often primarily in charge of daytime care of infants in many agricultural societies (Weisner & Gallimore, 1977). The Leidermans (1974a, 1977) provide one of the most detailed reports on this arrangement and argue that the patterns of socialization that develop cannot be adequately accounted for by a theory that gives the mother an exclusive role. In the Hausa study by Marvin et al. (1977), the grandmother was found to play a significant and culturally defined role, in addition to siblings, leading to the observation that in naturally occurring situations, most babies demonstrated attachment to three or four people.

The developmental progression of attachment behaviors in various settings poses additional questions about which aspects of development are inherently connected. In Figure 2, for example, we can see, in addition to the similarity of emergence, considerable diversity in the amount and duration of distress to maternal departure. This diversity probably reflects the various social niches of the older infants, each of which will have its own adaptive requirements. At least one meaningful psychological comparison can be drawn from this diversity: as different as the American and !Kung samples are in physical contact, exposure to strangers, and many other factors, they share nearly exclusive maternal care, relatively common distress to maternal departure, and relatively slow decline in this distress. Decoupling aspects of the environment that are linked in our society is the most potent tool of cross-cultural research, and other rewarding comparisons could be drawn from attachment studies if multiple measures of behavior and environment were available in more settings. The discontinuity in Kagan's most isolated Mayan sample, if replicated elsewhere, could suggest a new set of questions.

*Socialization of interaction.* In contrast to studies that relate a few "diagnostic" measures to the specific contours of attachment theory, a number of reports attempt to analyze early infant-caretaker interaction as socialization toward culturally appropriate patterns. Whereas the early "culture and personality" literature followed this course in a qualitative way, more recent work has used intensive, quantitative observations of actual interactions in consort with detailed ethnographic information. Caudill and Weinstein's (1969) study in Japan and America was the first in this paradigm, and along with later reports it yields a comprehensive picture of social interaction in the first six years of life (Caudill, 1972; Caudill & Schooler, 1973). When observed in the home, Japanese mothers were seen to engage in a particularly close and solicitous relation with their infants—soothing, pacifying, and calming. The infants, in turn, were relatively quiet. Caudill contrasted this picture to the American mother who actively stimulated her baby, especially through lively vocalization. This contrast presages the expected patterns of interaction in later years. It is also consonant with the divergent folk theories—the need in the Japanese mother's mind to encourage social integration and mutual interdependence, and the American mother's intent to facilitate her baby's assertive individuality.

In light of the newborn results cited earlier, Freedman (1974) has proposed a reverse causal relationship. The quiet, accepting Japanese infant and the active, irritable Caucasian infant elicit different caretaking from their mothers and ultimately join a social pattern fashioned by like-tempered individuals. Kuchner (1978) has recently completed a study of Chinese-American infants that replicates major aspects of both Freedman's newborn results and Caudill's interaction observations, even at two weeks of age. She concluded that the temperament differences at birth contribute to the interactional results through different frequencies of changing state. In contrast, Caudill and Frost (1973) found Japanese-American mother-infant dyads to behave generally like Caucasian-Americans, rather than like native Japanese. In fact, on the major contrast of maternal talking and infant vocalization, they exceeded the Caucasian-American sample. A resolution of these conflicting results and interpretations must await Kuchner's detailed report and probably further research.

Socialization studies in this tradition have also been carried out in Africa. LeVine (1973, 1974a) has speculated that mothers in traditional agricultural societies of sub-Saharan Africa do not display the overt affection often thought to be "instinctively maternal" in European countries. He relates this tendency to adaptive needs in these hierarchical, face-to-face communities. Several reports would seem to be in agreement with this generalization, although they lack specific comparative data (Ainsworth, 1967; Goldschmidt, 1975). Preliminary results from LeVine's recent project among the Gusii of Kenya are more persuasive. Direct expression of intense affect is discouraged, and face-to-face interaction is avoided in many situations. Interviews and observations of infants and their mothers reveal relatively low levels of face-to-face interaction and intimate expressiveness (Keefer, Dixon, Tronick, & Brazelton, 1977; LeVine, personal communication).

In contrast, there are qualitative reports of exceptionally expressive interaction among other African groups (e.g., Kilbride & Kilbride, 1974; Mundy-Castle & Okonji, 1978), and quantitative comparisons to the same effect (Goldberg, 1977; Kilbride, 1976; Lusk & Lewis, 1972; Super & Harkness, 1974). Even though it might be argued that none of these cases exactly fits the type of community LeVine initially discussed, the more important point is that there is substantial variation in the overt character, at least, of early interaction, and that much of it may ultimately be related in an orderly way to larger aspects of the culture.


## Conclusions


Cross-cultural studies of infant development have yet to fulfill their potential contribution. This is partly for their small number, but also because of their frequent methodological inadequacy. The interdisciplinary complexity of the enterprise places an unusual burden on the three tasks of any social science. First, the accurate, quantitative description of infant behaviors under field conditions is noticeably more difficult than in the one-way-mirrored, wired-for-sound laboratory, but it still requires the technical skills of the psychometrician and the ethologist. Second, the theoretical perspectives of several disciplines are needed to conceptualize adequately the observed regularities and differences. Finally, understanding the causes and consequences of the regularities and differences can be treacherous without both the clinical insights of the ethnographer and the cold tools of the statistician.

Nevertheless, the literature as it stands already makes a substantial beginning toward sketching out the commonalities of our species' early ontogeny and the ways in which diversity is created around this core. The essential motor and mental competencies may become expressed in any particular behavior at slightly varying times, but they are strongly "built-in" in that they seem to develop similarly in all children in the diverse niches humankind has created for its infant young. The use of these abilities, still in infancy, to join in the social fabric becomes patterned in ways we are only beginning to recognize as cultural. Cultural diversity is as special to our species as the built-in plans, and it appears that infancy is not too early to study its workings also.

## Note

1. The author's research and preparation of this chapter were supported in part by funds granted by the William T. Grant Foundation, the Carnegie Corporation of New York, and the Spencer Foundation. All statements made and views expressed are the sole responsibility of the author.

## References

AINSWORTH, M. D. S. *Infancy in Uganda: Infant care and the growth of love.* Baltimore, Md.: Johns Hopkins Press, 1967.

——. Attachment theory and its utility in cross-cultural research. In P. H. Leiderman, S. R. Tulkin, & A. Rosenfeld (Eds.), *Culture and infancy: Variations in the human experience.* New York: Academic Press, 1977. (a)

——. Infant development and mother-infant interaction among Ganda and American families. In P. H. Leiderman, S. R. Tulkin, and A. Rosenfeld (Eds.), *Culture and infancy: Variations in the human experience.* New York: Academic Press 1977. (b)

ARAI, S., ISHIKAWA, J., & TOSHIMA, K. Développement psychomoteur des enfants Japonais. *Revue de Neuropsychiatrie Infantile et d'Hygiène Mentale de l'Enfance,* 1958, *6,* 262–269.

ATHAVALE, V. B., KANDOTH, W. K., & SONNAD, L. Developmental pattern in children of lower socio-economic group below 5 years of age. *Indian Pediatrics*, 1971, *8*, 313–320.

AYRES, B. Effects of infant carrying practices on rhythm in music. *Ethos*, 1973, *1*, 387–404.

BARDET, C., MASSÉ, G., MOREIGNE, F., & SENECAL, M. J. Application du test de Brunet-Lézine à un groupe d'enfants Ouolofs de 6 mois à 24 mois. *Bulletin de la Société Médicale d'Afrique Noire de Langue Française*, 1960, *5*, 334–356.

BARRY, H. III, & PAXSON, L. M. Infancy and early childhood: Cross-cultural codes 2. *Ethnology*, 1971, *10*, 466–508.

BARRY, H. III., & ROBERTS, J. M. Infant socialization and games of chance. *Ethnology*, 1972, *11*, 296–308.

BATESON, G., & MEAD, M. *Balinese character: A photographic analysis*. New York: New York Academy of Sciences, 1942.

BAYLEY, N. Comparisons of mental and motor test scores for ages 1–15 months by sex, birth order, race, geographical location, and education of parents. *Child Development*, 1965, *36*, 379–411.

BLOUNT, B. G. Parental speech and language acquisition: Some Luo and Samoan examples. *Anthropological Linguistics*, 1972, *14*, 119–130.

BOVET, M. C., DASEN, P. R., INHELDER, B., & OTHENIN-GIRARD, C. Étapes de l'intelligence sensori-motrice chez l'enfant Baoulé: Étude préliminaire. *Archives de Psychologie*, 1972, *41*, 363–386.

BOWLBY, J. *Attachment and loss* (Vol. 1): *Attachment*. New York, Basic Books, 1969.

BRAZELTON, T. B. Implications of infant development among the Mayan Indians of Mexico. *Human Development*, 1972, *15*, 90–111.

————. Implications of infant development among the Mayan Indians of Mexico. In P. H. Leiderman, S. R. Tulkin, & A. Rosenfeld (Eds.), *Culture and infancy: Variations in the human experience*. New York: Academic Press, 1977.

BRAZELTON, T. B., KOSLOWSKI, B., & TRONICK, E. Neonatal behavior among urban Zambians and Americans. *Journal of the American Academy of Child Psychiatry*, 1976, *15*, 97–107.

BRAZELTON, T. B., ROBEY, J. S., & COLLIER, G. A. Infant development in the Zinacanteco Indians of Southern Mexico. *Pediatrics*, 1969, *44*, 274–290.

BRAZELTON, T. B., TRONICK, E., LECHTIG, A., LASKY, R., & KLEIN, R. E. The Behavior of nutritionally deprived Guatemalan infants. *Developmental Medicine and Child Neurology*, 1977, *19*, 364–372.

BRAZELTON, T. B., TRYPHONOPOULOU, Y., & LESTER, B. M. A comparative study of Greek neonatal behavior. *Pediatrics*, in press.

BROWN, R. E., & HALPERN, F. The variable pattern of mental development of rural black children: Results and interpretation of results of studies on Mississippi children aged one week to three years by the Gesell Developmental Scales. *Clinical Pediatrics*, 1971, *10*, 404–409.

CAMPBELL, B. A., & SPEAR, N. E. Ontogeny of memory. *Psychological Review*, 1972, *79*, 215–236.

CAUDILL, W. A. Tiny dramas: Vocal communication between mother and infant in Japanese and American families. In W. P. Lebra (Ed.), *Transcultural research in mental health: Vol. II of mental health research in Asia and the Pacific*. Honolulu: University Press of Hawaii, 1972.

CAUDILL, W., & FROST, L. A comparison of maternal care and infant behavior in Japanese-American, and Japanese families. In W. Lebra (Ed.), *Youth, socialization, and mental health: Vol. III of mental health research in Asia and the Pacific.* Honolulu: University Press of Hawaii, 1973.

CAUDILL, W. A., & SCHOOLER, C. Child behavior and child rearing in Japan and the United States: An interim report. *Journal of Nervous and Mental Disease, 1973, 157,* 323–338.

CAUDILL, W. A., & WEINSTEIN, H. Maternal care and infant behavior in Japan and America. *Psychiatry, 1969, 32,* 12–43.

CHANG, N. Y. *Cross-cultural perspectives of motor development in infants.* Unpublished undergraduate thesis, Harvard University, 1976.

CHISHOLM, J. S. *Developmental ethology of the Navajo.* Unpublished doctoral dissertation, Rutgers University, 1978.

———. Development and adaptation in infancy. In C. Super & S. Harkness (Eds.), Anthropological perspectives on child development. *New Directions for Child Development, 1980, 8,* 15–30.

CHISHOLM, J. S., WOODSON, R. H., & DA COSTA-WOODSON, E. M. Maternal blood pressure in pregnancy and newborn irritability. *Early Human Development, 1978, 2*(2), 171:178.

CLARK, D. L., KREUTZBERG, J. R., & CHEE, F. K. W. Vestibular influence on motor development in infants. *Science, 1977, 196,* 1228–1229.

CLARKE, A. M., & CLARKE, A. D. B. *Early experience: Myth and evidence.* New York: Free Press, 1976.

COLL, C., SEPKOSKI, C. & LESTER, B. M. *Differences in Brazelton Scale performance between Puerto Rican and North American White and Black newborns.* Paper presented at the meeting of the Society for Research in Child Development, New Orleans, La., 1977.

———. *Differences in Brazelton scale performance between Puerto Rican and Mainland Black and Caucasian infants.* Manuscript submitted for publication, 1978.

CORMAN, H. H., & ESCALONA, S. K. Stages of sensorimotor development: A replication study. *Merrill-Palmer Quarterly, 1969, 15,* 351–362.

CRAVIOTO, J., BIRCH, H. G., DE LICARDIE, E., ROSALES, L., & VEGA, L. The ecology of growth and development in a Mexican preindustrial community: Report I. Method and findings from birth to one month of age. *Monographs of the Society for Research in Child Development, 1969, 34* (5, Serial No. 129).

CURTI, M. W., MARSHALL, F. B., & STEGGERDA, M. The Gesell schedules applied to one-, two-, and three-year-old Negro children of Jamaica, B.W.I. *Journal of Comparative Psychology, 1935, 20,* 125–156.

DAS, V. K., & SHARMA, N. L. Developmental milestones in a selective sample of Lucknow children: A longitudinal study. *Indian Journal of Pediatrics, 1973, 40,* 1–7.

DASEN, P. R. Preliminary study of sensori-motor development in Baoule children. *Early Child Development and Care, 1973, 2,* 345–354.

DASEN, P. R., INHELDER, B., LAVALLÉE, M., & RETSCHITZKI, J. *Naissance de l'intelligence chez l'enfant Baoulé de Côte d'Ivoire.* Berne: Hans Huber, 1978.

DASEN, P. R., LAVALLÉE, M., RETSCHITZKI, J., & REINHARDT, M. Early moderate malnutrition and the development of sensori-motor intelligence. *Journal of*

*Tropical Pediatrics and Environmental Child Health,* 1977, 23, 145–157. (Monograph)

DEVRIES, M. W., & SUPER, C. M. Contextual influences on the Brazelton Neonatal Behavioral Assessment Scale and implications for its cross-cultural use. In A. Sameroff (Ed.), Organization and stability of newborn behavior: A commentary on the Brazelton Neonatal Behavioral Assessment Scale. *Monographs of the Society for Research in Child Development,* 1979, 43, (5–6, Serial No. 177), 92–101.

DU BOIS, C. *The people of Alor.* Minneapolis: University of Minnesota Press, 1944.

FALADÉ, S. *Le développement psycho-moteur de jeune Africain originaire du Senegal au cours de sa première année.* Paris: Foulon, 1955.

————. Le développement psycho-moteur de l'enfant Africain du Senegal. *Concours Médical,* 1960, 82, 1005–1013.

FALMAGNE, J.-C. Étude comparative du développement psychomoteur pendant les six premièrs mois de 105 nourrissons blancs (Bruxelles) and 78 nourrissons noirs (Johannesburg). *Mémoirs de L'Academie Royale des Sciences d'Outre-Mer. Classes des Sciences Naturelles et Médicales,* 1962, 13, fasc. 5.

FANTZ, R. L. Pattern vision in young infants. *Psychological Record,* 1958, 8, 43–47.

FIELD, C. E., & BABER, F. M. *Growing up in Hong Kong.* Hong Kong: Hong Kong University Press, 1973.

FINLEY, G. E., KAGAN, J., & LAYNE, O. JR. Development of young children's attention to normal and distorted stimuli: A cross-cultural study. *Developmental Psychology,* 1972, 6, 288–292.

FOX, N. A. *Developmental and birth-order determinants of separation protest: A cross-cultural study of infants on the Israeli Kibbutz.* Unpublished doctoral dissertation, Harvard University, 1975.

————. Attachment of Kibbutz infants to mother and metapelet. *Child Development,* 1977, 48, 1228–1239.

————. The relationship of ordinal position to attachment behaviors on the Israeli Kibbutz. Paper presented at meeting of the Society for Cross-cultural Research, New Haven, Conn., 1978.

FREEDMAN, D. G. Genetic influences on development of behavior. In G. B. A. Stoelinga & J. J. Van der Werff Ten Bosch, *Normal and abnormal development of behavior.* Leiden: Leiden University Press, 1971.

————. *Human infancy: An evolutionary perspective.* Hillsdale, N. J.: Earlbaum, 1974.

FREEDMAN, D. G., & FREEDMAN, N. C. Behavioral differences between Chinese-American and European-American newborns. *Nature,* 1969, 224, 1227.

GADDINI, R. Transitional objects and the process of individuation: A study in three different social groups. *Journal of the American Academy of Child Psychiatry,* 1970, 9, 347–365.

GEBER, M. Développement psycho-moteur de l'enfant africain. *Courrier,* 1956, 6, 17–29.

————. L'enfant africain occidentalisé et de niveau social supérieur en Ouganda. *Courrier,* 1958, 8, 517–523. (a)

————. Tests de Gesell et de Terman-Merrill appliqués en Uganda. *Enfance,* 1958, 11, 63–67. (b)

————. The psycho-motor development of African children in the first year, and the influence of maternal behavior. *Journal of Social Psychology*, 1958, 47, 185–195. (c)

————. Problèmes posés par le développement du jeune enfant africain en fonction de son milieu social. *Le Travail Humain*, 1960, 23, 97–111.

————. Longitudinal study and psychomotor development among Baganda children. In *Proceedings of the Fourteenth International Congress of Applied Psychology* (Vol. 3). Copenhagen: Munksgaard, 1962.

————. L'environnement et le développement des enfants africains. *Enfance*, 1973, 3-4, 145–174.

————. La recherche sur le développement psychomoteur et mental à Kampala. *Compte-rendu de la XII Reunion des Equipes Chargées des Études sur la Croissance et de développement de l'enfant normal*. Paris: Centre International de l'Enfance,1974.

GEBER, M., & DEAN, R. F. A. The state of development of newborn African children. *Lancet*, 1957, 272(1), 1216–1219). (a)

————. Gesell tests on African children. *Pediatrics*, 1957, 20, 1055–1065. (b)

————. Psychomotor development in African children: The effects of social class and the need for improved tests. *Bulletin of the World Health Organization*, 1958, 18, 471–476.

————. Le développement psychomoteur et somatique des jeunes enfants africains en Ouganda. *Courrier*, 1964, 14, 425–437.

GEWIRTZ, J. L. The course of infant smiling in four child rearing environments in Israel. In B. M. Foss (Ed.), *Determinants of infant behavior* (Vol. 3). New York: Wiley, 1965.

GOLDBERG, S. Infant care and growth in urban Zambia. *Human Development*, 1972, 15, 77–89.

————. Infant development and mother-infant interaction in urban Zambia. In P. H. Leiderman, S. R. Tulkin, & A. Rosenfeld (Eds.), *Culture and infancy: Variations in the human experience*. New York: Academic Press, 1977.

GOLDSCHMIDT, W. Absent eyes and idle hands: Socialization for low affect among the Sebei. *Ethos*, 1975, 3, 157–163.

GRAHAM, F. K., MATARAZZO, R. G., & CALDWELL, B. M. Behavioral differences between normal and traumatized newborns: II: Standardization, reliability, and validity. *Psychological Monographs*, 1956, 70(21, Whole No. 428).

GRANTHAM-MCGREGOR, S. M., & HAWKE, W. A. Developmental assessment of Jamaican infants. *Developmental Medicine and Child Neurology*, 1971, 13, 582–589.

GREENBAUM, C. W., & LANDAU, R. Mothers' speech and the early development of vocal behavior: Findings from a cross-cultural observation study in Israel. In P. H. Leiderman, S. R. Tulkin, & A. Rosenfeld (Eds.), *Culture and infancy: Variations in the human experience*. New York: Academic Press, 1977.

GRIFFITHS, J. Development of reflexes in Bantu children. *Developmental Medicine and Child Neurology*, 1969, 11, 533–535.

HARKNESS, S. The cultural context of child development. In C. Super and S. Harkness (Eds.), Anthropological perspectives on child development. *New Directions for Child Development*, 1980, 8, 7–13.

HARKNESS, S., & SUPER, C. M. Why African children are so hard to test. In L. L.

Adler (Ed.), Issues in cross-cultural research, *Annals of the New York Academy of Sciences*, 1977, *285*, 326–331. Reprinted in L. L. Adler (Ed.), *Cross-cultural research at issue.* New York: Academic Press, in press.

HARLOW, H. & HARLOW, M. K. The affectional systems. In A. M. Schrier, H. Harlow, & F. Stollnitz (Eds.), *Behavior of non-human primates: Modern research trends* (Vol. 2). New York: Academic Press, 1965.

HARRIS, M. *The rise of anthropological theory: A history of theories of culture.* New York: Crowell, 1968.

HONG, K. M., & TOWNES, B. D. Infants' attachment to inanimate objects: A cross-cultural study. *Journal of the American Academy of Child Psychiatry*, 1976, *15*, 49–61.

HOPKINS, B. Culturally determined patterns of handling the human infant. *Journal of Human Movement Studies*, 1976, *2*, 1–27.

————. The early development of black and white infants living in Britain. Paper presented at the meeting of the International Association for Cross-cultural Psychology, Tilburg, 1978.

HOROWITZ, F. D., ASHTON, J., CULP, R., GADDIS, E., LEVIN, S., & REICHMANN, B. The effects of obstetrical medication on the behavior of Israeli newborn infants and some comparisons with Uruguayan and American infants. *Child Development*, 1977, *48*, 1607–1623.

HUNT, J. McV., PARASKEVOPOULOS, J., SCHICKENDANZ, D., & UŽGIRIS, I. C. Variations in the mean ages of achieving object permanence under diverse conditions of rearing. In B. Z. Friedlander, G. Sterritt, & G. E. Kirk (Eds.), *The exceptional infant II: Assessment and intervention.* New York: Brunner/Mazel, 1975.

IVANANS, T. Effect of maternal education and ethnic background on infant development. *Archives of Disease in Childhood*, 1975, *50*, 454–457.

JANES, M. D. Physical and psychological growth and development. *Journal of Tropical Pediatrics and Environmental Child Health*, 1975, *21*, 26–30.

KAGAN, J. The determinants of attention in the infant. *American Scientist*, 1970, *58*, 298–306.

————. *Change and continuity in infancy.* New York: Wiley, 1971.

————. Emergent themes in human development. *American Scientist*, 1976, *64*, 186–196.

KAGAN, J., KEARSLEY, R. B., & ZELAZO, P. R. *Infancy: Its place in human development.* Cambridge, Mass.: Harvard University Press, 1978.

KAGAN, J., & KLEIN, R. E. Cross-cultural perspectives on early development. *American Psychologist*, 1973, *28*, 947–961.

KAGAN, J., KLEIN, R. E., FINLEY, G., ROGOFF, B., & NOLAN, E. A cross-cultural study of cognitive development. *Monographs of the Society for Research in Child Development*, 1979, *42*, Serial No. 180.

KAGAN, J., & MOSS, H. A. *Birth to maturity: A study in psychological development.* New York: Wiley, 1962.

KANDOTH, W. K., SONNAD, L., & ATHAVALE, V. B. Milestones in lower socioeconomic group. *Indian Pediatrics*, 1971, *8*, 176–183.

KARDINER, A. Conclusions to the autobiographies. In C. Du Bois, *The people of Alor: A social-psychological study of an East Indian island.* Minneapolis: University of Minnesota Press, 1944.

KEEFER, C. H., DIXON, S., TRONICK, E., & BRAZELTON, T. B. A cross-cultural study of face to face interaction: Gusii infants and mothers. Paper presented at meeting of the Society for Research in Child Development, New Orleans, 1977.

————. Gusii infants' neuromotor behavior. Paper presented at the International Conference on Infant Studies, Providence, R. I., 1978.

KILBRIDE, J. E. Mother-infant interaction and infant sensorimotor development among the Baganda of Uganda. Unpublished doctoral dissertation, Bryn Mawr College, 1976.

KILBRIDE, J. E., & KILBRIDE, P. L. Sitting and smiling behavior of Baganda infants: The influence of culturally constituted experience. Journal of Cross-cultural Psychology, 1975, 6, 88–107.

KILBRIDE, J. E., ROBBINS, M. C., & KILBRIDE, P. L. The comparative motor development of Baganda, American white, and American black infants. American Anthropologist, 1970, 72, 1422–1428.

KILBRIDE, P. L., & KILBRIDE, J. E. Sociocultural factors and the early manifestation of sociability behavior among Baganda infants. Ethos, 1974, 2, 296–314.

KNOBLOCH, H., & PASAMANICK, B. The relationship of race and socioeconomic status to the developmental of motor behavior patterns in infancy. Psychiatric Research Reports, 1958, 10, 123–133.

KOGA, Y. MCC baby test. Tokyo: Dobunshoin, 1967.

KOHEN-RAZ, R. Scalogram analysis of some developmental sequences of infant behavior as measured by the Bayley Infant Scale of Mental Development. Genetic Psychology Monographs, 1967, 76, 3–21.

————. Mental and motor development of Kibbutz, institutionalized, and home-reared infants in Israel. Child Development, 1968, 39, 489–504.

KONNER, M. J. Aspects of the developmental ethology of a foraging people. In N. Blurton Jones (Ed.), Ethological studies of child behavior. Cambridge, England: Cambridge University Press, 1972.

————. Infants of a foraging people. Unpublished doctoral dissertation, Harvard University, 1973.

————. Maternal care, infant behavior and development among the !Kung. In R. B. Lee & I. DeVore (Eds.), Kalahari hunter-gatherers: Studies of the !Kung San and their neighbors. Cambridge, Mass.: Harvard University Press, 1976.

————. Infancy among the Kalahari Desert San. In P. H. Leiderman, S. R. Tulkin, & A. Rosenfeld (Eds.), Culture and infancy: Variations in the human experience. New York: Academic Press, 1977.

KOPP, C. B., KHOKA, E. W., & SIGMAN, M. A comparison of sensorimotor development among infants in India and the United States. Journal of Cross-cultural Psychology, 1977, 8, 435–452.

KUCHNER, J. A cross-cultural study of Chinese-American and European-American mothers and their infants. Paper presented at the International Conference on Infant Studies, Providence, R. I., 1978.

LAGERSPETZ, K., NYGARD, M., & STRANDVIK, C. The effects of training in crawling on the motor and mental development of infants. Scandanavian Journal of Psychology, 1971, 12, 192–197.

LAMBERT, W. W., TRIANDIS, L. M., & WOLF, M. Some correlates of beliefs in the malevolence and benevolence of supernatural beings: A cross-societal study. *Journal of Abnormal and Social Psychology,* 1959, *58,* 162–169.

LANDAU, R. Extent that the mother represents the social stimulation to which the infant is exposed: findings from a cross-cultural study. *Developmental Psychology,* 1976, *12,* 399–405.

———. Spontaneous and elicited smiles and vocalizations of infants in four Israeli environments. *Developmental Psychology,* 1977, *13,* 389–400.

LANDAUER, T. K., & WHITING, J. W. M. Infantile stimulation and adult stature of human males. *American Anthropologist,* 1964, *66,* 1007–1028.

LASKY, R. E., KLEIN, R. E., & MARTINEZ, S. Age and sex discriminations in five- and six-month-old infants. *Journal of Psychology,* 1974, *88,* 317–324.

LASKY, R. E., LECHTIG, A., DELGADO, H., KLEIN, R. E., ENGLE, P., YARBROUGH, C., & MARTORELL, R. Birth weight and psychomotor performance in rural Guatemala. *American Journal of Diseases of Children,* 1975, *129,* 566–569.

LEBOYER, F. *Loving hands: The traditional Indian art of baby massaging.* New York: Knopf, 1976.

LEIDERMAN, P. H., BABU, B., KAGIA, J., KRAEMER, H. C., & LEIDERMAN, G. F. African infant precocity and some social influences during the first year. *Nature,* 1973, *242,* 247–249.

LEIDERMAN, P. H., & LEIDERMAN, G. F. Affective and cognitive consequences of polymatric infant care in the East African Highlands. In A. D. Pick (Ed.), *Minnesota symposia on child psychology* (Vol. 8). Minneapolis: University of Minnesota Press, 1974. (a)

———. Familial influences on infant development in an East African agricultural community. In E. J. Anthony & C. Koupernik (Eds.), *The child and his family: Children at psychiatric risk* (Vol. 3). New York: Wiley, 1974. (b)

———. Economic change and infant care in an East African agricultural community. In P. H. Leiderman, S. R. Tulkin, & A. Rosenfeld (Eds.), *Culture and infancy: Variations in the human experience.* New York: Academic Press, 1977.

LESTER, B. M., & BRAZELTON, T. B. Cross-cultural assessment of neonatal behavior. In H. W. Stevenson & D. A. Wagner (Eds.), *Cultural perspectives on child development.* San Francisco: Freeman, in press.

LESTER, B. M., KOTELCHUCK, M., SPELKE, E., SELLERS, M. J., & KLEIN, R. E. Separation protest in Guatemalan infants: Cross-cultural and cognitive findings. *Developmental Psychology,* 1974, *10,* 79–85.

LEVINE, R. A. Culture, personality, and socialization: An evolutionary view. In D. A. Goslin (Ed.), *Handbook of socialization: Theory and research.* New York: Rand McNally, 1969.

———. Patterns of personality in Africa. *Ethos,* 1973, *1,* 123–152.

———. Comment on the note by Super and Harkness. *Ethos,* 1974, *2,* 382–386. (a)

———. Parental goals: A cross-cultural view. *Teachers College Record.* 1974, *76,* 226–239 (b)

———. Child rearing as cultural adaptation. In P. H. Leiderman, S. R. Tulkin, & A. Rosenfeld (Eds.), *Culture and infancy: Variations in the human experience.* New York: Academic Press, 1977.

————. Anthropology and child development. In C. M. Super & S. Harkness (Eds.). Anthropological perspectives on child development. *New Directions for Child Development*, 1980, *8*, 71–86.

LEWIS, M., & BAN, P. Variance and invariance in the mother-infant interaction: A cross-cultural study. In P. H. Leiderman, S. R. Tulkin, & A. Rosenfeld (Eds.), *Culture and infancy: Variations in the human experience.* New York: Academic Press, 1977.

LÉZINE, I., STAMBAK, M., & CASATI, I. *Les étapes de l'intelligence sensori-motrice.* Paris: Centre de Psychologie Applique, 1969.

LIDDICOAT, R. Development of Bantu Children. (Letter to the Editor). *Developmental Medicine and Child Neurology*, 1969, *11*, 821–822.

LIDDICOAT, R., & GRIESEL, R. D. A scale for the measurement of African urban infant development: Preliminary report. *Psychologia Africana*, 1971, *14*, 65–75.

LIDDICOAT, R., & KOZA, C. Language development in African infants. *Psychologia Africana*, 1963, *10*, 108–116.

LUSK, D., & LEWIS, M. Mother-infant interaction and infant development among the Wolof of Senegal. *Human Development*, 1972, *15*, 58–69.

MARVIN, R. S., VANDEVENDER, T. L., IWANAGA, M. I., LEVINE, S., & LEVINE, R. A. Infant-caregiver attachment among the Hausa of Nigeria. In H. McGurk (Ed.), *Ecological factors in human development.* Amsterdam: North-Holland, 1977.

MASON, W. A. Early social deprivation in the non-human primates: Implications for human behavior. In D. C. Glass (Ed.), *Environmental influences.* New York: Rockefeller University Press, 1968.

MASSÉ, G. *Croissance et développement de l'enfant à Dakar.* Paris: Centre International d'Enfance, 1969.

MEAD, M. *Growing up in New Guinea: A comparative study of primitive education.* New York: William Morrow, 1930.

MINTURN, L., & LAMBERT, W. W. *Mothers of six cultures: Antecedents of child rearing.* New York: Wiley, 1964.

MOREIGNE, F. Le développement psycho-moteur de l'enfant Wolof en milieu Dakarois de 6 mos à 6 ans. *Revue de Neuropsychiatrie Infantile et d'Hygiène Mentale de l'Enfance*, 1970, *18*, 765–783.

MOSS, H. A. Sex, age, and state as determinants of mother-infant interaction. *Merrill-Palmer Quarterly*, 1967, *13*, 19–36.

MUNDY- CASTLE, A. C., & OKONJI, M. O. Mother-infant interaction in Nigeria. Paper presented at the meeting of the International Association for Cross-cultural Psychology, Tilburg, 1978.

MUNROE, R. H., & MUNROE, R. L. Household density and infant care in an East African society. *Journal of Social Psychology*, 1971, *83*, 3–13.

MUNROE, R. L., MUNROE, R. H., & WHITING, J. W. M. The couvade: A psychological analysis. *Ethos*, 1973, *1*, 30–74.

NAIDR, J. Psychomotorický vývoj africkýchv děti. *Ceskoslovenska Pediatrie*, 1975, *30*, 173–176.

PALTI, H., GITLIN, M., & ZLOTO, R. Psychomotor development of two-year-old children in Jerusalem. *Journal of Cross-cultural Psychology*, 1977, *8*, 453–464.

PATEL, N. V., & KAUL, K. K. Behavioral development of Indian rural and urban infants in comparison to American infants. *Indian Pediatrics*, 1971, *8*, 443–451.

PHATAK, P. Motor and mental development of Indian babies from 1 month to 30 months. *Indian Pediatrics,* 1969, *6,* 18–23.

———. *Mental and motor growth of Indian babies (1–30 months).* Final Report, Department of Child Development, M. S. University of Baroda, Baroda, India, 1970. (a)

———. Motor growth patterns of Indian babies. *Indian Pediatrics,* 1970, *7,* 619–624. (b)

POOLE, H. E. The effect of Westernization on the psychomotor development of African (Yoruba) infants during the first year of life. *Journal of Tropical Pediatrics,* 1969, *15,* 172–176.

PRESCOTT, J. W. Abortion or the unwanted child: A choice for a humanistic society. *The Humanist,* 1975, *35*(2), 11–15.

RABIN, A. I. Behavior research in collective settlements in Israel: 6 infants and children under conditions of "intermittant" mothering in the kibbutz. *American Journal of Orthopsychiatry,* 1958, *28,* 577–584.

RAMARASAONA, Z. *Psychomotor development in early childhood in the Tananarive region.* Report of the CSM Meeting of Specialists on the basic psychological structures of African and Madagascan Populations. London: CCTA/CSA Publication No. 51, 1959.

REBELSKY, F. First discussant's comments: Cross-cultural studies of mother-infant interaction: Description and consequence. *Human Development,* 1972, *15,* 128–130.

———. Infancy in two cultures. In F. G. Rebelsky & L. Dormon (Eds.), *Child development and behavior* (2nd ed.). New York: Alfred A. Knopf, 1973. (Reprinted from *Nederlands Tijdschrift voor de Psychologie,* 1967, *22,* 379–385.)

ROSENBLITH, J. F. Newborn characteristics of infants who became victims of the Sudden Infant Death Syndrome (SIDS). *JSAS Catalog of Selected Documents in Psychology,* 1978, *8,* 60. (Ms. No. 1716)

ROSENBLITH, J. & ANDERSON-HUNTINGTON, R. B. Defensive reactions to stimulation of the nasal and oral regions in newborns: relations to state. In J. F. Bosma & J. Showacre (Eds.), *Development of upper respiratory anatomy and function: Implications for sudden infant syndrome.* Bethesda, Md.: Department of Health, Education, and Welfare Publication VIH 76-941, 1975.

SCARR-SALAPATEK, S. An evolutionary perspective on infant intelligence: Species patterns and individual variations. In M. Lewis (Ed.), *Origins of intelligence.* New York: Plenum, 1976.

SELLERS, M. J., KLEIN, R., KAGAN, J., & MINTON, C. Developmental determinants of attention: A cross-cultural replication. *Developmental Psychology,* 1972, *6,* 185.

SMILANSKY, E., SHEPHATIA, L., & FRENKEL, E. *Mental development of infants from two ethnic groups* (Research Report No. 195). Jerusalem: Henrietta Szold Institute, 1976.

SOLOMONS, G., & SOLOMONS, H. C. Motor development in Yucatecan infants. *Developmental Medicine and Child Neurology,* 1975, *17,* 41–46.

SPIRO, M. E. Ghosts: An anthropological inquiry into learning and perception. *Journal of Abnormal and Social Psychology,* 1953, *48,* 376–382.

SPIRO, M. E., & D'ANDRADE, R. G. A cross-cultural study of some supernatural beliefs. *American Anthropologist,* 1958, *60,* 456–466.

SSENGOBA, C. M. E. B. *The effects of nutritional status on the psychomotor development of rural Kenyan infants.* Unpublished doctoral dissertation, University of Michigan, 1978.

SUPER, C.M. Patterns of infant care and motor development in Kenya. *Kenya Education Review,* 1973, *1,* 64–69.

————. Environmental effects on motor development: The case of African infant precocity. *Developmental Medicine and Child Neurology,* 1976, *18,* 561–567.

————. Behavioral development in infancy. In R. L. Munroe, R. H. Munroe, & B. B. Whiting (Eds.), *Handbook of cross-cultural human development.* New York: Garland Press, 1980.

SUPER, C. M., & HARKNESS, S. Patterns of personality in Africa: A note from the field. *Ethos,* 1974, *2,* 377–381.

————. The development of affect in infancy and early childhood. In H. Stevenson & D. Wagner (Eds.), *Cultural perspectives on child development.* San Francisco: Freeman, in press. (a)

————. The infant's niche in rural Kenya and metropolitan America. In L. L. Adler (Ed.), *Cross-cultural research at issue.* New York: Academic Press, in press. (b)

TAKAHASHI, K., & HATANO, G. Mother-child interaction and cognitive development. Paper presented at the meeting of the Japanese Psychological Association, Nagoya, 1976.

TAKAHASHI, M. The cross-sectional study of infants' smiling, attention, reaching, and crying responses to the facial models. *Japanese Journal of Psychology,* 1973, *44,* 124–134.

————. The longitudinal study of infants' smiling responses in relation to neonatal spontaneous smiles. *Japanese Journal of Psychology,* 1974, *45,* 256–267.

THEUNISSEN, K. B. *A preliminary comparative study of the development of motor behavior in European and Bantu children up to the age of one year.* Unpublished master's dissertation, Natal University College, 1948.

UKLONSKAYA, R., PURI, B., CHOUDHURI, N., DANG, L.; & KUMARI, R. Development of static and psychomotor functions of infant in the first year of life in New Delhi. *Indian Journal of Child Health,* 1960, *9,* 596–601.

VALANTIN, S. *Le développement de la fonction manipulatoire chez l'enfant senegalais au cours des deux premières années de la vie.* Unpublished doctoral thesis, Université de Paris, 1970.

VARKEVISSER, C. M. *Socialization in a changing society: Sukuma childhood in rural and urban Mwanza, Tanzania.* Den Haag: Center for the Study of Education in Changing Societies, 1973.

VINCENT, M., & HUGON, J. L'insuffisance ponderale du premature africain au point de vue de la santé publique. *Bulletin of the World Health Organization,* 1962, *26,* 143–174.

VOUILLOUX, P. D. Étude de la psychomotoricité d'enfants africains au Cameroun: Test de Gesell et réflexes archaïques. *Journal de la Société des Africainists,* 1959, *29,* 11–18. (a)

————. Test moteurs et réflexe plantaire chez de jeunes enfants camerounais. *Presse Médicale,* 1959, *67,* 1420–1421. (b)

WALTERS, C. E. Comparative development of Negro and white infants. *Journal of Genetic Psychology,* 1967, *110,* 243–251.

WARREN, N. African infant precocity. *Psychological Bulletin,* 1972, *78,* 353–367.

WARREN, N., & PARKIN, J. M. A neurological and behavioral comparison of African and European newborns in Uganda. *Child Development,* 1974, *45,* 966–971.

WEISNER, T. S., & GALLIMORE, R. My brother's keeper: Child and sibling caretaking. *Current Anthropology,* 1977, *18,* (2) 169–190.

WERNER, E. E., BIERMAN, J. M., & FRENCH, F. E. *The children of Kauai: A longitudinal study from the prenatal period to age ten.* Honolulu: University Press of Hawaii, 1971.

WERNER, E. E., SIMONIAN, K., & SMITH, R. S. Ethnic and socioeconomic status differences in abilities and achievement among preschool and school-age children in Hawaii. *Journal of Social Psychology,* 1968, *75,* 43–59.

WHITING, J. W. M. Socialization process and personality. In F. L. K. Hsu (Ed.), *Psychological anthropology.* Homewood, Ill.: Dorsey Press, 1961.

———. Causes and consequences of mother-infant contact. Paper presented at meeting of the American Anthropological Association, New York, 1971

———. A model for psychocultural research. In P. H. Leiderman, S. R. Tulkin, & A. Rosenfeld (Eds.), *Culture and infancy: Variations in the human experience.* New York: Academic Press, 1977.

WHITING, J. W. M., CHASDI, E. H., ANTONOVSKY, H. F., & AYRES, B. C. The learning of values. In E. Z. Vogt & E. M. Albert (Eds.), *People of Rimrock: A study of values in five cultures.* Cambridge, Mass.: Harvard University Press, 1966.

WHITING, J. W. M., & CHILD, I. L. *Child training and personality.* New Haven, Conn.: Yale University Press, 1953.

WOLFF, P. H. Observations on the early development of smiling. In B. Foss (Ed.), *Determinants of infant behavior* (Vol. 2). New York: Wiley, 1963.

———. Biological variations and cultural diversity: An exploratory study. In P. H. Leiderman, S. R. Tulkin, & A. Rosenfeld (Eds.), *Culture and infancy: Variations in the human experience.* New York: Academic Press, 1977.

WUG DE LEON, E., DE LICARDIE, E., & CRAVIOTO, J. Operación Nimiquipalq VI: Desarrollo psicomotor del niño en una población rural de Guatemala. *Guatemala Pediatrica,* 1964, *4,* 92–106.

YAMADA, Y. Effects of stimulus novelty on visual and manipulative exploration in infancy. *Japanese Journal of Educational Psychology,* 1978, *1,* 41–51.

ZELAZO, P. R., ZELAZO, N. A., & KOLB, S. "Walking" in the newborn. *Science* 1972, *176,* 314–315.

ZERN, D. The influence of certain child-rearing factors upon the development of a structured and salient sense of time. *Genetic Psychology Monographs,* 1970, *81,* 197- 254.

———. The relationship between mother-infant contact and later differentiation of the social environment. *Journal of Genetic Psychology,* 1972, *121,* 107–117.

# 3

# Issues in the Cross-Cultural Study of Bilingual Development

*Norman S. Segalowitz*

## Contents

## Abstract

This chapter begins with a discussion of the major factors that investigators have suggested may be sources of variability in second language learning success. The factors discussed include: linguistic differences between the languages learned, language learning aptitude, the learner's attitude towards language learning, personality variables, and the social context in which the bilingual development takes place. These factors are considered as potential sources of cross-culture variation in second language learning success. Following this discussion is an outline of some approaches to language acquisition and their relevance to bilingual development. The final section of the chapter considers the social and psychological implications of bilingualism for the individual, with specific reference to the cognitive organization of the languages an individual knows (the consequences of knowing more than one language for general cognitive functioning as indicated by, say, measures of intelligence or creativity), and for the social adjustment of the bilingual individual. Possible sources of variation across cultures in the extent and nature of the impact of bilingualism on the individual are discussed.

## Introduction

The cross-cultural psychologist can look at bilingualism from two perspectives. The first concerns the nature of bilingual development from the point of view of the bilingual individual. By virtue of knowing two languages, bilinguals locate themselves at the interface between cultures in contact. This situation gives rise to a number of interesting questions. How do the two native language communities act toward bilinguals in their midst? Are bilinguals accepted as full-fledged members of one or both communities? How do the reactions of the native language communities affect the bilingual's social and cognitive development? Does bilingualism confer on the individual the special role of acting as a mediator or communication link between the two linguistic communities? How do bilinguals feel with respect to ethnolinguistic identity? Are they alienated from one or both language groups or do they feel enriched by dual membership? Does bilingualism lead to the internalization of the cultural values of both ethnolinguistic communities whose languages are spoken? If so, does this present any special problem for the bilingual?

From a more cognitive point of view, one can also raise questions about the nature of language development, the representation of multiple languages in the brain, and the impact of bilingualism on cognitive functioning. Does multiple language acquisition proceed in the same manner as single language acquisition? How do different language acquisition environments affect this development? Does bilingual development affect intellectual skills positively by providing the individual with an enriched linguistic capacity or does it have a negative effect by providing cross language interference? Do bilinguals perceive the world differently from monolinguals because of the additional linguistic-semantic system at their disposal? Does bilingualism facilitate the mastery of other languages?

The second perspective concerns the nature of cross-cultural variation in bilingual development. This involves an examination of bilingualism as it manifests itself in different bilingual settings. For example, is bilingual development in an industralized society different from that of other societies? Do societies differ in the way they value bilingual skills among their members? Do societies differ in the degree to which bilingual skills are achieved by their members, and if so, what sociocultural factors are responsible for such differences?

The present review examines bilingual development primarily from the point of view of the social and cognitive factors regarding the bilingual individual, drawing mostly from "single-setting" studies. Unfortunately, there has been little research work to date allowing for direct comparison of bilingual development data across different societies. Although data from a wide variety of social and linguistic settings do exist, it is often difficult to make direct comparisons between settings because so many factors are confounded. Consequently, little can really be said at this time about the reasons for cross-cultural variation in bilingual development other than to identify relevant factors in a very general way. It is hoped, however, that by identifying the salient social and cognitive issues in bilingualism research, this review will facilitate the translation of "single setting" research into comparative studies across communities that possess widely differing sociocultural characteristics. Such studies will make a central contribution to our understanding of bilingual development because, as we shall see, social and cultural variables are known to be important determinants of the rate and extent of second language development.

A word about the term *bilingual* is in order at this point. In common usage, the term *bilingual* usually refers to a person able to use two or more languages, and the term often implies equal ability in all the languages spoken. Such perfectly balanced linguistic skills are rare, however, for a very basic reason. Social settings that promote the learning of two languages generally do so because each language serves a different communicative function. In such cases, second language users will, naturally, acquire somewhat different skills in each language. One language may be used extensively for one set of purposes (e.g., communication at home, or at work, or with a particular social group) while the other language may be used for other purposes. Each communicative function places different linguistic demands on the speaker (such as vocabulary and speech style) and so, as a rule, mastery of the languages will not be absolutely balanced. Thus, speakers may sound nativelike in each of their languages when they use them in their usual contexts, but careful testing will often reveal significant asymmetries in the language skills (e.g., d'Anglejan & Tucker, 1973).

The ordinary definition of *bilingual* is unsatisfactory for the further reason that it excludes the great number of speakers who may be limited in their second language skills (they must speak slowly; they have an accent; they are limited to a few topics) but for whom the second language is an important medium of communication. Indeed, it is probable that such bilinguals actually constitute the majority of the world's second language users. For purposes of this paper, then, the term *bilingual* will refer to anyone who is able to use and frequently does use at least two languages for communication, regardless of that person's fluency.

Note, however, that by considering nonfluent speakers as bilingual, the number of different levels and types of bilingualism that one can imagine becomes very large indeed. A bilingual's skill may range from the rudimentary to the very fluent. The bilinqual's skill may vary in different facets of the language (syntax, vocabulary, phonology) and in different social settings where the language is used. Measuring a speaker's level of knowledge of a second language can thus become a very complex matter, especially if one is interested in a full appreciation of the strengths and limitations of the speaker's skill. See Fishman and Cooper (1971), Kelley (1969) and the references cited there for a fuller discussion of the issues involved in measuring second language proficiency. Jakobovits (1970) also presents detailed discussions of theory and practice regarding second language assessment.

A description of individuals' skills with a second language provides only part of what is needed to characterize bilingualism in a given group. For a fuller account, it is also necessary to consider the uses and functions of the languages in the speech community under consideration. Elucidating the relationship between the functions of language in the speech community and observed speech patterns is now considered to be one of the primary tasks of linguistic analysis (see Hymes, 1972; Labov, 1969, 1970, 1971). Most theoretical work in this area has focused on monolingual communities, and contributions have come not only from linguists, but also from anthropologists and sociologists. For example, among linguists Labov (1971) and Cedergren (Cedergren & Sankoff, 1974) have been concerned with the elaboration of linguistic tools (viz., the use of variable rules) that permit one to relate linguistic descriptions to the social contexts in which the speech under analysis has occurred. Sociologists and anthropologists have written extensively about the social functions of language (e.g., functions other than the communication of factual information) and about the social forces that act on speech communities and the way their impact is reflected in individuals' speech patterns (e.g., Fishman, 1971; Giles, 1977; Giles & Powesland, 1975: Giles & St. Clair, 1979; Gumperz, 1968; Gumperz & Hymes, 1972, appendix for additional bibliography; Hymes, 1962, 1971, 1972). Similar approaches have been taken regarding bilingual communities (see, for example, Blom & Gumperz, 1972; Fishman, 1968, 1972; Gumperz, 1964; Haugen, 1956, 1970, 1972; Nida & Wonderly, 1971; Rubin, 1962). For specific case studies from Africa, Asia, and Latin America, see Ladmiral (1973), Parkin (1977), Rice (1962), and Whiteley (1971). These sociolinguistic considerations are of the utmost importance for the psychological study of bilingualism since they touch on the social factors directly relevant to an understanding of attitudes, beliefs, and motivations relevant to language development.

This paper is divided into three main sections. The first section deals with five major factors that have been closely studied in research on bilingualism and that may be important to an understanding of cross-cultural variation in bilingual development: linguistic, aptitude, attitude, personality, and social factors. The second section deals briefly with theories of language development that are relevant to bilingualism. The third section deals with the social and cognitive impact of bilingualism on the individual with reference to possible sources of cross-cultural variation.

Two major topics that are not discussed further in this review deserve mention: bilingual education and language planning. These fields represent the applied aspects work on bilingual development. All of the issues discussed here are relevant to the problems language planners and educators face, but the relative importance of these factors in any given situation will depend largely on local linguistic, social, political, and psychological considerations. Recent reviews concerning developments in bilingual education and second language instruction, methodology, and theory can be found in Burt and Dulay (1975) and Ritchie (1978). The volume by Spolsky and Cooper (1977a) contains theoretical perspectives on bilingual education and Spolsky and Cooper (1977b) presents case studies of bilingual education programs in over twenty countries. Rubin and Jernudd (1971) and Fishman, Ferguson and DasGupta (1968) contain important papers and further references on language planning.

## Factors in Bilingual Development

*Linguistic Factors*

A large body of linguistic literature on bilingual development is concerned with predicting the features of any given second language that should be difficult to master due to interference from the features of the learner's first language (e.g., see Ferguson, 1959; Lado, 1957; Nickel, 1971). The magnitude of such interference (which, naturally, is absent in monolingualism) may vary from one linguistic setting to another. For instance, the mastery of English as a second language where Chinese is the first language may take a different course from the acquisition of English by French speakers because of the different extent to which features of the mother tongue will interfere or facilitate mastery of English.

Recently, however, some writers have suggested that not all features of bilingual development are attributable to interference effects (see Richards, 1971a and b; Sampson & Richards, 1973; Wardaugh, 1970, for surveys of some of the literature and issues in this area). The view is emerging that the second language learner may have certain cognitive propensities that shape the course of bilingual development quite apart from those habits and processes that can be directly attributed to influences of the particular languages involved (Anderson, 1978; Corder, 1971; Nemser, 1971; Selinker, 1971). Cross-cultural research that provides detailed linguistic descriptions of the patterns of development in a variety of bilingual settings may thus help us distinguish language-specific from language-independent cognitive influences.

One proposal about how cross-cultural research might be conducted in this vein is suggested by Slobin (1973). He indicates how it may be possible by studying bilingual children in order to discover some of the cognitive and perceptual strategies that guide language development in general (whether monolingual or bilingual). For example, he reports a study in which Hungarian Serbocroatian bilingual children demonstrated mastery of locative constructions (into, at, out of) earlier in Hungarian than in Serbocroatian. This finding was interpreted as indicating that the syntactic device used for locatives in Hungarian—the use of different noun suffixes—is easier to learn than that used in Serbocroatian—prepositions coordinated with noun suffixes. From these and other data, Slobin concludes that children have a perceptual strategy that leads them to focus on the ends of words for important grammatical information earlier than on other parts of words. This use of bilingual learners enables the researcher to control variation due to environmental and individual differences that would be introduced from comparisons of monolingual children learning one or the other language, but not both.

McLaughlin (1978) provides a major review of the case studies of bilingual children, including both those who acquired their two languages simultaneously and those who acquired them successively. This literature is relatively small given the diversity of the world's languages, and it involves relatively few cases of bilingualism with non-Indoeuropean languages. McLaughlin's review makes clear that the evidence to date suggests that bilingual and monolingual language acquisition follow the same basic developmental pattern. Even though the overall pattern of development may be similar, however, certain structures may be acquired in one language before the analogous structure is acquired in the other because of differences in their syntactic complexity. Also, the acquisition of certain structures in one language by a bilingual child may lag behind its acquisition by a monolingual child. There may also be, of course, interference between languages in which a structure from one language "appears" in the other. The amount and kind of interference can vary greatly, however, depending on the degree to which the two languages are well differentiated in the environment (e.g., one language at home, the other at school) and the extent to which the languages are balanced (whether the child experiences them with equal frequency). It should be clear that comparisons of language development in bilingual children judiciously selected from a wide variety of language settings can yield valuable information about the processes underlying both single and multiple language development.

This topic is discussed further in the section on theories of bilingual development.

## Aptitude

Most societies have folklore about the language learning abilities of other national groups. English-speaking peoples have a notorious reputation for being unable to master foreign languages, while it is believed that many continental Europeans have no difficulty whatsoever. Such beliefs reflect a view that language learning aptitude is an important determinant of success in bilingual development and that variations exist in the way this aptitude is realized in different cultural settings.

Language learning aptitude has been defined in terms of abilities to manipulate symbols, sound discriminations, memory for speech sequences, and so on. The study of such skills had received considerable attention in North American research (Carroll, 1963b; Jakobovits, 1970). The findings generally indicate that, even though such an aptitude factor can be reasonably identified, it still does not account for a great part of the variation in language learning success. This is important to note because it implies that differences across communities in the incidence and level of bilingual development may depend on factors other than inherent abilities favoring multilingualism. This does not appear to be the case with first language learning where high levels of mastery are nearly universal despite diversity in human cultures.

Gardner (1979) reviews literature indicating that in some communities the predictive value of aptitude and intelligence measures for second language achievement is greater than it is in other communities. He find that the relation between individual difference factors and achievement is greater in monolingual communities and weakest in those settings where bilingualism exists to a great degree. This suggests that social factors (community expectations and support) are probably the really significant ones leading to differences between communities in second language learning success and that cross-cultural differences in so-called aptitude (if such differences exist) are less important.

Related to the issue of aptitude is the topic of age and its effect on second language learning. Many authors have argued that language learning is easier before the age of twelve or so when cerebral lateralization is not yet supposed to be complete (Lenneberg, 1967; Penfield & Roberts, 1959; Scovel, 1969; Seliger, 1978; but see Krashen, 1973, for a dissenting view). If this is correct, an important source of cross-cultural variation may be the age at which individuals are exposed to effective second language learning situations. The difficulty with this approach, however, is that age may be correlated with other factors that may more directly determine the pattern of language development (Asher & Price, 1967; Hill, 1970; Macnamara, 1973; McLaughlin, 1978). For example, older people may have less time to spend on language learning and they may typically be exposed to inefficient or inappropriate methods of learning (certain types of classroom regimes may be less efficient than the street learning to which children are often exposed). In many Western industrial societies, these factors are greatly confounded. It would be useful to know if age appears to be a determinant of bilingual development in all societies; Hill (1970) suggests not, and the weight of evidence concerning social factors that are clearly confounded with age also supports the view that age per se may have little to do with second language learning success.

*Attitudes*

Studies conducted three or four decades ago suggested that attitudinal factors may be as important or more important than aptitude in determining children's language learning success (Jordan, 1941; Pritchard, 1935). For example, Jones (1949, 1950, 1959) found that among children learning Welsh as a second language, attitudes towards learning a second language were more closely related to language learning success than was intelligence. Their results, together with observations of individual bilinguals, such as those reported by Lambert (1967), Nida (1956) and Whyte and Holmberg (1956), encouraged researchers to undertake more systematic investigations of the relationship between attitudes and motivation in second language learning.

One of the more important and influential series of studies in this area is the work of Lambert and Gardner and their co-workers. Their factor analytic studies revealed some interesting patterns in the relative contribution of language learning aptitude and verbal intelligence, motivation for studying a second language, attitudes toward speakers of the second language, and other factors (e.g., Gardner & Lambert, 1965, 1972). They found that aptitude and attitude are relatively independent determinants of level of language attainment. Moreover, in their studies they identified two principal types of language learning motivation that were strongly related to learning success. One they called "instrumental motivation" in reference to the learner's desire to learn the language for its usefulness (e.g., in obtaining employment; dealing with clients, customers, shopkeepers; travel). The other they called "integrative motivation" because of the learner's desire to be liked by members of the other language group. They found that integratively motivated learners have a somewhat higher degree of second language attainment, demonstrating that type of motivation as well as strength of motivation is a relevant factor in language learning success. This type of research has revealed similar results in a number of different settings with learners of various language back-grounds including English-speaking Canadians learning French, English-speaking Jews learning Hebrew, Franco-Americans learning French, and Filipinos learning English (Anisfeld & Lambert, 1961: Gardner & Lambert, 1972; Randhawa & Korpan, 1973).

In some cultures, the integrative motivation may be relatively stronger or easier to generate among learners either because of the close proximity of the other language group or because of the desire of learning to emigrate to the country of that group. In some cultures, it is also possible that instrumental functions are more important because there are relatively few native speakers around or because, despite the need to interact with speakers of the other group language, there is social hostility between the two groups. Such differences between communities, in the extent to which either of these types of motivations are important, can be responsible for different patterns of bilingual development. There may be differences between groups in the level of bilingualism attained and the number of bilinguals in the community. Such motivational factors may also necessitate the selection of different teaching strategies or the selection of particular language learning goals in accordance with the motivations of the learners (Gardner & Lambert, 1972). For example, in developing countries the learning of a European language may serve primarily instrumental goals whereas in Europe or North America integrative goals may be particularly relevant.

Gardner (1979) has elaborated a model that considers the interactions of attitudes, motivations, and second language learning achievement in the social milieu. His hypothesis was that attitudes affect language acquisition success "because they serve as motivational support rather than as direct determinants of achievement" (Gardner, 1979, p. 218). In support of this, he presents evidence from a study of English-speaking Canadians learning French in which learners' attitudes (as indexed by interest in the language and culture and by ethnocentrism) ceased to correlate with achievement when the effect of motivation (indexed by effort expended to learn) was statistically removed. Motivation, however, did correlate with achievement even with the contribution of attitudes statistically removed. Furthermore, expected differences between monolingual and bilingual settings were also found.

Such results have interesting implications for cross-cultural research if one considers a finer classification of environments beyond Gardner's admittedly crude monolingual versus bilingual types. For example, one can distinguish between what Lambert (1975, 1977) has referred to as "additive" and "subtractive" bilingualism. In the additive situation, acquisition of a second language is viewed by the learner as a source of enrichment (e.g., it provides access to another culture), whereas in the subtractive situation it is viewed negatively (e.g., it threatens the learner with cultural alienation). One would expect the interplay of attitudes and motivations to be different in these situations, and support for this idea is cited by Gardner from studies by Clément, Gardner, and Smythe (1977a and b).

Of particular value to cross-cultural work in this area would be a typology or classification system that enabled researchers to compare environments in terms of the relative strengths of ethnolinguistic variables such as status of the language groups, number and kind of social institutions that support each group, and so on. Giles, Bourhis, and Taylor (1977) have proposed such a schema that may prove valuable for studies comparing second language acquisition achievement in different communities as a function of attitudinal and motivational variables. Their typology would enable one to more precisely define the relevant point of similarity and difference that characterize the communities under study.

*Personality*

Related to the work on the role of attitudes in second language learning is speculation on the relationship between personality and bilingual devel-opment. For example, Gardner and Lambert (1959) and Lambert, Hodgson, Gardner, and Fillenbaum (1960) found that individuals who are successful in bilingual development have weaker tendencies towards authoritarianism than those with lower degrees of success. Gardner and Lambert (1972) and Gardner and Smythe (1975) mention other possible determinants of second language learning success; they suggest that factors such as Machiavellianism and need achievement may be relevant, although to date there is little empirical work relating these factors to bilingualism (see e.g., Frasure-Smith, Lambert, & Taylor, 1975). The fact that such factors are known to be subject to considerable variation from one society to another (e.g., McClelland, 1961, on need achievement) suggests that cross-cultural research will aid in the assessment of the importance of these factors.

There has been some attempt to relate theories of ego development to bilingualism, but the literature here is small and highly speculative. Guiora and his colleagues (Guiora, 1967; Guiora, Brannon, & Dull, 1972; Guiora, Lane, & Bosworth, 1968; Taylor, Catford, Guiora, & Lane, 1971) view language as a symbolic system that is involved in ego formation, the process of representing the self. In their view, language is important because its symbolism provides a means for integrating the various representations of self. Pronounciation is considered particularly important because it defines the boundaries of the language ego; you identify yourself by the way you speak, and to speak like someone else implies some distortion or flexibility in the language ego. Since early ego development is marked by a great deal of flexibility, young children more easily acquire nativelike pronunciation in a foreign language than adults do. In more advanced stages of ego development, flexibility is diminished and so the older child or adult is more likely to speak a second language with an accent. Individuals who are relatively more flexible in extending their ego boundaries—those who are highly empathic—should be better able to master pronunciation in a foreign language than those who have more rigid ego boundaries. Some of the studies reported by Guiora and his colleagues lend support to these hypotheses. However, apart from the papers produced by these researchers and several psychoanalytically oriented papers (see Wolff, 1967, and references in Diebold, 1968; Haugen, 1956; and Marcos, Eisma, & Guimon, 1977), there is very little systematic work on the relation between ego development factors and bilingual language acquisition.

Although these references to the place of personality in language development come from disparate sources, a common thread runs through them. They all involve factors dealing with how individuals view themselves and the types of interactions they seek with others. They may be sensitive to others' feelings (empathic), may desire to use them or manipulate them (instrumental motivation, Machiavellianism), or may wish to be liked by them or become one of them (integrative motivation). All of these points of view suggest that bilingual development may be strongly affected by factors of sensitivity to others and the need for affiliation, especially with others who speak the second language (Findling, 1969). Research on this topic will, however, have to consider sociolinguistic factors that determine the opportunities available to an individual in a given society to fulfill his or her affiliative needs through second language speech. The next section deals with this topic.

*Social Factors*

Recent theoretical literature dealing with the factors that promote and hinder bilingual development and that are responsible for the difference between child and adult bilingualism have drawn attention to the learning *situation* and its contribution to the process of second language acquisition. For example, Macnamara (1973) has emphasized the importance of the cognitive requirements of the situation: the need to convey some specific information at some particular moment. In the classroom, second language speech use is highly ritualized in the sense that the speech is not really uttered for communicative purposes but rather to satisfy some rules of classroom behavior agreed on by teacher and student. According to Macnamara's approach, since classroom speech does not always fulfill genuine psychological needs, the learning is much less effective than it might otherwise be. Learning a second language in the street, on the other hand, is characterized by a very real desire to fulfill clearly defined cognitive needs, such as those involved in explaining the rules of a game, obtaining some object from someone, or imparting or receiving information (see also Tucker & d'Anglejan, 1970).

This view—that language learning is facilitated by an environment in which the messages to be communicated are psychologically important to the speaker—converges with some sociolinguistic views of what it takes to be competent to communicate. Hymes (1971), for example, points out that normally one needs to learn not only what to say and how to say it (this involves knowing the vocabulary, syntax, and phonology of the language), but also what the appropriate form of speech is for the situation. Such knowledge is referred to as *sociolinguistic communicative competence.* In different situations, different ways of speaking are appropriate. For example, sometimes one must use polite forms of speech that include both certain lexical items and certin pronunciation patterns for all words. In other situations, it is appropriate to use only one language and not another, while the reverse can be true for the same individuals in some other context. Yet in still others it may be appropriate to use a mixture of the languages—either by alternating between languages or using constructions in one language that borrow heavily from the other (as in Filipino Tagalog–English "mix-mix"; see also Cooper & Greenfield, 1969; Fishman, 1968; Gumperz & Hernandez, 1971; Haugen, 1977).

Several points can be made about this factor of appropriateness and its relation to language learning. First, it is certainly true that even first language development is heavily influenced by sociolinguistic considerations. Every learner has to learn what to watch for in the situation that determines the appropriate way to speak. These factors include, among other things, the topic of discussion, the type of speech used by the interlocutor, the social status of the interlocutor, and the physical setting (Fishman, 1972; Gumperz, 1972). Most such learning is unconscious; that is to say, speakers in a given culture are usually not very aware of the ways they modulate their speech according to the way features of the situation are arranged. One implication for second language learning is that the situations in which bilinguals have to use their second language often are quite restricted compared to those encountered with the first language. For example, some bilinguals might only use their second language when speaking to superiors, with classmates, or with workmates. Each of these situations carries with it certain sociolinguistic demands to speak in a particular way. The learner may master the speech registers appropriate for these situations but be unable to fulfill the sociolinguistic requirements in less familiar contexts. A typical example is that of the bilingual English speaker in North America who has learned French or Spanish at school and rarely uses it outside the classroom. When the situation requires a register of speech that is less formal than the classroom register, the bilingual may find himself in difficulty because he is unable to fulfill the sociolinguistic requirements of the situation, even though he has the vocabulary and syntax skills for conveying the appropriate conversational information. This possibility raises the interesting question about how the bilingual will react when he finds he cannot speak appropriately in the sociolinguistic sense. One study of this type of situation suggests that the bilingual's perception of the interlocutor is altered in a way that may lead the bilingual to avoid such situations again (Segalowitz, 1976, 1977a). This phenomenon may be expected to vary across different communities since different societies will present their bilingual speakers with different types of situations with which to cope.

A second aspect of the sociolinguistic nature of bilingual development concerns the variety of second language learning environments available and the impact that these different types of environments have on learning success. In many industrialized societies, the typical pattern is early monolingualism followed by formal language instruction in adolescence or adulthood (Tucker, 1974, describes some of the variations in methods of second language exposure at school; see also Burt & Dulay, 1975). In addition, some individuals may be born of linguistically mixed parentage or be immigrants to a new linguistic region and thus become bilingual. But there are other patterns of exposure and reasons for multilingual skills that are quite different from those encountered in industrialized countries.

For example, Sorensen (1967) writes about a South American Indian group living in the northwest Amazon basin. The area contains speakers of a great many mutually unintelligible languages. Each local tribe, identified by the language spoken, is exogamous and so consequently marriages involve speakers of two different languages. Each community will thus have several languages spoken: the language of the males (residence is patrilocal) and the languages of the wives. The children are exposed to many different languages and it appears that the norm in that society is for everyone to be multilingual, not bilingual. Children learn the language of their father, that of their mother, and the languages spoken by the wives taken by other males in the tribe. Mothers will sometimes teach the children their language by rather formal devices (such as list learning), and when a male wants to marry a girl whose language he does not know, he learns the language first from the mother-in-law to be.

Salisbury (1962) reports about groups in New Guinea where bilingualism is common and a source of great prestige. In many public gatherings, speeches are translated into the various local languages even though this is not always done strictly to facilitate the audience's comprehension. The use of translation marks the occasion as formal and important and thereby increases the status of the main speaker. Bilingual skills also are useful in a variety of social situations among these people, such as in engaging in competitive one-upmanship or in flattering one's hosts or guests. When individuals learn a new language while outside their group, on their return they give classes in the new language to the other members. In general, bilingualism is very widespread among these people and is actively and successfully cultivated.

In both of these examples, it appears that the functions of language and the conditions of exposure to language are in many respects extremely different from the patterns commonly found in industrialized societies. It is therefore natural to expect that in these societies the relationship between language mastery and factors of personality, motivation, and attitude may be somewhat different from the patterns usually reported in the literature. As Hill (1970) points out, these examples may provide evidence against the view that adults cannot as a rule master second languages to a high degree of proficiency. Closer examination of the variety of patterns of bilingualism will allow us to better understand the interactions between the functions of language, types of language training to which the learner has been exposed, and the value systems of the learner (see also Torres, 1974).

There is still a third way bilingual development may vary cross-culturally in its social aspects. This concerns the choice of language as a function of the situation. In many societies, bilingual members use one language at home and another at work, even with the same individuals. Sometimes one language is used for discussing some topics while another is used for others (Fishman, 1971). The interesting questions raised here concern the variety of language mixes possible and the process by which a child learns the rules for language selection. There are few data concerning this latter topic, but studies in this area would be extremely useful (see Cazden, 1970). First, they would enable us to learn when a child has the ability to perceive certain social features of a situation (e.g., the status of an individual or importance of a topic). If a culture marks situations of certain types by prescribing which language is appropriate to use, one can discover when children understand the social convention by noting if their speech correctly reflects the distinctions made. Such a study would also enable the impact of social factors on language development to be measured. In monolingual societies, situations are often marked by the selection of the appropriate speech register. However, it is sometimes difficult to observe this marking precisely because the differences between registers are often very subtle (involving only slight and occasional shifts in pronunciation). Bilingual situations, on the other hand, involve very distinct marking systems: either one or the other language is used, and this may provide us with a useful tool for studying sociolinguistic development. (Fantini, 1978; Swain, 1971, also notes the similarities between the learning of two registers in one language and the learning of two languages).

Finally, in connection with sociolinguistic considerations, mention should be made of the incidence of cross-linguistic communication among bilinguals. In regions where two linguistic groups share the same social setting and have many opportunities to interact, one might expect that those who are functionally bilingual would have more extended social contact with members of the other language group than would those who share their mother tongue. This does not always turn out to be the case. Simard and Taylor (1973) report that Montrealers who have learned basic communication skills in the language of the other major group (English or French) in the city have relatively little contact across mother tongue boundaries. Taylor and Gardner (1970) found that moderately skilled bilinguals may be pessimistic about their ability to communicate effectively across linguistic boundaries even though they do in fact have sufficient skills (also Taylor & Simard, 1972). Such negative expectations, together with the more situationally determined sociolinguistic factors mentioned earlier may operate to hinder functional bilinguals from using their skills in some societies. Of course, even so-called balanced bilinguals who appear to be equally fluent in each language may have communication difficulties at a more sophisticated level when speaking with the second language group. Tucker and Gedalof (1970) and d'Anglejan and Tucker (1973) found that balanced bilinguals still communicate in a more native-like fashion using their mother tongue than in their second language. This suggests that subtle cultural differences that really have more to do with ethnic origin rather than with language can still operate as a communication barrier even among fluent bilinguals. It again goes without saying that in certain cultural contexts such inhibitory influences on cross-linguistic communication may operate at only a very weak level.

In summary, it can be said that a number of social factors determine the incidence of bilingualism and the level of language mastery attained and that these factors may be subject to considerable variation. Cross-cultural work in this area will have the important function of clarifying the role of factors relating to attitudes, motivation, and personality in determining patterns of bilingual language development (see Gardner, 1979). Such work will, of course, have to overcome the normal confoundings in any given society of these factors with each other, with age, and with sociolinguistic factors.

## Theories of Bilingual Development

The literature does not contain many well-developed theories about the processes underlying bilingual development. Unfortunately, this limits our ability to generate hypotheses about cross-cultural issues in bilingual development in a systematic fashion and to organize in a useful way observations from case studies of language learning in bilingual settings. Even though the literature does contain a number of case studies (see, for example, references cited in McLaughlin, 1978), no really comprehensive theory about how this development takes place and how it differs from monolingual development has emerged from them. Some of the major approaches that have guided research on bilingual development are mentioned in the following paragraphs.

Taylor (1974) presents a cognitive network theory approach that is conceived in the framework of neoassociationist theories currently popular in cognitive psychology. It was directly inspired by the semantic memory theory of Rumelhart, Lindsay, and Norman, (1972) and Lindsay and Norman (1972) (see especially Norman & Rumelhart, 1975). This approach was itself an attempt to provide a model of human memory and meaning systems that was at once consistent with well-accepted associationistic principles and yet also free of some of the more persistent shortcomings of earlier associationistic formulations of language and meaning. The account of language development provided by Taylor involves the construction by the learner of a network of concepts and relationships between concepts. By describing the interactions that can take place between features of the network when two languages are being acquired, Taylor is able to make some predictions about the course of bilingual development.

Taylor's theory begins with the development of low-level concepts in the network. These are the simple concepts for various features of the environment, defined in sensory terms (lines, contours, colours, elementary acoustic features, and so on). Patterns in the environment will activate a network of such features. For example, the perception of an apple will involve the perception of a particular shape, color, and other features. Over a period of time, the recurrence of the given pattern of features comes to define a higher order concept; in this case "apple." In this manner, a series of feature concepts are built up into a highly elaborate network of concepts.

The building up of higher order networks is not restricted to the representation of physical properties only. Relationships between physical objects can also emerge as stable recurrent patterns and thus gain the status of a concept in the network (e.g., relationships such as "lives in"; agent of an action; is the sister of). Taylor attempts to account for the acquisition of concepts that are important to language development in this way. Included among these is the concept of "label," that certain noises (that people utter) are names for concepts already acquired. In Taylor's treatment of this issue, a prediction is made that the course of bilingual development necessarily retards the initial acquisition of the concept of "label" in relation to its speed of acquisition by monolinguals and that this will result in a slower early vocabulary growth. On the other hand, he predicts more successful coordination of vocabulary growth in two languages once the bilingual child has overcome an early slow start. Monolinguals should, according to the theory, find it more difficult to begin acquisition of a second language once they have already developed a well-defined concept of "label" since learning a second language involves disrupting and differentiating structures in the network that already function in a well-coordinated manner. Taylor also predicts from his theory that a bilingual would be better prepared than a monolingual to learn yet another language (see Davine, Tucker & Lambert, 1971, on this topic).

The cognitive network theory offers an interesting perspective on bilingual development, but there is at present little experimental work that speaks directly to the issues it raises. Part of the problem is that the theory is not very precise in terms of specifying which concepts should be easier or more difficult to learn or what conditions most facilitate learning. It is hoped that further development of the theory will address these issues.

The second major psycholinguistic approach to bilingual development is Slobin's (1973). Slobin's work represents an interesting departure from earlier psycholinguistic theories of development in which the emphasis was on discovering the underlying competence or knowledge children possess that enables language learning to take place at all. Slobin has redirected the focus of attention away from the content of the child's knowledge about the nature of language (the content of the competence contained in the "language acquisition device" postulated by Chomsky, 1965) to the *process* by which the child deals with significant linguistic information in the environment. Slobin outlines a number of perceptual strategies or predispositions that characterize what children attend to first in language learning situations. As mentioned earlier, the study of bilingual children can be a particularly important aspect of the research procedure that Slobin advocates. He demonstrates how one can develop hypotheses about potential universal perceptual strategies that children use and then test their validity with children in very different language learning contexts.

Roger Brown (1973) has also presented an approach to language development stressing early cognitive factors that guide the course of acquisition. Brown's work has dealt primarily with monolingual development, but the principles involved may be useful for making predictions about the course of bilingual development, especially in early childhood. Brown and his students (e.g., De Villiers & De Villiers, 1973, 1974, 1978) have described factors in early cognitive growth, especially in the sensorimotor period, that may be responsible for the particular patterns of words and syntax capabilities that appear at the two- and three-word stage in early development. They also have investigated the role of the factors of word order and other aspects of the child's early awareness of the structure of language. These findings have yet to be integrated into a fuller picture of the processes that obtain in bilingual development.

More recently, there have been developments in theories of adult second language acquisition and the processes underlying language learning in formal instructional settings. Two major themes characterize this literature at the moment. One is that the acquisition of new structures follows a systematic pattern and the other is that the learner uses particular cognitive strategies in mastering a second language.

A major concept underlying the notion of systematic patterning in second language development is *interlanguage* (Richards, 1972; Selinker, 1972). Here the idea is that a linguistic system—an interlanguage—develops from the learner's attempt to acquire a second language. The interlanguage is different from the linguistic system underlying either the native language or the target language (as spoken by its native speakers). Evidence for the interlanguage come from studies of learners' errors, errors that are believed to result from the learners' application of particular cognitive strategies. For example, Selinker, Swain, and Dumas (1975) report evidence, from English-speaking children learning French, of errors due to language transfer, overgeneralization, and simplification. The version of French these learners spoke differed systematically from the French of native language speakers, yet nevertheless it provided an acceptable medium of communication among the learners themselves. In principle, the interlanguage would be expected to change over time and approximate more closely the target language, but usually learners, especially adults, often stop progressing well before achieving nativelike competence. Their second language output contains, therefore, many elements of the interlanguage that are not to be found in the target language. This process of retaining interlanguage structures is called "fossilization."

Gatbonton (1978) reports a study that looked at the stages through which an interlanguage passes in the case of native French speakers acquiring the English phonological targets voiced TH (as in *the*), voiceless TH (as in *three*), and the voiceless velar glide/h/ (as in *hot*). She employed a model of language development derived from theories of linguistic variation and of the processes underlying the formation of creole languages (e.g., Bickerton, 1973). Essentially she found that the acquisition of nativelike production of target sound followed a regular pattern, which she called a gradual diffusion process (Gatbonton, 1978). Nativelike elements appeared in the learners' speech in one particular phonetic environment and then spread across to other environments in an orderly fashion. The patterning observed allowed her to identify particular stages of development and to make certain predictions about the future course of the learner's phonological development.

Dulay and Burt (1974, 1978) have focused on what they refer to as the creative construction process. This is the "process by which learners gradually reconstruct rules for speech they hear, guided by innate mechanisms which cause them to formulate certain types of hypotheses about the language system being acquired, until the mismatch between what they are exposed to and what they produce is resolved" (Dulay & Burt, 1978, p. 67).

They note that language acquisition—whether of a first or a second language—is creative in the sense that there is a degree of learner independence from external input factors. They wish to address the problem: when does speech input *not* affect learning and when does it exert its influence? In approaching this question, they identify five general sources that may account for discrepancies between the learners' speech output and the input they receive. One of these is called by them the "socioaffective filter." This refers to the learners' unconscious needs, attitudes, and motivations (discussed earlier in this chapter). A second source they call the "cognitive organizer." This refers to the learner's basic cognitive processes, the strategies that systematically create certain kind of errors and other cognitive factors that affect the order in which structures are acquired (see e. g., Anderson, 1978; d'Anglejan & Tucker, 1975; Dulay & Burt, 1974). A third source is called the "monitor" (Krashen, 1977; 1978), and this refers to the learners' conscious editing of their own speech. The degree of conscious self-correction will depend on the cognitive and sociolinguistic demand characteristics of the situation. Some tasks naturally focus speakers' attention on the way they sound, whereas others do not do this to the same degree. It is reasonable to expect that, depending on the kinds of situations learners generally find themselves in when acquiring their second language, the "monitor" will assume some particular level of importance in shaping language development. These three sources—the socioaffective filter, the cognitive organizer, and the monitor—will interact with the two remaining sources: personality factors and first language experience. For a fuller discussion of evidence regarding these factors and their interactions, see Dulay and Burt (1978).

These approaches should be of interest to the cross-cultural psychologist because they provide a framework in which one can think about universal cognitive mechanisms underlying language development and the role social and affective factors play in the process. The careful comparison of the course of language development, particularly bilingual development, in different cultures may enable the researcher to separate those processes that are context-specific from those that are common to all learners.

## Impact of Bilingualism on the Individual

Lambert distinguishes between what he calls additive and subtractive bilingualism. His idea is that under some circumstances, bilingualism can have an enhancing effect on the individual; the addition of a second language allows the person access to another group and may possibly have generally beneficial effects on cognitive functioning. In other circumstances, bilingualism may have an overall negative effect; the individual may only add a new language at the cost of losing contact with his own mother tongue and culture (see, for example, Lambert, 1975, 1977). Indeed, several theories of language and thought support the view that bilingualism may have a special impact on the social and cognitive functioning of the individual. The mediational theories of Vygotsky (1962) and Ervin and Osgood (1954) clearly fall into this group, as do theories of "linguistic relativity" (Whorf, 1956). In this section, these and other approaches to the relation of language to thought will be discussed. First, mediational theories and the research that stems from them will be considered, but only briefly, since the results of such studies have not been very conclusive. This discussion will be followed by a review of the work that explores hypotheses that the bilingual's general overall cognitive functioning is either enhanced or diminished by bilingualism. Finally, there will be a discussion of the impact of bilingualism on the social behavior and social adjustment of the bilingual.

*Mediational Theories*

There is a large literature concerning the impact of bilingualism on cognitive processes that stems from mediational views of language and thought (see Albert & Obler, 1978; Segalowitz, 1977b, for a more detailed presentation). One of the early important papers in this area (Ervin & Osgood, 1954) presented a neobehaviorist theory of bilingual development and made specific predictions concerning the effects of different patterns of bilingual development on the cognitive organization of the languages. Two types of bilingualism were identified by the theory according to whether one or two associative networks underlie the two languages. Compound bilingualism, in which there is only one underlying network, was hypothesized to result from acquisition of the two languages at the same time in the same context. Coordinate bilingualism, which is supposed to result when the languages are acquired sequentially and/or in different contexts, has different and relatively more independent meaning systems subserving each language. One prediction that stems from this theory is that compound bilinguals should show more difficulty in keeping the languages separated under certain experimental conditions. Numerous studies have attempted to find evidence for the two types of bilingualism, but the results to date provide only equivocal support for the compound-coordinate distinction. A number of studies support the predictions made by the theory (Ervin, 1964; Jakobovits & Lambert, 1961; Lambert, Havelka, & Crosby, 1958; Lambert & Rawlings, 1969; Segalowitz & Lambert, 1969), while a number fail to do so (Arkwright & Viau, 1974;

Dillon, McCormack, Petrusic, Cook, & Lafleur, 1973; Kolers, 1963). It is probable that much of the confusion in these findings stems from inconsistencies in the way subjects have been classified as coordinate or compound (Diller, 1967; see also Macnamara, 1967, 1970). For example, speakers may be classified as compound bilinguals if they acquired their languages simultaneously; but if some of them have learned the languages in two different contexts, they should be relatively more like coordinate bilinguals than those acquiring the languages in the same contexts. Similarly, some coordinate bilinguals may be more bicultural than others, depending on how different the learning contexts were. Researchers have not always paid close attention to the different ways the factors of time and place of learning may combine. Thus, the lack of consistent support for the specific proposals of Ervin and Osgood may indicate that the relationship between acquisition pattern and cognitive organization of language is not as simple as originally thought.

That bilingualism has a cognitive impact is also predicted by theories of linguistic relativity (Whorf, 1956; see also Fishman, 1960; Alatis, 1970, pp. 40–45; Carroll, 1963a; Christophersen, 1973). The principle here is that, to an important extent, the language we use determines the way we categorize events and objects in the world (Brown & Lenneberg, 1954; Carroll & Casagrande, 1958; Lantz & Stefflre, 1964). Thus, a person who possesses two languages should, in theory at least, have two ways of categorizing experiences. Such additional powers may be an advantage in that they provide an individual with a richer set of optional ways of perceiving, or they may be viewed as a liability if the two classification systems interfere with each other. Now, even though the experimental support for the Whorfian thesis that language shapes perception is not very strong, there is some evidence that perception and categorization of social events can be influenced by the language used. For example, studies by Ervin (1964; Ervin-Tripp, 1967) show that bilinguals will speak about social events and people with different underlying value systems according to which language they use. This finding has interesting implications incidentally for therapeutic work with bilinguals where the choice of language can be a critically important factor in the attitude patients express towards their symptoms (see also Peck, 1974).

*General Cognitive Effects*

Early theorizing and research on the cognitive impact of bilingual development on the individual stressed the potential negative side effects. For example, Weinreich (1953) reviews a large literature that claims to show that bilingualism leads to lowered intelligence, moral degradation, and personality disorders. As Weinreich himself points out, most of this research was methodologically unsound. Often, the authors neglected to take into account cultural differences between monolingual control subjects and the bilinguals. Differences in social class background and proficiency in the language of the test were often overlooked. Moreover, the notion of intelligence itself was used very crudely and uncritically. Intelligence was what intelligence tests measured, and little attempt was made in the early studies to distinguish between possible component skills that may underlie intelligence and those that may be selectively affected by bilingualism (for a survey of the work in bilingualism and intelligence, see also Arsenian, 1945; Balkan, 1970; Darcy, 1953, 1963; Haugen, 1956; Jones, 1959, 1966; Macnamara, 1966; Peal & Lambert, 1962).

Peal and Lambert (1962) reported one of the first studies in which attempts were made to avoid some of the more obvious shortcomings of the earlier research. They considered a number of hypotheses about the way bilingualism might affect intellectual functioning. First, they suggested that bilingualism may free one from the tyranny of words. That is, a bilingual child may more easily dissociate the idea behind a thought from the form it takes when verbalized. Second, and in contrast to the point just made, bilingualism might lead to linguistic interference and hence impose a burden on the individual to devote extra attention to keeping the effects of interference to a minimum. Third, they suggested that a bilingual person may have a richer cultural experience than a monolingual and this richness may enhance the early development of processes that are important for general intellectual functioning. Finally, they suggested (see also Anisfeld, 1964) that the bilingual may be cognitively more flexible because of his or her practice in switching back and forth between languages. They hypothesized that bilinguals and monolinguals should perform differently on a number of subtests of intelligence, reflecting the notion that the structure of intellect will be different for the two groups. In general, they found support for the hypothesis that bilingualism would enhance cognitive functioning. The bilinguals they tested had higher verbal and nonverbal IQ and they performed better on tests of nonverbal flexibility. This they attribute to the bilingual's relative freedom from the tyranny of words.

Balkan (1970), working with Swiss children, also found that bilinguals scored higher than monolinguals on tests of numerical aptitude, verbal flexibility, perceptual flexibility, and general reasoning, even though they were matched on general intelligence with the monolinguals. Ben-Zeev (1972, 1977) derived a number of hypotheses from Piaget's theory of cognitive development that predict superior verbal flexibility in bilinguals and the results of her studies support these contentions. Other support for heightened verbal and cognitive flexibility in bilinguals has been presented by a number of researchers (Cummins & Gulutsan, 1974; Feldman

& Shen, 1971; Ianco-Worrall, 1972; Jacobs & Pierce, 1965; Landry, 1974; and Torrance, Wu, Gowan, & Aliotti, 1970).

One important problem in this area of research is the following. A growing number of theorists maintain that the concepts of intelligence and creativity subsume complexes of different cognitive processes. It is very possible that these cognitive skills may receive differential emphasis in different cultures (see Lloyd, 1972, for a general discussion of these issues and further bibliographic sources). In future cross-cultural studies of bilingualism and intellectual abilities, it will be important to ask whether this can account for variation in the impact of bilingualism from one cultural setting to another. At the moment, few data speak directly to this issue. The more recent studies, which were cited earlier, were conducted in different settings (Canada, Israel, South Africa, Switzerland, United States), but the cultures involved do not appear to value radically different kinds of intellectual skills. What remains to be done is to explore further the specific components of intellectual development with a view to discovering how they may be affected by bilingualism and to what extent this influence is dependent on cultural variables.

One interesting area in which cross-cultural studies of bilingualism could shed light on an important problem concerns the representation of mutiple languages in the brain. Very little is known about this topic, as indeed researchers are still groping with the problem of how single languages are represented. The basic neurological issue here is to what extent multiple languages are represented in the brain in shared or separate neurological systems.

The little insight that we do have on this issue stems from research on aphasia with bilinguals. There are three basic approaches to language recovery in bilingual aphasics. The first approach is known as the "rule of Ribot" (see Weinreich, 1953), which claims that the first language to return will be the first language learned. Lambert and Fillenbaum (1959) found support for this type of aphasic syndrome in their study of French Canadian and European French bilinguals. The second type of pattern is known as "Pitres' rule" (Pitres, 1895). This is a habit strength rule that claims that the language most used will be the one most resistant to impairment in aphasia. Pitres (1895), Lambert and Fillenbaum (1959), and to some extent Weisenburg and McBride (1964) report examples of this type of pattern. Note, however, that often the first learned language is also the most used and so it is sometimes difficult to find cases that permit one to distinguish between Ribot's rule and Pitres' rule. A third approach is Minkowski's (1928), which predicts that the language to recover first will be the one with which the patient had the strongest emotional bond. Support for this pattern comes from Leischner (1948) (cited in Lambert &

Fillenbaum, 1959) and Hécaen and Angelergues (1968); but again the potential for confounding first language, most used language, and language of emotional attachment is very great. Research in a wide variety of cultural settings in which there are different configurations of these three factors may make it possible to separate out these different influences (see Albert & Obler, 1978; Paradis, 1977; Whitaker, 1978 for reviews in this area).

*Bilingualism, Biculturalism, and Social Adjustment*

So far, the discussion has focused on the cognitive impact of bilingualism. However, we might expect bilinguals to be affected socially—both in their social behavior and their social cognitions—since bilinguals are to some extent bicultural. In learning a second language, one learns the conceptual tools used by a group of people that live in a socially distinct environment. Even if the mastery of the second language is very weak and contact with the culture of the second language group is small, it is still possible that bilinguals will be *perceived* as bicultural or potentially bicultural people and hence treated differently by those around them. In this area, we can expect a great deal of cross-cultural variation. Not only may there be variation in the extent to which bilingualism actually implies biculturalism, but there may also be variation in the way individuals in the mother tongue and other language group react to bilinguals in their midst. These factors may in turn have an important impact on the course of bilingual development in the individual. The following discussion reviews some of the evidence for these sorts of influences and presents some issues that merit exploration.

It is often thought that bilinguals are caught between two cultures and suffer a great deal of unhappiness in learning to cope with their ambiguous identity. There is no doubt that such problems are genuine. The question is whether the problem is inherent in bilingualism. Those who believe it is argue that social values and feelings of ethnic loyalty are so wrapped up in linguistic experiences that if one knows two languages extremely well, one necessarily possesses the cultural values and identity features that are encoded in the two languages (see references cited in Weinreich, 1953). Early theorists thus argued that bilinguals are likely to be continually caught in a competition between two sets of loyalties. An alternative view is that it is not bilingualism *per se* that is responsible for such adjustment problems when they occur, but that it is the reactions of the surrounding community or communities that cause difficulties. Considerable support is emerging in the literature for this latter contention. For example, Bossard (1945), Soffietti (1955), and Spoerl (1943) discuss observations of bilinguals who have experienced adjustment problems, and they conclude that the reactions of the people with whom the bilinguals interact matter more than the fact of bilingualism as such. Aellen and Lambert (1969) compared the ethnic identification and personality adjustment of bilingual children of mixed English-French parentage in Montreal with monolingual children of French or English parentage only. They found no differences between the children of mixed background and single language background on measures of parental identification, ethnic identification, self-esteem, and stability. If anything, they found that the bilinguals appeared to enjoy healthier relationships with their parents and felt that their parents took more interest in them than did monolinguals. Thus, this study indicates that bilingualism does not necessarily lead to poor social adjustment (see also Findling, 1969; Kuo, 1974a and b; and Lambert, Gardner, Barik, & Turnstall, 1962).

It is possible to argue that the bicultural component of bilingualism, especially fluent bilingualism, may result in a weakening of bonds between language and cultural values. That is, constellations of cultural attitudes and values may become less intimately linked to a particular form of linguisitic expression. For example, the differences and similarities between two cultures may become psychologically more salient for bilinguals because they actually experience these differences and similarities as they switch from one language to another. Monolinguals, on the other hand, can only learn about the similarities and differences through the medium of one language, that is, indirectly through translation. Because of this increased experiential salience, bilinguals may be able to escape from the linguistic aspects of cultural values and develop representations of values and attitudes that are not closely tied to particular ways of expressing them verbally. In this sense, the bilingual may be less dependent on words than is the monolingual.

This loosening of the bonds between language and cultural values may have different consequences in different settings. For example, in one setting it may be that members of the mother tongue group perceive the bilinguals among them as potential defectors to the other group. In this case, there may be pressures to limit the extent to which the other language is learned lest it proceed too far and the speaker begin to pass too easily as a member of the other group. Presumably such reactions would exist where the two language groups in question are in competition or conflict (Segalowitz & Gatbonton, 1977).

Another possibility is that native speakers of the bilingual's second language might be suspicious of outsiders who learn their language too well. Lambert (1967) refers to the "linguistic spy," the individual who actually passes as a member of the other language group. Again, whether such feelings arise may depend on the social, political, and cultural aspects of the situation. If they do arise, they may affect the pattern of bilingual development by constraining the way bilinguals from outside the group are received. Negative reactions would tend to discourage others from developing high levels of fluency.

It is possible, too, for groups to have little or no strong feelings at all about bilingualism and that individuals may freely pass from one group to another. In such conditions, one would expect to see much more widespread and much higher levels of fluency in second languages than in the previously described situations (e.g., Sorensen, 1967).

There is yet another interesting way in which such factors of ethnic identification may be related to bilingualism. In sociolinguistic studies of first language speech, it is found that speakers modify the way they speak by choosing one or another register depending on the person they are speaking with, the topic, and the situation (Ervin-Tripp, 1967, 1972). It is possible that bilinguals, especially those with accented speech in the second language, will also vary the way they speak in their second language according to the characteristics of the situation. For example, imagine a context in which there is a great deal of nationalistic rivalry between the two language groups in question (as, for example, in Quebec or Belgium). Individuals speaking in their second language before a mixed group may find it appropriate to use more heavily accented speech than they would normally use in order that the members of the audience who share their mother tongue do not suspect them of weak linguistic loyalties. In other situations, the same individuals might speak differently, while in some cultures this issue may never even arise.

The evidence supporting the hypothesis that bilinguals may vary their speech in this way is, at the moment, very sparse and largely inferential. The possibility of this occurring is suggested by studies on the reactions of people to accent (Anisfeld, Bogo, & Lambert, 1962; Lambert, Hodgson, Gardner, & Fillenbaum, 1960; Strongman & Woosley, 1967) language choice (Blom & Gumperz, 1972; Herman, 1968) and linguistic accommodation (Bourhis, Giles, & Lambert, 1975; Giles & Powesland, 1975; Simard, Taylor, & Giles, 1976). It would thus be useful to know whether members of a given community make particular judgments about the bilinguals among them on the basis of their speech and whether the bilinguals modify their use of their second language speech in front of their own group in reaction.

If bilinguals in some settings do behave this way, there may be an interesting consequence for bilingual development itself. In cultures where there are large groups of second language speakers with the same language background and where members of the group are likely to use the second language often in the presence of other members of their own group, it is possible that some community-wide patterns of bilingual development will evolve. This might occur for example among Puerto Rican Spanish-English bilinguals in New York, French-English bilinguals in Montreal, or Georgian-Russian speakers in Tbilisi. Certain patterns of pronunciation may be shared by such a second language speaking community that might not appear in the speech of isolated individuals learning the same language. In other words, there may be sociolinguistic factors shaping the patterns of second language speech just as there are in first language speech (Segalowitz & Gatbonton, 1977). Research on this topic would need to examine the phenomenon in a variety of cultural settings to see how factors of ethnic identification, frequency of occasions to hear others speaking the language as a second language, and social and linguistic rivalry influence this process.

## Summary

This chapter has tried to outline the major issues and findings in the area of bilingual development. Two broad categories of issues were discussed. The first concerned the factors that are responsible for the existence of bilingualism in a community and the level of bilingual ability achieved. Material was presented to show that the primary factors affecting bilingualism are those that are subject to variation from social influences. For example, personality, attitudinal, and motivational characteristics of the individual have all been found to be positively related to bilingual proficiency. This suggests that many of the differences in patterns of bilingual development that are observed in different cultural settings—differences in terms of how widespread bilingualism is and in the levels of proficiency attained—might be attributable to these factors. Extensive cross-cultural comparisons should strongly sensitize us to the variety of patterns of bilingual development that can and do exist. In addition to these socially conditioned characteristics of the individual, there are sociolinguistic determinants of bilingual development. Each culture places certain requirements on the individual to use one particular language or variety of that language in specific situations. These sociolinguistic demands can pose barriers to bilingual development if they are very restrictive (demanding very special speech skills) or if the culture imposes penalties for failing to observe the sociolinguistic conventions.

The second major issue concerns the impact of bilingualism on the individual. Evidence was reviewed that shows that general cognitive functioning may be enhanced by bilingualism, especially general intelligence and factors of cognitive flexibility. However, it is possible that these characteristics only manifest themselves in particular ways, depending on the intellectual skills that are valued highly by the culture. It is possible, therefore, that the findings reviewed present a very narrow view of the possible impact of bilingualism on intellectual skills, since they were obtained primarily from European and North American sources. Cross-cultural work in this area will help broaden our view about how bilingualism affects general cognitive skills as well as reveal to us which aspects of this impact are culture specific and which are universal. Such findings will, of course, also be relevant to the general issue of the relationship between language and thought.

In addition, a number of hypotheses and findings were presented concerning the impact of bilingualism on the social adjustment of the individual. Evidence was presented that bilingualism as such need not necessarily have a negative impact, but that under certain conditions it is possible for a bilingual person to experience conflicts of cultural identity. It was suggested that the surrounding culture can engender this identity problem in a number of ways and that such problems may in turn affect the way bilingual development proceeds in a given community. Cross-cultural studies of the ways individuals adapt to the social stress that may accompany bilingualism will help provide a fuller understanding of the impact of bilingualism on the individual.

Finally, careful attention to the linguistic details of bilingual development may reveal to us a great deal about the processes underlying language development in general. In this sense, the study of bilingualism is a useful source of information that complements what is learned from the study of single language development. As Slobin (1973) attempts to show, certain questions in developmental psycholinguistics may be better answered by reference to bilingual development than to monolingual development. The widest possible studies in this area will teach us about those features of language learning, in both the adult and child, that reflect universal cognitive mechanisms and those that are specific to the conditions under which language is being learned.

## References

AELLEN, C., & LAMBERT, W. E. Ethnic identification and personality adjustments of Canadian adolescents of mixed English-French parentage. *Canadian Journal of Behavioral Science,* 1969, *1,* 123–128.

ALATIS, J. E. (Ed.) *Monograph Series on Languages and Linguistics.* Washington, D.C.: Georgetown University Press, 1970.

ALBERT, M., & OBLER, L. *The bilingual brain.* New York: Academic Press, 1978.

ANDERSON, J. Order of difficulty in adult second language acquisition. In W. Ritchie (Ed.) *Second Language Acquisition Research.* New York: Academic Press, 1978.

ANISFELD, E. *A comparison of the cognitive function of monolinguals and bilinguals.* Unpublished doctoral dissertation, McGill University, Montreal, 1964.

ANISFELD, M., BOGO, N., & LAMBERT, W. E. Evaluational reactions to accented speech. *Journal of Abnormal Social Psychology,* 1962, *65,* 223–231.

ANISFELD, M., & LAMBERT, W. E. Social and psychological variables in learning Hebrew. *Journal of Abnormal and Social Psychology,* 1961, *63,* 524–529.

ARKWRIGHT, T., & VIAU, A. Les processus d'association chez les bilingues. *Working Papers in Bilingualism,* 1974, (2), 57–67.

ARSENIAN, Seth, Bilingualism in the post-war world. *Psychological Bulletin,* 1945, *42,* 65–85.

ASHER, J. J. & PRICE, B. S. The learning strategy of the total physical response: some age differences. *Child Development,* 1967, *38,* 1119–1227.

BALKAN, L. *Les effets du bilinguisme français-anglais sur les aptitudes intellectuelles.* Brussels: Aimav, 1970.

BEN-ZEEV, S. *The influence of bilingualism on cognitive development and cognitive strategy.* Unpublished doctoral dissertation, University of Chicago, Illinois, 1972.

————. Mechanisms by which childhood bilingualism affects understanding of language and cognitive structures. In P. Hornby (Ed.), *Bilingualism: Psychological, Social and Educational Implications.* New York: Academic Press, 1977.

BICKERTON, D. Quantitative versus dynamic paradigms: The case of Montreal "Que." In C. J. Bailey & R. Shuy (Eds.), *New Ways of Analyzing Variation in English.* Washington, D.C.: Georgetown University Press, 1973.

BLOM, J. P., & GUMPERZ, J. J. Social meaning in linguistic structures: code-switching in Norway. In J. J. Gumperz & D. Hymes (Eds.), *Directions in Sociolinguistics: The Ethnography of Communication.* New York: Holt, Rinehart & Winston, 1972.

BOSSARD, A. The bilingual individual as a person. *American Sociological Review,* 1945, *10,* 699–709.

BOURHIS, R. Y., GILES, H., & LAMBERT, W. E. Social consequences of accommodating one's style of speech: A cross-national investigation. *International Journal of the Sociology of Language,* 1975, *6,* 55–72.

BROWN, R. *A first language: The early stages.* Cambridge, Mass.: Harvard University Press, 1973.

BROWN, R., & LENNEBERG, E. H. A study in language and cognition. *Journal of Abnormal and Social Psychology,* 1954, *49,* 454–462.

BURT, M., & DULAY, H. *New directions in second language learning, teaching and bilingual education.* Washington, DC: TESOL, 1975.

CARROLL, J. B. Linguistic relativity, contrastive linguistics and language learning. *International Review of Applied Linguistics,* 1963, *1,* 1–20. (a)

————. Research on teaching foreign languages. In N. L. Gage (Ed.), *Handbook of Research on Teaching.* Chicago: Rand McNally, 1963. (b)

CARROLL, J. B., & CASAGRANDE, J. B. The function of language classification in behavior. In E. Macoby, T. M. Newcomb & E. L. Hartley, (Eds.), *Readings in Social Psychology* (3rd ed.). New York: Holt, Rinehart & Winston, 1958.

CAZDEN, C. B. The situation: A neglected source of social class differences in language use. *Journal of Social Issues,* 1970, *26,* 35–60. (Reprinted in J. B. Pride & J. Holmes [Eds.], *Sociolinguistics.* Harmondsworth, England: Penguin Books, 1972).

CEDERGREN, H., & SANKOFF, D. Variable rules: performance as a statistical reflection of competence. *Language,* 1974, *50,* 333–355.

CHOMSKY, N. *Aspects of the theory of syntax.* Cambridge, Mass.: M.I.T. Press, 1965.

Theodore Lownik Library
Illinois Benedictine College
Lisle, Illinois 60532

CHRISTOPHERSEN, P. *Second-language learning: Myth & reality*. Harmondsworth, England: Penguin Books, 1973.

CLÉMENT, R., GARDNER, R., & SMYTHE, P. Motivational variables in second language acquisition: a study of francophones learning English. *Canadian Journal of Behavioral Sciences*, 1977, 9, 123–133. (a)

CLÉMENT, R., GARDNER, R., & SMYTHE, P. Motivational characteristics of francophones learning English. *Research Bulletin, University of Western Ontario*, 1977, No. 408. (b)

COOPER, R., & GREENFIELD, L. Language use in a bilingual community. *Modern Language Journal*, 1969, 53, 166–172.

CORDER, S. Idiosyncratic dialects and error analysis. *International Review of Applied Linguistics*, 1971, 9, 146–160.

CUMMINS, J., & GULUTSAN, M. Bilingual education and cognition. *The Alberta Journal of Educational Research*, 1974, 20, 259–269.

D'ANGLEJAN, A., & TUCKER, G. R. Communicating across cultures: An empirical investigation. *Journal of Cross-Cultural Psychology*, 1973, 4, 122–130.

D'ANGLEJAN, A., & TUCKER, G. The acquisition of complex English structures by adult learners. *Language Learning*, 1975, 25, 281–293.

DARCY, N. T. A review of the literature on the effects of bilingualism upon the measurement of intelligence. *Journal of Genetic Psychology*, 1953, 82, 21–57.

————. Bilingualism and the measurement of intelligence: Review of a decade of research. *The Journal of Genetic Psychology*, 1963, 103, 259–282.

DAVINE, M., TUCKER, G. R., & LAMBERT, W. E. The perception of phoneme sequences by monolingual and bilingual elementary school children. *Canadian Journal of Behavioral Science*, 1971, 3, 72–76.

DE VILLIERS, J. G., & DE VILLIERS, P. Development of the use of word order in comprehension. *Journal of Psycholinguistic Research*, 1973, 2, 331–341.

————. Competence and performance in child language: Are children really competent to judge? *Journal of Child Language*, 1974, 1, 11–22.

————. *Language acquisition*. Cambridge, Mass.: Harvard University Press, 1978.

DIEBOLD, R. A. The consequences of early bilingualism in cognitive development and personality formation. In E. Norbeck, D. Price-Williams, & W. M. McCord (Eds.), *The study of personality: An interdisciplinary appraisal*. New York: Holt, Rinehart and Winston, 1968.

DILLER, K. C. 'Compound' and 'coordinate' bilingualism—a conceptual artifact. Paper presented to the Linguistic Society of America, Illinois, 1967.

DILLON, R. F., McCORMACK, P. D., PETRUSIC, W. M., COOK, M., & LAFLEUR, L. Release from proactive interference in compound and coordinate bilinguals. *Bulletin of the Psychonomic Society*, 1973, 2, 293–294.

DULAY, J., & BURT, M. A new perspective on the creative construction process in child second language acquisition. *Language Learning*, 1974, 24, 253–278.

DULAY, H., & BURT, M. Some remarks on creativity in language acquisition. In W. Ritchie (Ed.), *Second language acquisition research*. New York: Academic Press, 1978.

ERVIN, S. Language and TAT content in bilinguals. *Journal of Abnormal and Social Psychology*, 1964, *68*, 500–507.

―――. An Issei learns English. *Journal of Social Issues*, 1967, *23*, 78–90.

―――. On sociolinguistic rules: Alternation and co-occurrence. In J. J. Gumperz, & D. Hymes (Eds.), *Directions in sociolinguistics: The ethnography of communication.* New York: Holt, Rinehart & Winston, 1972. (Revised version of: Sociolinguistics. In L. Berkowitz [Ed.], *Advances in experimental social psychology* [Vol. 4]. New York: Academic Press, 1969.)

ERVIN, S., & OSGOOD, C. E. Second language learning and bilingualism. *Journal of Abnormal and Social Psychology* (supplement), 1954, *49*, 139–146. Also in C. E. Osgood and T. A. Sebeok (Eds.), *Psycholinguistics.* Bloomington, Indiana: Indiana University Press, 1965.

FANTINI, A. Bilingual behavior and social cues: Case studies of two bilingual children. In M. Paradis (Ed.), *Aspects of bilingualism.* Columbia, South Carolina: Hornbeam Press, 1978.

FELDMAN, C., & SHEN, M. Some language-related cognitive advances of bilingual five-year olds. *The Journal of Genetic Psychology*, 1971, *118*, 235–244.

FERGUSON, C. (Ed.). *Contrastive Structure Series.* Washington, D.C.: Center for Applied Linguistics, 1959.

FINDLING, J. Bilingual need affiliation and future orientation in extragroup and intragroup domains. *The Modern Language Journal*, 1969, *53*, 227–231.

FISHMAN, J. A. A systematization of the Whorfian hypothesis. *Behavioral Science*, 1960, *5*, 323–339.

―――. Sociolinguistic perspective on the study of bilingualism. *Linguistics*, 1968, *39*, 21–50.

―――. The sociology of language: An interdisciplinary social science approach to language in society. In J. A. Fishman (Ed.), *Advances in the sociology of language* (Vol. 1). The Hague: Mouton, 1971.

―――. Domains and the relationship between micro- and macro-sociolinguistics. In J. J. Gumperz & D. Hymes (Eds.), *Directions in sociolinguistics: The ethnography of communication.* New York: Holt, Rinehart & Winston, 1972. (Revised and extended version of: Who speaks what language to whom and when. *La Linguistique*, 1965, *2*, 67–88.)

FISHMAN, J., FERGUSON, C. & DASGUPTA, J. (Eds.). *Language problems of developing nations.* New York: John Wiley & Sons, 1968.

FISHMAN, J., & COOPER, R. The interrelationships and utility of alternative bilingualism measures. In W. Whiteley, (Ed.), *Language use and social change*, London: Oxford University Press, 1971.

FRASURE-SMITH, N., LAMBERT, W. E., & TAYLOR, D. M. Choosing the language of instruction for one's children: A Québec study. *Journal of Cross-Cultural Psychology*, 1975, *6*, 131–155.

GARDNER, R. C. Social psychological aspects of second language acquisition. In H. Giles & R. St. Clair (Eds.), *Language and social psychology.* Oxford: Basil Blackwell, 1979.

GARDNER, R. C., & LAMBERT, W. E. Language aptitude, intelligence and second-language acquisition. *Canadian Journal of Psychology*, 1959, *13*, 266–272.

―――. Language aptitude, intelligence and second language achievement. *Journal of Educational Psychology*, 1965, *56*, 191–199.

————. *Attitudes and motivation in second language learning.* Rowley, Mass.: Newbury House, 1972.

GARDNER, R. C., & SMYTHE, P. C. Motivation and second language acquisition. *Canadian Modern Language Review*, 1975, *31*, 218–230.

GATBONTON, E. Patterned phonetic variability in second-language speech: A gradual diffusion model. *Canadian Modern Language Review*, 1978, *34*, 335–347.

GILES, H. (Ed.). *Language, ethnicity and intergroup relations.* London: Academic Press, 1977.

GILES, H., BOURHIS, R., & TAYLOR, D. Toward a theory of language in ethnic group relations. In H. Giles (Ed.), *Language, ethnicity, and intergroup relations.* London: Academic Press, 1977.

GILES, H., & POWESLAND, P. *Speech style and social evaluation.* New York: Academic Press, 1975.

GILES, H., & ST. CLAIR, R. (Eds.). *Language and social psychology.* Oxford: Blackwell, 1979.

GUIORA, A. Z. Toward a systematic study of empathy. *Comprehensive Psychiatry*, 1967, *8*, 375–385.

GUIORA, A. Z., BRANNON, R. C., & DULL, C. Y. Empathy and second language learning. *Language Learning*, 1972, *22*, 111–130.

GUIORA, A. Z., LANE, H. L., & BOSWORTH, L. A. An exploration of some personality variables in authentic pronunciation of a second language. In E. Zale (Ed.), *Proceedings of the conference on language and language behavior*, New York: Appleton-Century-Crofts, 1968.

GUMPERZ, J. J. Linguistic and social interaction in two communities. In J. Gumperz & D. Hymes (Eds.), The ethnography of communication. *American Anthropologist*, 1964, *66*(6), Part II, 137–154.

————. Types of linguistic communities. In J. Fishman (Ed.), *Readings in the sociology of language.* The Hague: Mouton, 1968.

————. Sociolinguistics and communication in small groups. *Working Paper No. 33.* Language Behavior Research Laboratory, University of California, 1970. (Reprinted in J. B. Pride & J. Holmes [Eds.], *Sociolinguistics.* Harmondsworth, England: Penguin Books, 1972).

GUMPERZ, J. J., & HERNANDEZ, E. Cognitive aspects of bilingual communication. In W. Whiteley (Ed.), *Language use and social change.* London: Oxford University Press, 1971.

GUMPERZ, J. J., & HYMES, D. (Eds.). *Directions in the ethnography of communication.* New York: Holt, Rinehart & Winston, 1972.

HAUGEN, E. *Bilingualism in the Americas: A Bibliography and Research Guide.* American Dialect Society, Publication No. 26, University of Alabama: University of Alabama Press, 1956.

————. On the meaning of bilingual competence. In R. Jakobson & S. Kawamoto, (Eds.), *Studies in general and oriented linguistics: presented to Shiro Hattori.* Tokyo: TEC Co. Ltd., 1970.

————. *The ecology of language.* Stanford: Stanford University Press, 1972.

————. Norm and deviation in bilingual communities. In P. Hornby (Ed.), *Bilingualism: Psychological, social and educational implications.* New York: Academic Press, 1977.

HÉCAEN, H., & ANGELERGUES, R. *Pathologie du Language, l'aphasie.* Paris: Librairie Larousse, 1968.

HERMAN, S. R. Explorations in the social psychology of language choice. In J. Fishman (Ed.), *Readings in the sociology of language.* The Hague: Mouton, 1968.

HILL, J. H. Foreign accents, language acquisition and cerebral dominance revisited. *Language Learning,* 1970, *20,* 237–248.

HYMES, D. The ethnography of speaking. In T. Gladwin & W. Sturtevant (Eds.), *Anthropology and human behavior.* Washington: Anthropological Society of Washington, D.C., 1962. Reprinted in F. Fishman (Ed.), *Readings in the sociology of language.* The Hague: Mouton, 1968.

HYMES, D. H. *On communicative competence.* Philadelphia: University of Philadelphia Press. (Reprinted in J. Pride & J. Holmes [Eds.], *Sociolinguistics.* Harmondsworth, England: Penguin Books, 1971.)

———. Models of interaction of language and social life. In J. Gumperz & D. Hymes (Eds.), *Directions in sociolinguistics.* New York: Holt, Rinehart & Winston, 1972.

IANCO—WORRALL, A. D. Bilingualism and cognitive development. *Child Development,* 1972, *43,* 1390–1400

JACOBS, J. F., & PIERCE, M. L. Bilingualism and creativity. *Elementary English,* 1965, *42,* 499–503

JAKOBOVITS, L. *Foreign language learning.* Rowley Mass.: Newbury House, 1970.

JAKOBOVITS, L., & LAMBERT, W. E. Semantic satiation among bilinguals. *Journal of Experimental Psychology,* 1961, *62,* 576–582

JONES, W. R. Attitude towards Welsh as a second language. A preliminary investigation. *British Journal of Educational Psychology,* 1949, *19,* 44–52.

———. Attitude towards Welsh as a second language. A further investigation. *British Journal of Educational Psychology,* 1950, *20,* 117–132.

———. *Bilingualism and intelligence.* Cardiff: University of Wales Press, 1959.

———. *Bilingualism in Welsh education.* Cardiff: University of Wales Press, 1966.

JORDAN, D. The attitude of central school pupils to certain subjects, and the correlation between attitude and attainment. *British Journal of Educational Psychology,* 1941, *11,* 28–44.

KELLEY, L. G. (Ed.). *Description and measurement of bilingualism.* Toronto: University of Toronto Press, 1969.

KOLERS, P. A. Interlingual word associations. *Journal of Verbal Learning and Verbal Behavior,* 1963, *2,* 291–300.

KRASHEN, S. D. Lateralization, language learning, and the critical period: some new evidence. *Language Learning,* 1973, *23,* 63–74.

———. The monitor model for adult second language performance. In M. Burt, H. Dulay, & M. Finocchairo (Eds.), *Personal viewpoints on aspects of ESL.* New York: Regents, 1977.

———. Individual variation in the use of the monitor. In W. Ritchie (Ed.), *Second language acquisition research.* New York: Academic Press, 1978.

KUO, E. C. Y. Bilingual pattern of a Chinese immigrant group in the United States. *Anthropological Linguistics,* 1974, *16,* 128–140. (a)

————. The family and bilingual socialization: A sociolinguistic study of a sample of Chinese children in the United States. *The Journal of Social Psychology,* 1974, *92,* 181–191. (b)

LABOV, W. Contraction, deletion and inherent variability of the English copula. *Language,* 1969, *45,* 715–762.

————. The study of language in its social context. *Studium Generale,* 1970, *23,* 30–87.

————. Methodology. In W. Orr Dingwall (Ed.), *Survey of linguistic science.* Maryland: University of Maryland Linguistic Program, 1971.

LADMIRAL, J. R. (Ed.). Bilinguisme et francophonie. Special Issue of *Ethnopsychologie,* 1973, *28,* 129–340.

LADO, R. *linguistics across culture.* Ann Arbor: University of Michigan Press, 1957.

LAMBERT, W. E. A social psychology of bilingualism. *Journal of Social Issues,* 1967, *23,* 91–109.

————. Culture and language as factor in learning and education. In A. Wolfgang (Ed.), *Education of immigrant students.* Toronto: Ontario Institute of Studies in Education, 1975.

————. The effects of bilingualism on the individual: Cognitive and sociocultural consequences. In P. Hornby (Ed.), *Bilingualism: Psychological, social and educational implications.* New York: Academic Press, 1977.

LAMBERT, W. E., & FILLENBAUM S. A pilot study of aphasia among bilinguals. *Canadian Journal of Psychology,* 1959, *13,* 28–34.

LAMBERT, W. E., GARDNER, R. C., BARIK, H. C., & TURNSTALL, K. Attitudinal and cognitive aspects of intensive study of a second language. *Journal of Abnormal and Social Psychology,* 1962, *66,* 358–368.

LAMBERT, W. E., HAVELKA, J., & CROSBY, C. The influence of language acquisition contexts on bilingualism. *Journal of Abnormal and Social Psychology,* 1958, *56,* 239–244.

LAMBERT, W. E., HODGSON, R. C., GARDNER, R. C., & FILLENBAUM, S. Evaluational reactions to spoken languages. *Journal of Abnormal and Social Psychology,* 1960, *60,* 44–51.

LAMBERT, W. E., & RAWLINGS, C. Bilingual processing of mixed-language associative networks. *Journal of Verbal Learning and Verbal Behavior,* 1969, *8,* 604–609.

LANDRY, R. G. A comparison of second language learners and monolinguals on divergent thinking tasks at the elementary school level. *Modern Language Journal,* 1974, *58,* 10–15.

LANTZ, D., & STEFFLRE, V. Language and cognition revisited. *Journal of Abnormal and Social Psychology,* 1964, *69,* 472–481.

LEISCHNER, A. Über die Aphasie der Mehrsprachigen. *Archiv für Psychiatric,* 1948, *180,* 731–775. (Cited in Lambert, W. E., & Fillenbaum, S. A pilot study of aphasia among bilinguals. *Canadian Journal of Psychology,* 1959, *13,* 28–34).

LENNEBERG, E. H. *Biological Foundations of Language.* New York: John Wiley and Sons, 1967.

LINDSAY, P. H., & NORMAN, D. A. *Human information processing.* New York: Academic Press, 1972.

LLOYD, B. B. *Perception and cognition: A cross-cultural perspective.* Harmondsworth: Penguin Books, 1972.

MACNAMARA, J. *Bilingualism in primary education*. Edinburgh: Edinburgh University Press, 1966.

————. The bilingual's linguistic performance—a psychological overview. *Journal of Social Issues*, 1967, *23*, 58–77.

————. Bilingualism and thought. In J. Alatis (Ed.), *Monograph Series on Languages and Linguistics*. Washington, D.C.: Georgetown University Press, 1970.

————. The cognitive strategies of language learning. In J. Adler, Jr. & J. Richards (Eds.), *Focus on the learner*. Rowley, Mass.: Newbury House, 1973.

MARCOS, L. R., EISMA, J., & GUIMON, J. Bilingualism and sense of self. *American Journal of Psychoanalysis*, 1977, *37*, 285–290.

McCLELLAND, D. C. *The achieving society*. Princeton, N.J.: Van Nostrand, 1961.

McLAUGHLIN, B. *Second language acquisition in childhood*. Hillsdale, N.J.: Lawrence Erlbaum Associates, 1978.

MINKOWSKI, M. Sur un cas d'aphasie chez un polyglotte. *Revue Neurologique*, 1928, *35*, 361–366.

NEMSER, W. Approximative systems of foreign language learners. *International Review of Applied Linguistics*, 1971, *9*, 115–123.

NICKEL, G. Contrastive linguistics and foreign language teaching. In G. Nickel (Ed.), *Papers in contrastive linguistics*. Cambridge, England: Cambridge University Press, 1971.

NIDA, E. A. Motivation in second language learning. *Language Learning*, 1956, *7*, 11–16.

NIDA, E., & WONDERLY, W. Communication roles of language in multilingual societies. In W. Whiteley (Ed.), *Language use and social change*. London: Oxford University Press, 1971.

NORMAN, D., & RUMELHART, D. *Explorations in cognition*. San Francisco: W.H. Freeman, 1975.

PARADIS, M. Bilingualism and aphasia. In H. A. Whitaker and H. Whitaker (Eds.), *Studies in neurolinguistics*. New York: Academic Press, 1977

PARKIN, D. Emergent and stabilized multilingualism: Polyethnic peer groups in urban Kenya. In H. Giles (Ed.), *Language, ethnicity and intergroup relations*. London: Academic Press, 1977.

PEAL, E., & LAMBERT, W. E. The relation of bilingualism to intelligence. *Psychological Monographs*, 1962, *76*, (27)

PECK, E. JR. The relationship of disease and other stress to second language. *International Journal of Social Psychiatry*, 1974, *20*, 129–133.

PENFIELD, W., & ROBERTS, L. *Speech and brain mechanisms*. Princeton: Princeton University Press, 1959.

PITRES, A. Étude sur l'aphasie chez les polyglottes. *Revue de Médecine*, 1895, *15*, 873–879.

PRITCHARD, R. A. The relative popularity of secondary school subjects at various ages. *British Journal of Educational Psychology*, 1935, *5*, 157–179.

RANDHAWA, B. S., & KORPAN, S. M. Assessment of some significant affective variables and the prediction of achievement in French. *Canadian Journal of Behavioral Science*, 1973, *5*, 24–33.

RICE, F. (Ed.). *Study of the role of second language in Asia, Africa and Latin America*. Washington, D.C.: Center for Applied Linguistics, 1962.

RICHARDS, J. A noncontrastive approach to error analysis. *English Language Teaching,* 1971, *25,* 204–219. (a)

———. Error analysis and second language strategies. *Language Sciences,* 1971, *17,* 12–22. (b)

———. Social factors, interlanguage, and language learning. *Language Learning,* 1972, *22,* 159–188.

RITCHIE, W. (Ed.). *Second language acquisition research.* New York: Academic Press, 1978.

RUBIN, J. Bilingualism in Paraguay. *Anthropological Linguistics,* 1962, *4,* 52–58.

RUBIN, J., & JERNUDD, B. *Can language be planned?* Honolulu: University Press of Hawaii, 1971.

RUMELHART, D. E., LINDSAY, P. H., & NORMAN, D. A. A process model for long term memory. In E. Tulving & W. Donaldson (Eds.), *Organization of memory.* New York: Academic Press, 1972.

SALISBURY, R. F. Notes on bilingualism and linguistic change in New Guinea. In J. B. Prides & J. Holmes (Eds.), *Sociolinguistics.* Harmondsworth, England: Penguin Books, 1972. (Reprinted from *Anthropological Linguistics,* 1962, *4,* [7], 1–13).

SAMPSON, G., & RICHARDS, J. C. The study of learner language systems. *Language Sciences,* 1973, *19,* 18–25.

SCOVEL, T. Foreign accents, language acquisition and cerebral dominance. *Language Learning,* 1969, *19,* 245–253.

SEGALOWITZ, N. Communicative incompetence and the nonfluent bilingual. *Canadian Journal of Behavioral Science,* 1976, *8,* 122–131.

———. Bilingualism and social behavior. In W. Coons, D. Taylor, & M. A. Tremblay (Eds.), *The individual, language and society in Canada.* Ottawa: Canada Council, 1977. (a)

———. Psychological perspectives on bilingual education. In B. Spolsky & R. L. Cooper (Eds.), *Frontiers of bilingual education.* Rowley, Mass.: Newbury House, 1977. (b)

SEGALOWITZ, N., & GATBONTON E. Studies of the nonfluent bilingual. In P. Hornby (Ed.), *Bilingualism: Psychological, social and educational implications.* New York: Academic Press, 1977.

SEGALOWITZ, N., & LAMBERT, W. E. Semantic generalization in bilinguals. *Journal of Verbal Learning and Verbal Behavior,* 1969, *8,* 559–566.

SELIGER, H. Implications of a multiple critical periods hypothesis for second language learning. In W. Ritchie (Ed.), *Second language acquisition research.* New York: Academic Press, 1978.

SELINKER, L. The psychologically relevant data for second language learning. In P. Pimsleur & T. Quinn (Eds.), *The psychology of language learning.* Cambridge, England: Cambridge University Press, 1971.

———. Interlanguage. *International Review of Applied Linguistics.* 1972, *10,* 209–231.

SELINKER, L., SWAIN, M., & DUMAS, G. The interlanguage hypothesis extended to children. *Language Learning,* 1975, *25,* 139–152.

SIMARD, L., & TAYLOR, D. The potential for cross-cultural communication in a dyadic situation. *Canadian Journal of Behavioural Science,* 1973, *5,* 211–225.

SIMARD, L. M., TAYLOR, D. M., & GILES, H. Attribution processes and interpersonal accommodation in a bilingual setting. *Language and Speech*, 1976, *19*, 374–387.

SLOBIN, D. Cognitive prerequisites for the development of grammer. In C. A. Ferguson and D. Slobin (Eds.), *Studies of child language development*. New York: Holt, Rinehart & Winston, 1973.

SOFFIETTI, J. P. Bilingualism and biculturalism. *Journal of Educational Psychology*, 1955, *46*, 222–227.

SORENSEN, A. P., JR. Multilingualism in the Northwest Amazon. In J. B. Pride & Janet Holmes (Eds.), *Sociolinguistics*. Harmondsworth, England: Penguin Books, 1972. (Revised version from *American Anthropologist*, 1967, *69*, 670–684.)

SPOERL, D. T. Bilinguality and emotional adjustment. *Journal of Abnormal and Social Psychology*, 1943, *38*, 37–57.

SPOLSKY, B. Attitudinal aspects of second language learning. *Language Learning*, 1969, *19*, 271–285.

SPOLSKY, B., & COOPER, R. (Eds.). *Frontiers of bilingual education*. Rowley, Mass.: Newbury House, 1977. (a)

————. *Case studies in bilingual education*. Rowley, Mass.: Newbury House, 1977. (b)

STRONGMAN, K., & WOOSLEY, J. Stereotyped reactions to regional accents. *The British Journal of Social and Clinical Psychology*, 1967, *6*, 164–167.

SWAIN, M. Bilingualism, Monolingualism and Code Acquisition. Paper presented at the Child Language Conference, Chicago, November 22–24, 1971.

TAYLOR, D. T., & GARDNER, R. C. Bicultural communication. A study of communicational efficiency and person perception. *Canadian Journal of Behavioral Science*, 1970, *2*, 67–81.

TAYLOR, D. T., & SIMARD, L. The role of bilingualism in cross cultural communication. *Journal of Cross-Cultural Communication*, 1972, *3*, 101–108.

TAYLOR, L. L., CATFORD, J. C., GUIORA, A. Z., & LANE, H. H. Psychological variables and ability to pronounce a second language. *Language and Speech*, 1971, *14*, 146–157.

TAYLOR, M. Speculations on bilingualism and the cognitive network. *Working Papers in Bilingualism*, 1974, *2*, 68–124.

TORRANCE, E., WU, J., GOWAN, J., & ALIOTTI, N. Creative functioning of monolingual and bilingual children in Singapore. *The Journal of Educational Psychology*, 1970, *61*, 72–75.

TORRES, D. Types of bilingual education in Peru. *Lenguaje y Ciencias*, 1974, 14, (2), 77–84. (*Language and Language Behavior Abstracts*, January 1975, 9 [1], 126, No. 7500546).

TUCKER, G. R. Methods of second-language teaching. *The Canadian Modern Language Review*, November 1974, *31*, 102–107.

TUCKER, G. R., & D'ANGLEJAN, A. Language learning processes. In D. Lange (Ed.), *Britannica review of foreign language education* (Vol. 3). Chicago: Encyclopedia Britannica, 1970.

TUCKER, G. R., & GEDALOF, H. Bilinguals as linguistic mediators. *Psychonomic Science,* 1970, *20,* 369–370.

VYGOTSKY, L. S. *Thought and language.* Cambridge, Mass.: M.I.T. Press. 1962.

WARDAUGH, R. The contrastive analysis hypothesis. *TESOL Quarterly,* 1970, *4,* 123–130.

WEINREICH, U. *Languages in contact.* New York: Linguistic Circle of New York, 1953.

WEISENBURG, T., & MCBRIDE, K. E. *Aphasia, a clinical and psychological study.* New York: Harper, 1964.

WHITAKER, H. Bilingualism: A neurolinguistics perspective. In W. Ritchie (Ed.), *Second language acquisition research.* New York: Academic Press, 1978.

WHITELEY, W. (Ed.). *Language use and social change: Problems of multilingualism with special reference to Eastern Africa.* London: Oxford University Press, 1971.

WHORF, B. *Language, Thought and reality,* Cambridge, Mass.: John Wiley & Sons, 1956,

WHYTE, W. F., & HOLMBERG, A. R. Human problems of U.S. enterprise in Latin America. *Human Organization,* 1956, *15,* 1–40.

WOLFF, P. H. Cognitive considerations for psychoanalytical theory of language acquisition. *Psychological Issues,* 1967, *5,* 299–343.

# 4

# Language Development

*Melissa Bowerman*

## Contents

## Abstract

"How does a child learn to talk?" Cross-cultural research that examines this problem is reviewed in this chapter.[1] The focus is on three major content areas: the acquisition of the linguistic code (including syntactic, morphological, and semantic structure), the development of rules for socially appropriate language use (the emergence of different speech acts, speech variants, and discourse conventions), and the role of the environment (speech to children, other social factors). Methodological problems in studying child language cross-culturally are also discussed. The chapter emphasizes how cross-cultural research contributes towards understanding the process of language development by disentangling possible explanatory variables that are confounded in any one linguistic community, thereby showing how the child's characteristic ways of approaching the language-learning task interact with the properties of the language to be acquired and with the child's social environment.

## Introduction

The mastery of a first language is one of the most striking achievements of early childhood. Although scholars have pondered how language is acquired for centuries, the intensity with which it has been scrutinized over the last two decades is unprecedented. As Brown (1974) puts it, "all over the world the first sentences of small children are being painstakingly taped, transcribed, and analyzed as if they were the last sayings of great sages" (p. 123). This surge of interest stems in part from an increasing appreciation among social scientists for the complexity of the child's task and for the challenge it poses to current conceptions of learning. It also reflects a growing awareness that language acquisition is linked in intricate and as yet little-understood ways with human perceptual and cognitive abilities and with the structure of natural languages.

The inspiration for the "modern" study of child language can be traced rather directly to the work of the linguist Chomsky (1957, 1959, 1965), who argued cogently that existing theories of both language structure and language acquisition were grossly inadequate. Two of his claims particularly influenced subsequent research. First was his argument that knowing a language does not mean simply knowing a repertoire of sentences. Rather, being a fluent speaker of a language entails having internalized a set of rules that underlies sentence construction. According to this view, the task of the language-learning child can be seen as a problem in rule formulation: from the limited sample of speech to which he is exposed the child must somehow arrive at a set of rules that will enable him to produce and comprehend an infinite number of possible sentences.

Chomsky's second influential claim was that the structure of language is intimately related to the child's capacity to acquire it. He argued that the rules governing sentence construction are so abstract and complex that the child could not "discover" them from the superficial characteristics of the speech he hears unless he were guided by some inborn knowledge of what to look for. What Chomsky attributed to the child was an innate knowledge of linguistic universals, that is, of whatever structural principles are common to all languages. Indeed, the very existence of linguistic universals, according to Chomsky and his followers, is a direct consequence of the child's capacity for language: whatever characterizes this capacity has left its mark on the structure of all natural languages by restricting the form of language to that which is learnable by humans (McNeill, 1966b, p. 50).

Much of the early "post-Chomskian" research was specifically aimed at the question of whether children's early linguistic progress could indeed be characterized accurately in terms of rule formulation (e.g., Berko, 1958; Brown & Berko, 1960; Brown & Fraser, 1963; Braine, 1963; Miller & Ervin, 1964). This research quickly resulted in a number of empirically based generalizations about the early syntactic systems of children learning English, and a limited amount of evidence from children learning other languages suggested tantalizingly that the observed phenomena might be universal (Slobin, 1966a, 1968, 1969, 1970). Questions began to proliferate. Would putative universals of language development hold up against further cross-cultural scrutiny? What other as yet unsuspected similarities might there be among children learning different languages? For example, do all children pass through a similar sequence of "stages" on their way to adult mastery of the language? How does the structure of the language being acquired affect the learning process? What could account for any observed universals of language acquisition? In particular, could an innate knowledge of universals of language be effectively invoked as an explanation for commonalities among children learning different languages? The era of cross-cultural research on child language development had begun.

Comparative work with existing material proved difficult, however. Although child language had been studied by researchers in a number of European countries and in the Soviet Union, much of the material was inaccessible to English-speaking investigators. In addition, adequate comparison was thwarted by differences both in data collection techniques and in the particular problems that had been investigated. Finally, most of the non-English studies dealt with the acquisition of languages that share an Indo-European ancestry with English. How language acquisition proceeds in languages with totally different structural properties was little understood. New data that could provide a firmer basis for comparative analysis were clearly called for.

An important reflection of this need was the 1967 publication of *A Field Manual for Cross-Cultural Study of the Acquisition of Communicative Competence.* This volume, edited by Slobin and collaborated on by several psychologists and anthropologists at the University of California at Berkeley, presented an admirably eclectic view of the range of phenomena that should be studied, a summary of existing research techniques, and specific suggestions for the conduct of cross-cultural research on language development.

In the years since the *Field Manual* came out, the cross-cultural study of child language has mushroomed. The vigor of the approach is attested to by the appearance of many detailed reports on language acquisition by children learning languages other than English,[2] the instigation of child language projects at universities and research centers in a number of countries by investigators interested in the work going on elsewhere, the convocation of several international conferences on child language, and the founding of the *Journal of Child Language,* a publication with an international advisory board that explicitly encourages the submission of articles on languages other than English. During this period, considerable progress has been made in our understanding of how language acquisition takes place. Much of this progress would not have been possible without the input provided by studies of children in non-English-speaking communities.

The discussion in this chapter of the role of cross-cultural research in the study of language development is organized in the following way. The first major section provides an overview of what is studied in research on language development and outlines the major goals of cross-cultural investigation in this field. Following this is a section on methodological problems in studying child language cross-culturally. Then come two major sections that discuss cross-cultural perspectives on selected aspects of the acquisition of the *linguistic code* and of competence in *language use,* respectively. "Selected" must be stressed because in a chapter-length review the coverage is necessarily limited. The most notable omissions are cross-cultural perspectives on babbling and speech perception during the first year of life and on phonological development.[3] These have been neglected in the interests of providing a more thorough review of the development of *form-meaning* relationships, or how children acquire an understanding of the referential and social meanings that underlie language and how they master the linguistic devices their language employs to express these meanings.

Following the sections on the linguistic code and on language use is a discussion of the role of the child's social milieu in the acquisition of language. The chapter concludes with a brief consideration of directions for future research and some comments about the value of research on language development for investigators in other fields.

### Cross-Cultural Research on Language Development: An Overview of Content and Goals

The ultimate motivation for doing cross-cultural research on language development, as in any content area, is to determine what is universal and what is specific to particular groups and to formulate, on the basis of this information, both very general principles that apply to individuals in all cultures and detailed accounts of how these principles are realized under different kinds of conditions. Of course, the goals of any particular cross-cultural study are much more specific. Before we consider what some of these goals are in the case of child language research, a general review of the subject matter of the study of language development is in order.

## Acquiring Communicative Competence

A general theory of language development must be able to account for both what the child acquires—the nature of the information the child must have to qualify as a fluent speaker—and how he acquires it. One important function of Slobin's (1967) *Field Manual* was to heighten awareness among students of child language of the different types of information a speaker must master.

*The linguistic code.* During most of the 1960s, investigators focused heavily on one particular kind of linguistically relevant knowledge—knowledge of the *linguistic code*, or the structure of language itself insofar as it is an instrument for expressing referential or ideational content (propositions about events, objects, actions, spatial relationships, feelings, and so on). Even within this general category, research efforts were mainly limited to the exploration of how children learn morphological and syntactic rules, that is, rules governing the way in which morphemes combine to form words and sentences. The investigation of the acquisition of other aspects of language structure, including semantics and phonology, has begun to flourish only more recently.

The initial restriction of research to the child's learning of the structural characteristics of his language was primarily due to the influence of the distinction Chomsky drew between *competence*, or "the speaker-hearer's knowledge of his language," and *performance*, or "the actual use of language in concrete situations" (1965, p. 4). According to Chomsky, performance is affected by "such grammatically irrelevant conditions as memory limitations, distractions, shifts of attention and interest, and errors (random or characteristic)" (1965, p. 3); competence, in contrast, is the "mental reality underlying actual behavior" (1965, p. 4). Chomsky argued that performance is irrelevant for linguistic theory; linguists should be concerned with characterizing competence.

*Rules for language use.* By the late 1960s, a small but growing number of investigators had voiced objections to Chomsky's notion of competence (e.g., Hymes, 1964; 1971a; Slobin, 1967; Campbell & Wales, 1970). They pointed out that the domain of linguistic knowledge with which Chomsky was concerned constitutes only *one* component, albeit critical, of what the speaker must know in order to be fluent in his language. In particular, they argued that in ignoring "the actual use of language in concrete situations" Chomsky was overlooking all the knowledge that speakers must draw on in order to produce utterances that are not only grammatically well formed but also *appropriate* to the particular social contexts in which they occur. As Hymes put it, "it is not enough for the child to be able to produce any grammatical utterance. It would have to remain speechless if it could not decide which grammatical utterance here and now, if it could not connect utterances with situations" (1964, p. 110).

Norms governing the contextually appropriate use of language are no less binding than rules governing syntactic or phonological well-formedness. For example, departures from "grammaticality" can readily be detected in both cases. For this reason, such norms can be formalized as *rules for language use*. These rules, which have been termed "sociolinguistic" or "pragmatic," depending on the investigator's orientation and emphasis, specify how language is used in particular social settings to accomplish specific goals such as eliciting or imparting information, making requests, telling stories or jokes, negotiating a conversation, emphasizing or highlighting some parts of a message and backgrounding others, and so on. How speakers cast their sentences and how listeners interpret them is systematically related to a host of social and contextual factors such as the attributes and interpersonal history of the participants in the speech event, the setting, the topic of conversation, and the details of the preceding discourse, (Hymes, 1972).

The totality of knowledge that enables a speaker to produce utterances that are structurally well formed, referentially accurate, and contextually appropriate, and to understand the speech of others as a joint function of its structural characteristics and social context, has become known as *communicative competence* (Gumperz & Hymes, 1964; Slobin, 1967). To provide a comprehensive account of the acquisition of communicative competence under a full range of social and linguistic conditions must be the ultimate goal of any theory of language development.

### Learning the Mapping Between Form and Meaning

Consider from the child's perspective what is involved in acquiring communicative competence. From those around her, she hears sequences of sounds varying simultaneously along a number of dimensions. At the same time, she is experiencing continual changes in her external environment, both physical and social, and shifts in her internal or subjective reactions. Her problem, to a borrow a construct from Bruner, Wallach, and Galanter (1959), is to identify *recurrent regularities* and to build a model isomorphic with the redundancy of the environment.

What are the "regularities" in question? First are regularities or patterns in the linguistic signal itself. For example, recurrent sounds, words, intonational patterns, and so forth, must begin to be recognized as "the same" despite superficial variation. Restrictions on how linguistic forms are patterned must be discovered (e.g., *put the hat on, put on the hat, put it on,* but not *put on it*). Second are regularities in the child's social and physical environment and in her internal experiences or reactions. Identifying regularities of this second type entails nothing less than building up a complex system of *meanings*—ways of categorizing and interpreting the significance of events in the world. Third and most critical, the child must discover the *contingencies* between linguistic forms and physical and social meanings, that is, how the two sets of variables covary. For example, she must determine which linguistic variations are insignificant and which are linked in a regular way to variation in meaning. Conversely, she must learn which discriminable differences in meanings are matched by differences in language forms and which are not. And, most centrally, she must work out precisely what the connections are, that is, which meanings are associated with which linguistic forms. The child's task of discovering how language forms and meanings covary is often called the *mapping* problem (e.g., Clark, 1975).

Determining how children accomplish the mapping between form and meaning requires the joint exploration of a number of problems. For example: 1) How does the child approach the analysis of the linguistic signal itself? Does she come equipped with strategies specific to language, for example, knowledge of some of the structural properties of language? Or does her analysis depend only on more general information-processing abilities? How does she determine what behaviors on the part of others are relevant to language (coughs? clicks? gestures?) and which are not? 2) How does the child categorize and interpret the nonlinguistic events of her environment, that is, build up a repertoire of meanings? Does she start out as a *tabula rasa* or does she have inherent predispositions to categorize in certain ways, for example, to attend to certain stimuli and not others as a basis for classification? Does language influence her way of conceptualizing her physical and social surroundings or does she organize and interpret the environment relatively independently of language? 3) How does the child tackle the mapping problem itself? Are there priorities in the hypotheses she entertains about what meaning might be associated with language form X, or, conversely, what language form might be used to express meaning Y? What factors make the mapping problem difficult and what factors facilitate it? For example, what is the effect of inconsistency or irregularity (noise) in the system of mapping itself? Does speech to children have special tutorial properties that help them discover connections between forms and meanings? How does the frequency with which the child is exposed to various forms affect the rate and order of acquisition? Questions like these cannot be answered without input from cross-cultural research, for reasons that are outlined below.

## Goals of Cross-Cultural Research on Language Acquisition

For heuristic purposes, three broad, interrelated goals of cross-cultural research relevant to language acquisition may be distinguished. First is the goal of obtaining a deeper understanding of what children must learn in order to be fluent in their native language, and of the social contexts in which they may be called on to learn it. What in fact is the range of variability in the structure and use of language? How much cross-cultural variation is there in the socialization practices that are relevant to language acquisition?

Information about whether there are constraints on the form that language structures and rules for language use can take is of particular importance for the study of language development because of the possibility that universals of language may be linked to the inherent knowledge, strategies, or expectations of the language-learning child, as Chomsky (1965) suggested and as will be discussed later. Information about variability in the social contexts of language acquisition is also essential for exploring questions of innateness, for two reasons. First, as Campbell and Wales (1970) point out, universals of language might stem at least in part from universal experiences of early childhood rather than from innate predispositions. Second, biologically given predispositions should show up as similarities among language-learning children even if there are gross differences in their environments and in the language socialization practices to which they are exposed. Conversely, to the extent that language development is dependent on environmental rather than biological factors, cross-cultural variability in language socialization should result in different patterns of acquisition.

The second goal of cross-cultural research is to determine what is universal and what is variable in the course of language development itself. Do generalizations based on children learning one particular language apply to children everywhere? Or do differences of language structure and environment exert such strong effects that few commonalities can be found?

The first and second goals of cross-cultural research on language acquisition feed directly into the third goal: to arrive at a theory of *how* children acquire language that not only accounts for any observed universals of development but that also is sufficiently flexible and abstract to explain variability by reference to the way the knowledge, learning principles, or strategies that the child brings to the task *interact* with the particular language rules that must be acquired and with the characteristics of the social milieu.

Aspects of these three broad goals of cross-cultural research on language development are overviewed below; themes raised here are pursued in more detail in subsequent sections.

*Cross-cultural perspectives on acquiring the linguistic code.* Differences among languages are found at every level of structure: phonological, morphological, syntactic, and semantic. For example, English relies heavily on word order to distinguish between nouns with different syntactic functions such as subject, direct object, and indirect object (cf. *John hit Jim* versus *Jim hit John; give the dolly a baby* versus *give the baby a dolly*). In contrast, Hungarian and Russian mark these relations by case endings on the nouns, leaving word order free to vary in the service of other goals, such as emphasizing new information and backgrounding old information. To take a second example, Spanish uses intonation (rising versus falling) to distinguish between yes/no questions and declaratives, whereas Finnish signals this distinction with word order rearrangements and the addition of a question particle without accompanying intonational changes. English uses both changes in intonation *and* in word order; Tarascan (an Indian language spoken in Mexico) uses neither, but instead distinguishes questions from declaratives by voicing the normally whispered sentence-final vowel. Languages also differ in the way they categorize or divide up the world of experience through their lexicon and syntactic structure. Some semantic categories found in one language may have no counterpart in another, or the categories of the two languages may overlap in complex ways.

As these examples indicate, individual languages represent particular "solutions" from among a range of possible solutions to the problem of how meanings and formal devices for expressing meanings are to be related to each other (see Bates, 1976a, p. 161 ff. for relevant discussion). Similarly, the various structural characteristics (e.g., syntactic, semantic) of a language are themselves interrelated in specific ways. The problem that this language-specific "packaging" of characteristics poses for the student of child language is that it creates a confounding of the factors that might be invoked to explain why children learning a certain language proceed as they do. For example, if children learning English tend to observe word-order constraints in their earliest sentences, is this because of a built-in tendency of all language-learning children to prefer rigid word order? Or might it instead simply reflect exposure to a language in which word order plays a critical role in expressing basic semantic/syntactic relations? Similarly, if children learning a particular language acquire a given set of language forms in a certain order, does the explanation lie in the relative difficulty of the *meanings* these forms express? Or is it perhaps due instead to the relative difficulty of the formal devices that are used to encode these meanings?

Disentangling confounding factors so that questions like these can be answered requires comparing the progress of children learning languages that differ structurally in key respects. Only when we know that children behave similarly with regard to a particular aspect of acquisition even though there may be critical differences in the structures being acquired can we speculate sensibly about universality. On the other hand, when we find that children learning different languages proceed differently, a careful analysis of their behaviors against the structural features of their languages often allows us to infer determining factors. In short, information on the learning of a wide variety of languages must be compared and integrated in efforts to move beyond the simple description of how acquisition takes place in particular linguistic communities to a universally applicable account of how children approach the structure of language.

*Cross-cultural perspectives on rules for language use.* Nowhere is cross-cultural research more essential than in helping investigators identify and characterize what the child must learn in order to use his knowledge of the structural aspects of language in contextually appropriate ways. Fourteen years ago, Ervin-Tripp (in Slobin, 1967) noted that the study of rules for language use, or "the ethnography of speaking," was "in its infancy," and observed that an important first step must be "to obtain sufficient ethnographic data to provide a basis for comparative discussion among . . . field workers" (p. xi).

Much of the literature that has been published to date on the ethnography of speaking, by sociolinguists, anthropologists, and child language specialists alike, has been aimed not only at presenting specific research findings but also, perhaps even more importantly, at "consciousness raising"—increasing our level of awareness that, just as there are important structural differences from one language to another, so also is there significant cross-cultural variation in patterns of language use.

A central fact that must be dealt with in studying situationally appropriate speech is that language, even within a relatively homogeneous linguistic community, is not a single monolithic entity. Rather, it comprises a set of linguistic variants—alternative ways to express approximately the same ideational content or to accomplish a given aim, such as requesting a service. Variation takes place at every level of language structure, including pronunciation (e.g., *eating* versus *eatin'*, *What are you doing?* versus *Whatcha doin'?*), lexicon (e.g., *woman* versus *lady*, *Mr. Smith* versus *Bob*, *Mary loves John* versus *she loves him*), prosody, (e.g., *Hárry killed Jim* versus *Harry killed Jím*), and syntax (e.g., *open the window* versus *I wonder if there's some way to cool off this room?*).

The choices speakers make between competing variants are systematically linked to a variety of factors. One important goal of ethnographic research on rules for language use has been to formulate a universally applicable vocabulary for identifying, describing, and interrelating these factors. Hymes suggests that at least sixteen or seventeen components of speaking situations must be distinguished in order to account for the way people talk and interpret the talk of others, for example, for the choices they make between alternate ways to express more-or-less the same message. He notes that these components combine in different ways in different cultures; thus, "these features and dimensions, more than particular constellations of them, will be found to be universal, and hence elementary to descriptive and comparative frames of reference" (1972, p. 49). Among the components that Hymes and other have emphasized are the attributes of the *participants* in the speech event (e.g., their sex, relative and absolute age, social status, role relative to one another in the context of speech [e.g., waiter-diner, doctor-patients], their assumptions about each other's prior state of knowledge, their past interpersonal history [e.g., friendly or quarrelsome], the *topic* of the message, and the *setting* (including the time, place, and "situation," e.g., a dinner party or a date) (see Hymes, 1972; Ervin 1964a; Rubin, 1974).

Cultural specificity is found not only in the way in which such factors cluster (are "emicized") to constrain the production and interpretation of speech but also in the way each factor is defined within the culture. For example, the relative ages of the speaker and listener may be important in most or all cultures, but the degree of discrepancy in age that is required to make a difference linguistically varies considerably (Ervin-Tripp, 1971). Similarly, how relative social status is defined and what contrasts between settings are linguistically important are subject to wide cultural variation (Rubin, 1974).

Cross-cultural variation is also found in the specific ways that speech is affected by factors such as social status and setting. For example, probably all languages have less versus more "formal" ways of talking (with "formality" being culturally defined but usually including some reference to variables like absolute and relative social status, degree of social distance, and setting). But the way in which degrees of formality are marked linguistically varies greatly from one social group to another. Sometimes the variants are options within the same language or dialect (e.g., *eatin'* versus *eating; buck* versus *dollar; tu* versus *vous; gimme your coat* versus *it's cold out tonight* as alternate ways to obtain a coat). In other communities, contrasts in formality may be marked by a shift between a local dialect and a standard language. In still others, the same effect may be obtained by shifting between distinct languages (Rubin, 1962). Because the communicative ends that are served by shifting between alternate linguistic forms may be similar despite differences in the "level" at which the shifting takes place, several sociolinguists have suggested that the tradition of thought that equates one language, one culture sets up artificial boundaries and should be abandoned in favor of a theory that treats monolingualism, bidialectalism, and bilingualism within a common sociolinguistic framework (Gumperz & Hymes, 1964; Hymes, 1971b; Rubin, 1974).

Acquiring language entails not only learning how to form sentences that are grammatical and contextually appropriate one at a time, and to interpret such sentences by others, but also learning *discourse* conventions, or how successive sentences are integrated into coherent longer sequences. Discourse conventions, like rules governing the alternation between linguistic variants, are culturally variable. For example, social groups differ with regard to the types of discourse they stress and the elaboration or systematization of the knowledge required to successfully participate in them. Examples of genres that vary in their social significance and degree of elaboration from culture to culture and even among subgroups within a culture include story-telling, joking, insult-exchange or verbal dueling, indirect speaking or innuendo, and political or rhetorical speaking.

Even when genres of discourse are widespread or universal, there may be significant variability in their specific content and/or in the sequencing of material. For example, Mitchell-Kernan and Kernan (1975) and Dundes, Leach, and Özkök (1972) note that there are cross-cultural differences in the content of insults. Godard (1977) has analysed differences in the content and sequencing of telephone conversations in France and the United States. And Philips (1976), who compared the regulation of conversation among Indian speakers on an Oregon reservation and among "Anglos," found differences in the use of devices for regulating conversational turn-taking such as gaze direction and body alignment and in the speakers' degree of control over their own turns and those of their addressees.

Discourse conventions may vary across cultures in even more subtle ways. For example, Keenan (1976) has recently presented a thought-provoking analysis of possible cross-cultural differences in the underlying assumptions that speakers and listeners bring to linguistic interactions. Her analysis uses the influential work of Grice (1975) as a jumping-off point. According to Grice, participants in conversation expect each other to conform to a certain implicit code of behavior; this code can be formalized in terms of *conversational maxims,* such as "be informative" (meet the informational needs of your listener) and "be relevant" (keep your utterances relevant to the topic at hand). These maxims guide both the speaker's behavior and the listener's interpretation of what the speaker says. Of course, the maxims are in fact often violated, but the context will usually hold some clue to the possibility of violation; in the absence of counterindications, interlocutors will ordinarily assume that the maxims are being followed.

Are Gricean conversational maxims universal? Grice did not discuss this, but the assumption that they are is implicit in his work. Keenan, however, presents counterevidence based on her analysis of expectations and practices regarding "informativeness" among Malagasy villagers (Madagascar), and observes that "In some societies, meeting the informational needs of a conversational partner may be relatively unmarked or routine behavior. In other societies, meeting another's informational needs may be relatively unexpected or marked behavior" (1976, p. 69). Despite Grice's inattention to the possibility of cultural differences in underlying assumptions about conversation, an important value of his work, as Keenan stresses, is that it "orients us to pursue the . . . goal of assessing universal conversational principles," and "offer[s] a framework in which the conversational principles of different speech communities can be compared" (p. 79).

Most studies to date on the acquisition of rules for language use have been conducted in single cultures and have concentrated primarily on describing what the child learns and when he learns it. Explicitly comparative studies are only recently beginning to appear (e.g., Ervin-Tripp, 1977; Hollos & Beeman, 1978; Mitchell-Kernan & Kernan, 1975). As these studies multiply, researchers will gradually become better equipped to tackle the difficult question of *how* children learn the socially appropriate use of language.

*Cross-cultural perspectives on the role of the social milieu.* What role does the child's environment play in language development? In traditional behaviorist psychology, the environment has been considered paramount, with the child's caretakers supplying models of correct speech patterns, encouraging imitation, and shaping the child's speech efforts by differential reinforcement to more closely approximate the norms of the community.

If we look beyond middle-class Western societies, however, it becomes clear that this view is parochial in its assumptions about the social context in which language learning takes place. For example, in many cultures, toddlers are cared for primarily by slightly older children rather than by attentive parents (Slobin, 1975a). In some social groups, children's verbal efforts are met with relative indifference rather than encouragement (e.g., Hymes, 1972; Ward, 1971). And high tolerance for error, that is, failure to provide corrective feedback, appears to be the rule not only in other cultures but even in our own (see Brown & Hanlon, 1970; Radulovic, 1975; Blount, 1972a; and Kernan, 1969, for evidence on this matter with regard to American, Yugoslavian, Luo, and Samoan parents, respectively).

Despite great cultural variation in general child-raising practices and in the specific treatment of language development, the overall course of language acquisition is very similar from one social group to another. For example, Lenneberg (1966) noted the striking absence of reports by anthropologists about "discrepancies between the vocalizations or communicative behavior among the children of 'primitive' and 'western' man" (p. 230). He reported additionally that recent field work in several cultures confirmed the concordances between speech and motor behavior that had previously been observed in western cultures, for example, first words at about the time of walking, fluency (despite minor inaccuracies) by the time the child can tiptoe or walk backwards three yards. Lenneberg and others have used these findings to support the view that language development is to a large extent maturationally controlled and therefore robust against a wide variety of environmental conditions, some of which would necessarily be seen as highly adverse from a behaviorist's standpoint.[4]

Additional arguments for the importance of biological factors in language development are provided by Slobin (1970). Observing that children everywhere seem to pass through a "two word stage" of development, he notes that "There is no a priori reason why child speech, at a certain stage, should be limited to utterances of two words in length, for children can babble much longer strings of sound. The universality of this phase suggests the maturation of a 'language acquisition device' with a fairly fixed programming span for utterances at the start" (p. 176).

Despite these indications that language acquisition has a significant biological component, there is increasing evidence that children's inherent capacity interacts in complex ways with environmental factors. The prime support for this view comes from recent studies of the nature of talk to children. According to the nativist view of the mid-1960s, speech to children cannot serve as a sufficient basis for extracting rules of grammar because it is random, haphazard, and full of disfluencies and ungrammatical sentences. But careful scrutiny has demonstrated that this assumption is invalid. Speech to children is not only admirably fluent and free of errors, but also different in a number of potentially important ways from the speech that adults address to each other. For example, it is characterized by shorter, slower, and syntactically simpler sentences, modifications of word choice and phonological structure, and special interaction patterns. Most detailed studies of caretaker speech have been carried out in English-speaking communities (see Snow, 1977, and de Villiers & de Villiers, 1978, for reviews), but the phenomenon of special, simplified speech to language learners appears to be universal (Ferguson, 1977).

The generality of special speech to infants, coupled with its simplicity, clarity, and redundancy relative to speech among adults, has led many researchers to suggest that it plays an important tutorial role in language acquisition (e.g., Snow, 1972; Garnica, 1977). To the extent that this proposal is substantiated, arguments for a strong innate component to the language acquisition capacity that are based on the supposed degeneracy of the child's language input are correspondingly weakened (Brown, 1977; Newport, Gleitman, & Gleitman, 1977).

Interest in the role of the social milieu in language acquisition has not been limited to caretaker speech patterns, although this topic has received the most intense examination in recent years. Investigators have also pointed to the existence of cultural differences in general *style* of child socialization, particularly socialization with respect to language. Style is in part a function of beliefs about how babies should be treated and what should be expected of them. There is significant cultural and subcultural variation in these beliefs (see Tulkin & Kagan, 1972; Blount, 1972a; Hymes, 1971b). For example, in some cultures it is assumed that infants can understand speech from birth or even before (Blount, 1972a), whereas in others the child is credited with comprehension only much later. How might this differentially affect the kind of speech infants are exposed to? A study by Bingham (1971) suggests an answer: she found that adults who believe that babies can understand a great deal simplify their speech to prelinguistic children more than those who believe that comprehension begins later. It is not yet known whether exposure to simplified speech during the first year of life affects subsequent language acquisition, but, if so, this could result in systematic differences among social groups in qualitative or quantitive aspects of language development. Other cultural factors that affect the speech the young child hears include attitudes about the *social role* of the child within the family or the society (Blount, 1972b; Bernstein, 1972; Fischer, 1970).

The nature of communication between child and caretaker will be examined more fully in cross-cultural perspective in a subsequent section, along with discussions of the effects of environmental variation on the course of language development. Most studies of the latter topic have been carried out only within homogeneous social groups or at best across social classes; there are still few explicitly cross-cultural studies. However, whether carried out across individuals within social classes, across social classes within a culture, or across cultures, the advantage of the comparative approach is that it allows the role of environmental factors to be assessed in the context of "natural experiments" that would be unethical if set up deliberately (Ervin-Tripp, in Slobin, 1967, p. 138).

## Methodological Problems in Studying Child Language Cross-Culturally

*Methodological Bias*

Comparing the language acquisition of children in different linguistic communities raises certain methodological problems that do not affect the comparative study of children within relatively homogeneous groups. A warning that has by now been raised in connection with so many areas of psychological investigation that it requires little elaboration here is that what one finds when looking for particular kinds of knowledge or ability is greatly affected by how one looks for it. Methods of data collection that work well enough in one cultural setting are often inadequate in another because they fail to engage the relevant knowledge or skill. Thus, what may at first appear to be a deficiency on the part of members of one culture relative to members of another culture may actually stem from factors irrelevant to the ability under investigation. A simple shift in the task or in the content area to which the task is applied will sometimes produce surprisingly different results (see Cole, Gay, Glick, & Sharp, 1971, for a careful exploration of this general theme as it affect the cross-cultural conduct of cognitive psychology).

The possibility of cultural bias in the application of methods for studying language development are obviously of both theoretical and practical concern. The theoretical problem is that methodological factors may lead one to identify differences in the language development of children in different social groups where differences do not exist. The most important practical problems raised by questions of methodological adequacy concern educational practices in countries whose children are linguistically and/or culturally heterogeneous.

Two types of methodological bias that can threaten the validity of comparative studies of language development have been discussed by Ervin-Tripp (1972). She termed these *linguistic bias* and *sociolinguistic bias.*

*Linguistic bias.* Linguistic bias arises when the linguistic materials that are selected for testing or as targets for observation are not potentially equally accessible or familiar to the children being compared. This problem is particularly serious when the children involved are ostensibly speakers of the "same" language but are acquiring dialects that treat the linguistic forms under study differently. In this case, the blanket use of the same forms (usually taken from the "standard" dialect) for all subjects virtually guarantees a poorer performance by the children for whom the forms are less familiar (see Ervin-Tripp, 1972, and Dale, 1976, p. 305, for some examples from the literature).

*Sociolinguistic bias.* "Each community, even subgroups within communities like teenage gangs, may develop its own patterns of language use, its own set of speech events, its own valuing of skill" (Ervin-Tripp, 1972, p. 265 in Ervin-Tripp, 1973). This means that the social situations in which the investigator collects data and the particular techniques he uses may have very different kinds of significance for members of different groups. The term *sociolinguistic bias* refers to bias that arises when an investigator's methods of data collection do not tap the intended linguistic ability equally in members of different social groups because of differences in rules for language use or in reactions to the investigator's tasks.

Consider the cultural factors that may affect attempts to collect representative samples of children's spontaneous speech. Most of the English-speaking children whose speech has served as a basis for cross-cultural comparison have come from middle-class families where the display of verbal skill to friends and strangers alike is encouraged and where interactions with strangers may be commonplace. Such children tend to be relaxed and talkative in a wide range of settings, even when confronted with demands for unfamiliar types of performance (e.g., psycholinguistic tests). Compare this happy situation with the one that met Blount (1969), who studied language development among the Luo of east Africa. There, despite visiting extensively in the children's homes, varying the time of day at which the visits took place, and providing props for stimulating speech, Blount was able to collect less than 200 spontaneous utterances from a total of six children—barely enough to even suggest the nature of the children's verbal abilities. Blount attributed the children's silence to a number of cultural factors, including the promotion and encouragement of children's fear of strangers by both ecological conditions and social practices, the fact that children are taught to be silent in the presence even of welcomed visitors so that adults can talk, and the fact that children are taught to speak to adults in certain respectful ways. Even when the children were encouraged to talk by their parents they found it difficult to overcome these culturally induced strictures. Blount's perceptive analysis nicely illustrates Hymes's (1971b) observation that the difficulties anthropologists experience in gathering ethnographic data can provide valuable cues to the local rules of language use.

Even when children are not severely reluctant to talk, cultural differences in adult-child interaction patterns can affect data collection. For example, parents in some social groups are accustomed to conversing with their children and have well-developed techniques for eliciting speech on a variety of topics. In other groups, adults may typically speak with children primarily to direct and control their behavior, or may interact with them relatively little because caretaking responsibilities are typically assigned to other, slightly older children. The latter situation confronted Kernan (1969) in his study of language acquisition by Samoan children. The spontaneous speech samples collected from one of his two subjects consisted primarily of short labeling responses to "what's that?" questions from the child's mother and aunt, who were hard-pressed to think of ways to engage the child in conversation.

The traditional western technique of taping mother-child interactions in the home seems quite unsuited to such cultures. Obtaining maximally informative speech samples requires following children to the settings in which their most representative and varied speech takes place. Schieffelin

(1980) has recently provided an interesting account of the ethnographic work that went into her identification of such settings for the Kaluli children she studied in New Guinea, along with thoughtful analyses of how unexamined assumptions in the Western approach to scientific study have hampered attempts to collect useful language data from non-Western children.

Transplanting experimental techniques for probing children's linguistic knowledge to social groups other than those in which they were developed is an even greater challenge than trying to collect representative speech samples. A first problem, of course, is that how children perform on such tasks is influenced by how they perceive them and what they think is expected of them; cross-cultural differences in these factors is inevitable. But beyond this, the use of certain techniques may present specific problems in some cultures but not in others. For example, many studies of how English-speaking children comprehend various words and sentence structures have required that the subjects distinguish between two or more pictured stimuli and pick out the one referred to or described by an utterance produced by the experimenter (e.g., Fraser, Bellugi, & Brown, 1963). But interpreting the meaning of two-dimensional representations is governed to a large extent by learned and culturally variable conventions (Davidoff, 1975, p. 90). Moreover, children's access to such representations and their opportunity to learn interpretive conventions vary considerably across cultures. Thus, experimental techniques involving pictures may be impossible to employ in some cultures.

A second example of a technique that may be relatively unsuited to some cultures is elicited imitation. This method can often provide information about the nature of children's grammatical rule systems (e.g., Slobin & Welsh, 1973; Kuczaj & Maratsos, 1975; and Menyuk, 1963), and it has been successfully used with Mayan children (Stross, 1969). However, Ervin-Tripp and Mitchell-Kernan (1977, p. 19) report that researchers have had trouble using it in Italy, apparently because children's imitation of the speech of others is censured.

Sometimes cultural differences in the way children "take to" a technique can be overcome by special adaptations. Kernan and Blount's (1966) attempt to test Mexican children with Berko's (1958) technique for studying children's knowledge of morphological rules provides a good example. This method entails showing the child cartoon-like pictures and asking her to complete utterances about the pictures. Thus, the child might first be presented with a picture of a "wug," then a picture of two of them along with the sentence "Now there are two―――." Nonsense words are used to insure that correct performance ("wugs" in this case) can be attributed to true knowledge of morphological rules rather than to memorization of the inflected forms of familiar words. Berko's middle-class American subjects were not bothered by the nonsense words and readily inflected them, but Kernan and Blount found their lower-class Mexican subjects reluctant to use them. They interpreted this as a difference in the degree to which the children had been exposed to formal testing situations. Eventually Kernan and Blount were able to induce the children to respond to nonsense items by presenting them with warm-up examples using real words, a preliminary not found necessary by Berko.

### Reappraising Existing Generalizations in Light of Cross-Cultural Evidence

Suppose that cross-cultural work has revealed some differences between children in another culture and those "at home," and that special care has been taken to ensure that the new data are not biased and misleading for reasons of the sort just discussed. Can we now conclude with confidence that true cross-cultural differences exist? Clearly not. Another possibility must first be considered: that our assumptions about children in the familiar culture are in error.

One important contribution that cross-cultural research can make to the study of language development, as to any discipline, is to force investigators to question the accuracy of existing generalizations. Reappraisal on the basis of cross-cultural information can lead to the identification and elimination of erroneous or unwarranted assumptions. When this is done, apparent cross-cultural differences may disappear. Notice that the outcome in this case is the opposite of the outcome of removing cultural bias: eliminating bias makes members of the "other" culture seem more similar to members of the known culture, whereas revising assumptions about the known culture in light of new cross-cultural information makes members of the known culture appear more similar to members of the "other" culture.

The power of cross-cultural research to force reevaluations of existing assumptions has been realized in connection with at least two English-based generalizations about children's early language, the "pivot grammar" and "telegraphic speech." These will be considered in a later section.

### Problems in Identifying Causes of Variability Among Children

Cross-cultural research has great potential for separating confounded factors and allowing researchers to determine how variation in patterns of language acquisition is linked to variation in social milieu and in rules governing language structure and use. However, realizing this potential has been more difficult than investigators at first envisioned. In particular, efforts to link differences in acquisition to differences in the language being learned or to variability in social practices have often failed because the variation among children *within* linguistic and cultural boundaries has often turned out to be just as great as the variation across them.

One illustration will suffice. Children differ with respect to how rigidly they order words in their sentences. Some used fixed order for words performing such basic syntactic functions as subject, verb, and direct object, whereas others use flexible order. A reasonable hypothesis would be that such variation is determined by the way in which word order is treated in the language being learned. Children learning languages that have fairly fixed word orders, such as English, would be expected to observe word order constraints consistently in their own speech, whereas children learning languages with relatively flexible word orders, such as Turkish, would be expected to adhere to word order constraints less rigorously or not at all.

As it turns out, this hypothesis is accurate only in a rough, probabilistic sort of way: most children learning fixed-order languages do observe word order constraints from early on, but some do not. Similarly, many children learning flexible-order languages use relatively flexible order, but some use very rigid order (see Brown, 1973, for a review of relevant data). Some of this variability can be accounted for by a more detailed characterization of the exact properties of the language being learned (e.g., Slobin, 1976; see discussion later in this chapter, p. 130). However, even children learning the *same* language may differ considerably in their treatment of word order (e.g., see Braine, 1971, and Ramer, 1976, for data on English-speaking children). Obviously, then, factors in addition to the particular language being learned must influence children's handling of word order. These factors must be sought at a level beneath the relatively coarse variable of "language." For example, subtle differences in the way children's caretakers *use* the resources of a given language may account for at least some of the differences among children learning that language. This possibility was suggested by Bowerman's (1973a) analysis of word order in two Finnish children of middle-class, academically oriented homes: one child's mother used very flexible word order in speaking to her child, and the child's treatment of word order was correspondingly flexible, whereas the word order patterns of both the other mother and her child were considerably more constrained.

In summary, determinants of variability in the course of language acquisition may often be relatively subtle and will not be revealed unless investigators go beyond the gross linguistic and social differences that characterize cultures as a whole in order to explore the way in which details of language use and socialization practices are distributed within the society (see Hymes, 1964). Efforts to do this at the level of social class have met with some success (e.g., Bernstein, 1971; Hess & Shipman, 1965).

However, even at the subcultural level of social class, group members are heterogeneous with respect to certain variables that affect the pattern of language acquisition. Thus, given types of variation are found among children *within* the same subgroup as well as across groups and across cultures. However, the proportions of children doing one thing as opposed to another may vary across class and cultural lines in accordance with the degree to which the causal factors are concentrated in and typical of the different groups.

*Equating Children: A Prelude to Comparison*

When researchers want to make detailed comparisons of the language development of different children, they must have some way to equate the children for level of development so that they can distinguish "real" differences from differences in degree of linguistic maturity. What can be used as a developmental yardstick? Chronological age is far too rough a guide; even children learning the same language often differ radically in ability at a given age (Brown & Fraser, 1963). A more useful index for equating English-speaking children has proved to be "mean length of utterance" or MLU, which is usually calculated in morphemes (rather than words) on the basis of a sample of a hundred or more consecutive utterances. MLU is a particularly valuable developmental index early in language development; it becomes more variable and therefore less useful as it increases (Brown, 1970).

Could MLU also be used as a metric to equate speech samples from children learning different languages? At first this was unknown. Even if it were established that MLU provides a universally reliable index to development among children learning the same language, this would not resolve the question of whether similar MLUs signal similar developmental levels across languages. In addition to this theoretical uncertainty there was a practical one. Calculating MLUs for children's speech samples requires a number of relatively arbitrary decisions. Certain conventions or rules of thumb have been worked out to guide those who are working with English speech samples (see Slobin, 1967; Brown, 1973), but these are often inadequate for researchers dealing with other languages, particularly more highly inflected ones like German (see Park, 1970), Dutch (Arlman-Rupp, van Niekerk de Haan, & van de Sandt-Koenderman, 1976), and Finnish (Bowerman, 1973a) (see Brown, 1973, for discussion). How such researchers resolve particular dilemmas can considerably influence the MLU values they assign to given speech samples.

Despite these uncertainties about the cross-linguistic application of MLU, the metric has, on the whole, proved to do a remarkably good job of equating children learning different languages at least in the early stages of development. However, Brown (1973) warns that MLU and other possible quantitative guides to level of development "are only intended as interim external indices, known to be better than chronological age. . . . When we have found evidence of reliable internal semantic and grammatical change . . . we can identify a child's construction level in these terms and ignore the various external indices" (p. 72).

### Acquiring the Linguistic Code: Syntactic and Semantic Development

*What Could Be Innate?*

Chomsky's (1965) hypothesis that there is an explicit connection between universals of language structure and children's capacity for language acquisition (see p. 94, Introduction to this chapter) generated enormous interest and controversy; debate on LAD, the postulated inborn "language acquisition device," was the dominant theoretical issue of the 1960s. Discussion centered on three questions. First, what could such a device be like, that is, how would it operate? Second, what kind of evidence is there for a genetic preprogramming of language ability? And third, what is the nature of "linguistic universals"—are they such that they cannot be explained except by invoking an innate language faculty?

Early debate on the first question—how might LAD operate—focused on whether the device was best conceived in "content" or "process" terms. According to the content approach, LAD could be characterized as a storehouse for information about language universals (e.g., that words fall into certain syntactic classes, that sentences are composed of a subject and a predicate, that language is characterized by certain kinds of formal properties and operations; Chomsky, 1965, pp. 28–30). The content approach to LAD was pursued most vigorously by McNeill (1966a, b, 1970, 1971), who proposed, for example, that children's earliest attempts at sentence construction are guided by an innate grasp of the "basic grammatical relations" (subject, predicate, main verb, direct object, modifier).

Proponents of the process approach (Slobin, 1966b; Fodor, 1966), in contrast, suggested that what is innate is not a set of categories, structural relationships, or rules, but rather a set of *procedures* for analyzing linguistic input (Fodor cautioned, however, that such procedures might be learned rather than innate). Universals of language structure would result from the interaction of linguistic input with these analytic procedures, but would not in themselves be part of the child's biological endowment.

The second question—whether there is evidence for a genetic preprogramming of language—was addressed most compellingly by Lenneberg (1966, 1967). As noted earlier, Lenneberg argued that language has deep biological roots and that language acquisition is, in contrast to other more clearly "learned" behaviors, largely controlled by maturational factors. In support of these claims, Lenneberg presented evidence that there is a "critical period" for language acquisition from birth to puberty and that the ages at which children reach certain basic "milestones" of language development are consistent from one culture to the next despite great differences in environmental conditions (see the discussion of social milieu presented earlier in this chapter, pp. 105–106).

Although Lenneberg's work obviously suggests that there is a significant biological substratum to the capacity for language acquisition, it does not actually support the strong claim to which it has often been applied, that this substratum is specific to *language*. Lenneberg himself became increasingly explicit in his view that the biological foundation for language is not limited to language alone; rather, it inheres in the general cognitive organization and dispositions of mankind and manifests itself in other capacities, such as mathematical ability (Lenneberg, 1971).

Lenneberg's position on this takes us directly to the third question, whether explaining linguistic universals requires appeal to an innate language-specific faculty. This question involves perhaps the most complex issues and has aroused the most heated controversy. Lyons (1966) pointed out early in the debate that existing views on what aspects of language structure are universal were based on little cross-linguistic evidence and would no doubt undergo radical change. He proposed further that those features of language standing a fair chance of being universal could probably be learned by the child on the basis of his general cognitive knowledge. Both of these remarks presaged future lines of research and hypothesizing.

Within the field of linguistics itself, there was growing discontent with Chomsky's separation of syntax and semantics and his claim that the former is more basic to sentence structure than the latter. By the early 1970s several investigators had proposed that syntactic and semantic structure are intricately intertwined, with semantic elements actually being the more fundamental (e.g., Fillmore, 1968; G. Lakoff, 1971; McCawley, 1971; Postal, 1971). Some linguists suggested that certain aspects of sentence structure held by Chomsky and others to be universal, such as the subject-predicate relationship, are in fact not universal at all but instead are best seen as resulting from language-specific transformational operations on underlying semantic materials (Fillmore, 1968). These new conceptions of language structure cast doubt on the need to credit children with innate knowledge of at least some of the formal syntactic structures that had been nominated as candidate components of LAD (Bowerman, 1973b).

Even as questions were being raised in the field of linguistics about what aspects of language structure are in fact universal, investigators in other fields were suggesting that many purported linguistic universals are not *sui generis* but rather have striking correlates in the universal *nonlinguistic* modes of organizing and conceptualizing experience that the child builds up during the early months of life (Sinclair-de Zwart, 1969, 1971, 1973; Greenfield, Nelson, & Saltzman, 1972; Goodson & Greenfield, 1975; see Bowerman, 1974, for discussion).

Both the introduction of grammatical frameworks that treat semantic structure as primary and the proposal that many syntactic structures have nonlinguistic counterparts lent strength to the growing feeling that much or all of language acquisition can be accounted for by reference to children's general cognitive abilities without invoking a language-specific capacity. By the late 1960s and early 1970s, many researchers had adopted a cognitive-perceptual orientation towards what is biologically "given" to the child, and towards accounting for linguistic universals. Supporting materials have proliferated. For example, there is evidence from studies of both children and adults, some of it cross-cultural, that human beings are predisposed towards categorizing some domains of experience in certain ways and that these predispositions are reflected in universals of semantic structure (e.g., Berlin & Kay, 1969; Rosch, 1973, 1974, 1975; E. Clark, 1977; H. Clark, 1973). Similarly, it has been argued that certain concepts are inherently less "complex," that is, more salient or basic—than others to adults and children alike, and that differences in complexity show up both in language structure and in the relative ease with which children acquire various linguistic forms (E. Clark, 1973b; H. Clark, 1973). Still other universals of language structure have been explained in terms of constraints on the human capacity to process information received in a temporally ordered, rapidly fading medium (Vennemann, 1975; Bever & Langendoen, 1971; Lehmann, 1973; Kuno, 1974; see Slobin, 1975a, for an overview).

Despite the current widespread emphasis on the important role played by cognitive-perceptual factors in the acquisition of language, the question of whether there might nevertheless be some preprogramming for language that is purely *linguistic* and cannot be related to a more general cognitive capacity is far from settled (see Cromer, 1974, 1976, for discussion). Recent evidence in support of this possibility has been presented by Leonard, 1975; Roeper, 1976; and Lust, 1977; among others. However, explicit attempts to link children's linguistic predispositions to universals of language structure have been very few, and for the most part either highly speculative (e.g., Dowty, 1976, on causative verb constructions), open to alternative interpretations (see, for example, Brown, 1973, and Bowerman, 1973a and b, on McNeill's hypothesis that children come equipped with knowledge of the basic grammatical relations), or not borne out by further study.[5] In summary, then, clear-cut support is still lacking for the hypothesized relationship between children's capacity for language acquisition and any universals of language structure that cannot be viewed as manifestations of more general cognitive universals.

### Early Studies of Language Acquisition: From Form to Meaning

Most empirical studies of language acquisition have been conducted not in hopes of relating language acquisitional processes to linguistic universals but rather in order to discover, quite concretely, what children know about various aspects of language structure at different stages of development. What are their early utterances like? What is the best way to characterize the knowledge that underlies these utterances? Is there a consistent order in which various forms emerge?

The first child language studies of the post-Chomskian era were attempts to describe English-speaking children's first sentences and to characterize the rules for word combination that might underlie them. Existing cross-linguistic material was quickly brought in for comparison, with the result that several hypothesized "universals of language acquisition" were soon ripe for the testing. New cross-linguistic material introduced in the late 1960s supported some of the more general of these proposals, for example, that early child language everywhere is patterned and productive. That is, children are clearly not just memorizing sentences or sentence fragments, but rather are learning something that allows them to go beyond what they have heard to create and comprehend novel utterances. However, certain more specific hypotheses about universal characteristics of early child language were found untenable. These hypotheses and the analyses that led to their rejection are considered below, in connection with more recent studies that bear on the same and related problems.

*The pivot grammar.* Following Chomsky's (1959) compelling arguments that knowing a language involves having internalized a set of rules governing sentence construction, researchers began to investigate whether in fact children's earliest sentences could be characterized as rule-governed, and, if so, what the rules were like. Studying these questions required dropping preconceptions based on knowledge of the categories and relationships of *adult* grammar (e.g., noun, verb, subject, predicate) to approach child language like a linguist studying the structure of an unknown language.

Three independent studies soon suggested that early sentences are indeed patterned and systematic, and, moreover, that they could be described in terms of simple rules specifying the temporal sequencing of words in different syntactic classes (Braine, 1963; Brown & Fraser, 1963; Miller & Ervin, 1964). The findings of the three studies were remarkably similar and soon formed the basis for an influential model of children's earliest syntactic knowledge known as the "pivot grammar" (McNeill, 1966b, 1970; Slobin, 1968).

According to the rules of the pivot grammar, children's early words can be divided into two syntactic classes on the basis of differences in the way they behave in sentences. A relatively small number of words, known as "pivots," occur with high frequency relative to other words, have fixed position (first or last in two-word utterances), can combine freely with all nonpivot words but not with other pivots, and do not occur as single-word utterances. The residual (nonpivot) words in the child's vocabulary, known as "open class" words, occur with lesser frequency, do not have fixed position, combine either with pivots or with each other, and also occur as one-word utterances. Children appeared to differ with respect to which of their words were "pivots" and which were "open" (e.g., *want* or *more* might be pivots for one child, open for another), but at a more abstract level their grammars were said to be identical.

Slobin (1966a, 1968), who was interested in the generality of the pivot grammar, examined several studies of children learning languages other than English. After finding that all the children had used certain words with relatively high frequency and fixed position, he concluded that the pivot grammar might characterize the first stage of syntactic development everywhere (Slobin, 1968, 1969). McNeill (1966a and b, 1970) proposed that the pivot grammar might be the outcome of children's innate knowledge of certain putative linguistic universals.

The universality of the pivot grammar was still uncertain, however, so investigators launching new cross-linguistic studies of language acquisition in the late 1960s looked at their data with interest to see whether the model would be supported. To summarize a long story, the new data provided clear counterevidence (e.g., Bowerman, 1973a, on Finnish; Kernan, 1969, on Samoan (see analysis in Bowerman, 1973a); Rydin, 1971, on Swedish). The various criteria used in differentiating word classes in a pivot grammar analysis (differences in relative frequency, fixed versus flexible position, occurring versus not occurring as single-word utterances, and so on) simply did not converge on two distinct word classes (see Bowerman, 1973a, and Brown, 1973, for discussion). When taken beyond English, then, the pivot model proved descriptively inadequate.

But what about its adequacy for English-speaking children? Bowerman (1973a) was struck by the fact that despite the failure of her two young Finnish subjects to adhere to the rules of the pivot grammar, their utterances were remarkably similar to those that had been reported for English-speaking children. After reanalyzing the data from the American children on whose speech the pivot model had been based, she found that not a single child's speech conformed fully to the rules of the pivot grammar. Deviations from the model were no greater for the Finnish children than for the American children. Bowerman concluded that the pivot grammar model, which was an abstraction from the findings of three different studies, distorted the original data and neglected important individual differences among the children who had been studied. Results from analyses of other American children (Bloom, 1970; Bowerman, 1973a) have confirmed that the pivot grammar provides an inaccurate account of the early syntax of children learning English. Little wonder that the pivot grammar failed its test of universality! This example illustrates how an important benefit of the cross-cultural approach can be to force a reappraisal of our conceptions of what takes place in our own culture.

*Beyond the pivot grammar.*  The pivot grammar model suffered from a deeper flaw than descriptive inaccuracy, however. In an influential study of three American children, Bloom (1970) argued compellingly that the pivot grammar is in principle incapable of representing what children know about language because it does not take *meaning* into account, but only the superficial form and arrangement of words in sentences. Bloom illustrated the point with her now-famous *Mommy sock* example. This utterance was produced by her subject Kathryn on two different occasions: once as Mommy put Kathryn's sock on Kathryn and once as Kathryn picked up Mommy's sock. A pivot grammar for Kathryn would have assigned both utterances identical structural representations: open class word + open class word. But, argued Bloom, surely the two utterances *meant* very different things to Kathryn, so the structural relationships between *Mommy* and *sock* were not in fact identical. In one, the word *sock* represented an object acted on by an agent represented by the word *Mommy*, and in the other it represented an object owned by Mommy.

Bloom presented various kinds of evidence for her argument that differentiated meanings underlay her subjects' superficially similar utterances. The most important of these was that the children used *word order* patterns that were consistent with the meanings one would attribute to their utterances, given knowledge of the nonlinguistic contexts in which they were spoken. Thus, for example, agents and possessors were consistently placed first in two-word utterances, while objects acted on or possessed were placed second. Working independently of Bloom, Schlesinger (1971) also concluded that word order consistencies in children's first two-word sentences are a function of underlying meaning.

Brown (1973) has termed the method of Bloom and Schlesinger (and many others since then) the "method of rich interpretation," since it requires using clues from behavior and nonlinguistic context to make judgments about children's probable semantic intentions. Despite the inherent risks and uncertainties of the method (one can never be certain that the intentions underlying given utterances have been judged correctly; see Brown, 1973, for discussion), the method of "rich interpretation" has opened up a new and remarkably productive phase of research on child language. Use of the method has, among other things, resulted in the discovery of previously unrecognized similarities in the speech of children learning different languages. These are discussed in the following section.

*Stage I: First Word Combinations*

*Characterizing the early sentences.* Cross-linguistic perspectives on the structure of children's first sentences are provided by Brown (1973) and Bowerman (1973a, 1975), who compared the speech of children in a variety of linguistic communities. Both studies looked at children in the early period of word combining, which has become widely known as "Stage I," following Brown's (1973) terminology. Stage I is defined as the period beginning when MLU first rises above 1 (that is, when the child first starts to combine morphemes) and ending when MLU reaches 2 (an arbitrary cut-off point), at which time utterances of three and four morphemes are common and sentences as long as seven morphemes sometimes occur. Brown's study is based on nineteen Stage I spontaneous speech samples collected by himself and others from thirteen children learning one of five languages: English, Finnish, Samoan, Spanish, and Swedish. In Bowerman's investigation, Stage I was broken down into "early" and "late" substages and the speech of Finnish, Samoan, English, and Luo speaking children was compared at each of these.

What is Stage I speech like? Its most striking aspect is that it is limited, or almost limited, to the expression of a small set of meanings that is the same from one language to the next. As Slobin (1970) notes, "if you ignore word order, and read through transcriptions of two-word utterances in the various languages we have studied, the utterances read like direct translations of one another" (p. 177). Brown (1973) calculated that a list of eight "prevalent semantic relations" would account for about 70 percent of the multiword utterances in the samples of the children he studied. These include Agent and Action (e.g., *Adam hit, man dance,* and translation equivalents), Action and Object, (*hit ball, bite finger*), Agent and Object (with an implied action linking them, e.g., *Adam ball,* and see Bloom's *Mommy sock* example, p. 119 above), Action and Location (e.g., *go store, sit bed*), Entity and Location (*ball table, car garage*), Possessor and Possessed (*Mommy hat, candy mine*), Entity and Attribute (*big bed, more juice, other cookie, hair wet*), and Demonstrative and Entity (*this/that doggie, here/there cookie, it clock*). Also common are utterances referring to or requesting the disappearance or nonexistence of an object or event (e.g., *juice all gone, no more walk, no pocket, ant away*) and rudimentary questions about location (e.g., *where X [go]?*) and identity (e.g., *what dat?*). Somewhat less common are utterances referring to instruments (*sweep broom, cut knife*), indirect objects (*give Mommy, show me*), experiencers and states (*Adam see*), and a few others.

Brown noted that these few meanings by no means exhaust the range of possible meanings that languages can express. He hypothesized that the reason for their frequency and apparent universality early in development is that they constitute the linguistic expression of *sensorimotor intelligence,* or the kind of basic understanding of the world that children everywhere construct during the first two years of life, according to Piagetian theory (see also D. Edwards, 1974).

It is instructive to notice what is missing from the early sentences as well as what is present: prepositions, definite and indefinite articles, copulas (forms of *be*), noun and verb inflections, conjunctions, and verbal auxiliaries. The absence of these forms from the early speech of English-speaking children led Brown and Fraser (1963) and Brown and Bellugi (1964) to characterize this speech as "telegraphic." Telegraphic speech was described in terms of a distinction between "content" words and "functors." Content words are primarily nouns, verbs and adjectives. These reference-making words belong to large syntactic classes that readily admit new members. Functors, in contrast, primarily serve grammatical rather than referential functions and belong to small, closed syntactic classes. In a comparison of cross-linguistic data Slobin (1970) reported that "telegraphic speech" seemed to be a universal of early language development. We will return to the aptness of this description shortly.

The first major complications that lengthen children's utterances from two to three morphemes appear to take place in a similar way across a variety of languages (Brown, 1973; Bowerman, 1973a, 1975). Rather than adding in the various functors that would be required by the adult language (e.g., *ball table* expanding to *ball on table, that ball* to *that's the ball*), children begin to *combine* the meanings expressed earlier in two-word utterances. In one type of elaboration, major constituents (Agent, Action, Location, etc.) that occurred two-at-a-time earlier begin to combine to form three-constituent strings like Agent-Action-Object (e.g., *Adam hit ball* [English]; *Rina eats cake, piggy drives bicycle* [both Finnish]); and Agent-Action-Location (e.g., *bunny walks sand* [Finnish]; *goes Usa there* [Samoan]). In a second type of elaboration, a major constituent, such as Agent, Object, Location, or "Demonstrated Entity," undergoes expansion as an attributive or possessive construction. For example, *monkey come* might now be realized as *big monkey come, lift stone* as *lift big stone, sit chair* as *sit Daddy chair* (= in Daddy's chair), *that soup* as *that Mommy soup,* and *there cookie* as *there more cookie.* The approximately simultaneous emergence of three-morpheme strings of both kinds (three major constituents versus two major constituents, one of which is a modified noun) led Brown (1973) and Bowerman (1973a) to conclude that the two types of syntactic elaboration are equivalent in cognitive complexity.

*Readjusting our model of Stage I speech.* New data and reanalyses of earlier data require that our notions of the characteristics of Stage I speech be continually modified. However, evidence that at first appears to challenge the cross-linguistic validity of the description often ends up exposing oversimplifications in the original conclusions, just as in the case of the pivot grammar (see discussion earlier, pp. 118–119). That is, when researchers suggest ways in which their subjects, learning language D, depart from the "universal" characterization of child speech that was developed on the basis of children learning languages A, B, and C, closer analysis often reveals that at least some children learning A, B, and C also depart from the model in similar ways.

Brown (1973), for example, used an apparent departure from the "telegraphic speech" characterization of early sentences as a starting point for a reevaluation of the general adequacy of this description. In analyzing speech corpora from young German children, Park (1970) had found that a number of functors were used frequently and appropriately. He concluded that "apparently functors do not operate in the same manner in American and German children" (p. 6). Brown (1973) makes the following observation:

> At first sight Park's paper suggests the breakdown, just in the case of German, of a description of Stage I speech, otherwise universally apt. In fact, however, his data are not so very different from data reported by other investigators. After all, no one found functors invariably absent from Stage I, only usually so. What is different about the German study is the stance Park takes up. Most of us, especially students of English, have taken the position that Stage I speech is, in the main, telegraphic and have tried to explain away the exceptions in one way or another. Park, in not committing himself to the maintenance of the generalization, turns us back to the data of the other studies to see what the *exceptions* to the rule have been like. (p. 80)

Brown then reminds us that many of the functors found in Park's German data are also present in early child English and other languages. For example, personal and demonstrative pronouns, prolocatives like *here* and *there*, and words like *on* and *off* (used as verbal particles equivalent to "take off" and "put on" rather than as prepositions) are common; these are technically functors because, like *a, the,* and present progressive *-ing* (for example), they belong to small, closed syntactic classes.

Why are functors like these present in early sentences whereas others are not? Brown argues that the gross dichotomy between "functors" and "content words" has obscured important differences among words. He observes that the category "functor" in American English is defined "by the partial convergence of a large number of characteristics or variables. Some, at least, of these variables affect the probability that a given form will occur in Stage I speech" (p. 82). According to Brown, "what the study of languages other than English does ... is to change the correlations among variables and so help to force us to think not in terms of a class but of variables" (p. 82).

After a review of available evidence on the presence or absence of functors in the early speech of children in a variety of linguistic communities, Brown proposed that the likelihood that a particular functor will be present in early speech is a combined function of four determinants: relative perceptual salience, relative frequency in adult input, whether the form taken by the functor is constant or is conditioned by verbal context, and whether the functor expresses a basic semantic role (e.g., agent, object, possessor, location) or instead marks a "modulation" of meaning such as plurality or past time. More specifically, Brown hypothesized that functors that have high perceptual salience, high frequency in adult speech, are unconditioned by context, and express basic roles will be "fully controlled" in early speech. Functors that have high salience and frequency but that are conditioned by context and/or express modulations of meaning will occur, but only in "prefabricated routines" rather than under full control. And functors that have low salience and frequency, are conditioned, and express modulations will be absent (Brown, 1973, p. 88).

Brown's revised analysis of telegraphic speech comes much closer to accounting for all the data than did the earlier version, but further modifications will still be needed. For example, Lindhagen (1976) has challenged the hypothesis that only functors expressing "basic semantic roles" will be used "freely and correctly" in Stage I. Her two Swedish subjects, who clearly qualified as Stage I speakers on many other grounds, showed good control of certain functors expressing "modulations" of meaning, including markers for the definite form of nouns and for the present and future tense of verbs. Similarly difficult to square with Brown's formulations are Burling's (1959) report on his 2-year-old son's learning of Garo, a Tibeto-Burman language, and Varma's (1979) observations on a Stage I Hindi-speaking child. From the very beginning of word combination, both children used, productively and appropriately, a variety of verb suffixes marking modulations such as "imperative," "past," "present progressive" (Hindi) or "present/habitual" (Garo); other functors such as possessive suffixes and the copula (Hindi) soon followed.

Arlman-Rupp et al. (1976) advance still further challenges to the universal aptness of Brown's characterization of "telegraphic speech" during Stage I. They found that the Stage I Dutch children they studied used a large number of "modal elements" expressing modulations of meaning involving certainty, probability, possibility, and so on (e.g., in translation *now, now again, just, then, really, indeed, must,* and *may*). They disagree with Brown's (1973) conclusion that when such forms occur in Stage I they are used idiosyncratically, inflexibly, and uncomprehendingly: their subjects appeared to use them appropriately and with understanding. Arlman-Rupp et al. also found that only about 50 percent of their subjects' multiword utterances could be described in terms of Brown's "prevalent semantic relations," as opposed to the average of 70 percent reported by Brown for children learning other languages. Even those utterances that could be classified in terms of one or another of the prevalent relations contained a great deal of "surplus material," such as copulas, articles, and prepositions. They conclude that "the concept of prevalent semantic relations would seem to be a much less powerful way of describing the early stage of language acquisition in Dutch than in English or in the other languages Brown studied" (p. 272).

Arlman-Rupp et al.'s study certainly underlines some weaknesses of the existing characterization of Stage I speech, but the conclusion that there is some *systematic* difference between Dutch children and the speakers of English, Finnish, Samoan, Swedish, and Spanish on whose data Brown drew is probably unwarranted. In the twelve samples Brown analyzed, the percentage of utterances acounted for by the prevalent semantic relations ranged from 30 to 81; the percentage was 58 or under for four samples. Obviously Brown's description of Stage I speech fits some children better than others, but it is not at all clear that its adequacy can be predicted on the basis of the language being learned. At the least, however, it appears that Stage I children *are* capable of conceptualizing and verbally expressing certain "modulations of meaning." The exact conditions under which they do this have yet to be worked out, however.

### Operating Principles for Language Acquisition

Simply describing what children do linguistically is a necessary first step in accounting for language acquisition. But beyond this it is essential to ask why they do it in this way and not in some other. Identifying consistencies in the way children approach linguistic material is often difficult beyond Stage I because any such consistencies interact in complicated ways with other factors such as the particular structures that must be learned. The end result is that underlying regularities are obscured by the surface appearance of wide variability in patterns of acquisition from one language to the next or even among children learning the same language.

*Slobin's 1973 "Cognitive Prerequisites" paper.* In a 1973 paper entitled "Cognitive prerequisites for the acquisition of language," Slobin made a seminal contribution to the study of language development by pulling order out of masses of cross-linguistic data. Taking into account reports on the acquisition of about forty different languages, Slobin inductively formulated seven very general "operating principles" that "guide the child in

developing strategies for the production and interpretation of speech and for the construction of linguistic rule systems" (p. 194). Each operating principle, which is phrased as a self-instruction to the child, accounts for a number of observed "universals" of grammatical development. Each universal, in turn, is a summary statement based on information about the acquisition of various kinds of structures in a number of different languages.

Slobin's analysis of children's operating principles is founded in part on a working hypothesis about semantic acquisition: that "the rate and order of development of the semantic notions expressed by language are fairly constant across languages, regardless of the formal means of expression employed" (p. 187). If this "very strong developmental psycholinguistic universal" is true, argues Slobin, "and if communicative intentions can be reliably assessed from a combination of contextual and partial linguistic cues [i.e., by the method of "rich interpretation" described earlier, see p. 119], then we have a powerful research tool for probing the information processing devices used and developed by children to understand speech and to construct grammars" (p. 187). In essence, the method Slobin proposes is to measure the lag between a child's first (linguistic) attempts to express a given meaning and his later mastery of the conventional linguistic device(s) for encoding that meaning. Systematic variation in length of time to mastery as a function of the type of device involved (e.g., inflections versus word order versus intonation) would reflect the relative difficulty of the devices for the child and so provide clues to the child's strategies for linguistic data-processing.

Slobin illustrates this method with a test case involving two children who were bilingual in Hungarian and Serbo-Croatian. Before the age of two, these children were appropriately using a variety of Hungarian case endings to express such locative notions as "into," "out of," and "onto." Yet at the same time they were barely beginning to develop equivalent locative forms in Serbo-Croatian, which are prepositions governing various (nonlocative) case endings on the following nouns. Slobin notes that the lag in development in Serbo-Croatian cannot be attributed to immaturity of semantic intentions, since if a child can express such notions as "into" in one language (e.g., by saying *doll drawer-into* as she puts a doll into a drawer), we can infer that she is capable of the same semantic intentions when speaking the other language even though she may say only *doll drawer*. The difficulty presented by Serbo-Croatian is thus not a semantic one; rather, it has to do with the nature of the linguistic devices the language uses to *express* locative meanings. Slobin's point does not depend on the child's bilingualism. He uses this example merely to demonstrate the claim, supported by other data as well, that semantic intentions can develop in advance of knowledge of the necessary linguistic devices to encode these intentions.

After consideration of this and other material, Slobin concludes that (all else being equal) children find suffixes, postverbal particles, and post-positions easier to learn than prepositions for expressing locative relationships. Moreover, this tendency is "not limited to the expression of locatives. In fact, it seems to reflect a generally early tendency on the part of the child to attend to the ends of words when scanning linguistic input in a search for cues to meaning" (p. 191). The operating principle that Slobin proposes to account for this is *Pay attention to the ends of words*. A language developmental universal that flows from this is: "For any given semantic notion, grammatical realizations in the form of suffixes or post-positions will be acquired earlier than realizations in the form of prefixes or prepositions" (p. 192).

Slobin's six other proposed operating principles, arrived at in the same way from examination of language-specific data, are as follows (each principle is illustrated by one or two of the developmental universals that the principle is designed to account for). (1) *Pay attention to the order of words and morphemes* (e.g., "The standard order of functor morphemes [inflections, prepositions, etc.] in the input language is preserved in child speech"). (2) *Avoid interruption or rearrangement of linguistic units* (e.g., "Structures requiring permutation of elements will first appear in non-permuted form," as in "Where I can go?"). (3) *Underlying semantic relations should be marked overtly and clearly* (e.g., "A child will begin to mark a semantic notion earlier if its morphological realization is more salient perceptually (ceteris paribus)"; "When a child first controls a full form of a linguistic entity which can undergo contraction or deletion, contractions or deletions of such entities tend to be absent"). (4) *Avoid exceptions* (This is illustrated in the discussion of the acquisition of morphological rules). (5) *The use of grammatical markers should make semantic sense* (e.g., "Semantically consistent grammatical rules are acquired early and without significant error"). (6) *The phonological forms of words can be systematically modified.*

Inevitably, these operating principles require continuing revision, tightening, and supplementing as ongoing work reveals counterexamples and unexplained phenomena. Maratsos (1979), for example, notes that the principle that *Underlying semantic relations should be marked overtly and clearly* seems particularly weak: young children often do not make semantic relations explicit even when they have the capacity to do so. Acknowledging this, Slobin (in press) suggests that this operating principle may function to guide *discovery* rather than, as the original formulation indicates, production. That is, "surface marking that is 'overt' and 'clear' is more easily discovered and acquired by the child."

Slobin (in press) goes on to elaborate on the notion of what constitutes "overt and clear grammatical marking," drawing on recent findings from cross-linguistic studies in which children learning English, Italian, Serbo-Croatian, and Turkish served as participants in a battery of experiments

testing their grasp of a variety of sentence patterns and words (see Slobin, in press, for an overview and Slobin, 1976; Ammon & Slobin, 1978; Johnston & Slobin, 1979; and Slobin & Bever, to appear, for details on the studies). In particular, Slobin now stresses the importance of *local cues*, or "signals to underlying meaning which occur at localized points in the sentence," such as grammatical particles indicating notions like causation and aspect (Slobin, in press).

As the previous paragraph suggests, the commonalities in the course of language development that Slobin's operating principles are designed to capture are not for the most part common patterns of acquisition at the level of form and content, but rather factors that influence ease of acquisition (Slobin, in press). Taken together, they provide a partial explication of what constitutes formal complexity for the child. Thus, a child will acquire given syntactic devices more or less readily according to whether they involve preword or postword marking, whether the devices are regular or subject to many exceptions, whether they are semantically arbitrary or mark underlying meaning distinctions, whether they do or do not require the interruption of linguistic material, and so on.

Formal complexity, defined in this way, interacts with the complexity of underlying meanings to determine the order in which children will begin to produce and understand linguistic forms. The relative difficulty of meaning is the ultimate constraint, since regardless of how simple a syntactic device is it will not be acquired unless the meaning it encodes is within the child's grasp. However, a given meaning may be relatively easy, but if a particular language encodes this meaning in a way that is formally difficult for children, children learning that language will not acquire the conventional means for expressing the idea until relatively late.

Children's acquisition of devices for marking yes-no questions provides a good example of this phenomenon. As noted earlier, many languages offer a distinctive intonation pattern that distinguishes questions from declarative sentences. Children learning such languages typically begin to use intonation to mark questions by the two-word stage or even earlier. But asking a question in Finnish cannot be accomplished by manipulation of intonation; rearrangements of word order and the addition of a question-particle are required instead. Correspondingly, children learning Finnish do not begin to ask formally marked yes-no questions until long past the two-word stage, even though we can assume that entertaining an interrogative intent is within their cognitive capacity earlier (Bowerman, 1973a; see Slobin, 1970, 1973, for discussion).

The operating principles that determine what aspects of language are difficult or easy for a child to acquire may reflect constraints on human information processing and rule formation and storage that are not limited to children. Slobin (1975b) has recently proposed that children's operating principles reflect very general psychological laws that constrain the form

natural languages can take, guide the way in which languages change over time, and determine the way in which languages affect each other when they are in bilingual contact. Thus, for example, those aspects of the structure of a particular language that are easy for children to learn tend to persist over time in the historical evolution of the language and are resistant to erosion by bilingual contact; conversely, those aspects that are hard for children to acquire are less stable over time and are susceptible to rapid modification in the event of continued bilingual contact.

*Word order.* The workings of several of Slobin's operating principles, including the way in which they interact with each other and with the structure of the language being learned, can be seen with particular clarity in the processes by which children learn word order patterns and inflectional morphology. These two syntactic devices have long interested students of language acquisition, and have been the subject of considerable cross-linguistic attention, because they constitute two major mechanisms that languages can call on, either singly or in combination, to distinguish between nouns in different syntactic roles such as subject and direct object.

First hypotheses about children's approach to word order were based on studies of children learning English. These children, it was noted, tend to observe adult-like word order constraints both in imitations of adult utterances and in spontaneous speech. Observing that English relies heavily on word order to convey basic syntactic information, Brown and Bellugi (1964) speculated that the child learning English preserves word order because he intends the meanings conveyed by these orders. But, they cautioned, "it is also possible that he preserves word order just because his brain works that way and that he has no comprehension of the semantic contrasts involved" (p. 137). They called for data from children learning languages that do not use word order as a major syntactic device to help evaluate these alternatives.

When Slobin (1966a) reported that a child learning Russian, a language with relatively free word order, also used a fixed order for subject-verb-object sentences, it seemed as though rigid word order might indeed be characteristic of all early child speech. Slobin proposed that "there must be something in LAD, the built-in 'language acquisition device' . . . that favors beginning language with ordered sequences of unmarked classes, regardless of the degree of correspondence of such a system with the input language" (1966a, pp. 134–35). McNeill (1966a) hypothesized that children's rigid word order reflects their innate knowledge of the "basic grammatical relations" (subject, predicate, verb, direct object, modifier) and their search to express these in their speech. Both Slobin and McNeill suggested that children learning highly inflected languages with relatively flexible word orders might use rigid word order in their own

speech up until the time they acquire inflections; then they would learn rules for reordering sentence elements.

Further cross-linguistic data soon proved these hypotheses wrong. Children learning highly inflected, flexible languages do not necessarily preserve word order either in imitating the utterances of others or in their own spontaneous sentences in the period before they acquire inflections to mark subject, object, and so on (see, for example, Bowerman, 1973a, on Finnish; Slobin, 1973, on Polish and Russian; Slobin, 1976, in press, on Turkish).

Even though children do not universally rely on fixed word order in the initial stages of word combination, they clearly come equipped to consider the possibility that word order may be important (hence Slobin's operating principle, *Pay attention to the order of words and morphemes.*) Children learning relatively inflexible languages like English and Samoan tend to acquire appropriate ordering rules very early, although there are some exceptions (e.g., Burling, 1959; Braine, 1971). And even those learning more flexible languages seem to rely on word order to an extent. For example, Braine (1976), who compared speech corpora from children learning English, Finnish, Samoan, Hebrew, and Swedish for clues to children's early rules for sentence construction, concluded that for all children "the first productive structures are formulae of limited scope for realizing specific kinds of meanings. They define how a meaning is to be expressed by specifying where in the utterance the words expressing the components of meaning should be placed" (p. 4). Some of these "positional patterns" are word-based (e.g., *there* + X, *want* + X, *have* + X, *big* + X), while others involve the placement of words representing more abstract categories of meaning such as actor or possessor.

Bates (1976a) and MacWhinney (1975), who studied Italian and Hungarian children respectively, found that many or most of their subjects' first word combinations could be accounted for by word-based positional patterns of the type described by Braine (1976). But word-order regularities in the rest of their sentences reflected not underlying semantic distinctions (e.g., actor first, action second), but rather *focusing* principles such as "new information first, old (or given) information second" (Bates, 1976a) or "more important information (whether new or old) first, less important information second" (MacWhinney, 1975). Adult speakers of Italian and Hungarian also do not rely heavily on order to convey basic semantic information, but use word-order contrasts for the pragmatic purpose of foregrounding and backgrounding sentence constituents instead. Bates (1976a) proposes that children adopt semantic ordering principles when there are clear-cut models for this in the adult input, but use pragmatic ordering principles when there are not (although their first pragmatic ordering principles may not correspond with those of adults).

Besides focusing, a second factor that influences how word order is handled by children learning "flexible order" languages is the relative difficulty of the language's inflectional system. Turkish has a system of agglutinative inflectional morphology that is so clear and regular that it is "a joy to descriptive linguists . . . and to the Turkish child as well," who masters the entire system before the age of two (Slobin, 1975b, p. 7). In contrast, the inflectional system of Serbo-Croatian is exceedingly complex, with many irregularities and with case endings varying on the basis of gender, animacy, number, and phonological shape of the stem. Mastering this system is a drawn-out process that continues at least until the age of five (Slobin, 1975b; Radulovic, 1975). Slobin (1976, in press) reports that young Turkish and Yugoslavian children performed very differently on a comprehension task that required them to manipulate toys to act out sentences composed of two nouns and a verb in various order permutations and with inflections variously present or absent (e.g., "calf touches bird"). The Turkish children relied on case endings from a very young age and never developed word-order strategies to guide their assignment of subject and object roles to the nouns (the use of word order strategies for interpreting sentences is typical of both young American children, cf. Bever, 1970; Fraser, Bellugi & Brown, 1963; and French children, cf. Sinclair & Bronckhart, 1972; it has also been documented in older Tamil-speaking children, Garman, 1974). The Yugoslavian children, in sharp contrast to the Turkish youngsters, seemed at first to require redundant cues from both inflections *and* word order, and went on depending heavily on word order for some time.

The spontaneous speech of Turkish and Yugoslavian children parallels their comprehension strategies. The former vary order freely virtually from the beginning of word combination, whereas the latter adhere to a far more rigid word order than do their parents, even long after they have acquired inflections (Slobin, 1976; Radulovic, 1975). Children learning other Slavic languages, which have inflectional systems similar to that of Serbo-Croatian, also show a heavy reliance on word order (Slobin, 1976).

Slobin (1976) concludes that "given a reliable case inflection system [i.e., like that of Turkish], children are not constrained to orient to word order as a guide to underlying semantic relations." (He leaves open the question of whether they may instead formulate pragmatic word order rules of the type discussed by Bates and MacWhinney). In contrast, children whose language provides a complex, irregular, and unreliable case system may "find it hard to believe that what they are exposed to is a case system . . . they suspect that the real marker to underlying relations in their language is word order." Slobin (1975b, 1976) relates the difference in the ease with which children learn the inflectional systems of Turkish versus Slavic (and, more generally, Indo-European) languages to differences in the persistence of these systems over time: the former have endured with little change for centuries whereas the latter have progressively decayed and been partially replaced by analytic devices that are apparently easier than the original system (although still harder than the Turkish system) not only for children to master but also for adults to process in speaking and comprehending.

*Morphology.* Despite the existence of gross disparities in the elaboration and complexity of the inflectional systems of different languages, the pattern of acquiring inflectional morphology is remarkably similar everywhere. Slobin (1973, p. 205) sketches the following stages of inflectional marking of a semantic notion: (1) no marking, (2) appropriate marking in limited cases, (3) overgeneralization of marking (often accompanied by redundant marking), and (4) full adult system. Stage 3, which is fairly straightforward in English (e.g., characterized by the production of overgeneralizations like *comed, breaked, foots,* and redundant forms like *wented, toastses* and *feetses*) is often marked in languages with more complex inflectional systems by "substages of successive overgeneralizations, in which one form drives out another. . . . For example, Russian children first use the masculine and neuter *-om* inflection for all singular noun instrumentals; then replace this with the feminine *-oy;* and only later sort out the two inflections" (Slobin, 1973, p. 205). Slobin (1968) has termed this phenomenon "inflectional imperialism." Nowhere is it clearer than in the acquisition of inflections that children are seekers of *broad patterns.* No matter how well practiced a language form may be, if it is irregular with respect to a particular rule it will be eclipsed for a time by a regularized form once the child discovers the rule. This is the essence of Slobin's (1973) operating principle *Avoid exceptions.*

Another of Slobin's operating principles, *The use of grammatical markers should make semantic sense* (1973, p. 206), is reflected in various other aspects of the acquisition of morphology. Children attempt to link markers to meaning distinctions as directly as possible. This means that they have relatively little difficulty with semantically consistent inflections. For example, English speakers very early appear to grasp the meaning distinction that determines whether a verb can take present progressive *-ing* or not ("process" verbs can, "state" verbs cannot), and rarely or never make overgeneralizations such as *liking, wanting,* and *needing* (Brown, 1973). However, when semantically arbitrary factors, such as the phonological shape of the stem to which an inflection is attached, determine what inflection should be used to perform a given semantic function, children initially ignore such factors and apply a single inflectional form in all formal contexts in which the function must be marked.

The operating principle *Underlying semantic relations should be marked overtly and clearly* is illustrated by other aspects of morphological development. For example, children initially avoid inflections that are homonymous, that is, that express more than one meaning, preferring to express a given meaning with a phonologically unique form wherever possible. Thus, Russian children first bypass the Russian inflection -oy in favor of -om as a marker for instrumental nouns; the former is more frequent in adult speech, but it expresses four meanings in addition to instrumentality, whereas the latter has only one homonym.[6]

*Unconfounding Within-Language Variables to Determine*
*Sources of Complexity*

Implicit in much of the foregoing discussion is that cross-linguistic research can serve to clarify sources of relative difficulty or complexity *within* a single language as well as across languages. It does this by allowing possible explanatory variables that are confounded within the language to be separated so their independent effects can be assessed. For example, cross-cultural research has allowed researchers to conclude that English-speaking children's early observation of word-order constraints is related primarily to the structure of the language they are learning rather than to a very general strategy of the language-learning child, since children learning at least certain flexible-order languages show no tendency towards rigid word order.

The point that cross-cultural research can profitably be applied to the solution of within-language problems is important enough to merit further illustration. An excellent example of research of this nature is provided by Hakuta's (1976) study of how Japanese children interpret sentences containing relative clauses.

English-speaking children's comprehension and production of sentences with relative clauses has been extensively studied (see de Villiers, Tager Flusberg, Hakuta, & Cohen, 1979, for review). Although findings are somewhat mixed, a common observation is that sentences such as "the horse that bit the cow ran away" are both harder to comprehend and later to be produced than those like "the horse bit the cow that ran away." What does this difficulty stem from? One possible line of explanation would focus on the *syntactic roles* of the nouns involved: the former sentences involve an operation on the *subject* noun while the latter involve one on the *object* noun. Perhaps for some reason operations on subjects are harder than operations on objects. A second quite different type of explanation makes reference to the *positioning* of the relative clause within the sentence. In the former, more difficult type of sentence, the relative clause is *center-embedded* and interrupts the main clause, while in the latter, easier type of sentence it is *right-branching* and leaves the main clause undisturbed.

If we stick solely to English, it is difficult to determine whether syntactic role or positioning is the more important source of difficulty, since in simple sentences right-branching relative clauses always operate on object nouns and center-embedded relative clauses always operate on subject nouns. But in Japanese this confounding of factors is absent. Sentences can easily be constructed in which syntactic role and positioning (center-embedded versus left-branching, in this case) vary independently. And Hakuta's (1976) to-the-point study of Japanese children's comprehension of relative clause-containing sentences indicates that the more important factor is *positioning:* center-embedded sentences were more difficult than left-branching sentences *regardless* of whether the relative clause was attached to the subject noun or the object noun.[7] Notice that this finding accords with Slobin's (1973) operating principle *Avoid interruption or rearrangement of linguistic units,* and particularly with one of its associated developmental universals: "There is a tendency to preserve the structure of the sentence as a closed entity, reflected in a development from sentence-external placement of various linguistic forms to their movement within the sentence" (p. 200).

Studies like Hakuta's, in which a within-language problem is explored with the help of information on the acquisition of a language that is structurally dissimilar in key ways, should become increasingly common as investigators formulate more precise hypotheses about possible sources of complexity or difficulty. Further existing research along these lines includes Lust and Wakayama's (1979) comparison of the acquisition of conjoining operations (with "and") in Japanese and English and MacWhinney's (1976) and Radulovic's (1975) data on the order in which various "grammatical morphemes" (that is, functors such as case endings, other inflections, and prepositions) emerge in Hungarian and Serbo-Croatian, respectively (cf. Brown, 1973, for discussion of the order of emergence in English and the confounding of semantic and syntactic complexity as possible explanations).

*A Closer Look at Semantics*

As the discussions of the semantics of children's early sentences and of operating principles for language acquisition indicate, there is presently considerable interest in the role played by cognitive growth in the acquisition of language. Earlier in this century it was common to view cognitive development as heavily dependent on language learning (see Cromer, 1974, for discussion). For example, Sapir, Whorf, and their followers argued that language is the medium through which children learn to categorize and organize their experience of the world. This stance has been strikingly reversed in a currently popular position on the relationship between cognitive and linguistic growth. This view holds that cognitive growth is prior to and relatively independent of language acquisition; moreover, the acquisition of language itself depends heavily on previous conceptual development. Thus, children are seen as expressing verbally only those meanings that they have already worked out on a nonlinguistic basis. Their task is regarded as one of learning conventions for mapping or translating from one representational system (i.e., nonlinguistic conceptual organization) to another (i.e., language) (see Schlesinger, 1971; Slobin, 1973; Bloom, 1973; Nelson, 1974; Wells, 1974, for various versions of this hypothesis). Recall in this connection the working assumption that guided Slobin in making sense of a patchwork quilt of language acquisition data from many cultures: that semantic intentions develop in advance of knowledge of the formal linguistic means to express them, and that the rate and order in which they develop is fairly constant (as discussed earlier, p. 125).

Even though there can be no question that the recent emphasis on cognitive development has led to important insights into language acquisition, the hypothesis that language is initially learned only to encode previously formulated meanings may be a considerable oversimplification. At the least, it has certainly tended to discourage interest in a problem about which little is yet known—how children work out the fine details of the semantic systems of their own language, insofar as these details differ from one language to another. This problem will be considered shortly, after a look at the nature of the evidence that cognitive growth precedes language.

*Evidence for the primacy of cognitive development.* One important source of support for the "cognition-first" hypothesis has already been mentioned (p. 125)—that children often show signs from both behavior and immature linguistic constructions (as analyzed through the method of "rich interpretation") of wanting to communicate certain meanings before they have acquired the conventional linguistic devices for doing so. After presenting evidence for this phenomenon, Slobin (1973) concluded that "new [linguistic] forms first express old functions [meanings]" (p. 184). Conversely, when new *meanings* enter, the child expresses them with whatever "old forms" he has available, since he still lacks the conventional devices for encoding them. Cromer (1968, 1974) hypothesized that the development of new meanings or semantic intentions may in fact precipitate an active search for the relevant linguistic forms.

A second line of evidence for the primacy of cognitive development over linguistic development comes from numerous studies indicating that in the absence of full knowledge of the meanings of words or of syntactic patterns children rely on nonlinguistic strategies to direct their *interpretations* of these forms in the speech of others. For example, when 2-year-olds are told to "put X in/on/under Y," they behave according to expectations about how things should be spatially related (E. Clark, 1973a; Wilcox & Palermo, 1974; see also E. Clark, 1975; Chapman & Miller, 1975; R. Clark et al., 1974, for other examples of strategies based on nonlinguistic expectations).

Still further support for the "cognition-first" hypothesis comes from evidence that once a child has acquired a given language form, she may use it to express a range of meanings that differs systematically in some way from the range of meanings in connection with which she has heard it modeled. A plausible explanation for this phenomenon is that the child has identified the form with a concept of her own devising and uses this concept as her hypothesis about the meaning encoded by that form. Sometimes the concept is *overextended* relative to the adult concept tagged by that word; that is, it encompasses the adult meaning and more besides. For example, a child may use *doggie* to refer to all four-legged animals or *ball* to refer to all small round objects (E. Clark, 1973b). Alternatively, sometimes the range is *underextended.* For example, Antinucci and Miller (1976) found that both American and Italian children initially use past-tense markers not to refer indiscriminately to any event in the past, as in adult speech, but only for that subset of past events that result in a *change of state* that persists up to the time of speech.

What about Slobin's hypothesis that the rate at which and order in which semantic intentions develop in children learning different languages is fairly constant? This has been relatively little studied as yet. What little evidence is available is somewhat mixed. For example, on the positive side, Clancy, Jacobsen, and Silva (1976) found that children's intentions to link propositions together in various ways develop in the same order regardless of language (e.g., simple conjoining first, causal linkages later, temporal sequencing with *before* and *after* still later; American, Turkish, German, and Italian children were studied). Similarly, Johnston and Slobin (1979) found that the order in which children learning English, Italian, Turkish, and Serbo-Croatian acquired locative markers (*in, on, between,* etc., and their translation equivalents) could be predicted to a large extent on grounds of conceptual difficulty (where *conceptual* was defined in terms both of cognitive difficulty of the spatial notions involved and relative salience in communicative settings). Discrepancies among orders of acquisition, where they existed, could be explained in terms of special facilitating or retarding effects of the linguistic devices used by the different languages to encode the locative notions.

On the negative or at least "not yet explained" side, however, is the fact that the order of emergence of two-word utterances expressing various semantic relationships (e.g., possession, agent-action) is somewhat variable across children learning both the same and different languages Bowerman, 1975; Braine, 1976). Reasons for this variability are not yet clear, but it cannot easily be accounted for by reference to the complexity of the formal encoding devices offered by the language (see Bowerman, 1975). Thus, it is possible that it reflects a *variable order of emergence* of the relevant semantic notions.

*Origins of prelinguistic concepts.* If children's acquisition and use of language forms depend heavily on concepts formulated prior to language, where do these concepts originate? Some are undoubtedly idiosyncratic (e.g., see Nelson, 1974; Bowerman, 1980), but others appear to be very general and may well reflect universal cognitive processes. Such processes could be expected to manifest themselves not only in the course of language development but also in the structure of language itself. A number of observations and hypotheses about this possibility have been made. For example, several investigators have remarked on the striking correspondence between the relational meanings of children's Stage I sentences and the set of "cases" or basic meanings that Fillmore (1968) proposed as universal primitives of underlying sentence structure (e.g., Brown, 1973; Bowerman, 1973a). As Brown (1974) notes, "This is surprising since Fillmore did not set out to say anything at all about child speech but simply to provide a universal framework for adult grammar" (p. 130). The "fit" between child speech and Fillmore's case grammar is not perfect (see Bowerman, 1973a; Brown, 1973; Braine, 1976; and Lindhagen, 1976, for discussion), but it is close enough to suggest that the types of meanings that are universally basic to language structure are also universally among the earliest meanings to emerge in child speech.

Evidence linking the acquisition of *word meaning* to the semantic structure of languages, and ultimately tying both to underlying cognitive processes, has been advanced by E. Clark and Rosch. Clark first tried to identify the types of semantic distinctions that children's early words encode, and then to determine the ontogenetic origin of these distinctions. In the first phase of research, Clark (1973b) examined diary study reports on the way children in many different language communities extended words to novel objects. In a later study (Clark, 1977), she compared children's bases for word extension with the semantic distinctions encoded by the obligatory classifier systems found in many natural languages.[8] She found that:

> Visual perception plays an important role [in] both. . . . In both cases, objects are categorized primarily on the basis of shape, and the same properties of shape appear to be relevant in acquisition and in classifier systems. Roundness and length . . . appear to be very salient. (p. 460)

Clark concluded that word acquisition and the classifier systems of natural languages are similar because both depend on a universal, "a priori, nonlinguistic categorization process." Her conclusion is strengthened by Allan's (1977) independent claim, based on study of the semantics of classifier systems in more than 50 languages, that, counter to strong Whorfian claims, "diverse language communities categorize perceived phenomena in similar ways" (Allan, 1977, p. 285).

Rosch, who has explored category structure cross-linguistically and ontogenetically, reports various additional kinds of evidence for the hypothesis that human beings are predisposed to categorize in certain ways and that these predispositions influence both language structure and language development. One cogent line of work has involved color categorization. Anthropologists had long supposed that the way in which different cultures cut up and label the color spectrum is highly arbitrary. But recent research has shown this to be untrue: even though the boundaries of color categories do vary considerably from language to language, speakers of different languages tend to agree in the color instances they select as being *best exemplars* for given categories (Berlin & Kay, 1969). In other words, best exemplars ("focal colors") for color categories of different languages cluster in certain areas of color space rather than being randomly distributed across it.

Rosch found that focal colors are more easily remembered than non-focal colors both by Americans, whose language has a highly differentiated color vocabulary, and by the Dani, a stone-age people of New Guinea whose language encodes only a simple distinction between light and dark (Heider [Rosch's former name], 1972). Moreover, names could more easily be taught to the Dani for focal than for nonfocal colors (Rosch, 1973), focal colors attract the attention of young children more readily than nonfocal colors (Heider, 1971), and focal colors are recognized by children as instances of their color category earlier than nonfocal colors (Mervis, Catlin, & Rosch, 1975). Rosch (1974) has proposed that focal colors are perceptually more salient than nonfocal ones for certain physiological reasons and that they serve as "natural prototypes" around which the historical development and ontogenetic learning of color names revolve. Rosch (1974) also discusses evidence that there are similar perceptually salient natural prototypes in other category domains (shape, emotion) and suggests further that certain broad "psychological principles of categorization may apply to the formation of all categories, even in culturally relative domains" (p. 119).

*Some cautions: interactions between language and cognition.* To summarize the preceding discussion, there is now considerable evidence that, contrary to earlier views, cognitive development to a large extent paces the acquisition of language forms and constrains the way in which they are used. However, it is becoming increasingly clear that attempts to *explain* language development by reference to nonlinguistic conceptual development are doomed to failure. A first critical problem is that this approach overlooks essential differences between "knowing" something nonlinguistically, for example, having a sensorimotor understanding of events in the world, and having the kinds of semantic categories needed for language (Bloom, 1973; Bowerman, 1976; Schlesinger, 1977; Slobin, 1979). The former cannot simply be mapped directly into the latter; as Dore (1979) puts it, "Propositions are not merely tacked onto conceptual schemata, as some investigators would have it, they are themselves cognitive reorganizations of those schemata on the plane of linguistic expression" (p. 136).

The "cognition-first" hypothesis also suffers from an inability to account for cross-linguistic semantic variability. If language forms are mapped onto already formulated meanings, how are concepts that are needed for some languages but not for others constructed? It is clearly implausible that children formulate on a nonlinguistic basis all the concepts that are required by all the world's languages and then, depending on their local language, proceed to map some of these into language but not others. Much more likely is that experience with language must often instruct the child on the necessary concepts. But exactly how?

The "cognition-first" hypothesis also cannot account for the learning of semantic categories in the case of those categories whose "core meanings" may be universal but whose boundaries are variable. For example, even assuming that children generate the core meanings independently of language and then identify them with received language forms, how do they adjust the boundaries of these concepts to conform with the local adult norms?

It is tempting to relegate problems of learning language-specific categories and of adjusting category boundaries to a "later" stage of language acquisition, beyond the early period of word acquisition and sentence construction during which one can reasonably assume that autonomous cognitive development exerts its maximum influence. But this is unsatisfactory, not only because it provides no solution, of course, but also because there is growing reason to suspect that language plays a more important role even in early concept formation than the "cognition-first" hypothesis allows for. For example, Bowerman (1976, 1980) presents data suggesting that children at the one-word stage attend to language forms whose meanings they do not yet know and attempt to build meanings to match the usage they have observed. The meanings they construct, often erroneous by adult standards, reflect a complex interaction between the child's own predispositions to categorize in certain ways and the categorization schemes suggested by adult usage.

If children even at the one-word stage are influenced in their categorizations by the nature of the adult input, we might expect to see some systematic differences in the speech of young children learning different languages that have thus far been overlooked in the recent emphasis on very general cognitive precursors to language development and on "universal" aspects of the meanings of children's early utterances. An intriguing question in this connection is whether children's first (Stage I) sentences already exhibit language-specific properties that have gone unremarked because existing schemes for classifying them semantically are too coarse.

In studies of adult language, Talmy (1975, 1976) has shown that languages differ in the characteristic ways they bundle or "conflate" semantic material into words. For example, English routinely allows the semantic notions of *motion* and *manner* to conflate such that they are expressed by a single verb, as in sentences like *The bottle FLOATED into the cove* (= by floating move, or move in a floating manner). In contrast, Spanish does not routinely allow this conflation; instead, motion and path (direction) conflate while manner must be expressed separately: *The bottle ENTERED* (= *moved into*) *the cove floating.*

Do Stage I speakers of languages that typically conflate motion and manner produce sentences like *man run house* (= runs into the house), *birdie fly up*, etc., whereas those whose languages are not characterized by this pattern do not? This seems likely (see Farwell, 1976, 1977, and Johnston 1976, for relevant observations and Slobin, 1979, for related discussion). But the use of descriptive categories like "action" and "location" that do not discriminate between sentences like *man run house* on the one hand and *man go house* or *man enter house* on the other would obscure such differences. As this example illustrates, the exploration of interactions between linguistic and cognitive development will necessitate much finer-grained comparisons of children learning different languages than have thus far been performed.

The preceding pages have examined the child's acquisition of the semantic and syntactic structure of the language to which he is exposed. Cross-linguistic studies have helped illuminate both general strategies the child brings to the task of mastering the linguistic code and the differential effects of exposure to different kinds of structures. A linguistic code is not mastered in social isolation, however. As the child acquires knowledge of the formal aspects of language, he is also learning how to *use* language to accomplish various ends in specific contexts, and how to interpret the meanings of the utterances of others as a function of the circumstances in which they are produced. Cross-cultural perspectives on the development of skill at language use are explored below.

## Acquiring Rules for Language Use

What problems confront the child in learning to use his language in contextually appropriate ways? The child's task is parallel in many respects to the task reviewed in the last section, that of learning the mapping between language forms and referential or propositional meanings. However, in the present case the "meanings" that the child must learn to express are not concepts such as "possession," "location," or "agency," but rather social intentions such as the desire to direct the listener's behavior or to inform him of something, to insult him or show him deference, and so on.

In learning how to convey his social intentions effectively and appropriately, the child must acquire a repertoire of speech variants, or alternative ways to say more or less the same thing, and he must learn the social implications of these variants. He must learn the socially appropriate use of language not only in order to use language effectively himself—which includes knowing how to break the rules to achieve certain effects such as humor or insult—but also in order to interpret the utterances of others. For example, when his companion says *it's cold out tonight*, does she mean it as a statement of opinion or as a request for his coat? When he is asked *do you know any stories?* is a *yes* or *no* answer expected, or should he begin to tell one? When the speaker called him *Mr. Jones* instead of *Bob* was this a sign of respect or an attempt to increase the social distance between them? The correct interpretation of how others intend their utterances to be taken and of how they view the relationship between the speaker and listener depends on the ability to process utterances *in conjunction with the situations* in which they are uttered.

In addition to learning how to deal with the social implications of language one sentence at a time, both as a speaker and as a listener, the child must learn conventions governing longer stretches of language; for example, he must learn the rules regulating conversational turn-taking. He must learn how to anticipate his listener's needs by emphasizing new information and backgrounding old information that is already shared by virtue of the preceding discourse or other mutual knowledge. He must learn the "sequencing rules" (Ervin-Tripp, 1969) that govern how one greets, takes leave, changes the topic, responds to an insult, tells a joke or story, participates in courtroom procedures, conducts a telephone call, and so on. Knowledge of sequencing rules is just as essential for interpreting the meaning of other people's utterances as is knowledge of the social implications of speech variants. For example, *hello?* in the middle of a telephone conversation has quite a different meaning from *hello?* at the beginning of it.

How children go about acquiring the pragmatic/sociolinguistic skills they need in order to be fluent speakers of their native language is less well understood than how they acquire knowledge of the linguistic code. Studies of such topics have begun to appear only recently, and information about children's behavior in particular social settings is still too limited to allow more than preliminary guesses about what "universals" of pragmatic/sociolinguistic development might be like, and about what kinds of factors may influence the rate, order, and qualitative nature of learning. The following subsections single out three topics for discussion in cross-linguistic perspective: the acquisition of speech acts, speech variants, and discourse skills. These are followed by a more general attempt to look at what factors may be operating to determine when and how children acquire particular pragmatic/sociolinguistic abilities.

*The Development of Speech Acts*

*Functions of speech.* The child's first step in learning how to use language appropriately is to acquire some reasons for using it at all. What does he wish to accomplish through words? Does he want to request help? Report an observation? Direct someone's attention?

A speaker's goal or communicative intent in using language is designated by the term "speech act," first introduced by Austin (1962) (the terms *performative* and *illocutionary force* are now often used roughly synonymously, see Bates, 1976b). Speakers' goals can be classified in different ways or at different levels of abstraction, according to the investigator's purposes (Mitchell-Kernan & Kernan, 1977). Informal listings at a fairly low level of abstraction include such intents as reporting, announcing, insulting, instructing, requesting, interpreting, commanding, praying, cursing, taunting, and inquiring (Hymes, 1971b). More abstractly, requesting, commanding, praying, and inquiring can all be construed as attempts to influence the behavior of another. Similarly, issuing a command may serve not only an immediate communicative purpose of influencing someone's behavior but also a more subtle one—which could also be served by other types of speech acts—of establishing or reestablishing social superiority (Mitchell-Kernan & Kernan, 1977).

Are speech acts universal? At a relatively specific level of categorization there is no doubt cross-cultural variability (Ervin-Tripp, 1973). However, Searle (1976) has recently proposed a tentatively universal listing of five major categories of speech acts (*illocutionary acts* in his terminology) that subsume more specific ones: *representatives* or assertives (telling people how things are); *directives* (trying to get people to do things); *commissives* (committing oneself to doing things, e.g., promising); *expressives* (expressing feelings and attitudes); and *declarations* (bringing about changes through speech, e.g., "you're fired," "I resign"). 

The concept of speech acts has played a central role in many analyses of rules for language use. This is because it provides a framework within which the contingent relationships between formal linguistic structures and social-contextual factors can be worked out. For example, one can ascertain how the formal realization of a given speech act varies as a function of the relative social status of the speaker and listener, the presence or absence of shared background information, the topic, and so on.

*Order of emergence of speech acts.* What communicative functions are served by children's earliest utterances? Do different types of speech acts emerge in a consistent order across children and across languages? How are the early speech acts related to nonlinguistic communicative signals and to level of cognitive development? Questions like these have so far been explored extensively only with middle-class English- and Italian-speaking infants, so generalizations must be considered preliminary.

Several researchers have found that the period preceding the emergence of real words is characterized by the use of syllables that are idiosyncratic but phonetically relatively stable. These occur as an integral part of some action pattern, such as *mm* while reaching for something, *brrr* while pushing a toy vehicle, *bam* while knocking something over, *da* while pointing at something (Bates, Camaioni, & Volterra, 1975; Bates, Benigni, Bretherton, Camaioni, & Volterra, 1977, (Italian, American children); Dore, Franklin, Miller, & Ramer, 1976; Carter, 1975, 1978 (both American) ). The first recognizable words are also tied to action, e.g., *bye bye* or *hi* accompanied by a wave; *da* ("give" in Italian) while handing over or receiving an object. These words have been called "pure performatives" (Greenfield & Smith, 1976) because they lack propositional content; that is, they do not appear to make reference.

Two kinds of early words and word-like sounds are particularly common and have been singled out for special analysis by several investigators because of their communicative importance: those used in eliciting an adult's help in obtaining an object and those used in pointing out an object or event for the adult's attention. These seem to be primitive versions of Searle's speech act categories of "directives" and "representatives," respectively (Clark & Clark, 1977). Bates and her colleagues (Bates et al., 1975, 1977), studying both Italian and American babies, tried to trace the precursors of these speech acts back into the prelinguistic period and to identify their cognitive prerequisites. They found that the intentions of indicating and requesting something were already being systematically expressed in the prelinguistic period (by about 10–12 months) by points or palm-up reaches coupled with eye contact.

Bates et al. (1975, 1977), curious to determine whether there might be specific cognitive prerequisites for the development of the prelinguistic "requesting" and "declaring" communicative routines, performed a number of formal and informal cognitive tests on their subjects. They found that the emergence of the routines (which they termed "proto speech acts") coincided with the attainment of Piaget's sensorimotor Stage 5, which is characterized by the child's ability to use novel means, such as tools, in pursuit of familiar goals. Bates et al. conclude that communication through pointing or reaching coupled with eye contact can be considered a form of tool use just as is pulling on a cloth to obtain an object on the other side: the first is the use of an object as the means to obtain adult attention, the second is the use of an adult as the means to obtain a desired object, and the third is the use of an object to obtain another object.

As the child matures, he develops linguistic means to express his communicative intents. What he once expressed with gestures and eye contact alone, he later conveys with these gestures plus a vocalization such as *da* or *mm*. Still later he adds words such as *doggie* or *more*, perhaps with distinctive intonations for different speech acts (Dore, 1975),[9] and later yet he formulates word combinations such as *there doggie* and *more cookie* to express the same basic speech acts.

Notice that this account of the acquisition of speech acts or communicative intentions parallels Slobin's account of the acquisition of the "semantic intentions" underlying referential speech (as discussed earlier; see p. 125); in both cases, it is hypothesized that "intentions" (either semantic ones such as "possession" and "location" or communicative ones such as "directing" and "asserting") emerge prior to the acquisition of conventional devices for expressing them (Bates, 1976a, b). Development consists of both gradually replacing linguistically immature methods of expression with more mature, elaborated ones and of learning alternative ways of encoding acts along with the social bases for selecting between them.

With maturation also comes an expansion in the child's repertoire of speech acts. Whether speech acts of various kinds emerge in a consistent order across all children is not yet clear. After reviewing several recent studies on the development of speech acts and pointing out some conflicting claims, Nelson (1978) observes that there is no reason to expect a universal course of development because "the set of possible [speech acts] is open" and because many of the communicative goals that a speaker can achieve through language can also be achieved through nonlinguistic means such as pointing, reaching, and so on. However, certain general developmental trends may turn out to hold up if speech acts are categorized broadly enough. For example, after reviewing the admittedly limited cross-cultural evidence on the order of emergence of speech acts, Clark and Clark (1977) tentatively concluded that speech acts are acquired in the following order: directives and representatives (Searle's [1976] terminology; these correspond to the requesting and pointing out or remarking forms examined earlier); then commissives; then expressives (although a few types of expressives appear at an early age). Evidence on the relative difficulty of commissives (promising, committing oneself) relative to directing others comes from both American children (C. Chomsky, 1969) and German children (Grimm, 1975; Grimm & Schöler, 1975); see Clark and Clark, 1977, for a brief review.


*Acquiring Speech Variants*

When do children begin to acquire more than one way to express the same speech act? Is alternation between speech variants random, or are children sensitive to the social correlates of alternative forms right from the beginning? What social features are they responsive to first? When do children begin to recognize the social import of stylistic variation in the speech of others, regardless of whether they themselves use the forms in question? When do they acquire a sense of norms for socially appropriate speech that is firm enough to allow them to detect violations? When do they begin to recognize cues to social background in the speech of others? When do they acquire evaluative attitudes towards stylistic variants? (See Ervin-Tripp, 1972, for a general discussion of these and related questions.)

*When do speech variants emerge?* Research relevant to some of these "when" questions has provided surprises. Until fairly recently it was widely assumed that in both speech and other behaviors preschool children are "egocentric," that is, insensitive to listener and contextual variations and unable to tailor their behavior to fit the occasion or the perspective of others (Piaget, 1926). However, recent studies show, counter to this view, that very young children are capable of attending to the characteristics and needs of their companions and of framing their speech accordingly. For example, in the United States (evidence is not yet available from elsewhere), children as young as two (Ervin-Tripp, 1977) and clearly by four (Shatz & Gelman, 1973; Sachs & Devin, 1976) speak differently to younger children than they do to peers and adults. The adjustments they make for infants (higher pitch, syntactic simplification, and so on) are similar to those made by adults in talking to babies. These speech modifications appear to reflect a real sense of conventions for talking to young children rather than merely the effects of listener feedback, because they occur even when the addressee is a doll whom the child has been instructed to treat like a baby (Sachs & Devin, 1976).

Studies of how young children interpret the sentences of others have also revealed a surprising sensitivity to the social correlates of speech variants. For example, Bates (1976a) found that Italian children as young as three were capable of judging the relative "niceness" or politeness of certain request forms, while Jacobs (cited in Ervin-Tripp, 1977) found that five-year-old English speakers were able to accurately identify potential speakers for a variety of directives.

Young children are not only able to distinguish among speech variants and identify them with certain social features, but they are also capable of developing *evaluative* attitudes towards these variants quite early. Cremona and Bates (1977) found that when lower-class rural Italian children were presented with pairs of sentences in dialect versus standard Italian and asked to choose which one was "better," by first grade they already selected the standard variant over 80 percent of the time. As Bates (1975) points out, this finding has interesting implications for the study of the development of self-esteem, since the sentences the children evaluated negatively were cast in a dialect they themselves spoke.

*Social determinants of directives.* A particularly fruitful method for getting at young children's sensitivity to features of the social context has been through the study of children's production and comprehension of *directives*. Directives are perhaps especially sensitive to social features because they make a demand on the listener for services; these services may or may not be rendered depending on how the directive is put (Ervin-Tripp, 1977). For adults, issues of cost to the addressee, normal or expected duties versus special favors, relative status and the like enter into computing how to issue a directive, with less direct forms typically being used with social superiors and to request tasks outside of normal duties (see Ervin-Tripp, 1976a, for discussion). Indirectness is regarded as more "polite" because it leaves options open for the addressee, who can fail to "hear" the utterance as a directive and so refuse compliance without a direct confrontation (R. Lakoff, 1973b).

How children acquire directive forms is one of very few questions in the pragmatic/sociolinguistic study of language development that has been explicitly investigated cross-culturally (Ervin-Tripp, 1977; Hollos & Beeman, 1978). Ervin-Tripp compared studies of the production, comprehension, and evaluation of various directive forms by children learning English, Turkish, Italian, and Hungarian and was able to identify a number of shared features of development. She reports that the earliest request forms are gestures, vocalizations, and names of desired objects, followed towards the end of the second year by word combinations with words like *want* and *more*. Between 2 and 3 years (and sometimes even earlier), children begin to develop more elaborate repertoires for making requests. Variants are not distributed randomly across contexts: even children as young as 2 frame their directives differently depending on factors such as the age and familiarity of the addressee and the content of the request. For example, direct commands (e.g., *Give me . . .*) are typically used with peers or younger children, whereas commands softened with *please* and less direct forms like *Can I have. . ?, Would you give me . . . ?* are addressed to older children and adults. Languages differ in the "softening" devices they provide (e.g., inflections, particles, syntactic additions and rearrangements, special intonations), so the particular ones children learn and the time of their emergence is somewhat language-specific. Most indirect directives (i.e., those that do not explicitly command) at least include mention of the desired object or action, e.g., *We haven't had any candy in a long time; Mom, don't you have any pickles?* Directives that do not mention what is desired (e.g., *Do you have a broken arm?* as a request for help in carrying in groceries) emerged very late in all the children studied (Ervin-Tripp, 1977).

In comprehension, the sequence of emergence is similar—although in advance of production—with more direct forms being understood as directives before less direct forms and with oblique hints understood only very late. However, certain conventionalized indirect forms (e.g., *Would you shut the door?*) appear to be comprehended as directives just as early as direct command are (e.g., Bates, 1971; Shatz, 1974). Bates (1976a and b) suggests that these may be so routine that their meaning can be acquired before the child has worked out the elaborate interpretive strategies that the comprehension of indirect speech normally requires.

Although there are certain cross-cultural similarities in the acquisition of directives (e.g., the early sensitivity to social features of the addressee; the gradual elaboration of indirect, polite ways to request), there are also differences. Hollos and Beeman's (1978) comparative study of directives among rural Hungarian and Norwegian children indicates that there is variability in the way directives are handled in different cultures and that children begin to "take on" the style of their community by at least 4 or 5 (the youngest age group studied). Hollos and Beeman's Hungarian subjects were capable of requesting help, permission, and so on efficiently from family, playmates, and strangers alike, although they had different styles for dealing with intimates and nonintimates. The Norwegian children also distinguished intimates from nonintimates, but in a different way: by becoming more and more indirect as social distance increased. They preferred, in fact, not to issue directives to nonintimates at all, but rather to gain the help of an intermediary. Hollos and Beeman note that the direct versus indirect styles (and reliance on middlemen in the case of the latter) are typical of adults as well as children in the Hungarian versus Norwegian villages they studied. They conclude that:

> there is a 'cultural communicative style' which operates in the issuing of directives—a kind of qualitative contour for this particular set of related communicative acts which is distinct for different societies . . . children learn the contours of this communicative style before they acquire the complete lexical and behavioral repertoire which helps them to adapt specific communicative acts to criteria of effectiveness and appropriateness. (pp. 353–354)

Boggs (cited in Ervin-Tripp & Mitchell-Kernan, 1977, p. 21) has raised similar considerations about cultural differences in directives. He notes that most of the cultures in which the acquisition of directives has been studied (specifically, American, Italian, Hungarian) "positively value the individual's manipulation of others, and appear to train children positively to engage in such strategies." But in other cultures (e.g., Hawaiian, Ojibwan) "manipulation among adults, as among children, is anathema." This results in different requesting styles. Boggs states that Hawaiian children "risk . . . a slap" if they repeat requests with increasing emphasis, so their repetitions involve "a withdrawal of urgency." Hollos and Beeman (1978), in contrast, found that their Hungarian subjects *intensified* requests when they had to repeat them.

## Discourse

Cultures vary tremendously in the types of discourse they stress, the content of specific genres of discourse, and the sequencing of materials (see p. 104 above). Whether there are universals in the acquisition of discourse conventions, what form such universals might take, and how acquisition is affected by specific kinds of variability is still largely unknown. However, preliminary research on children from a variety of cultures has begun to suggest some patterns.

*Conversation.* The development of skill at conversation involves knowing how to take turns rather than talking simultaneously or interrupting, how to sustain dialogue by responding appropriately to the utterances of the conversational partner and then adding relevant new comments (Keenan, 1974), how to initiate and terminate interactions (see Schegloff, 1972, for analysis of "opening" sequences), and how to negotiate successful transactions (Cook-Gumperz, 1977). A major finding of recent work on child dialogue is that children begin to develop skill at conversation as early as the second year of life. Documentation of early conversational ability comes mostly from studies of American and English children (Greenfield & Smith, 1976; Keenan, 1974; Bloom, Rocissano, & Hood, 1976; Dore, 1977; Halliday, 1975; Garvey, 1975, Ervin-Tripp, 1978), but data from children learning other languages are corroborative (e.g., Shugar, 1978, on Polish; Slama-Cazacu, 1977, on Rumanian). Recent studies of interaction patterns and reciprocal vocalizations between caretakers and prelinguistic children (e.g., Stern, Jaffe, Beebe, & Bennett, 1975; Bruner, 1975; Freedle & Lewis, 1977) indicate that the roots of conversational skill, e.g., turn-taking and joint focus on a topic, may extend back even further, into the first year of life. Evidence for the early onset of conversational responsiveness, like that of the early development of socially conditioned speech variants (see p. 144 above), strongly challenges Piagetian assumptions about the egocentricity of young children (see Keenan, 1974; Keenan & Klein, 1975).

Little is yet known about how children adopt the conversational conventions of their social group. Most of the work that has been done on this topic concerns the acquisition of devices for highlighting new information and backgrounding shared or presupposed information in the dialogue between child and interlocuter. Studies of American children (Greenfield, 1978; Greenfield & Zukow, 1978) and Italian children (Bates, 1976a) at the one-word stage of development indicate that children first mark the distinction between given and new by their choice of which element of the nonlinguistic context to encode linguistically. They select elements that are new, or salient by virtue of undergoing change. This choice reflects the *child's* point of view, however, rather than an understanding of the addressee's perspective. The sequencing of given and new information can also be accomplished through dialogue at the one-word stage. For example, the adult introduces a topic and the child adds a one-word comment (Greenfield & Smith, 1976), or the child introduces something, waits and repeats it if necessary until the adult acknowledges it, and then adds a comment about it (Scollon, 1976).

By the two-word stage, at around the age of 2, cultural/linguistic differences in the handling of old versus new information begin to appear. Children learning languages with relatively flexible word order manipulate word order to distinguish beween words encoding new and old information (Bates, 1976a, Italian children; MacWhinney, 1975, Hungarian children), whereas children learning languages that rely on word order to convey basic semantic information may use *contrastive stress* to mark old versus new (Wieman, 1976; American children).

Although some cultural specificity in conversational skill emerges early, it is likely that complete socialization into the local conventions takes a long time. For example, Cook-Gumperz (1977) found that even though dyads of 10-year-old American children were skillful at negotiating verbal interactions of certain kinds, their exact methods differed from those typically used by American adults. For instance, they used intonation to express certain meanings that adults would tend to "lexicalize" (express with words). In a related example, Keenan (1974) reported that by at least the age of 2 years, 9 months, her English-speaking twin sons had learned that responses to a prior speaker's utterances should "be relevant" (see Grice, 1975, and the discussion in this chapter, pp. 104–105, on conversational maxims); however, they apparently interpreted "relevance" differently from adult speakers. For example, their responses were often tied to the phonological form of the previous speaker's utterance, rather than to its content as in adult speech. Keenan's notational system for representing the conversational interactions of young children should prove useful to researchers interested in detecting cross-cultural similarities and differences in the development of dialogue.

*Disputing.* A number of special genres of discourse have been singled out recently for close study by students of language development; these include verbal play (Kirshenblatt-Gimblett, 1976, cross-cultural; Garvey, 1977, American children) and narration and joke-telling (Watson-Gegeo & Boggs, 1977, Boggs & Watson-Gegeo, 1978, Hawaiian children). Some of the most intriguing cross-cultural comparisons to date have involved the acquisition of patterns for verbal disputing. Verbal disputing is a natural choice for cross-cultural study because it almost surely occurs in every culture, but its patterning and content appear to be rather culture-specific. In some cultures disputing procedures are exceedingly elaborate and ritualized (cf. Dundes et al.'s [1972] study of verbal dueling among young Turkish boys, participation in which requires both general cultural knowledge and skill at returning an insult with a rhyme, and Labov, Robins, & Lewis's [1968] analyses of dueling games such as "playing the dozens" among black American adolescents).

Children's disputing has been studied in several different cultures. Analyses indicate that even by the age of 4 to 6 children have mastered the general structure of dispute sequences and some culturally specific ways of realizing it. For example, Boggs (1978) found that among his part-Hawaiian subjects, routines for direct allegations and contradictions, escalating to insults, appeared by as early as four. He notes that these routines were similar to those found among Massachusetts youngsters by Lein and Brenneis (1978), although the latter children differed from the former in that their claims were often far-fetched and unsupportable.

Mitchell-Kernan and Kernan (1975) report interesting cross-cultural differences in the content of children's disputes. They found that young Samoan children's insults and retorts were typically based on allegations about parents or about deviance in personal attributes such as cleanliness and appearance. The ultimate insult, for which no effective retort was possible, was to accuse the other of stinginess. Young black American children from Oakland, in contrast, often accused each other of being babies but did not derogate each other's parents (until they were much older) or refer to stinginess. Mitchell-Kernan and Kernan conclude that the analysis of disputing can give important insights into the acquisition of cultural values that are rarely discussed directly.

*Determinants of Pragmatic/Sociolinguistic Learning*

In studying the development of pragmatic/sociolinguistic knowledge, as in studying the acquisition of grammatical rules, it is necessary to go beyond simply describing what children learn and when they learn it in order to determine why learning proceeds in certain ways and not in others. For example, why are certain links between linguistic forms and social-contextual variables relatively easy to acquire and others harder?

*The role of formal factors.* Differences in time of acquisition are undoubtedly related in part to the nature of the formal linguistic devices through which social meanings are conveyed, just as the time at which children express given semantic intentions linguistically is partially a function of the relative difficulty of the structural devices used to encode those meanings. In fact, many of the variables that facilitate or hamper the child's acquisition of syntactic and morphological rules undoubtedly affect pragmatic/sociolinguistic learning in similar ways.

Consider, for example, the finding that children acquire very early the ability to produce and understand directives in which the desired action is explicitly mentioned, but that they are relatively old before they produce hints that omit mention of the action (e.g., *it's cold in here* as a request for someone to shut the door) or begin to "hear" the directive intent behind such utterances (Ervin-Tripp, 1977). This sequence of development accords fully with Slobin's (1973) operating principle. *Underlying semantic relations should be marked overtly and clearly* (see p. 126 above); although in this case the underlying meanings are *communicative intents* rather than semantic relations.

Other aspects of pragmatic/sociolinguistic learning also conform with Slobin's operating principles, indicating that these principles are at work beyond the semantic-grammatical domain to which Slobin's examples are restricted. For instance, in their analysis of American and Samoan children's disputes, Mitchell-Kernan and Kernan (1975) note that certain errors stem from children's applications of given types of insult too broadly, failing to take into account distinctions in context that determine whether the insult is really appropriate (e.g., "she got a baby," said censuringly of a married woman, and "your father sleeps with your mother"). Mitchell-Kernan and Kernan observe that these errors are overgeneralizations similar to those made in the acquisition of lexical items and grammatical structure. With development, children "will, presumably, progress towards a more complete knowledge of their culture by learning to make those finer distinctions and to differentiate cases according to culturally relevant contextual factors" (pp. 313–314). This statement is clearly a pragmatic  counterpart to one of the universals of grammatical development that Slobin's *Avoid exceptions* principle was designed to account for: "Rules applicable to larger classes are developed before rules relating to their subdivisions, and general rules are learned before rules for special cases" (Slobin, 1973, p. 205).

Another of Slobin's operating principles is: *The use of grammatical markers should make semantic sense.* This principle was based on (among other things) the general finding that "semantically consistent grammatical rules are acquired early and without significant error" (see p. 131 above for discussion). The principle that form-meaning pairings are easier to acquire if they are consistent rather than inconsistent can be invoked to account for certain findings reported by Edelsky (1977). Drawing on R. Lakoff's (1973a) analysis of the difference between men's and woman's speech in English, Edelsky studied the ability of American grade-schoolers to guess the probable sex of speakers of sentences containing various sex-linked items such as *adorable, oh dear, damn,* and *just* (as an intensifier). She found that the earliest words to be associated with speakers of a given sex were those that adult subjects had previously judged to be highly or "categorically" sex-linked, that is, almost exclusively used by either male or female speakers. Words that were "variably" sex-linked—that is, only probabilistically associated with males or females—did not take on sexual connotations for the children until later.

This example, which shows the effect of consistency on time of acquisition of forms *within* a language, has interesting cross-cultural implications. Probably every language has speech variants that are sensitive to the sex of participants in the speech event, but languages differ considerably with respect to where, how, and how consistently sexual distinctions are marked linguistically. The English system is not very elaborate. There are relatively few sex-linked forms, and most of these are only probabilistically associated with speakers or hearers of a given sex. In many languages, however, the sex of the speaker, hearer, or both is *obligatorily* marked in a number of places in the system, for example, by the choice of syntactic markers, lexical items, and/or pronunciation (see Haas, 1964, for a typology of languages and discussion). If degree of consistency is an influential determinant of time of acquisition, children learning such languages should acquire a sense of appropriate speech to and/or from male and female speakers much earlier than those whose languages, like English, mark sex less consistently.

Evidence on this is fragmentary, but it accords with the prediction. For example, the American children in Edelsky's study were relatively slow to recognize that some forms are associated with female rather than male speakers and *vice versa:* first graders had little success at the task. In contrast, Braine (1976, p. 42) and Bar-Adon (1971, pp. 438–439) report that children who were learning Hebrew, a language in which the sex of speaker or listener (or both) is obligatorily marked in certain sentence patterns, were capable of selecting the proper sex-linked imperative verb form at least for certain verbs in their very earliest word combinations (e.g., *tire* versus *tiri,* imperative "see" for male versus female addressees).

Even though these studies of English- and Hebrew-speaking children are not directly comparable for a variety of reasons, they nevertheless suggest that the process of acquiring linkages between language forms and contextually given social meanings—including but not limited to the sex of the participants in a speech event—may be affected by formal factors such as degree of consistency. Of course, other factors are undoubtedly at work simultaneously, such as the relative difficulty of the denotational meanings of the particular linguistic forms that have socially conditioned variants. Future cross-cultural studies that explore how formal factors influence the acquisition of knowledge about socially appropriate language will have to control for such factors carefully.

*The role of meaning.* Another factor that must be taken into account in attempts to determine how children acquire conventions governing socially appropriate language is the nature of the *social meanings* to which alternation between linguistic variants is sensitive. Are some social meanings inherently easier than others to learn, regardless of how they are marked linguistically or what their cultural importance is? Or is the time at which children become aware of given social distinctions affected by language-structural and/or cultural practices?

Slobin (1973) has convincingly argued that the child's intention to communicate semantic concepts such as possession and location can precede the acquisition of the conventional linguistic devices for encoding these concepts. Presumably the same is also true for social meanings. That is, a child could be well aware for example of distinctions among settings and in the attributes of his interlocutors (sex, age, relative familiarity, and so on), and perhaps modify his speech in some way in response to these distinctions (e.g., silence with strangers versus volubility among intimates, Gleason, 1973) well before he learns the conventional linguistic devices for marking the distinctions. But is this always the case? Can we set up a working hypothesis for social distinctions that is parallel to Slobin's (1973) hypothesis that "the rate and order of development of the semantic notions expressed by language are fairly constant across languages, regardless of the formal means of expression employed" (p. 187, see p. 125 above)? Or might the learning of social distinctions instead be significantly influenced by social practices and by the characteristics of the language that the child is learning, such that time and order of acquisition are highly variable?

As noted previously, there is evidence that language may influence some aspects of the child's early formation of semantic concepts, despite claims to the contrary. The possibility that language plays an instrumental role in teaching children social concepts is even stronger. This is because many of the social concepts to which rules for language use are sensitive are not based directly on variables like sex and age that have observable nonlinguistic correlates—correlates that could presumably be noticed by the child independently of language. Rather, their existence is part and parcel of the communicative system. Gumperz (1972) states it this way:

Just as the meaning of words is always affected by context, social categories must be interpreted in terms of situational constraints.

Concepts such as status and role are thus not permanent qualities of speakers, instead they become abstract communicative symbols, somewhat like phonemes and morphemes. . . . The division between social and linguistic categories is thus obliterated. Communication is not governed by fixed social rules; it is a two-step process in which the speaker first takes in stimuli from the outside environment, evaluating and selecting from among them in the light of his own cultural background, personal history, and what he knows about his interlocutors. He then decides on the norms that apply to the situation at hand. These norms determine the speaker's selection from among the communicative options available for encoding his intent. (p. 15)

To the extent that socially important concepts can be inferred *only* through communicative interactions, and have no direct nonlinguistic correlates, their acquisition could not take place independently of language. In other words, only by observing how the selection of language forms varies as a function of complex interactions among factors such as sex, age, setting, topic, etc., could a child formulate the relevant concepts. One way in which such social learning might take place is discussed by Ervin-Tripp (1976b).

Social alternations [between language forms] are rarely single sets for single social variables. [For example,] the forms which signal male-female contrasts in Japanese also signal higher-lower. Thus, whenever a woman speaks to a man she not only tells him he is male; she tells him he is of higher rank. . . . The social significance of equivalence structures is that some meanings from one set of contrasts carry over to the other as a kind of metaphor. (p.145)

Ervin-Tripp goes on to hypothesize that the *first* meanings that children ascribe to alternations may be social features they already recognize, such as age or sex contrasts.

In the more ambiguous cases, where similar contrasts are used, we can assume the child will search for the social features that account for a formal contrast he has already found to be significant. For instance, once the child discovers differences that correlate with age of addressee in many features of language, he will see these same features extended to rank contrasts when no age differences exist. He may never be explicitly told there is a rank difference, but the metaphor of power will instruct him that X is treated like an elderly adult and Y is treated like a child. (pp. 151–152)

On the basis of such considerations Ervin-Tripp (1976b) concludes that the system of alternations in realizing speech acts may provide "an instructional milieu for learners regarding the major social dimensions and categories of the groups they join." Ferguson (1977) makes a further relevant observation here: he notes that the special features of the speech that caretakers address to children ("Baby Talk") in themselves "delineate . . . roles: typically caretakers use them to the child, not to one another; older children use them to younger children, not to still older children; female caretakers use them more often than male caretakers and so on. Age, sex and kin roles are thus signaled insistently by [Baby Talk]" (p. 234).

To summarize, there is good reason to believe that many of the social concepts that are expressed by alternation among linguistic variants are learned through language itself rather than independently of language. This means that the rate and order of acquiring these meanings will vary across cultures (no doubt within some as yet undetermined limits) as a function of differences in the way the categories manifest themselves linguistically. For example, all else being equal, we would expect meanings linked consistently with given forms to be learned earlier than those linked only probabilistically.

*Tutoring and motivation.* What might affect patterns of acquiring pragmatic/sociolinguistic rules, in addition to formal factors and the nature of the social meanings signaled by choices between variants? Two other factors that must also be considered include explicit adult *teaching* and the child's *motivation* to learn given forms.

Tutoring appears to be an insigificant factor in the child's learning of syntactic and morphological rules. As noted earlier (p. 105 above), adults around the world seldom correct children's grammatical errors or supply explicit instructions. However, the picture is different with respect to the socially appropriate use of language; here, instruction is evidently much more common. Gleason and Weintraub (1976), who studied the acquisition of politeness formulas in English (along with certain other routines), suggest that unlike most language structures these are learned through explicit teaching and prompting ("What do you say?" "Say please"). Societies differ in the emphasis they put on early socialization into politeness. Bates (1976a), for example, observes that Italian parents are relatively tolerant in this respect. Thus, degree of adult pressure may considerably influence the age at which children master politeness routines. Similar cross-cultural variability in tolerance may also affect the learning of other conventions for appropriate language use, such as the avoidance of taboo words or the restriction of discussions of certain topics to certain settings (e.g., "where do babies come from?" as a topic for the privacy of the home). Of course, many aspects of socially appropriate language use, like much of language structure, are below the adult's level of conscious awareness and so are not available for explicit teaching.

When a child is exposed to competing speech styles, e.g., dialects, which one does he "select" to learn? Factors such as frequency of exposure and adult instruction may be important, but equally or even more important, as Hymes (1971b) emphasizes, are motivational factors. Motivation is not influenced only, or even necessarily, by evaluative attitudes, i.e., by which speech variant the child perceives to be socially "better." More important may be the child's attachment of emotional importance to one variant over another (which is related to the larger issue of the role of language in maintaining a sense of "solidarity" among speakers). Which speech variants a child adopts may also, by some unknown age, be influenced by his identification with a certain social role (e.g., masculine, tough) (Hymes, 1971b).

The preceding discussion has considered a number of variables that may influence the acquisition of rules for language use: formal factors such as the consistency with which social distinctions are marked, the nature of the social concepts themselves, the degree to which rules are inculcated through explicit teaching, and the child's motivation to acquire certain speech variants over others. Sorting out the relative contribution of these factors to the patterns by which children learn to use language in socially appropriate ways will be exceedingly difficult. Cross-cultural studies in which independent variables are carefully controlled will be essential to such efforts.

## The Role of the Environment

How is a child's language development affected by the social milieu in which learning takes place, for example, by who takes care of her, how the caretaker speaks to her and interacts with her, how many people she encounters in the daily course of events, where she spends her time, who she needs to talk to and for what reasons, and so on? The discussion below takes up the three aspects of the role of the environment that have been most studied within a comparative (although not always cross-cultural) framework: a major independent variable, the nature of talk to children, and two important dependent variables, *rate* of development and the way the child *uses* what language she knows as a function of environmental influences.

### Talking to Children Around the World

Ethnographic research in widely scattered societies has established that "in all speech communities there are probably special ways of talking to young children which differ more or less systematically from the more 'normal' form of the language used in ordinary conversation among adults" (Ferguson, 1977, p. 209).[10] This special style of language has been termed "Baby Talk" by researchers with a cross-cultural orientation (Ferguson, 1977) and "motherese" by researchers focusing on English (Newport, 1976).

Most of the features that distinguish the Baby Talk register from "normal" adult-to-adult speech are not found in every community, but many are very widespread. Ferguson (1977) proposes that the various features reflect three different types of underlying processes, which he terms "simplifying," "clarifying," and "expressive." Common simplifying processes, for example, include the substitution of simpler sounds for more complex ones, the reduction of syllable structure to "simple canonical forms," the reduction of inflectional affixes, the avoidance of second person pronouns in favor of other address forms, and the use of special terms for kin, body parts and functions, animals, foods, evaluative attributes, and so on. Widespread clarifying processes include repetition, exaggeration of intonational contours, and slow speech. And expressive processes very often include diminutives or other hypocoristic affixes, the "softening" or palatalization of consonants, labialization of consonants and vowels, and—probably a universal feature—the use of raised pitch. Brown (1977) suggests that simplifying and clarifying processes probably both derive from a desire to communicate and be understood, whereas expressive processes have as their main motivation the expression of affection.

Despite gross similarities in Baby Talk from one social group to the next, there are important cross-cultural differences as well. Most obviously, features that are present in some societies may be entirely lacking in another. More subtle, however, is variation that involves not the categorical presence or absence of given features of Baby Talk but rather differences in the frequency with which these features occur. A study by Blount and Padgug (1977) illustrates this phenonomenon clearly, and provides an excellent jumping-off point for future fine-grained comparative work on the characteristics of Baby Talk. Blount and Padgug formulated a checklist of thirty-four paralinguistic, prosodic, and interactional features that are often found in Baby Talk and used this in rating samples of speech from five English-speaking and four Spanish-speaking sets of parents to their one-word-at-a-time stage children. (The Spanish speakers came from several countries.) The investigators found consistent profiles of feature usage within each language, and both similarities and differences across languages.

Among the ten most frequently used features in each language, six were shared: exaggerated intonation, repetition, high pitch, instructionals (e.g., "that's a ball" after a child's incorrect identification), lower volume, and lengthened vowels. However, the level of usage of some of these features differed. Most strikingly, English-speaking parents used high pitch more than Spanish-speaking parents did (it figured in consistently over 60 percent of their utterances, versus 42–60 percent), and they relied on it more heavily in proportion to the total number of Baby Talk features (20–25 percent versus 10–14 percent). Features that ranked among the top ten for English but not Spanish included breathiness, creaky voice, tenseness, and falsetto, whereas those for Spanish but not English included attentionals (*hey!*, *look!*, child's name), fast tempo, raised volume, and personal pronoun substitution. Overall, the Spanish-speaking parents used a higher rate of Baby Talk features than the English-speaking parents.

What can account for such differences in speaking to young children? Blount and Padgug propose that they reflect cultural differences in style of interaction. Specifically, they suggest that the English style is more heavily affective, since there is a greater reliance on affectively marked features such as intonation. In contrast, Spanish is more directly interaction-oriented, relying on structural devices such as attention-getting devices, repetition, instruction, and special pronoun usage.

Elsewhere, Blount (1972a) has stressed the wide variety of cultural variables that go into making up a social group's style of "language socialization," by which is meant not only the nature of Baby Talk but also such factors as when Baby Talk is used (in what contexts and for what age of children), what kind of language is expected of the child at various stages of development, how the child's verbal efforts are received, and so on. After describing the social and physical environment of language-learning Luo children, Blount concluded that "three features—practicality, absence of direct negative sanctions, and emphasis on individual freedom—appear to be the defining characteristics of what might be labeled the *Luo Type* of linguistic socialization" (p. 247). He noted that other studies "may serve to define additional types and provide a basis on which the nature, range, and causes of differing types can be explained" (p. 248).

One cultural dimension that may have a particularly important effect on the way adults interact verbally with children is the prevailing attitude towards the role of children in society. This may influence not only the extent to which Baby Talk features are used but also such variables as how often children are spoken to and what kinds of verbal interactions they are engaged in. For example, according to Blount (1972b), children are regarded as socially subordinate to adults in Luo and Samoan culture. This attitude manifests itself in the language of the adult in a very high proportion of imperatives and interrogatives, which effectively forestall conversational equality. Analyses by Blount of samples of Black English parent-child interactions revealed a different pattern, whereby children were treated more as conversational partners and were asked many yes-no questions designed to tap their preferences. Questions of this type were rare in the Luo and Samoan samples.

Another study implicating the social status of children as an important factor in language socialization practices is Fischer's (1970) comparison of Japanese school children and their parents to their American counterparts.

Although both cultures can be considered "child centered," Fischer found that the Japanese parents put more stress on the child's position as a child and tended to indulge dependency more than American parents. Communicative correlates of these attitudes included less talking to children on the part of the Japanese parents, more use of nonverbal communication, longer use of Baby Talk and a more favorable attitude toward it, and greater willingness to interpret children's deviant utterances as meaningful.

The study of cross-cultural similarities and differences in the way members of a society communicate with children is an important ethnographic pursuit in its own right. But the ultimate question that begs for an answer is whether variation in communicative patterns leads to differences in the course of language development, and if so, how? For example, does the use of the Baby Talk register actually facilitate language development, such that children who are exposed to more of it (or more of certain features of it, or more of it at certain stages of development) acquire language more rapidly than those who do not? Are some aspects of language acquisition more influenced by the speech the child hears than others? Does variation in linguistic input that reflects different attitudes towards children's social role affect language development differentially? And so on. Questions like these have increasingly interested students of child development, but although a number of relationships between linguistic input and language acquisition have been proposed, most evidence must still be regarded as preliminary or suggestive rather than conclusive. Some possible relationships are examined.

### Environmental Influences on Rate of Development

*Language input and rate of development in socially homogeneous groups.* The most detailed studies of rate of development as a function of exposure to different kinds of verbal input have been conducted with socially homogeneous groups of English-speaking children. Although initial investigations failed to reveal the predicted differences (e.g., Cazden, 1965; Feldman, 1971), more recent studies examining a wider range of input variables have begun to suggest that rate differences related to input do exist (e.g., Nelson, Carskaddon, & Bonvillian, 1973; Cross, 1975, 1978; Newport, 1976; Newport, Gleitman, & Gleitman, 1975, 1977).

Most reported relationships do not involve those features of input that typically distinguish speech to children from speech among adults (e.g., high pitch, exaggerated intonation contours), although these features have rarely been explicitly investigated. Rather, the putative relationships hold between rate of acquisition and the relative frequency with which caretakers use various kinds of structures and interaction patterns that occur in speech to both children and adults. For example, Cross (1978) reports that "acceleration in linguistic acquisition is associated with an input that is substantially matched to the child's own communicative intentions" (p. 214). Newport et al. (1975) found evidence that "the frequencies of certain kinds of structures in maternal speech do predict learning of related structures by the child" (p. 112), although they caution that frequency often *interacts* with children's language processing strategies (Slobin, 1973) to produce patterns of outcome not predictable from *absolute* frequencies alone.

Most interestingly from a cross-cultural perspective, Newport et al. (1977) found that only certain aspects of language development are affected by frequency differences in the input, and that whether a given language structure is affected is related to how fundmental it is. Universals such as the expression of semantic relations among agents, actions, objects, locations, and so on are the least affected, whereas language-specific structures like the English auxiliary system are the most affected. This finding provides preliminary support for Cazden's (1971) hypothesis:

> Variation in a child's experience will affect acquisition along [a continuum from language-universal to language-specific] in different ways or to different degrees. The acquisition of components towards the . . . more universal . . . end should require less exposure to samples of speech, show less variability across children, and be reflected in a shorter learning period and fewer errors on the part of any one child. Conversely, acquisition of the more language-specific components of competence . . . should require more exposure, show greater variability across children, and be reflected in a longer learning period and more fluctuations and errors by each child. (pp. 42–43)

*Social variables and rate of acquisition.*  If rate of acquisition can be affected by differential patterns of caretaker speech even within socially relatively homogeneous groups, it is plausible to hypothesize that systematic rate differences may obtain across cultural boundaries as a function of systematic differences in how caretakers interact with children. Any cross-cultural differences that do exist in rate of development cannot be too great, since children everywhere seem to follow roughly the same developmental timetable (see p. 106 above). Nevertheless, relatively small systematic differences might well have escaped notice thus far because studies as fine-grained as those of Cross (1975, 1978) and Newport et al. (1975, 1977) have not yet been conducted cross-culturally.

One formidable obstacle to cross-cultural research on rate of development is the difficulty of finding satisfactory ways to compare and equate levels of development when different languages are involved. The mean length of children's utterances provides a rough overall guide to the earlier stages of development (see p. 113 ff. above), but it is insensitive to differences in ability that do not affect sentence length and it becomes an unreliable index to linguistic maturity at later stages of development. Despite the absence of cross-cultural studies, certain within-culture studies (where the variable of language is held constant) have hinted at input-rate relationships that might be expected to differentiate children cross-culturally.

The social variable that has received the most attention over the years as a possible determinant of rate of language development is *social class membership*. Social class differences in mother-child interaction patterns have been documented in a number of studies (e.g., Hess & Shipman, 1965; Bee, Van Egeren, Streissguth, Nyman, & Leckie, 1969, in the United States; and Snow, Arlman-Rupp, Hassing, Jobse, Joosten, & Vorster, 1976, in the Netherlands),[11] and many investigators have reported differences in rate of language learning favoring the middle-class child. This has led to the concept of "verbal deprivation" and its associated effects on educational policy.

However, evidence for verbal deprivation is highly controversial. For example, many findings of differences can be explained away as artifacts resulting from linguistic bias in the testing materials and from sociolinguistic bias in the settings in which data were collected (see p. 107 ff, above; Cazden, 1970, 1971; Ervin-Tripp, 1971. Dale, 1976, p. 317 ff., provides a brief review of the evidence pro and con on social class differences in rate of development). On the basis of these and other considerations, a number of researchers have suggested that the effects of social class on language acquisition are to be found not in rate of development or size of the repertoire but rather in differences in the typical *uses* to which language is put (Cazden, 1970; Ervin-Tripp, 1971; Cole & Bruner, 1972). We will return to this topic shortly.

A second social variable with important implications for the cross-cultural study of differences in rate of development is the *source of linguistic input* to the language-learning child. As noted earlier, children in some cultures are cared for primarily by adults and in others by slightly older children. Is rate of development affected differentially by the age of the caretaker?

In a preliminary consideration of this question, Slobin (1975a) concluded that the answer is no, since researchers in Samoa, Kenya, and a black United States ghetto, all cultures in which toddlers spend most of their time with other children, found the course and rate of language development to be similar in overall outline to that described for middle-class western children who are tended primarily by their mothers. Absence of rate differences between children cared for by adults and those tended by other children has been attributed to the fact that children as well as adults speak a special, simplified language to language learners (Slobin, 1975a).

More recent studies have suggested that rate differences related to age of primary caretaker do exist, and that these may be traced to differences in the way children and adults interact verbally with toddlers. In a within-culture study in a Kipsigis community in Kenya, Harkness (1977) compared the rate of language development of children who spent most of their time with adults versus with other children. She found that faster development (as judged by mean length of utterance) was associated with spending more time with adults. In an attempt to determine why, Harkness analyzed and compared the speech addressed to her subjects by mothers and by 4- to 8-year-old children. The groups did not differ in the use of repetitions of various kinds or in efforts to elicit speech, and both adjusted the length of their sentences to the mean length of utterance of their younger conversational partners, although the mothers used somewhat longer and syntactically more complex sentences than the 4- to 8-year-olds. However, mothers engaged language learners in longer dialogues on a given topic and asked more questions, whereas children more often simply made statements. Harkness concluded that the faster rate of learning associated with adult conversational partners is due to the higher rate of verbal interaction maintained by adults.

Bates (1975), drawing on studies of the effects of birth order, twinship, and institutionalization on rate of development, also suggests that children are less effective than adults as language socializers. Bates interprets this differently from Harkness, however. She attributes it not to differences in rate of interaction but rather to the relatively lesser ability of children to take the perspective of their interlocutor in both constructing their own utterances and in interpreting the other's utterances. Less ability to see things as your partner does, for example, to provide him with the background information that he must have if he is to interpret your speech, results in a higher proportion of failed communication attempts.

These findings and interpretations are suggestive, but they are not conclusive. Brown (1977) reminds us that measures of rate of development can be misleading. With reference to Harkness's (1977) study, he notes that the fact that children who associate primarily with adults produce longer sentences on the average than those who spend time mostly with children may not reflect a truly greater linguistic ability. It might stem instead from the success of adults at keeping children "responding at the upper end of their competence range." With peers, children may have "attempted less" (p. 23). Further investigation is clearly needed before questions about the effect of age of caretaker on language development can be satisfactorily answered.

*Environmental Influences on the Child's Use of Language*

*Elaborated versus restricted codes.* The most complex and comprehensive arguments about differences in language use as a function of social group membership have been presented by Bernstein (1966, 1971, 1972). Bernstein, whose work has been conducted in England, postulates that although members of the middle and working classes command more or less the same body of grammatical knowledge, there are systematic differences in the way they call on the resources of their language in everyday life.

Bernstein termed the language of the working class the *restricted code* and that of the middle class the *elaborated code.* The functional difference between them is that the restricted code depends heavily on immediate context and past shared experience and expectations to convey meaning whereas the elaborated code communicates meaning much more explicitly. In terms of specific behavioral differences, speakers of the restricted code allegedly use more pronouns and more deictic forms (words with shifting, context-based reference, for example, *here-there, this-that*), whereas speakers of the elaborated code use more nouns and noun modifiers. In addition, restricted code users employ more idioms and clichés and simpler syntactic structures and tend to qualify and elaborate meanings less than elaborated code users. Finally, restricted code users rely more heavily on paralinguistic communicative signals like intonation, facial expression, and gestures. In early versions of his theory, Bernstein argued that middle-class speakers can also use the more context-based restricted code where social conditions call for it, but he proposed that members of the working class are largely limited to the restricted code and do not have the option of becoming more verbally explicit.

What cultural factors underlie use of the two codes? Bernstein hypothesized that the restricted code will emerge "where the culture or subculture raises the 'we' above 'I'. . . . The use of a restricted code creates social solidarity at the cost of the verbal elaboration of individual experience" (1972, p. 476). The elaborated code, in contrast, "will arise wherever the culture or subculture emphasizes the 'I' over the 'we.' It will arise wherever the intent of the other person cannot be taken for granted . . . an elaborated code encourages the speaker to focus on the experience of others as different from his own" (1972, pp. 476–477).

Bernstein has developed these cultural concepts by reference to the *role relations* within societies and families. Restricted codes are considered characteristic of "closed role" or "position-oriented" systems, in which judgments and decisions are made on the basis of ascribed roles such as sex, age, and family role (father, daughter, and so on). Conversely, elaborated codes are found in "open role" or "person-oriented" systems that refer less to ascribed status and position than to individual characteristics.

The codes are transmitted largely through the modes of social control characteristic of the two systems, according to Bernstein. Closed role system parents typically either legislate action ("shut up," "stop that," and so on) or appeal to the child on the basis of age, sex, or role norms (e.g., "little boys don't cry," "Daddy doesn't expect to be spoken to like that")

(Bernstein, 1972, p. 486). In contrast, open role system parents more often appeal to personal characteristics and give explanations based on motivations, intentions, consequences, and the like.

Bernstein's theory has generated considerable interest and research since its initial formulation, but it has remained highly controversial. Controversy has centered on two basic issues. First, does the speech of members of the middle and working classes really differ in the way Bernstein hypothesized? Second, if there really are differences in speech, are there cognitive consequences associated with the use of one code or the other? This latter question arose because of the "neo-Whorfian" position espoused by Bernstein in his earlier writings, according to which the linguistic differences that develop between children of different classes differentially affect the course of intellectual growth in favor of the middle-class child. More recently Bernstein (1972) has disavowed the implication of cognitive deficiency on the part of the working-class child, adopting a "different but equal" view. He does continue to argue, however, that the restricted code "directs the child to orders of learning and relevance that are not in harmony with those required by the school . . . between the school and the community of the working-class child there may exist a cultural discontinuity based upon two radically different systems of communication" (1972, p. 473).

With regard to the first question, whether members of different classes really differ in their typical patterns of speech, findings are mixed. Some researchers have reported code-related differences in speech collected in various situations from both adults and school-age children (e.g., Brandis & Henderson, 1970; Rackstraw & Robinson, 1967; Hawkins, 1969; Cook-Gumperz, 1973 [all in England]; Williams & Naremore, 1969 [U.S.]. And a study of Italian children by Parisi and Gianelli (1974; reported in Bates, 1976b) disclosed differences linked to social class as early as 1½ to 2½ years of age, with the working-class children depending more heavily on pronouns coupled with context to carry meaning and the middle-class children using more nouns. On the other hand, other studies have failed to uncover significant class differences (e.g., A. D. Edwards, 1976, England).

Many researchers have argued that even when such differences are found, they are not compelling evidence for a difference in underlying *ability* to exploit the resources of language but stem instead from class differences in speakers' relative familiarity with given situations and in their notions of what kind of speech is appropriate or called for in different settings (e.g., Labov, 1970; van der Geest, Gerstel, Appel, & Tervoort, 1973). This interpretation finds support in studies indicating that social class differences in apparent ability diminish or disappear when the conditions of the task or the setting in which speech samples are collected are slightly altered (e.g., Heider, Cazden, & Brown, 1968; Williams & Naremore, 1969;

van den Broeck, 1977; see Ervin-Tripp, 1972, for discussion). The interpretation of social-class speech differences in terms of differing rules for
language use rather than differences in underlying ability with elaborated
speech has been adopted by Bernstein himself in his more recent work
(see, for example, Bernstein, 1971, pp. 179–180).

*Effects of schooling on linguistic and cognitive ability.* Many investigators have
explored the relationship between schooling and the child's ability to use
language. Bernstein's approach, and that of many researchers in the
United States who are concerned with educational policy, has been to examine how differences in language ability related to social class or ethnic
background affect children's ability to behave effectively in school situations. Other investigators have come at it from the opposite direction, trying to determine how schooling influences children's language skills, and,
through these, their more general cognitive abilities.

A cross-cultural approach to the effects of schooling on language and
cognition was taken by Bruner, Olver, and Greenfield (1966), who reported on experiments carried out in a variety of settings. These investigators concluded that going to school, and particularly learning to read
and write, increases children's ability to use language in ways that are
relatively abstract and removed from immediate context. This greater linguistic ability, in turn, frees them from the need to attend to the concrete,
perceptual attributes of objects. Thus, on tests of cognitive development
such as picture sorting and conservation tasks they usually perform in a
more abstract, less percept-bound way than children from the same culture who have not attended school. Goody and Watt (1962) present related arguments that the achievement of literacy provides people with intellectual tools.

A number of researchers in recent years have criticized proposals like
these, arguing that many apparent differences in the cognitive functioning
of schooled and nonschooled individuals are artifacts of the kind of testing done and the materials used. For example, Cole et al. (1971) concluded
on the basis of their studies among the Kpelle of Liberia that "cultural differences in cognition reside more in the situations to which particular
cognitive processes are applied than in the existence of a process in one
cultural group and its absence in another" (p. 233). More specifically, with
reference to educated and noneducated Kpelle children,

> We suggest that there is a different likelihood that a given situation will evoke
> a general, as opposed to a specific, mode of problem-solving. It is *not* the case
> that the noneducated African is incapable of concept-based thinking. . . . In-
> stead, we have to conclude that the situations in which he applies general,
> concept-based modes of solution are different and perhaps more restricted
> than the situations in which his educated age mate will apply such solutions.
> (p. 225)

This argument is exactly parallel to the one presented immediately above to the effect that differences in language use among members of different social groups reflect differences not in underlying *ability* but rather in the social settings that evoke particular uses.

The existence of such diverse opinions on whether and how schooling influences linguistic and cognitive abilities indicates that the problem is exceedingly complex. As Ginsberg (1977) puts it in a brief overview of aspects of the problem,

> It is naïve and imprecise to think of the general "effects of schooling on cognition." Schooling takes many forms and involves many components, some facilitative of certain kinds of cognition and some not. Cognition and its transfer are similarly multifaceted. It is therefore imperative to examine the nature of both schooling and cognition in far more detail than has been done to date. (p. 10)

*Other Environmental Variables*

The preceding discussion of the influence of environmental factors on rate of language development and on patterns of language use has been selective, concentrating primarily on the impact of variation in linguistic input and caretaker-child interaction patterns rather than on ecological factors such as the types of activities the child typically engages in, the frequency with which she leaves the home, interacts with people outside the immediate family, witnesses novel events, etc. Such factors may well have systematic effects on language development[12] and are obviously dimensions along which cultures vary, but, with the exception of schooling, they have as yet been little investigated from a cross-cultural perspective.

## Conclusions

"How does a child learn to talk?" This little question looks so deceptively simple that almost every parent has a ready answer for it. Yet it is still one of the most challenging problems confronting social scientists. Contemporary efforts to achieve a better understanding of the process of language acquisition have benefited immensely from the input from cross-cultural research, as the discussions in the preceding pages have emphasized. Many pieces are still missing from the puzzle, however.

The problems that have been most thoroughly explored cross-culturally are, in general, those that have interested researchers right from the start of the post-Chomskian era; for example, the structure of children's early sentences, morphological acquisition, the handling of word order.

Within the domain of semantics, cross-cultural work has concentrated primarily on the relational meanings of the first sentences (e.g., agent, action), on possible semantic universals, and on the earliest period of acquiring word meanings. Even though some aspects of later semantic development have been extensively studied among English-speaking children, little comparative material is yet available. How children approach those aspects of semantic structure that are language-specific rather than universal has been little studied either within or across cultures.

The most recent topics to receive intensive within-culture scrutiny are how children learn to use language in contextually appropriate ways and what role is played by the language the child hears. Cross-cultural research in these areas is still relatively sparse but rapidly gathering momentum, as demonstrated by three recent publications: Snow and Ferguson (1977) on talk to children and Ervin-Tripp and Mitchell-Kernan (1977) and an issue of *Language in Society* (1978, 7, 3) on child discourse.

Most problems in language acquisition that have attracted extensive within-culture interest have sooner or later been explored cross-culturally. However, there are exceptions: certain problems with long histories of research in English-speaking countries have received surprisingly little cross-cultural attention. Two such problems—the role of imitation and the relationship between comprehension and production—are mentioned here to illustrate some directions in which future cross-cultural research might go.

The role of imitation in language development has been debated by American psychologists for years. According to many behaviorist theorists, imitation is an essential component of the language acquisition process. Post-Chomskian psycholinguists of the 1960s, in contrast, presented evidence that imitation plays a negligible role (e.g., Ervin, 1964b; Lenneberg, 1966; McNeill, 1970). The most recent studies indicate that although language acquisition is not dependent on imitation (some children almost never imitate), imitation may for some children serve an important function in processing new linguistic materials (Bloom, Hood, & Lightbown, 1974) or in storing up speech fragments for later analysis (R. Clark, 1978).

If children vary in their tendency to use imitation as strategy for language acquisition, it is possible that there are systematic cross-cultural differences in reliance on this strategy. The data needed to examine this possibility are not yet available, but fragmentary evidence of cultural differences in the sanctioning of children's imitation is suggestive. Recall that, according to Ervin-Tripp and Mitchell-Kernan (1977), speech imitation by children is discouraged in Italy; in contrast, Schiefflin (1980) reports that the Kaluli in New Guinea continually elicit imitation from language-learning children and have a special linguistic routine for doing so.

A second factor that may influence whether children adopt an imitation strategy is the extent to which caretakers *model* imitation as a speech act. In a study of American mother-child dyads, Folger and Chapman (1978) found that "the relative frequency with which children imitated mothers reflected the relative frequency with which mothers imitated children" (p. 25). If cross-cultural differences exist in how often caretakers repeat children's utterances, as seems likely, there may be accompanying systematic cultural differences in children's reliance on an imitation strategy for language acquisition.

A second problem that has interested researchers for many years but that has not yet received systematic cross-cultural study is the developmental relationship between comprehension and production. At one time it was widely assumed, with some experimental support (Fraser, Bellugi, & Brown, 1963), that the ability to comprehend given linguistic forms always precedes the ability to produce them. However, more recent evidence indicates that the relationship between comprehension and production is far more complex than this. For example, although comprehension apparently precedes production among English-speaking children for some forms, the reverse is true for other forms (see Bloom, 1974, and Chapman, 1978, for review and discussion).

Determinants of the developmental relationship between comprehension and production (e.g., which one precedes for a given form, length of the lag) are not well understood yet. However, a recent study by Hollos (1977), which explores rural versus urban Hungarian children's ability with personal pronouns, suggests that environmental factors may at least in some cases play a significant role. Hollos found that both sets of children did better at comprehending the social implications of various pronouns than they did at producing the appropriate pronouns in role-playing situations, and that the urban children were more advanced than the rural children in both skills. Hollos attributes this latter finding to the urban children's greater opportunities for social-verbal interactions with a variety of other people. What is interesting for present purposes is that the difference between the two sets of children was considerably *greater* for production than for comprehension; in other words, the ability to comprehend was less affected by environmental factors than was the ability to produce. Even though Hollos's study of course is not cross-cultural, the rural-urban distinction has entered into many discussions of cross-cultural differences. The results of her study thus indicate the potential fruitfulness of cross-cultural explorations of the developmental relationship between comprehension and production.

Throughout this chapter the emphasis has been on how cross-cultural research can help us better understand the process of language development. In closing, let us look briefly at child language research from another perspective: What can the study of language acquisition, enriched as it has been and will continue to be by cross-cultural comparisons, contribute to research in other fields?

In acquiring language, the child must draw on a variety of different kinds of knowledge and ability. And child language researchers, increasingly aware of this, have profited immensely in recent years from taking into account information on children's perceptual, cognitive, and social development. But information can flow both ways: studies of child language in turn provide excellent clues to these aspects of child development.

Information about children's cognitive and perceptual abilities is found in a number of different types of studies. For example, many investigations of children's comprehension of words and sentence structures have shown that when children lack a full understanding of the forms in question their interpretations are guided in systematic ways by cognitively based strategies of various sorts, including assumptions about "how things are" in the world (e.g., E. Clark, 1973a, 1975; Wilcox & Palermo, 1974; Chapman, 1978).

How children speak—particularly deviations from adult norms in their use of words, inflections, and sentence structures—provides further important evidence on matters of interest to developmental psychologists: what is cognitively or perceptually salient for children (e.g., Bloom, 1970, 1973; Brown, 1973; E. Clark, 1973b, 1977; Bowerman, 1973a, 1976, 1980), what conceptual distinctions children make (Antinucci & Miller, 1976), what categorizational principles are available to them in the second year of life (Bowerman, 1978, 1980), and how cognitive and linguistic development are related (Slobin, 1973; Cromer, 1974; Schlesinger, 1977; Bowerman, 1976, 1980).

Studies of language development offer a variety of clues to social development. For example, as Ervin-Tripp and Mitchell-Kernan observe, "there is no way to study the acquisition of norms for sociolinguistic rules without at the same time learning about the child's socialization into the role system" (1977, p. 11). These authors point out that in learning the proper use of address terms, pronouns, and directives, "children systematically must come to attend to the features of age and power and familiarity of addressees" (1977, p. 11). The order in which these features begin to influence children's selection of speech variants, along with errors children make on the path to adult competence, are excellent sources of information about the development of social concepts. Besides offering clues to children's knowledge of social roles, children's speech provides insight into their developing understanding of cultural values. This important point was emphasized by Mitchell-Kernan and Kernan (1975) in their pioneering investigation of cross-cultural similarities and differences in disputing (see p. 149 above).

The preceding paragraphs indicate ways in which child language research provides information on processes of cognitive, perceptual, and social development. But the study of language acquisition has broader implications. As Chomsky hypothesized and as recent research increasingly demonstrates, there are close connections between children's characteristic ways of approaching the task of language acquisition and the properties of the linguistic structures they must acquire. Thus, the relevance of the study of language acquisition extends to linguists and to all scholars who are interested in the nature of higher mental processes.

# Notes

1. This research was supported in part by Grant HD00870 from the National Institute of Child Health and Human Development. Some of the writing was carried out during a year at the Netherlands Institute for Advanced Study in the Humanities and Social Sciences. The support of these institutes is gratefully acknowledged.

2. For example, Blount (1969, Luo); Kernan (1969, Samoan); Stross (1969, Tzeltal); Bowerman (1973a) and Argoff (1976) (Finnish); Omar (1973, Egyptian Arabic); Schaerlaekens (1973, Dutch); Lange and Larsson (1973) and Lindhagen (1976) (Swedish); MacWhinney (1974, 1976, Hungarian); Aksu (1978, Turkish); Miller (1979, German); see Slobin (1972) for a more complete listing broken down by language.

3. The interested reader is referred to Ingram (1974), Ferguson and Garnica (1975), and Ferguson (1976) for overviews of phonological development that take cross-linguistic data into account.

4. Kagan and Klein (1973) report on a culture in the Guatemala highlands in which both cognitive and language development are considerably slowed down by the practice of keeping infants inside dim huts, holding them constantly and not allowing them to crawl about, and rarely talking or interacting with them. First words for these children apparently emerge at about 2½ years of age, or 1½ years later than for children in most cultures. Nevertheless the subsequent course of language and cognitive development is apparently normal, which led the authors to revise their earlier opinion that the nature of the early environment is a critical factor in later development. Instead, they now suggest that cognitive (and presumably linguistic) development is maturationally controlled and resilient even in the face of extremely adverse environmental conditions.

5. Cf. Cromer's (1975) unsuccessful attempt to replicate, with English-speaking children, a study by McNeill, Yukawa, and McNeill (1971) on how Japanese children comprehend slightly deviant sentences with direct and indirect objects. McNeill et al. had interpreted their findings as indicating that the children expected a marked linguistic form to be the indirect object, in accordance with a putative linguistic universal favoring the explicit marking, e.g., by inflection, of indirect objects over direct objects.

6. Consult Maratsos (1979) for a consideration of ways in which certain aspects of morphological acquisition do not accord with Slobin's operating principles, and MacWhinney (1978) for a comprehensive model of the processes involved in the learning of morphophonology based on experimental and diary data on the acquisition of ten different languages.

7. Actually, things are somewhat more complex than this. Some investigators of English-speaking children have found that center-embedded relatives are easier to understand than right-branching relatives at certain ages (H. Brown, 1971; Lahey, 1974); Aller (1977), studying Arabic-speaking children, also found center-embedded relatives easier. Some of the discrepancies between different researchers' findings may be attributable to important differences in the construction of stimulus sentences, as de Villiers, Tager Flusberg, Hakuta, and Cohen (1979) discuss. Sorting out the relative contribution of various structural properties to the complexity of relative clause-containing sentences will undoubtedly require both careful control of all possible sources of processing difficulty in constructing stimuli sentences and further cross-linguistic work.

8. Classifiers are linguistic forms used in conjunction with the predication of something about objects, e.g. when they are counted ("nine round-things balls") or when they are acted on (e.g., "he caused round-solid-thing-to-move upwards stone"—he lifted the stone).

9. The role of intonation in the one-word period is highly controversial. See Dore (1975) for one viewpoint, discussion, and references to investigators with differing positions.

10. Some language that have been studied include English, Arabic, Comanche, Gilyak, Latvian, Spanish, Marathi, and Japanese. See Ferguson (1977) for a listing of major sources on these and other languages.

11. Interestingly, however, these differences apparently take place *beneath* the level of overall simplification of speech to children, which, to judge from Snow et al.'s data on Dutch mother-child dyads, is general across social class lines.

12. See, for example, Nelson (1973) on the effects of frequency of television watching, "outings," etc. on rate of language development among middle-class American children and Hollos (1977 and p. 167) on differences between rural and urban Hungarian children's ability with the complex system of personal pronouns in Hungarian.

# References

AKSU, A. *Aspect and modality in the child's acquisition of the Turkish past tense.* Unpublished doctoral dissertation, University of California at Berkeley, 1978.

ALLAN, K. Classifiers. *Language,* 1977, *53,* 285–311.

ALLER, S. K. The acquisition of relative constructions in Arabic. Paper presented at the 6th Annual University of Wisconsin-Milwaukee Linguistics Symposium. Milwaukee, March 18–19, 1977.

AMMON, M. S., & SLOBIN, D. I. A cross-linguistic study of the processing of causative sentences. *Papers and Reports on Child Language Development* (Stanford University Department of Linguistics), 1978, *15*, 114–128.

ANTINUCCI, F., & MILLER, R. How children talk about what happened. *Journal of Child Language*, 1976, *3*, 167–189.

ARGOFF, H. D. *The acquisition of Finnish inflectional morphology.* Unpublished doctoral dissertation, University of California at Berkeley, 1976.

ARLMAN-RUPP, A. J. L., VAN NIEKERK DE HAAN, D., & VAN DE SANDT-KOENDERMAN, M. Brown's early stages: Some evidence from Dutch. *Journal of Child Language*, 1976, *3*, 267–274.

AUSTIN, J. L. *How to do things with words.* New York: Oxford University Press, 1962.

BAR-ADON, A. Primary syntactic structures in Hebrew child language. In A. Bar-Adon & W. F. Leopold (Eds.), *Child language: A book of readings.* Englewood Cliffs, N.J.: Prentice-Hall, 1971.

BATES, E. *The development of conversational skill in 2, 3, and 4 year olds.* Master's thesis, University of Chicago, 1971 (Reprinted in Pragmatics Microfiche, 1975, 1[2], Cambridge University.)

————. Peer relations and the acquisition of language. In M. Lewis & L. Rosenblum (Eds.), *The origins of behavior* (Vol. 4): *Friendship and peer relations.* New York: John Wiley & Sons, 1975.

————. *Language and context: The acquisition of pragmatics.* New York: Academic Press, 1976. (a)

————. Pragmatics and sociolinguistics in child language. In D. Morehead & A. Morehead (Eds.), *Directions in normal and deficient child language.* Baltimore: University Park Press, 1976. (b)

BATES, E., CAMAIONI, L., & VOLTERRA, V. The acquisition of performatives prior to speech. *Merrill-Palmer Quarterly*, 1975, *21*, 205–226.

BATES, E., BENIGNI, L., BRETHERTON, I., CAMAIONI, L., & VOLTERRA, V. From gesture to the first word: On cognitive and social prerequisites. In M. Lewis & L. Rosenblum (Eds.), *The origins of behavior* (Vol. 5): *Interaction, conversation, and the development of language.* New York: John Wiley & Sons, 1977.

BEE, H. L., VAN EGEREN, L. F., STREISSGUTH, A. P., NYMAN, B. A., & LECKIE, M. S. Social class differences in maternal teaching strategies and speech patterns. *Developmental Psychology*, 1969, *1*, 726–734.

BERKO, J. The child's learning of English morphology. *Word*, 1958, *14*, 150–177.

BERLIN, B., & KAY, P. *Basic color terms.* Berkeley: University of California Press, 1969.

BERNSTEIN, B. Elaborated and restricted codes: Their social origins and some consequences. In A. G. Smith (Ed.), *Communication and culture.* New York: Holt, Rinehart & Winston, 1966.

————. *Class, codes, and control* (Vol. 1): *Theoretical studies towards a sociology of language.* London: Routledge & Kegan Paul, 1971.

————. A sociolinguistic approach to socialization, with some reference to educability. In J. J. Gumperz & D. Hymes, *Directions in sociolinguistics.* New York: Holt, Rinehart & Winston, 1972.

BEVER, T. The cognitive basis for linguistic structures. In J. R. Hayes (Ed.), *Cognition and the development of language.* New York: John Wiley & Sons, 1970.

BEVER, T. G., & LANGENDOEN, D. T. A dynamic model of the evolution of language. *Linguistic Inquiry*, 1971, 2, 433–461.

BINGHAM, N. E. Maternal speech to pre-linguistic infants: Differences related to maternal judgments of infant language competence. Unpublished paper, Cornell University, 1971.

BLOOM, L. *Language development: Form and function in emerging grammars.* Cambridge, Mass.: MIT Press, 1970.

―――. *One word at a time: The use of single-word utterances before syntax.* The Hague: Mouton, 1973.

―――. Talking, understanding, and thinking. In R. L. Schiefelbusch & L. L. Lloyd (Eds.), *Language perspectives—Acquisition, retardation, and intervention.* Baltimore: University Park Press, 1974.

BLOOM, L., HOOD, L. & LIGHTBOWN, P. Imitation in language development. *Cognitive Psychology*, 1974, 6, 380–420.

BLOOM, L., ROCISSANO, L. & HOOD, L. Adult-child discourse: Developmental interaction between information processing and linguistic knowledge. *Cognitive Psychology*, 1976, 8, 521–552.

BLOUNT, B. G. *Acquisition of language by Luo children.* Unpublished doctoral dissertation, University of California at Berkeley, 1969.

―――. Aspects of Luo socialization. *Language in Society*, 1972, 1, 235–248. (a)

―――. Parental speech and language acquisition: Some Luo and Samoan examples. *Anthropological Linguistics*, 1972, 14, 119–130. (b)

BLOUNT, B. G., & PADGUG, E. J. Prosodic, paralinguistic, and interactional features in parent-child speech: English and Spanish. *Journal of Child Language*, 1977, 4, 67–86.

BOGGS, S. T. The development of verbal disputing in part-Hawaiian children. *Language in Society*, 1978, 7, 325–344.

BOGGS, S. T., & WATSON-GEGEO, K. A. Interweaving routines: Strategies for encompassing a social situation. *Language in Society*, 1978, 7, 375–392.

BOWERMAN, M. *Early syntactic development: A cross-linguistic study with special reference to Finnish.* Cambridge, England: Cambridge University Press, 1973. (a)

―――. Structural relationships in children's utterances: Syntactic or semantic? In T. E. Moore (Ed.), *Cognitive development and the acquisition of language.* New York: Academic Press, 1973. (b)

BOWERMAN, M. Discussion summary: Development of concepts underlying language. In R. L. Schiefelbusch & L. L. Lloyd (Eds.), *Language perspectives—Acquisition, retardation, and intervention.* Baltimore: University Park Press, 1974.

―――. Cross-linguistic similarities at two stages of syntactic development. In E. H. Lenneberg & E. E. Lenneberg (Eds.), *Foundations of language: A multidisciplinary approach.* New York: Academic Press, 1975.

―――. Semantic factors in the acquisition of rules for word use and sentence construction. In D. Morehead & A. Morehead (Eds.), *Directions in normal and deficient child language.* Baltimore: University Park Press, 1976.

―――. The acquisition of word meaning: An investigation into some current conflicts. In N. Waterson & C. Snow (Eds.), *The development of communication.* New York: John Wiley & Sons, 1978.

————. The structure and origin of semantic categories in the language learning child. In M. L. Foster & S. Brandes (Eds.), *Symbol as sense*. New York: Academic Press, 1980.

BRAINE, M. D. S. The ontogeny of English phrase structure: The first phase. *Language*, 1963, *39*, 1–14.

————. The acquisition of language in infant and child. In C. Reed (Ed.), *The learning of language*. New York: Scribners, 1971.

————. Children's first word combinations. *Monographs of the society for research in child development*, 1976, *41* (1, Serial No. 164).

BRANDIS, W., & HENDERSON, D. *Social class, language, and communication*. London: Routledge and Kegan Paul, 1970.

BROWN, H. D. Children's comprehension of relativized English sentences. *Child Development*, 1971, *42*, 1923–1936.

BROWN, R. The first sentences of child and chimpanzee. In *Selected papers by Roger Brown*. New York: Free Press, 1970.

————. *A first language: The early stages*. Cambridge, Mass.: Harvard University Press, 1973.

————. The development of the human child's native language. In A. Silverstein (Ed.), *Human communication: Theoretical explorations*. Hillsdale, N.J.: Lawrence Erlbaum, 1974.

————. Introduction. In C. E. Snow & C. A. Ferguson (Eds.), *Talking to children: Language input and acquisition*. Cambridge, England: Cambridge University Press, 1977.

BROWN, R., & BELLUGI, U. Three processes in the child's acquisition of syntax. In E. H. Lenneberg (Ed.), *New directions in the study of language*. Cambridge, Mass.: MIT Press, 1964.

BROWN, R., & BERKO, J. Word association and the acquisition of grammar. *Child Development*, 1960, *31*, 1–14.

BROWN, R., & FRASER, C. The acquisition of syntax. In C. H. Cofer, & B. S. Musgrave (Eds.), *Verbal behavior and learning*. New York: McGraw-Hill, 1963.

BROWN, R., & HANLON, C. Derivational complexity and order of acquisition in child speech. In J. R. Hayes (Ed.), *Cognition and the development of language*. New York: John Wiley & Sons, 1970.

BRUNER, J. S. The ontogenesis of speech acts. *Journal of Child Language*, 1975, *2*, 1–19.

BRUNER, J. S., WALLACH, M. A., & GALANTER, E. H. The identification of recurrent regularity. *American Journal of Psychology*, 1959, *72*, 200–209.

BRUNER, J. S., OLVER, R. R., & GREENFIELD, P. M. *Studies in cognitive growth*. New York: John Wiley & Sons, 1966.

BURLING, R. Language development of a Garo and English speaking child. *Word*, 1959, *15*, 45–68.

CAMPBELL, R., & WALES, R. The study of language acquisition. In J. Lyons (Ed.), *New horizons in linguistics*. Harmondsworth, England: Penguin Books, 1970.

CARTER, A. The transformation of sensorimotor morphemes into words: A case study of the development of 'more' and 'mine'. *Journal of Child Language*, 1975, *2*, 233–250.

————. The development of systematic vocalizations prior to words: A case study. In N. Waterson & C. Snow (Eds.), *The development of communication.* New York: John Wiley & Sons, 1978.

CAZDEN, C. B. *Environmental assistance to the child's acquisition of grammar.* Unpublished doctoral dissertation, Harvard University, 1965.

————. The neglected situation in child language research and education. In F. Williams (Ed.), *Language and poverty: Perspectives on a theme.* Chicago: Markham Publishing Co., 1970.

————. The hunt for independent variables. In R. Huxley & E. Ingram (Eds.), *Language acquisitions: Models and methods.* London: Academic Press, 1971.

CHAPMAN, R. S. Comprehension strategies in children. In J. F. Kavanagh, & W. Strange (Eds.), *Implications of basic speech and language research for the school and clinic.* Cambridge, Mass.: MIT Press, 1978.

CHAPMAN R. S., & MILLER, J. F. Word order in early two and three word utterances: Does production precede comprehension? *Journal of Speech and Hearing Research,* 1975, *18,* 355–371.

CHOMSKY, C. S. *The acquisition of syntax in children from 5 to 10.* Cambridge, Mass.: MIT Press, 1969.

CHOMSKY, N. *Syntactic structures.* The Hague: Mouton, 1957.

————. Review of Skinner (1957). *Language,* 1959, *35,* 26–58.

————. *Aspects of the theory of syntax.* Cambridge, Mass.: MIT Press, 1965.

CLANCY, P., JACOBSEN, T., & SILVA, M. The acquisition of conjunction: A cross-linguistic study. *Papers and Reports in Child Language Development* (Stanford University Department of Linguistics), 1976, *12,* 71–80.

CLARK, E. V. Non-linguistic strategies and the acquisition of word meanings. *Cognition,* 1973, *2,* 161–182. (a)

————. What's in a word? On the child's acquisition of semantics in his first language. In T. E. Moore (Ed.), *Cognitive development and the acquisition of language.* New York: Academic Press, 1973. (b)

————. Knowledge, context, and strategy in the acquisition of meaning. In D. Dato (Ed.), *Georgetown University round table on languages and linguistics.* Washington, D.C.: Georgetown University Press, 1975.

————. Universal categories: On the semantics of classifiers and children's early word meanings. In A. Juilland (Ed.), *Linguistic studies offered to Joseph Greenberg: On the occasion of his sixtieth birthday.* Saratoga, Calif.: Anma Libri, 1977.

CLARK, H. H. Space, time, semantics, and the child. In T. E. Moore (Ed.), *Cognitive development and the acquisition of language.* New York: Academic Press, 1973.

CLARK, H. H., & CLARK, E. V. *Psychology and language.* New York: Harcourt, Brace & Jovanovich, 1977.

CLARK, R. Some even simpler ways to learn to talk. In N. Waterson & C. Snow (Eds.), *The development of communication.* New York: John Wiley & Sons, 1978.

CLARK, R., HUTCHESON, S., & VAN BUREN, P. Comprehension and production in language acquisition. *Journal of Linguistics,* 1974, *10,* 39–54.

COLE, M., & BRUNER, J. S. Some preliminaries to some theories of cultural difference. *Yearbook of the National Society of the Study of Education.* Chicago: University of Chicago Press, 1972.

COLE, M., GAY, J., GLICK, J., & SHARP, D. *The cultural context of learning and thinking.* New York: Basic Books, 1971.

COOK-GUMPERZ, J. *Social control and socialization: A study of class differences in the language of maternal control.* London: Routledge & Kegan Paul, 1973.

————. Situated instructions: Language socialization of school age children. In S. Ervin-Tripp & C. Mitchell-Kernan (Eds.), *Child discourse.* New York: Academic Press, 1977.

CREMONA, C., & BATES, E. The development of attitudes toward dialect in Italian children. *Journal of Psycholinguistic Research,* 1977, *6,* 223–232.

CROMER, R. F. *The development of temporal reference during the acquisition of language.* Unpublished doctoral dissertation, Harvard University, 1968.

————. The development of language and cognition: The cognition hypothesis. In B. Foss (Ed.), *New perspectives in child development.* Baltimore, Md.: Penguin, 1974.

————. An experimental investigation of a putative linguistic universal: Marking and the indirect object. *Journal of Experimental Child Psychology,* 1975, *20,* 73–80.

————. The cognitive hypothesis of language acquisition and its implications for child language deficiency. In D. Morehead & A. Morehead (Eds.), *Directions in normal and deficient child language.* Baltimore, Md.: University Park Press, 1976.

CROSS, T. Some relationships between motherese and linguistic level in accelerated children. *Papers and Reports on Child Language Development* (Stanford University Department of Linguistics), 1975, *10,* 117–135.

————. Mother's speech and its association with rate of linguistic development in young children. In N. Waterson & C. Snow (Eds.), *The development of communication.* New York: John Wiley & Sons, 1978.

DALE, P. *Language development: Structure and function* (2nd edition). New York: Holt, Rinehart & Winston, 1976.

DAVIDOFF, J. B. *Differences in visual perception: The individual eye.* New York: Academic Press, 1975.

DE VILLIERS, J. G., & DE VILLIERS, P. A. Semantics and syntax in the first two years: The output of form and function and the form and function of the input. In F. D. Minifie & L. L. Lloyd (Eds.), *Communicative and cognitive abilities—Early behavioral assessment.* Baltimore, Md.: University Park Press, 1978.

DE VILLIERS, J. G., TAGER FLUSBERG, H. B., HAKUTA, K., & COHEN, M. Children's comprehension of relative clauses. *Journal of Psycholinguistic Research,* 1979, *8,* 499–518.

DORE, J. Holophrases, speech acts, and language universals. *Journal of Child Language,* 1975, *2,* 21–40.

————. 'Oh them sheriff': A pragmatic analysis of children's responses to questions. In S. Ervin-Tripp & C. Mitchell-Kernan (Eds.), *Child discourse.* New York: Academic Press, 1977.

————. What's so conceptual about the acquisition of linguistic structures? *Journal of Child Language,* 1979, *6,* 129–137.

DORE, J., FRANKLIN, M., MILLER, R., & RAMER, A. Transitional phenomena in early language acquisition. *Journal of Child Language,* 1976, *3,* 13–28.

DOWTY, D. Montague grammar and the lexical decomposition of causative verbs. In B. H. Partee (Ed.), *Montague Grammar.* New York: Academic Press, 1976.

DUNDES A., LEACH, J. W., & ÖZKÖK, B. The strategies of Turkish boys' verbal dueling rhymes. In J. J. Gumperz & D. Hymes (Eds.), *Directions in sociolinguistics.* New York: Holt, Rinehart & Winston, 1972.

EDELSKY, C. Acquisition of an aspect of communicative competence: Learning what it means to talk like a lady. In S. Ervin-Tripp & C. Mitchell-Kernan (Eds.), *Child discourse.* New York: Academic Press, 1977.

EDWARDS, A. D. Speech codes and speech variants: Social class and task differences in children's speech. *Journal of Child Language,* 1976, *3,* 247–265.

EDWARDS, D. Sensory-motor intelligence and semantic relations in early child grammar. *Cognition,* 1974, *2,* 395–434.

ERVIN, S. An analysis of the interaction of language, topic, and listener. In J. J. Gumperz & D. Hymes (Eds.), The ethnography of communication. *American Anthropologist,* 1964, *66* (6, Pt. 2), 86–102. (a)

————. Imitation and structural change in children's language. In E. H. Lenneberg (Ed.), *New directions in the study of language.* Cambridge, Mass.: MIT Press, 1964. (b)

ERVIN-TRIPP, S. Sociolinguistics. In L. Berkowitz (Ed.), *Advances in experimental social psychology.* New York: Academic Press, 1969. (Reprinted in B. G. Blount [Ed.], *Language, culture, and society.* Cambridge, Mass.: Winthrop Publishers, 1974.)

————. Social background and verbal skills. In R. Huxley & E. Ingram (Eds.), *Language acquisition: Models and methods.* London: Academic Press, 1971.

————. Children's sociolinguistic competence and dialect diversity. In I. J. Gordon (Ed.), *Early childhood education: The seventy-first yearbook of the National Society for the Study of Education.* Chicago: University of Chicago Press, 1972.

————. The structure of communicative choice. In A. S. Dil (Comp.), *Language acquisition and communicative choice: Essays by Susan M. Ervin-Tripp.* Stanford, California: Stanford University Press, 1973.

————. Is Sybil there? The structure of American English directives. *Language in Society,* 1976, *5,* 25–66. (a)

————. *Speech acts and social learning.* In K. H. Basso & H. A. Selby (Eds.), *Meaning in anthropology.* Albuquerque: University of New Mexico Press, 1976. (b)

————. Wait for me, roller-skate! In S. Ervin-Tripp & C. Mitchell-Kernan (Eds.), *Child discourse.* New York: Academic Press, 1977.

————. Some features of early adult-child dialogues. *Language in Society,* 1978, *7,* 357–373.

ERVIN-TRIPP, S., & MITCHELL-KERNAN, C. (Eds.), *Child discourse.* New York: Academic Press, 1977.

FARWELL, C. B. The early expression of motion and location. Paper presented at the first annual Boston Conference on Language Development. Oct. 2, 1976.

————. The primacy of goal in the child's description of motion and location. *Papers and Reports on Child Language Development* (Stanford University Department of Linguistics), 1977, *13,* 126–133.

FELDMAN, C. The effects of various types of adult responses in the syntactic acquisition of two- to three-year-olds. Unpublished paper, Department of Psychology, University of Chicago, 1971.

FERGUSON, C. A. Learning to pronounce: The earliest stages of phonological development in the child. In *Papers and Reports on Child Language Development* (Stanford University Department of Linguistics), 1976, *11*, 1–27.

————. Baby talk as a simplified register. In C. E. Snow & C. A. Ferguson (Eds.), *Talking to children: Language input and acquisition.* Cambridge, England: Cambridge University Press, 1977.

FERGUSON, C. A., & GARNICA, O. K. Theories of phonological development. In E. H. Lenneberg & E. Lenneberg (Eds.), *Foundations of language development: A multidisciplinary approach.* New York: Academic Press, 1975.

FILLMORE, C. J. The case for case. In E. Bach & R. T. Harms (Eds.), *Universals of linguistic theory.* New York: Holt, Rinehart & Winston, 1968.

FISCHER, J. L. Linguistic socialization: Japan and the United States. In R. Hill & R. König (Eds.), *Families in east and west.* The Hague: Mouton, 1970.

FODOR, J. A. How to learn to talk: Some simple ways. In F. Smith & G. A. Miller (Eds.), *The genesis of language: A psycholinguistic approach.* Cambridge, Mass.: MIT Press, 1966.

FOLGER, J. P., & CHAPMAN, R. S. A pragmatic analysis of spontaneous imitations. *Journal of Child Language,* 1978, *5*, 25–38.

FRASER, C., BELLUGI, U., & BROWN, R. Control of grammar in imitation, comprehension, and production. *Journal of Verbal Learning and Verbal Behavior,* 1963, *2*, 121–135.

FREEDLE, R., & LEWIS, M. Prelinguistic conversations. In M. Lewis & L. Rosenblum (Eds.), *The origins of behavior* (Vol. 5): *Interaction, conversation, and the development of language.* New York: John Wiley & Sons, 1977.

GARMAN, M. On the acquisition of two complex syntactic structures in Tamil. *Journal of Child Language,* 1974, *1*, 65–76.

GARNICA, O. K. Some prosodic and paralinguistic features of speech to young children. In C. E. Snow & C. A. Ferguson (Eds.), *Talking to children: Language input and acquisition.* Cambridge, England: Cambridge University Press, 1977.

GARVEY, C. Requests and responses in children's speech. *Journal of Child Language,* 1975, *2*, 41–63.

————. Play with language and speech. In S. Ervin-Tripp, & C. Mitchell-Kernan (Eds.), *Child discourse.* New York: Academic Press, 1977.

GINSBERG, H. Some problems in the study of schooling and cognition. *The Quarterly Newsletter of the Institute for Comparative Human Development* (Rockefeller University), 1977, *1*, 7–10.

GLEASON, J. B. Code switching in children's language. In T. E. Moore (Ed.), *Cognitive development and the acquisition of language.* New York: Academic Press, 1973.

GLEASON, J. B., & WEINTRAUB, S. The acquisition of routines in child language. *Language in Society,* 1976, *5*, 129–136.

GODARD, D. Same setting, different norms: Phone call beginnings in France and the United States. *Language in Society,* 1977, *6*, 209–219.

GOODSON, B. D., & GREENFIELD, P. M. The search for structural principles in children's manipulative play: A parallel with linguistic development. *Child Development,* 1975, *46*, 734–746.

GOODY, J., & WATT, I. The consequences of literacy. *Comparative Studies in Sociology and History,* 1962, *5*, 304–345.

GREENFIELD, P. M. Informativeness, presupposition, and semantic choice in single-word utterances. In N. Waterson & C. Snow (Eds.), *The development of communication.* New York: John Wiley & Sons, 1978.

GREENFIELD, P. M., NELSON, K., & SALTZMAN, E. The development of rulebound strategies for manipulating seriated cups: A parallel between action and grammar. *Cognitive Psychology,* 1972, *3,* 291–310.

GREENFIELD, P. M., & SMITH, J. H. *The structure of communication in early language development.* New York: Academic Press, 1976.

GREENFIELD, P. M., & ZUKOW, P. G. Why do children say what they say when they say it?: An experimental approach to the psychogenesis of presupposition. In K. Nelson (Ed.), *Children's language* (Vol. 1). New York: Gardner Press, 1978.

GRICE, P. Logic and conversation. In P. Cole & J. L. Morgan (Eds.), *Syntax and semantics* (Vol. 3): *Speech acts.* New York: Academic Press, 1975.

GRIMM, H. Analysis of short-term dialogues in 5–7 year olds: Encoding of intentions and modifications of speech acts as a function of negative feedback. Paper presented at the Third International Child Language Symposium, London, September, 1975.

GRIMM, H., & SCHÖLER, H. Erlauben—Befehlen—Lassen: Wie gut verstehen kleine Kinder kausativierende Beziehungen? In H. Grimm, H. Schöler, & M. Wintermantel (Eds.), *Zür Entwicklung sprachlicher Strukturformen bei Kindern.* Weinheim, W. Germany: Julius Beltz Verlag, 1975.

GUMPERZ, J. J. Introduction. In J. J. Gumperz and D. Hymes (Eds.), *Directions in sociolinguistics: The ethnography of communication.* New York: Holt, Rinehart & Winston, 1972.

GUMPERZ, J. J., & HYMES, D. Ethnography of communication. *American Anthropologist,* 1964, special issue no. 6.

HAAS, M. R. Men's and women's speech in Koasati. In D. Hymes (Ed.), *Language in culture and society.* New York: Harper & Row, 1964.

HAKUTA, K. The role of word order in children's acquisition of Japanese. Paper presented to the New England Child Language Association, Brown University, Dec. 4, 1976.

HALLIDAY, M. A. K. *Learning how to mean—Explorations in the development of language.* London: Edward Arnold, 1975.

HARKNESS, S. Aspects of social environment and first language acquisition in rural Africa. In C. E. Snow & C. A. Ferguson (Eds.), *Talking to children: Language input and acquisition.* Cambridge, England: Cambridge University Press, 1977.

HAWKINS, P. R. Social class, the nominal group, and reference. *Language and Speech,* 1969, *12,* 125–135.

HEIDER, E. R. 'Focal' color areas and the development of color names. *Developmental Psychology,* 1971, *4,* 447–455.

———. Universals in color naming and memory. *Journal of Experimental Psychology,* 1972, *93,* 10–21.

HEIDER, E. R., CAZDEN, C. B., & BROWN, R. Social class differences in the effectiveness and style of children's coding ability. *Project Literacy Reports, No. 9.* Ithaca, N.Y.: Cornell University Press, 1968.

HESS, R. D., & SHIPMAN, V. C. Early experience and socialization of cognitive modes in children. *Child Development,* 1965, *36,* 869–886.

HOLLOS, M. Comprehension and use of social rules in pronoun selection by Hungarian children. In S. Ervin-Tripp & C. Mitchell-Kernan (Eds.), *Child discourse*. New York: Academic Press, 1977.

HOLLOS, M., & BEEMAN, W. The development of directives among Norwegian and Hungarian children: An example of communicative style in culture. *Language in Society*, 1978, 7, 345-355.

HYMES, D. Formal discussion. In U. Bellugi and R. Brown (Eds.), The acquisition of language. *Monographs of the Society for Research in Child Development.*, 1964, 29 (1, Serial No. 92).

————. Competence and performance in linguistic theory. In R. Huxley & E. Ingram (Eds.), *Language acquisition: Models and methods*. London: Academic Press, 1971. (a)

————. Sociolinguistics and the ethnography of speaking. In E. Ardener (Ed.), *Social anthropology and linguistics*. Association of Social Anthropologists, Monograph 10. London: Tavistock, 1971. (b) (Reprinted in B. G. Blount [Ed.], *Language, culture and society*. Cambridge, Mass.: Winthrop Publishers, 1974.)

————. Models of the interaction of language and social life. In J. J. Gumperz & D. Hymes (Eds.), *Directions in sociolinguistics*. New York: Holt, Rinehart & Winston, 1972.

INGRAM, D. Phonological rules in young children. *Journal of Child Language*, 1974, 1, 49-64.

JOHNSTON, J. R. The growth of propositional complexity: New data and critique. Unpublished paper, University of California at Berkeley, 1976.

JOHNSTON, J. R., & SLOBIN, D. I. The development of locative expressions in English, Italian, Serbo-Croatian and Turkish. *Journal of Child Language*, 1979, 6, 529-545.

KAGAN, J., & KLEIN, R. E. Cross-cultural perspectives on early development. *American Psychologist*, 1973, 28, 947-961.

KEENAN E. O. Conversational competence in children. *Journal of Child Language*, 1974, 1, 163-183.

————. On the universality of conversational postulates. *Language in Society*, 1976, 5, 67-80.

KEENAN, E. O., & KLEIN, E. Coherency in children's discourse. *Journal of Psycholinguistic Research*, 1975, 4, 365-380.

KERNAN, K. T. *The acquisition of language by Samoan children*. Unpublished doctoral dissertation, University of California at Berkeley, 1969.

KERNAN, K. T., & BLOUNT, B. G. The acquisition of Spanish grammar by Mexican children. *Anthropological Linguistics*, 1966, 8, 1-14.

KIRSHENBLATT-GIMBLETT, B. (Ed.). *Speech play: Research and resources for studying linguistic creativity*. Philadelphia: University of Pennsylvania Press, 1976.

KUCZAJ, S., & MARATSOS, M. What a child *can* say before he *will*. *Merrill-Palmer Quarterly*, 1975, 21, 89-111.

KUNO, S. The position of relative clauses and conjunctions. *Linguistic Inquiry*, 1974, 5, 117-136.

LABOV, W. The logic of nonstandard English. In F. Williams (Ed.), *Language and poverty*. Chicago: Markham, 1970.

LABOV, W., ROBINS, C., & LEWIS, J. *A study of the non-standard English of Negro and*

*Puerto Rican speakers in New York City. Final Report, OE–6–10–059.* New York: Columbia University, 1968.

LAHEY, M. Use of prosody and syntactic markers in children's comprehension of spoken sentences. *Journal of Speech and Hearing Research,* 1974, *17,* 656–668.

LAKOFF, G. *Irregularity in syntax.* New York: Holt, Rinehart & Winston, 1971.

LAKOFF, R. Language and woman's place. *Language in Society,* 1973, *2,* 45–80. (a)

———. The logic of politeness: Or minding your P's and Q's. *Papers from the 9th Regional Meeting of the Chicago Linguistic Society,* 1973. (b)

LANGE, S., & LARSSON, K. Syntactical development of a Swedish Girl Embla, between 20 and 42 months of age. Part I: Age 20–25 months. Report No. 1 *Project Child Language Syntax, Institutionem för Nordiska Språk,* Stockholms Universitet, 1973.

LEHMANN, W. P. A structural principle of language and its implications. *Language,* 1973, *49,* 47–66.

LEIN, L., & BRENNEIS, D. Children's disputes in three speech communities. *Language in Society,* 1978, *7,* 299–309.

LENNEBERG, E. H. The natural history of language. In F. Smith & G. Miller (Eds.), *The genesis of language: A psycholinguistic approach.* Cambridge, Mass.: MIT Press, 1966.

———. *The biological foundations of language.* New York: John Wiley & Sons, 1967.

———. Of language, knowledge, apes, and brains. *Journal of Psycholinguistic Research,* 1971, *1,* 1–29.

LEONARD, L. B. On differentiating syntactic and semantic features in emerging grammars: Evidence from empty form use. *Journal of Psycholinguistic Research,* 1975, *4,* 357–364.

LINDHAGEN, K. *Semantic relations in Swedish children's early sentences.* Studia Psychologica Upsaliensis 3. Uppsala, Sweden: Acta Universitatis Upsaliensis, 1976.

LUST, B. Conjunction reduction in child language. *Journal of Child Language,* 1977, *4,* 257–287.

LUST, B., & WAKAYAMA, T. The structure of coordination in children's first language acquisition of Japanese. In F. Eckman & A. Hastings (Eds.), *Studies in first and second language acquisition.* Rowley, Mass.: Newbury House, 1979.

LYONS, J. In 'General Discussion' to McNeill's paper, The creation of language by children. In J. Lyons & R. J. Wales (Eds.), *Psycholinguistics papers.* Edinburgh: University of Edinburgh Press, 1966.

MACWHINNEY, B. *How Hungarian children learn to speak.* Unpublished doctoral dissertation, University of California at Berkeley, 1974.

———. Pragmatic patterns in child syntax. *Papers and Reports on Child Language Development* (Stanford University Department of Linguistics), 1975, *10,* 153–165.

———. Hungarian research on the acquisition of morphology and syntax. *Journal of Child Language,* 1976, *3,* 397–410.

———. The acquisition of morphophonology. *Monographs of the Society for Research in Child Development,* 1978, *43* (1–2, Serial No. 174).

MARATSOS, M. How to get from words to sentences. In D. Aaronson & R. Rieber

(Eds.), *Perspectives in psycholinguistics*. Hillsdale, N.J.: Lawrence Erlbaum, 1979.

McCawley, J. D. Prelexical syntax. In R. J. O'Brien (Ed.), *Georgetown University round table on languages and linguistics*. Washington, D.C.: Georgetown University Press, 1971.

McNeill, D. The creation of language by children. In J. Lyons & R. J. Wales (Eds.), *Psycholinguistics papers*. Edinburgh: Edinburgh University Press, 1966. (a)

――――. Developmental psycholinguistics. In F. Smith & G. Miller (Eds.), *The genesis of language: A psycholinguistic approach*. Cambridge, Mass.: MIT Press, 1966. (b)

――――. The development of language. In P. H. Mussen (Ed.), *Carmichael's manual of child psychology* (3rd. ed). New York: John Wiley & Sons, 1970.

――――. The capacity for the ontogenesis of language. In D. I. Slobin (Ed.), *The ontogenesis of language*. New York: Academic Press, 1971.

McNeill, D., Yukawa, R., & McNeill, N. B. The acquisition of direct and indirect objects in Japanese. *Child Development*, 1971, *42*, 237–249.

Menyuk, P. A preliminary evaluation of grammatical capacity in children. *Journal of Verbal Learning and Verbal Behavior*, 1963, *2*, 429–439.

Mervis, C., Catlin, J., & Rosch, E. Development of the structure of color categories. *Developmental Psychology*, 1975, *11*, 54–60.

Miller, M. *The logic of language development in early childhood*. Berlin: Springer-Verlag, 1979.

Miller, W., & Ervin, S. The development of grammar in child language. In U. Bellugi & R. Brown (Eds.), The acquisition of language. *Monographs of the Society for Research in Child Development*, 1964, *29*, (1, Serial No. 92).

Mitchell-Kernan, C., & Kernan, K. T. Children's insults: America and Samoa. In M. Sanches & B. G. Blount (Eds.), *Sociocultural dimensions of language use*. New York: Academic Press, 1975.

――――. Pragmatics of directive choice among children. In S. Ervin-Tripp & C. Mitchell-Kernan, *Child discourse*. New York: Academic Press, 1977.

Nelson, K. Structure and strategy in learning to talk. *Monographs of the Society for Research in Child Development*, 1973, *38* (1–2, Serial No. 149).

Nelson, K. Concept, word, and sentence: Interrelations in acquisition and development. *Psychological Review*, 1974, *81*, 267–285.

――――. Early speech in its communicative context. In F. D. Minifie & L. L. Lloyd (Eds.), *Communicative and cognitive abilities—Early behavioral assessment*. Baltimore: University Park Press, 1978.

Nelson, K. E., Carskaddon, G., & Bonvillian, J. D. Syntax acquisition: Impact of experimental variation in adult verbal interaction with the child. *Child Development*, 1973, *44*, 497–504.

Newport, E. L. Motherese: The speech of mothers to young children. In N. J. Castellan, D. B. Pisoni, & G. R. Potts (Eds.), *Cognitive theory* (Vol. II ). Hillsdale, N. J.: Lawrence Erlbaum, 1976.

Newport, E. L., Gleitman, H., & Gleitman, L. R. Mother, I'd rather do it myself: Some effects and non-effects of maternal speech style. In C. A. Ferguson &

C. E. Snow (Eds.), *Talking to children: Language input and acquisition.* Cambridge, England: Cambridge University Press, 1977.

———. A study of mothers' speech and child language acquisition. *Papers and Reports on Child Language Development* (Stanford University Department of Linguistics), 1975, *10*, 111–115.

OMAR, M. E. *The acquisition of Egyptian Arabic as a native language.* The Hague: Mouton, 1973.

PARISI, D., & GIANELLI, W. Language and social environment at two years. Unpublished manuscript, Institute of Psychology, National Council of Research, Rome, Italy, 1974.

PARK, T. The acquisition of German syntax. Unpublished paper, University of Bern, Switzerland, Psychological Institute, 1970.

PHILIPS, S. U. Some sources of cultural variability in the regulation of talk. *Language in Society,* 1976, *5*, 81–95.

PIAGET, J. *The language and thought of the child.* London: Routledge & Kegan Paul, 1926.

POSTAL, P. On the surface verb 'remind.' In C. J. Fillmore & T. D. Langendoen (Eds.), *Studies in linguistic semantics.* New York: Holt, Rinehart & Winston, 1971.

RACKSTRAW, S. J., & ROBINSON, W. P. Social and psychological factors related to variability of answering behavior in five-year-old children. *Language and Speech,* 1967, *10*, 88–106.

RADULOVIC, L. *Acquisition of language: Studies of Dubrovnik children.* Unpublished doctoral dissertation, University of California at Berkeley, 1975.

RAMER, A. Syntactic styles in emerging language. *Journal of Child Language,* 1976, *3,* 49–62.

ROEPER, T. Children's syntax. Unpublished paper, University of Massachusetts, 1976.

ROSCH, E. On the internal structure of perceptual and semantic categories. In T. E. Moore (Ed.), *Cognitive development and the acquisition of language.* New York: Academic Press, 1973.

———. Linguistic relativity. In A. Silverstein (Ed.), *Human communication: Theoretical explorations.* Hillsdale, N. J.: Lawrence Erlbaum, 1974.

———. Universals and cultural specifics in human categorization. In R. Brislin, S. Bochner, & W. Lonner (Eds.), *Cross-cultural perspectives on learning.* New York: Halsted Press, 1975.

RUBIN, J. Bilingualism in Paraguay. *Anthropological Linguistics,* 1962, *4*, 52–58.

———. Sociolinguistics. In J. J. Honigmann (Ed.), *Handbook of social and cultural anthropology.* New York: Rand McNally College Publishing Company, 1974.

SACHS, J., & DEVIN, J. Young children's knowledge of age-appropriate speech styles in social interaction and role playing. *Journal of Child Language,* 1976, *3,* 81–98.

SCHAERLAEKENS, A. M. *The two-word sentence in child language development: A study based on evidence provided by Dutch-speaking triplets.* The Hague: Mouton, 1973.

SCHEGLOFF, E. A. Sequencing in conversational openings. In J. J. Gumperz & D. Hymes (Eds.), *Directions in sociolinguistics.* New York: Holt, Rinehart & Winston, 1972.

SCHIEFFELIN, B. B. Getting it together: An ethnographic approach to the study of the development of communicative competence. In E. Ochs & B. B. Schieffelin (Eds.), *Developmental pragmatics.* New York: Academic Press, 1980.

SCHLESINGER, I. M. The production of utterances and language acquisition. In D. I. Slobin (Ed.), *The ontogenesis of grammar.* New York: Academic Press, 1971.

––––––. The role of cognitive development and linguistic input in language development. *Journal of Child Language,* 1977, 4, 153–169.

SCOLLON, R. *Conversations with a one-year-old.* Honolulu: University of Hawaii Press, 1976.

SEARLE, J. The classification of illocutionary acts. *Language in Society,* 1976, 5, 1–23.

SHATZ, M. The comprehension of indirect directives: Can two-year-olds shut the door? Paper presented to the Linguistic Society of America, 1974.

SHATZ, M., & GELMAN, R. The development of communication skills: Modifications in the speech of young children as a function of listener. *Monographs of the Society for Research in Child Development,* 1973, 38 (5, Serial No. 152).

SHUGAR, G. W. Text analysis as an approach to the study of early linguistic operations. In N. Waterson & C. Snow (Eds.), *The development of communication.* New York: John Wiley & Sons, 1978.

SINCLAIR-DE ZWART, H. Developmental psycholinguistics. In D. Elkind & J. H. Flavell (Eds.), *Studies in cognitive development.* New York: Oxford University Press, 1969.

––––––. Sensorimotor action patterns as a condition for the acquisition of syntax. In R. Huxley & E. Ingram (Eds.), *Language acquisition: Models and methods.* New York: Academic Press, 1971.

––––––. Language acquisition and cognitive development. In T. E. Moore (Ed.), *Cognitive development and the acquisition of language.* New York: Academic Press, 1973.

SINCLAIR, H., & BRONCKHART, J. P. S.V.O. a linguistic universal? A study in developmental psycholinguistics. *Journal of Experimental Child Psychology,* 1972, 14, 329–348.

SLAMA-CAZACU, T. *Dialogue in children.* The Hague: Mouton, 1977. (Originally published in Rumanian in 1961.)

SLOBIN, D. I. The acquisition of Russian as a native language. In F. Smith & G. A. Miller (Eds.), *The genesis of language: A psycholinguistic approach.* Cambridge, Mass.: MIT Press, 1966. (a)

––––––. Comments on McNeill's 'Developmental psycholinguistics.' In F. Smith & G. A. Miller (Eds.), *The genesis of language: A psycholinguistic approach.* Cambridge, Mass.: MIT Press, 1966. (b)

––––––. (Ed.). *A field manual for cross-cultural study of the acquisition of communicative competence.* Berkeley: A.S.U.C. Bookstore, 1967.

––––––. Early grammatical development in several languages, with special attention to Soviet research. Working Paper No. 11, Language-Behavior Research Laboratory, Berkeley, 1968.

––––––. Questions of language development in cross-cultural perspective. In The structure of linguistic input to children. Working Paper No. 14, Language-Behavior Research Laboratory, Berkeley, 1969.

––––––. Universals of grammatical development in children. In W. Levelt &

G. B. Flores d'Arcais (Eds.), *Advances in psycholinguistic research*. Amsterdam: North Holland Publishing Co., 1970.

————. (Ed.). *Leopold's bibliography of child language*. Bloomington: Indiana University Press, 1972.

————. Cognitive prerequisites for the development of grammar. In C. A. Ferguson & D. I. Slobin (Eds.), *Studies of child language development*. New York: Holt, Rinehart & Winston, 1973.

————. On the nature of talk to children. In E. H. Lenneberg & E. Lenneberg (Eds.), *Foundations of language: A multidisciplinary approach*. New York: Academic Press, 1975. (a)

————. The more it changes. . . : On understanding language by watching it move through time. In *Papers and Reports on Child Language Development* (Stanford University Department of Linguistics), 1975, *10*, 1–30. (b) (Revised version appears as Language change in childhood and in history. In J. Macnamara [Ed.], *Language learning and thought*. New York: Academic Press, 1977.)

————. Evidence for syntactic change in child speech: Word order in Serbo-Croatian and Turkish. Unpublished manuscript, University of California at Berkeley, 1976.

————. The role of language in language acquisition. Unpublished paper, University of California at Berkeley, 1979.

————. Universal and particular in the acquisition of language. In L. Gleitman & E. Wanner (Eds.), *Language acquisition: State of the art*. New York: Academic Press, in press.

SLOBIN, D. I., & BEVER, T. G. Cross linguistic acquisition of canonical arrangements of word order and inflections (to appear).

SLOBIN, D. I., & WELSH, C. A. Elicited imitation as a research tool in developmental psycholinguistics. In C. A. Ferguson & D. I. Slobin (Eds.), *Studies of child language development*. New York: Holt, Rinehart & Winston, 1973.

SNOW, C. E. Mothers' speech to children learning language. *Child Development*, 1972, *43*, 549–565.

————. Mothers' speech research: From input to interaction. In C. E. Snow & C. A. Ferguson (Eds.), *Talking to children: Language input and acquisition*. Cambridge, England: Cambridge University Press, 1977.

SNOW, C. E., ARLMAN-RUPP, A., HASSING, Y., JOBSE, J., JOOSTEN, J., & VORSTER, J. Mother's speech in three social classes. *Journal of Psycholinguistic Research*, 1976, *5*, 1–20.

SNOW, C. E., & FERGUSON, C. A. (Eds.), *Talking to children: Language input and acquisition*. Cambridge, England: Cambridge University Press, 1977.

STERN, D., JAFFE, J., BEEBE, B.,& BENNETT, S. Vocalizing in unison and in alternation: Two modes of communication within the mother-infant dyad. In D. Aaronson and R. W. Rieber (Eds.), *Developmental psycholinguistics and communication disorders*. New York: New York Academy of Sciences, 1975.

STROSS, B. *Language acquisition by Tenejapa Tzeltal children*. Unpublished doctoral dissertation, University of California at Berkeley, 1969.

TALMY, L. Semantics and syntax of motion. In J. P. Kimball (Ed.), *Syntax and semantics* (Vol. 4). New York: Academic Press, 1975.

————. Semantic causative types. In M. Shibatani (Ed.), *Syntax and semantics* (Vol. 6): *The grammar of causative constructions*. New York: Academic Press, 1976.

TULKIN, S., & KAGAN, J. Mother-child interactions in the first year of life. *Child Development*, 1972, 43, 31–42.

VAN DEN BROECK, J. Class differences in syntactic complexity in the Flemish town of Maaseik. *Language in Society*, 1977, 6, 149–181.

VAN DER GEEST, T., GERSTEL, R., APPEL, R., & TERVOORT, B. *The child's communicative competence.* The Hague: Mouton, 1973.

VARMA, T. L. Stage I speech of a Hindi-speaking child. *Journal of Child Language*, 1979, 6, 167–173.

VENNEMANN, T. An explanation of drift. In C. N. Li (Ed.), *Word order and word order change.* Austin: University of Texas Press, 1975.

WARD, M. C. *Them children: A study in language learning.* New York: Holt, Rinehart & Winston, 1971.

WATSON-GEGEO, K. A., & BOGGS, S. T. From verbal play to talk story: The role of routine in speech events among Hawaiian children. In S. Ervin-Tripp & C. Mitchell-Kernan (Eds.), *Child discourse.* New York: Academic Press, 1977.

WELLS, G. Learning to code experience through language. *Journal of Child Language*, 1974, 1, 243–269.

WIEMAN, L. A. Stress patterns of early child language. *Journal of Child Language*, 1976, 3, 283–286.

WILCOX, S., & PALERMO, D. S. "In," "on," and "under" revisited. *Cognition*, 1974, 5, 245–254.

WILLIAMS, F., & NAREMORE, R. C. Social class differences in children's syntactic performance: A quantitative analysis of field study data. *Journal of Speech and Hearing Research*, 1969, 12, 778–793.

# 5

# Culture and Memory Development

*Daniel A. Wagner*[1]

## Contents

## Abstract

Social scientists have noted the important and diverse effects of culture and society on cognition and memory in individuals. Research undertaken in this country and in other, sometimes very different cultural settings, has led to the hypothesis that certain aspects of memory seem to be a function of socialization, whereas others appear to be relatively immune to societal influence. This chapter reviews research on memory development in children and adults that led to this thesis. Cross-cultural studies of recall and recognition memory are considered in the light of theoretically related work undertaken in more "controlled" experimental settings, mainly in the United States. The question of whether particular cultural settings favor the development of particular memory skills is considered in a section on "cultural specificity." The issue of competence and performance in the measurement of an individual's abilities is also given serious attention.

In the final section, a summary is provided that includes a number of likely directions for further research in this domain of inquiry.

## Introduction

In every case where [the Africans'] memorizing power could relieve them of the effort of thinking and reasoning, they did not fail to make use of it. (Levy-Bruhl, 1910 [1966], p. 25).

My own experience [in South Africa] is that primitives who possess less than a five-digit span [over 50% of the subjects tested] are incapable of profiting from school instruction except to a very limited extent. (Porteus, 1937, p. 301).

I myself, having listened to numerous stories about the marvellous word-perfect memory of the Swazi from his childhood up, . . . arranged a simple test. Choosing at random a boy of eleven or twelve years of age, a native interpreter and myself concocted a brief message of about twenty-five words which the boy was to take from one end to another of a village. . . . The results were much the same as they would have been for similar tests in a typical European group, neither better nor worse. (Bartlett, 1932 [1967], pp. 248–249).

But it is worth mentioning that among the Iatmul [in New Guinea] definite efforts are made to increase the memory endowment of individuals, by means of magical techniques. Soon after birth, a male child is made to inhale smoke from a fire which has been bespelled, in order that the boy shall grow up to be erudite in the totemic names of his clan; and later in life a man may be treated with spells which are believed to act on his heart (the seat of memory) giving him facility in the memorizing of name-cycles and spells. (Bateson, 1936 [1958] p. 221).

As these quotes indicate, the influence of culture on the development of memory has been a topic of interest to a broad spectrum of social scientists over the last several decades. These citations attest also to the diversity of opinion about culture's potential impact on memory. Even though the general topic of culture and thinking has historically tended to pit anthropologists (who believed that "the functions of the human mind are common to the whole of humanity" [Boas, 1911, p. 135]) against the psychologists who, with the advent of standardized intelligence tests, sought to find those groups who were more or less intelligent (see Kamin, 1974), the study of memory has been an exception. Not only have there been mixed opinions among investigators from each of these fields, but also people besides memory experts have been interested in differences in memory ability, as can be readily seen in the initiation ceremony described by Bateson (1936).

Memory is one of the "basic" cognitive abilities that is virtually always included in tests concerned with cognitive or intellectual development. Indeed, in recent years the study of memory skills in children has increased dramatically (e.g., Kail, 1979; Kail & Hagen, 1977; Ornstein, 1978). Theories of memory development have been derived to a great extent from laboratory research with adults; the obvious parametric change was the study of children's memory skills at various ages. There is, at present, an interface between the adult and child research on memory, reviewed by Brown (1975); Flavell (1977); Hagen, Jongeward, Kail (1975); and Wagner and Paris (in press). One outcome of this increase in laboratory studies of memory development has been an increase in cross-cultural studies of memory in children. As seems often the case in cross-cultural research, investigators have been interested primarily in two problem areas: (1) to test the *generality* of a given laboratory theory with other, sometimes "exotic," populations; and (2) to gather information on the variety of memory abilities and mnemonics (or memory strategies) that may be found in different societies.

Interestingly, the four rather dated descriptions of memory that began this section provide many of the cues for present-day investigation and discussion of cultural influences on memory development. Levy-Bruhl (1910) implies that rote memorizing precludes higher level thinking processes, while Porteus (1937) seems to believe that some basic memory ability (i.e. the digit span) is crucial for thinking in school settings. Bartlett (1932) in his very informative book, provides a more balanced view, but does suggest that some cultures are likely to have individuals that are "rote" memorizers. Anthropologist Bateson (1936) appears to be suggesting that certain cultures make a conscious effort to develop memory skills among those who will need them in the society.

With the large variety of studies that have been carried out in numerous cultures, there is a serious problem of organizing the material so that a unified picture may be produced. The present reviewer chose to select and describe cross-cultural memory research through a theoretical perspective. That is, most of the investigations that will be discussed here appear to have some relevance towards developing a comprehensive or general model of memory development. This theoretical view was clearly *not* always the stated purpose of each study described. Some research was carried out before contemporary memory models were available. In other cases, researchers were more interested in studying the variations in memory ability than the commonalities that might lead to theory construction. Equipped with a theoretical model of memory, we may be better able to discern what aspects of memory are likely to be culturally influenced. Even though this approach has the advantage of promoting a coherent line of reasoning, there are also other good reasons for making this decision. First, several excellent reviews of some of this literature have appeared in recent years. A historical view of memory aids in Europe was published

by Yates (1966); the cross-cultural literature on adult memory was reviewed by Cole and his colleagues in several places (Cole & Gay, 1972;
Cole, Gay, Glick & Sharp, 1971; Cole & Scribner, 1974; and Cole &
Scribner, 1977) and a review of Soviet research on the socio-historical determinants of memory has been provided by Cole and Scribner (1977),
and Meacham (1977). Second there are a number of studies that violate
Campbell's (1961, p. 344) important argument that "No comparison of a
single pair of natural objects is interpretable" across cultures, since there
are many alternative hypotheses for the differences or similarities discovered. In other words, "multiple indicators" (Campbell, 1961) are necessary
in order to triangulate on "causal" factors, and in order to reduce the number of "tenable rival explanations."

The present paper will focus on developmental research as well as on
nondevelopmental (nonontogenetic) research that may be interpreted
within developmental theory. In the latter case, factors such as schooling,
urbanization, cultural values, and the like—usually *within* a given cultural
group—may be thought of as being related to or underlying memory development. Finally, there are certain aspects of memory which we still
know little about, theoretically or empirically. For example, eidetic imagery is a fascinating topic, but there is simply not enough known about it
for Doob's (1966, 1970) studies to be considered in a reasonable theoretical context. Despite these caveats, there remains a fairly substantial body
of research that is playing an increasingly important role in the general
memory literature.

This chapter is organized to reflect the theoretical perspective mentioned. An overview of contemporary theories of memory development
will be presented first. Next, two cross-cultural studies that have had an
impact on theory in memory development will be reviewed. The following two sections will provide general reviews of the cross-cultural literature on recall and recognition memory. The results of these studies will be
viewed then from the perspective of cultural diversity or "cultural specificity" in memory and mnemonic processes. In the last major section, the
difficult methodological issue of assessment of comparative differences is
addressed, along with the contemporary issues of "production deficiency"
and "spontaneity." The final summary reviews the main points of the
present discussion and considers future directions in the area of culture
and memory.

## Brief Theoretical Outline of Memory
## Development

In recent years, researchers working primarily in the United States have
arrived at considerable agreement concerning the course of memory de-

velopment in children and up through adulthood. Recent reviews of experimental studies of children's memory have been provided by Brown (1975), Hagen et al. (1975), Flavell (1977) and in the extensive volume by Kail and Hagen (1977). Following, in part, on models of adult memory (e.g., Atkinson & Shiffrin, 1968), developmentalists have carried out a wide range of controlled experiments designed to determine those aspects of memory which appear to undergo ontogenetic change and those that do not. According to these observers there are "structural" features of memory (after Atkinson & Shiffrin, 1968; or "hardware," after Morrison, Holmes, & Haith, 1974) that emerge early in life and remain relatively unchanged through the life span. These features include relatively fixed capacities of sensory (Morrison et al., 1974) and short-term memory (Chi, 1976; Hagen et al., 1975), and invariance in forgetting rates in visual recognition memory tasks (Brown, 1975; Wickelgren, 1975). Aspects of memory that are more variable across age have been called "control processes" (Atkinson & Shiffrin, 1968) or memory strategies that children acquire and are able to employ in increasingly diversified ways. Both acquisition (e.g., rehearsal, clustering) strategies and retrieval strategies (e.g., cued recall) have been extensively studied and have been found to increase dramatically between about four and fourteen years of age in Western schoolchildren (for reviews, see Kail & Hagen, 1977).

There are, of course, many variants on this rather elementary sketch, and these may depend importantly on the nature of the memory task itself. For example, performance on some recognition tasks has been found to vary little with age, apparently due to the fact that strategic behavior may not be effective for high performance (Brown, 1975). However, a number of recent studies have demonstrated improvement in recognition memory across age groups. In some studies, use of verbal encoding was implicated (e.g., Perlmutter & Myers, 1976), whereas in other studies (Dirks & Neisser, 1977; Mandler & Robinson, 1978), increased performance on complex pictorial tasks seemed to indicate the development of perceptual scanning strategies in older children and adults. Also, there are certain tasks, such as recall of stories or connected discourse, in which the structure of the story may have an impact on performance (Mandler & Johnson, 1977). Furthermore, there is a fair amount of evidence that children encode or "take in" stimulus information in ways that vary (at least) with age, and that stimulus encoding is an important variable in how much a child can remember (see Kail & Siegel, 1977; Tversky & Teiffer, 1976). Finally, an alternative to the Atkinson-Shiffrin model has been developed by Craik and Lockhart (1972), who emphasize the "depth" of processing or encoding that subjects use in memory tasks.

The cross-cultural strategy is often used to "test" laboratory-based theories and hypotheses. However, there is a more fundamental relationship between developmental and cross-cultural (comparative) research on memory. As in the study of child and adolescent development, the researcher is often unable to determine just what develops. Is age (i.e., biological maturation) or some other age-related factor (e.g., schooling, societal experience, and so on) responsible for the "developmental" changes that the investigator finds? Though the term *developmental* usually means ontogenetic, the study of memory development makes it particularly clear that ontogeny is not the source of all (even age-related) development. The question addressed by this paper and in many cross-cultural studies is: How do nonmaturational or cultural/experiential factors impact on an individual's memory ability? Soviet psychology's emphasis on sociohistorical determinants of memory provides an important perspective in attempting to answer this question (Meacham, 1977; Smirnov, 1973). Soviet psychologists focused on the role of societal intellectual activities that an individual engages in, and subsequent impact on cognitive actions of the individual. Basically, this point of view suggests that cultural variability in intellectual activities is the basis for both developmental and cross-cultural differences in memory. This seems to be so because of the important role played by memory strategies, mnemonics or other memory activities (e.g., verbal encoding, perceptual scanning, depth of processing, and so on), that may vary across individuals and contexts for remembering, as well as across societies. Thus, it is not surprising that many studies have focused on the sorts of memory strategies that seem to be used increasingly by older children and by those individuals who have had certain kinds of lifetime experiences. For example, since schooling provides an important and intellectually strenuous experience for most children, this experience would seem likely to produce significant change. A number of researchers have studied just such effects.

As mentioned, structural features have been said to be relatively invariant where they can be separated from control processes. It would seem reasonable, therefore, to search for "universals" or evidence of little variability across cultures in these aspects of memory. Some studies (e.g., Wagner, 1978a) have taken this approach. Also, we may note that developmental research on recall and recognition memory have often been studied separately (apparently due to paradigmatic problems, and large differences in performance). Even though this tendency has begun to change in the laboratory (e.g., Perlmutter & Lange, 1978), we shall see that only a very few cross-cultural studies have studied these two performance variables together.

It seems, therefore, that many cross-cultural studies parallel laboratory studies in significant ways. We shall see studies of recognition and recall memory that are based on laboratory paradigms and that add significantly to our knowledge about memory and its variability. Both laboratory and cross-cultural studies are based on research involving an interaction between memory tasks (and contexts) and individuals. If we accept, for the moment, the assumptions that (1) memory tasks can be constructed which measure with validity across individuals and groups, and (2) human beings have (on the average; i.e., across groups) equal potential, then it follows that group differences in memory are likely to be a function of the lifetime experiences that interact with each individual's potential. Thus, there need be no conceptual distinction between laboratory-based developmental studies and cross-cultural studies, either empirically or theoretically. But, as we shall see, there remain a number of understudied and unresolved areas that limit the extent and generality of theories of memory development.

## Two Contemporary Studies

### Cole et al. (1971): Free Recall Learning

The work of Michael Cole and his colleagues on cross-cultural memory and cognition is especially instructive because it exemplifies the important interaction (some would say dialectic) between the theory-builders in psychology and the discoverers in ethnography. Their research spans a period of more than ten years in Liberia and Mexico and has been extremely influential in the general area of cross-cultural methodology as well as in its contribution to the literature on culture and memory.

With the publication of *The Cultural Context of Learning and Thinking*, Cole, Gay, Glick, and Sharp (1971) provided perhaps the most diverse and in-depth study of memory in a non-Western society undertaken to date. Working primarily among the Kpelle in Liberia (West Africa), these researchers set out systematically to investigate some of the traditional statements about prodigious memory among illiterate Africans. Indeed, the authors provide the following statement by Bartlett (1932) with respect to the "rote" memory of nonliterate people:

> According to the general theory of remembering which has been put forward, there is a low level type of recall which comes as nearly as possible to what is often called rote recapitulation. It is characteristic of a mental life having relatively few interests, all of them somewhat concrete in character and no one of which is dominant. (Bartlett, 1932, p. 114).

Cole and his associates decided to test such assertions with a standard free recall paradigm in which a list of words is read to the subject, and then the subject is requested to recall as many words as possible. The free recall task has the advantage of being relatively easy to administer, but more importantly, "the subject is free to remember in any manner he

chooses; the way in which subjects reorder to-be-learned lists when recalling them in this unconstrained fashion gives important insight into the
mechanisms of memory" (Cole & Gay, 1972, p. 1069). Cole and his colleagues also noted that a number of investigators (e.g., Bousfield, 1953)
had consistently found that American adult subjects showed a strong tendency to cluster semantically or reorganize the material at the time of recall. Furthermore, over repeated trials with a single list, subjects who performed well on this task usually showed a high degree of clustering,
whereas poor performers did not (see Tulving, 1967).

In order to study the nature of clustering in memory output, Cole et al.
(1971) used a variety of verbal and nonverbal categorizing techniques to
produce a list of well-known Kpelle language nouns that belonged to four
semantic ("clusterable") categories (food, tools, clothes, and utensils). A
list of nonclusterable nouns (i.e., those for which no apparent semantic
category was a useful superordinate) was also constructed for comparison.
Several variations on the successive or multitrial free recall paradigm were
used in these studies, but the basic task proceeded as follows: A list of
twenty clusterable or nonclusterable words or the objects themselves are
presented to the subject, who is asked to recall as many items as possible
following the presentation of the last list item. This procedure is repeated
over five presentations; on each, the order of the words is rearranged.
Also, experiments often included variation between stimulus materials
(e.g., words versus objects); one or more of the population variables of
age, culture (California versus Kpelle), schooling (schooled versus nonschooled), and urbanization (rural versus urban), and task (e.g., recall
freely or according to an experimenter-determined procedure).

In a series of three experiments, Kpelle subjects from three age groups
(6–8, 10–14 and 18–50 years) were tested on the free recall task. Schooled
and nonschooled children were compared in the two younger age groups;
educated tribal adults were difficult to find, so that only nonschooled
adults were included. California school children of the same age were included for cross-cultural comparison, primarily to study the relationship
between the two populations on process variables (such as clustering, serial position effects, and rote learning).

The major results of these experiments were summarized in a later
review:

1. As American children grow older, the number of words recalled and the
   rate at which the list is learned increase markedly; older Liberian Kpelle
   subjects recall only slightly more than younger subjects. Most striking
   is the fact that, on the whole, learning is very slow for Liberian subjects;
   only a few more words are recalled on the fifth presentation of the list
   than were recalled on the first presentation.

2. Clusterable lists are learned a little more easily by all the Kpelle groups, and by all the American groups as well.
3. The American children, especially those 10 years and older, cluster their recall, that is, items from the same taxonomic category are said together, but the Kpelle show little or no semantic clustering.
4. The Kpelle subjects all recall objects better than spoken words, but so do the Americans. (Cole & Scribner, 1974, p. 129)

In addition, none of the Kpelle groups appeared to be "rote" memorizing on this task, since, in virtually all conditions, the relation (or correlation) between input order and output order (i.e., serial order of words or objects recalled) was negligible. In a separate condition, potential effects of motivation were studied by providing Kpelle subjects with varying material reinforcements. Thus, in the same free recall task, ten nonschooled adults received up to almost twice the monetary award (final amount was set by level of performance) that ten other adults received. In this and another motivational variant, Cole et al. found virtually no change in number of words recalled or in clustering. Interestingly, with such increased incentive, the Kpelle subjects apparently did try harder—many more responses were given at the time of recall, but these were mostly repeated items or items not on the original list!

In a second series of experiments, Cole and his collegues looked at a number of population and task variables that they thought might affect memory performance. In the first set of these experiments, a group of subjects from the Vai (also in Liberia) were studied, because some of them had become literate in the Vai (indigeneous) form of writing. Samples of literate and nonliterate Vai adults were tested on the standard free recall task. Even though the results of the illiterate Vai varied little from the Kpelle of earlier experiments in terms of low recall, little improvement over trials, and lack of effects of clusterable lists, the literate Vai recalled significantly more words than the nonliterate Vai, and showed some evidence of clustering in recall. It was noted, however, that the Vai were more "Westernized" than the typical Kpelle population, since less than half of the former were farmers (the others were in various skilled trades). In another study, urban and rural school children (10–14 years of age) were compared. Though the urban Kpelle remembered significantly more than the rural children (10.2 versus 8.7 items, out of 20 total items), little clustering or learning over trials was found in either group. Though the effect of formal schooling seemed of little importance in earlier experiments with younger children (up to 14 years of age), another experiment was undertaken to compare older (18–20 year old) nonschooled and schooled adolescents. In this comparison, there was a large and consistent difference in performance, with the schooled group superior on the first trial and subsequent trials of recall, and clustering which increased over trials. The nonschooled Kpelle did show clustering on initial trials (which is somewhat discrepant from earlier studies), but showed no improvement over trials.[2] In summarizing these studies, Cole et al. (1971) distinguished between the varied effects of urbanization/Westernization and schooling in concluding that "simply living in an urban environment does not *qualitatively* change the major features of free recall learning, but that *qualitative, as well as quantitative,* changes in learning occur at the level of education represented by our high-school subjects" (p. 130, emphases added). The effect of urbanization produced a moderate quantitative (but not qualitative) improvement in recall for most Kpelle; a similar phenomenon will be discussed later in the work of Wagner (1978a).[3]

In a second set of experiments in this series, Cole et al. tried to determine whether nonliterate/nonschooled subjects lacked some "general memory skill" or whether they could perform as well as high school students "but under different conditions" (p. 131). In what has been called the "chairs" experiment, an attempt was made at making the experimental task more meaningful to African subjects (who, earlier anthropoligists had sometimes claimed, had "concrete mentalities"). In a pilot study, involving twenty 10–14-year-old school children, the twenty objects (used in the earlier word versus object recall experiment), were presented one at a time, above one of four chairs facing the child. For half the subjects, the objects of a given semantic category (cluster) were presented above the *same* chair (the "rule" condition); the other half of the subjects saw the objects with semantic categories broken up, hence the "random" condition. A set of five items was, in each condition, held up over a particular chair over all five trials, but the subjects were not instructed to recall by chair or category. The results of this pilot study were dramatic: the rule condition produced superior performance in terms of both number of words recalled over trials, and in clustering over trials.

In a large follow-up experiment, an attempt was made to determine whether the rule condition provided a clustering cue by organizing the semantic unit over a specific concrete "tag" (i.e., the chair). The "rule" and "random" conditions were repeated, and a third condition was added: presenting the items above a single chair (the other three chairs were not used). Surprisingly, the results of the replication showed that recall was equally good in all three conditions, even including presentation over a single chair! Also, both recall and clustering were very high (over seventeen items out of twenty), beginning on the first trial. Furthermore, there was an interesting interaction between the results for each condition and which of the two testers was collecting the data. In a recent review of this study, Cole and Scribner (1977) suggest that "having a 'concrete reminder' is more critical for good recall than the particular form the reminder takes" (p. 257). Unfortunately, the lack of replication across conditions and the unexplained variability across experimental testers make further interpretation hazardous. As Cole et al. add, *"something produced excellent recall"* (p. 134), but no clear explanation is apparent.

Following up on the question of retrieval cues, Cole et al. designed an experiment (based on earlier work by Tulving & Osler, 1968) in which verbal cues were used to enhance recall in 10- to 14-year-old school children. There were five different conditions in which semantic category cues (clothes, tools, food, and utensils) were provided verbally at designated moments of the experiment: (1) cued at both presentation and recall; (2) cued at presentation, but not at recall; (3) cued at recall, but not during presentation; (4) never cued; and (5) "constrained" recall: same as condition (1) except that the subject was asked to name as many items as possible from a given category, whereupon the tester would provide the next category name (for example, "food") and the subject would try to name all the food items. This procedure was repeated for the first four trials with the order of recall categories varying from trial to trial. On the fifth trial, condition (4) was imposed, such that the subject was given no cues at presentation or recall, and no constraints were imposed on recall output.

Based on the prior work of Tulving and Osler (1968), it would be hypothesized that cues at presentation would be somewhat more effective than cues at recall, because of the association in storage between the item to be recalled and the category (retrieval) cue. However, the results showed that none of the cue conditions (1 to 3) were effective in increasing recall beyond the typical number found in earlier studies. In contrast, the "constraint" condition produced a dramatic increase in recall beginning with the first trial, and remained high through trial 4. Interestingly, on trial 5, where recall was neither cued nor constrained, subjects still tended to cluster items, and recall dropped slightly but remained significantly higher than in any other condition. A slightly modified replication of this experiment was undertaken with third and sixth graders in the United States. The results were generally similar in that the cues in conditions 1 to 3 were of little help to children. As in Liberia, the "constrained" condition produced increased recall on trials 1 to 4. On trial 5, apparently clustering remained high but recall dropped. Since mean scores of performance are not provided for either the Liberia or United States data, it is impossible to speculate on the origin of this cross-cultural difference. Nonetheless, Cole et al. have demonstrated that the Kpelle *can* show memory abilities similar to those of American children on a complex task, and this was an important step in refuting simplistic notions that Africans are only rote memorizers.[4] Clearly, the Kpelle had the to-be-remembered items in memory storage, but could not retrieve them.

The final study in this series carried out by Cole et al. was designed to discover the conditions in which the Kpelle *would* be likely to be rote memorizers and the conditions in which they would use strategies such as category clustering. (The previous "constrained" experiment, though inducing high recall was not an adequate test for "true" clustering, since subjects were required to respond category by category [on trials 1 to 4]—leading to "perfect" clustering.) Derived from Bartlett's (1932) classic research on story memory, an ingenious experiment was developed in which different story contexts were created along traditional Kpelle themes into which the twenty basic clusterable items were embedded. Groups of ten nonliterate/nonschooled adults were tested in each of five story conditions, where the main conditions were as follows: (1) a story that ended with the list of twenty basic clusterable items in randomized order; (2) a second story where the list was still randomized, but each five items were associated with a particular person in the story; (3) the same story as in condition 2, but where each person was associated with a given semantic category of items; and finally (4) two additional stories that were highly constrained in that each item was meaningfully linked to the neighboring item in the story. Each story was presented five times to each group, as in the standard paradigm. With the connected stories (condition 4), no changes could be made in the order of presentation since the items could not be displaced without affecting the sense of the story, but in the other conditions, items were randomized across trials.

In summarizing the results of the study, Cole et al. (1971) state: "it was found that the structure of subjects' recall mirrored the way in which the to-be-recalled items were structured within the story. If the items were structured in a linear manner . . . [as in condition 4], then a very high correlation between input and output was observed. However, if presentation structure was clustered [as in conditions 2 and 3] so was the structure of recall" (p. 140). Indeed, the correlations were 0.56 and 0.51 between input and output in the connected stories of condition 4, indicating a great degree of rote recapitulation. However, there is a distinction that may be made between rote memory and learning a story by understanding its sense—developing a "schema" (to use the term of Bartlett, 1932). Since, in condition 4, subjects were apparently asked by the tester to "tell the story over for me" (p. 267), it is unclear whether the items appeared in order due to some rote memory method, or because the gist of the story dictated that items come earlier or later (a form of reconstruction).

Furthermore Cole et al. suggested that conditions 2 and 3 indicated structured recall, but the available data (most of the means, clustering scores and correlations of input and output have not been published) seem to indicate that performance was extremely poor in these conditions (about half the typical level of 9 or 10 items), and input-output correlations averaged about $r = .15$ (for a control group and conditions 1 to 3). This correlation is somewhat higher than in previous experiments and adds a possible confounding factor to the clustering condition (condition

3). That is, it is possible that the clustering observed was a function of either rote learning or story reconstruction as discussed above in the case of condition 4. Clustering, in this case, may not be a function of using semantic organization, but of other factors. There is also some indication that some subjects focused on a particular story person in conditions 2 and 3, thereby reducing the utility of the twenty item test. It is difficult to agree, therefore, with the statement that "for the first time one observes the high degree of organization that is characteristic of typical American subjects" (Colby & Cole, 1973, p. 81), because performance was so low and artifacts may explain some of the clustering in the data.

Finally, it might seem that the compelling input-output correlation of condition 4 would be an important finding regardless of rote or schema interpretations; but this may not be so. The task requirements may be fundamentally different if the subject perceives and performs as if he is to retell the story rather than merely recall the items.[5] Semantic discourse processes may differ greatly from those skills used in restricted ("episodic") list-learning tasks (Tulving, 1972). In sum, we have seen some interesting data in this study, but definitive interpretation is elusive.

Despite some of these criticisms, the Cole et al. (1971) studies led to a number of important findings in culture and memory. In terms of methodology, Cole and his colleagues demonstrated that adapting the experimental task to the cultural context could not only lead to improved performance, but also to increased understanding of the memory processes of differing subject populations. Discussion of some of the more recent work of Cole and his collaborators is provided in later sections of this chapter.

*Wagner (1978a): Short-term and Recognition Memory*

In a number of ways, Wagner's work followed conceptually on that of Cole et al. (1971). First, Wagner was concerned with "appropriate" methodology, using tasks designed to engage subjects' interests and motivation. In Mexico, for example, Wagner (1974, 1975) used a well-known children's game (*loteria*) as the material for a memory task. In Morocco, Wagner (1978a) chose stimuli for a recognition task from pictures of Oriental rugs that were of particular interest to Moroccans, who consider rugs to be one of the most valuable items in their society. Second, Wagner was concerned with the problem of making inferences from overall memory scores and so used tasks where process variables could be studied, such as serial position effects. Also like Cole, Wagner was interested not only in the influence of general factors, such as formal schooling and urbanization, but also in the discovery of memory ability among relatively nonschooled populations, such as the rug sellers of Marrakech, or students of the Quran who never attended government schools. Finally, an attempt was made to extend our theoretical knowledge of memory, across a variety of tasks and populations.

As mentioned earlier, Atkinson and Shiffrin (1968) proposed a model of memory that distinguished between structural features and control processes in memory. The related development models of Brown (1975) and Hagen et al. (1975) proposed that memory structure developed early in life, whereas control processes develop more slowly through young and middle childhood. Wagner's (1978a) working hypothesis was that control processes might be considerably more sensitive to environmental events than structural features, which should appear in relatively stable fashion, from an early age in all population groups.

To gather evidence, Wagner went to Morocco, where wide variation in schooling and degree of urbanization within a single culture provided an excellent setting for studying such global factors. Two main experiments (short-term recall and recognition memory) were conducted on a sample of 384 Moroccan males, who were selected so as to complete a three-way factorial design: age (7, 11, 14, and 19 mean years of age) × schooling (schooled versus nonschooled) × environment (urban versus rural). Thus, there were sixteen groups and twenty-four subjects in each group. Additional groups of subjects were also tested in order to study possible culture-specific influences on mnemonics: traditional Quranic scholars; Moroccan rug sellers; and University of Michigan students. The memory tasks used in the experiments were chosen because they each tapped into aspects of structure and control processes.

The first experiment explored the development of short-term recall. A serial memory task, used extensively in the developmental literature, required the subject to locate the position of an animal drawing in a series of seven briefly presented drawings, where the to-be-remembered drawing varied in position from trial to trial over fourteen trials. The subject was first shown each of the seven cards, which were then placed face down after a brief presentation. Following the presentation of the seven cards, the subject was shown a single "probe" card with an animal drawing on it, and had to find the location of the same animal in the linear array of face-down cards.

The task has been particularly useful because it provides a serial position curve, where the primacy effect has been shown to be a function of verbal rehearsal strategies (Hagen et al., 1975). Also, the recency effect provides a measure of short-term store, considered to be a structural feature of memory. Finally, the task provides an overall recall measure by the percent correct over fourteen trials.

Analyses of variance showed that recency recall was stable and relatively invariant across all population groups studied, regardless of age, schooling, and environment. Primacy recall developed with age *only* for schooled subjects, and in a somewhat diminished form for nonschooled children who lived in an urban setting. Also, primacy recall was the most important factor in improved overall recall in the older schooled groups. The Quranic scholars' performance was similar to that of rural non-schooled subjects, who showed little primacy effect and no increase in recall with age. As in one of the Cole et al. (1971) studies, the influence of urbanization did not interact with age but did result in increased recall for urban subjects of all ages. In an earlier experiment undertaken in Mexico, Wagner (1974) found similarly that urbanization had an effect on overall recall, but that number of years in school seemed to be the more important factor in producing the primacy effect and increased overall recall.

In general, the first experiment provided evidence that formal schooling and urbanization may contribute independently and positively to the development of control processes or mnemonics. It was suggested that the use of mnemonic strategies, such as rehearsal, may be linked to certain (as yet not well understood) cultural experiences, whereas short-term store— a structural feature measured by the recency effect—seems to be present in all individuals, regardless of age or special cultural experiences.

Developmental studies of recognition memory—in contrast to recall—have been often characterized by a lack of age-related trends in performance (Brown, 1975). Such invariance with age is often considered to be evidence of the degree to which recognition memory does *not* require mnemonic strategies (Brown, 1975). As mentioned earlier, some recent recognition studies have demonstrated developmental increases, usually by using complex tasks where verbal or perceptual strategies may be used (e.g., Perlmutter & Myers, 1976; Dirks & Neisser, 1977; Mandler & Robinson, 1978). On the other hand, studies have consistently shown that forgetting rates (the continuous decay of information from memory as a function of time or intervening information to be remembered) are invariant from childhood through adulthood (e.g., Wickelgren, 1975). The second experiment was designed to look at overall pictorial recognition performance as well as forgetting rates.

The subjects for the second experiment were the same as those in the first experiment, except for the addition of two groups: adult Moroccan rug sellers and University of Michigan students. All subjects were tested on a modified version of the continuous recognition memory task of Shepard and Teghtsoonian (1961), which provides a measure of forgetting rate as well as overall recognition performance. The stimuli consisted of 207 black and white photographs of Oriental rugs. The experiment included a practice test of over 30 trials, followed by the experimental task of 177 trials. The experimental task consisted of 88 different rug patterns and 88 exact duplicates, which were arranged in a sequential array so that duplicates formed "lags" of 1, 5, 10, and 25 intervening items. Both practice and experimental stimuli were arranged in large notebooks, so that when the next pattern was exposed, it covered the previous pattern. The subject was instructed to look at each rug carefully, and say whether the present pattern was appearing for the first or second time. The subject was allowed about five seconds to look and respond to each item before turning to the next item.

Results of the second experiment were analyzed on the basis of five derived measures of performance: total correct (sum of hits and correct rejections); and $d'^6$ for each of the four lags. For each of these measures, three-way analyses of variance were performed. The most important results of these analyses were: (1) chronological age produced little or no reliable effects for any of the measures; (2) schooling produced a significant effect, but primarily at longer lags; (3) the effect of environment was highly significant, but contrary to the recall task, the rural subjects were superior on total correct recognition; and (4) Michigan students and rug sellers performed as well as the best rural subjects whereas the Quranic students scored near the bottom. Statistical profile analyses of forgetting rates (the decline in $d'$ over the four lag conditions) showed that the curves were, in general, invariant or parallel to one another across both age and population groups, including the traditional Quranic scholars, Moroccan rug sellers, and University of Michigan students.

In general, these data on recognition memory supported previous research that indicated little age-related change in forgetting rates. Furthermore, forgetting rates were invariant with respect to schooling and environment. Although it was unclear why rural subjects performed so much better than urban subjects on total correct, one potential hypothesis is that rural subjects were more familiar with rugs than urban subjects (more discussion of familiarity effects are provided later in this chapter). Finally, the rug sellers (with little formal education) scored as well or better than all other Moroccan groups. Even though familiarity might again be invoked as a hypothesis, Wagner hypothesized that rug sellers might be able to pick out distinctive features in rugs as a function of occupational experience. Furthermore, other evidence suggested that some rug sellers also use categorization strategies to aid in recall of rugs as a part of daily commerce. For example, rug sellers label individual rugs to be bought or sold (in the daily market) by regional origin, thus providing categorical labels for memory storage. They also *literally* store the rugs by these categories in their shops! Here we see a close relationship between the everyday activities of the rug sellers and outcomes of memory activity (a point often made in Soviet psychology, e.g., Smirnov, 1973).

Quranic students were originally thought to have special memory abilities, either by their selection for study at the Quranic school, or as a function of daily memorization of the Quran. In both experiments, however, Quranic students showed poor memory performance and little use of memory strategies or mnemonics. Wagner suggests that this poor performance may be due to the fact that Quranic students' everyday memory tasks involve related and meaningful verbal material. Thus, the recall and recognition tasks, which used pictorial stimuli, may not make use of the subject's knowledge, semantic network (as opposed to "episodic" memory) or schemas (after Bartlett, 1932). Although young Moroccan children may learn the Quran by rote methods and sometimes not comprehend the words they are repeating (i.e., without a knowledge of Arabic), older Quranic students may use mnemonic skills on oral or written narrative texts (for a discussion of study in Quranic schools, see Wagner & Lotfi, 1980). Thus, Quranic students may have well-developed schemas for embedding new information about the Quran, even though such schemas are relatively nonfunctional for the processing of spatially presented pictures, as in the recall task. In contrast, school children may often memorize a large array of more-or-less meaningful items and may have developed skills for episodic memory to a greater extent than Quranic students. A follow-up study (with different subjects at the same Quranic school in Morocco) showed that beginning students learn quickly how to use chanting as a way of "keeping track" of Quranic verse. Only later do more advanced students learn to "chunk" passages into units to aid in remembering.[7] In Liberia, Scribner and Cole (1978) found that Quranic students used mnemonics, but only when the task made use of serial ordering skills. Such evidence suggests that we should be careful in our intuitions about the availability of cognitive skills in differing populations; the particular task used may be a crucial determinant of memory performance.

In general, the combined results of the two experiments appeared to support the hypothesis that experiential factors, such as formal schooling and living in an urban environment, may influence the development of control processes in memory. The results of the recall experiment showed that verbal rehearsal appeared to be used only by older schooled subjects, and to some extent by urban nonschooled subjects. These data, reflecting the stable use of rehearsal strategies by about age 13, are consistent with data collected among American schoolchildren. From the recognition experiment, there was some further evidence that encoding strategies may be used by rug sellers to aid in recognition. The acquisition of these strategies was less than clear, because age-related changes were not observed among these subjects.

Wagner also found that certain features of memory were *not* evidently influenced by the experiential contrasts of this study. Specifically it seemed that structural features of memory were least affected: a relatively fixed-capacity short-term store was found in all groups; and forgetting rates were also found to be relatively invariant. Interestingly, sociodemographic background data, collected for each subject, was found to be of little help in predicting memory performance when schooling and urbanization were controlled.

Wagner concluded his paper as follows:

> Stated in its strongest form, the present study supports the hypothesis that the structure of memory is a *universal* in cognition, while control processes seem to be more culture-specific, or a function of the particular experiences that surround each growing child. While the pattern of results appears to support this hypothesis, it is obviously difficult to claim a completely universal structure of memory because: (1) Only certain structural features of memory were studied; and (2) behavioral universals—like behavioral theories—are impossible to prove. Additional research might find qualitative differences in structural features of memory in other cultures or with other types of tasks. With respect to control processes, large differences appear to be found as a function of children's lifetime experiences. However, we cannot claim that children growing up in some cultures are unable to use certain control processes or that such processes do not exist in some cultures, for the present study has dealt with the kinds of control processes used on specified tasks. (1978a, p. 25)

This statement was based on Wagner's studies, on other cross-cultural research, and on a large body of relevant laboratory work, primarily in the United States. As in the work of Cole et al. (1971), a variety of assumptions were made about the relation between control processes or strategies (such as clustering, and verbal rehearsal) and overall scores on the experimental tasks. In Cole's experiments in Liberia, and in a large number of American laboratory studies, category clustering was found to be related to higher recall. Further, by the manipulation of subjects' behavior, various experiments indicated that clustering led to higher recall. In a similar vein, Wagner (1974, 1978b) inferred (with only a small amount of observational data) that high primacy and subsequent high overall recall was a function of verbal rehearsal or related strategies. Such an inference, though not conclusive, seemed reasonable in the light of laboratory studies in which experimenters observed, and, at times, manipulated children's memory strategies to produce higher recall (e.g., Flavell, 1970; Kingsley & Hagen, 1969). The problem of determining underlying processes from outcomes on cognitive tasks is not specific to cross-cultural research. Indeed, concern with this problem arises often in laboratory research and such research is of considerable utility in increasing the validity of cross-cultural findings.

In summing up this section, we may now have a theoretical frame in which to organize the remaining studies to be reviewed. The most interesting questions appear to be: What sorts of influences seem to affect memory performance, and are control processes implicated in such variations? Are there culture-specific skills that develop under only special circumstances, such as in the individual mnemonists (Luria, 1968) or eidetic imagery (Doob, 1966)? And how do such factors as experimental task, stimulus familiarity, and culture relevancy interact in memory performance?

## Further Studies of Recall Memory

The use of strategies in certain recall tasks seems to be the main source of variability in memory performance across age and experience. We now turn to a number of other studies that have explored the topic of the development of strategies in recall.

In the research of Cole et al. (1971), it was found that nonschooled Kpelle showed little use of semantic clustering strategies in free recall, unless the experimenter imposed retrieval constraints. Scribner (1974) decided to explore how these subjects might exhibit the use of category structures when they were allowed to make up their own taxonomic categories opposed to those *considered* to be semantically "appropriate" in the Kpelle language (such as "food," "clothes," and so on, discussed above, and in Cole et al., 1971). To determine the categories that Kpelle preferred, Scribner had them perform a sorting task of twenty-five objects that would be used in a subsequent test of recall. Subjects were presented with the twenty-five clusterable items on a table and told to classify and reclassify the objects on repeated trials in which they were reshuffled; that is, the subject was required to "put these things back into the same groups you made before." A minimum of three items had to be in a category, so that the maximum number of categories was eight. When the subject met the criterion of identical category sorts on two consecutive trials, the twenty-five objects were covered up, and recall of the items was requested. As in Cole et al. (1971), taxonomically clusterable and nonclusterable objects were used as conditions in the experiment. Since Scribner was interested in the nature of antecedent experiences on categorization and recall, she included in her study: schooled and nonschooled children at ages 6 to 8 years and 10 to 14 years; and adults from 16 to 60 years of age from four differing "modernization" levels—high school students (most urbanized); "cash" workers (unskilled, but paid trades); "road" farmers (with access to roads and urban centers); and traditional "bush" farmers.

In Scribner's view, the major finding was that subjects in each of these populations *made use of their own groupings* to structure their recall (Scribner, 1974). This is especially important because in these earlier studies by Cole et al. (1971), only the older schooled Kpelle—and none of the non-schooled Kpelle groups—made use of category clustering in recall. Scribner concluded from these results that the Kpelle can show organized recall following "required" classification and reordering tasks. Although high school subjects showed the highest clustering and the highest recall, in general, little relationship was found between output organization and number of objects recalled. Also, even though all adult groups showed higher clustering and recall for the clusterable list than the nonclusterable list, higher clustering did not always lead to higher recall (as in the case of schooled 10- to 14-year-olds). From this complex picture, two general points may be made.

First, when psychologists look at the effects of clustering, standard taxonomic categories may limit the subject's categorizing capabilities. Second, as was found in the story recall in Cole et al. (1971), if category clustering is not systematically related to recall output, then conclusions about memory processing may be uncertain. In the present case, however, the fact that the clusterable list led to higher recall following the required categorization trials seems to imply that the taxonomic ordering of materials can be efficiently processed by subjects from extremely varied backgrounds. Finally, as in the studies by Cole et al. (1971) and Wagner (1974, 1978a), schooling and urbanization appeared to be important antecedent factors in the development of both strategic organization and recall.

Other studies of free recall have also noted the effects of experiential factors such as education on memory performance. In a cross-cultural replication of Cole et al. (1971), Sharp, Cole, and Lave (1978) studied memory performance in five adult populations (12 subjects per group) in Yucatan (Mexico) which varied in age, education and cultural background: younger, nonschooled Mayans (mean age = 28 years); older, nonschooled Mayans (mean age = 58 years); younger, slightly schooled Mestizos (mean age = 29 years; mean education = 2 years); younger, moderately schooled Mestizos (mean age = 28 years; mean education = 5 years); and students and schooled adults (mean age = 21 years; mean education = 10 years). The design allowed for both age and education comparisons within the adult sample. The free recall task was quite similar to that employed in the earlier Liberian studies. Twenty common nouns were selected to form four basic taxonomic categories; no nonclusterable list was presented. As in earlier studies, the list was presented five times, with recall assessed after each presentation. Results showed that recall was related to increased schooling, although the effect of chronological age was insignificant. Furthermore, extensive use of category clustering to aid recall was observed only in the most educated group of Mestizos. Also as in Wagner (1978a), Sharp and his colleagues found that other sociodemographic variables (e.g., parental occupation, age, sex, and language) were of little predictive utility beyond the variable of years of schooling when a regression analysis was performed.

Pollnac and Jahn (1976) have recently tried to replicate taxonomic clustering behaviors in several samples of school children (about 13 to 15 years of age) in Uganda. Through the method of triad sorts, a list of eighteen clusterable words was constructed, and read twice to the subjects, after which recall was requested. Since the subjects had been selected from three different schools (two were public; one was religious and required children to recite long prayers), the data was analyzed separately by school. The most unusual outcome was that both clustering and higher recall were exhibited by the students in the religious school although only a little clustering was evidenced in the other schools. As Pollnac and Jahn point out, the religious school may have been providing the skills necessary for increased recall, though other studies of religious schools (e.g., Wagner & Lofti, 1980; Scribner & Cole, 1978) showed that the effects are generally small. The study also provides support for the hypothesis that it is not schooling per se that activates cognitive skills, but the *activities* that children undergo when in school. More research on variation in schooling would seem to be important. For a review of the general and specific effects of schooling on cognitive skills, see Rogoff (chapter 6, this volume).

Parker (1977) explored the general question of whether "concrete" or "abstract" words were easier to remember. In America, laboratory studies (e.g., Paivio, Yuille, & Rogers, 1969) had shown that concrete (imageable) nouns were better recalled than abstract words. Parker hypothesized that earlier, anecdotal references to the "concreteness" of African thought could be tested by seeing whether Africans would show an even greater effect than Americans in a cross-cultural comparison. Parker tested twenty-seven university students in Ghana and twenty-nine American university students. About half of each group was tested on the "concrete" fifteen-word list (which consisted of high concrete/imagery words from norms collected by Paivio et al., 1969), and half on the "abstract" fifteen-word list. Each subject was tested across four trials. The results indicated no differences in words recalled by Ghanaian and American students, but a significant (positive) effect for concreteness across trials. Thus, the "concrete" versus "abstract" distinction was replicated cross-culturally, but was not found to interact with culture. Parker suggested that the fact that both subject groups were highly schooled may explain the similarity across cultures (see also Yavus, 1971). Two other experimental results were of interest. First, an examination of input-output recall organization—a measure of "rote" serial learning—showed that American subjects displayed more "rote" memorization behavior than the Ghanaian students! Second, an analysis of serial position curves of the free recall output showed considerable variability across conditions and cultures, whereas the recency effect was uniformly high. As Parker noted, this adds some support for the suggestion that the recency effect is a structural (or universal) feature of memory (Wagner, 1974, 1978b).

As part of a highly publicized study on the developmental resiliency of Guatemalan children, Kagan and Klein (1973) included a study of free recall among 5- to 12-year-old children from two somewhat contrasting Guatemalan villages. One village was Mayan, and had neither school nor contact with written language; the other village was more "modern" and had a school. The memory task consisted of twelve miniature objects from three conceptual categories that were covered up with a cloth after a brief inspection period. The child tried to recall as many objects as he could over two trials. Recall varied from five to ten items, with a significant increase with age even for the nonschooled children. Also, clustering (in this case, the consecutive output of two conceptually related items) was better than chance for almost all children. Although these results for non-schooled children seem in contrast with Cole et al. (1971), the Guatemala study used objects while the Liberia study used words. One curious aspect of recall was that the clustering index remained constant over age even though recall increased. As mentioned earlier, in the studies of Cole et al. (1971) and Scribner (1974), the lack of correspondence between clustering and recall raises questions about the validity of clustering as an effective strategic process in recall among such populations. It should be noted also that Kagan and Klein claim that these recall results compare favorably with data collected on American children by Appel, Cooper, McCarrell, Sims-Knight, Yussen, and Flavell (1972). Unfortunately, such a comparison would seem unwarranted, since modality of stimuli (object versus pictures), number of stimuli (12 versus 15), and number of conceptual categories (3 versus 5) varied across Guatemalan and American studies, and all such factors are known to have possible effects on recall. Two additional studies undertaken in Latin America include that of Hall (1972) in Colombia and Stevenson, Parker, Wilkinson, Bonnevaux and Gonzalez (1978) in Peru. Both studies found that even a small increase in years of schooling could effect recall on a variety of verbal and nonverbal memory tasks.

Finally, Wagner has used the short-term recall task mentioned earlier to study *incidental* recall in Yucatan (Wagner, 1974) and Morocco (Wagner, 1976). In the recall task described earlier, there were two stimuli on each of the cards to be remembered. One was the "target" picture that the subjects were told to remember; the other picture was "incidental" to the intended recall task. In the manner of Hagen and his associates (Hagen et al., 1975), Wagner tested for incidental recall by requesting the subject to name which target picture "went with" which nontarget stimulus. In earlier American studies, a curvilinear trend was found, with incidental recall increasing until about age 12 to 14 whereupon incidental recall dropped as a function of greater selective attention abilities in the children. In the Yucatecan study, schooled and urban subjects were superior to nonschooled and rural subjects and incidental recall followed a pattern similar to that in the United States, except that the drop-off occurred several years later in

Yucatan. In Morocco, the results were more complex. Again, urban and schooled subjects remembered more incidental information than their rural and nonschooled counterparts. The curvilinear trend was not apparent for any single group though the age range was more restricted in Morocco (7 to 19 mean years) than in Yucatan (7 to 27 mean years). In a recent review, Cole and Scribner (1977) have suggested that Wagner's data support Soviet research indicating "that the difference between incidental and intentional recall should increase with development" (p. 252). Although an analysis of the mean values of incidental and intentional recall would support this statement, mean recall scores are misleading since the notion that intentional recall increases *at the expense* of incidental recall in the *individual* implies that a trade-off in processing must occur. However, neither the Yucatan data nor the Morocco data indicate that there is a negative correlation between intentional and incidental recall. In fact, in the Morocco study, intentional and incidental recall were correlated positively ($r = .29$, $p < .01$). A recent study of incidental memory in Peru (Wilkinson, Parker, & Stevenson, 1979) also found a significant positive correlation between intentional and incidental memory in 5- and 6-year-old children who had or had not attended school. In summary, incidental recall seems to be subject to the same experiential influences as intentional recall, and the consistency of curvilinear developmental trends will have to await further research.

## Recognition Memory

Compared to research on recall, there have been remarkably few cross-cultural studies of recognition memory. It is not clear why this should be so, but it is perhaps due to the fact that recognition memory ability has been found to be generally excellent across age and subject populations, as in Wagner's (1978a) study discussed earlier. Even though overall recognition was very good and forgetting rates were found to be quite parallel, Wagner did find that recognition accuracy varied from one group to another. One hypothesis considered was that stimulus familiarity (e.g., with Oriental rugs) may have provided cues for better retention of the complex stimulus configuration.

A study by Shepherd, Deregowski, and Ellis (1974) was based on the same principle of stimulus familiarity. The investigators were concerned with anecdotal evidence suggesting that persons of one racial group have difficulty in recognizing persons of another racial group. Shepherd et al. compared groups of white British adults (moderately schooled) with Negro adults (minimally schooled) living in Rhodesia (Zimbabwe) on a recognition task in which twenty photographs of black and white faces were presented. Then, following a twenty-four hour delay, the twenty photographs were again presented, embedded in twenty "foil" or distractor photographs. The subjects were required to say whether they had "seen an item before." Since there were significant differences in response bias between the samples, a $d'$ analysis was used. Results showed that, even though Europeans were superior in overall recognition, Africans were superior in recognizing Caucasian faces. This study not only shows the importance of stimulus but also the potential cognitive origins of social stereotypes. Another study by the same authors (Deregowski, Ellis, & Shepherd, 1973), using similar, but nonidentical samples did *not*, however, find the same general results. There were no racial differences in recognition performance. Shepherd et al. (1974) suggest that the lack of correspondence in the results of the two studies was due to sample selection. Clearly more work needs to be done in this area.

An interesting developmental study of recognition memory for simple objects and complex scenes was undertaken in Guatemala (Newcombe, Rogoff, & Kagan, 1977). Three groups of rural Mayan villagers were selected from mean ages 6, 9, and 19 years. The older Mayans had considerably more schooling than the younger children. The recognition test consisted of pictures of six familiar objects and six familiar scenes that the subjects were allowed to study, one by one, at their own pace (usually a few seconds for each picture). Immediately after presentation, the twelve pictures were each paired with a single "foil" that was similar to the original picture except for a change in any one of three ways: rearrangement (one element in a changed position); addition (a plausible addition to the original picture); or perspective change (the picture was taken from a 45-degree change in angle). Since subjects always made a binary choice between the original and a foil, chance level was 50 percent correct. As would be expected, pictures of objects were recognized better than pictures of scenes (80 percent versus 71 percent correct, respectively). The percentage correct overall recognition increased with age: 63 percent, 72 percent, 92 percent. But only the adults scored significantly better than the younger two groups. Variation in foil type had no effect on correct recognition. As a part of the same project, Newcombe et al. compared same-aged subjects in the United States. Trends were found to be similar with age and type of stimulus (objects were better recognized than scenes), but foil type was also an important factor. Cross-cultural comparison of Guatemalan and American subjects with respect to mean levels of performance was not calculated due to differences in methodology across populations.

The finding of age-related increases in recognition memory for complex pictorial stimuli corresponds quite well with the laboratory findings reported earlier (Dirks & Neisser, 1977; Mandler & Robinson, 1978). Even though no clear explanation for increase in recognition is provided, it is possible that perceptual scanning strategies are increasingly available to older children (see Vurpillot, 1968). Also, in the Guatemala research, older Mayans were more educated than the younger Mayans,·thus allowing no separation of age and schooling. This is important since we have noted earlier than mnemonic strategies are more likely to be available to schooled subjects. This study raises the possibility that perceptual scanning strategies may be added to the list of cognitive and mnemonic skills that are influenced by schooling. However, the Guatemalan results failed to confirm the investigators' hypothesis that type of foil would interact with performance over age and type of stimulus. Nonetheless, this line of work seems to be interesting.

A study in Liberia by Cole and his colleagues (reported in Cole & Scribner, 1977) compared recognition memory of orally presented words and visually presented objects. Schooled (6–8, 10–14 years old) and non-schooled (6–8-, 10–14-year-old, and adult) Kpelle were tested five times on a list of sixteen items-to-be-recognized among a set of twenty-four foil or distractor items. For the two comparable sets of children (no educated adults were included), scores of overall correct recognition for words and objects were virtually identical among schooled and nonschooled children. However, there was a strong interaction between type of stimulus and amount of education. Thus, schooled Kpelle recognized more words than objects, whereas nonschooled Kpelle more objects than words. These data correspond somewhat to the Newcombe et al. (1977) study in that schooling seems to have its greatest effect on verbally encodable material. Surprisingly, however, Cole found that recognition for words decreased with age (in contrast to Newcombe et al.), but hypothesized that a possible change in decision criterion among older subjects may be the cause of this trend. Changes in criterion are a particular problem in recognition studies, since decision criteria (for saying "yes" or "no" to an old or new stimulus) may vary greatly between individuals and groups of individuals. Cross-cultural studies such as Shepherd et al. (1974) and Wagner (1978a) have tried to eliminate decision bias by using paradigms that allow the calculation of $d'$. For a discussion of some remaining problems, see Wagner and Davis (1978).

Rogoff (1977) has reported on research in which several measures of memory were observed among sixty 9-year-old Guatemalan school children. Each child was presented with four different memory tests: visual recognition (observe small arrangement of objects, and later distinguish it from a similar foil); visual reconstruction (recreate a complex scene of twenty objects from a pool of eighty familiar objects after a short delay); verbal recognition (distinguish originally presented stimulus sentence from a foil that was syntactically similar, but different in meaning); and verbal recall (listen to a folk story, and repeat it to an adult). The results showed that the memory measures were intercorrelated in such a way that children high on visual memory were generally lower on verbal memory (the exception was a positive correlation between verbal reconstruction and visual recognition). These data, then, point to a possibility that individual children may be more adept with one modality or presentation than another. Another interesting aspect of Rogoff's study was her attempt to relate memory performance of a sample of these children with induced teaching styles of the children's mothers. In a realistic but constructed teaching situation, mothers were rated as being either "verbal" or "demonstrative" in teaching their child two trials of a single learning task. Analyses indicated that mothers who were most verbal had children who performed best on the verbal memory tasks, whereas demonstrative mothers had children who scored low on verbal memory. Visual memory was unrelated to maternal teaching style. The data (though only correlational) seem to suggest that children's verbal skills are at least partly a function of cultural patterns in mother-child interaction. Since mothers' teaching styles were also related to years of formal schooling (the more schooled mothers had a more verbal style), we again see the potential mediating importance of schooling. Given the limited sample size and analyses available, the present study should be considered as suggestive that mother's teaching style may be one of a number of experiential factors that may interact with differing memory and cognitive skills.

Clearly, there is a paucity of cross-cultural research on recognition memory. Few studies have looked at the interrelation of recognition and recall skills. Neither Rogoff (1977) nor Wagner (1978a) found consistent relationships between several recognition and recall variables, and, thus, it may be the case that mediating variables (such as perceptual or semantic skills, or modality of stimuli) may be obscuring such interrelationships. Nonetheless, the topic of individual differences has been given increased attention in laboratory studies, and it seems only a matter of time until the findings of individual differences research and cross-cultural research are integrated and synthesized.

## Cultural Specificity in Memory

In his famous work among Swazi cattleherders in Africa, Bartlett (1932) pointed to the importance of social knowledge and social tendencies as a partial explanation of the excellent recall of earlier cattle transactions that he had observed. Bartlett proposed that significant social (or cultural) experience with a certain restricted body of material could lead to prodigious memory feats with that material. Such an assertion, which leads to the notion of cultural specificity in memory, may be broken down into two component parts: aspects of culture that may lead to special or differential memory skills, and the question of stimulus familiarity and encoding in memory.

In a first attempt at testing Bartlett's hypothesis that social tendencies affect recall, Nadel (1937a and b) sought to compare story recall in two Nigerian groups that were similar in language and general environment but apparently differed dramatically on certain cultural dimensions. Thus, the Yoruba had a "complex, rationalized religious system," which emphasized "logical coherence" and "meaning oriented interpretation"; whereas the Nupe were described as a group whose religious beliefs involved "magical" principles, and who were "psychologically . . . more enumerative . . . and given to . . . circumstantial details" (p. 431). Nadel proposed that such cultural contrasts would lead to similar contrast in recall of stories. He selected groups of 16- to 18-year-old school children from each group. The subjects were read a story that Nadel created, but that was based on a native folktale common to both the Yoruba and the Nupe. The story was presented in the morning, and several hours later (and one week later) each subject was tested for recall. Nadel was concerned with recall of structural or logical elements of the story, as well as of the detail or facts. By analyzing additions and omissions in output, Nadel claimed that his prior cultural analysis was reflected in recall. The Nupe were overly concerned with circumstantial detail and added or elaborated on "facts," whereas the more "rational" Yoruba emphasized the logic of the story and provided extra structure where necessary. Little forgetting was noted over the one week delay. The Nupe were relatively unconcerned with "logical coherence." Even though Nadel's study is in some ways a good example of the cultural specificity hypothesis, his conclusions are considerably weakened because his global definitions of "tribal personality" are difficult to relate to the specific memory outcomes described by Bartlett. Nonetheless, these experiments provide a rich body of information on individual story output that is not often available from laboratory studies (see especially Nadel, 1937b).

A more recent study by Ross and Millsom (1970) has looked at story recall among college students in Ghana and New York City. Three folk stories were used for testing (two were taken from the work of Bartlett, 1932). Unlike earlier studies, subjects in this experiment were not explicitly told that they were to remember the story. Each subject was read one of the three stories and was tested about forty minutes after presentation, and then twice more over (unannounced) intervals of several weeks. Recall was measured by a theme analysis, and by counting total words recalled. Results showed that Ghanaian students recalled more words and themes than the New York City students. Little loss in retention was noted over an interval of several weeks. Also, it was found that the themes recalled by Ghanaian subjects were very much the same as those remembered by the Americans (rank-order correlation of 0.69). Ross and Millsom argue that special cultural features (e.g., magical, supernatural) of the folktales were not responsible for differential recall. They propose that the well-known *oral* tradition in Africa may be the underlying factor that explains superior African performance. Similar consequences of an oral tradition have been suggested by Greenfield (1972) and Goody (1977).

Two recent studies concerning story recall bear on the issue of cultural specificity. In the first (Kintsch & Greene, 1978), undertaken with American university students, it was found that recall performance was highly dependent on the nature of the story "schemata" or structure. An unusual (e.g., Apache Indian) story tended to produce much lower recall than a story whose structural features derived from Euro-American folktales. The authors proposed that story schemata may be culture specific, in a manner similar to Bartlett (1932). However, the second study (Mandler, Scribner, Cole, & DeForest, 1980) supports the contrary proposition by showing that diverse story structures produce similar qualitative outcomes across differing cultural groups. More specifically, the study compared children and adults in both America and Liberia who were schooled, and additional Liberian groups who varied greatly on schooling and literacy experience. All subjects were required to recall five different stories with origins ranging from Greek and European to Liberian (Vai). The results of this interesting study were complex, but the primary conclusion was that recall of the various substructures or "nodes" of the story was qualitatively very similar across the different stories and across the different groups of subjects (though there were some quantitative differences in total recall by age, schooling, and literacy). Mandler et al. conclude that the structure or schemata of the story is more important than its specific content in determining recall; and that culture-specific content, while affecting overall recall, should not greatly affect the pattern of recall across diverse cultural groups. They suggest that the contrasting findings of Kintsch and Greene were artifactual, in that the Apache story might have been particularly difficult for *any* group of subjects even, presumably, for Apache subjects who had not previously heard the story). In sum, the study by Mandler et al. does not refute the assertion that story content may influence subsequent memory of the stories, but it does support the hypothesis that folktales may possess an inherent structure that influences the pattern of recall similarly across diverse subject groups.

Further support for the notion that cultural or social tendencies determine memory performance comes from a pair of studies that deal with the concept of time. In the first study, Deregowski (1970) notes that "anecdotal evidence suggests that the concept of time differs from society to society, and that in some societies less attention is paid to time than in others" (p. 37). In a story recall task, Deregowski expected that temporal concepts would be better remembered by groups of subjects who grow up in an environment in which time is "stressed"; that is, in which punctuality and speed of activity are important. Undertaken in Zambia, the subjects of his experiment were: forty urban primary school boys (mean age = 13 years; mean schooling = 6 years), and forty-four rural adult women, who had seldom or never been to the city. Each subject heard a tape recording of a story that contained eight important elements, of which four were temporal and four were numerical but not temporal (e.g., quantities of money or bananas). Even though schoolchildren recalled almost twice as much numerical information as the rural women, most of their advantage was on temporal elements of the story, as Deregowski hypothesized. For the numerical, but nontemporal, elements the difference was very slight. Deregowski concluded that the evidence supported Bartlett's observation that even the recall of digits is not independent of cultural significance or social tendency.

Price and Tare (1975) undertook a replication of Deregowski's (1970) study in Papua New Guinea. The procedure was the same as that of the earlier study. Five subject populations were tested: urban second-grade schoolchildren (aged 6 to 7 years) of indigenous or European background; urban fourth-grade schoolchildren of either background; and fourth-grade children from an indigenous traditional school where the students are drawn from families recently migrated from the rural countryside. In general, the New Guinea results support very closely the results from Zambia. The younger (grade two) European group of children performed like their indigenous counterparts, *except* for the temporal elements of the story where the European children were superior. By grade four, this difference disappeared as a result of increased schooling, with concomitant emphasis on time values. The more traditional children forming the fifth group were inferior to the urban fourth-grade children, and their overall recall scores were quite similar to the Zambian data in Deregowski's research. Price and Tare suggest that increased schooling is the cause for the decrease in indigenous versus European temporal recall between grades two and four, but they also point out that home background variables may be the best explanation for the modern versus traditional *school* differences in temporal recall. It is also interesting to note that numerical values for quantities of *money* were consistently the best-recalled aspect of the nontemporal story elements, across all groups of subjects. This seems to be a clear indication of the social importance that money had attained in still traditional societies.

The effects of ecological and environmental factors on memory has also been a subject of study. For example, Kleinfeld (1971) hypothesized that rural Eskimo childdren would have superior *visual* memory when compared to Caucasians because a substantial body of literature had indicated superior perceptual skills as a function of traditional Eskimo hunting activities and the like. Rural Eskimo and urban Caucasian school children, ages 9 to 16 years, were tested on a drawing reproduction task of various complex geometrical designs that had been briefly portrayed on the blackboard of a classroom. After testing, judges rated each of the drawings on a 0 to 5 scale of correctness for the four drawing stimuli, such that a perfect score would be 20. An analysis of variance showed that performance increased with age in both groups, and that, overall, the Eskimo children (mean correctness = 16.7) were considerably superior to the urban Causasian children (mean correctness = 14.3). Based on these results and on a *post hoc* questionnaire, in which teachers often remarked on Eskimo children's tendency to pay attention to visual detail, Kleinfeld concluded that these children have, indeed, "unusual ability in visual memory." She suggested that schools might take advantage of such ability to make up for "weakness . . . [in] verbal abstract skills." Since this study is the only one of its kind, further research is needed to help tease apart the underlying factors that may have produced the intriguing differences between these groups of children.

One other study examined the effects of environment on memory for location. Meacham (1975) compared rural Guatemalan children and urban American children (mean ages 5 and 7 years). The memory task consisted of a set of toy objects and a piece of cardboard on which were drawn six familiar "locations," such as a garden or a tree. On each of four trials, the experimenter placed each of the six objects in a particular location. When doing so, he would say, for example, "I'm hiding the chair in the garden," and so on. After all objects were hidden (i.e., placed out of view, under a cloth), each child was asked either to name the objects that went with each place, or to name the places that went with each object. A further condition allowed Meacham to separate verbal (imagined) from actual presentation of the objects and places. Results showed that although American children performed better overall, there as an important interaction between cultural group and type of recall. American children remembered objects and places equally well, but the Guatemalan children remembered locations better than objects. As Meacham points out, testing conditions might account for the overall cross-cultural differences but are unlikely to be responsible for the interaction. Interestingly, there were similar age-related increases in recall for both objects and places in both cultural groups. This leaves open the question of whether the Guatemalan children have a developmental "lag" or whether such differences will be maintained through development. A replication of Meacham's study was carried out by E. Hurlow-Hannah (reported in Cole & Scribner, 1977) in Liberia with schooled and nonschooled children aged 5 to 14 years. All groups of children showed better location memory than object memory, even though it was hypothesized (based on Meacham's work) that older educated Liberians would appear more like American children and thus show less difference between object and location performance. Other analyses in the Liberian study indicate that the development of object and place memory may be more complex than originally thought.

One major problem with the studies described is that they include little discussion of the mechanisms that might produce variable memory skills. It has already been suggested that cultural and developmental differences in memory may be primarily a function of mediational or mnemonic strategies. The studies concerned with religion, visual ecology, and spatial location provide us with limited understanding as to how the memory skills might be influenced, although they have provided clues about where to look. We shall return to this question a little later.

Consider now the question of familiarity and its importance to cross-cultural memory research. It has sometimes been said that cross-cultural differences based on an experimental task are simply due to lack of familiarity with task materials in the life experience of some cultural groups. To make such an assertion, we must first look at how familiarity is supposed to interact with task performance. Surprisingly, the literature on familiarity and memory is not very large. In a review of laboratory recall and recognition research with *verbal* materials, Kintsch (1970) concluded that familiarity led to higher recall, but lower recognition memory. In a well-known paper, Craik and Lockhart (1972) proposed that differences in memory performance are, in part, a function of how easily the material is encoded by the individual. Familiarity may, therefore, allow some material to be better encoded in memory and better remembered. The effects of familiarity are not necessarily tied to process variables (such as strategies), but appear to interact with the processing that the subject already employs.

In many of the studies discussed in this paper, an attempt was made to use stimulus materials familiar to all groups of subjects. Obviously, equivalent familiarity is virtually impossible across groups as well as across individuals. In Wagner's (1978a) study of recognition memory for Oriental rugs, differences in correct recognition were suggested to be a function of better encoding by subjects more familiar with the stimuli. Three major pieces of evidence supported this assertion: (1) nonschooled Moroccan rug sellers scored better than all other groups, regardless of education; (2) rural subjects (possibly more familiar with rugs) were superior to urban subjects, and this was in sharp contrast to a recall task using pictures of simple animals; and (3) there was little effect of these supposed differences in familiarity on forgetting rates, as predicted by the memory model. In contrast, another study of pictorial recognition memory was conducted by Kagen, Klein, Haith, and Morrison (1973) in Guatemala. The stimuli were pictures cut out from American magazines, and thus, virtually guaranteed of being less familiar to the Guatemalan children than to the American children in the study. In part of the study, pictures were ranked by Guatemalans on degree of familiarity into three categories, and recognition performance was analyzed in terms of these categories. Kagan et al. found that correct recognition was unrelated to the category of familiarity. This was an intriguing result, but possible ceiling effects made other aspects of the study difficult to interpret.

The notion of cultural specificity in memory is, of course, not limited only to experimental cross-cultural research. A variety of other studies supports the hypothesis that culture and experience may influence memory, primarily in the area of the utilization of strategies or mnemonics. It is well known that remembering the words to a song is greatly facilitated by singing the song—the tune and rhythm serve as mnemonics. Among the Kpelle in Liberia, Lancy (1977) has reported that "my informants had great difficulty recalling the songs unless they were singing *and dancing*" (p. 9, emphasis added). Thus, we see a motoric or kinesthetic mnemonic that aids recall. Similar evidence was recently gathered in a study of memory in deaf children (Liben & Drury, 1977). In this study, deaf children created their own, apparently culture-specific or deaf-specific mnemonics for remembering. The authors observed the use of finger spelling and the use of mime representations as mnemonics. A considerable body of historical information is available in Yates (1966) and in case studies of mnemonists, such as the classic study by Luria (1968). Finally, there is a variety of historical and ethnographic information on mnemonics as used in diverse cultures (see Baddeley, 1976; Wagner, 1978b). In sum, it would seem that cultural variation in memory—if it could be adequately measured—would appear relatively large. It seems that memory has been one of the mental faculties that has been of crucial importance to many peoples and societies throughout human history and it is not at all surprising to find significant differences due to content familiarity as well as to process or mnemonics.

## Assessing Comparative Differences in Memory

In cross-cultural as well as laboratory research on memory development, investigators have been concerned with the general issue of performance and competence. As pointed out by Cole and Bruner (1971), this distinction refers to the fact that what a person does (behaviorally) in a given context (his or her performance) is not necessarily, and often is not, an adequate estimate of what he or she is capable of doing in that context or somewhat altered contexts (his or her competence). Based on a large body of research with American children, Flavell (1970) made a similar point when he suggested that many children who show poor memory performance do not suffer from some "structural" (or cerebral) deficit, but seem merely not able to bring into *use* memory strategies in the appropriate context. When he constructed experimental situations in which children were given certain requisite behaviors (such as "repeat the names of these animals"), such children showed much more typical or grade-level performance. Flavell termed this phenomenon "production deficiency," since inducing the production of task-appropriate strategies in low-scoring children was usually sufficient to produce increased performance.

In cross-cultural research, it has been suggested, similarly, that "production deficiency" is an appropriate way to view lower memory performance among certain (often nonschooled) groups of people (Cole & Scribner, 1977b; Wagner, 1974, 1978a). To test for production deficiency, at least three (not mutually exclusive) areas of manipulation of memory performance among low-scoring subjects have been used in cross-cultural research: acquisition strategies, retrieval strategies, and stimulus encoding. Strategies of acquisition involve skills that are induced in subjects that lead to increased memory input and to subsequent output. One good example is provided by Scribner (reported in Cole & Scribner, 1977, pp. 260–261) in which Liberian subjects were asked to arrange taxonomically clusterable items "in any way that would help them remember." Only a few uneducated subjects provided taxonomic organization spontaneously, whereas about 25 percent were able to do so under "extra prodding" instructions. Although the advantage of organization on recall in Scribner's experiment is not provided, it seems probable from a number of similar experiments by Flavell (1970) and others (e.g., Hagen & Stanovich, 1977), that induced organization at acquisition leads to increased performance. Wagner (1975) found, for example, that requiring Yucatecan schoolchildren to label to-be-remembered items helped them focus on a remembering task. In this study, rehearsal of previously presented items (an acquisition strategy) was actually impeded by the labeling, but the advantage of better selective attention and increased echoic (recency effect) store led to overall superior recall.

Another way to manipulate subjects' recall significantly is by inducing various retrieval strategies. As Kobasigawa (1977) has suggested, constrained recall is one important way of producing increased recall because taxonomic categories may not be known to the subject and/or each category may not be exhaustively searched at the time of recall. We have seen in the studies of Cole et al. (1971) that constrained taxonomic recall is one of the few methods in which categorized and high recall was obtained in nonschooled subjects. By providing the taxonomic categories at the time of recall, Cole and his associates provided the retrieval cues or "routes" that aided Kpelle subjects in gaining access to previously stored information.

Finally, we have seen a number of examples in which providing for better stimulus encoding of the to-be-remembered items served to change memory output. As Scribner (1976) has suggested, the free recall task (as well as many other memory tasks) often "requires the subject to produce internal cues or structure" (p. 319) in order to achieve good performance. Thus, one way to achieve better stimulus encoding is to "build-in" semantic information into the memory task. Sharp et al. (1979) have undertaken a study along these lines by looking at paired-associate learning among schooled and nonschooled Yucatecans. Subjects were read one of two possible lists of paired nouns: a "within-category" list contained word pairs that were taxonomically related (e.g., root-branch); the "between-category" list contained word pairs that were not taxonomically related (e.g., root-sheep). Subjects were read the fourteen-item paired lists and, when presented with a given item, the subject had to recall the item's pair. Analyses of errors showed that all groups produced superior performance on the within-category list when compared to the between-category list, and that the largest increase in performance was among the *least* educated group (the Mayan nonschooled adults)! As in some of the earlier training studies (e.g., Flavell, 1970), the lowest performers may benefit most from experimenter-provided aids. Another example of providing the necessary task structure was evident in the experiments of story recall by Cole et al. (1971) discussed earlier. In these studies, the structure of the story appeared to alter significantly the way in which subjects performed on recall measures. Finally, the study of recognition memory for rugs in Morocco (Wagner, 1978a) showed that certain stimuli may have a special salience that is useful to given populations of subjects, such as the Moroccan rug sellers. As Gibson (1969) has pointed out, perceptual learning may lead to an increased ability to pick out distinctive features in stimuli; and it seems likely that such ability provides increased encoding and better subsequent recall.

It has been suggested that various mnemonics or strategies such as those discussed above demonstrate that individuals who perform poorly on memory tasks are often capable of "remediation . . . by such interventions as direct instruction or changing task environments" (Brown & Campione, 1978, p. 47). In the context of their discussion of typical or "modal" training studies with low-performing children, Brown and Campione add, furthermore, that "the aim of training is to achieve not only maintenance but generalization" (p. 49). Maintenance of training refers to the fact that the subject does not provide the required strategy *spontaneously,* and the training is seldom long-lasting (but see Brown, Campione, & Barclay, 1979, for a training study with some success in terms of both generalization and maintenance).

The question of spontaneity is one that has been particularly troublesome in comparative research. When an individual does not spontaneously produce a certain mnemonic strategy on a given task, there are a number of ways to interpret the results. As mentioned, most contempo-

rary comparative researchers seem to prefer invoking the production deficiency hypothesis—that the individual has no structural problem, but
often needs some guidance or change in task context for good mnemonic
behavior to be evidenced. Thus, we find Cole et al. (1971) concluding that
"cultural differences in cognition reside more in the *situations* to which
particular cognitive processes are applied than in the existence of a process in one cultural group and its absence in another" (p. 233; emphasis
added). Such an assertion—particularly given the checkered history of
cross-cultural cognitive research—may not only be fairly accurate but also
be a necessary reminder that we should be cautious about cross-cultural
inferences. Are differences in spontaneity evidence of "real" comparative
differences in memory? In the study (described earlier) in which Kpelle
were given instructions to do "anything" to remember better, Scribner
found that these subjects produced almost no evidence of measurable,
Western-like mnemonic behavior, whereas another similar study (Moely,
Olson, Halwes, & Flavell, 1969) indicated that most fifth graders in the
United States did so spontaneously. In their review of this work, Cole and
Scribner (1977) refer to these results as evidence for a "genuine cultural
difference" (p. 261). The problem here is that it is seldom clear whether
the *spontaneous* production of a given mnemonic behavior is in some important sense distinguishable from an induced (with ease?, with difficulty?) behavior. Indeed, the *leit motif* of the Cole et al. (1971) studies of
Kpelle memory is that if spontaneous mnemonic production is not obtained in a given task, then the experimenter should try another task—
implying that spontaneity is not a particularly important issue. The utility
of the production deficiency model is that it removes statements of comparative differences from the (probably incorrect) realm of biogenetic deficits in memory and leads the investigator to discover what training or task
structure may lead to adequate production or performance.

The remaining problem with the notion of production deficiency is to
determine whether spontaneity, per se, is evidence for differences in
memory that are superficial and remedial, or whether constant intervention is required for maintenance of behavior. Using a linguistic metaphor,
one could term this distinction "surface" versus "deep" differences in
memory. Surface differences would be those that are relatively easily and
permanently remediated through some type of intervention, training, task
reformulation, or contextual change; deep differences would be those that
are not so easily changed or maintained by intervention. It should be further noted that the surface-deep distinction is meant to subdivide categories of behavior that fall into the larger category of production deficiency.
Clearly there should be some way to distinguish between the performance
of educably retarded children (Brown, 1977) and of nonschooled Liberians
as in the studies of Cole et al. (1971). Even though their performance characteristics (e.g., amount recalled, lack of spontaneous strategic behavior)

may be similar, these groups are probably fundamentally different in that the latter could probably attain maintenance of task-appropriate behavior, whereas the retardates are unlikely to do so. Also, nonschooled Kpelle are likely to be able to demonstrate excellent memory skills in areas that are of special significance to them (as in Bartlett's "social tendency" hypothesis), whereas retardates will not. At present, there seems to be no easy way to decide unerringly whether a production deficiency is to be labeled "surface" or "deep." In an interesting study of the same problem, Cox and Paris (1979) found that elderly subjects needed much less "coaching" than young children in producing good mnemonic mediators, even though both groups were "production deficient" on an earlier memory task. In the sense of the above argument, we might say that the elderly group showed a "surface" or superficial production deficiency that was relatively easy to remediate.

In their review, Cole and Scribner (1977) argue convincingly that differences in memory performance between schooled and nonschooled subjects may be a function of the former's repeated exposure to situations in which decontextualized and quite variable material is presented in schools for deliberate memorizing. Furthermore, they suggest that nonschooled subjects do poorly on memory tasks particularly when the tasks are not related to the individual's cultural experience. Such a viewpoint is particularly acceptable in the light of recent American laboratory studies that have focused on the importance of knowledge in children's memory development. For example, Brown (1977) has proposed that knowledge base may affect "the rules, strategies and operations which can be used to make more efficient use of a limited capacity system" (pp. 104–105). She goes on to say that:

> In addition the child's knowledge base is deficient in at least three ways: (a) amount of information it contains; (b) organization and internal coherence of that information; and (c) the number of available routes by which it can be reached. (p. 105)

Even though it is sometimes inappropriate to make the developmental versus comparative (cross-cultural) analogy, it seems clear that differences in knowledge base are also much akin to Bartlett's (1932) notion of "social tendency," in which experience with material and/or a memory task leads to superior performance. The argument of Cole and Scribner is similar in that nonschooled subjects have a different knowledge base from which to process information. Interestingly, the notion of comparative differences in knowledge base, while believable, poses a problem for the argument of Cole and Scribner (1977) that the basis of cross-cultural differences in memory resides in the "distribution of situations posing different demand characteristics vis-à-vis memory" (p. 268). For the term *situation* applies to context, whereas knowledge base applies to kinds of antecedent information (linguistic, cognitive, experiential, and so on) that the individual has previously acquired. Even though it would be difficult to support any claim about cultural or societal differences in *general* knowledge, it may be said that *specific* areas of knowledge do vary across societies or cultures (in fact, this represents one of the basic defining features of "culture"). That variation in specific knowledge can influence memory performance has been illustrated in several recent studies (e.g., Chi, 1978).

In earlier sections of this paper, it was argued that structural features of memory seem invariant across a wide range of experiential backgrounds. Control processes or mnemonic strategies were proposed as the source of cultural specificity in memory, that is, the origin of most cross-cultural comparative differences. It should be added here that knowledge base may provide an important interactive element, either through its relationship with stimulus encoding at the microlevel or at the macrolevel in the subject's activity within society (see Meacham's discussion of Soviet research on this topic, 1975, 1977). The issue of knowledge base is also related to current research on the role of metamemory, or the subject's self-awareness of what he or she needs to do to remember (see Flavell & Wellman, 1977). There has, to date, been little cross-cultural work in this area, although it would seem to be an area of considerable usefulness. It may be the case, for example, that schoolchildren's experience with varieties of decontextualized memory tasks enables them to generalize their skills across more tasks. This question brings us back to the surface-deep distinction since the ability to generalize from school-trained skills is difficult to measure with laboratory research methods.

In this section, we have noted the difficulty of distinguishing between certain kinds of production deficiency. To make this further and rather subtle distinction may make the memory researcher's job more difficult. There has been a trend in recent years to consider evidence of good memory performance among those who were poor performers as sufficient to demonstrate equivalency in memory and other cognitive competencies. The present discussion has argued that equivalency—at least as discussed in terms of production deficiencies—is an oversimplification of the available evidence.

## Summary

The issue of culture and memory has generated considerable interest over many years. Early writings on this topic mainly concentrated on anecdotal accounts from world travelers, missionaries, and anthropologists, who provided mixed accounts of memory abilities in "other" cultures. Some of this evidence and more recent evidence was based on case studies of individuals with great mnemonic prowess and also was from research on groups of individuals who have developed various mnemonic techniques for the retention of information. More recent studies of culture's influence on memory has focused on how various cultural and environmental factors impact on memory as it is described in terms of memory models derived from laboratory studies.

The studies of Cole et al. (1971) and Wagner (1978a) were described in considerable depth, since each provided a number of avenues to explore not only cultural variation, but also the generality of laboratory-based theories of memory development. Among other things, the Cole et al. research found that increased memory performance could be induced in nonschooled as well as in schooled subjects by altering the task or the task context. This point is particularly important in the light of earlier statements that nonschooled or illiterate individuals were only capable of simple "rote" memory performance. Wagner (1978a), in selecting samples from Moroccan populations that varied on schooling and environment, and working with several measures of memory performance, was able to demonstrate a theoretically interesting variation in memory output. Structural features of memory were much less variable across groups than were control processes, as expected from theoretical predictions. The performance of Quranic scholars and Moroccan rug sellers provided support for the hypothesis that mnemonic abilities may be, to some extent, culture-specific or a function of particular environmental experiences. Support for the notion of culture-specific control processes was also found in studies ranging from historical and ethnographic accounts, to experimental research in diverse cultures.

In general, recall memory was found to vary primarily as a function of the subjects' utilization of task-appropriate strategies or mnemonics. Recognition memory was much less malleable, apparently because these tasks required few if any subject-controlled strategies. These results tend to fit well with a variety of laboratory studies that are the bases for developmental models of memory.

In a discussion of problems in assessing comparative differences in memory, it was suggested that the term *production deficiency* may be of limited usefulness. Although helpful in dispelling erroneous notions of structural learning deficiencies, the term *production deficiency* is too general to discriminate between certain comparative differences in memory. This seems to be particularly crucial in judging whether differences in the spontaneous use of strategies are superficial or require some sort of constant intervention for maintenance. The categories of "surface" and "deep" differences in memory were suggested in order to make this distinction clear, though at present there does not appear to be an adequate procedure for making accurate surface–deep distinctions.

There seem to be a number of directions that the area of culture and memory development may take in the years to come. First, there is a need for more in-depth ethnographic studies of memory in naturalistic contexts, because culturally determined intellectual activities (including schooling, literacy training, oral history, and many others) are likely to be major sources of cross-cultural differences in memory. The study of metamemory, in particular, would seem to fit quite well into an ethnographic design, since information is elicited from subjects on their everyday use of memory. Also, naturalistic research will lead to a better understanding of everyday memory skills that often escape psychologists' attention (see Neisser, 1978) and may provide a more valid way to compare memory skills across cultures, without the imposition of Western-derived tasks. Second, as we find out more about individual differences in memory, an integration or interface will have to be made with comparative group differences. Also, relatively little is currently known about the interrelationship between various everyday and laboratory memory skills. New and creative memory tasks should be developed to tap into culture-specific and situation-specific abilities. Third, terms such as *production deficiency* that gloss over relevant comparative distinctions, and such troublesome issues as spontaneity, will have to be given more serious consideration in future studies. Finally, there is little written that integrates the cross-cultural and ontogenetic research with other memory research on atypical or clinical differences in memory (see Wagner and Paris, in press), but it is certain that any general theory of memory will have to take into account this entire range of inquiry.

One general question remains to be addressed: Is there an "appropriate methodology" in cross-cultural research on memory that will guide us in the future? Investigators using laboratory-derived tasks, adapted to the cultural context (which includes much of the research described in this paper), have made an important contribution to our knowledge of memory. However, even cultural adaptation of such tasks is, in the final analysis, *only* an adaptation and is unable to meet the anthropological critique that suggests completely within-culture or "emic" methods. Although this is a general issue that is pertinent to all domains of psychological research, its ramifications for future research are still being debated (e.g., Laboratory for Comparative Human Cognition, 1979).

It seems apparent that the concern about inferences made from data collected using laboratory paradigms cannot be easily resolved by simply adopting other (say, ethnographic) paradigms. Undertaking careful ethnography and making careful observations would certainly help in avoiding erroneous inferences that may occur in cross-cultural research. However, without the experimental skills adequately to measure memory (or any other cognitive) abilities, the ethnographer may be led to erroneous judgments from either key informants or uninformed observation. The resolution of this concern for validity does not seem to lie within a single domain or discipline, but within the careful use of the investigatory tools of a general social science. In the study of cultural influences on memory, as in any interdisciplinary research domain, it is becoming increasingly evident that overspecialization in a single paradigmatic area may lead to increased error. The concern about ecological validity, appropriate methods, and cultural relativity are not new topics in social science, but they become more salient as our methods for empirical research become more sophisticated. It is hoped that the next review of research in culture and memory will be able to encompass a broader range of multidisciplinary investigations into this basic area of human intellect.

## Notes

1. The author would like to thank B. Rogoff, J. Stigler, and the editors and reviewers of this volume for their helpful comments on earlier drafts of this chapter.

2. It should be noted here that there is an assumption, in this free recall paradigm, that increased recall over trials is a function of increased clustering over trials. However, in the data supplied by Cole et al. (1971) in Figures 4–7 and 4–8 (p. 129), it appears that nonliterate (nonschooled) Kpelle demonstrate increasing performance over the first five trials, but clustering does not increase systematically. The lack of relationship between these two variables (clustering and number of words recalled) casts some doubt on the necessity of clustering for increased recall in some contexts. However, laboratory studies have in general shown a consistent relationship between these variables (Tulving, 1967).

3. The distinction between qualitative and quantitative change in behavior has been, and continues to be, a particularly thorny issue in psychology. In the context of memory research, it is often assumed that qualitative change may be said to occur if it can be shown that some *underlying* operation (e.g., clustering strategy) can be related to some observed quantitative change.

4. Kpelle schoolchildren were used in this experiment, so that the question is still open with respect to performance of nonschooled/nonliterates in such a task situation.

5. Since Kpelle were tape recorded in condition 4, they may well have tried simply to recall the entire story as a way of recalling the items. While this may be a useful mnemonic, it is *not* considered to be rote recapitualation.

6. The $d'$ score is an essentially unbiased measure of accuracy derived from signal detection theory, and is calculated as the $z$-score distance separating two theoretically normal distributions of new and old items. For more detail, see Wagner (1978a).

7. For an interesting discussion of the societal role of memory in Moroccan Quranic schools, see Eickelman, 1978. Also, Roskies (1978) provides a fascinating look at alphabetic memorization in the traditional European "heder" (Hebrew) schools.

# References

APPEL, L. F., COOPER, R. G., McCARRELL, N., SIMS-KNIGHT, J., YUSSEN, S. R., & FLAVELL, J. H. The development of the distinction between perceiving and memorizing. *Child Development*, 1972, *43*, 1365–1381.

ATKINSON, R. C., & SHIFFRIN, R. M. Human memory: a proposed system and its control processes. In K. W. Spence & J. T. Spence (Eds.), *The psychology of learning and motivation: Advances in theory and research* (Vol. 2). New York: Academic Press, 1968.

BADDELEY, A. D. *The psychology of memory.* New York: Basic Books, 1976.

BARTLETT, F. C., *Remembering.* London: Cambridge University Press, 1932 (1967).

BATESON, G. *Naven.* Palo Alto: Stanford Univerity Press, 1936 (1958).

BOAS, F. *The mind of primitive man.* New York: The Free Press, 1911 (1965).

BOUSFIELD, W. A. The occurrence of clustering in the recall of randomly arranged associates. *Journal of General Psychology*, 1953, *49*, 224–240.

BROWN, A. L. The development of memory: knowing, knowing about knowing, and knowing how to know. In H. W. Reese (Ed.), *Advances in child development and behavior* (Vol. 10). New York: Academic Press, 1975.

———. Knowing when, where, and how to remember: A problem of metacognition. In R. Glaser (Ed.), *Advances in instructional psychology.* Hillsdale, N. J.: Erlbaum, 1977.

BROWN, A. L., & CAMPIONE, J. C. Permissible inferences from the outcome of training studies in cognitive development research. *Quarterly Newsletter of the Institute for Comparative Human Development*, 1978, *2*, 46–53.

BROWN, A. L., CAMPIONE, J. C., & BARCLAY, C. R. Training self-checking routines for estimating self-readiness: Generalization from list learning to prose recall. *Child Development*, 1979, *50*, 501–512.

CAMPBELL, D. T. The mutual methodological relevance of anthropology and psychology. In F. L. K. Hsu (Ed.), *Psychological anthropology.* Homewood, Ill.: Dorsey Press, 1961.

CHI, M. T. H. Short-term memory limitations in children: Capacity or processing deficits? *Memory & Cognition*, 1976, *4*, 559–572.

———. Knowledge structures and memory development. In R. Siegler (Ed.), *Children's thinking: What develops?* Hillsdale, N. J.: Erlbaum, 1978.

COLBY, B. N., & COLE, M. A cross-cultural analysis of memory and narrative. In R. Horton and R. Flannegan (Eds.), *Modes of thought.* London: Faber, 1972.

COLE, M., & BRUNER, J. Cultural differences and inferences about psychological processes. *American Psychologist*, 1971, *26*, 867–876.

COLE, M., & GAY, J. Culture and memory. *American Anthropologist*, 1972, *74*, 1066–1084.

COLE, M., GAY, J., GLICK, J., & SHARP, D. *The cultural context of learning and thinking.* New York: Basic Books, 1971.

COLE, M., & SCRIBNER, S. Cross-cultural studies of memory and cognition. In R. V. Kail, Jr. and J. W. Hagen (Eds)., *Perspectives on development of memory and cognition.* Hillsdale, N. J.: Erlbaum, 1977.

Cox, G. L., & Paris, S. G. Memory skills of young and elderly: What is a production deficiency? Paper presented at the annual meeting of the Gerontological Society, Dallas, 1978.

Craik, F. I. M., & Lockhart, R. S. Levels of processing: A framework for memory research. *Journal of Verbal Learning and Verbal Behavior,* 1972, *11,* 671–684.

Deregowski, J. B. Effect of cultural value of time upon recall. *British Journal of Social and Clinical Psychology,* 1970, *9,* 37–41.

Deregowski, J. B., Ellis, H. D., & Shepherd, J. W. A cross-cultural study of recognition of pictures of faces and cups. *International Journal of Psychology,* 1973, *8,* 269–273.

Dirks, J., & Neisser, U. Memory for objects in real scenes: The development of recognition and recall. *Journal of Experimental Child Psychology,* 1977, *23,* 315–328.

Doob, L. W. Eidetic imagery: A cross-cultural will-o-the-wisp? *Journal of Psychology,* 1966, *63,* 13–34.

———. Correlates of eidetic imagery in Africa. *Journal of Psychology,* 1970, *76,* 223–230.

Eickelman, D. F. The art of memory: Islamic education and its social reproduction. *Comparative Studies in Society and History,* 1978, *20,* 485–516.

Flavell, J. H. Developmental studies of mediated memory. In H. W. Reese & L. P. Lipsett (Eds.), *Advances in child development and behavior* (Vol. 5). New York: Academic Press, 1970.

———. *Cognitive development.* Englewood Cliffs, N. J.: Prentice-Hall, 1977.

Flavell, J. H., & Wellman, H. M. Metamemory. In R. V. Kail, Jr. & J. W. Hagen (Eds.), *Perspectives on the development of memory and cognition.* Hillsdale, N. J.: Erlbaum, 1977.

Gibson, E. J. *Principles of perceptual learning and development.* New York: Appleton-Century-Crofts, 1969.

Goody, J. Mémoire et apprentissage dans les sociétés avec et sans écriture: La transmission du Bagre. *L'Homme,* 1977, *17,* 29–52.

Greenfield, P. M. Oral or written language: The consequences for cognitive development. *Language and Speech,* 1972, *15,* 169–178.

Hagen, J. W., Jongeward, R. H., & Kail, R. V., Jr. Cognitive perspectives on the development of memory. In H. W. Reese (Ed.), *Advances in child development and behavior* (Vol. 10). New York: Academic Press, 1975.

Hagen, J. W., & Stanovich, K. G. Memory: Strategies of acquisition. In R. V. Kail, Jr. & J. W. Hagen (Eds.), *Perspectives on the development of memory and cognition.* Hillsdale, N. J.: Erlbaum, 1977.

Hall, J. W. Verbal behavior as a function of schooling. *American Journal of Psychology,* 1972, *85,* 277–288.

Kagan, J., & Klein, R. E. Cross-cultural perspectives on early development. *American Psychologist,* 1973, *28,* 947–961.

Kagan, J., Klein, R. E., Haith, M. M., & Morrison, F. J. Memory and meaning in two cultures. *Child Development,* 1973, *44,* 221–223.

Kail, R. *The development of memory in children.* San Francisco: W.H. Freeman, 1979.

Kail, R. V., Jr., & Hagen, J. W. (Eds.). *Perspectives on the development of memory and cognition.* Hillsdale, N. J.: Erlbaum, 1977.

KAIL, R. V., JR., & SIEGEL, A. W. The development of mnemonic encoding: From perception to abstraction. In R. V. Kail, Jr. & J. W. Hagen (Eds.), *Perspectives on the development of memory and cognition*. Hillsdale, N. J.: Erlbaum, 1977.

KAMIN, L. *The science and politics of I.Q.* Hillsdale, N. J.: Erlbaum, 1974.

KEENEY, T. J., CANIZZO, S. E., & FLAVELL, J. H. Spontaneous and induced verbal rehearsal in a recall task. *Child Development*, 1967, *28*, 953–966.

KINGSLEY, P. The development in Zambian children of strategies for doing intellectual work. Paper presented at the African Regional Conference of the International Association of Cross-cultural Psychology, Ibadan (Nigeria), April, 1973. (Also reported in Wober, M. *Psychology in Africa*. London: International African Institute, 1975.)

KINGSLEY, P. R., & HAGEN, J. W. Induced versus spontaneous rehearsal in short-term memory in nursery school children. *Developmental Psychology*, 1969, *1*, 40–46.

KINTSCH, W. Models for free recall and recognition. In D. A. Norman (Ed.), *Models of memory*. New York: Academic Press, 1970.

KINTSCH, W., & GREENE, E. The role of culture-specific schemata in the comprehension and recall of stories. *Discourse Processes*, 1978, *1*, 1–13.

KLEINFELD, J. Visual memory in village Eskimo and urban Causcasian children. *Artic*, 1971, *24*, 132–137.

KOBASIGAWA, A. Retrieval strategies in the development of memory. In R. V. Kail, Jr. & J. W. Hagan (Eds.), *Perspectives on the development of memory and cognition*. Hillsdale, N. J.: Erlbaum, 1977.

LABORATORY OF COMPARATIVE HUMAN COGNITION. Cross-cultural psychology's challenges to our ideas of children and development. *American Psychologist*, 1979, *34*, 827–833.

LANCY, D. F. Studies of memory in culture. In L. L. Adler (Ed.), *Issues in cross-cultural research*. Annals of the New York Academy of Sciences, 1977.

LEVY-BRUHL, C. *How natives think*. New York: Washington Square Press, 1910 (1966).

LIBEN, L. S., & DRURY, A. M. Short-term memory in deaf and hearing children in relation to stimulus characteristics. *Journal of Experimental Child Psychology*, 1977, *24*, 60–73.

LURIA, A. R. *The mind of a mnemonist*. New York: Basic Books, 1968.

MANDLER, J. M., & JOHNSON, N. S. Remembrance of things parsed: Story structure and recall. *Cognitive Psychology*, 1977, *9*, 111–151.

MANDLER, J. M., ROBINSON, C. A. Developmental changes in picture recognition. *Journal of Experimental Child Psychology*, 1978, *26*, 122–136.

MANDLER, J. M., SCRIBNER, S., COLE, M., & DEFOREST, M. Cross-cultural invariance in story recall. *Child Development*, 1980, *51*, 19–26.

MEACHAM, J. A. Patterns of memory abilities in two cultures. *Developmental Psychology*, 175, *11*, 50–53.

―――. Soviet investigations of memory development. In R. V. Kail, Jr., & J. W. Hagen (Eds.), *Perspectives on the development of memory and cognition*. Hillsdale, N. J.: Erlbaum, 1977.

MOELY, B. E., OLSON, F. A., HALWES, T. G., & FLAVELL, J. H. Production deficiency in young children's clustered recall. *Developmental Psychology*, 1969, *1*, 26–34.

MORRISON, F. J., HOLMES, D. L., & HAITH, M. M. A developmental study of the effect of familiarity on short-term memory. *Journal of Experimental Child Psychology*, 1974, *18*, 412–425.

NADEL, S. F. Experiments on culture psychology. *Africa*, 1937, *10*, 421–435. (a)

———. A field experiment in racial psychology. *British Journal of Psychology*, 1937, *28*, 195–211. (b)

NEISSER, U. Memory: What are the important questions? In M. M. Gruneberg, P. Morris & R. N. Sykes (Eds.), *Practical aspects of memory*. New York: Academic Press, 1978.

NEWCOMBE, N., ROGOFF, B., & KAGAN, J. Developmental changes in recognition memory for pictures of objects and scenes. *Developmental Psychology*, 1977, *13*, 337–341.

ORNSTEIN, P. A. *Memory development in children*. Hillsdale, N. J.: Erlbaum, 1978.

PAIVIO, A., YUILLE, J. C., & ROGERS, T. B. Noun imagery and meaningfulness in free and serial recall. *Journal of Experimental Psychology*, 1969, *79*, 509–514.

PARKER, J. F. Free recall of abstract and concrete words by American and Ghanaian college students. *International Journal of Psychology*, 1977, *12*, 243–252.

PERLMUTTER, M., & LANGE, G. A developmental analysis of recall-recognition distinctions. In P. A. Ornstein (Ed.), *Memory development in children*. Hillsdale, N. J.: Erlbaum, 1978.

PERLMUTTER, M., & MYERS, N. A. A developmental study of semantics effects on recognition memory. *Journal of Experimental Child Psychology*, 1976, *22*, 438–453.

POLLNAC, R. B. & JAHN, G. Culture and memory revisited: An example for Buganda. *Journal of Cross-Cultural Psychology*, 1976, *7*, 73–86.

PORTEUS, S. D. *Intelligence and environment*. New York: Macmillan, 1937.

PRICE, J. R., & TARE, W. A cross-cultural study of recall of time-related and non-time-related verbal material. *International Journal of Psychology*, 1975, *10*, 247–254.

ROGOFF, B. Mother's teaching style and child memory: A highland Guatemala study. Paper presented at the annual meeting of the Society for Research in Child Development, New Orleans, March, 1977.

ROSKIES, D. Alphabet instruction in the East European heder. *YIVO Annual of Jewish Social Science*, 1978, *17*, 21–53.

ROSS, B. M., & MILLSOM, C. Repeated memory of oral prose in Ghana and New York. *International Journal of Psychology*, 1970, *5*, 173–181.

SCRIBNER, S. Developmental aspects of categorized recall in a West African society. *Cognitive Psychology*, 1974, *6*, 475–494.

———. Situating the experiment in cross-cultural research. In K. F. Riegel & J. A. Meacham (Eds.), *The developing individual in a changing world*. Chicago: Aldine, 1976.

SCRIBNER, S., & COLE, M. Effects of constrained recall training on children's performance in a verbal memory task. *Child Development*, 1972, *43*, 845–857.

———. Unpackaging literacy. *Social Science Information*, 1978, *17*, 19–40.

SHARP, D., COLE, M., & LAVE, C. Education and cognitive development: The evidence from experimental research. *Monographs of the Society for Research in Child Development*, 1978, 44, 1–112.

SHEPARD, R. N., & TEGHTSOONIAN, M. Retention of information under conditions approaching a steady state. *Journal of Experimental Psychology*, 1961, 62, 55–59.

SHEPHERD, J. W., DEREGOWSKI, J. B., & ELLIS, H. D. A cross-cultural study of recognition memory for faces. *International Journal of Psychology*, 1974, 9, 205–211.

SMIRNOV, A. A. *Problems of the psychology of memory*. New York: Plenum, 1973.

STEVENSON, H. W., PARKER, T., WILKINSON, A., BONNEVAUX, B., & GONZALEZ, M. Schooling, environment, and cognitive development: A cross-cultural study. *Monographs of the Society for Research in Child Development*, 1978, 43, No. 175.

TULVING, E. Theoretical issues in free recall. In T. R. Dixon & D. L. Horton (Eds.), *Verbal learning and general behavior theory*. Englewood Cliffs, N. J.: Prentice-Hall, 1967.

————. Episodic and semantic memory. In E. Tulving & W. Donaldson (Eds.), *Organization of memory*. New York: Academic Press, 1972.

TULVING, E., & OSLER, S. Effectiveness of retrieval cues in memory for words. *Journal of Experimental Psychology*, 1968, 77, 593–601.

TVERSKY, B., & TEIFFER, E. Development of strategies for recall and recognition. *Developmental Psychology*, 1976, 12, 406–410.

VURPILLOT, E. The development of scanning strategies and their relation to visual differentiation. *Journal of Experimental Child Psychology*, 1968, 6, 632–650.

WAGNER, D. A. The development of short-term and incidental memory: A cross-cultural study. *Child Development*, 1974, 45, 389–396.

————. The effects of verbal labeling on short-term and incidental memory: A cross-cultural and developmental study. *Memory and Cognition*, 1975, 3, 595–598.

————. *Memories of Morocco: A cross-cultural study of the influence of age, schooling and environment on memory*. Ph.D. dissertation, University of Michigan, Ann Arbor, 1976.

————. Memories of Morocco: The influence of age, schooling and environment on memory. *Cognitive Psychology*, 1978, 10, 1–28. (a)

————. Culture and mnemonics. In M. M. Gruneberg, P. Morris & R. N. Sykes (Eds.), *Practical aspects of memory*. New York: Academic Press, 1978. (b)

WAGNER, D. A., & DAVIS, D. A. The necessary and the sufficient in cross-cultural research. *American Psychologist*, 1978, 33, 857–858.

WAGNER, D. A., & LOTFI, A. Traditional Islamic education in Morocco: Sociohistorical and psychological perspectives. *Comparative Education Review*, 1980, 24, 238–251.

WAGNER, D. A., & PARIS, S. G. Problems and prospects in comparative studies of memory. *Human Development*, in press.

WATKINS, M. J., & TULVING, E. Episodic memory: When recognition fails. *Journal of Educational Psychology: General*, 1975, 104, 5–29.

WELLMAN, H., RITTER, A., & FLAVELL, J. H. Deliberate memory behavior in the delay reactions of very young children. *Developmental Psychology*, 1975, 11, 780–787.

WICKELGREN, W. A. Age and storage dynamics in continuous recognition memory. *Developmental Psychology*, 1975, 11, 165–169.

WILKINSON, A., PARKER, T., & STEVENSON, H. W. Influence of school and environment on selective memory. *Child Development*, 1979, *50*, 890–893.

YATES, F. A. *The art of memory.* Chicago: University of Chicago Press, 1966.

YAVUS, H. S. Development of retention and organization occurring in free recall in Turkish children. *Journal of Genetic Psychology*, 1971, *118*, 203–210.

# 6

# Schooling and the Development of Cognitive Skills

~~~~~~~~~~~~~~~~~~~~~~~~~~~~~~~~~~~~~

*Barbara Rogoff*

~~~~~~~~~~~~~~~~~~~~~~~~~~~~~~~~~~~~~

## Contents

## Abstract

Research in societies in which schooling is not compulsory or not universally available provides an opportunity to compare the cognitive test performance of people who have and have not been to school, controlling for age. This chapter first reviews research comparing schooled and nonschooled (or less schooled) samples' performance on perception, memory, classification and concept development, logical problem-solving, and Piagetian tests. Many of the studies suffer from limitations in generalizability since they often (a) do not control for factors covarying with schooling, (b) are not concerned with the unfamiliarity of the materials used or the test situation itself, and (c) assume that the behavior which has been sampled has generality beyond the specific competence observed. The chapter discusses possible effects of selection bias and test bias and of limits on the generalizability of the findings. Finally, the chapter considers various speculations regarding the processes by which schooling may have its effect: the possible importance of verbal instruction out of context, the emphasis on searching for general rules to fit all situations, and facility with specific skills taught in school, especially literacy.

## Introduction

Investigators of cognitive development have become concerned that cognitive changes frequently observed to occur over the school years may be due to experience in school rather than to maturational changes (Brown, 1977; Cole & Scribner, 1975). Research exploring changes with age in Western children is confounded by entrance into school at about age 5 and by a high correlation between age and grade in school thereafter to adulthood. Indeed, the Laboratory of Comparative Human Cognition (1979) notes that "to some people it seems that cognitive-developmental research in the United States has been measuring *years of schooling*, using *age* as its proxy variable" (p. 830).

In many nontechnological societies, formal schooling has been imported from Western (technological) nations but is not yet universal. Although the teaching methods in such schools are probably different from current Western educational practices, the relative independence of age and amount of schooling provides investigators with a natural laboratory for investigating the effects of increasing age unconfounded by schooling, or the effects of schooling when age is held constant.

Psychologists look to such cross-cultural studies to determine which cognitive developmental phenomena, evidenced in standard experiments or tests, are influenced by the schooling "confound," rather than by maturation and general experience with the world. If a consistent effect of schooling on cognitive activities were found, psychologists would need to consider carefully the implications for both the generality and the developmental source of such cognitive phenomena.

Looking at schooling and cognition from a different angle are those who, rather than regarding schooling as a disturbance of otherwise natural development, are interested specifically in the cognitive consequences of schooling. Cross-cultural studies are essential to this interest as well, since societies in which schooling is not compulsory, or not universally available, provide an opportunity to compare the test performance of people who have and have not been to school, controlling for age.

This review will first provide a comprehensive survey of studies that have explicitly compared the performance of schooled and nonschooled populations on cognitive tests. Almost all of the studies derive from a decidedly Western viewpoint. The topics that have received attention in comparisons of schooled and nonschooled populations are perception, memory, classification and concept development, logical problem-solving, and Piagetian tasks. The studies will be described in that order—in a progression from what is considered more basic to higher-order cognitive activities—with a summary of findings at the end of each section. Unfortunately a large number of the studies were not motivated by any theoretical perspective suggesting reasons to expect a schooling effect or leading to thoughtful, in-depth exploration of cognitive processes, but rather by an interest in trying standard psychological tasks in other cultures. (Another recent review of the cognitive consequences of schooling appears in Nerlove & Snipper, in press.)

Many of the studies suffer from limitations in generalizability since they often (a) do not control for covarying factors, (b) are not concerned with the unfamiliarity of the materials used or the test situation itself, and (c) assume that the behavior that has been sampled has generality beyond the specific competence observed.

Is the schooling effect an artifact due to nonrandom selection of which people go to school? Although in the studies reviewed, groups of schooled and nonschooled children have been at least roughly equated in terms of age, other variables that covary with schooling are usually left uncontrolled (e.g., urban/rural differences, family wealth and occupations, familiarity with Western technology, and aspirations). It is thus likely that some of the apparent schooling effects are due to covarying factors instead.

Are schooling effects due to test bias? Nonschooled children may be less comfortable than schooled children in the unusual social situation of testing. They are likely to be less familiar with various aspects of the test: the language or materials used, the specific activities in which they are required physically or mentally to manipulate the materials, and even the requirement of performing for the purpose of being evaluated. These problems are compounded because of the Western derivation of most of the tests given. Western schooling may thus serve as culture contact, providing schooled people with familiarity with superficial features of the tests, which gives them a performance edge over nonschooled people.

Are the effects of schooling on cognitive test performance real but limited in generality? Two versions of this question will be considered in the final section of this chapter: that tests tap skills related to those taught in school but unrelated to everyday cognitive activities; and that the skills tapped by the tests are so specific that they cannot be safely generalized even to other school-like cognitive activities. Although most authors assume that tests measure important underlying cognitive competences, there is little empirical work to decide the issue of the generality of the behavior observed in tests. Since these questions apply to most of the research on the cognitive consequences of schooling, discussion of them will be deferred until after the literature is reviewed.

A serious shortcoming of the research reviewed is the lack of consideration of the processes by which schooling may have its effect. Some speculations have been offered that are considered in the concluding pages of this chapter: the possible importance of verbal instruction out of context, the emphasis on searching for general rules to fit all situations, and facility with specific skills taught in school, especially literacy. However, the majority of studies merely compare individuals who have or have not received Western-style schooling. With few exceptions (e.g., Fobih, 1979; Lancy, 1978; Minuchin, Biber, Shapiro, & Zimiles, 1969; and Pollnac & Jahn, 1976), there has been little investigation of the effect of varying type or quality of Western schooling. Most studies have also ignored the issue of how much schooling is necessary to influence performance (an exception is Cole, Gay, Glick, & Sharp, 1971).

Furthermore the schooled versus nonschooled comparisons have seriously overlooked other forms of education. Traditional societies have a number of different kinds of educational mechanisms, including bush schools, apprenticeships, and various informal educational experiences (Fortes, 1938; Gearing & Tindall, 1973; Middleton, 1970; Spindler, 1955). Very interesting discussion of dimensions of difference between various forms of education appears in Scribner and Cole (1973); Greenfield and Lave (in press); and Lave (in press). Few studies have explored the cognitive consequences of educational experiences other than Western-style schooling: Lave (1977) studied tailoring apprenticeship; Childs and Greenfield (in press) explored weaving instruction; Scribner and Cole (1978a), Wagner (1978b), and Bennett (1979) investigated Qur'anic schooling; and Scribner and Cole (1978a) studied informal literacy training.

## Research Testing the Relationship
## Between Schooling and Cognition

*Perception*

The perceptual studies that have tested for the effects of schooling have been generally limited to the understanding and analysis of two-dimensional visual stimuli. One area of inquiry has been the perception of depth in two-dimensional pictures. Strictly speaking, this is a reading or a translation skill, interpreting depth in something flat. However, in much of the literature the skill is referred to as a perceptual ability—what the natives are able (or unable) to see when looking at pictures. A second topic is susceptibility to visual illusions, many of which use perspective cues like those in pictures. The third topic that has been explored with samples varying in amount of schooling is perceptual analysis of stimuli (most of which are two-dimensional). This includes pattern matching and disembedding figures from background.

*Depth perception in pictures.* An early paper by Hudson (1960) specifies several artistic or graphic conventions used in Western illustrations and photographs to indicate depth: relative sizes of objects (an object nearer to the observer appears larger than one that is the same size but further away); object superimposition or overlap (when one object overlaps or obscures another the superimposed object appears further away); and perspective cues (parallel lines seem to converge in the distance).

Hudson investigated the reading of depth in pictures using a drawing of a hunting scene with a man pointing a spear in the direction of both an elephant and an antelope. The pictures contain two-dimensional and three-dimensional information. In the two-dimensional plane of the paper both the elephant and the antelope are in line with the man's spear and the elephant is closer to the spear than the antelope. However, the elephant appears some distance back from the man and antelope when three-dimensional depth cues are considered (e.g., the elephant is much smaller and on a higher plane of the picture). [One of these pictures is shown on p. 30 of Volume 3, this *Handbook.*] To probe the subject's perception, the tester asked, "Which is nearer to the man, the elephant or the antelope?" Subjects who reported the antelope to be nearer were classified as three-dimensional (3D) perceivers. Other responses were coded as two-dimensional (2D). Hudson claims that the main population difference in percentage of 3D South African viewers is illiterate versus school-going. He suggests that the determining factor is experience viewing photographs or drawings, either in formal education or in informal teaching at home.

Hudson argues that the results were not due to misunderstanding of the question "Which is nearer to the man, elephant or antelope?" since (a) subjects classified as 2D on the basis of the "nearness" question also identified the elephant as the hunter's quarry, and (b) most samples answered the question immediately, whether they gave 2D or 3D responses. However, high school and graduate teacher samples hesitated greatly in responding, sometimes taking as long as one hour per picture. They asked the tester for information on the mode of perception because they considered both the possibility of 2D and 3D. Hudson interprets this as occupational cautiousness and a problem in perceptual organization, though it seems likely instead that the highly schooled samples were the only ones willing to point out the ambiguity to the tester.

A positive relationship between amount of schooling and 3D responding to pictures was also reported by Dawson (1967a, 1967b), Kilbride and Leibowitz (1975), Kilbride, Robbins, and Freeman (1968), and Wagner (1977). Kilbride and Robbins (1968) asked subjects to identify the roads in Hudson's drawings which are represented by converging lines. Subjects who identified the road as a hill, stone, ladder, or letter "A" (not using linear perspective) had less formal schooling than subjects who identified the road on a three-dimensional basis.

*Illusions involving perspective cues.* The Ponzo illusion (Figure 6–1) has also been used as a measure of use of perspective cues in viewing two-dimensional materials. The illusion resembles the road in Hudson's drawings. Viewers who are susceptible to the illusion report that the upper horizontal line appears longer than the lower one, presumably because perspective cues make the upper part of the illusion appear further away. A relation between illusion susceptibility and three-dimensional interpretation of pictures was found by Kilbride and Leibowitz (1975) and by Wagner (1977). However, the effect of schooling is uncertain. Leibowitz and Pick (1972) found greater susceptibility to the illusion accompanying schooling. Wagner's reports of Ponzo illusion susceptibility are inconsistent with each other as well as with the findings of Leibowitz and Pick (1972): he reports no effect of schooling (1977) as well as decreased susceptibility for schooled compared to nonschooled subjects (Wagner & Heald, 1979).

Adding background depth cues to the Ponzo illusion, by superimposing it on a photograph of a railroad track or a plowed field, had no effect on the illusion susceptibility of relatively nonschooled Ugandan villagers (their judgments of line length were *accurate* under all conditions) but in-

PONZO

Figure 6–1. The Ponzo illusion.

creased the susceptibility of Ugandan college students from the same environment (Leibowitz & Pick, 1972). Graphs provided by Wagner (1977) show that with depth cues added, nonschooled subjects showed significantly *less* susceptibility to the illusion than schooled subjects, who showed only slightly more susceptibility with the added depth cues than without. Leibowitz and Pick postulate that education increases familiarity of pictorial depth cues and also increases ability to disregard or inhibit rival "flatness" cues (absence of binocular disparity, visibility of surface and edge of the picture, and awareness that the image is simply on a piece of paper). However, an attempt to diminish flatness cues by presenting the pictures in a viewing box did not make the rural 2D viewers any more susceptible to the illusion (Kilbride & Leibowitz, 1975).

Pick and Pick (1978) point out that in the Ponzo illusion the subjects are explicitly instructed to compare the actual 2D length of the lines. They suggest that, rather than increasing the ability to use 3D cues or to ignore flatness cues, extensive use of 3D pictorial representation may hamper one's ability to use the two-dimensional information provided in pictures.

Results have been inconsistent for other illusions that are presumed to depend on perspective cues. With the Müller-Lyer illusion, Davis (1970) found less illusion susceptibility with greater schooling, whereas Wagner and Heald (1979) found greater susceptibility in schooled samples. No schooling effect was found for the horizontal-vertical illusion (Pollnac, 1977). As in common for research on illusions, results are difficult to interpret. A possible reason is that susceptibility to these illusions is influenced both by familiarity with 2D depth cues and by experience analyzing two dimensional figures. Schooling differences in the latter skill are described in the next section.

*Perceptual analysis.* Several studies have found that when a task requires analytic discrimination of stimuli, schooled subjects perform better than nonschooled subjects. Schooled Peruvian children were more accurate in matching a line drawing to a standard from among a series of transformations of the standard than nonschooled children (Stevenson, Parker, Wilkinson, Bonnevaux, & Gonzalez, 1978). Myambo (1972) argues that differences in "analytic attitude" were responsible for education-related differences in a shape constancy task. For some reason, she considers responses closer to the retinal image shape to be more analytic, but as Pick and Pick (1978) point out, the uneducated subjects performed the task most accurately since they gave shape constancy responses.

Greenfield and Childs (1972) found that schooled Mexican boys were more accurate than nonschooled boys in constructing stick representations of patterns familiar to them in their everyday clothing. The authors suggest that formal schooling may induce an analytic self-consciousness about familiar aspects of one's culture. More likely, in their opinion, is that schooling may facilitate the translation of information from one context (woven material) to a different one (the stick pattern). They suggest that this kind of translation is similar to that provided by schooling's introducing a written language into an oral culture.

The tests used as measures of cognitive style include the Embedded Figures Test (EFT) and Koh's Block Test, which involve disembedding one component of a two-dimensional figure from the rest of the figure, usually with a speed criterion. As Serpell (1976) has pointed out, in non-Western societies these tests may simply be measures of skill at perceptual analysis. Most studies using these tests cross-culturally have not been specifically concerned with the effects of schooling. However, a few studies do test the effects of schooling, generally without controlling for other factors. Positive correlations have been reported between schooling and performance on the EFT and Koh's Block Test by Dawson (1967a, 1967b), Witkin and Berry (1975), and Berry (1976) for a large number of cultural groups.

It is unclear from these studies what might account for the improved performance of the school-attenders. Suggestions include the use of "analytic functioning"; familiarity with task parameters such as the use of two-dimensional materials and the criterion of speed; and possible confounding with covarying factors uncontrolled in the correlations reported above (e.g., age, urbanization). However, the latter interpretation is not supported by studies that have found schooling differences when controlling for age and urban/rural differences (Fahrmeier, 1975; Wagner, 1978a).

*Summary.* Schooling seems to have an influence on the reading of depth cues in two-dimensional representations. Nonschooled subjects, who usually have less contact with books and pictures, are less familiar with graphic conventions used in Western pictures to represent depth in two dimensions. Some of the difficulty of nonschooled subjects on these tasks may come from lack of communication of task demands, such as whether they are supposed to be answering a question about nearness in two-dimensional or in three-dimensional space.

The effect of schooling on susceptibility to visual illusions involving perspective cues is inconsistent. Perhaps this is because schooled subjects are more familiar with 2D depth cues (which would increase susceptibility) but also more familiar with analytic discrimination of 2D stimuli (which would decrease susceptibility).

Tasks involving analytic perceptual discrimination (comparing similar stimuli, analyzing patterns, and disembedding figures from background) also show schooling effects. It is unclear how much of the difference in performance is influenced by unfamiliarity of the form of representation (often two-dimensional) and by speeded tests.

*Memory*

The memory tasks that have been given cross-culturally have generally involved deliberate remembering of unrelated bits of information. Schooled Western subjects usually devise organizational strategies to aid memory in such tasks (paired associate learning, free recall, serial recall). A few studies have involved tests of recognition memory, a task that has been proposed not to allow the use of mnemonic strategies. (See Wagner's chapter in this volume of the *Handbook* for discussion of cultural "universals" and "differences" in memory.) Before examining results with the tasks just mentioned, we will consider the work done on eidetic imagery—a task that carries predictions of better performance on the part of *nonschooled* subjects.

*Eidetic imagery.* Eidetic images are visual images that persist for a period following stimulation, that are fairly accurate and detailed, and that can be scanned by the viewer. Various writers (reported by Doob, 1964) have thought that the incidence of eidetic imagery would be higher among nonliterate populations than among the literate, who place emphasis on verbal memory. Eidetic imagery might be another way besides writing in which information could be stored. In his 1964 study in Nigeria, Doob found a slight but nonsignificant difference between subjects varying in amount of schooling, with more eidetic imagery associated with less schooling. Doob (1970) summarizes several studies, saying that the research provides "tenuous wisps of evidence" for the position that eidetic imagery is negatively correlated with acculturation (including education).

*Paired associate learning.* In the paired associate task, the subject must learn associations between pairs of stimuli, one furnished by the tester as a stimulus (cue) item, and the other that the subject learns as the response. School grade predicts performance on this task for Yucatan subjects (Anglin & Skon, cited in Sharp, Cole, & Lave, 1979). Colombian children with more schooling learned paired asssociate lists faster than did children with less schooling (Hall, 1972). However, when learning was brought to equal levels (requiring six trials for the low-schooling group and three for the high-schooling group), there was no difference between the two groups in retention of the material.

Sharp, Cole, and Lave (1979) report a greater schooling effect when there was little relationship between items in the pairs (e.g., bull-root), as opposed to when there was an explicit relationship between items (from the same semantic category, e.g., bull-sheep). They conclude that if some connection between items is structured into the task, populations with little schooling will have a relatively easier time learning the material than if the connections are less obvious and have to be actively constructed by the subject.

*Free recall.* In the free recall task, subjects are required to repeat a list of items (often words read aloud) in any order. As in the paired associate learning task, recall is usually improved if there is some organization to the list, such as using items that belong to a limited number of semantic categories (e.g., animals, furniture). Subjects who make use of the existing structure of the list (e.g., clustering words by categories) or who invent some organizing principles generally recall more words.

Studies comparing nonschooled subjects and subjects with a few years of schooling have found inconsistent results (Bennett, 1979; Cole, Gay, Glick, & Sharp, 1971; Fahrmeier, 1975; Lancy, 1978). However, when high school students are compared with nonschooled subjects, a striking superiority in recall as well as more clustering of items by semantic category are found for the schooled subjects (Cole et al., 1971; Sharp, Cole, & Lave, 1979).

Cole et al. (1971) suggest that since effects show up for high-school-educated Kpelle as well as for American subjects after about three years of United States education, "some features of recall may be the result of something connected with literacy when combined with the detached learning of the book and schoolroom" (p. 130). A study reported in an appendix of the same book also suggests that literacy is important: subjects from the Vai tribe who were literate in Vai but had little formal schooling recalled and clustered more than Vai subjects who were not literate in the Vai script (and also had little schooling).

By manipulating task demands, Cole et al. (1971) attempted to determine the aspects of the task that provided difficulty for the nonliterate subjects. Recall and clustering increased when the category structure of the lists was marked by holding items from each category over a specific chair, compared to holding the items randomly over different chairs. Verbal cuing of the categories also improved performance, but only when the subjects were told the category names at the time of presentation of the list and at the time of recall were asked to remember all the items from one category, then given the name of another category and asked to recall those items, and so on. When cuing was discontinued, recall and clustering remained high. Forcing the use of cues was successful in enhancing recall and semantic clustering even after the cued constraints were removed. When organization of the free recall items was imposed by embedding the items in stories, subjects recalled the items according to the organization provided by the stories: with a story involving a "linear" adventure, the items were very likely to be recalled in the order in which they occurred in the story; if the story involved clusters of items, so did the structure of recall.

From this series of studies, Cole et al. (1971) conclude that at some time in the fifth- to eighth-grade range in Liberia, students begin to use semantic categories to control memorization of lists. People who have not had extensive schooling produce semantic categorization and high levels of performance when the task is constructed in such a way that the organizational structure (semantic categories, story line) is made explicit. They suggest that nonliterates (and those with a small amount of schooling) have not learned to engage in activities that provide structure for material that appears unrelated.

Scribner (1974) found that if a personally meaningful organization of items was made available to nonliterate subjects, they could make use of it in structuring free recall. Subjects sorted items into piles until the same organization was repeated on subsequent sorts, and then were tested for recall. Semantic categories were more often used by subjects with more schooling, but all groups made use of their personal sorting structure to organize their free recall of the items.

*Serial recall.* Tests of memory span (repeating lists of digits or words in order) yield better performance on the part of schooled than of non-schooled subjects (Fahrmeier, 1975; Stevenson et al., 1978).

In the serial short-term recall task, a series of cards with pictures are shown briefly to the subject and then turned face down in linear order. The subject is then shown a "probe card" with a picture corresponding to one of the face-down cards, and asked to point to the location of its mate. With United States subjects, heightened recall for the first items shown ("primacy effect") has been explained in terms of the use of rehearsal as a recall strategy. Heightened performance on the last item(s) shown ("recency effect") has been attributed to the echoic or sensory memory store.

Wagner (1974) found greater recall and a more striking primacy effect for Yucatan subjects with greater amounts of schooling than for those with less schooling. Differences in the recency effect were not striking. Wagner concludes that "higher-level mnemonic strategies [such as verbal rehearsal, which was not measured but only inferred] in memory may do more than 'lag' by several years—the present data indicate that without formal schooling, such skills may not develop at all" (p. 395).

In a later study with Moroccan males differing systematically in age, schooling, and urbanization, Wagner (1978b) found that schooled subjects at older ages (over 13 years) showed greater recall, much greater primacy, and only slightly greater recency. He concludes that control processes (e.g., rehearsal) are much more subject to environmental influences than are structural features of memory (e.g., sensory or echoic store, as inferred from minimal differences in recency effect). However, this formulation is challenged by Bennett's (1979) findings that the control processes (as inferred from the primacy effect) remain relatively constant, whereas the recency effect varies greatly with differences in educational background.

The serial recall task is complicated by the fact that the cards contain incidental information in addition to the pictures on which the subject expects to be tested. Schooled subjects show greater recall for both central and incidental information than do nonschooled subjects, as well as a larger difference between central and incidental memory (Cole & Scribner, 1977, analyzing Wagner's 1974 data; Wilkinson, Parker, & Stevenson, 1979). Cole and Scribner interpret such findings as evidence of the greater number of strategies that schooled people spontaneously apply to intentional memory tasks.

*Recognition memory.* Recognition memory has been suggested by Brown (1975) as a memory task in which strategy use does not enter. Since the spontaneous use of mnemonic strategies seems to be one of the most striking differences in memory performance between schooled and nonschooled groups, it is of interest to consider the few recognition memory studies that have made schooling comparisons. The only study that might support Brown's view is that of Wagner (1978b), showing similar forgetting *rates* for schooled and nonschooled Moroccan males in a continuous recognition task for rug patterns. However, schooled subjects had more total items correct and, in a replication with Michigan college students, some subjects reported using strategies in this task (e.g., counting the number of discrete shapes in the rug patterns, comparing differences in rectangularity of the patterns). The other studies that have made schooling comparisons with recognition memory tasks have found better performance by schooled subjects (Hall, 1972; Rogoff, in press).

Several authors have discussed the difficulty of communicating the task demands of recognition tests to non-Western subjects. For subjects who are used to true-false and multiple-choice tests, the recognition paradigm is very familiar. Greenfield and Childs (1972) discuss their unsuccessful efforts to teach Zinacanteco children how to handle multiple-choice materials in a pattern analysis task. Rogoff (1977b) describes great difficulty in communicating task demands to Guatemalan Mayan children in a sentence recognition task. Nine-year-old children who had more schooling performed much better than children of the same age who had less schooling. In a forced-choice recognition task with groups of objects, the task demands were more comprehensible to the children, and grade in school was less predictive of performance. In Wagner's (1978b) continuous recognition task with rug designs, the experimenter occasionally had to go through the practice task in detail with younger nonschooled subjects, and 3 percent of the subjects were eliminated from the sample for lack of task comprehension. As reported, schooled children recognized the rug patterns more accurately in this task than did nonschooled children. It is possible that schooling differences in performance on recognition tasks are related to ease of understanding the school-like response demands. A related argument given by Cole and Scribner (1977) is that performance on cross-cultural recognition tests may reflect changes toward a stricter criterion in decision processes for judging an item to be "new" or "old," and be relatively uninfluenced by memory processes.

A recognition memory study with Colombian children supports the idea that differences in judgment criteria affect the performance of subjects with different amounts of schooling (Hall, 1972). Recognition of common words was tested in lists consisting of the "old" (originally presented) words mixed with "new" words that were similar to the old words and "new" words that were unrelated to the old words. Groups differing in schooling correctly recognized the old words with equal facility. However, subjects with little schooling falsely recognized the unrelated new words more frequently than did the subjects with more schooling. The low-schooling group falsely recognized unrelated new words as often as related new words. Hall mentions that twenty out of sixty-one subjects failed to "catch on" to the procedure, often identifying all words in the test list as "old." The fact that subject loss was twice as great for the low-schooling group again supports the conclusion that schooling differences on recognition tests may involve difficulty in communicating task demands.

*Summary.* From a large number of studies using memory tests, it appears that nonschooled subjects generally have less success than do schooled subjects on these tasks and are unlikely to engage spontaneously in strategies that provide greater organization for unrelated items. However, under conditions in which an appropriate organizational strategy is made explicit, nonschooled subjects are able to make use of it. Since differences do not generally appear until the schooled sample has received several years of schooling, it seems that some experience at school influences learning of organizational strategies. The lack of facility of nonschooled people in actively constructing connections between unrelated items should perhaps not be regarded as a difference in memory, but rather as a difference in a particular problem-solving skill that may seldom be necessary for subjects who do not have to learn to remember lists of initially unrelated items (as in school). Although nonschooled subjects take longer to learn associations between words, once learning is achieved, retention in memory is equal for subjects with different amounts of schooling.

Cole and Scribner (1977) point out that in contrast to poor performance on Western memory tests, anthropological accounts suggest that the memory of non-Western people is quite impressive for information that is culturally important, and philological studies suggest that illiterate bards show phenomenal recall for narrative material, which carries its own organization to aid memory. Mack (1976) reports that Howeitat shaykhs had detailed accurate memory of battles and raids fifty years after the events and cites T. E. Lawrence as speculating that "their very illiteracy has trained them to a longer memory and a closer hearing of the news" (Mack, 1976, p. 206).

Unfortunately, few studies have specifically compared the memory of schooled and nonschooled people for material that is important to them or that carries its own organization. An interesting study by Dubé (cited in Nerlove & Snipper, in press) found no differences in story recall for literate and nonliterate African adolescents. However, Mayan children with more schooling recalled stories better than did age-mates with less schooling (Rogoff, in press). Differential familiarity with telling stories may be responsible for this discrepancy. On tests involving reconstruction of organized three-dimensional scenes and recall of meaningful actions, subjects with more schooling showed better performance (Rogoff, 1980; Stevenson et al., 1978). As will be discussed later in this chapter, the fact that an activity occurs in the context of a test may give an advantage to schooled children, no matter what the content.

It has been suggested that strategy use is not involved in recognition memory, but cross-cultural recognition memory tests generally find better performance on the part of schooled subjects. This appears to be because schooled subjects understand the unusual task demands of the test with greater ease. Here again we see differences in facility with handling the demands of testing, rather than with the cognitive skill the test was intended to tap.

*Classification and Concept Development*

The studies in this section examine the organization that subjects impose on individual objects, words, or pictures. The dimensions commonly used are: taxonomic categorization based on semantic class (such as dog-cat); functional categorization on the basis of being used together (such as hatchet-log); and perceptual categorization on the basis of color, size, shape, and number. The preferred dimension used by a group is usually taken as evidence of the "abstractness" of their thinking. Classifying by color or number ("concrete" or perceptual features) is considered a more immature response, on the basis of developmental studies with United States children, than grouping by form (requiring abstraction of features from the stimuli rather than reacting to a "superficial" unidimensional feature). Grouping by function is in turn considered more abstract, and taxonomic categorization is regarded as the most advanced response (on the basis that it shows understanding of species-genus relationships). The nature of the stimuli (geometric stimuli, words, pictures, objects) limit the dimensions that can be used in any one study. Mode of organization has been investigated using three basic tasks: free association, classification, and concept learning.

*Free association.* Subjects are asked to respond with the first word that comes to mind on hearing a stimulus word. A common finding with United States schooled children is that with increasing age, there is a shift from syntactic responding (response word could follow the stimulus word in a sentence, e.g., red-house) to paradigmatic responding (response word is of the same grammatical form class as the stimulus word, e.g., red-black, dog-cat).

Several studies report that paradigmatic responding increases with increasing age and schooling. Subjects with more schooling also are more likely to give taxonomic responses (responses belonging to the same category, e.g., shirt-pants) and superordinate terms (e.g., pineapple-fruit) (Hall, 1972; Sharp & Cole, 1972; Sharp, Cole & Lave, 1979). Hall attributes the schooling effect to an emphasis in the early school years on conceptual and associative relationships among words.

However, as Sharp, Cole, and Lave (1979) point out, it is not clear whether increased paradigmatic responding represents differences in verbal development or in response patterns to a specific task. In standard free-association instructions, subjects are given examples that correspond to the stimulus word in both grammatical (paradigmatic) class and taxonomic class ("if I hear the word 'house,' I think of building, post office, store, shoe shop, tortilla shop"). The authors varied the nature of the examples, giving (for instance) hypothetical responses of "red, to live, or store" to the hypothetical stimulus word, "building." All subject groups were influenced by the instructions, giving noun responses to noun stimuli, and adjective responses otherwise. However, it is interesting that the change in instructions had the greatest effect on the secondary students, suggesting that education affects sensitivity to nuances of the instructions. In many of the studies of classification and concept learning, it will be important to consider differences in understanding of the task by different subject groups.

*Classification.* Studies of classification require subjects to sort objects (or pictures of them) and geometric stimuli into groups that "go together" or "are alike." Some studies have given subjects the names of objects orally and asked them to tell which two of three (for example) are alike and in what way. Populations vary in the preferred dimensions of classification, as well as ease of changing dimensions of categorization (taken as evidence of flexible organization), the exhaustiveness of their sorts, and the ease of verbalization of the dimensions used. A discussion of cultural and schooling differences in classification is found in Glick (1975).

*Familiarity of materials.* Price-Williams (1962) very early emphasized the importance of using indigenous materials, and he attributes his findings of no schooling differences in classification to familiarity of materials. Differences in classification on the basis of familiarity of materials were found by Okonji (1971a) and by Deregowski and Serpell (1971).

Irwin and McLaughlin (1970) tested the hypothesis that if subjects often differentiate objects in daily life, they will show little difficulty separating those objects into functional (as opposed to perceptual) groups in a free-sort task. Subjects sorted geometric stimuli (differing in color, shape, and number) or bowls of rice (differing in size of bowl, type of rice, and cleanness of grains). Nonliterate Liberian adults were able to shift dimensions more successfully when sorting rice than when sorting geometric stimuli, and did so as well as Liberian students did when sorting geometric stimuli. They could accurately describe the basis of their sorts more frequently with rice than with geometric figures. An extension of that study (Irwin, Schafer, & Feiden, 1974) reports that United States undergraduates responded to requests to sort bowls of rice with the same hesitance and bewilderment as shown by Liberian nonliterates when asked to sort cards decorated with squares and triangles. United States subjects were able to perform more sorts of the geometric figures than were Liberian nonliterates, who were able to perform more rice sorts than were the United States subjects. Both groups, when tested with an unfamiliar task, sorted most readily by perceptually salient and unidimensional stimulus features and had difficulty shifting dimensions.

An attempt to replicate this finding with Yucatan subjects sorting maize versus sorting geometric stimuli, however, found no differences in performance on the basis of familiarity of materials (Sharp et al., 1979). Greenfield (1974) also failed to find a difference favoring familiar materials in a sorting task with flowers (familiar) and rods (unfamiliar). However all subjects were given the flower-sorting task first, so there may have been a practice or instructional effect of the flower-sorting task on the rod-sorting task.

Greenfield provides important distinctions between levels of familiarity that might affect classification: familiarity with *mode of representation* (i.e., the geometric figures and pictures are two-dimensional); familiarity with the *objects;* familiarity with the relevant *features* of the object (e.g., blue, triangle); familiarity with a *dimension* (e.g., color or shape as culturally relevant dimensions); and familiarity of an *object-dimension relationship* (if people in the culture actually categorize these particular objects according to that dimension). A task can be culturally appropriate in meeting one of these criteria while being arbitrary in failing to meet another one of the criteria.

Since familiarity of materials may play a role in the performance of schooled versus nonschooled populations, we will separate studies that have used geometric stimuli from those using natural objects (or pictures of them) in the following discussion of schooling effects, remembering that familiarity of objects does not ensure cultural appropriateness of the task.

*Classification of geometric figures.* Serpell (1969) found that Zambian university students matched a standard predominantly on the basis of form, whereas illiterate women showed a slight tendency to prefer color. A similar finding was reported by Schmidt and Nzimande (1970), with schooled children showing a shift from color to other dimensions with increasing age/schooling, whereas nonschooled subjects showed no shift away from color preference. In addition, schooled subjects were more able than nonschooled to sort by all the available dimensions and to reclassify according to a different dimension. Gay and Cole (1967) also found schooled subjects to shift dimensions more readily than do nonschool children.

More sorting by form, greater ability to shift dimensions, and more facility in expressing reasons for the sorts accompanied greater schooling for Liberian Mano subjects (Irwin & McLaughlin, 1970). However, there was a familiarity problem: in Mano there are no words for triangle or square, and subjects had to express these concepts by analogy or description ("the ones with three corners"). This unfamiliarity of features of the stimuli would likely have an influence on performance.

Yucatan subjects with more schooling showed increasing ability to classify cards and to reclassify them according to a different dimension (Sharp et al., 1979). However, these data do not support the notion of a color-to-form or color-to-number shift as a function of schooling (contrary to the studies previously listed).

*Classification of pictures or objects.* Price-Williams (1962) gave classification tasks using plants and models of familiar animals to Tiv (Nigerian) children. There was no difference between the literate and the nonliterate children in the number of reclassifications by different dimensions, nor in the dimensions used for classification (including both perceptual features such as color, size, or situation, and functional aspects of the stimuli such as edibility).

In contrast, Greenfield, Reich, and Olver (1966) found differences in classification between schooled and nonschooled rural Wolof children of Senegal. The children were presented with sets of three drawings of common objects that could be grouped in pairs sharing either color, form, or function. Neither the schooled nor nonschooled children classified on the basis of function, but schooled children decreased in the use of color and increased in form groupings, whereas nonschooled children increased in color grouping and did not use form as a basis for grouping. With increasing age/grade, the schooled children increased in the use of superordinate explanations (naming a category that includes the pair chosen and excludes the odd member of the set), whereas the nonschooled children seldom used such explanations. This set of results may best be explained by the fact that the nonschooled children had great difficulty identifying the pictures. The authors state that even the youngest schooled children (who had attended school for only a few months) showed facility in identifying the pictures when compared with nonschooled children of any age.

Evans and Segall (1969) similarly found that nonschooled Ugandan children sorted pictures by color, whereas their schooled counterparts began sorting by function at about grade three. However, in this study, too, some of the children had difficulty recognizing the pictures. When real objects were employed, both schooled and nonschooled children sorted by color. A discrepant result is reported by Philp and Kelly (1974), who found that both schooled and nonschooled New Guinea children preferred sorting photographs by function rather than by perceptual or taxonomic dimensions.

The use of taxonomic categorization has been found consistently with subjects with more than a fourth-grade education (Cole et al., 1971; Scribner, 1974; Sharp et al., 1979). Subjects with less schooling use some taxonomic categorization, but in addition often classify on the basis of "functional entailment" in which objects act on each other (e.g., the file and the hammer sharpen the cutlass).

On the basis of extensive interviewing using verbal classification problems, Luria (1976) concluded that illiterate Central Asian peasants (in contrast with literate peasants) did not use words as symbols of abstract categories useful for categorizing objects. Instead, they grouped objects functionally, in terms of their role in a practical situation. When the interviewer tried to suggest grouping by taxonomic category, they generally rejected the suggestion, insisting that a person who used it would be "stupid" and that it did not reflect the intrinsic relationships among the objects. The responses of Luria's illiterate subjects suggest that rather than being unable to use taxonomic categorization, they felt that it was a trivial solution and that functional categorization was more appropriate. This is a difference in how the subjects define the task rather than in abstractness of thought. A transcript of an interview illustrates the point.

An illiterate peasant is given the problem of choosing which three of the following items are similar: hammer-saw-log-hatchet.

"They all fit here! The saw has to saw the log, the hammer has to hammer it, and the hatchet has to chop it. And if you want to chop the log up really good, you need the hammer. You can't take any of these things away. there isn't any you don't need!"

. . . [Interviewer suggests that another] fellow said that the saw, hammer, and hatchet are all alike in some way, while the log isn't.

"So what if they're not alike? They all work together and chop the log. Here everything works right, here everything's fine."

[Interviewer] Look, you can use one word—tools—for these three but not for the log.

"What sense does it make to use one word for them all if they're not going to work together?" (Luria, 1976, p. 58)

*Concept learning.* Concept learning (discrimination learning) tasks resemble the classification tasks in that they consider the subject's use of various dimensions and ability to shift dimensions. They differ in that the subject's task is to "guess" which stimulus the tester "has in mind." After some guesses and information about correctness, the subject is presumably able to detect the dimension that underlies the "correct" stimuli. A subject who has detected this concept will require fewer trials to predict accurately which stimulus is "correct" than will a subject who is simply learning the correctness of each stimulus through trial and error, without the benefit of using a concept as a simplifying principle.

Schooled Peruvian 6-year-olds were more proficient than were non-schooled age-mates at learning to use the concept of fruit when shown colored drawings of fruits and animals, and the concept "twoness" when shown geometric figures varying in number and shape (Stevenson et al., 1978). Concept-learning on the basis of color was equally easy for schooled and nonschooled Ganda subjects, whereas the concept of function was only used by schooled groups (Evans & Segall, 1969). However, since nonschooled subjects had difficulty identifying the pictures, and the word for "alike" in the instructions implies "alike in physical appearance" differences on the basis of schooling may have more to do with difficulties identifying the stimuli and the task than in using an abstract concept.

Difficulty in identifying the task also seems to enter into a study reported by Cole et al. (1971) in which nonliterate Kpelle adults performed a category discrimination task with tree leaves versus vine leaves (a familiar distinction). In one condition, the subjects were told to identify which leaves were from trees and which were from vines. In another condition, the same discrimination was involved, but subjects were not told that the distinction was tree versus vine leaves, but rather leaves that "belong to Sumo" versus leaves that "belong to Togba" (personal names). In the third condition, tree and vine leaves were split between Sumo and Togba, so that subjects had to learn which leaves belonged to which name one-by-one, rather than being able to make use of the rule to simplify the task. Learning was very rapid (one trial) when the tree-vine distinction was made explicit. However, when the distinction was not appropriately identified, learning was slightly slower even than when assignment of leaves to names was random. It is unclear from these results whether the problem was that the dimension was not specified, or whether the use of personal names actually misled the subjects.

*Summary.* Studies of classification and concept development generally show that compared to nonschooled subjects, schooled subjects are more likely to classify systematically on the basis of taxonomic category rather than function, or by form rather than color of geometric or unfamiliar stimuli. Schooled populations also show greater facility at shifting to alternative dimensions of classification, and at explaining the basis of their classifications.

Results of a number of studies suggest that differences between schooled and nonschooled groups may reside in differences in understanding of the task, identifying two-dimensional stimuli, and familiarity with the materials rather than in any cognitive propensity to classify the world in more or less abstract dimensions. Schooling may simply increase the likelihood that subjects consider the aim of the task to be the same as that assumed by the experimenter.

Cognitive anthropologists suggest that one cannot know the meaning of a question until observing the answer it elicits; the answer defines the question (Frake, 1977). In many classification tasks, differences in performance may reflect differences in what question subjects have decided to answer. An anecdote reported by Glick (1975) illustrates the point that task performance does not necessarily reveal ability on the construct the experimenter hopes to test, but instead shows the subject's most elegant solution to the problem as he sees it. Kpelle subjects sorted twenty objects into functional groups (e.g., knife with orange, potato with hoe) rather than into categorical groups, and would often volunteer, on being further questioned, that this is the way a wise man would do things. "When an exasperated experimenter asked finally, 'How would a fool do it,' he was given back sorts of the type that were initially expected—four neat piles with foods in one, tools in another, and so on" (p. 636).

### Logical Problem-Solving

To determine whether populations vary in the way they combine information to come to conclusions, researchers have given problems of rule learning and verbal logical problems.

*Rule learning.* These studies resemble the concept learning studies reviewed in the previous section in that they present problems for which there are simplifying rules or concepts. The studies reviewed under con cept learning emphasized ease of learning particular dimensions, whereas the studies in this section explore the ways that subjects combine dimensions or shift rules.

Ciborowski and Cole (1971) and Cole et al. (1971) report a concept learning experiment in which subjects had to apply either a conjunctive rule (e.g., choose the stimulus that is red *and* large) or a disjunctive rule (e.g., choose the stimulus if it is red *or* if it is large *or* both at once). Schooled subjects made fewer errors than did nonschooled subjects in learning the task, regardless of which rule was being learned. However, the authors noticed that the task arrangement had allowed correct responding on the unintended basis of position, rather than conceptual rules. In reanalyzing the results, the authors found that the effects of education were localized in the position bias parameter rather than in the application of the rules. In other words, it appears that the schooled and nonschooled subjects did not differ in effectiveness of learning conceptual rules, but rather in outsmarting the experimenters, making use of regularities in their concrete behavior. Other studies (Ciborowski & Cole, 1973; Cole et al., 1971) have replicated the finding of no differences on the basis of education in the learning of conjunctive and disjunctive rules in a variety of tasks.

A comparison between rule learning (how to combine known attributes) and concept learning (determining which dimensions are relevant) gave results congruent with others reported previously (Ciborowski, 1977). Education produced no effects on rule learning (for either a conjunctive or a disjunctive rule), but educated subjects showed better performance than did noneducated subjects on the concept learning problems. This latter task corresponds roughly to the tasks used in studies reported in the previous section on concept learning, in which education effects were also noted.

*Verbal logical problems.* In work done during the early 1930s, Luria (1976) used verbal syllogisms (see the following example) to probe the use of logical "devices" that allow the use of deduction and inference without reliance on direct experience. He found that Central Asian subjects did not treat the syllogism as if the premises constituted a logical relation, but rather treated them as unrelated, separate judgments. When asked simply to repeat the syllogisms, the illiterate peasants modified their form:

> [Syllogism] Precious metals do not rust. Gold is a precious metal. Does it rust or not?
>
> [Subject's repetition] "Do precious metals rust or not? Does gold rust or not?" (p. 104)

It is clear from many recall transcripts that the illiterate subjects do not perceive the problem in the manner in which the experimenter expects.

The experimenter is imposing a problem with rules running counter to the usual demands involved in asking an opinion. Subjects with some schooling repeated the syllogisms with no special difficulties.

When asked to make inferences on the basis of the premises of syllogisms, literate subjects solved the problems in the expected manner, but many illiterate subjects refused, not accepting the major premise as a "given," and instead protesting that they "could only judge what they had seen," or "didn't want to lie."

> [Syllogism] In the Far North, where there is snow, all bears are white. Novaya Zemlya is in the Far North and there is always snow there. What color are the bears there?
>
> ... "We always speak only of what we see; we don't talk about what we haven't seen."
>
> [E:] But what do my words imply? [The syllogism is repeated.]
>
> "Well, it's like this: our tsar isn't like yours, and yours isn't like ours. Your words can be answered only by someone who was there, and if a person wasn't there he can't say anything on the basis of your words."
>
> [E:] ... But on the basis of my words—in the North, where there is always snow, the bears are white, can you gather what kind of bears there are in Novaya Zemlya?
>
> "If a man was sixty or eighty and had seen a white bear and had told about it, he could be believed, but I've never seen one and hence I can't say. That's my last word. Those who saw can tell, and those who didn't see can't say anything!" (At this point a young Uzbek volunteered, "From your words it means that bears there are white.")
>
> [E:] Well, which of you is right?
>
> "What the cock knows how to do, he does. What I know, I say, and nothing beyond that!" (pp. 108–109)

From this transcript it appears that the subject and the experimenter are having a disagreement about what kind of evidence one should accept as truth. The subject insists that truth should be based on first-hand knowledge, or perhaps on the word of a reliable, experienced person. He obviously does not include the experimenter in the latter category, either because the experimenter does not claim to have had the experience himself of verifying the color of the bears, or because the experimenter is not considered an authority. (Triandis [personal communication] points out that the peasant's replies may also reflect the conflict between Russians and Central Asians, who were conquered by the Russians.) Given differing criteria for determining truth, the peasant's treatment of the syllogism cannot be taken as evidence of his logical functioning. Luria notes that the illiterate subjects' reasoning and deduction follow the rules when dealing with immediate practical experience, making excellent judgments and drawing all the implied conclusions. However, in a system of "theoretical thinking," they show several differences from the literate subjects. They refuse to accept the premise as a point of departure for subsequent reasoning; they treat the premise as a particular message about some particular phenomenon rather than as a "universal" given; they treat the syllogism as a collection of independent particular statements rather than as a unified logical problem.

Cole et al. (1971) found that when the problem format was changed to evaluating a stated conclusion of the premises, rather than answering a question on the basis of the premises, nonschooled subjects had much less difficulty. This supports the argument that the illiterate subjects are uncomfortable with having to answer a question for which they cannot verify the premises. When the answer was provided by the experimenter, the subjects were willing to consider whether that answer was a logical conclusion, and examined the hypothetical premises and conclusion to see if they fit logically.

Luria's findings have been replicated by Cole et al. (1971), Scribner (1975), Fobih (1979) and Sharp et al. (1979). Scribner characterized the reasons given by schooled subjects as "theoretic"—explicitly relating the conclusions to the premises—and the reasons given by nonschooled subjects as "empiric"—justifying the conclusion on the basis of personal experience or personal belief. She also examined the recollections of the subjects for the syllogism itself, and found very fragmentary recall on the part of the nonschooled subjects, as Luria found. However, the schooled subjects also showed a great deal of error in reproduction of the syllogism (though not as extreme as the nonschooled). Scribner emphasizes that the differences in accuracy of recall and the evidence that the problem was transformed by the nonschooled subjects preclude making conclusions about their logical processes on the basis of solution data alone.

Examining the use of theoretic reasons versus empiric reasons, Scribner (1977) found that it was very rare for a theoretical reason to be given for a wrong answer. However, use of empirical reasons was associated with correct answers at a rate that was only slightly better than chance. This effect was observed for both schooled and nonschooled populations from various studies (including Sharp et al., 1979). Thus, when nonliterate individuals treat the problem as a self-contained logical unit, they show the same logicality as literate individuals.

Scribner also points out that most nonliterate subjects respond theoretically to some of the problems, indicating that even though they use the empirical mode more frequently, that they are not dominated by it. She argues, in addition, that the nonliterate person's frequent failure to react to the syllogism as a logical problem should not be confused with a failure to think hypothetically. She cites a transcript of a subject using the hypothetical mode to explain his reason for not being able to answer the question: "If you know a person, if a question comes up about him, you are able to answer." He reasoned hypothetically about the practical situation in denying the possibility of reasoning hypothetically about information of which he had no experience.

*Summary.* Though there have not been many studies of logical problem-solving, the results are quite consistent. Schooled and nonschooled groups do not differ in their skill at learning conjunctive and disjunctive rules in rule learning tasks. Schooling does affect subjects' handling of verbal logical problems. There is no evidence that the difference is in terms of logical reasoning, but rather in willingness to accept a syllogism as a contained problem from which a conclusion may be drawn. The nonschooled groups are uncomfortable answering a question for which they cannot verify the premises. They generally give empiric answers to the problem, justifying the conclusion on the basis of personal experience rather than by relating the conclusions to the given premises. When nonschooled subjects are willing to treat the problem as a logical unit, they show the same logicality as the schooled subjects.

Scribner (1977) suggests that verbal syllogisms represent a specialized language genre that is recognizably different from other genres. Through practice with the genre, individuals become able to handle more complex versions of it, and understand the form of the problem. In Western schooling, people may become familiar with the genre through experience with story problems and other verbal problems in which the answer must be derived from the relationships presented in the problem.

Olson (1977) emphasizes that what is at issue is whether or not the meaning is assumed to be fully explicit and autonomous in the problem. He comments that if logic is defined as drawing "correct" conclusions from explicit premises, then performance that brings in personal experience would be evidence of illogical reasoning. On the other hand, if logic is defined as operating on premises as they have been personally interpreted, then such performance is completely logical.

## Piagetian Tasks

Piaget's theory of cognitive development focuses on the progress made in understanding the world by children as they mature and gain experience. It concentrates on understanding of the physical world (some would say, the physical world as conceived by the Western scientist), dealing with concepts such as causality, space, time, quantity, volume, and multiplication of classes. According to the theory, children progress through a series of stages (sensorimotor, preoperational, concrete operational, formal operational) in a regular sequence.

The tests that have been used to compare schooled and nonschooled groups are from the concrete operational and formal operational periods, comparing test performance at various ages to determine rate of development. It should be noted that these studies do not directly test Piaget's theory, since the theory is concerned with the sequence of development rather than the rate. However cross-cultural research has borrowed the tests, interpretations of performance, and concept of developmental stages from Piaget.

The research uses tests he developed to probe the thinking of Western European children. For example, the test for liquid conservation involves pouring equal amounts of liquid into identical containers, having the child verify that they contain the same amount, then pouring the contents of one of the containers into another of a different shape. A child who answers that they are still the same amount is considered a conserver, and one who maintains that there is more water in one container is considered a nonconserver. Piaget was most interested in understanding how the child reasoned, rather than in whether the child knew the right answer. He used a "clinical method" in which children's answers were probed and questions reworded in a very individual fashion in order to understand *how* the children came to their answers. Cross-cultural research using Piaget's tests has generally not followed the clinical method, but has standardized the questions and sometimes not even asked the children to explain their answers. This facilitates comparison of populations, but uses Piaget's tasks as intelligence test items in which reasoning is not probed but simply assessed for correctness.

In borrowing Piaget's tests and administering them in a standardized fashion, researchers have also borrowed Piaget's interpretation of what the test indicates: underlying development in logical thinking. There is reason to doubt that comparing quantities of water necessarily taps the same process in all cultures. Since the child's reasoning is seldom explored, all one can safely conclude from most studies is that the child has compared two glasses of water and answered "the same" or "not the same." Whether this is an important test of the child's understanding of the world is another matter.

In addition to borrowing the specific tests and the interpretation of performance, cross-cultural researchers have made use of the theoretical concept of "development." If nonschooled 9-year-olds do not conserve and nonschooled 13-year-olds do conserve, the researcher concludes that not until age 13 do the nonschooled children enter the stage of concrete operations, which implies more than simply whether a child can conserve or not. It implies a generalized structure of thought that is assumed to permeate much, if not all, of the child's intelligence. This is a far bigger inferential leap than simply concluding that the nonschooled children do not learn a particular skill or concept until age 13 (e.g., to impose organization spontaneously on material to be remembered, to explain the dimensions used in classifying geometric stimuli). Borrowing the concept of generalized cognitive development along a time line, the researcher may claim that one population is retarded relative to another, or even that one population is stunted in cognitive development (if adults do not pass the test either). With the tremendous amount of work done using the clinical method as well as the standardized approach in Western nations, it may be fair (though some would disagree) to talk about generalized cognitive development for these populations. However, when giving the same tests in standard form to populations for which the materials, the questions, and even testing itself is unfamiliar, it is quite a jump in inference to make conclusions about the logical stage of the people tested.

*Concrete operations.* The most commonly used tests that are presumed to tap children's concrete operational thought are the conservation tests, which involve a transformation of some object such that it appears perceptually different but conserves some essential quality. One test for conservation of *quantity* (liquid) has been described. Another conservation of *quantity* test involves changing the shape of one of two balls of clay, and asking the child if there is still the same amount. The clay may also be used to see if the child considers the *weight* or the *volume* to remain the same though the shape is changed. Conservation of *number* requires the child to ignore the varying length of rows of equal numbers of objects. Conservation of *length* involves changing one of two straight paths to a crooked path, or displacing them so the ends no longer line up. Conservation of *area* involves judgments of relative surface area of two fields with equal numbers of houses, either in neat compact rows or in scattered positions. A few other concrete operations tasks that do not involve conservation will be described as encountered.

An early study by Goodnow (1962; Goodnow & Bethon, 1966) is widely cited as finding no schooling effect on conservation (e.g., Ashton, 1975; Dasen, 1972; deLemos, 1969; Furby, 1971; Mermelstein & Shulman, 1967; Nyiti, 1976; Okonji, 1971b). However, there are problems with coming to such a conclusion from Goodnow's data. First, both populations (Chinese boys of low socioeconomic status) whose performance was analyzed to determine schooling effects, were schooled. Those labeled "schooled" were apparently drawn mostly from schools and partly from boys' clubs. Those labeled "semischooled" generally had at least one year of schooling and were drawn from boys' clubs. The problem is that the clubs for this sample, organized by the Department of Social Welfare, have an educational emphasis and provide "the three Rs" as well as other activities for the boys on a half-day basis five days a week. Whatever results may be found for these two populations cannot be interpreted as testing the effects of amount of schooling, but only the effects of different types of schooling. The second difficulty is that sampling of subjects was done on the basis of performance on the Ravens Matrices test, which the authors used as a measure of IQ. It has been demonstrated that performance on Piagetian tests is correlated with performance on IQ tests (e.g., Fahrmeier, 1978; Goodnow & Bethon, 1966), so the attempt to control for IQ would necessarily reduce the variability in performance on Piagetian tests. Thus, with both samples receiving some kind of formal schooling, and with only individuals having comparable "IQ" scores sampled, one would expect few differences in performance on conservation tests.

Indeed, Goodnow reports that her data (on conservation of weight, volume, space) show how little effect the schooling variable may have. She explains her results in terms of the deleterious effects of some of the school programs on the children's judgments. The Chinese children who were in school were apparently influenced by a special science program and justified their judgments of inequality with statements such as: "Because there's no center of gravity in this one," or "Because all the air has been pushed out of the round one" (p. 9). From the frequency of justification on such bases, the author concluded that such schooling leaves the boys with an unquestioning respect for booklearning and a feeling that the obvious answer must be wrong. In effect, Goodnow is arguing that schooling makes no difference in success on the tasks but does influence the boys' reasoning.

An early study by Greenfield (1966), on the other hand, shows large differences in conservation of liquids by rural schooled and nonschooled Wolof children in Senegal. The schooled children showed a pattern of improvement with age similar to that found with Genevan children, whereas the nonschooled children even at age 11 to 13 did not go beyond 50 percent conserving responses, with no significant increase over the 8- to 9-year-old nonschooled children. Greenfield suggests that "without school, intellectual development, defined as *any* qualitative change, ceases shortly after age nine" (p. 234).

Greenfield notes that the nonschooled children frequently justified their choice on the basis of the action of the experimenter ("There is more in this glass because you poured it"). This never occurred among the children who had been in school at least seven months. When the nonschooled children were allowed to pour the liquid themselves, they showed dramatically greater conservation. Greenfield interprets this finding as evidence of "magical" causal thinking—attributing special powers to intervening human agents—an interpretation that she did not substantiate. The children were observed to be very quiet and patient in the testing situation, with which they had had no prior experience. Nonschooled children are used to being commanded by adults, not to having their opinions asked. Perhaps the results merely indicate that the nonschooled children were acting in a respectful manner to this strange adult who had come all the way from her own country to pour water back and forth.

Would she have gone to all that trouble if she thought nothing was changing by her action? Furthermore,

> Outside the schoolroom, it is rare for a Wolof adult to ask another adult, or even a child more than six or seven years old, a question to which he or she already knows the answer. Where this kind of questioning does occur it suggests an aggressive challenge, or a riddle with a trick answer. . . . [S]ubjects unaccustomed to schoolroom interrogation would be in a poor position to understand the researcher's motives or to guess what sort of response was wanted of them. (Irvine, 1978, p. 304)

The nonschooled children may thus simply be responding to the strange situation involving a powerful adult by trying to give an answer that the adult might be presumed to expect. When the nonschooled children themselves poured the water, their conservation responses were essentially equal to those of the schooled children. Greenfield has more recently (1976) discussed these findings as showing similar underlying competences of all groups tested, though their performance differs according to the situation.

Mermelstein and Shulman (1967) found no differences in conservation of quantity between 9-year-olds from a Virginia community which had been without schooling for several years and 9-year-olds from a community which had had regular schooling. Six-year-olds (who had not attended school) from each community served as controls for differences between the two communities. There were no differences between them. The authors point out that the nonschooled 9-year-olds had in fact had eight months of formal schooling prior to the testing, and that this might have accounted for the finding of no differences (though the "schooled" 9-year-olds would presumably have had several years more schooling).

A study by deLemos (1969) is also cited frequently as support for a lack of schooling effects. Although deLemos made no formal comparison, the performance of schooled and nonschooled Australian Aborigine children (aged 10 to 14 years) can be extracted from tables that deLemos presented. For conservation of quantity and length, respectively, 12 percent and 18 percent of the nonschooled children show conservation, while 42 percent and 44 percent of the schooled children show conservation. It is thus quite surprising that deLemos states in the discussion that "there does not therefore appear to be a direct relationship between the development of conservation concepts and Western-type schooling" (p. 266). This argument seems to be based on the observation that there were some subjects who did not conserve even after eight years of schooling, whereas others showed clear conservation with no schooling at all. Though it is likely true that schooling is not a necessary nor sufficient cause for conservation, the data do seem to show some relationship between attending school and succeeding on conservation tasks.

Several studies have found schooled children more likely to conserve than nonschooled children of the same age. Okonji (1971b) found that schooled Ugandan children showed increasing conservation of length with increasing age/grade, whereas nonschooled children showed no such increase. Page (1973) classified most nonschooled Zulu subjects as preconcrete operational, and half of the schooled population (age 11 to 20 years) as concrete operational, on the basis of tasks tapping concepts of length and distance. Philp and Kelly (1974) and Kelly (1977) report that conservation of quantity and length increase with number of years of schooling for schooled New Guinea children, whereas there is no increase for a nonschooled group matched roughly in age. Laurendeau-Bendavid (1977) found schooling differences for Rwandan children on tests of conservation of number and of area and a seriation test (ordering sticks of slightly different lengths.) In the schooled group, performance improved in a regular fashion with increasing age; but for the nonschooled and partially schooled groups, there was no apparent improvement beyond the age at which they quit school. The author concludes that:

> School attendance not only has an effect on the development of concepts related to school subjects, but accelerates the development as a whole. . . . When schooling is lacking or is interrupted at some point, it appears that this slows development to such a degree that no evolution can be detected between the age of school termination and the upper age limit used. (p. 165)

Stevenson et al. (1978) also found schooled Peruvian 6-year-olds to perform better on a seriation task than did their nonschooled counterparts.

Fahrmeier (1978) reports somewhat inconsistent results with schooled and nonschooled Hausa children on seven conservation tests. With one sample, schooled children showed better performance only on conservation of number and of time, and with another sample, only on conservation of length and quantity. Response bias and selection bias problems complicate interpretation of these results, though it appears that schooling has small and inconsistent effects on conservation in this study.

A study matching Nigerian subjects on the basis of age and rural/urban residence (Owoc, 1973) found that schooled subjects after age 8–9 performed better on a test of conservation of liquid than did their nonschooled counterparts, whose performance leveled off after this age. A problem with this study involves the fact that the conservation question was worded such that conservation responses were not explicitly allowed ("Which of these has more water now—the calabash or the bottle?"). It may be that the older nonschooled subjects were more respectful of their interrogators and hesitated to suggest that neither of the stated alternatives had more water.

A careful study by Nyiti (1976) controlled some methodological problems that Nyiti feels are responsible for many findings of differences between schooled and nonschooled populations. He was familiar with the subjects' culture and language (himself a native speaker), and he did not follow a standardized procedure but rather a more clinical method, giving the child "as much chance as possible to manifest his available structures." Nyiti found no difference between schooled and nonschooled Tanzanian 8- to 14-year-olds in conservation of quantity, weight, and volume. The ages at which conservation was attained were very similar to those reported in other studies for European and United States children. The author cites an unpublished study by Kamara with the Themne of Sierra Leone that used the same careful method and similarly found no influence of schooling on the development of conservation.

A training study that attempted to teach nonconserving children to conserve also provides some suggestion that there are no differences on the basis of schooling and that what differences have been observed may be due to lack of understanding of task demands. On the basis of a pretest, Pinard, Morin, and Lefebvre (1973) chose nonconserving children from groups of schooled and nonschooled Rwandan and schooled Canadian 7-year-olds. (Unfortunately, figures are not given regarding relative performance of the three groups as a whole on this selection pretest.) Control groups evidenced little increase in conservation over the period of the study, which included posttests at two to four days and at two months following training. Training (which emphasized anticipation and compensation) produced large increases in conservation for each of the three groups, with no differences among the three. From this, it appears that the schooled and nonschooled subjects were equally able to profit from training in conservation. (It should be noted that the schooled groups had received little schooling—five to six months for the Rwandans and one year for the Canadians.)

The only difference between the three groups was the number of children who were successful on the compensation training session after a single session. Among the Canadian children, there were none, among the Rwandan schooled there were three out of sixteen, and among the Rwandan nonschooled seven out of fifteen children showed this immediate effect. Dasen (1977) suggests that these children had a "latent competence" for conservation of quantity, which was "activated" by very short training. It seems plausible that what these subjects learned in one training session was not conservation, but rather the nature of the problem being posed. Once clear as to what the question was, they could answer it. This argument suggests that among the nonschooled subjects in this study (and probably in others) who were classified as nonconservers, a large proportion were falsely classified because they had an unclear idea of what question they had been asked.

The previous conservation studies have predicted equal or better performance by schooled compared with nonschooled groups. There are a few authors who expect schooled children to do *worse* on conservation tests. Kiminyo (1977) discusses methodological reasons why schooled children would *appear* to do better on conservation tests and experiential differences that he feels would favor the nonschooled children. He suggests that Western education in African settings teaches language skills and rules for performance in examinations, and that school children may seem to give more conserving responses than nonschool children but based only on rote use of rules and guesswork. Schooling teaches children to give answers to questions, whereas nonschool children may be more susceptible to traditional cues implying that their statements are incorrect when an adult asks "Why?"—and therefore change their statements, appearing not to conserve. Kiminyo feels that nonschooled children have more experience with the environment and predicts that they would actually be more likely to conserve. However, he finds no schooling differences with 7- to 12-year-old Kenyan children on tests of conservation of quantity, weight, and volume. He concludes by suggesting that improvement in the content or teaching of the schools is needed, which seems somewhat at odds with his original hypothesis.

Armah and Arnold (1977) argue that schooling prevents Ghanaian girls from manipulating different objects and seeing their possible transformation—experience that they suggest is common in traditional families engaged in producing or selling pottery or foodstuffs. They predicted greater conservation of quantity and amount for nonschooled girls than for schooled girls, particularly for those in traditional families. They found no significant schooling effect, though the direction of results was as predicted.

Strauss, Ankori, Orpaz, and Stavy (1977) found that during the early school years, schooled Arab children made *more* errors in problems of understanding proportional reasoning than did nonschooled Arab children. The children were asked to determine the relative sweetness of solutions (proportion of sugar to water) when varying amounts of sugar and/or water were added to standard solutions. The schooled children did slightly better when dealing with the simple situation in which sugar was added (requiring the judgment "sweeter"). However, for more complicated problems in which water was added ("not as sweet"), both sugar and water were added ("just as sweet"), or two equal solutions were poured together ("just as sweet"), the younger schooled children (age 5 through 9) had much more difficulty than their nonschooled counterparts who began solving these problems at age 6-7. Graphs show that the 10- to 13-year-old schooled children are able to solve these problems, surpassing the nonschooled children. The authors suggest that early schooling promotes a general additive set in which addition leads to more and subtraction leads to less. The schooled children may be overapplying this rule to the problems that require coordinated relations between the amounts of water and of sugar. Schooling would thus be interfering with the young child's correct everyday concept, as shown by the nonschooled population.

*Formal operations.* Formal operational thought is expected to begin during adolescence. It involves hypothetical-deductive reasoning, with systematic exploration of all possible combinations. Cross-cultural studies using tasks intended to tap these abilities have  generally indicated much less success on the part of  non-Western and nonschooled populations than of Western schooled groups (Ashton, 1975).

Goodnow (1962) found that schooled Chinese youth did better than less formally schooled Chinese youth on a task of combinatorial reasoning (making all possible pairs of colors with no repetition of pairs). Methodological problems with this study (discussed earlier) would only have attenuated the differences found. Philp and Kelly (1974) found that neither schooled nor nonschooled New Guinea children had any success at all in predicting results and stating principles involved in the functioning of a pendulum. Laurendeau-Bendavid (1977) found that only Rwandan children whose education had extended beyond sixth grade (and only a few of those) were at the formal operational level of performance in a task involving understanding of probabilities. She concludes that schooling is necessary but not sufficient for the attainment of formal operational thinking.

Both the nature of the tasks used and the differences in performance between schooled and nonschooled subjects suggest that formal operational performance may be considered a product of high levels of Western schooling, but that even large amounts of Western schooling do not guarantee success on these tasks. It has been noted (e.g., Ashton, 1975) that even in Western European and United States populations the incidence of formal operational performance is much lower than would be expected of a universal stage.

*Summary.* The studies based on Piagetian concrete operational tests have obtained inconsistent results, compared to other topics reviewed. A large group of studies found no difference between schooled and nonschooled populations. However, a considerably greater number of studies found better performance on the part of schooled children than of nonschooled children. Only one study found nonschooled children performing better than schooled children, and this occurred only until age 10, when the schooled surpassed the nonschooled.

Several authors assume that, in fact, there should be differences on the basis of schooling. They have suggested at least three reasons to account for the findings of no difference. One is that if the schools were better, the schooled children would have the advantage in concrete operational tests that the authors expect them to have (Kiminyo, 1977). Goodnow (1962) suggests that the schools teach a lack of reliance on one's own thought and too great a respect for book learning. Fahrmeier (1978) proposes that schooling may make a difference only if there are "specific elements" in the curriculum. The inclusion in the curriculum of activity involving manipulation of concrete materials has been emphasized (Ashton, 1975; deLemos, 1969).

A second suggestion to account for findings of no differences involves insufficient differences in the extent of schooling of the two groups. Mermelstein and Shulman (1967) found no differences between schooled and "nonschooled" 9-year-olds, but the latter group had received eight months of schooling prior to the tests. Pinard et al. (1973) found no differences on the basis of schooling, but the schooled populations had received only a few months to a year of schooling.

A third argument is that differences between schooled and nonschooled groups should show up only in populations in which other influences (e.g., teaching at home, experience acting on the environment) would not provide the appropriate background experiences (whatever they might be) for attainment of concrete operations (Armah & Arnold, 1977). Okonji (1971b) claims that if the cultural environmental properties for the development of a certain concept are adequate, schooling will have a minimal effect. DeLemos (1969) suggests that less difference should be found on the basis of schooling for children living in an industrialized society as compared to a rural, nontechnical society. Ginsburg (1978) has demonstrated that schooling affects computational skills in one cultural group in which numerical concepts are not emphasized, but not in another group in which numerical concepts are important in the everyday economics. (Note, however, that a recent study [Ginsburg, Posner, & Russell, manuscript] using more complex arithmetic problems shows small but significant schooling effects for the latter cultural group as well.)

On the other hand, another group of arguments can be made to account for the findings of differences in performance on the basis of schooling, if it is assumed that there should be no real differences. The task used may be culturally inappropriate; if a more appropriate task were used, the schooled children (who have, through schooling, received more contact with Western concepts) would no longer have an advantage.

It is interesting that two studies that employed indigenous concepts found no differences between schooled and nonschooled groups. Greenfield and Childs (1977) explored the development of Piagetian concepts involving relational thought through interviews of Zinacanteco (Mexican) children regarding their own kinship network. Clear developmental trends were indicated for understanding of kinship terms from one's own perspective (egocentrism), understanding kinship terms involving reciprocal relations between two of one's siblings (reciprocity), and understanding kin terms from two points of view even when one is part of it personally (reversibility). Schooled and nonschooled children did not differ in the development of these concepts.

A class inclusion problem involving indigenous botanical classifications (Kelly, 1977) asked New Guinea children such questions as: Are there more instances of leaf vegetable A or leaf vegetable B? Are there more of leaf vegetable A or of leaf vegetables? The children were shown instances of each category, and questioning continued up the hierarchy of vegetables, food plants, living things. Kelly found no differences between schooled and nonschooled children tested in the vernacular in understanding the principles of class inclusion.

Schooling effects have been attributed to methodological defects involving lack of knowledge on the part of the experimenter of the child's language and culture, and lack of clinical probing of the child's thought (reliance on standardized methods, Nyiti, 1976). In several studies it appeared that the standard method may be more easily understood by the schooled populations. Pinard et al. (1973) found that with minimal training in a conservation task, nonschooled children showed far more spontaneous switches to conserving responses than did schooled children, supporting the idea that the nonschooled were simply learning what it was that they were being asked, whereas the schooled may have already understood the question even if they could not answer it correctly. Nonschooled children, having less experience with a testing situation, may be concerned with showing respectful behavior to the tester and trying to figure out the tester rather than to figure out the problem. Kiminyo (1977) points out that the nonschooled child will be more likely to change an answer when asked "why?" by an adult, since this traditionally means that the adult considers the child's answer incorrect.

The formal operational tasks given cross-culturally have provided fairly consistent results, with large amounts of schooling apparently necessary (though not sufficient) for successful performance. Ashton (1975) attributes this to the emphasis on symbolic thinking in the schools. However, it may simply be the case that the content of the formal operational tasks is taught in science and mathematics classes in higher education. Super (1979) elaborates these points in an interesting discussion of the implicit and explicit teaching of formal operational skills in Western culture.

In the view of the present author, the most valuable direction for cross-cultural Piagetian work to take would be to apply Piaget's philosophy and method of inquiry, rather than filling more suitcases with standardized versions of his tests to try on more populations. It is not a simple task for a person from one society to attempt to understand the logical processes of people from another; it requires intimate knowledge of the language and culture. However, Piaget made progress in understanding the system of reasoning of people who think far differently from him (e.g., infants and small children) by carefully observing and probing their behavior and explanations. Such an approach could be applied to understanding the (possibly different) logical system of people in other cultures.

## Explanations for the Relationship
## Between Schooling and Cognition

Now that the research on the relationship between schooling and cognitive test performance has been reviewed, alternative explanations for the observed relationships will be considered. Two categories of explanation (selection biases and test biases) suggest that methodological problems may be responsible for the relationship. The remainder of the chapter deals with speculations on schooling's influence on cognition. This involves, first, a discussion of what is meant by cognition—how general or specific are cognitive activities—and second, what aspects of schooling might mediate the relationship between schooling and cognition.

*Selection Biases*

As noted in the introduction, differences between schooled and non-schooled groups are likely to include other factors besides experience with schooling. Most of the studies reviewed in previous sections of this chapter did not attempt to control for such other variables. In fact, most did not mention selection biases as a possibility in discussing their sample or their results.

Parents who allow or encourage their children to go to school may be wealthier, have more modern attitudes, or hold different aspirations for their children than parents who do not. Schmidt and Nzimande (1970) note that schooled children came from less traditional families than non-schooled children. Arab children have been found to receive more schooling if their fathers express a strong orientation toward the future, have more education, and are somewhat dissatisfied with life as a farmer, compared with fathers of children who received less schooling (Sutcliffe, 1978). Parental education, occupations, and financial status predicted the amount of schooling received by subjects in Guatemala, the Yucatan, and Peru (Rogoff & Lave, 1979; Sharp, Cole, & Lave, 1979; Wilkinson, 1979).

Children who go to school may be more precocious, obedient, disobedient, daring, interested in schooling, well nourished, and so on than children who do not. Stevenson et al. (1978) report that Peruvian parents of nonschooled children believe that their children are "too young" for school, indicating selection of children for school on the basis of maturity. An informant of Greenfield and Childs (1972) claimed that parents send their stupid children to school so that the teacher can make them smart.

A few studies examined patterns of performance to determine whether schooled and nonschooled samples differed before experiencing different amounts of schooling. Laurendeau-Bendavid (1977) and Mermelstein and Shulman (1967) found that at ages prior to divergence in amount of schooling, groups showed comparable performance. On the other hand, Fahrmeier (1975) found differences between schooled and nonschooled groups after only a week or a few months of schooling. He attributes this difference to a motivational selection bias and notes great difficulty in recruiting nonschooled subjects to participate in his study. Stevenson et al. (1978) similarly found large differences between schooled and nonschooled children after only a few months of schooling (and had similar problems in recruiting nonschooled rural subjects), but interpret the results as showing the great effects on cognitive performance that only a few months of schooling can provide.

Longitudinal studies of children's characteristics before and after school experience indicate that differences in cognitive test performance exist even before any schooling has occurred. Super (1977) reports that Kipsigis children who later attended school had a greater advantage over nonschool children *before* school entry than after a year of schooling. This selection bias was accompanied by differences in parental education and religion for the two groups of children. Similarly, Irwin, Engle, Yarbrough, Klein, and Townsend (1978) found that Guatemalan Ladino children who later attended school showed better performance on a large battery of cognitive tests *before* they began school than children of the same age who did not attend. Attendance at school was also predicted by family economic level, parental education, and parental modernity. These results suggest that it is important to pay more attention to controlling for other factors that accompany differences in schooling.

Although selection biases have an influence on amount of schooling received, they may be insufficient to account for the demonstrated effects of schooling on test performance. When family background is controlled statistically, schooling has an important independent effect on test performance (Rogoff, in press; Wilkinson, 1979). Preliminary analyses of the Irwin et al. (1978) data base also appear to show an effect of schooling over and above the effects of family background and initial test performance differences (Irwin, personal communication, 1979).

## Test Biases

*Familiarity of materials.* Some authors have suggested that, to a large extent, the differences found between schooled and nonschooled individuals may be explained by greater familiarity of the schooled populations with the materials presented. This issue was presented in some depth in the section of this chapter dealing with classification, and other discussions of the problem appear in Pick (Volume 3, this series), Glick (1975), and Cole et al. (1971).

With unfamiliar materials, nonschooled populations may have more difficulty showing capacities that they can show with familiar materials. However, at least three sources of unfamiliarity must be considered: the materials; the operations to be performed; and the assemblage of the operations and materials, which is influenced by knowledge of what is expected for adequate performance (Cole et al., 1976; Lave, 1977). The rarity of studies successfully handling these problems means that this alternative cannot be ruled out as a major determinant of the findings of better performance on the part of schooled than nonschooled subjects.

*Familiarity of language.* In some studies, the language used in testing has been more familiar to the schooled groups than to the nonschooled. This may be justified by the researchers on the basis of "controlling" for language differences by using the official language of the country, which is generally also the school language. For example, Stevenson et al. (1978) tested Peruvian Quechua children in Spanish, the official school language. The nonschooled Quechua were screened for inclusion in the study on the basis of being able to answer several questions in Spanish. However, it was sometimes necessary for the tester (who was partially bilingual) to translate words into Quechua during the tests. It is interesting that there was a very high rate of refusal to participate on the part of these nonschooled Quechua children. The authors also report that the intercorrelations among their large battery of tasks was higher for nonschooled than schooled groups. They suggest that schooling imparts a variety of specific skills, increasing differentiation of cognitive processes. Another interpretation, however, is that the nonschooled children's performances correlated to a higher degree because of a large influence on their performance of understanding of the tasks. Within the nonschooled group, children with greater Spanish language skills (as well as familiarity with testing or comfort with strangers) would likely have shown consistently better performance across all tasks than those who had not figured out what was going on.

Hall, Reder, and Cole (1975) have demonstrated that differences in dialect have an effect on test performance. Recall of stories was equal for white United States children tested in standard English and black United States children tested in black English vernacular, though white children recalled more than black children when they were tested in standard English, and black children did better than white when they were tested in black English vernacular. Such findings emphasize the importance of equating task demands in terms of familiarity rather than administering an identical test to all groups.

*Familiarity with the test situation and demands.* An obvious difference between schooled and nonschooled groups is in familiarity with being tested per se. McNemar (1940) emphasizes the likelihood that differences in rapport with adults account for performance differences of schooled and nonschooled children. As suggested several times earlier in this chapter, differences in understanding of the task may account for many of the findings of difference in performance on the basis of schooling. Scribner (1976) cites Orne as finding it impossible to design an experiment *without* demand characteristics, that is, an experiment in which subjects do not construct hypotheses regarding the "problem" under investigation. Goodnow (1976) proposes that differences between groups may be due largely to interpretation of what problem is being solved in the task, and different values regarding "proper" methods of solution (e.g., speed, reaching a solution with the minimum of moves or redundancy, physically handling materials versus "mental shuffling," original solution versus deference to authority). Schooled children are likely to have had more practice figuring out what an adult is really asking when the adult does not reveal all aspects of performance that will be evaluated. Sharp et al. (1979) found that schooled subjects were more sensitive to nuances of their instructions. Vernon (1969) and Mehan (1976) discuss a large number of extrinsic factors that may influence performance for subjects unfamiliar with testing.

Schooled people are more familiar with an interview or testing situation in which a high-status adult, who already knows the answer to the question, requests information of a lower status person, such as a child. It is not uncommon in traditional societies for the interaction between adults and children to be characterized in terms of commands by the adult and compliance by the child (Harkness & Super, 1977). In such a society, a year of school dramatically increases children's ability to finish a test—regardless of correctness of answers—and increases the number of words used in responding (Super, 1977). Blount (1972) has pointed out that in traditional cultures, children are unlikely to be allocated "conversational peer" status, in which either person may initiate conversation. The traditional adults seldom ask children's opinions. In addition, individual performance may be unfamiliar to nonschooled children in cultures in which children form cohesive groups somewhat independent of adult society (Jordan, 1977).

Schooling also provides practice with certain conventions and genres, such as Western conventions for representing depth in two-dimensional pictures; the genre of the story problem (similar to the syllogism) in which one must rely only on information given in the problem to reach the answer; and the common format of test items (e.g., multiple choice). Schooling may also provide students with a common view of what is "clever" (e.g., classification of objects by taxonomic category rather than by their function).

Students become familiar with other aspects of testing. An emphasis on fast performance, as in a timed test, may be unusual outside of school in many cultures. Cazden and John (1971) note that in some cultures, it is uncommon to be tested at an arbitrary point in the learning process, but rather that learners begin to participate in an activity when they feel competent at the skill being learned. Schooling would clearly provide familiarity with having to answer a question before the content has been fully mastered. Students learn that answers are to be reached by working independently from neighbors rather than by collaborating (otherwise known as cheating). Students may have more experience exploring strange materials, so that strange apparatus may be less likely to evoke fear (as has been observed among nonschooled subjects in one study, Cole et al, 1971).

These arguments suggest that schooling affects familiarity with aspects of the test situation that are common to both schooling and cognitive testing, rather than affecting anything that could be called a more general cognitive skill. In the next section of the paper, we will consider the issue of the generalizability of cognitive skills, especially cognitive skills evidenced in tests.

## The Issue of the Generality of Cognitive Skills

Before discussing the effects that specific aspects of schooling might have on cognitive skills, it is necessary to consider what we mean by cognitive skills—especially the issue of how far we are willing to generalize performance in a particular situation to a more general underlying ability. For example, what conclusions about generality can be drawn from successful performance on a syllogism problem? That the individual (a) will do well on the next syllogism? (b) will do well on other kinds of logic problems? (c) will be logical in many situations? or (d) is smart?

The studies reviewed in this chapter have varied in the degree to which they generalize performance on particular tasks to specific skills versus general underlying abilities (e.g., the perception of depth in pictures, the ability to think abstractly or logically). Researchers seem to make decisions regarding the generality of their findings on the basis of assumptions rather than of evidence of generality or specificity of skills. Three aspects of this assumption will be discussed: the generalizability of test skills to cognitive skills used in everyday life, the relation of test skills to skills used in school, and the separability of underlying cognitive processes from the contexts in which they are used.

*Generalizability of test skills to everyday cognitive skills.* This issue relates to the previous section on test bias, in that some populations have less familiarity with the demands of testing than others, so the tests may not be equally ecologically valid for both populations. Scribner (1976) provides a thoughtful discussion of the role of the experiment in cross-cultural research. She points out that subjects who perform poorly on tests often can be observed to use elegant reasoning processes in situations outside of the experiment. Cole (1975) and Labov (1970) similarly describe subjects who seem to lack an ability such as taking the listener's point of view or talking fluently, but exhibit sophisticated cognitive skills in the same domain outside of the experimental setting.

The question of the ecological validity of tests is important not only to comparisons of populations differing in experience with tests (as in the cross-cultural studies) but also to research in which the subjects are familiar with tests but the skills they use in tests may nevertheless not generalize to the skills they use in everyday life, because of the situational specificity of skills (Mehan, 1976). Charlesworth (1976) documents a long history of studies demonstrating that performance on intelligence tests does not predict (or has not been validated on) intelligent behavior in everyday life. (It should be noted that intelligence tests were invented to predict school performance.) Charlesworth proposes that psychologists should observe intelligent behavior in everyday life—studying both environments and persons—in order better to identify basic cognitive skills that are involved in successful adaptation to the environment and thus to construct more "ecologically valid" measures to identify these skills. Others (Cole, Hood, & McDermott, 1978; Kessel, 1979; Laboratory of Comparative Human Cognition, 1979; Mehan, 1976) argue that we should be studying cognitive activities in the contexts in which they naturally occur, taking into account the richness of the situation (including the test situation) that people use to support their cognitive activities.

*The relationship between cognitive skills used in tests and those taught and used in school.* Versions of most of the cognitive tasks given in cross-cultural experiments can be found in Binet's early work searching for behavior that predicted performance in school.

The correlation between successful performance on Binet's tasks and success in school was a tautology; the items were picked because they discriminated between children at various levels of academic achievement. Might we not be witnessing the converse of that process when we observe people with educational experience excelling in experimental tasks whose form and content are like those they have learned to master in school? (Cole et al., 1976, p. 227)

Psychologists commonly assume that the skills tapped in cognitive tests develop rather independently from such environmental factors as schooling, and that they measure underlying capacities that are not specifically taught in school. When a connection between test performance and schooling is found, this is interpreted as showing that schooling is "a powerful agent for changing the direction in which the course of human cognitive development will flow" (Schmidt & Nzimande, 1970, p. 147). This interpretation suggests that tests tap something far more profound than simply skills that are taught in school.

School and test skills are often given a place of honor in the cognitive repertoire although we have no evidence that they deserve such a position on the basis of being more basic or general in intellectual functioning than are cognitive skills used in everyday life. Interest in cognitive activities manifested in tests may be due to their importance for success in the academic environment rather than because of any general importance for humans in other environments. Neisser (1976) points out that academicians construct the tests, and by definition have done well themselves in school:

> This is one reason why academic people are among the stoutest defenders of the notion of intelligence, and why the tests seem so obviously valid to us who are members of the academic community. . . . There is no doubt that Academic Intelligence [in which he includes performance in experiments on cognition] is really important for the kind of work that we do. We readily slip into believing that it is important for *every* kind of significant work. . . . Thus, academic people are in the position of having focused their professional activities around a particular personal quality, as instantiated in a certain set of skills. We have then gone on to *define* the quality in terms of this skill set, and ended by asserting that persons who lack these special skills are unintelligent altogether. (p. 138)

Outside the academy, Neisser points out, this specialized definition of intelligent behavior is not agreed with—academicians are not regarded as having generalized intelligence, but instead as being ineffectual, lacking good sense, and overly concerned with trivia. Academicians, on the other hand, can be heard bemoaning the fact that academic reasoning is not used in everyday life (see, for example, the transcript of an open discussion on schooling and the acquisition of knowledge, Anderson, Spiro, & Montague, 1977, pp. 255–257).

*The separability of cognitive processes from the contexts in which they are used.* Conceptions of cognitive ability have ranged from a broad unitary ability to innumerable skills inseparable from situations. The most general view is that test performance is indicative of a unitary cognitive ability (like a trait) characteristic of each person; that is, characteristic of all of the individual's cognitive processes.

An intermediate position is that several (or even many) cognitive abilities rather than just one can be identified, but each subability is fairly general across a large number of situations for any one individual. For example, Stevenson et al. (1978) selected a broad battery of memory and cognitive tasks for testing Peruvian children, because they were convinced that cognitive functioning is specific rather than general (on the basis of what they consider to be low intercorrelations among cognitive tasks).[1] They state, however, that they did not test material directly taught in school, since they were interested in the development of cognitive abilities rather than in the acquisition of specific information. This view seems to differ from the unitary ability stance only in assuming a larger (but still finite) number of abilities and in giving a variety of tests, instead of one, to get a more accurate measurement of the rate of cognitive development.

The most specific view of cognitive activities is that they are not separable from their use in particular situations, that performance does not represent an underlying ability but rather a learned skill in handling a particular situation, and that transfer from one situation to another is limited. Individuals thus would not differ in the "power" of their thinking, but simply in the contexts in which they apply their cognitive processes. Those with experience in one context will be fluent in the application of that skill to that kind of problem, but not necessarily to another problem with which they are less familiar. Test performance may not generalize to the treatment of everyday problems, and intelligent behavior in one everyday problem may not generalize to another, even though we might be able to name some processes (e.g., memory, logical thinking, referential communication) that all the activities have in common. Individual (or cultural) differences may not lie in one's "ability" to apply certain processes (across situations or contexts), but rather in the contexts in which those processes are habitually applied. This would produce differences between individuals or groups in facility with the process in any one context, but lack of consistency in the application of processes across contexts.

Psychologists have long debated the amount of transfer expected from specific activities to other activities (Vygotsky, 1962). Thorndike (1914) described the common view that:

> The words accuracy, quickness, discrimination, memory, observation, attention, concentration, judgment, reasoning, etc., stand for some real and elemental abilities which are the same no matter what material they work upon;

that . . . in a more or less mysterious way learning to do one thing well will make one do better things that in concrete appearance have absolutely no community with it. (p. 272)

Thorndike's issue of "mental discipline" is the same question as the degree of transfer of processes involved in one cognitive activity to another context. An interesting discussion of generalization from one domain to another appears in Cole et al. (1976), and a paper by Ginsburg (1977) treats some problems in determining the nature of transfer of skills from one situation to another.

Cole and Scribner (1975) point out that most psychologists think that it is possible (in principle and in practice) to examine cognitive processes without concern for the content of what is being processed, i.e., to neutralize the task so that performance reflects "pure process." Cole and Scribner question the feasibility of ever separating process and content and suggest further that there is no such thing as process divorced from content (or context). (Relevant discussion of the distinguishability of the processes and products of thought appears also in Price-Williams's chapter in Volume 2 of this *Handbook*.)

The question of separating content and process is important not only to psychologists interested in group or individual differences in cognitive functioning, but also to theorists (e.g., Piaget) who suggest that various task performances relate to each other in an integrated structure. Piaget's theory needs the concept of horizontal décalage to account for the fact that each individual does not simultaneously acquire all skills that are theoretically related. Flavell (1971) discusses difficulties in determining whether different cognitive performances are indeed bound together in a structured system of thought as the theory suggests. Dasen and Heron (this volume) also discuss Piaget's concept of "structure d'ensemble" in cross-cultural research.

I have discussed the issue of the degree of generality of cognitive performance observed in tests in some depth because it pervades the research and the conceptions of the effects of schooling on cognitive abilities. No resolution of alternate views is possible here. However, we should be cautious about assuming generality across situations without evidence of transfer, in order to avoid misleading ourselves and in order to keep from reaching overbroad conclusions regarding the thinking processes of some populations. Our sample of performance may be too narrow (if general abilities exist but need to be sampled more broadly) or may be based on performance in an activity that is irrelevant to the conclusions we wish to make (if process and content cannot be separated).

In the following discussion of the mechanisms by which schooling might affect cognition, it will be apparent that some authors assume generality or extensive transfer of test and school skills, whereas others propose that specific skills taught in school produce specific effects on cognitive performance. It is especially interesting that it has been suggested that schooling teaches the ability to transfer information and skills from one context to another and to make use of general rules by which specific instances may be understood (Brown, 1977; Scribner & Cole, 1973).

*Speculations on the Mechanism of Schooling's Influence on Cognition*

Most of the studies reviewed in this chapter have suggested that something about schooling promotes cognitive development, but they seldom specify what it is about schooling that might have an effect. Bovet (1974) proposes that schooling develops an analytic approach useful in conservation tasks. Furby (1971) claims that Western schooling teaches children to reason logically on the basis of empirical observation, thus diminishing "magical thinking."

There is a remarkable lack of empirical research studying the mechanism for schooling's presumed effect. Assuming that the results reporting a connection between schooling and cognitive test performance are not simply a function of selection and test bias, it is crucial to specify what *aspects* of schooling might influence particular cognitive skills.

*Schooling's emphasis on searching for general rules.* It has been proposed that schooling emphasizes the use of explicitly stated rules, and that schoolchildren are taught to look for rules from which specific instances can be understood. Schooling may emphasize the search for universals and for principles by focusing on classification of knowledge and use of formal symbol systems, such as mathematics and logic, that are applied to a large range of materials and even applied within the system itself, as in algebra (Cole et al., 1971; Goodnow, 1976; Munroe & Munroe, 1975).

Scribner and Cole (1973) suggest that practice applying common operations (e.g., counting, classifying) to a multitude of tasks underlies the tendency of schooled people to generalize rules across situations. Being repeatedly exposed to problems of the same type produces learning-to-learn. Cole et al. (1971) found that schooled subjects were more likely to treat individual discrimination-learning stimulus presentations as evidence from which the general problem can be induced, whereas nonschooled subjects more frequently treated each new stimulus presentation as a separate problem. (The nonschooled subjects may not realize that the experimenter would structure trials according to an underlying rule.) The urge to find a general schema was so strong for schooled American subjects that they insisted on trying to apply general rules even if it meant violating the instructions of the task, or when in fact, no obvious concept was involved. This tendency *interfered* with their learning of information that was random rather than rule-governed—they went to great lengths to discover a rule when there was none, and their learning was slowed in the process. Ginsburg (1977) also makes the point that transfer of learning is not always desirable. Children make errors in overextending the rules of grammar ("I goed to the park"); in arithmetic, transferring the rule that order makes no difference from addition to subtraction would be an unwise generalization. These authors suggest that the school emphasis on search for rules may at times be counterproductive.

Other authors question the idea that schooled subjects are more proficient at transfer of skills to new situations. Irwin et al. (1974) suggested that, if formal schooling does enhance generalization to new situations, then Western schooled subjects should show less disparity in performance on culturally appropriate and on unfamiliar versions of a cognitive task than do nonschooled subjects. Their results show this not to be the case. Both groups showed facility with the familiar version of the task, and schooled subjects showed a slightly *greater* difference between culturally appropriate and unfamiliar variants of the task than the nonschooled subjects.

Lave (1977) tested the relative transfer of school-based learning and non–school-based learning by studying the use of mathematics skills by Liberian tailors varying in amount of experience in school and in tailoring. She gave mathematics problems resembling problems encountered in tailoring and others similar to school mathematics problems. Although both involved the same mathematical operations, years of tailoring experience was the best predictor (in a multiple regression analysis) of tasks resembling those performed by tailors, whereas years of schooling was the best predictor for school-like arithmetic problems. Both sets of skills had restricted generalizability, suggesting that school skills do not transfer more broadly than nonschool skills.

*Instruction in the verbal mode, out of context.* Several authors have suggested that what distinguishes school learning from informal instruction outside of school is that school instruction takes place largely through the use of language removed from its everyday context. Informal learning occurs through activities (including language) that are embedded in the context in which the information and skills are to be used (Bruner, Olver, & Greenfield, 1966; Scribner & Cole, 1973). Note that this distinction is somewhat overdrawn: all teaching involves a mixture of verbal instruction and demonstration.

Descriptions of informal instruction (e.g., Fortes, 1938; Kenyatta, 1953; Mead, 1964; Redfield, 1943) suggest that children learn by observing their elders and by participating in the simpler aspects of the activity as they become competent. The teaching adult more often provides a demonstration of the skill than a verbal rule, and the emphasis is on the learner's becoming a good observer and not asking questions. It is rare in many cultural settings to find an interaction that can be identified as an explicit teaching session (Bruner, Olver, & Greenfield, 1966; Rogoff, 1977a). Nash (1967) describes the way Mayan adults learn to weave on factory footlooms: they silently watch an experienced weaver perform the process over and over for several weeks, and then take up the equipment themselves and competently perform the entire process. Goody (1978) notes that Gonja pupils learning to weave virtually never ask questions of the teacher. Learning by observation may require different skills on the part of the learner than does learning by verbal rules (Childs & Greenfield, in press; Lave, in press).

In school instruction, most lessons involve information or skills in which the concrete referent is not present (e.g., geography) or in many cases no concrete referent exists (e.g., in school arithmetic, children learn to add numbers rather than numbers of things). Vygotsky (1962) suggested that in school, "scientific" concepts are transmitted by learning a general definition (e.g., for "exploitation") and then learning to apply it to instances. He contrasted these concepts with "spontaneous" concepts that characterize learning outside of school, in which we build concepts (e.g., "brother") through experience with many concrete instances of it. Schooling's emphasis on learning "scientific" concepts apart from context may relate to the findings that schooled people are more likely to use taxonomic categories and nonschooled people use more functional categories.

Greenfield (1972) and Greenfield and Bruner (1969) have proposed that practice using language out of context makes mental manipulations and organization of concepts possible, and increases the use of abstract thought. Ashton (1975) similarly suggests that schoolchildren learn to appreciate the process, rather than the specific product, of thought through talking about objects in their absence, and that they acquire a consciousness of what it is they actually "know" and how they solve problems from being forced to code and recode information along abstract dimensions.

Scribner and Cole (1973) state that informal learning is not likely to promote verbal formulation on the part of the learner any more than it does on the part of the model. This would account for frequent findings that schooled subjects have an easier time explaining their reasoning than do nonschooled subjects. In addition, it relates to the ease with which subjects can communicate with each other when the immediate context is removed, as when subjects are asked to describe some stimulus objects so that a person on the other side of a screen could tell which of an identical set of objects was being described. Cole and Scribner (1974) report that nonliterate Kpelle adults had difficulty communicating unambiguously about objects that they did not view in common. Triandis (personal communication) points out that in ordinary situations, the most effective communication may involve interdependent verbal and nonverbal messages (e.g., saying "this stick" and pointing at it), rather than a highly specified verbal statement by itself.

A few studies have investigated the relationship between mode of instruction and children's cognitive skills. Rogoff (1977a) explored the relationship between performance on memory tests and experience with verbal instruction versus demonstration outside of school (in maternal instruction). The Mayan children whose mothers used predominantly verbal instruction performed better on verbal memory tests than did children whose mothers predominatly used demonstration. It is interesting that this effect was limited to verbal memory tests; there was no relationship between mode of instruction and spatial memory test performance. Jordan (1977) reports a similar relationship (with Hawaiian children) between verbal instruction by mothers and children's performance on the verbal scale of an intelligence test. Although these studies were correlational, the results are consistent with the hypothesis that mode of instruction may be one mechanism by which formal schooling influences performance on school-like tests. However, no relationship was found between mode of instruction and test performance for two United States populations (Jordan, 1977; Rogoff, 1980), perhaps because of more widespread reliance on verbal instruction than on demonstration by the United States mothers relative to the Mayan and Hawaiian mothers.

It should be noted that the speculations and research on mode of instruction confound three dimensions that could be separated in future research: use of verbal versus nonverbal instructions, use of general rules versus examples (given either verbally or nonverbally), and instruction embedded in participation, or out of the context in which the skill will be used.

*Consequences of specific skills taught in school.* Some effects of schooling may be due to specific skills that are taught in school and used directly in cognitive tests. For example, school is one of the few situations in which a person has to remember information deliberately, as a goal in itself, and make initially meaningless information make sense. Many of the strategies used in memory test performance (which shares those task demands) may be taught or encouraged by schooling.

Similarly, schooling may have an influence on classification tasks, especially those involving geometric stimuli, through the emphasis on form discrimination necessary to learn to read and write the alphabet. Glick (1975) proposes that training in reading alters the manner in which form discriminations are made and may affect attention to form when there are a number of possible dimensions of classification. Schooling's emphasis on defining, organizing, and classifying, and on learning concepts starting from general definitions rather than from exemplars may contribute to the preference of schooled people to classify on the basis of taxonomic categories (Luria, 1976; Munroe & Munroe, 1975; Vygotsky, 1962).

The particular format of school problems may provide specific background necessary to solve problems in similar format met in cognitive tests. For example, Scribner (1977) points out that the logical syllogism fits a specific genre of problem in which the listener is supposed to make judgments on the basis only of information presented in the problem, and that this genre is common in school (e.g., arithmetic story problems). Neisser (1976) refers to such problems as "puzzles" and points out that they are very different from the problems of everyday life. Olson (1976) argues that problems in which the text is scrutinized to determine whether it contains truth are a product of the development of written essayist prose. Since several authors have suggested particular consequences of learning the written form of language, we will consider it separately.

*Literacy.* Some authors argue that literacy allows new modes of thought that have widespread consequences; others propose that literacy provides specific skills that may or may not be important in a particular culture.

Greenfield (1972) argues that written speech is at a higher level of abstraction than is oral speech, in that writing requires independence from situational context. She claims that the implications for manipulability are great:

> Linguistic contexts can be turned upside down more easily than real ones. Once thought is freed from the concrete situation, the way is clear for symbolic manipulation and for Piaget's stage of formal operations, in which the real becomes but a sub-set of the possible. (p. 175)

The invention of literacy has been suggested to have had profound historical cognitive effects. With the possibility of written records, the importance of memory in preserving chronicles in the form of narrative diminished. At the same time, the concept of remembering information word for word (rather than gist) may also have arisen with the possibility of checking recall against written records (Cole & Scribner, 1977). Olson (1976) claims that some kinds of statements (definitions, logical principles) that are not easily memorized appeared with literacy. Goody and Watt (1968) attribute the concept of "logic"—an immutable and impersonal mode of discourse—to the invention and widespread use of the phonemic alphabet, which allowed recording of words unambiguously. Examination of inconsistencies in statements was made possible when written records replaced oral accounts, and Greek citizens became more conscious, comparative, and critical of historical and theological accounts. Scribner and Cole (1978a) point out that this historical/societal analysis cannot necessarily be taken as evidence for an effect of literacy on the contemporary individual. The individual in a literate society may not personally have to engage in writing in order to develop "literate modes of thought."

In a fascinating account of the uses and historical development of literacy, Goody (1977) argues that the graphic representation of communication "is a tool, an amplifier, a facilitating device . . . which encourages reflection upon and the organisation of information" (p. 109) not only for those who can write and read but also for nonreading people of societies with writing. Using illustrations from early written records, Goody suggests that the making of lists is dependent on writing, and that comparison, classification, and hierarchical organization of items is greatly facilitated by their visuo-spatial arrangement in a list. He points out, in addition, that lists of decontextualized words dominate psychological tests and suggests that familiarity with lists and with the classification systems that lists promote (e.g., alphabetic, taxonomic) influence the ability to recall such material. He points out that such facility may be irrelevant for people in oral cultures, "who are less adapted to this form of activity and who participate neither in its gains nor in its costs" (p. 111).

In Olson's (1976, 1977) speculations on the cognitive consequences of literacy, he emphasizes that human intellect cannot be separated from the technologies (e.g., writing, speech, numerical systems) invented to extend cognitive processes. He states that the conception of a general quality of mind (underlying ability) is useless, since it is only in the interaction with the technology (writing, navigational system, and so on) that cognitive processes operate. A similar argument is made by Luria (1971): intellectual processes do not exist outside of the social-historical (material) conditions in which they operate. This view argues that cognitive processes are cultural inventions and vary according to the cognitive supports and demands placed by the technology of the culture. Literacy and schooling are instrumental in the construction of a particular form of knowledge relevant to a particular set of culturally valued activities.

> All tasks or performances that we require from children in intelligence tests reflect competence with our technologies. They assess the level of competence of a child or an adult in using some artifact that we find important in our culture. . . . If it is agreed that our measures of intelligence reflect different kinds of symbolic competencies, it is perfectly legitimate to measure this level of competence to determine, for example, if a child requires more practice, but it is illegitimate to draw any inferences about so-called underlying abilities. (Olson, 1976, p. 195)

Note that although this view does not assume the existence of a general cognitive ability, the effects of the technology (writing in particular) are considered to have a profound effect on the thought of those who use this tool, transforming not only their written thinking, but also their treatment of oral language by transfer of the literate mode of thought.

Written language frees mental resources from the memory of the statement to be able to reflect on its implications. The written statement may be examined for consistency, and in the case of essayist prose, the reader can treat the statement as if the meaning were autonomous (contained in the text itself) and independent from the social context of the writer and reader. In oral language, the context and the interaction between speaker and listener help to establish the meaning, which can be "negotiated" in the interaction.

Olson argues that cognitive activity in the literate use of language (both written and oral) cannot be generalized to the everyday use of language and other cognitive skills, since their technologies and purposes are different. In literate thought, the meaning and truth is to be ascertained in the statement itself, whereas in everyday thought, social information is taken into account to determine meaning. People who are literate and schooled are competent (through practice with written technology) in examining statements in isolation for logical meaning (as with logical syllogisms), whereas those without this experience do not examine reality in this manner.

Olson does not suggest the corollary, that people without literate experience might be more competent at determining the meaning of contextual and interpersonal cues. Various suggestions of two parallel "ways of knowing"—analytic versus holistic or relational; field dependent versus field independent—might imply that training in the literate mode of thought could have a tradeoff in everyday intellectual functioning emphasizing embeddedness in context. The possibility that acquiring literacy produces changes in hemispheric lateralization of the brain has been suggested by Bogen (1975), McLuhan (1978), and Vargha-Khadem, Genesee, Seitz, and Lambert (1977).

Olson (1976) suggests that in cultures lacking written prose, people are less concerned with the formulation of general statements than in cultures with widespread literacy. He suggests that this difference is responsible for differences observed between cultures in the tendency to search for generalizations. He also attributes the cognitive changes that have been observed near the onset of schooling (White, 1965) to the familiarity gained with literacy at that age.

The only work that tests the effects of literacy per se on performance on cognitive tests is that of Scribner and Cole (1978a, 1978b). They point out that most of our ideas about the importance of writing are tied up with school-based writing—the production and comprehension of essayist text (expository writing).

The assumption that logicality is in the text and the text is in school can lead to a serious underestimation of the cognitive skills involved in non-school, non-essay writing, and, reciprocally, to an overestimation of the intellectual skills that the essayist [text] "necessarily" entails. This approach binds the intellectual and social significance of writing too closely to the image of the "academic" and the professional member of society. (1978a, p. 24)

Scribner and Cole examined the cognitive activities of the people of a traditional, non–school-going society who use an indigenous writing system. The Vai people of Liberia have independently developed a phonetic writing system, widely available throughout the society, consisting of a syllabary of 200 characters with a common core of 20–40. Alternatively, some Vai individuals are literate in Arabic or in English. English is the official national language and is learned in Western-style schools; Arabic is the religious script and is learned in traditional Qur'anic schools emphasizing the rote memorization or reading aloud of religious passages usually without understanding of the language; Vai script is used for the majority of personal and public needs in the villages and is transmitted outside of any institutional setting, with a nonprofessional literate teaching a friend or relative over a period of two weeks to two months.

The Vai script has diverse and important uses, but Vai literacy does not lead to learning of new knowledge nor expository writing concerned with examining ideas. Scribner and Cole (1978a) predicted that such literacy would not have the general intellectual consequences that have been suggested to be the result of high levels of school-based literacy. They found little difference between nonschooled Vai literates and nonliterates in performance on logical and classification tasks.

To test the effects of learning and use of the various scripts, they proceeded to examine the component skills involved in literacy in the various scripts, using tasks having different content but apparently similar skills. Results of three of the tasks are described in the following. (It should be noted that all subjects are Vai people, varying in experience with different scripts and with schooling.)

In a *communication* task, in which the object is to describe a board game in its absence, they expected that Vai literates (who frequently write letters requiring communication carried in the text and not supported by context) to be more successful than Arabic literates and people not literate in any script. The English literates, who were high school students, were expected to be highly successful in this task as well. The groups ranked as follows: high school students literate in English, Vai literates, Arabic literates, and nonliterates.

The authors demonstrated specific consequences of Qur'anic schooling with a *memory* task resembling learning of the Qur'an (learning a string of words in order, adding one word to the list on each trial). On this task, English students again ranked first, but here the Arabic literates showed better performance than either the Vai literates or the nonliterates. On other memory tests (Scribner & Cole, 1978a; Wagner, 1978b), Arabic literates showed no superiority in performance over the Vai literates and the nonliterates, suggesting a very specific transfer of learning rather than a general transfer.

Since Vai script is written without word division, the authors suspected that Vai literates might have skills in integration of syllables into meaningful linguistic units. They gave a *language analysis* test involving listening to meaningful sentences broken into syllables that were presented at a slowed rate. Vai literates were better at comprehending and repeating such sentences than were Arabic literates and nonliterates. When the sentences were presented word by word instead of syllable by syllable, the Vai literates had no advantage over the other literates.

Results of these and other experimental tasks suggest that components of reading and writing may in fact promote very specific language-processing and cognitive skills, but that skills in classification and logic problems are not the inevitable outcome of learning to use alphabetic scripts or to write any kind of text. Whether the important influence on these tasks is experience with expository text is unresolved, since such experience is confounded with experience with Western schooling. Scribner and Cole expect that there would be specific but not general transfer from essayist text to some cognitive skills.

> Nothing in our data would support the statement . . . that reading and writing entail fundamental "cognitive restructurings" that control intellectual performance in all domains. Quite the contrary: the very specificity of the effects suggests that they may be closely tied to performance parameters of a limited set of tasks. (1978a, pp. 36–37)

Scribner and Cole (1978b) point out that the formulations of general cognitive development have not explained the processes by which general effects of literacy or schooling would be achieved. Nor have they tested literacy per se as distinct from schooling (which is likely to teach other things besides literacy). Scribner and Cole propose that specific activities promote specific skills. With increased practice under varying conditions, with a variety of materials of wide applicability, skills involved in literacy would become increasingly free from the specific conditions of the original practice.

Scribner and Cole (1978a) suggest that researchers begin more functional analysis of how literacy is used outside of school, to understand school-based and non–school-based literacy practices, and their implications for cognitive activity. They propose linking reading and writing activities to the competencies desired as outcomes, such as those required for participation in a technological society. The kind of writing that is emphasized in school (essayist text) may have a very specific role in meeting academic requirements but perhaps may not fulfill any other purpose.

## Summary

This chapter has reviewed research investigating the effects of formal Western-style schooling on cognitive test performance and considered explanations for the observed effects. Research suggests that schooled individuals have gained skills both in the use of graphic conventions to represent depth in two-dimensional stimuli and in the fine-grained analysis of two-dimensional patterns. They have increased facility in deliberately remembering disconnected bits of information, and spontaneously engage in strategies that provide greater organization for the unrelated items. Schooled people are more likely to organize objects on a taxonomic basis, putting categorically similar objects together, whereas nonschooled people often use functional arrangements of objects that are used together. Schooled groups show greater facility in shifting to alternative dimensions of classification and in explaining the basis of their organization. Schooling appears to have no effect on rule learning nor on logical thought as long as the subject has understood the problem in the way the experimenter intended. Nonschooled subjects seem to prefer, however, to come to conclusions on the basis of experience rather than by relying on the information in the problem alone. The results of Piagetian tests are somewhat inconsistent, but they suggest that schooled children are more likely to show conservation and that schooling may be necessary for the solution of formal operational problems.

A number of procedural problems were discussed that make it difficult to be confident about some of these conclusions. It is likely that schooling is not randomly assigned to individuals, but that the schooled and nonschooled groups differ in a number of other ways as well. In addition, a number of aspects of testing may be sufficient to account for the observed performance differences between schooled and nonschooled groups: differential familiarity with materials and operations used in the tasks, with language used by the tester, and with features of the test situation, such as understanding implicit instructions, comfort in talking to strange adults, and anticipating what the experimenter considers "proper" methods of solution. These problems limit the strength of the conclusions that can be drawn from the fairly consistent findings of better performance on Western tests by schooled than nonschooled subjects.

Assuming that these difficulties do not completely account for the findings, alternative mechanisms for the effect of schooling on cognition

were considered. The speculations vary in the degree to which they assume that the performance tapped in tests represents general versus specific cognitive skills, and the degree of generality of cognitive activities
across different contexts (e.g., tests, school, everyday life). Four influences
were discussed as possible mechanisms for the schooling effect: (a)
schooling's emphasis on searching for general rules; (b) the use of verbal
instruction out of context from everyday activities; (c) the teaching of specific skills in school, such as memory strategies, taxonomic categorization,
and the  treatment of "puzzles" in which the answer is to be derived from
information in the problem; and specifically (d) literacy, which may allow
the examination of statements for consistency or may simply teach some
specific cognitive skills.

Since the evidence is not strong for general rather than specific effects
of schooling on cognitive skills, it is suggested that the effects of schooling
be considered in the light of the uses to which skills learned in school are
to be put. The following account gracefully illustrates the issue of the generality of effects of Western education. It is the reply of the Indians of the
Five Nations to an invitation in 1744 by the commissioners from Virginia
to send boys to William and Mary College:

> You who are wise must know, that different nations have different concep-
> tions of things; and you will therefore not take it amiss, if our ideas of this
> kind of education happen not to be the same with yours. We have had some
> experience of it: several of our young people were formerly brought up at the
> colleges of the northern provinces; they were instructed in all your sciences;
> but when they came back to us . . . [they were] ignorant of every means of
> living in the woods . . . neither fit for hunters, warriors, or counsellors; they
> were totally good for nothing. We are, however, not the less obliged by your
> kind offer . . . and to show our grateful sense of it, if the gentlemen of Virginia
> will send us a dozen of their sons, we will take great care of their education,
> instruct them in all we know, and make *men* of them. (Drake, 1834, Book I,
> Chapter III, p. 27)

## Note

1. Some readers may wonder if the level of intercorrelations among tasks would
   provide resolution to the question of generality or specificity of cognitive activities. This is unlikely, since on the one hand, lower-than-expected correlations
   may be explained by the believer in generality as due to idiosyncratic aspects
   of the tasks, and on the other hand, higher-than-expected correlations may be
   explained by the believer in specificity as reflecting only the common demands
   of testing necessary for performance on all the tasks used.

# References

ARMAH, K., & ARNOLD, M. Acquisition of conservation in Ghanaian children. Paper presented at the meeting of the Society for Research in Child Development, New Orleans, 1977.

ASHTON, P. T. Cross-cultural Piagetian research: An experimental perspective. *Harvard Educational Review*, 1975, 45, 475–506.

ANDERSON, R. C., SPIRO, R. J., & MONTAGUE, W. E. (Eds.), *Schooling and the acquisition of knowledge.* Hillsdale, N.J.: Erlbaum, 1977.

BENNETT, J. H. B. *Schooldays: An ethnography of education.* Unpublished doctoral dissertation, University of Cambridge, 1979.

BERRY, J. W. *Human ecology and cognitive style.* New York: John Wiley & Sons, 1976.

BLOUNT, B. G. Parental speech and language acquisition: Some Luo and Samoan examples. *Anthropological Linguistics*, 1972, 14, 119–130.

BOGEN, J. E. Some educational aspects of hemispheric specialization. *UCLA Educator*, 1975, 17, 24–32.

BOVET, M. C. Cognitive processes among illiterate children and adults. In J. W. Berry & P. R. Dasen (Eds.), *Culture & cognition: Readings in cross-cultural psychology.* London: Methuen, 1974.

BROWN, A. L. The development of memory: Knowing, knowing about knowing, and knowing how to know. In H. W. Reese (Ed.), *Advances in child development and behavior* (Vol. 10). New York: Academic Press, 1975.

————. Development, schooling, and the acquisition of knowledge about knowledge. In R. C. Anderson, R. J. Spiro, & W. E. Montague (Eds.), *Schooling and the acquisition of knowledge.* Hillsdale, N.J.: Erlbaum, 1977.

BRUNER, J. S., OLVER, R. R., & GREENFIELD, P. M. (Eds.), *Studies in cognitive growth.* New York: John Wiley & Sons, 1966.

CAZDEN, C. B., & JOHN, V. P. Learning in American Indian Children. In M. L. Wax, S. Diamond, & F. O. Gearing (Eds.), *Anthropological perspectives on education.* New York: Basic Books, 1971.

CHARLESWORTH, W. R. Human intelligence as adaptation: An ethological approach. In L. B. Resnick (Ed.), *The nature of intelligence.* Hillsdale, N.J.: Erlbaum, 1976.

CHILDS, C. P., & GREENFIELD, P. M. Informal modes of learning and teaching. In N. Warren (Ed.), *Studies in cross-cultural psychology,* (Vol. 2). London: Academic Press, in press.

CIBOROWSKI, T. The influence of formal education on rule learning and attribute identification in a West African society. *Journal of Cross-Cultural Psychology*, 1977, 8, 17–32.

CIBOROWSKI, T., & COLE, M. Cultural differences in learning conceptual rules. *International Journal of Psychology*, 1971, 6, 25–37.

————. A developmental and cross-cultural study of the influences of rule structure and problem composition on the learning of conceptual classifications. *Journal of Experimental Child Psychology*, 1973, 15, 193–215.

COLE, M. An ethnographic psychology of cognition. In R. W. Brislin, S. Bochner, & W. J. Lonner (Eds.), *Cross-cultural perspectives on learning.* New York: John Wiley & Sons, 1975.

COLE, M., GAY, J., GLICK, J. A., & SHARP, D. W. *The cultural context of learning and thinking.* New York: Basic Books, 1971.

COLE, M., HOOD, L., & McDERMOTT, R. P. Concepts of ecological validity; their differing implications for comparative cognitive research. *The Quarterly Newsletter of the Institute for Comparative Human Development,* 1978, *2,* 34–37.

COLE, M., & SCRIBNER, S. *Culture and thought.* New York: John Wiley & Sons, 1974.

———. Theorizing about socialization of cognition. *Ethos,* 1975, *3,* 250–268.

———. Cross-cultural studies of memory and cognition. In R. V. Kail, Jr. & J. W. Hagen (Eds.), *Perspectives on the development of memory and cognition.* Hillsdale, N.J.: Erlbaum, 1977.

COLE, M., SHARP, D. W., & LAVE, C. The cognitive consequences of education. *Urban Review,* 1976, *9,* 218–233.

DASEN, P. R. Cross-cultural Piagetian research: A summary. *Journal of Cross-Cultural Psychology,* 1972, *3,* 23–40.

———. Are cognitive processes universal? A contribution to cross-cultural Piagetian psychology. In N. Warren (Ed.), *Studies in cross-cultural psychology* (Vol. 1). London: Academic Press, 1977.

DAVIS, C. M. Education and susceptibility to the Muller-Lyer illusion among the Banyankole. *Journal of Social Psychology,* 1970, *82,* 25–34.

DAWSON, J. L. M. Cultural and physiological influences upon spatial-perceptual processes in West Africa, Part I. *International Journal of Psychology,* 1967, *2,* 115–128.(a)

———. Cultural and physiological influences upon spatial-perceptual processes in West Africa, Part II. *International Journal of Psychology,* 1967, *2,* 171–185. (b)

DeLEMOS, M. M. The development of conservation in Aboriginal children. *International Journal of Psychology,* 1969, *4,* 255–269.

DEREGOWSKI, J. B., & SERPELL, R. Performance on a sorting task: A cross-cultural experiment. *International Journal of Psychology,* 1971, *6,* 273–281.

DOOB, L. W. Eidetic images among the Ibo. *Ethnology,* 1964, *3,* 357–363.

———. Correlates of eidetic imagery in Africa. *Journal of Psychology,* 1970, *76,* 223–230.

DRAKE, S. G. *Biography and history of the Indians of North America.* Boston: O. L. Perkins and Hilliard, Gray & Co., 1834.

EVANS, J. L., & SEGALL, M. H. Learning to classify by color and by function: A study of concept-discovery by Ganda children. *Journal of Social Psychology,* 1969, *77,* 35–53.

FAHRMEIER, E. D. The effect of school attendance on intellectual development in Northern Nigeria. *Child Development,* 1975, *46,* 281–285.

———. The development of concrete operations among the Hausa. *Journal of Cross-Cultural Psychology,* 1978, *9,* 23–44.

FLAVELL, J. M. Stage-related properties of cognitive development. *Cognitive Psychology,* 1971, *2,* 421–453.

FOBIH, D. K. *The influence of different educational experiences on classificatory and verbal reasoning behaviour of children in Ghana.* Unpublished doctoral dissertation, University of Alberta, 1979.

FORTES, M. *Social and psychological aspects of education in Taleland.* Oxford: Oxford University Press, 1938.

FRAKE, C. O. Plying frames can be dangerous: Some reflections on methodology in cognitive anthropology. *Quarterly Newsletter of the Institute for Comparative Human Development,* 1977, *1,* 1–7.

FURBY, L. A theoretical analysis of cross-cultural research in cognitive development: Piaget's conservation task. *Journal of Cross-Cultural Psychology,* 1971, *2,* 241–255.

GAY, J., & COLE, M. *The new mathematics and an old culture.* New York: Holt, Rinehart & Winston, 1967.

GEARING, F. O., & TINDALL, B. A. Anthropological studies of the educational process. In B. J. Siegal, A. R. Beals, & S. A. Tyler (Eds.), *Annual Review of Anthropology* (Vol. 2). Palo Alto, Calif.: Annual Reviews, 1973.

GINSBURG, H. Some problems in the study of schooling and cognition. *The Quarterly Newsletter of the Institute for Comparative Human Development,* 1977, *1,* 7–10.

―――. Poor children, African mathematics, and the problem of schooling. *Educational Research Quarterly,* 1978, *2,* 26–42.

GINSBURG, H., POSNER, J. K., & RUSSELL, R. L. The development of mental arithmetic in schooled and unschooled people: A cross-cultural study. Unpublished manuscript.

GLICK, J. Cognitive development in cross-cultural perspective. In F. Horowitz et al. (Eds.), *Review of Child Development Research* (Vol. 4). Chicago: University of Chicago Press, 1975.

GOODNOW, J. J. A test of milieu effects with some of Piaget's tasks. *Psychological Monographs,* 1962, *76* (36, Whole No. 555).

―――. The nature of intelligent behavior: Questions raised by cross-cultural studies. In L. B. Resnick (Ed.), *The nature of intelligence.* Hillsdale, N.J.: Erlbaum, 1976.

GOODNOW, J. J., & BETHON, G. Piaget's tasks: The effects of schooling and intelligence. *Child Development,* 1966, *37,* 573–582.

GOODY, E. N. Towards a theory of questions. In E. Goody (Ed.), *Questions and politeness: Strategies in social interaction.* Cambridge, England: Cambridge University Press, 1978.

GOODY, J. *The domestication of the savage mind.* Cambridge, England: Cambridge University Press, 1977.

GOODY, J., & WATT, I. The consequences of literacy. In J. R. Goody (Ed.), *Literacy in traditional societies.* Cambridge, England: Cambridge University Press, 1968.

GREENFIELD, P. M. On culture and conservation. In J. S. Bruner, R. R. Olver, & P. M. Greenfield (Eds.), *Studies in cognitive growth.* New York: John Wiley & Sons, 1966.

―――. Oral or written language: The consequences for cognitive development in Africa, the United States, and England. *Language and Speech,* 1972, *15,* 169–178.

―――. Comparing dimensional categorization in natural and artificial contexts: A developmental study among the Zinacantecos of Mexico. *Journal of Social Psychology,* 1974, *93,* 157–171.

―――. Cross-cultural research and Piagetian theory: Paradox and progress. In K. F. Riegel & J. A. Meacham (Eds.), *The developing individual in a changing world* (Vol. 1). Chicago: Aldine, 1976.

GREENFIELD, P. M., & BRUNER, J. S. Culture and cognitive growth. In D. A. Goslin (Ed.), *Handbook of socialization theory and research.* New York: Rand McNally, 1969.

GREENFIELD, P. M. & CHILDS, C. P. Weaving, color terms, and pattern representation: Cultural influences and cognitive development among the Zinacantecos of Southern Mexico. Paper presented at the meeting of the International Association for Cross-Cultural Psychology, Hong Kong, 1972. *Interamerican Journal of Psychology,* in press.

―――. Understanding sibling concepts: A developmental study of kin terms in Zinacantan. In P. R. Dasen (Ed.), *Piagetian psychology: Cross-cultural contributions.* New York: Gardner Press, 1977.

GREENFIELD, P. M., & LAVE, J. Cognitive aspects of informal education. In H. Stevenson & D. Wagner (Eds.), *Child development in cross-cultural perspective.* San Francisco: Freeman Press, in press.

GREENFIEL,D, P. M., REICH, L. C., & OLVER, R. R. On culture and equivalence: II. In J. S. Bruner, R. R. Olver, & P. M. Greenfield (Eds.), *Studies in cognitive growth.* New York: John Wiley & Sons, 1966.

HALL, J. W. Verbal behavior as a function of amount of schooling. *American Journal of Psychology,* 1972, *85,* 277–289.

HALL, W. S., REDER, S., & COLE, M. Story recall in young black and white children: Effects of racial group membership, race of experimenter, and dialect. *Developmental Psychology,* 1975, *11,* 628–634.

HARKNESS, S., & SUPER, C. M. Why African children are so hard to test. In L. L. Adler (Ed.), *Issues in cross-cultural research. Annals of the New York Academy of Sciences,* 1977, *285,* 326–331.

HUDSON, W. Pictorial depth perception in African groups. *Journal of Social Psychology,* 1960, *52,* 183–208.

IRVINE, J. T. Wolof "magical thinking": Culture and conservation revisited. *Journal of Cross-Cultural Psychology,* 1978, *9,* 300–310.

IRWIN, M., ENGLE, P. L., YARBROUGH, C., KLEIN, R. E., & TOWNSEND, J. The relationship of prior ability and family characteristics to school attendance and school achievement in rural Guatemala. *Child Development,* 1978, *49,* 415–427.

IRWIN, M. H., & MCLAUGHLIN, D. H. Ability and preference in category sorting by Mano schoolchildren and adults. *Journal of Social Psychology,* 1970, *82,* 15–24.

IRWIN, M. H., SCHAFER, G. N., & FEIDEN, C. P. Emic and unfamiliar category sorting of Mano farmers and U.S. undergraduates. *Journal of Cross-Cultural Psychology,* 1974, *5,* 407–423.

JORDAN, C. Maternal teaching, peer teaching, and school adaptation in an urban Hawaiian population. Paper presented at the meetings of the Society for Cross-Cultural Research, Michigan, 1977.

KELLY, M. Papua New Guinea and Piaget—An eight-year study. In P. R. Dasen (Ed.), *Piagetian psychology: Cross-cultural contributions.* New York: Gardner Press, 1977.

KENYATTA, J. *Facing Mt. Kenya.* London: Secker & Warburg, 1953.

KESSEL, F. S. Research in action settings: A sketch of emerging perspectives. *International Journal of Behavioral Development,* 1979, *2,* 185–205.

KILBRIDE, P. L., & LEIBOWITZ, H. W. Factors affecting the magnitude of the Ponzo perspective illusion among the Baganda. *Perception & Psychophysics,* 1975, *17,* 543–548.

KILBRIDE, P. L., & ROBBINS, M. C. Linear perspective, pictorial depth perception and education among the Baganda. *Perceptual and Motor Skills,* 1968, *27,* 601–602.

KILBRIDE, P. L., ROBBINS, M. C., & FREEMAN, R. B., JR. Pictorial depth perception and education among Baganda school children. *Perceptual and Motor Skills,* 1968, *26,* 1116–1118.

KIMINYO, D. M. A cross-cultural study of the development of conservation of mass, weight, and volume among Kamba children. In P. R. Dasen (Ed.), *Piagetian psychology: Cross-cultural contributions.* New York: Gardner Press, 1977.

LABORATORY OF COMPARATIVE HUMAN COGNITION. Cross-cultural psychology's challenges to our ideas of children and development. *American Psychologist,* 1979, *34,* 827–833.

LABOV, W. The logic of non-standard English. In F. Williams (Ed.), *Language and Poverty.* Chicago: Markham, 1970.

LANCY, D. F. Cognitive testing in the indigenous mathematics project. *Papua New Guinea Journal of Education,* 1978, *14,* 114–142.

LAURENDEAU-BENDAVID, M. Culture, schooling, and cognitive development: A comparative study of children in French Canada and Rwanda. In P. R. Dasen (Ed.), *Piagetian psychology: Cross-cultural contributions.* New York: Gardner Press, 1977.

LAVE, J. Tailor-made experiments and evaluating the intellectual consequences of apprenticeship training. *The Quarterly Newsletter of the Institute for Comparative Human Development,* 1977, *1,* 1–3.

————. *Tailored learning: Education and cognitive skills among tribal craftsmen in West Africa.* Cambridge, Mass.: Harvard University Press, in press.

LEIBOWITZ, H. W., & PICK, H. A., JR. Cross-cultural and educational aspects of the Ponzo perspective illusion. *Perception and Psychophysics,* 1972, *12,* 430–432.

LURIA, A. R. Towards the problem of the historical nature of psychological processes. *International Journal of Psychology,* 1971, *6,* 259–272.

————. *Cognitive development: Its cultural and social foundations.* Cambridge, Mass.: Harvard University Press, 1976.

MACK, J. E. *A prince of our disorder: The life of T. E. Lawrence.* Boston: Little, Brown, 1976.

McLUHAN, M. The brain and the media: The "Western" hemisphere. *Journal of Communication,* 1978, *28,* 54–60.

McNEMAR, Q. A critical examination of the University of Iowa studies of environmental influences upon the IQ. *Psychological Bulletin,* 1940, *37,* 63–92.

MEAD, M. *Continuities in cultural evolution.* New Haven: Yale University Press, 1964.

MEHAN, H. Assessing children's school performance. In J. Beck, C. Jenks, N. Keddie, & M.F.D. Young (Eds.), *Worlds apart.* London: Collier Macmillan, 1976.

MERMELSTEIN, E., & SHULMAN, L. S. Lack of formal schooling and the acquisition of conservation. *Child Development,* 1967, *38,* 39–52.

MIDDLETON, J. (Ed.), *From child to adult.* New York: Natural History Press, 1970.

MINUCHIN, P., BIBER, B., SHAPIRO, E., & ZIMILES, H. *The psychological impact of school experience.* New York: Basic Books, 1969.

MUNROE, R. L., & MUNROE, R. M. *Cross-cultural human development.* Monterey, Calif.: Brooks/Cole, 1975.

MYAMBO, K. Shape constancy as influenced by culture, Western education, and age. *Journal of Cross-Cultural Psychology,* 1972, *3,* 221–232.

NASH, M. *Machine age Maya.* Chicago: University of Chicago Press, 1967.

NEISSER, U. General, academic, and artificial intelligence. In L. B. Resnick (Ed.), *The nature of intelligence.* Hillsdale, N.J.: Erlbaum, 1976.

NERLOVE, S. B. & SNIPPER, A. S. Cognitive consequences of cultural opportunity. In R. L. Munroe, R. H. Munroe, & B. B. Whiting (Eds.), *Handbook of cross-cultural human development.* New York: Garland, in press.

NYITI, R. M. The development of conservation in the Meru children of Tanzania. *Child Development,* 1976, *47,* 1122–1129.

OKONJI, M. O. The effects of familiarity on classification. *Journal of Cross-Cultural Psychology,* 1971, *2,* 39–49. (a)

————. Culture and children's understanding of geometry. *International Journal of Psychology,* 1971, *6,* 121–128. (b)

OLSON, D. R. Culture, technology, and intellect. In L. B. Resnick (Ed.), *The nature of intelligence.* Hillsdale, N.J.: Erlbaum, 1976.

————. The languages of instruction: The literate bias of schooling. In R. C. Anderson, R. J. Spiro, W. E. Montague (Eds.), *Schooling and the acquisition of knowledge.* Hillsdale, N.J.: Erlbaum, 1977.

OWOC, P. J. On culture and conservation once again. *International Journal of Psychology,* 1973, *8,* 249–254.

PAGE, H. W. Concepts of length and distance in a study of Zulu youths. *Journal of Social Psychology,* 1973, *90,* 9–16.

PHILP, H., & KELLY, M. Product and process in cognitive development: Some comparative data on the performance of school age children in different cultures. *British Journal of Educational Psychology,* 1974, *44,* 248–265.

PICK, A. D., & PICK, H. L., JR. Culture and perception. In E. C. Carterette & M. P. Friedman (Eds.), *Handbook of perception* (Vol. 10). New York: Academic Press, 1978.

PINARD, A., MORIN, C., & LEFEBVRE, M. Apprentissage de la conservation des quantités liquides chez des enfants rwandais et canadiens-français. *International Journal of Psychology,* 1973, *8,* 15–23.

POLLNAC, R. B. Illusion susceptibility and adaptation to the marine environment. *Journal of Cross-Cultural Psychology,* 1977, *8,* 425–434.

POLLNAC, R. B., & JAHN, G. Culture and memory revisited: An example from Buganda. *Journal of Cross-Cultural Psychology,* 1976, *7,* 73–86.

PRICE-WILLIAMS, D. R. Abstract and concrete modes of classification in a primitive society. *British Journal of Educational Psychology,* 1962, *32,* 50–61.

REDFIELD, R. Culture and education in the midwestern highlands of Guatemala. *American Journal of Sociology,* 1943, *48,* 640–648.

ROGOFF, B. Mother's teaching style and child memory: A Highland Guatemala study. Paper presented to the meeting of the Society for Research in Child Development, New Orleans, 1977. (a)

———. *A portrait of memory in cultural context.* Unpublished doctoral dissertation, Harvard University, 1977. (b)

———. Mode of instruction and memory test performance. Manuscript submitted for publication, 1980.

———. Schooling's influence on memory test performance. *Child Development,* in press.

ROGOFF, B. & LAVE, J. General or specific effects of schooling on occupation, wealth, and offspring's schooling. Unpublished manuscript, 1979.

SCHMIDT, W. H. O., & NZIMANDE, A. Cultural differences in color/form preference and in classificatory behavior. *Human Development,* 1970, *13,* 140–148.

SCRIBNER, S. Developmental aspects of categorized recall in a West African society. *Cognitive Psychology,* 1974, *6,* 475–494.

———. Recall of classical syllogisms: A cross-cultural investigation of error on logical problems. In R. J. Falmagne (Ed.), *Reasoning: Representation and process in children and adults.* New York: John Wiley & Sons, 1975.

———. Situating the experiment in cross-cultural research. In K. F. Riegel & J. A. Meacham (Eds.), *The developing individual in a changing world* (Vol. 1). Chicago: Aldine, 1976.

———. Modes of thinking and ways of speaking: Culture and logic reconsidered. In P. N. Johnson-Laird & P. C. Wason (Eds.), *Thinking.* Cambridge, England: Cambridge University Press, 1977.

SCRIBNER, S., & COLE, M. Cognitive consequences of formal and informal education. *Science,* 1973, *182,* 553–559.

———. Unpackaging literacy. *Social Science Information,* 1978, *17,* 19–40. (a)

———. Literacy without schooling: Testing for intellectual effects. *Harvard Educational Review,* 1978, *48,* 448–461. (b)

SERPELL, R. Cultural differences in attentional preference for colour over form. *International Journal of Psychology,* 1969, *4,* 1–8.

———. *Culture's influence on behavior.* London: Methuen, 1976.

SHARP, D., & COLE, M. Patterns of responding in the word associations of West African children. *Child Development,* 1972, *43,* 55–65.

SHARP, D., COLE, M., & LAVE, C. Education and cognitive development: The evidence from experimental research. *Monographs of the Society for Research in Child Development,* 1979, *44,* (1–2, Serial No. 178).

SPINDLER, G. D. (Ed.), *Education and anthropology.* Stanford: Stanford University Press, 1955.

STEVENSON, H. W., PARKER, T., WILKINSON, A., BONNEVAUX, B., & GONZALEZ, M. Schooling, environment, and cognitive development: A cross-cultural study. *Monographs of the Society for Research in Child Development,* 1978, *43* (3, Serial No. 175).

STRAUSS, S., ANKORI, M., ORPAZ, N., & STAVY, R. Schooling effects on the development of proportional reasoning. In Y. H. Poortinga (Ed.), *Basic problems in cross-cultural psychology.* Amsterdam: Swets, 1977.

SUPER, C. M. Who goes to school and what do they learn? Paper presented at the meeting of the Society for Research in Child Development, New Orleans, 1977.

————. A cultural perspective on theories of cognitive development. Paper presented at the meeting of the Society for Research in Child Development, San Francisco, 1979.

SUTCLIFFE, C. R. Education as a dependent variable in the process of modernization. *Journal of Social Psychology,* 1978, *104,* 3–7.

THORNDIKE, E. L. *Educational psychology.* New York: Teachers College, 1914.

VARGHA-KHADEM, F., GENESEE, F., SEITZ, M. M., & LAMBERT, W. E. Cerebral asymmetry for verbal and nonverbal sounds in normal literate and illiterate children. Paper presented at the meeting of the Society for Research in Child Development, New Orleans, 1977.

VERNON, P. E. *Intelligence and cultural environment.* London: Methuen, 1969.

VYGOTSKY, L. S. *Thought and language.* New York: John Wiley & Sons, 1962.

WAGNER, D. A. The development of short-term and incidental memory: A cross-cultural study. *Child Development,* 1974, *45,* 389–396.

————. Ontogeny of the Ponzo illusion: Effects of age, schooling, and environment. *International Journal of Psychology,* 1977, *12,* 161–176.

————. The effects of formal schooling on cognitive style. *Journal of Social Psychology,* 1978, *106,* 145–151. (a)

————. Memories of Morocco: The influence of age, schooling, and environment on memory. *Cognitive Psychology,* 1978, *10,* 1–28. (b)

WAGNER, D. A., & HEALD, K. "Carpentered World" hypothesis vs. Piaget: Revisiting the illusions of Segall, Campbell, & Herskovits. In W. J. Lonner, Y. H. Poortinga, & L. H. Eckensberger (Eds.), *Cross-cultural contributions to psychology.* Lisse: Swets & Zeitlinger, 1979.

WHITE, S. H. Evidence for a hierarchical arrangement of learning processes. In L. P. Lipsitt & C. C. Spiker (Eds.), *Advances in child development and behavior* (Vol. 2). New York: Academic Press, 1965.,

WILKINSON, A. C. Cognition in school: Why children go and what they learn. Paper presented at the meeting of the American Psychological Association, New York City, 1979.

WILKINSON, A., PARKER, T., & STEVENSON, H. W. The influence of school and environment on selective memory. *Child Development,* 1979, *50,* 890–893.

WITKIN, H. A., & BERRY, J. W. Psychological differentiation in cross-cultural perspective. *Journal of Cross-Cultural Psychology,* 1975, *6,* 4–87.

# 7

# Cross-Cultural Tests of Piaget's Theory

*Pierre R. Dasen*
*and Alastair Heron*

## Contents

## Abstract

Piaget's theory contends that cognitive development occurs through a sequence of stages that are thought to be universal, cultural factors affecting only the age at which the stages are attained. How far is this universalist position justified by the available cross-cultural evidence? After a short introduction to the theory, this chapter examines this evidence stage by stage, without summarizing all the data but focusing on some selected but important issues.

In the first (sensori-motor) stage, the sequence of substages has been verified without any exception, although the evidence is limited by the small number of cross-cultural studies. Already at this very early age (below 2 years), some variation occurs in the rate of development through the substages. For the second major stage of development (the concrete operational stage), the data base is much larger, and it is usually found that the sequence of substages (and also generally speaking the "qualitative" aspects of operational development) are confirmed; a few possible exceptions are discussed, and it is suggested that the evidence for qualitative differences is not convincing. On the other hand, systematic quantitative differences occur (in the rate of development, or the age at which the various substages are attained), which suggest that cultural factors are more important than Piaget's theory would have predicted. Among the factors that affect these quantitative differences, urbanization, acculturation, schooling, ecocultural relevance, and cognitive ambience are considered in this review, and it is suggested that future research should turn away from these "packaged" variables towards a study of individual differences. The results of a series of training studies suggest that the cultural differences that have been found can be reduced or overcome through appropriate intervention techniques, should this be deemed desirable.

Although the data base concerning the concrete operational stage is extensive, its quality is clearly unsatisfactory; some methodological problems are summarized, and two important issues are selected for more detailed discussion: (1) the problem of ensuring that the performance on the tasks that are used in experimental situations really reflects the underlying capacity or competence; (2) the lack of a consistent relationship between tasks in which this consistency or "structure d'ensemble" is predicted by the theory. A consideration of these rather complex issues is necessary for the interpretation of the rather odd but consistent finding, that in some populations a proportion of the children and adults do not seem to reach the last substage of the concrete operational stage, which constitutes an important limitation to the universalist position.

Finally, the controversies as well as the scarce evidence concerning the end-stage of the developmental sequence, the stage of formal operations, are considered. Generally speaking, the authors take the view that both positions, universality and cultural relativism, receive empirical support, depending on which aspects of cognitive development are being examined. There also seems to be diversification of development with age: there is little doubt about the universality of the first stage, whereas it is much less certain for the last. The cross-cultural data do not support every aspect of Piaget's theory, nor do they disprove it; rather, they call for an expansion of the theory that will attribute a greater importance to cultural factors.

## Introduction

### Summary of Piaget's Theory

Piaget's genetic epistemology is one of the most influential theories in contemporary psychology. Like Freud, Piaget left a permanent imprint on the social sciences of this century, even if the details of his theory may be questioned and will be reorganized with the progress of science. Unlike Freud, however, Piaget has not appealed to the general public: without some serious effort it is difficult to penetrate his sometimes esoteric writings, and of course sex is more interesting to most people than is logic! But in psychological science, which is characterized by a multiplicity of independent micro-theories, Piaget's system is the most complete and coherent attempt to discover the general laws governing the human mind.

In this generality, and its implication of universality, is to be found the main attraction of Piaget's theory to the cross-cultural psychologist and the anthropologist. Beyond the diversities in the cultural traditions of human groups, there must be some commonality, the expression of humanity itself, which is possibly best characterized by the basic mechanisms of human cognition.

But Piaget's theory is not, strictly speaking, a psychological theory; it is an epistemology, a philosophy of knowledge, although based on empirical evidence: the painstaking observation of hundreds of children in various phases of their development. Its ultimate aim is to establish a theory of scientific knowledge. But in order to understand the thinking processes of a scientist, or of any adult, for that matter, Piaget claimed that one has to understand how these processes develop, one has to look at their genesis—hence the appellation "genetic" epistemology, which refers to development and has nothing to do with genetics. A complementary method is the study of the history of science. Thus, even though Piaget was without any doubt one of the most influential personalities in developmental and child psychology, he was not in fact a psychologist but an epistemologist. This distinction is not trivial, because it explains the whole thrust of his work, as well as some of the difficulties and misunderstandings that occur—as we shall see in later sections—when the theory is used by psychologists.

What are the main characteristics of this theory? Despite the disappointment we are bound to generate in the reader, we cannot fully answer this question: the short summary provided in this introduction is bound to be misleading, but a more complete one would take too much space in a handbook that is not designed to be an introductory textbook of psychology. We shall therefore limit our answer to a few aspects of the theory that are directly relevant to the following discussion. This introduction should provide enough background information for a basic understanding of the main issues raised in this chapter, but the interested reader who encounters Piaget's theory here for the first time may want to consult one of the numerous introductory texts that this chapter cannot and should not replace. The initiated reader can move on at once to the next section, Summary of Cross-Cultural Findings.

Piaget's theory entails the existence of *stages* that are qualitatively different. The thinking processes of the child are not the same as those of the adult; development is not simply a matter of accumulating quantitative skills (such as an increase in memory span or in the number of words available for use) but follows a series of qualitative restructurings. These stages are *sequential*, that is, they appear in a fixed order of succession, because each one is necessary for the formation of the following one. There are three major stages of development: (a) the sensori-motor stage; (b) the stage of representative intelligence that leads to concrete operations; and (c) the stage of propositional or formal operations. We shall examine these stages in more detail shortly.

However, development does not occur in sudden jumps. A child is not at the concrete operational stage one day, and at the formal stage the next; rather, in moving from one major stage to the next, the child goes through a succession of *substages*, each of which—if the observational methods and analyses are fine enough—could be broken down into further substages. The passage from one of these substages to the next occurs through *assimilation* and *accommodation*. At any given time, the organism has at its disposal a certain number of *schemes* (or possible actions) that are organized or combined into *structures*. If the organism is presented with a slightly new problem, it accommodates or modifies the existing structure to suit the new situation, or it assimilates new elements into the existing schemes, thus creating new structures. Accommodation and assimilation are present in all activity, and their constant interaction Piaget calls *adaptation* or *equilibration*. Piaget borrowed these concepts from his background in biology, and more particularly embryology; according to Piaget, basic similarities exist between the laws of biological adaptation and those of psychological development.

This rooting of the theory in biology has led to the misconception that Piaget considered development to be innate. This is *not* the case. Except for the very first reflexes in the neonate, all subsequent schemes (we could say: behaviour) are the result of the interaction between the maturation of the organism and its environment. Why, then, do all individuals follow the same sequence of stages in their development? Is that not proof that the stages are innate? Not at all, answered Piaget; the interaction with the physical and social environments occurs at such a general level (the law of adaptation or equilibration), that differences in the environments are unlikely to affect the structure of the stages and their sequence. The prediction of *universality* of the sequence of stages is based on these assumptions: differences in the physical and social environments, as well as educational and cultural influences, are expected to influence the chronological age at which the stages are attained, but not their basic structure nor their sequence.

If development were determined by maturation alone, then the stages would occur at the same chronological age in every population. But this is not what Piaget (1966) expected. What he did expect was the universality of the developmental sequence, which can be explained by the fact that every environment has objects and people with which to interact. For cognitive development, the most important type of interaction with the environment is *logico-mathematical experience*, in which knowledge is not derived from the physical properties of objects (as in so-called physical experience) but from the properties of actions that are exerted on them. For example, if a child is counting stones or sticks, he may discover that if he counts them from left to right he finds the same number as when he counts from right to left, and again when he puts them in a circle; the child has thus discovered an important property of number, a relation derived from the action of putting the objects in a certain order and counting them, but not a property belonging to the objects themselves. Such logico-mathematical experience is therefore expected to be independent of the environment.

On the other hand, factors such as cultural differences, language, and education are expected to accelerate or delay the average chronological ages at which the stages are attained (Piaget, 1970), or "the detail of the conceptualizations (e.g., content of classifications, relations)" but not the operations themselves (Piaget 1966). The words *detail* and *content* may be seen as emphasizing the secondary role attributed by Piaget to this "diachronic (divergent or culturally relative) factor" (Piaget, 1966). For a more detailed discussion of the various factors of development posited by Piaget, and how cross-cultural studies are expected by Piaget (1966) to tease out their relative importance, the reader is referred to Jahoda's chapter in this *Handbook* (Volume 1, Chapter 4).

What, then, are the main stages of development? The *sensori-motor* period lasts from birth to approximately 2 years of age, during which the initial reflexes are extended and combined into "schemes" (actions that can be repeated) of increasing complexity; the individual, through interaction with the environment, builds up a practical (i.e., nonverbal) knowledge of the world around it. For example, only gradually does a baby acquire the understanding that an object is "permanent," i.e., that it remains an object even if it is hidden; in earlier stages, the infant makes no attempt to reach for a hidden object, even though it would be capable of doing so. Similarly, the baby gradually learns to solve such problems as retrieving an object that is out of reach with the help of an instrument such as a stick, or by pulling on the cloth that supports the object. Piaget distinguished six substages within the sensori-motor period and claimed that the individual is capable of internal representation only at the sixth substage.

The possibility of using symbols and signs is related to the progress of imitation, which at the sensori-motor stage is a sort of representation through actions. As imitation becomes differentiated and interiorized in images, it becomes the *semiotic function*, which makes possible the acquisition of language, but also includes mental imagery, symbolic games (or games of imagination), drawing, and so on. Thus, according to Piaget, the origin of logical operations is to be found in the sensori-motor period, and is therefore developmentally prior to language, which itself depends on the laws of the general coordination of actions (equilibration). The appearance of the semiotic function marks the beginning of the second major stage, the period of representative intelligence. It is common practice, however, to distinguish two stages within this period: the *preoperational* stage, and the stage of *concrete operations*.

At the stage of concrete operations, the child is able to put objects into one-to-one correspondence, to seriate (to order objects, for example, according to their increasing size), to classify, or to use addition, subtraction, or logical multiplication. These actions are called *operations* because they are interiorized (they involve internal representation) and reversible (each action can be cancelled by a reversed action). These operations do not occur in isolation, but are related to each other in *structures* that can be described by mathematical or logical models. This aspect of formalization of the theory, however, need not concern us here. Of central importance for our discussion is the idea that the concepts typical of this stage, and the logical operations that they subsume, such as classification or the use of relations, are a necessary basis for later scientific reasoning, and develop spontaneously in every child. Some of these logical operations relate to pan-human activities, which have been of great interest to anthropologists—for example, the use of taxonomies (classification) or kinship systems (relations)—and their use is fairly obvious in daily activities. Other aspects of concrete operations are less obvious and can only be discovered in experimental situations. For example, Piaget considered the logical structure of classification to be completely developed only when the individual could handle what has been called the *quantification of class inclusion*. Given two subclasses (which we can label A and A', for example, eight cats and two dogs), and the generic class (B: cats and dogs are domestic animals), the child who begins to use concrete operations can compare the two subclasses: in our example, there are more cats than dogs. But the child finds it difficult to compare one of the subclasses with the generic class (i.e., A with B): the child will say that there are more cats than animals. Such an answer is called "preoperational," because it reflects the type of reasoning that is typical of the child before the development of concrete operations. Thus, the preoperational stage is practically defined by what the child cannot yet do (although more recent research has concentrated on what the child *can* do during that stage). It may be a surprising answer to us adults, and we would not have found out about it if we had not asked the child the rather odd question: "Are there more cats or more domestic animals?" In a way, the psychologist "tricks" the subject by asking such an insidious question, but this may be a necessary step to discover an important aspect of cognition.

Another "trick" needs to be explained here because it will be mentioned often in this chapter: the famous "conservation" concept, or what is also called the *construction of invariants* (Piaget, 1952). This refers to the fact that some properties of an object may remain constant even if the perceptual aspect of the object is changed. For example, a ball of clay can be flattened or rolled out, and yet its mass, weight, and volume do not change; the child at the preoperational stage, however, focuses on one perceptual dimension, and believes that the change in shape implies a change in other properties.

In practice, the experiment is carried out in the following way. The subject is given two identical balls of clay, and it is made certain that he understands that they contain the same "quantity" of clay. He is then told to roll out or flatten one of them, and he is asked if it still contains the same quantity of clay as the ball left unchanged, or whether it now contains more or less. Usually, the subject is also asked to give a reason for his answer. The child at the preoperational stage will say: "There is more in the flat one, because now it is bigger" or "there is less because it is thin." He concentrates on one of the dimensions and the perceptual illusion predominates over logical reasoning. The child at the concrete operational stage, on the other hand, will say: "Obviously it must be the same quantity, the balls were the same before, no clay has been added or taken away; it is now longer but also thinner, and if we made the ball again, it would be the same." This child is said to conserve quantity, sometimes called mass or substance, and this is an indicator or marker for concrete operational logic.

Several other conservation tasks deal with the concept of quantity; for example, the quantity of liquids poured from one glass to another glass of a different shape (called conservation of liquids, or of continuous quantities), or a similar situation with a number of beads instead of a liquid (conservation of discontinuous quantities), or the conservation of number, length, area, and so on. The details of the techniques need not concern us here, but it is interesting to note that although these are all markers for the concrete operational stage, they are not achieved at the same chronological age.

Conservation is, at the concrete operational level, the equivalent of the "object permanency" established during the sensori-motor stage: the same structure is repeated (or, rather, reconstructed) at a higher level. This is called a "vertical décalage." A "horizontal décalage" is the reconstruction of the same structure within a single stage at different chronological ages, depending on the "content" to which it is applied. For example, the child may give a "conservation" answer when asked about the quantity of clay, but a "nonconservation" answer when asked about its weight. Thus, the child is able to use concrete operations with the concept of quantity, but not with the concept of weight; one or two years later, the child may extend the concrete operational logic to weight, but not yet to volume. Similarly, a child may give a class-inclusion answer when asked about a bunch of flowers, but give a preoperational answer when asked about animals.

This limitation of the logic to particular contents is exactly what makes the reasoning at this stage "concrete." In practice, this phenomenon implies that it is not possible to classify an individual as preoperational or concrete operational, because the type of reasoning the child uses depends on the concept to which it is applied. In theory, however, Piaget does expect some consistency across different conceptual areas—at least at the end of the concrete operational stage, the individual should be able to apply logical operations to any content. This "domain consistency" or *structure d'ensemble* as Piaget called it, is a difficult and controversial issue, to which, as we shall see in this chapter, cross-cultural studies have contributed important data.

The final period in the sequence is the stage of *formal operations*, in which the individual is capable of using propositional logic (reasoning on possibilities or hypotheses instead of real situations only), combinatorial operations (working out all the possibilities), or of devising scientific experiments (e.g., by holding all factors constant except one). In theory, formal thought is not limited by content, but in practice it is obvious that adults apply formal operations only very occasionally in their daily lives. Confronted with increasing evidence that most adults do not use formal operations as often as expected, Piaget (1972) revised his position; he came to think that all adults have the possibility, or competence, to use formal operations even though they may not use that potential in every case. He also suggested that "they reach this stage in different areas according to their aptitudes and their professional specializations" (p. 10). Occasionally, Piaget (1966, 1971) also suggested that formal schooling and participation in a technological culture are prerequisites for the attainment of formal operations; this is another controversial issue in cross-cultural studies, which we will take up later in this chapter.

*Summary of Cross-Cultural Findings*

We are now ready to ask the question of major interest: How far is the universalist position justified by the available cross-cultural data? Here we must observe immediately that the vast majority of empirical cross-cultural Piagetian studies have been concerned with a single stage—that of concrete operations—and that until recently this has involved a concentration of attention on the conservations. More recently, a few studies have explored the sensori-motor and formal stages, but no longitudinal studies covering more than one of the major stages has been reported. Thus, cross-cultural studies have never addressed themselves to the whole of Piaget's theory, but only to selected issues in the psychological (as opposed to epistemological) aspect of the theory.

The cross-cultural literature related to Piaget's theory is nevertheless extensive, and we will not attempt to cover it fully. Several specific reviews of it are available (Ashton, 1975; Carlson, 1976a, 1976b; Greenfield, 1976; Lautrey & Rodriguez-Tomé 1976); and the Piagetian approach is discussed in the wider context of cross-cultural psychology by LeVine (1970), Lloyd (1972), Brislin, Lonner, and Thorndike (1973), Cole and Scribner (1974), Price-Williams (1975), Glick (1975), Serpell (1976), Warren (1978), and Furby (1980) as well as by Jahoda and by Pick in chapters of this *Handbook*. The reader's attention is also drawn to some books of readings or selected papers (Berry & Dasen, 1974; Warren, 1977; Dasen, 1977a) and to the extensive bibliography with summaries compiled by Modgil (1974) and Modgil and Modgil (1976).

The position revealed by one relatively comprehensive review (Dasen, 1972a) seemed fairly straightforward:

a. The qualitative aspects of the theory (the sequence of stages and substages, their structural properties, the types of explanations given by respondents) have found support in a great majority of studies;
b. The horizontal décalages (e.g., the sequential appearance of conservation of quantity, weight, and volume) characterize sample means, but are not found in all individual subjects;
c. The quantitative aspects (the rate of progress through the stages, or the chronological age at which these are attained) show considerable intercultural variations.

These conclusions still summarize the majority of the data, but since 1972 a number of issues have been raised that suggest that the overall picture is more complex than was then thought to be the case. We shall now turn to a discussion of some of these data and to some of these issues, without attempting a complete coverage—the alternative strategy will be adopted of considering in some detail a small number of selected issues, illustrated by a selection of empirical studies. The reports selected are—for reasons partly of familiarity and convenience—mainly those describing the work of the present authors and their co-workers.

### The Sensori-motor Stage

Only very recently have any cross-cultural studies of sensori-motor intelligence followed Piaget's theory. Most previous work on infancy had dealt with motor development or had used general developmental schedules based on Gesell's observations. Reviews have been provided by Werner (1972), Warren (1972), Dasen (1974a), and Super (1980, and his chapter in this volume).

The dearth of Piagetian studies is probably due to the lack of standardized observation techniques. However now several ordinal scales are based on Piaget's early observations (Casati & Lézine, 1968; Lézine, Stambak, & Casati, 1969; Kopp & Sigman, 1972; Kopp, Sigman, & Parmelee, 1974; Uzgiris & Hunt, 1975; Corman & Escalona, 1969), and these have been expertly characterized and discussed by Uzgiris (1976). A larger number of cross-cultural studies can be expected now that these instruments are available.

Goldberg (1972) reported the first cross-cultural study of sensorimotor intelligence, using the Corman-Escalona scale in Lusaka (Zambia); she found a slight advance on American norms at 6 months and a slight lag at 9 and 12 months, but on the whole the major finding is the confirmation of Piaget's observations. The slight lag may be attributed to the difficulties in establishing rapport in the testing situation, because of a very strong fear of strangers at this age. Bovet, Dasen, and Inhelder (1974) mention similar problems in a pilot study in rural Ivory Coast, but these difficulties were overcome in the later extensive longitudinal study (Dasen, Inhelder, Lavallée, & Retschitzki, 1978) through the careful training of observers and extensive contact with the subjects. In this study, using the Casati-Lézine scale, a statistically significant advance on French norms was found on three subscales (the use of an instrument to attain an object that is out of reach, and two problems involving the combination of objects) throughout all substages and the whole age range (from 5 to 31 months). On other subscales, there usually was some advance on French norms, but it was not statistically significant at all substages.

These differences apply to the rate of development through the substages and indicate that even in this first stage, progress is not completely determined by biological factors; it also depends on the particular activities stimulated and reinforced by the physical and social environments. In Dasen et al.'s study, the greatest precocity occurs in subscales that involve the handling of objects; this may come as a surprise in view of the majority of the literature that has tended to describe the African infant as passive in a physical environment that is poor in objects (Richards, 1932; Ashton, 1952; Knappen, 1962; Erny, 1972) and a social environment that stresses interpersonal interactions rather than object manipulation (Zempléni-Rabain, 1970). However, Dasen et al. (1978) carried out some naturalistic behaviour observations and found the African babies in their study frequently manipulated a large array of objects (sticks, stones, cooking implements, tins, and so on), exploring them, combining them, and using them in meaningful sequences. These observations do not support the passivity said to characterize African children, at least not at this early age, and the results of the testing with the sensori-motor scale rather suggest an advance of African babies in the concept of object permanency and other object-related cognitive behaviour.

Mundy-Castle and Okonji (1976), reporting a study carried out by Whiten and Whiten among rural Igbo children in Nigeria, also suggest that early object manipulation is similar in English and Igbo babies, though noting "however, later interactions of mother and baby with objects revealed what may be an important difference. In Oxford, a lot of mother-infant interaction is focussed on objects, whereas in (Nigeria) none of this type of interaction was seen, apart from the mother giving an object to play with. Mothers did not seem to play object-games with their children" (p. 5). Thus, Mundy-Castle (1976) claims that Euro-American babies, after a certain age, would have greater experience in handling objects, and their attention would be "more often deliberately focussed on objective properties of reality" whereas "African babies receive more social stimulation and early emotional support than European babies. The issue here is whether in the long run this divergent stimulation  brings about a differential patterning of cognitive development, with Africans acquiring an intelligence that is more socially oriented, Europeans one that is more technologically oriented (Mundy-Castle, 1974)" (pp. 19–20). This hypothesis certainly warrants further testing.

To return to sensori-motor intelligence proper, a study (Sieye, 1975) of urban and peri-urban infants in Abidjan (Ivory Coast) using the Casati-Lézine scale confirms the advance of African babies over French norms, whereas a study in India using an American adaptation of the same scale by Kopp and Sigman (1972) reports a slight delay (Kopp, Khoka & Sigman, 1977). Thus, differences in the chronological age at which the substages of sensori-motor intelligence are attained do occur. However, in emphasizing these cultural differences, we may overlook the amazing commonality reported by all these studies: in fact, the qualitative characteristics of sensori-motor development are identical in all infants studied so far, despite vast differences in their cultural environments. The substages all appear in the same hierarchical ordering and even the details of the behaviours (object manipulations, explorations, combinations, and so on) are exactly comparable. In some cases, the similarity is almost unbelievable. For example, in one item of the Casati-Lézine scale, the baby is given a red plastic tube and a chain of paperclips without any instruction on what to do with these objects. All French babies, once they have reached Piaget's substage 5, are observed to make some attempt to have the chain pass through the tube, and they gradually solve the problem in a series of successive adaptations. African babies (Dasen et al., 1978), although they have never seen such strange objects as a plastic tube and paperclips, combine them in exactly the same way, making the same errors and finding the same progressively adapted solutions. The example is striking, because at later stages familiarity with the test materials is found to be an important determinant of performance.

Thus, as Warren (1980) has remarked: "Whatever differences there may be rest on a remarkable and usually unacknowledged base of commonality. The same elements of infant development emerge wherever studies are conducted" (p. 293). Warren carries the argument further to make a very important point:

> It may well be that our received conceptions of scientific method give the wrong bias, for cross-cultural and for developmental problems: we are taught to respect quantitative over qualitative approaches, and that is clearly mistaken here; and our research designs and statistics are sensitized to differences and often ignore commonalities. (p. 293)

> It may be that you need an awful lot of commonality to pin down a difference—between individuals or between cultures. (p. 291)

In cross-cultural tests of Piaget's theory, some authors focus on the qualitative generalities and thus support the universality, whereas others focus on quantitative differences and thus claim to disprove the theory. This is why the dialectics of proving or disproving the theory may not be the most productive strategy; the outcome seems to depend mainly on the preconceptions of the investigator. On the other hand, the amount of commonality also depends on the type of behaviour investigated, and in Piagetian psychology it depends on the stage studied: At the sensori-motor stage, there are strong indications that universality predominates over differences.

Is this also true at later stages? Before we turn to an extensive discussion of the concrete operational stage, a few words must be said about the intermediate period between the sensori-motor and the concrete operational stage, a very important period that corresponds to the preschool age. Facilities such as day-care centres and preschools are beginning to be provided in many developing countries, yet very little is known on the cognitive development of the children involved, and much more information is needed to guide the development of adapted methods and programs for these institutions. Evaluation projects often use IQ tests, which are clearly unsuitable in cross-cultural situations. Unfortunately Piaget's theory is still poorly equipped to deal with this age range in any positive way, but here obviously is a potentially fruitful research area.

A modest start in this direction has been made by Dasen et al. (1978) with a study of some aspects of the development of the "semiotic function" in rural African babies, the same sample as in the study of sensori-motor intelligence. The subjects were observed in two situations: (1) In their natural environment, usually the compound or open area between the houses of an extended family, where most of the domestic life takes place. The observers tried to record all the activities of the child without interfering in any way. (2) In a more structured situation, in which the mother and the child came to an observation hut, and the baby was sat in front of an array of objects, all of which were local, except two (black) dolls and a mirror. No instructions were given, except that the child was free to play with these objects in any way it wanted. After a warm-up period, the child's behaviour was videotaped for fifteen minutes.

The young Western baby uses objects indiscriminately as part of its activities; for example, it bangs them on the floor; then it explores the properties of these objects, which thus progressively acquire meaning. The semiotic function emerges when the baby is able to use an object in a meaningful sequence of activities, either conventionally (i.e., using each object in its usual function) or symbolically (i.e., using an object to represent something else). This is achieved through the imitation of familiar models.

This sequence of development was found in the African subjects of the study in much the same way and about the same ages as in Western children (although no quantitative data is offered to support that claim). The various stages appeared on the average slightly earlier in the naturalistic observations, and Dasen et al. remark that the environment of these African babies is rich in unstructured objects (sticks, stones, tins, and so on) that are particularly conducive to symbolic use. Whereas the stages of development were identical in the Ivory Coast and the French children, the content of their symbolic activities was, of course, linked to cultural models. Thus, a young African child is likely to imitate the activities of carrying water on the head or pounding yams in a mortar, whereas the French child is more likely to sit a doll on the potty. Depending on our theoretical inclinations, we may be struck by the similarities or by the differences!

## The Concrete Operational Stage

In discussing the results of cross-cultural studies relevant to the stage of concrete operations, we have a similar problem of emphasis. The quantitative aspects of Piaget's theory (the ages at which concrete operations are attained) are of interest to the developmental psychologist and have important implications for the application of the theory (for example, in curriculum development), yet they are almost irrelevant to genetic epistemology as a theory. If we devote so much space in this chapter to a discussion of cultural differences, it is because their interpretation raises interesting, difficult, and controversial issues. In the wake of this, the most important finding of almost all studies may be overlooked—namely that the same sequence of substages has been found everywhere and for every concept in the concrete operational stage studied so far. Here, again, we have a commonality that supports strongly the universalist position of Piaget's theory.

### Possible Qualitative Differences

There have been, however, a few suggestions of qualitative differences in the development of concrete operations. For example, Greenfield (1966) found that unschooled Wolof children in Senegal gave an unusual reason for their nonconservation answers. In this case, the task was the "conservation of liquids," which is similar to the conservation of mass (or "quantity") described in our introduction. Two identical glasses are filled with identical quantities of liquid, and the experimenter makes sure that the subject understands this. Then the liquid of one of the glasses is poured into a glass of a different shape, for example, a long and narrow one. The child at the preoperational stage focuses on only one dimension of the display, the level of the liquid: in the narrow glass, the level is higher and the child believes that there is more liquid ("more to drink"). In other words, the perceptual features predominate over the logic of the situation. The child at the concrete operational stage, on the other hand, is convinced that the quantity of liquid does not change. Among several reasons it can give to justify this belief, it may say that the level is higher but the glass is narrower; in other words, pays attention to and coordinates two dimensions of the display.

Some Wolof children (20 percent) who were still at the preoperational stage said that "there is more because you have poured it," as if the action of pouring the liquid could magically change its quantity. This prompted Greenfield to try another experiment in which she asked the children to pour the liquid themselves. This small change in procedure changed the outcome of the experiment considerably: 70 percent of the 6–7 year olds now gave conservation answers, as opposed to only 25 percent when the experimenter did the pouring. Greenfield called this phenomenon "action magic," the attribution of magical powers to the actions of the experimenter (usually a strange adult!).

Another difference in the reasoning of unschooled Wolof children seemed to be their inability to distinguish between the statement about something and the thing itself. Thus, the question: "Why do you say that this glass has more water than this one?" would be met with uncomprehending silence. If, however, the question was changed in form to: "Why *is* there more water in this glass?" it could often be answered quite easily. The unschooled Wolof children seem to "lack Western self-consciousness" (Greenfield & Bruner, 1969, p. 637), because of a collective, rather than individual, value orientation that occurs when individuals lack power over the physical world. "Wolof children who lack self-consciousness when questioned about their 'thoughts' also seem to be hindered by a lack of experience in manipulating the physical world when they approach a problem relating to the conservation of quantity across transformations in its appearance" (Greenfield & Bruner, 1969, p. 640).

This difference in value orientation and the lack of experience postulated by Greenfield and Bruner may explain the quantitative aspects of the results. The unschooled Wolof children seem to develop conservation concepts later than the schooled Wolof or Western children; the results even suggest that half of them do not reach the last substage of the conservation of liquids. On the other hand, there is no qualitative difference in the logical operations they use; at least some of the unschooled and all the schooled Wolof children do reach this last substage, and there is no indication that they have not followed the usual sequence. They may indeed perceive the question: "Why do you *say* this?" as an implicit criticism of their answer, and they may attribute magical powers to the strange investigator, but these are affective rather than cognitive differences. Furthermore, a large number of studies of conservation concepts in African children (summarized by Ohuche & Pearson, 1974) have been made since Greenfield's early work, but none has reported "action magic."

Another "deviation" from the normal sequence of substages has been reported by Bovet (1974) under the name of "pseudo-conservation." When presented with the task of conservation of quantity (liquids), unschooled Algerian children aged 7–9 years were giving conservation answers, but could not give a reason for them. Slightly older children (8–10 year olds), on the other hand, gave nonconservation answers, and then the usual sequence appeared unchanged: 9–11 year olds gave "intermediate" answers (they fluctuated between nonconservation and conservation answers during the interview), and 12–13 year olds gave conservation answers that they could justify in the usual way. This surprising result with the younger subjects led Bovet to give them additional tasks involving the pouring of liquid from one container to the next, and predicting each time where the level of the water would be. After this, the children gave preoperational answers on the conservation task. It seems that, at first, they were not paying any attention to the perceptual features of the display, and thus they stuck to the initial equality; the additional tasks drew their attention to these perceptual features, inducing nonconservation. The initial conservation answer was therefore not a true indicator of concrete operations; there was no "compensation" between the perceptual features of the display since these features were disregarded—it was a nonoperational "pseudo-conservation."

Because the normal sequence of substages appears after this "temporary deviation," Bovet sees in these results a proof of the strength of the normal developmental path; but Lautrey and Rodriguez-Tomé (1976) rightly remark that if such a small and temporary deviation is possible, it is likely that more important ones may also occur. The phenomenon, therefore, is potentially interesting; however, like Greenfield's "action magic," it has never been reported by any other investigator, and the finding itself is based on a very small sample. There is also the possibility that this pseudo-conservation stage may actually be a normal substage, but that it occurs in Western children at a very young age, when questioning about conservation is difficult or impossible.

So far, then, we have no completely convincing example of qualitative differences in concrete operational development. But the search, of course, should continue!

*Horizontal Décalages*

A common misconception attributes to the horizontal décalages the status of substages within the concrete operational stage; Piaget himself occasionally seemed to support such an interpretation (e.g., Piaget, 1966), at least in the regular succession of the conservation of quantity, weight, and volume, probably because this sequence has been verified (as sample averages in cross-sectional studies) so often in Western populations. However, there is no reorganization of operations at successively higher levels, but simply the application of the same operations to contents of increasing difficulty. A difference in task difficulty can hardly be seen as a serious threat to the theory itself.

The cross-cultural data on horizontal décalages have been reviewed elsewhere (e.g., Lautrey & Rodriguez-Tomé, 1976), so we shall mention them only briefly. De Lemos (1969) found that the conservation of weight was, on the average, easier than the conservation of quantity in a sample of Australian Aboriginal children. However, she always presented the tasks in the same order, with the conservation of quantity at the beginning; in situations in which the subjects are not familiar with the tasks and the testing situation, order-effects may, of course, be quite important. Dasen (1972b) tried to replicate these results in the same location, but he controlled for the order of presentation and did not find this inversion. On the other hand, he did not find that the conservation of volume appeared later than the conservation of weight, as would normally be expected; and, more importantly, when looking at individual results rather than group averages, he found patterns that did not confirm the expected sequence in almost half of the Aboriginal sample, and in 10 percent of the Western comparison group.

Thus, future studies of this question should concentrate on individual rather than on group results, and longitudinal studies would, of course, be even more to the point.

*Quantitative Differences*

Quantitative differences in the attainment of concrete operations are usually expressed in terms of the proportion of children who reach the last substage on any given concrete operational task; if these proportions are plotted over age, development curves such as the ones illustrated in Figure 7-1 are obtained.

Examples of such development curves, gleaned from the cross-cultural literature, appear in Dasen (1973, 1977b), Lautrey and Rodriguez-Tomé (1976), and in Kamara and Easley (1977) who also suggest a scheme to test the statistical significance of the observed differences. Curves of type (a) reflect a "rate" of development that is in advance; type (b) are similar to that found in Western children (w); and type (c) reflect a rate that is slightly slower, leading to a "delay" or "time lag"; but all children eventually reach the substage in question. These development curves do not show the rate of development of a concept in an individual child, but in the sample as a whole, a distinction that is important to remember. Curves of types (a), (b), and (c) present no problem to the theory and simply reflect "the fact that the stages . . . are accelerated or retarded in their aver-

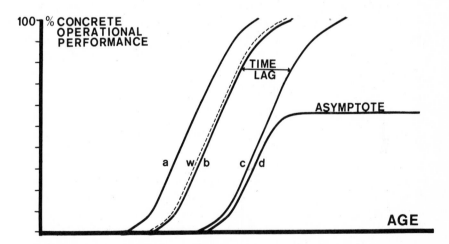

Figure 7–1. Theoretical development curves representing the percentage of concrete operational performance over age. Curve (w) is assumed to be the developmental curve for a sample of children from a Western, technological background, on any particular Piagetian task of the concrete operational stage. Curves (a), (b), (c), and (d) are possible developmental curves from cross-cultural studies; their interpretation is discussed in the text.

age chronological ages according to the child's cultural and educational environment" (Piaget, 1970, p. 721). Detailed studies are needed, of course, to examine with more precision which aspects of the cultural environment produce these quantitative variations. We shall examine some of these in the next section.

Curves of type (d), those that show a levelling off or "asymptote," *do* present a problem to the theory, because they reflect the fact (if we take the results at face value) that some individuals do not reach the concrete operational stage—at least not as far as the particular concept being studied is concerned. As we shall see, it is not uncommon to find in the same population a type (d) curve for some concepts, and types (a), (b), or (c) for other concepts. Thus, a development curve never reflects an "operational level" or any other such global construct, but is limited to the concept being studied and to the particular experimental setting in which the measures are obtained. Many type (d) curves have been reported in the literature; the fact that they occur can hardly be questioned, but their interpretation has given rise to several controversies, which we shall examine in subsequent sections of this chapter.

*Factors Affecting Quantitative Differences*

Most cross-cultural studies in the Piagetian area have attempted to study which factors affect the rate of development. Pick (Volume 3, Chapter 3 of this *Handbook*) has summarized several of these, in particular in relation to conservation, classification (but without mentioning the central role of "class inclusion" in Piaget's theory), and space concepts (but without mentioning Piaget). Rogoff, in this volume, discusses the influence of schooling. We shall therefore not dwell on the details of the findings but will only mention the major trends.

*Urbanization, acculturation, and schooling.* Several studies have compared urban with rural samples within the same cultural groups (e.g., Greenfield, 1966; Mohseni, 1966; Peluffo, 1967; Poole, 1968; Kiminyo, 1977; Opper, 1977). Usually, type (c) or (d) curves are found in the rural samples with almost every task, whereas no time lag or only a small one is found in urban environments. Similarly, the time lag is reduced with increasing contact with a Western, technological culture (de Lacey, 1970; Dasen, 1974b, 1977b) and disappears completely if the children are brought up in a completely Western context (Dasen, de Lacey, & Seagrim, 1973; Seagrim, 1977). The effects of schooling are less systematic. In Greenfield's (1966) study, as we have seen, a type (d) curve was found in the unschooled Wolof sample, whereas a type (c) curve occurred in both the urban and the rural schooled samples (with, contrary to most other findings, a faster rate of development in the rural sample). Laurendeau-Bendavid (1977) also finds a significant impact of schooling in a study carried out in Rwanda. On the other hand, schooling is reported to have no effect in some other studies (e.g., Goodnow, 1962; Kelly, 1977; Kiminyo, 1977).

Furby (1971) proposed that the seemingly contradictory results of various studies could be accounted for by a model comprising two environmental dimensions: (1) the degree of magical thinking versus empirical reasoning permitted in the culture (basically a non-Western versus Western dimension), and (2) the degree of interaction with objects leading to perceptual flexibility, or manual versus automated environment (basically the rural versus urban dimension). Her prediction that conservation would develop faster in a rural environment was based mainly on Greenfield's (1966) results, which are, however, at odds with most other findings; similarly, the magical thinking is derived from Greenfield's "action magic," which has not been confirmed by later studies. At least one study attempting to test the model (Skanes, 1976) has not supported it. The attempt, however, is an interesting one, because it points to the need for analyzing environmental characteristics *in relation* to the task characteristics (Furby, 1980). Similarly, Kiminyo (1977), in a study among the Kamba of Kenya, describes the daily activities of rural and urban, schooled and unschooled children and predicts that rural and unschooled children will attain conservation concepts earlier because they have more opportunities for an active interaction with the physical environment (Furby's "manual" environment). The results of the study only bear Kiminyo out insofar as no differences were found between the urban and rural, the schooled and unschooled children.

*Ecocultural relevance.* Another important factor producing quantitative differences in concrete operational development is the "ecocultural relevance" of particular conceptual areas. According to Berry (1976), people develop those skills that are useful for their survival in a particular ecology and its associated subsistence economy. In particular, Berry predicted and showed that nomadic, hunting-and-gathering people (such as the Eskimo, and to a somewhat lesser degree the Australian Aborigines) develop spatial skills to a higher degree than do sedentary, agricultural people (such as many African populations). In Berry's study, spatial skills were measured through such tests as Raven's (1938, 1949) Progressive Matrices (a nonverbal test that also includes items related to the logic of classification) and Koh's Blocks (also a measure of Witkin's construct of psychological differentiation—see Jahoda, Volume 1, Chapter 4, and Irvine & Carroll, Volume 2, Chapter 5, in this *Handbook*). Dasen (1975a) extended Berry's model to Piagetian psychology by predicting that spatial concrete operational concepts would be developed earlier and faster in a sample of

Eskimo children than in a sample of West African agriculturalists, with a sample of Australian Aborigines showing an intermediate rate of development.

According to Piaget's theory (Piaget & Inhelder, 1956), the child first acquires topological spatial concepts (inside/outside, open/closed, next to, and so on, leading to an understanding of the spatial order of objects), followed by projective (angles, points of view) and Euclidean spatial concepts (proportions and coordinates). Tasks that enable one to assess the development of these concepts are, for example, the location of an object on a model landscape that is rotated by 180 degrees in relation to a standard; or the prediction of the level of a liquid in a tilted bottle, which, according to Piaget, necessitates the coordination of two systems of Euclidean coordinates (referred to as a "horizontality" task).

Dasen's (1975a) predictions were fully sustained in a study of 190 rural, schooled, Central Eskimo, Australian Aboriginal (Aranda), and African (Ebrié) children aged 6 to 14 years. The development of the concept of "horizontality" in the Eskimo sample produced one of the few type (a) curves reported in the cross-cultural literature, whereas a type (d) curve was obtained for the same concept in the Ebrié sample. Other spatial concepts showed similar quantitative differences. Furthermore, Dasen predicted that, whereas nomadic people may require spatial concepts, agriculturalist people should need concepts of conservation of quantity, weight, and volume because food is stored and exchanged in markets. The results confirmed this prediction, at least in the age range 12–14 years; the ordering of the development curves for conservation of quantity, weight, and volume was exactly reversed from that found with spatial concepts, the African sample showing the fastest rate of development and the Eskimo sample the slowest rate, with intermediate results for the Australian Aboriginal sample. On the conservation of quantity (liquids), for example, a type (c) curve was found in the African sample, but type (d) curves in the two other samples.

The problem with all these variables, be they ecocultural relevance, urban/rural environment, or schooling, is that the mechanisms of their influence on cognitive development are not specified. Some authors, at best, speculate on what these mechanisms might be; these hypotheses, however, can hardly be tested because the factors are, in Whiting's (1976) telling phrase, "packaged variables." There are so many different aspects of living in a big city, as opposed to a rural area, that it is impossible to tell which one, or which combination of variables, is having an influence on cognitive development. One major task of cross-cultural research is now to unwrap these packages.

*Cognitive ambience.* A step in this direction could be made in the empirical study of "cognitive ambience," a concept first introduced briefly by Heron and Simonsson (1969) when discussing the potential importance for cognitive development of the language employed in the school as a medium of instruction from first grade onward:

> If the culture of which the indigenous language or languages form the main channel of social communication places value on concepts and behaviours important for full cognitive development, where "full" implies the goal specified by Piaget, then, by and large, the language will be consistent with those values in its capacity for encoding them. In such a case, the indigenous language is clearly a satisfactory medium, at least to start with, for primary education. If on the other hand, the opposite condition prevails, the case becomes strong for the employment as the educational medium of a language known to be favourable to full cognitive development, not solely or even mainly because it contains the appropriate concepts, but because its use will increase the probability of the child's exposure to the implicit "cognitively-relevant values" of the culture with which that language is associated. The extent to which this occurs will of course be considerably affected by the cultural-linguistic "integrity" of the teachers: clearly, an indigenous teacher whose own cognitively-relevant values are largely inconsistent with those implicit in the second language he is employing as a medium of education will not be an effective channel. (p. 290)

Ambience was there defined (p. 291) as "the total pattern of implicit cognitively-relevant cultural values, communicated through linguistic and other behaviour by adults and older children." The vital feature of this communication is the unintentionality, the day-to-day usualness, the taken-for-granted assumptions about what is and what is not important in life. Almost from birth—certainly from the prelinguistic phase towards the end of the first year—every child is provided automatically and usually without educational intent with a pattern of stimulation the quantity and quality of which is determined by the culturally shaped behaviour of parents, older siblings, and other adults and children. That culturally shaped behaviour necessarily involves what Maccoby and Modiano (1969) called "cognitive style." Although not accepting what we believe to be their oversimplified dichotomy between "peasant" and "urban" styles, their general approach is consistent with our present argument:

> It is our general hypothesis that cognitive style develops in childhood according to the demands of the culture, in terms of the mode of reasoning most functional for operating within the socio-economic conditions of the society or social class. (p. 22)

> Differences in cognitive style make it difficult for peasants to adapt to the urban-industrial world, where functional and abstract attributes are in the forefront of thought. These differences also have implications for the development of intellectual abilities. Urban children, at best, are able to synthesize concepts with accuracy and intellectual power. They have learned the basis of theoretical thought, of integrating diverse concepts in terms of superordinate structures and abstract reasoning. They have learned to free themselves from

the tyranny of the stimulus, its shape, color, and dominant  perceptible qualities. But their style runs the risk of stereotyping and overly formal reasoning.
Concepts are quickly put into boxes and the uniqueness of experience is lost.
(p. 31)

The concept of ambience finds circumstantial support in a study reported by Dasen, de Lacey, and Seagrim (1973). This involved the testing
(at ages ranging from 5 to 14 years) of a sample of children of Aboriginal
and mixed descent (total $N = 35$) who had been adopted or fostered from
a very early age (two-thirds of them before 1 year) by Australian families
of European descent. The performance of these children on four tasks
(horizontality, seriation, classification, and the Peabody Picture Vocabulary Test) was equal to that of comparison European groups and clearly
superior to that of comparison Aboriginal groups brought up on missions
or government settlements. Performance on conservation of quantity and
of weight was intermediate between that of the two comparison groups.

The fact that the "cognitive ambience" was more favourable for the
development of Piagetian concepts in the families of European descent
does not imply, in our view, that the more traditional Aborigines are "culturally deprived." It is a reflection, rather, on the cultural relativity of the
concepts studied; the values of the traditional Aboriginal culture are different, but it is meaningless to speak of cultural deprivation, except from
the ethnocentric point of view of the dominant, white, middle-class culture. The nomadic, hunting-and-gathering ecology of the Aborigines
seems to lead to a rather high level of spatial concept development (Dasen,
1975a), but little is known of the actual mechanisms of the ecocultural influence. What are the day-to-day activities and experiences of the Aboriginal child that favour spatial skills? A closer study of "cognitive ambience"
would give us the answer to that important question.

*Individual differences.* Unless "cognitive ambience" is broken down into
specific observations, however, it also remains a packaged variable. Furthermore, a major problem remains, one that was ignored almost completely by Piaget because of his epistemological approach: individual differences. Piaget was quite explicit about his position: "I have no interest
whatsoever in the individual. I am very interested in general mechanisms"
(Piaget, 1971, p. 211). Individual differences were completely ignored by
the Geneva school until Inhelder (1968) started to use Piagetian tasks in
clinical psychology, followed by Schmid (1969) and others.

For a correct interpretation of type (c) and (d) curves, attention to individual differences is now a necessary next step. As we have already mentioned, the asymptote in a type (d) curve does not mean that the cognitive
development of every individual is slowing down after a certain age, but it
does mean that some individuals reach a particular substage and others do

not, and that if an individual has not reached that substage before a certain age, he or she is unlikely to reach it later. Why does this happen? Why do these individual differences exist in samples that are often quite homogeneous in their physical, social, and cultural environment? None of the variables, such as urbanization, acculturation, schooling, or ecocultural relevance, can explain individual differences, because all of these are usually fairly homogeneous in any given population.

Interesting attempts to look at individual differences in terms of maternal teaching styles have been made by Adjei (1977) and Kirk (1977), both (but independently) in Ghana. The mothers were observed in an experimental situation, being asked to teach their child how to construct a puzzle. Some aspects of the mothers' teaching style were indeed related to the children's performance on Piagetian tasks. The problem with this type of approach is, first, that a few significant relationships appear among a large number of correlations, and much of the analysis appears to be post-hoc; and second, that this type of direct teaching situation is rather unusual in the traditional African context, where a great deal of learning occurs through observation and imitation of adults, usually in the context of daily routines. The approach, however, is potentially fruitful, especially if it were combined with more naturalistic behaviour observations. Studies like those of Nerlove, Roberts, Klein, Yarbrough, and Habicht (1974) and of Irwin, Klein, Engle, Yarbrough, and Nerlove (1977) have been looking for indicators of cognitive development (non-Piagetian) in the daily activities of children, observed through the technique of "spot" observations (a large number of "snapshots" on the whereabouts and activities of the child—a technique that reduces observer effects). This approach could possibly be used in the proposed search for the origins of individual differences.

*Training studies.* From the results we have reviewed in this section, it seems that only major differences in environmental conditions produce noticeable quantitative differences in concrete operational development. When we are comparing children brought up in a hunting-and-gathering economy to those who live in an agricultural setting, we are looking for extremes—large differences that can only be obtained through quasi-experimental cross-cultural designs, because no such variations can be found within our own culture, neither can they be produced or manipulated experimentally. Similarly, it is usually found that the time lag is reduced or is nonexistent in urban environments, in more Westernized contexts, or in children of the higher socioeconomic strata (e.g., Lloyd, 1971); but it is usually neither possible nor desirable to manipulate these variables.

The question then arises: Would it be possible to reduce the lag through a more direct, short-term intervention, without changing anything in the environment and culture? An answer to this question may, but need not, be motivated by a desire to "speed up" the spontaneous rate of development—a preoccupation that was much frowned on by Piaget himself. In fact, it is theoretically interesting to know how resistant to change these quantitative differences are. Training studies have been carried out to answer this question, the first one in the cross-cultural scene, by Pinard, Morin, and Lefebvre (1973). Three groups were trained for the conservation of quantity (liquids): unschooled and schooled children in Rwanda, and schooled children in Montreal, Quebec. All three groups showed a significant training effect and similar rates of learning, and it seems that the time lag was effectively reduced or bridged (although the publication does not actually provide the development-curve data).

Heron and Kroeger (1975) carried out a training experiment as part of a larger sequence of cross-cultural Piagetian studies. The sample consisted of 109 children (age range: 9–13 years, median: 11.6 years) of Yugoslav migrant workers who had been resident in West Berlin for periods ranging between six months and five years (median: 3.4 years). They were pretested on tasks of conservation (liquid quantity, weight, volume); class inclusion; and dichotomous and multiple classification. Experimental (training) and control groups were formed and posttested nine weeks later. No training effect was claimed in the case of conservation, since gains by experimental and control groups were not significantly different; but on multiple classification a highly significant training effect was evident at nine weeks, with significant generalization to selected items from Coloured Progressive Matrices (Raven, 1949).

Dasen (1975b; 1977b; Dasen, Lavallée, & Retschitzki, 1979; Lavallée & Dasen, 1980) and co-workers carried out a series of eight training studies, the results of which have been summarized by Dasen, Ngini, and Lavallée (1979). These studies dealt with the concepts of conservation of quantity (liquids), class inclusion, and horizontality and were carried out among a total of 132 Eskimo, West African (Baoulé), and East African (Kikuyu) children of various ages. A significant training effect was found in all the studies, the training was stable over time (delayed posttest after one month), and significant generalization to other concrete operational concepts occurred, showing that the training techniques indeed had activated a cognitive restructuring beyond the specific concept being trained. In most cases, the training effectively reduced or completely bridged the time lag.

These studies show that the quantitative variations are amenable to change. The time lags do not reflect some basic incapacity and can be bridged through adequate educational experiences if this is deemed worthwhile and desirable.

*Methodological Problems*

In the previous sections, we have taken the empirical data reported in the literature at face value. However, it is important to state unequivocally where we stand on the quality of this empirical basis. Quite simply, we regard it as highly unsatisfactory. We must therefore consider in detail some of the problems that have been raised about Piagetian theory, particularly in the cross-cultural context; this consideration will lead us, in this and the next two sections, into some technicalities. (The casual reader may want to avoid these by going forward to the section on adults, keeping in mind, however, that there are problems that must be faced in any serious evaluation of the theory.)

Our dissatisfaction arises partly from purely methodological considerations, such as those to which detailed attention has been given by Kamara and Easley (1977). In particular, these authors raise two important issues: the quality of the communication between experimenter and subject, and the necessity of using Piaget's "method of critical exploration," also called the "clinical" method.

According to Piagetian methodology, the experimental situation or "task" is only the point of departure for an extensive, in-depth dialogue between the experimenter and the child, each of the experimenter's questions being prompted by the preceding answer of the subject. In this way, the skilled interviewer can follow up the leads provided by the child's actions or answers; he constantly checks hypotheses about the underlying thought structures implied by the subject's reactions. Such a method is, of course, quite different from the standardized procedures so dear to most psychologists. In principle, this flexible method should be ideally suited to cross-cultural testing; in practice, however, its application requires not only an experimenter who is fully conversant with the theory (to guide on-the-spot hypothesis-testing), but he or she has also to be able to communicate with the subject at ease. In most cross-cultural studies, until very recently, the experimenter was a stranger; if he carried out the testing himself, difficulties of communication were unavoidable (not only linguistic but cultural), or else he standardized the procedures and trained assistants. It is only with the recent emergence of competent Piagetian psychologists in non-Western countries, who can carry out studies in their own culture, that this problem has been lessened if not solved (about half the contributions in Dasen's, 1977, edited volume are examples of this new trend).

However, the more basic source of dissatisfaction is to be found in the raw data themselves—the responses of subjects in various cultural settings to stimuli devised in another culture. This was brought to a focus in an article by Cole and Bruner (1971) that leaned heavily on the experimental anthropology approach of Cole, Gay, Glick and Sharp (1971) on the one hand, and on that of the psycholinguist Labov (1970) on the other, invoking en route the competence/performance model of Flavell and Wohlwill (1969). Leaving the latter for detailed attention in the next section, we can note here Labov's attack on the experimental method, as usually applied to the problem of subcultural differences in cognitive capacity:

> All children are asked . . . "tell me everything you can about this," but the speaker's (i.e. the child's) interpretation of this request, and the action he believes is appropriate in response is completely uncontrolled. One can view these test stimuli as requests for information, commands for action or meaningless sequences of words. . . . With human subjects it is also absurd to believe that identical stimuli are obtained by asking everyone the same question. Since the crucial intervening variables of interpretation and motivation are uncontrolled, most of the literature on verbal deprivation tells us nothing of the capacities of children. (Labov 1970, p. 171)

Cole and Bruner (1971) comment as follows:

> Here Labov is attacking the experimental method as usually applied to the problem of sub-cultural differences in cognitive capacity. We can abstract several assertions from this key passage: (a) formal experimental equivalence of operations does not ensure de facto equivalence of experimental treatments; (b) different subcultural groups are predisposed to interpret the experimental stimuli (situations) differently; (c) different subcultural groups are motivated by different concerns relevant to the experimental task; (d) in view of the inadequacies of experimentation, inferences about lack of competence among black children are unwarranted. (p. 869)

Both Kamara and Easley's (1977) and Cole and Bruner's (1971) methodological critiques support a strong universalist position. Kamara and Easley explicitly state that they would expect only type (b) curves if there were no methodological problems with the testing situations and procedures; thus, they deny any quantitative variations due to cultural influences (or any of the variables previously discussed), attributing them to methodological artifacts. Although we emphatically agree that some serious methodological problems must be resolved, we cannot accept such an extreme position.

Cole and Bruner's critique implicitly supports the universality of the competence for concrete operational reasoning, suggesting that the quantitative differences may be at the performance level. We shall now consider this issue in some detail.

*The Competence/Performance Distinction*

The model suggested by Flavell and Wohlwill (1969) introduces a distinction between competence and performance patterned on Chomsky's use of these terms in a psycholinguistic context. In their words:

A psychological theory that accounts for complex behaviour will have two principal components: a *competence* model, which is a formal, logical representation of the structure of some domain . . . an *automaton* model . . . , which represents the psychological processes by which the information embodied in competence actually gets accessed and utilized in real situations. The competence model gives an abstract purely logical representation of what the organism knows or could do in a timeless, ideal environment, whereas the automaton model has the job of describing a real device that could plausibly instance that knowledge or skill, and instance it within the constraints (memory limitations, rapid performance, etc.) under which human beings actually operate. (p. 71)

According to Flavell and Wohlwill, the probability that a given child will solve a given task can be formulated in the following equation:

$$P(+) = P_a \times P_b^{1-k}, \text{ where } 0 < P_a < 1;\ 0 < P_b < 1;\ \text{and}\ 0 < k < 1$$

where $P_a$ reflects the degree to which a given operation has become established in a particular child, in other words, the presence or absence of the operation structure (competence). An attribute of the task, $P_b$ represents the likelihood for any given task that the operation will in fact be called into play, and its end product be translated into the desired output. The parameter $k$ has to be introduced because these task-related variables vary with age. The values of all three factors are expected to vary between 0 and 1, which gives rise to a four-phase process of cognitive development. In the initial phase, $P_a = 0$, i.e., the child lacks the given operation. In a transitional phase $P_a$ changes from 0 to 1, whereas $k$ is assumed to remain equal to 0. In a period of stabilization the contribution of the task-related variables gradually decreases ($1 - k$ tends toward 0), and during the terminal phase the child "is able to bring the operation to bear on the problem successfully, regardless of the situational and task variables involved" (p. 101). The model is able to handle many empirical results on horizontal décalages and lack of intertask consistency.

However, in Flavell and Wohlwill's model, $P_b$ is an attribute of the task whereas what is needed to explain the competence/performance distinction in some cross-cultural situations is a variable that is an attribute of the culture. Thus (as advocated by Dasen, 1977c), one could introduce the variable $P_c$ representing the likelihood for any given task that the operation will in fact be called into play in a given cultural milieu. $P_c$ is likely to change with age, and its effect will probably increase with age, this is why it has to be raised to the power $k$. The complete equation now becomes:

$$P(+) = P_a \times P_b^{1-k} \times P_c^{k}$$

According to the competence/performance model, an initial answer a child gives to a Piagetian task may not necessarily reflect its "true" cognitive level, i.e., the underlying structure or competence. This situation seems to occur particularly frequently in cross-cultural situations.

There are indications that in some circumstances very little help is needed to "actualize" the latent competence (that is, to enable subjects to express their competence fully in their performance). A double example of this was provided in the West Berlin training study (Heron and Kroeger, 1975), in which the training elicited operational performance in multiple classification, and the experience of the pretest was sufficient to do the same for the control group in conservation of weight and volume. Another example is to be found in Bovet (1974), with  Algerian illiterate adults being tested for conservation of weight and of length. During  the testing  session, some of  Bovet's subjects went through the complete se-quence from pseudo-conservation through nonconservation to end up with an operational performance. Others changed from nonconservation to operational conservation after weighing the two pieces of clay once. But on other concepts, such as those of speed and of time (thought to be less culturally relevant), no such *Aktualgenese* occurred. The illiterate children in Bovet's study also gave more advanced answers after being exposed to some training situations. There are other examples of rapid learning of op-erational concepts. For example, Pinard, Morin, and Lefebvre (1973) re-port, on the average, similar rates of learning conservation of quantity (liq-uids) in French-Canadian, unschooled Rwandan, and schooled Rwandan children, aged 7 years. One difference, however, was found among the three groups: seven (of sixteen) subjects in the unschooled Rwandan group were successful on the training exercises after a single session, whereas only three in the schooled group and none in the French-Cana-dian group were successful. Dasen (1975b; 1977b) reports very rapid learning of conservation of quantity in Eskimo children aged 12 to 14; some children moved from nonconservation to full conservation after a mere exposure to other operational tasks and some moved from noncon-servation to the intermediate stage in the same way, and then acquired full conservation very rapidly during the training phase. On the other hand, subjects aged 10 and 11 remained at stage 1 despite exposure to other op-erational tasks, but then started to acquire the necessary operational structures during  the training phase.

We do not, however, wish to suggest that the apparent actualization of latent competence necessarily always occurs as in these examples. These subjects may have been at Flavell and Wohlwill's phase 3, where $P_a$ is equal or close to a value of 1, but $k$ is still zero. The immediate effect of the first test experience or of the training procedure is not to change the value of $P_a$ (the operational structure) but rather that of $P_b^{1-k}$ (the task-related variables that somehow prevented this operational structure from mani-festing itself): this is probably what occurred with the Eskimo children in

ment also follow the same general laws. Thus, one might expect wide-ranging consistencies. However, the empirical data base for each of these areas of development was obtained on different samples of children for each part of the research, and therefore the consistency was not tested empirically by Piaget himself. Psychometrically, functional and contextual aspects influence task performance and may obscure much of the consistency if it does exist. This is true intraculturally and possible even more interculturally.

2. A subperiod of *equilibrium,* which marks the achievement of concrete operational thinking in each conceptual area; thus, on Piagetian tasks of the concrete operational level, one expects systematic success or, in other words, a "ceiling" effect. Whenever type (d) curves occur, this consistency is obviously called into question.

A series of interlinked studies by Heron and his co-workers has paid particular attention to intertask consistency in a cross-cultural context. The two main Piagetian tasks were the conservation of weight and "matrices," a task of classification in which two or three attributes have to be considered at the same time. Theoretically, one would expect some relationship between the two tasks, not only because they are both assessing concepts of the concrete operational stage, but more specifically because both call for the coordination of two or more dimensions or attributes.

Heron and Simonsson (1969) used a nonverbal (miming) method of administrating the weight conservation task, based on Furth (1966), who developed it for use with deaf children in the United States. Their principal finding was that the proportion of Zambian children providing clear evidence of weight conservation performance did not continue to rise in the usual linear fashion, but that they reached a near asymptote of about 55 percent after the age of 11 years. They noted that this finding had a precedent in the data of Goodnow (1962) for Chinese children in a Hong Kong Anglo-Chinese school, and also in schools and clubs located in low-income districts. Heron (1971) used data from sixty-two of the original two hundred Zambian children to study the relationship between weight conservation performance and that on reasoning tasks of the induction and matrices type. He found very little connection between (a) the conservation and reasoning performance of these children, and (b) the conservation and the secondary school selection examination performance of thirty-one children in seventh grade. Performance on the induction and matrices tasks, however, correlated with examination performance.

These findings formed the basis for a subsequent study by Heron and Dowel (1973). This involved equal numbers of Papuan boys and girls in the Form 1 classes of an urban high school whose stated ages ranged from 10 to 16 years (median: 13 years). The aim of this study was twofold: to obtain data in a fresh cultural setting concerning weight conservation performance at the point of transition from primary to secondary education, and to explore the relationship between performance on conservation and on reasoning tasks of the matrix type. The latter involved fifteen items, drawn from a pool formed from those used by Heron in Zambia, Inhelder's items as used by de Lacey (1970) with Aborigines in Australia, and Progressive Matrices (Raven, 1938). The fifteen items were identified *a priori* as soluble (in ascending order of difficulty) by perceptual, counting, and operational means (five items in each category). Ten of the fifteen items fell in the predicted order of difficulty, without overlap, and no significant difference in performance or in the nature of errors made was found between those subjects (50 percent of the sample) who demonstrated weight conservation performance and those who did not do so. Several nonconservers in fact solved all fifteen of the matrix tasks.

Thus encouraged, Heron and Dowel (1974) took what appeared to be the logical next step. This consisted of broadening the Piagetian base from weight conservation to a wide range of concrete operational tasks, while focusing attention on the reasoning side solely on the multiple classification tasks used by Inhelder and Piaget (1964) as modified by de Lacey (1970). All tasks were administered in Serbo-Croat to the entire population of children in the age range 9.0–12.5 years (median: 10.5 years) who had arrived in Melbourne as permanent immigrants from Yugoslavia during the previous twenty-four months (range: 3–24 months). This group of children was found to be retarded on several aspects of concrete-operational performance by about two years as compared with Geneva data. Although on this occasion an association was found between performance on quantity and weight conservation and that on multiple classification, it was still the case that one-third of the nonconservers of weight could provide operational solutions to seven of the eight multiple classification tasks. As to the nonconserving group as a whole, no differences could be found (in terms of success/nonsuccess on multiple classification) in relation to age, sex, urban versus rural domicile or origin, more versus less recent arrival in Australia, or Macedonian versus Serbian ethnicity, nor did they differ systematically in approach to strategy to the multiple-classification tasks as evaluated by errors made. But on six of the eight multiple-classification tasks those in the *whole sample* who had immigrated sooner (12–24 months before administration of the tasks) did significantly better than the more recent arrivals (3–11 months).

Two years later Heron, Gardner, and Grieve (1976) retested thirty-four of those forty-nine Yugoslav children and also examined a quasi-control group of forty-nine children born and brought up in Australia, matched for age and father's occupation as closely as possible with the forty-nine children of the Heron and Dowel study. The performance of the Yugoslav children improved significantly in all tasks—very considerably on conservation (weight 56 to 77 percent, volume 44 to 74 percent)—less on multiple classification (64 to 79 percent in two-criteria tasks, 42 to

55 percent in three-criteria tasks). But at median age (now 12.5 years) these performances were still between two and four years retarded as compared with Geneva data. The Australian-born sample's performance differed significantly from that of the forty-nine Yugoslav children (at first testing) only on conservation, where it was superior (weight, 78 versus 55 percent; volume, 71 versus 45 percent). The association between weight conservation and multiple classification performance was similar to that observed in the original Yugoslav study.

Finally, Heron and Kroeger (1975) sought to extend the investigation of what could by now be described as uneven performance among children who should really be fully (concrete) operational by means of the training experiment summarized earlier. At the conclusion of the experiment, the presence or absence of weight conservation performance (in both training and control groups combined) was "both unaccounted for and essentially independent of current cognitive performance in other domains" (p. 229), including school mathematics grades.

It may be of significance to Piagetian theory that in cross-cultural studies the apparent rates of development are not uniform across the various aspects of concrete operations. Elsewhere (Heron, 1974) it has been noted:

> I find myself increasingly inclined to the view that the apparent unity (of the concrete operations stage) has been generated by the cognitively-relevant cultural homogeneity in development of the children serving as subjects in most European and North American studies. This possibility has been made more likely by the relative infrequency with which both conservation and other tasks subsumed under concrete operations have been included and compared across socially heterogeneous samples within such studies. (p. 100)

and elsewhere (Heron & Dowel, 1974):

> There seems to be a good case for not regarding the concrete operations stage as a formal unity: it may be more productive to view it as a set of structures without *necessary* interdependence. (p. 8)

In other words, the structure d'ensemble posited for the Genevan child does not necessarily hold elsewhere; two concepts that develop congruently in the average Genevan child may develop at very different rates in another culture, if one of them is more highly valued (i.e., is more relevant or adaptive) in that other culture.

The three-cultures study by Dasen (1975a), summarized previously, is an excellent illustration of this point; if a relationship exists between conservation concepts and spatial concepts, it is quite different in Eskimos (and Australian Aborigines) and in Ebrié (or Baoulé) Africans. One could assume, of course, that there is domain consistency, but that it is different in each culture. In any case, these results make it obvious that it is not possible to use any one task , or even a number of them, to assign a general developmental level, or a developmental status, to use Cole and Scribner's (1977) terms, to any individual and, *a fortiori*, to a whole population.

The lack (or cultural relativity) of domain consistency is seen by Cole and Scribner (1977) as a severe handicap to the cross-cultural application of a developmental theory such as Piaget's. But these authors place excessive demands on the theory, even if it were restricted to Western children. They ask for consistency over a wide "range of observations, tasks and spheres of activity," but one would want to see this assumption tested empirically *intra*culturally before it is extended to the cross-cultural arena.

The question of structure d'ensemble may also be linked to the competence/performance distinction that we have discussed in the previous section. Heron and Dowel (1973), referring to Flavell and Wohlwill's (1969) model for the first time in this context, wrote:

> It is possible to regard inter-task inconsistency as arising from the second (automaton performance) determinant—that is, the differential difficulties of the information-processing requirements of structurally equivalent tasks, or limitations as regards transfer and generalization, in contrast with the reasoning processes as such. For example, it is possible to explain the inability of conservers to co-ordinate relations in the matrix framework, although they presumably can do this in a conservation of quantity exercise by application of the above hypothesis. This particular example also raised the question of sequential patterning of cognitive structures. Piaget proposes an invariant sequence of acquisition and concomitantly functional relations between successive acquisitions such as co-ordination of relations and conservation. Flavell and Wohlwill speculate that some children may not acquire the concept of co-ordination before conservation, and, for those that do, the concept would perhaps help to mediate conservation. But some children may attain the latter in another way, perhaps by identity argument. Such a relationship would give rise to randomly distributed deviations from inter-task consistency in the study of structures in the process of formation. It is interesting to note here that only one conserver used a compensation argument on the conservation of weight test in the present study: the majority presented identity or reversibility justifications. (Heron & Dowel, 1973, p. 217)

*Concrete Operational Performance in Adults*

Here we should note the implications of the relatively scanty material on the nonappearance of some aspects of concrete operational performance even in adults. The first documented examples of nonconservation performance in a relatively large proportion of the adult population came from Australia (de Lemos, 1969; Dasen, 1974b) and Papua New Guinea (Prince, 1969; Kelly, 1970). Bovet (1974, 1975) found only 53 percent full conservation of weight in unschooled Algerian adults in the age range 25–50 years; there was a strong sex difference, most of the nonconservation answers being given by women. However, in 25 percent of the subjects, the nonconservation is described as being "of a particular nature": the subjects (all women) would say they could not answer the question, or they first gave a conservation answer but changed to nonconservation after the experimenter's prompting; four out of six subjects then changed to full conservation when they were allowed to weigh the two pieces of clay on a scale. Thus, Bovet does not attribute the lack of conservation performance to a lack of competence, but rather to the concurrent use of an "intuitive" mode, the "logical" mode remaining accessible but not spontaneously used.

Similarly, in Algeria (Bovet, 1975) and in the Ivory Coast (Bovet & Othenin-Girard, 1975), more adult illiterate women than men gave nonoperational answers to tasks assessing concepts of time and speed. "These difficulties seem to be linked to the low frequency of activities related to these concepts in everyday life. This seems to be particularly the case for the women, whose life is more sedentary than that of the men" (Bovet, 1975, p. 127, our translation). However, because of the lack of an adequate operational training method, it could not be established whether there was a real absence of competence for the concrete-operational structures of spatial-temporal relations, or whether latent structures were present but could not be readily used.

Thus, the "absence" of concrete-operational reasoning in some adults seems to be in many cases a question of performance rather than competence, and is not an absence of all concrete-operational reasoning, but only of those concepts that have little or no cultural relevance. One problem that remains to be more fully explained is that there are always some adults who do display the expected concrete-operational performance, even in concepts with little cultural relevance.

Furthermore, there is some evidence of a lack of concrete-operational performance in adults of low-socioeconomic level in Western countries. For example, in an important study by Graves (1972), the subjects were 120 adults, described as minimally educated, attending a further education course associated with the University of Mississippi. The sample consisted of four equal-sized groups of male and female whites and blacks (median age: 33 years). Even basing results on responses without explanatory justification from the subject, about 20 percent of these adult subjects could not demonstrate weight conservation, and the proportion of nonconservers rises steeply to 55 percent of white and 80 percent of black subjects for volume.

It is therefore probably the case that many adults in a variety of culturally and socially differing settings are unable to demonstrate full concrete-operational competence in terms of acceptable performance on Genevan tasks. But unfortunately we do not know whether this is so because:

a. The Genevan tasks are inappropriate without varying methodological safeguards, such as practice and/or training; the use of clinical interviews and structural analysis rather than treating the tasks as standard performance tests; lack of linguistic and cultural communication.
b. The basic competence for a given concept or structure is not universally present in the form originally described by Piaget: its lack in a substantial proportion of adults reflects a culture-specific value system that is favouring the development of those concepts or structures that are needed in a given ecocultural setting.

The implications of adult nonconservation—as established at the level of performance on Piaget's tasks—are considered fairly fully by Jahoda in his theoretical chapter in Volume 1 of this *Handbook*. He ends by saying:

> It can be stated quite categorically that no society could function at the preoperational level, and to suggest that a majority of any people are at that level is therefore nonsense almost by definition. (p. 116)

On the main issue, we find ourselves essentially in agreement with Jahoda and with Cole (1975), whom he quotes; however, we believe Jahoda's formulation to be incomplete and even misleading. One could wish that Jahoda had chosen to say "could function without competence in conservation," which would have taken into account two major issues raised in this chapter: (1) the competence/performance distinction; (2) the cultural relativity of "structure d'ensemble." In the absence of homogeneity within any individual, it is nonsense to consider the cognitive functioning of the society in terms of levels or stages.

It is unfortunate that Piaget's "conservations" have been turned into the major if not sole indicator of concrete operational reasoning. When Piaget (1952) considered conservation to be "a necessary condition for all rational activities" (p. 3), he did not have in mind the performance on any one of his tasks, but the fact that "any attempt by thought to build up a system of notions requires a certain permanence in their definitions" (p. 3). Thus, the underlying operations of identity and reversibility may be necessary in any rational conceptual system, but they need not be applied to every content, especially not if that content is not culturally relevant.

To make our position clearer, let us consider in some detail the very example chosen by Jahoda quoting Cole (1975):

> I am left wondering about the cognitive status of people who do not conserve. Consider, for example, research done among people who live in semi-arid locations where severe water shortages occur from time to time and natives' abilities to find water are legendary (e.g. Aborigines). Are we to believe that Aborigine adults will store water in tall thin cans in order to have "more water" . . . do they think they lose water when they pour it from a bucket into

a barrel? I am tempted to believe that they would have disappeared long ago were this the case. I also find it difficult to believe that they cannot think through an action and its reverse. Yet if we are to extrapolate the interpretations of poor performance from Genevan children to Aborigine adults . . . what else can we conclude? (p. 170)

This example specifically refers to the conservation of continuous quantity (liquids) in Australian Aborigines. The following performance results using the task of conservation of quantity were obtained in two studies that included some adult subjects: de Lemos (1969) found that only seven of twenty-six adults gave fully operational answers. Conservation of length, however, was achieved by three-quarters of the same adults. In a more natural situation, where women had to choose among unequal quantities of sugar poured into unequal shaped containers, eight of twelve subjects made a choice indicating nonconservation. Dasen (1974b) reports that only seven of a group of twenty adult Aborigines of Central Australia could demonstrate full conservation of liquids; eighteen of these, however, performed at the concrete-operational level on a task of spatial concepts ("horizontality") that, for European subjects, is much more difficult than the conservation of liquids.

The "poor" performance (we shall come back to the inadequacy of this value judgment) on conservation of quantity does not necessarily imply that competence for the conservation of quantity was absent in the adults tested, because additional techniques were not used to assess this. In any case, we would argue that these results do not imply that Australian Aborigines "cannot think through an action and its reverse" in an area that is relevant to them. But in traditional Aboriginal life, a precise comparison of amounts of liquids is not relevant, and the same could be said of weight and volume. Cole is right in saying that water is very important for their survival, as emphasized by Strehlow (1965):

> Each local group in the Western Desert had to know . . . all the locations of even the smallest rockholes and temporary waters in its own territory in order to survive. On travels over certain sandhill wastes, tree roots . . . often had to be tapped for water. During drought-enforced retreats from one safe water to the next, long distances had to be covered. . . . Moves like these were made with uncanny assurance, and without the aid of a compass. (p. 126)

To locate the water, the Aborigines needed concepts of space, not conservation of liquids, for once they had located the waterhole, comparison of quantities mattered little. In fact there were no buckets or barrels, no containers except *pitchis* (large wooden bowls generally used to carry objects or babies) and sometimes kangaroo skins or bark or plaited baskets (Berndt & Berndt, 1964, p. 101), none of which would allow any precise comparisons. The familiarity of present-day Aborigines with glass containers is not questioned, but the point is that traditional Aboriginal culture does not value quantity judgments. Therefore we see no reason that Aboriginal culture could not function without a need for conservation of quantity.

If that is so, is a nonconservation answer a "poor" performance? Would it be "better" or "more advanced" to give a concrete operational answer? In the case of a conceptual area that seems to have little adaptive value, there is no reason to attach a value system to the developmental sequence, and it is doubtful whether it is justified even in areas that are culturally relevant (Dasen, Berry, & Witkin, 1979).

## The Formal Operational Stage

Our discussion of concrete operational performance, and its occasional absence, in adults leads us on to consider the "end state" of Piaget's developmental sequence, the stage of formal operations. A very brief description of the characteristics of this stage has been given in the introduction, where we have also mentioned the increasing evidence that adults from Western technological societies do not automatically succeed at formal operational tasks (cf. Modgil & Modgil, 1976), a finding that prompted Piaget (1972) to revise his position to some extent. Although Piaget did not explicitly refer to Flavell and Wohlwill's (1969) competence/performance distinction, his revised position could be formulated in terms of that model: all adults have the competence for formal operations, although it may be reflected at the performance level only in some favourable circumstances.

Whether this statement should be restricted to adults in a Western technological environment (which implies a fair amount of formal schooling), or whether this competence can be expected to be universal, is a controversial issue on which empirical data is acutely lacking.

The very few cross-cultural studies that have included tasks of the formal operational stage have found very little evidence of formal operational performance. Recent reports include those of Philp and Kelly (1974) and Kelly (1977), who found no evidence whatever of formal operational thinking among adolescents at school in Papua New Guinea. The task used was Inhelder's and Piaget's (1958) "pendulum" task, in which the subject has to discover that the frequency of oscillation of a pendulum depends solely on the length of the string, excluding other factors such as the weight of the pendulum or the height from which it is released. To solve this problem, the subject has to design an experiment in which one of the factors is tested at a time, all others being held constant. Laurendeau-Bendavid (1977) found that only a few of the schooled adolescents in Rwanda could use formal operations in another of Inhelder's and Piaget's (1958) tasks, the "quantification of probabilities," which requires the comparison of two fractions. Using that same task, as well as others, all carefully adapted for group administration, Pearson (personal communication) found that only a small proportion of secondary school pupils in Ghana could use formal operations.

These findings may have important implications for teaching science and mathematics at the secondary school level, for Piaget's and Inhelder's tasks, although they are not directly drawn from the school curriculum, are obviously relevant to it. On the other hand, outside of that limited context, the tasks are clearly inappropriate to elicit formal operational reasoning in adults who have had a limited exposure to number problems and physics laboratories. In this respect, Feldman (1974) attributes the success of some Eskimo children on the first substage of formal operational thinking to her use of culturally familiar materials; but even in this case, a second level of formal operations did not seem to be reached. In any case, however, the negative results cannot demonstrate the absence of competence; in Cole et al.'s (1971) terms: "whenever we want to use an explanation that requires us to assume that one group 'has a process' while another does not, our interpretation is open to question. It is always possible that further experimentation would turn up evidence of the hypothetical process under proper circumstances" (p. 228).

Jahoda, in Volume 1 of this *Handbook*, puts forward clearly the hypothesis "that many individuals in traditional societies can function at the level of formal operations in spheres familiar to them" (p. 119) and in support of this view, he provides some anecdotal evidence in the areas of social relations and judicial processes. On the other hand, several commentators have questioned the universality of Piaget's developmental sequence by aiming their attack at the "developmental endpoint." Greenfield (1976), for example, remarks that scientific reasoning is not the valued endpoint in most cultures:

> One major criticism of Piaget's theory of development for cross-cultural research is that his notion of development is really the development of a Western scientist. (pp. 324–5)
>
> Cross-cultural researchers have failed to follow Piaget's own demonstration that, to study development, one must first understand the endstate toward which the developmental process is veering. An implication of Piaget's example for cross-cultural research is to ascertain the characteristics of an ideal type in a non-Western culture. (p. 325)

Similarly, Preiswerk (1976) sees Piaget's theory as a typical emanation of Western rationalism, and thus any cross-cultural extension of it as ethnocentrism:

> For Piaget, science is *ipso facto* progress: "reason" is intrinsically better than "primitive" thinking. . . . Rationalism is a fundamental aspect of Piaget's life work. The belief in decentered reason, in objective science, are elements which can possibly hinder cross-cultural communication. (Preiswerk, 1976, p. 504 and 509, our translation)

Buck-Morss (1975) goes a step further in identifying the Piagetian stages as reflecting specifically the social structure of the industrial and capitalistic West. According to her interpretation, Piaget was not so much interested in what the baby, at the sensori-motor stage, could do, as in how quickly it could do without it (p. 40); and according to her, Piaget's tasks of concrete operations "do not track concrete thinking at all . . . but progress toward formal abstraction" (p. 41). This "abstract, formal cognition may reflect a particular social structure, embodying the principles of exchange value, reification, and alienation which govern production and exchange in the industrialized West" (p. 35).

At the same time, as they tax Piaget's theory with ethnocentrism, these authors implicitly appeal for a revival of Levy-Bruhl's "primitive mentality." In their view, rationalism and scientific thinking, and the abstract, conceptual, or theoretic reasoning that they imply are typically Western; magical thinking (Greenfield, 1966), concrete or empiric modes of reasoning, are typically non-Western. Western man is an engineer; non-Western man a "bricoleur" (Lévi-Strauss, 1962). Is this not another form of ethnocentrism?

We are reviving here an age-old debate (cf. Berry & Dasen, 1974), and we have to admit that, as far as hard empirical evidence is concerned, we are hardly more advanced than fifty years ago. Most likely, both extreme positions (complete universality and radical cultural relativism) are equally far from the truth, but the controversy may perhaps lead to new and fruitful avenues of research. For example, there is no doubt that cross-cultural Piagetian research so far has sampled a very restricted set of skills. What we should be asking is, "How well can *they* do *their* tricks?" (Wober, 1969). The difficulty is to reach a sufficient degree of decentration in order to imagine what "their tricks" could be. Price-Williams (1975), for example, suggests that there are areas of knowledge (such as the understanding of altered states of consciousness) that require a different kind of thinking, a "mode of thought . . . which does in fact not sharply distinguish intellect and emotion" (p. 81), which could co-exist with the possibility of adopting strict logical criteria when the situation warrants, and that "the reason such thought has been labelled inferior is that we have no understanding of it" (p. 82). These are the areas of knowledge, in which Western thinking can be seen as "primitive," that may be most valued in other cultures. According to the position exemplified by Jahoda's statement (quoted earlier) one cannot reject off-hand the possibility that formal reasoning does occur in these yet unexplored areas of knowledge.

## Conclusion

It would certainly have been aesthetically more pleasing if we could now summarize a coherent body of empirical research, either supporting the universality of Piaget's theory or else clearly disproving it. But cross-cultural Piagetian psychology has not yet reached that final stage of equilibrium! Instead, we are faced with an intricate picture of universal elements moderated by cultural variation, with a suggestion of "diversification of development with age" (Greenfield, 1976); the picture, moreover, is blurred by unresolved methodological issues, and it is often incomplete because essential data are not yet available. Clearly, there is still a lot of work to be done.

## References

ADJEI, K. Influence of specific maternal occupation and behaviour on Piagetian cognitive development. In P. R. Dasen (Ed.), *Piagetian psychology: Cross-cultural contributions.* New York: Gardner Press, 1977, pp. 227–256.

ASHTON, H. *The Basuto.* New York: Oxford University Press, 1952.

ASHTON, P. T. Cross-cultural Piagetian research: An experimental perspective. *Harvard Educational Review,* 1975, 45 (4), 475–506.

BERNDT, R. M., & BERNDT, C. H. *The world of the first Australians.* Sydney: Ure Smith, 1964.

BERRY, J. W. *Human ecology and cognitive style: Comparative studies in cultural and psychological adaptation.* New York: John Wiley & Sons, 1976.

BERRY, J. W., & DASEN, P. R. *Culture and cognition: Readings in cross-cultural psychology.* London: Methuen, 1974.

BRISLIN, R. W., LONNER, W. J., & THORNDIKE, M. *Cross-cultural research methods.* New York: John Wiley & Sons, 1973.

BOVET, M. C. Cognitive processes among illiterate children and adults. In J. W. Berry & P. R. Dasen (Eds.), *Culture and cognition: Readings in cross-cultural psychology.* London: Methuen, 1974.

———. *Etude interculturelle de processus de raisonnement.* Doctoral thesis, University of Geneva, 1975.

BOVET, M. C., DASEN, P. R., & INHELDER, B. Etapes de l'intelligence sensori-motrice chez l'enfant Baoulé. Etude préliminaire. *Archives de Psychologie,* 1974, 41 (164), 363–386.

BOVET, M. C., & OTHENIN-GIRARD, C. Etude Piagétienne de quelques notions spatio-temporelles dans un milieu Africain. *Journal International de Psychologie,* 1975, *10* (1), 1–17.

BUCK-MORSS, S. Socio-economic bias in Piaget's theory and its implications for cross-cultural studies. *Human Development,* 1975, *18,* 35–49.

CARLSON, J. Kulturvergleichende Forschung sensu Piaget. In H. Walter (Ed.), *Sozialforschung, Band III, Sozialökologie. Neue Wege in der Sozialforschung.* Stuttgart: Frommann Verlag, 1976. (a)

————. Cross-cultural Piagetian studies: What can they tell us? In K. Riegel & J. Meacham (Eds.), *The developing individual in a changing world* (Vol. 1). The Hague: Mouton, 1976, pp. 334–345. (b)

CASATI, I., & LEZINE, I. *Les étapes de l'intelligence sensori-motrice (Manuel).* Paris: Centre de Psychologie Appliquée, 1968.

COLE, M. An ethnographic psychology of cognition. In R. W. Brislin, S. Bochner, & W. J. Lonner (Eds.), *Cross-cultural perspectives on learning.* New York: John Wiley & Sons, 1975.

COLE, M., & BRUNER, J. S. Cultural differences and inferences about psychological processes. *American Psychologist,* 1971, *26* (10), 867–876.

COLE, M., GAY, J., GLICK, J. A., & SHARP, D. W. *The cultural context of learning and thinking.* New York: Basic Books, 1971.

COLE, M., & SCRIBNER, S. *Culture and thought.* New York: John Wiley & Sons, 1974.

————. Developmental theories applied to cross-cultural cognitive research. *Annals of the N.Y. Academy of Sciences,* 1977, *285,* 366–373.

CORMAN, H. H., & ESCALONA, S. K. Stages in sensori-motor development: A replication study. *Merrill-Palmer Quarterly,* 1969, *15* (4), 351–361.

DASEN, P. R. Cross-cultural Piagetian research: A summary. *Journal of Cross-Cultural Psychology,* 1972, *3* (1), 23–39. (a)

————. The development of conservation in Aboriginal childen: A replication study. *International Journal of Psychology,* 1972, *7,* 75–85. (b)

————. Biologie ou culture? La psychologie inter-ethnique d'un point de vue Piagétien. *Psychologie Canadienne,* 1973, *14* (2), 149–166.

————. Le développement psychologique du jeune enfant Africain. *Archives de Psychologie,* 1974, *41* (164), 341–361. (a)

————. The influence of ecology, culture and European contact on cognitive development in Australian Aborigines. In J. W. Berry & P. R. Dasen (Eds.), *Culture and cognition.* London: Methuen, 1974, pp. 381–408. (b)

————. Concrete operational development in three cultures. *Journal of Cross-Cultural Psychology,* 1975, *6* (2), 156–172. (a)

————. Le développement des opérations concrètes chez les Esquimaux Canadiens. *Journal International de Psychologie,* 1975, *10* (3), 165–180. (b)

————. *Piagetian psychology: Cross-cultural contributions.* New York: Gardner Press (Halsted, Wiley), 1977. (a)

————. Are cognitive processes universal? A contribution to cross-cultural Piagetian psychology. In N. Warren (Ed.), *Studies in cross-cultural psychology* (Vol. 1). London: Academic Press, 1977, pp. 155–201. (b)

————. Cross-cultural cognitive development: The cultural aspects of Piaget's theory. *Annals of the N.Y. Academy of Sciences,* 1977, *285,* 332–337. (c)

DASEN, P. R., BERRY, J. W., & WITKIN, H. A. The use of developmental theories cross-culturally. In L. Eckensberger, Y. Poortinga, & W. Lonner (Eds.), Cross-cultural contributions to psychology. Amsterdam: Swets and Zeitlinger, 1979, pp. 69–82.

DASEN, P. R., DE LACEY, P. R., & SEAGRIM, G. N. An investigation of reasoning ability in adopted and fostered Aboriginal children. In G. E. Kearney et al. (Eds.), The psychology of Aboriginal Australians. Sydney: Wiley, 1973.

DASEN, P. R., LAVALLEE, M., & RETSCHITZKI, J. Training conservation of quantity (liquids) in West African (Baoulé) children. International Journal of Psychology, 1979, 14, 57–68.

DASEN, P. R., NGINI, L., & LAVALLEE, M. Cross-cultural training studies of concrete operations. In L. Eckensberger, Y. Poortinga, & W. Lonner (Eds.), Cross-cultural contributions to psychology. Amsterdam: Swets and Zeitlinger, 1979, pp. 94–104.

DASEN, P. R., INHELDER, B., LAVALLEE, M., & RETSCHITZKI, J. Naissance de l'intelligence chez l'enfant Baoulé de Côte d'Ivoire. Berne: Hans Huber, 1978.

DE LACEY, P. R. A cross-cultural study of classification ability in Australia. Journal of Cross-Cultural Psychology, 1970, 1, 293–304.

DE LEMOS, M. M. The development of conservation in Aboriginal children. International Journal of Psychology, 1969, 4, 255–269.

ERNY, P. L'enfant et son milieu en Afrique Noire. Paris: Payot, 1972.

FELDMAN, C. The development of adaptive intelligence. San Francisco: Jossey-Bass, 1974.

FLAVELL, J. H., & WOHLWILL, J. F. Formal and functional aspects of cognitive development. In D. Elkind & J. H. Flavell (Eds.), Studies in cognitive development. New York: Oxford University Press, 1969, pp. 67–120.

FURBY, L. A theoretical analysis of cross-cultural research in cognitive development: Piaget's conservation task. Journal of Cross-Cultural Psychology, 1971, 2, 241–255.

————. Implications of cross-cultural Piagetian research for cognitive developmental theory. In S. Modgil & C. Modgil (Eds.), Toward a theory of psychological development. Windsor: NFER, 1980, pp. 541–564.

FURTH, H. Thinking without language. New York: Free Press, 1966.

GLICK, J. Cognitive development in cross-cultural perspective. In F. D. Horowitz (Ed.), Review of child development research (Vol. 4). Chicago: University of Chicago Press, 1975, pp. 595–654.

GOLDBERG, S. Infant care and growth in urban Zambia. Human Development, 1972, 15, 77–89.

GOODNOW, J. J. A test of milieu effects with some of Piaget's tasks. Psychological Monographs, 1962, 76 (36, Whole No. 555).

GRAVES, A. J. The attainment of conservation of mass, weight and volume in minimally-educated adults. Developmental Psychology, 1972, 7, 223–224.

GREENFIELD, P. M. On culture and conservation. In J. Bruner, R. Olver, P. M. Greenfield et al. Studies in cognitive growth. New York: John Wiley & Sons, 1966, pp. 225–256.

————. Cross-cultural research and Piagetian theory: paradox and progress. In K. Riegel & J. Meacham (Eds.), The developing individual in a changing world (Vol. 1). The Hague: Mouton, 1976, pp. 332–333.

GREENFIELD, P. M., & BRUNER, J. S. Culture and cognitive growth. In D. A. Goslin (Ed.), *Handbook of socialization theory and research*. New York: Rand McNally, 1969, pp. 633–657.

HERON, A. Concrete operations, 'g' and achievement in Zambian children. *Journal of Cross-Cultural Psychology*, 1971, 2, 325–336.

————. Cultural determinants of concrete operational behaviour. In J. L. M. Dawson & W. J. Lonner (Eds.), *Readings in cross-cultural psychology*. Hong Kong: University Press, 1974, pp. 94–101.

HERON, A., & DOWEL, W. Weight conservation and matrix-solving ability in Papuan children. *Journal of Cross-Cultural Psychology*, 1973, 4, 207–219.

————. The questionable unity of the concrete operations stage. *International Journal of Psychology*, 1974, 9 (1), 1–9.

HERON, A., GARDNER, L., & GRIEVE, N. Concrete operational development in Yugoslav immigrant and Australian children. In Y. H. Poortinga (Ed.), *Basic problems in cross-cultural psychology*. Amsterdam: Swets and Zeitlinger, 1977, pp. 119–127.

HERON, A., & KROEGER, E. The effects of training on uneven concrete operational development in Yugoslav migrant children. In J. W. Berry & W. J. Lonner (Eds.), *Applied cross-cultural psychology*. Amsterdam: Swets and Zeitlinger, 1975, pp. 224–230.

HERON, A., & SIMONSSON, M. Weight conservation in Zambian children: A nonverbal approach. *International Journal of Psychology*, 1969, 4, 281–292.

INHELDER, B. *The diagnosis of reasoning in the mentally retarded*. New York: John Day, 1968.

INHELDER, B., & PIAGET, J. *The growth of logical thinking from childhood to adolescence*. London: Routledge and Kegan Paul, 1958.

————. *The early growth of logic in the child*. London: Routledge and Kegan Paul, 1964.

IRWIN, M., KLEIN, R. E., ENGLE, P. L., YARBROUGH, C., & NERLOVE, S. B. The problem of establishing validity in cross-cultural measurements. *Annals of the N.Y. Academy of Sciences*, 1977, 285, 308–325.

KAMARA, A. I., & EASLEY, J. A. JR. Is the rate of cognitive development uniform across culture? In P. R. Dasen (Ed.), *Piagetian psychology: Cross-cultural contributions*. New York: Gardner Press, 1977, pp. 26–63.

KELLY, M. R. Some aspects of conservation of quantity and length in Papua-New Guinea, in relation to language, sex and years at school. *Territory of Papua New Guinea Journal of Education*, 1970, 55–60.

————. Papua New Guinea and Piaget—An eight-year study. In P. R. Dasen (Ed.), *Piagetian psychology: Cross-cultural contributions*. New York: Gardner Press, 1977, pp. 169–202.

KIMINYO, D. M. A cross-cultural study of the development of conservation of mass, weight and volume among Kamba children. In P. R. Dasen (Ed.), *Piagetian psychology: Cross-cultural contributions*. New York: Gardner Press, 1977, pp. 64–88.

KIRK, L. Maternal and subcultural correlates of cognitive growth rate: The Ga pattern. In P. R. Dasen (Ed.), *Piagetian psychology: Cross-cultural contributions*. New York: Gardner Press, 1977, pp. 257–295.

KNAPPEN, M. T. *L'enfant Mukongo*. Louvain: Nauwelaerts, 1962.

KOPP, C. B., KHOKA, E., & SIGMAN, M. A comparison of sensori-motor development among infants in India and the United States. *Journal of Cross-Cultural Psychology*, 1977, *8*, 435–452.

KOPP, C. B., & SIGMAN, M. UCLA revision of the administration manual: The stages of sensori-motor intelligence in the child from birth to two years by Irène Casati and Irène Lézine. Manuscript, 1972.

KOPP, C. B., SIGMAN, M., & PARMELEE, A. H. A longitudinal study of sensori-motor development. *Developmental Psychology*, 1974, *10*, 687–695.

LABOV, W. The logical non-standard English. In F. Williams (Ed.), *Language and poverty*. Chicago: Markham, 1970.

LAURENDEAU-BENDAVID, M. Culture, schooling and cognitive development: A comparative study of children in French Canada and Rwanda. In P. R. Dasen (Ed.), *Piagetian psychology: Cross-cultural contributions*. New York: Gardner Press, 1977, pp. 123–168.

LAUTREY, J., & RODRIGUEZ-TOME, H. Etudes interculturelles de la notion de conservation. In J. Reuchlin (Ed.), *Cultures et conduites*. Paris: P.U.F., 1976, pp. 247–281.

LAVALLEE, M., & DASEN, P. R. Apprentissage de la notion d'inclusion de classes chez de jeunes enfants Baoulés (Côte d'Ivoire). *Journal International de Psychologie*, 1980, *15*, 27–41.

LeVINE, R. A. Cross-cultural studies in child psychology. In P. H. Mussen (Ed.), *Carmichael's Manual of Child Psychology* (Vol. II). New York: John Wiley & Sons, 1970.

LEVI-STRAUSS, C. *La pensée sauvage*. Paris: Plon, 1962.

LEZINE, I., STAMBAK, N., & CASATI, I. *Les étapes de l'intelligence sensori-motrice. Monographie No. 1.* Paris: Centre de Psychologie Appliquée, 1969.

LLOYD, B. B. The intellectual development of Yoruba children: A re-examination. *Journal of Cross-Cultural Psychology*, 1971, *2* (1), 29–38.

———. *Perception and cognition: A cross-cultural perspective*. Harmondsworth, England: Penguin, 1972.

MACCOBY, M., & MODIANO, N. Cognitive style in rural and urban Mexico. *Human Development*, 1969, *12*, 22–33.

MODGIL, S. *Piagetian research: A handbook of recent studies*. Windsor: NFER, 1974.

MODGIL, S., & MODGIL, C. *Piagetian research: Compilation and commentary* (Vol. 8): *Cross-cultural studies*. Windsor: NFER, 1976.

MOHSENI, N. *La comparaison des réactions aux épreuves d'intelligence en Iran et en Europe.* Thèse inédite. Paris: Université de Paris, 1966.

MUNDY-CASTLE, A. C. Social and technological intelligence in Western and non-Western cultures. *Universita* (University of Ghana), 1974, *4*, 46–52.

———. Psychology and the search for meaning. Manuscript, University of Lagos, 1976.

MUNDY-CASTLE, A. C., & OKONJI, M. O. Mother-infant interaction in Nigeria. Manuscript, University of Lagos, 1976.

NERLOVE, S. B., ROBERTS, J. M., KLEIN, R. E., YARBROUGH, C., & HABICHT, J. P. Natural indicators of cognitive development: An observational study of rural Guatemalan children. *Ethos*, 1974, *2*, 265–295.

OHUCHE, R. O., & PEARSON, R. E. Piaget and Africa: A survey of research involving conservation and classification in Africa. In Final Report, Seminar on the Development of Science and Mathematics Concepts in Young Children in African Countries. Nairobi: UNESCO-UNICEF, 1974, pp. 43–59. (Also in Modgil and Modgil, 1976, pp. 163–177.)

OPPER, S. Concept development in Thai urban and rural children. In P. R. Dasen (Ed.), *Piagetian psychology: Cross-cultural contributions.* New York: Gardner Press, 1977, pp. 89–122.

PELUFFO, N. Culture and cognitive problems. *International Journal of Psychology*, 1967, 2 (3), 187–198.

PHILP, H., & KELLY, M. Product and process in cognitive development. *British Journal of Educational Psychology*, 1974, 44, 248–265.

PIAGET, J. *The child's conception of number.* London: Routledge and Kegan Paul, 1952.

————. Nécessité et signification des recherches comparatives en psychologie génétique. *Journal International de Psychologie*, 1966, 1, 3–13. English trans. in J. W. Berry & P. R. Dasen (Eds.), *Culture and cognition.* London: Methuen, 1974, pp. 299–310.

————. Piaget's theory. In P. H. Mussen (Ed.), *Carmichael's Manual of Child Psychology* (Vol. I). New York: John Wiley & Sons, 1970, pp. 703–732.

————. *Le structuralisme.* Paris: P.U.F. (Que Sais-je), 1971.

————. Intellectual evolution from adolescence to adulthood. *Human Development*, 1972, 15, 1–12.

PIAGET, J., & INHELDER, B. *The child's conception of space.* London: Routledge and Kegan Paul, 1956.

PINARD, A., MORIN, C., & LEFEBVRE, M. Apprentissage de la conservation des quantités liquides chez des enfants rwandais et canadiens-français. *Journal International de Psychologie*, 1973, 8 (1), 15–24.

POOLE, H. E. The effect of urbanization upon scientific concept attainment among Hausa children in northern Nigeria. *British Journal of Educational Psychology*, 1968, 38, 57–63.

PREISWERK, R. Jean Piaget et les relations inter-culturelles. *Revue Européenne des Sciences Sociales*, 1976, 14 (38–39), 495–511.

PRICE-WILLIAMS, D. R. *Explorations in cross-cultural psychology.* San Francisco: Chandler and Sharp, 1975.

PRINCE, J. R. *Science concepts in a Pacific culture.* Sydney: Angus and Robertson, 1969.

RAVEN, J. C. *Progressive Matrices.* (Manual) London: Lewis, 1938.

————. *Coloured Progressive Matrices.* (Manual) London: Lewis, 1949.

RICHARDS, A. *Hunger and work in a savage tribe.* London: Routledge, 1932.

SCHMID, E. *L'examen des opérations de l'intelligence en psychopathologie de l'enfant.* Neuchâtel: Delachaux et Niestlé, 1969.

SEAGRIM, G. N. Caveat interventor. In P. R. Dasen (Ed.), *Piagetian psychology: Cross-cultural contributions.* New York: Gardner Press, 1977, pp. 359–376.

SERPELL, R. *Culture's influence on behaviour.* London: Methuen, 1976.

SIEYE, A. *Le développement psychobiologique de l'enfant ouest-africain.* Thèse inédite. Paris: Université René Descartes, 1975.

SKANES, G. R. Conservation and environment. *Canadian Journal of Behavioral Sciences*, 1976, 8 (3), 243–250.

STREHLOW, T. G. H. Culture, social structure and environment in Aboriginal Central Australia. In R. M. & C. H. Berndt (Eds.), *Aboriginal man in Australia.* Sydney: Angus and Robertson, 1965.

SUPER, C. M. Behavioral development in infancy. In R. L. Munroe, R. H. Munroe, & B. B. Whiting (Eds.), *Handbook of cross-cultural human development.* New York: Garland, 1980.

UZGIRIS, I. C. Organization of sensori-motor intelligence. In M. Lewis (Ed.), *Origins of intelligence.* New York: Plenum Press, 1976, pp. 123–164.

UZGIRIS, I. C., & HUNT, J. McV. *Assessment in infancy: Ordinal scales of psychological development.* Urbana: University of Illinois Press, 1975.

WARREN, N. African infant precocity. *Psychological Bulletin,* 1972, *78* (5), 353–367.

——. *Studies in cross-cultural psychology.* (Vol. 1). London: Academic Press, 1977.

——. Universality and plasticity, ontogeny and phylogeny: The resonance between culture and cognitive development. In J. Sants (Ed.), *Developmental psychology and society.* London: Macmillan & Co., 1978., pp. 290–326.

WERNER, E. E. Infants around the world. *Journal of Cross-Cultural Psychology,* 1972, *3* (2), 111–134.

WHITING, B. B. The problem of the packaged variable. In K. F. Riegel & J. A. Meacham (Eds.), *The developing individual in a changing world* (Vol. 1). The Hague: Mouton, 1976, pp. 303–309.

WOBER, M. Distinguishing centri-cultural from cross-cultural tests and research. *Perceptual and Motor Skills,* 1969, *28,* 488.

ZEMPLENI-RABAIN, J. L'enfant Wolof de 2 à 5 ans (Sénégal). Echanges corporels et échanges médiatisés par les objets. *Revue de Neuropsychiatrie Infantile,* 1970, *18* (10–11), 785–798.

# 8

# Studying Personality Development

*June Louin Tapp*[1]

## Contents

## Abstract

The vast and diffuse body of available personality-culture literature was not surveyed in detail in this chapter. Rather, an attempt was made to assess its significance theoretically and methodologically in order to construct heuristic and historically derived criteria for assessing past and future research. This was accomplished by selective analysis of landmark literature and examination of four significant issues that have persisted for almost half a century. One conclusion from this analytic review is that previous efforts were informative but incomplete. A new strategy is proposed, interdisciplinary and interdependent in approach, to gain perspective on the general problem of investigating the relationship of personality to culture and development *and* to answer the specific question: How could or should a cross-cultural researcher ask and answer questions about personality development? Called the Elephant Research Strategy

(ERS), the ERS has six elements and adapts ideas from *ecology*, techniques of *ethnography*, styles of *etiology*, concepts from *ethology*, attempts to avoid *ethnocentrism*, and forwards sentiments from *ethics* appropriate to the study of personality development cross-culturally.

## Ambiance and Aim

The 1970s witnessed a resurgence in the study of personality development cross-culturally. This decade also bore witness to the resiliency and tenacity of the topic. After almost forty years, personality and culture was again a legitimate area for those behavioral scientists—primarily psychologists and anthropologists—who remain preoccupied with investigating the relationship of individuals to societies and concerned with the interaction of personality, culture, and behavior.

### Ambiance

Anthropologists have long been concerned with describing mental processes (Tylor, 1871) and psychologists with explaining the effect of sociocultural systems on personality (Freud, 1930). By the 1920s, anthropologists actively pioneered the area of culture and personality and the topic gained momentum (Benedict, 1934; Kroeber, 1920; Malinowski, 1927; Mead, 1928; Sapir, 1934). For those scientists and scholars influenced by United States investigators, psychoanalytic theory provided the general framework; those influenced by British social anthropologists and French sociologists turned to structural-functional models. An important statement on personality in nature, society, and culture by Kluckhohn and Murray (1948a) came on the heels of a 1947 interdisciplinary conference on culture and personality that focused on four problem areas: defining terms, study techniques, evaluation, integration of future studies (Sargent & Smith, 1949).

The 1950s proved to be an abundant period; but the problems, particularly using psychoanalytic theory, only underscored the difficulty of examining the relationship of personality to culture and behavior (Erikson, 1950; Hallowell, 1953, 1955/1967; Haring, 1956; Mead, 1956; Spiro, 1958). In the 1960s, some researchers, dissatisfied with the state of theory and method in personality and culture assessment, wanted models and materials relevant to the special problems of personality study (Kaplan, 1961a, p. 2). Other researchers tried to fashion specific answers to the question:

"What, then, are the prospects for the psychologist in the cross-cultural study of personality development?" (Holtzman, 1965, p. 68). Still other researchers pursued the emergence of a productive cross-cultural methodology. These trends were fed as much by social psychologists as by anthropologists, psychiatrists, sociologists, or biologists (Adelson, 1969; Bruner, 1964; Campbell, 1961; Cohen, 1961, 1964; Hallowell, 1963; Hsu, 1961a; F. Kluckhohn & Strodtbeck, 1961; LeVine 1963; Mead, 1964; Pelto, 1967; Sears, 1961; Wallace, 1961a, 1961b; Whiting, 1968). A noticeable shift of interest from anthropology to psychology, as well as away from psychoanalytic modes, also occurred in the 1960s (Draguns, 1979; Klineberg, 1980).

By the 1970s, the increasing confusion surrounding the assessment of personality formation was readily articulated, and the need for a cross-disciplinary, cross-cultural research strategy was emphasized (Brislin, Lonner, & Thorndike, 1973; Butcher & Pancheri, 1976; LeVine, 1973a; Looft, 1973; Manaster & Havighurst, 1972; Munroe & Munroe, 1975; Price-Williams, 1974, 1975b; Triandis, 1972; Triandis, Malpass, & Davidson, 1972, 1973). During the same period, there was a call for more comparative child development research (LeVine, 1970). Social scientists interested in personality, culture, and behavior began addressing the importance of using cross-disciplinary paradigms beyond the traditional parameters of psychology and anthropology. For example, they explored multiple methods, cognitive-development variables, and mini-personality models. They also included data from biology and ethology. Such multidisciplinary activity seemed to refute one anthropologist's view that little had developed in the previous few years (Siegel, 1970, p. v), and one psychologist's description of the "magnificent failure" of cross-cultural studies in personality and culture (Bruner, 1974, p. 395). Rather the activity of the early 1970s, despite past disappointments, revealed an "amazing resilience" (Price-Williams, 1975a, p. 429) that previewed a renaissance of interest by the late 1970s (Draguns, 1979; Kiefer, 1977; Spindler, 1978a).

Even this scan of nearly half a century illuminates the changing emphases in research constructs for studying personality development cross-culturally. From the late 1920s to the mid-1950s, the area was dominated by psychoanalytically oriented anthropologists of the "old" culture and personality school. The more statistically or quantitatively oriented behavioral scientists prevailed from the late 1950s into the 1960s. In the late 1960s and the 1970s, the efforts of cross-cultural researchers (primarily psychologists) in the "new" personality and culture school were more evident. The latter group drew as readily on cognitive as on developmental processes, on ecological as on biological explanations, on social psychological as on psychoanalytic methods, in their reconceptualizations of research. Over this same time period, the issue of what constitutes personality and its relationship to culture and development remained a pre-eminent problem in terms of both definition and assessment.

## Aim

Given the complexity of such issues as definition and utility surrounding the study of personality and culture, a basic aim of this chapter is to address the general problem: How could or should a cross-cultural researcher ask and answer questions about personality development? To do this, one needs also to examine questions about the relationship of personality and culture *and* the "universality" of the dimensions underlying these constructs. This is a difficult task undertaken when the field of personality itself is in search of identity and much of science is in pursuit of a philosophy (Barber, 1961; Buss, 1975; Campbell, 1970, 1974b; Campbell & Naroll, 1972; Cronbach, 1975; Fiske, 1974, 1975b, 1978; Inkeles & Levinson, 1954; Kuhn, 1962; Meehl, 1967; Pedersen, 1977, 1979; Popper, 1963, 1968; Reese & Overton, 1970; Shweder, 1975; Tapp, 1980; Triandis, 1974a, 1974b; Vermeulen & deRuijter, 1975).

In the interim, research is published, policy is made, action taken, and programs are developed at national and international levels. Typically they are based on fragmented findings, drawn from areas where the majority of the world's population do not live (i.e., Europe and the United States). But, despite the limitations of generalizing Western models and measures and the questionable applicability of experimental or laboratory techniques, there remains the desire and need to study similarities and differences in the development of the human species world-wide and to distinguish the influences that make for personality. Indeed, the variability over time and place for definitions of personality, culture, and development (e.g., Allport, 1937/1961; Kroeber & Kluckhohn, 1952; LeVine, 1979; Murray, 1938; Werner, 1979) only underscores the need for a cross-cultural psychology of human development—a pan-cultural developmental life-span psychology—that would provide a common framework for assessing and mapping interactions between individual and institution, organism and environment, personality and culture, development and behavior. One aim of this chapter, then, is construction of a strategy for the investigation of what is enduring and characteristic for the individual and the context *and* to understand the interplay between them.

In undertaking this chapter, I want to emphasize that the topic of personality development cross-culturally cannot be treated as if it were an independent field or singular discipline removed from epistemological scrutiny, unblemished by ideological contexts, devoid of philosophical underpinnings, or ignorant of social obligation. Instead, it should be guided by the following kinds of cautions gleaned from the history of cross-cultural efforts, especially during the 1960s and 1970s: (a) that cross-cultural personality study is difficult and therefore requires adequate time and resources (Kaplan, 1961b, p. 310); (b) that multiple procedures should be employed to measure each disposition and must be revalidated in each new cultural setting (LeVine, 1973a, p. 83); (c) that generalizations about "universal" developmental phenomena are possible and can only be established after multiculture studies (Mussen, Conger, & Kagan, 1974, p. 23; Werner, 1979, p. 21); (d) that cross-cultural psychology's challenge to traditional developmental research demands more attention and analysis (Laboratory for Human Cognition, 1979a, p. 828); (e) that research and conceptualization on personality development focus on enduring individual and human characteristics across contexts (Draguns, 1979, pp. 180, 200); and (f) that more than one cultural or intellectual framework be used to explain and interpret finding so that personality development research is more international in its principles, premises, and promises (LeVine, 1979, p. 51; Werner, 1979, p. 2).

Rather than examine the study of personality development in a traditional way, this chapter adopts an unorthodox approach to the task, preferring not merely to catalog previous research reports or to review fragmentary findings from a large, diffuse literature. It offers a set of heuristic and historically derived criteria for assessing past and developing future research. Such an approach should foster psychological and pedagogical styles of inquiry and inference that expand the range and sophistication of theory and interpretation.

This approach is possible in part because of recent coverage on personality development in several substantial, although not exhaustive, reviews (Draguns, 1979; Klineberg, 1980; Laboratory, 1979b; LeVine, 1979; Malpass, 1977; Munroe & Munroe, 1975; Serpell, 1976; Spindler, 1978b; Triandis, Malpass, & Davidson, 1972, 1973; Thomae, 1979; Werner, 1979). Also, it is plausible because the histories and traditions of anthropology and psychology include personality and culture as coherent subjects for study and as explanations of human phenomena. Finally, it is preferable because the use of history—in this case, anthropology's and psychology's—is increasingly seen as a means to gain insight into contemporary psychological and scientific facts (Cronbach, 1975; Gergen, 1976; Smith, 1976).

To introduce the approach as well as to answer the general question of how should personality be studied cross-culturally, the chapter is divided into five parts:

1. *Changing Perspectives in Studying Personality Cross-Culturally* is an assessment of significant psychological and anthropological reviews on personality, comparative and otherwise.

2. *Landmark Literature: Precursors to a Model and a Method* is a discussion of historical commentaries, critical to the study of personality development cross-culturally.

3. *Significant Issues for an Emergent Model and Method* is an explication of ideas basic to a cross-cultural, interactive (biosocial), cognitive, and life-span developmental model.

4. *The Elephant Research Strategy: Approaches to Gain Perspective on the Whole Shape* is a description of six aspects, basic to studying personality development cross-culturally.

5. *Concluding Comment* includes a consideration of the implications for future inquiry and inference.

The reader is invited, as both critical scholar and enterprising student, to ponder the elusive realm of personality development using the framework outlined herein.

## Changing Perspectives in Studying Personality Cross-Culturally

To gain perspective on the nature of the problem, I describe some significant observations on the relationship of personality and culture. This is necessary because definitions in a field are as much phenomena of a culture (whether ethnic or national, scientific or social) as of a history (the decade 1940 versus 1950 or 1960 versus 1970). As such, they reflect the conceptual and methodological issues of a particular space and time. In this section, systematic reviews by United States psychologists are examined first; then, efforts among psychologists with a cross-cultural bent; third, anthropological analyses; and last, recent reactions to efforts in comparative child development.

### The State of the Art and Science in Reviews

To be consistent with the spirit of this chapter, the world's as well as the Western research literatures on personality should have been reviewed also. Unfortunately, space and time precluded this approach. Since inclusion of Asian research was beyond the scope of this work, the reader will find Pedersen's search for non-Western alternatives informative (1977, 1979). For example, Pedersen (1977) outlined some significant differences between Asian and Western psychology and psychotherapy. His exposition of the space-time culture of Asian psychology is instructive. He importantly cautions that, although psychology's cultural scope has broadened, it is perhaps the most culture-bound of the traditional disciplines. This view is supported by LeVine's analysis of child development research wherein, apparently, the most traditional interpretations and orthodox methods of Western psychology prevailed (1979).

A search of the Western–United States literature revealed that there may not be one review on personality research—psychological, cross-cultural, anthropological, or developmental—that does not contain a disclaimer as to bias, sprawl, and space or time limitations. Usually, too, there are demurs about the deficiency in theory and method for an adequate assessment of personality. The phenomenon, however, appears more as a statement on the disconcerting lack of a comprehensive integrated theory of personality development than a reflection on the synthesizing and analytic skills of the researcher. This seeming malady of the individual reviewer is symptomatic of the state of the art and science of personality.

*Psychology*

Recognizing the problematic nature of unicultural approaches, the patterns reported in the annals of United States psychology are, nevertheless, indicative of a major effort. Personality research, even in the 1950s, was described as proliferating semivalid, culturally inappropriate, and nonequivalent measures (Blake & Mouton, 1959; Kelly, 1954). The 1960s apparently brought slight relief either to psychology's "disconcerting sprawl" (Adelson, 1969, p. 217; Sanford, 1968) or to the psychologically oriented anthropologists' "continuing disenchantment" (Pelto, 1967, p. 141). The 1970s were little better. For example, Fiske (1974) described personality research as in a state of chaos and close to its limits; Carlson's (1975) optimism was contained by an eclectic search for theory; and Sechrest (1976) pessimistically documented identity and methodological crises. Only Cattell felt confident of getting beyond "past triviality" (1977a, p. 4). Near the end of the decade, Helson and Mitchell (1978) still reported brooding arguments about the existence of personality theory and the field itself.

From 1969 to 1978, review topics in the *Annual Review of Psychology* revealed a range of incomparable areas and little attention to cross-cultural work. For example, in 1969, Adelson's reports on cross-cultural personality research were basically nonexistent, although he covered four major areas (morality, effectiveness, conflict, aggression). Holzman (1974), recommending a unified field approach to examine the problem of change and continuity in personality development, adopted a developmental life-span framework (early childhood, late childhood, adolescence and young adulthood, and adulthood) to report on personality. However, the representation of cross-cultural personality work was sparse. Carlson (1975) too recognized the utility of biological-evolutionary, developmental life span, and cognitive approaches, but underscored the difficulty of organizing personality findings or posing significant, researchable questions in the absence of any widely shared theory (p. 396). Although she liked LeVine's psychoanalytic population-psychology paradigm, Carlson's report of cross-cultural personality work was lean.

After a ten-year comparison (1965–1974), Sechrest, too, concluded that personality research was extraordinarily complex. He basically thought that personality theory was in "sad shape" and most personality research was "inconsequential, trivial, and pointless" (1976, pp. 2–3). Furthermore, the difficulty in distinguishing among social, personality, and clinical psychology caused Sechrest, like Adelson and others, to argue that personality was suffering an identity crisis. His overall conclusion paralleled Fiske's: Current conceptions of personality and associated research paradigms were viewed as limited, suffering because "most of the data are the products of complex interpretive judgmental processes within the observers; the agreement between sets of observations is limited; [and] the ties between observations and concepts are tenuous and inadequate" (Fiske, 1974, p. 3).

Although Hoffman (1977) described the earlier interest and resurgent activity of psychologists about scientific concerns with "obvious social connotations" (p. 296) in the area of personality and social development (e.g., research on morality and equity), his review gives only limited attention to cross-cultural reports on the topics covered (e.g., development of role-taking skills, moral internalization, sex-role development, intrinsic motivations and external conditions). This lack is especially noticeable in the sections on cognitive aspects; in other areas, only two cross-cultural studies are reported. Nevertheless, Hoffman's observations reflected a major trend to respond to data and social influences when considering personality development from either an intra- or inter-cultural perspective. His analysis further recalled the influence of personal and professional as well as social values on scientific considerations.

Generally then the period from the 1960s into the 1970s, based on the coverage of personality in the *Annual Review of Psychology*, revealed a pessimistic agreement on the dearth of theory and method, loosely undergirded by a proliferation of noncomparable studies. The study of personality was seen by some as an organic and logical extension of clinical diagnosis, by others as complimentary to experimental social psychology, and by still others as defined by trait theories (Edwards & Abbott, 1973). But the period also experienced stronger pleas for other approaches to personality study such as cognitive, developmental, and ethological ones as well as pledges to cross-discipline and cross-cultural efforts (Ginsburg & Koslowski, 1976; Hetherington & McIntyre, 1975; Schaie & Gribbin, 1975). These views were fortified by a general divesting of fifty-year-old theories and twenty-five-year-old methods in a push toward "realistic eclecticism" in the mid-1970s (Carlson, 1975, p. 398) *and* in an effort to overcome the identity crisis in the field of personality, so distinctively felt in the late 1970s (Helson & Mitchell, 1978).

## Cross-cultural psychology

Despite the popularity of personality and culture research in the 1940s and 1950s, many psychologists during the 1960s period were discouraged by the immense complexity of both cross-cultural and personality theory. Some were challenged by the opportunity to resolve conceptual and methodological issues in the cross-cultural arena. This trend increased in the 1970s. Klineberg (1980) skillfully outlined the basic trends and issues before 1960 in the personality and culture field in his description of the historical antecedents of cross-cultural psychology. Some of the points affecting the emergence, decline, and renaissance of cross-cultural personality studies for psychology and anthropology are detailed herein.

The 1960s did nourish a "flowering of a new kind of empirical study and description of personality in nonliterate and non-Western societies" (Kaplan, 1968, p. 329). Some projects were heavily influenced by the pioneer work of such anthropologists as Boas, DuBois, Mead, Hallowell, and Henry. Many studies were primarily anthropological; several had theoretical and methodological problems, further exacerbated by the minimal participation of psychologists (Kaplan, 1968). A few were interdisciplinary in intent only; others were sadly short of a pan-cultural, longitudinal (developmental) component (Holtzman, 1965, 1968). For example, typically the culture-personality projects (e.g., Indian Education Research Project— Hopi, Navaho, Papago, Sioux, Truk, Zuni; Six Cultures Project) involved some personality tests, but usually the interdisciplinary procedures were less productive than planned. In part, this was the result of "a paucity of theoretical orientation"; in part, "the relative sparseness of the personality findings" (Kaplan, 1968, p. 335). Some psychologists viewed the studies of child rearing in the Six Cultures Project, for example, as not adding "a great deal to our present knowledge of personality development" (Holtzman, 1965, p. 68), despite their contribution to the cross-cultural survey approach.

Psychologists interested in universally applicable and durable theories for personality development research emphasized a pan-cultural approach and the need for highly trained, creative specialists in personality study (Kaplan, 1968, p. 332). These were not criticisms of the anthropologists who primarily had worked the culture-personality field, but rather caveats to psychologists wishing to investigate sociocultural factors in personality development. As Holtzman reasoned, "If the purpose of the cross-cultural study is to deal with biological, interpersonal, or environmental universals—that is, concepts which are appropriately applied to nearly any human culture—and if both variety and replication of cultural variables are essential for reaching a generalization, then the design must be pancultural" (1965, p. 69). Other pacesetters confirmed the necessity of psychologists and anthropologists working the field of culture and personality (Hsu, 1961a; Kaplan, 1961a). Such conclusions were basic to a new kind of cross-cultural psychology that emerged in the late 1960s (Holtzman, 1968). They laid the groundwork for a new interest in personality and culture and a new research approach that blossomed in the 1970s among both psychologists and anthropologists.

*Concurrent Anthropology*

The increasing emphasis by the 1970s on cross-cultural study as a research strategy and on a cross-disciplinary framework for obtaining sustainable theories, methods, and findings about human nature was more a phenomenon of psychology than anthropology. Yet some anthropologists courted the dismissal of false and artificial dichotomies between culture and personality, theory and method, similarity and difference. They saw them as disciplinary or culture-bound concepts that inhibited development of plausible alternative hypotheses and minitheories for explanation as well as multimethods for exploration.

Again, suffering the bias of my place and time, I survey reports by knowledgeable United States cultural anthropologists. The area of culture and personality has been ably and critically examined in the *Biennial Review of Anthropology* since 1959. For example, Honigmann (1959) saw psychologists as "more preoccupied than anthropologists with systematic psycho-cultural theory" (p. 69). Wallace and Fogelson (1961) traced significant trends, the most noteworthy dealing with the impact of cognition and physiological/biochemical processes. They underscored Honigmann's earlier report of "widespread dissatisfaction with the methodological and conceptual status of this subfield" (1961, p. 42).

LeVine (1963) lauded the contributions of the academic psychologists to culture-personality problems and their focus on the relation of cognition to culture and to personality (cf. 1979). As importantly, he maintained that the proposed new directions were actually renewed attempts to increase interdisciplinary connections and to link cognitive psychology, human biology, and sociology (1963, p. 111). Pelto's comprehensive chapter (1967) on psychological anthropology pointed to areas of interdisciplinary overlap and to major methodological developments (p. 140). He also recorded trends toward a sophisticated cross-cultural methodology, cognition and perception analysis, the data and theory of zoologists, and movement away from psychoanalysis. Above all, Pelto stressed the importance of asking questions about both the similarities and the differences to discern the " 'universal culture pattern' of human societies . . . the elements of psychic unity" (p. 188).

However, in 1969, editor Siegel omitted some more conventional fields (for example, psychological anthropology) that had "developed little, so far as could be judged, in the way of new departures during the past biennium" (1970, p. v). The omission, in the *Biennial Review of Anthropology* from 1969 until 1977, of cross-cultural personality research signified anthropology's general dismissal of the topic. Interest was partially revived by the double-duty contribution of social psychologists Triandis, Malpassi, and Davidson—first as a *Biennial* chapter entitled, "Cross-cultural Psychology" with a section on "Socialization, Personality, Psychopathology" (1972); then second, as an *Annual Review* chapter entitled, "Psychology and Culture" with a section on "Personality Dispositions" (1973). Also there was evidence of pertinent research in Arensberg's 1972 "Culture as Behavior," Udy's 1973 report on "Cross-cultural Analysis: Methods and Scope," Draper's 1974 "Comparative Studies of Socialization," Firth's 1975 "Appraisal of Modern Social Anthropology," and Fox and Fleising's 1976 "Human Ethology." In 1977, Kiefer's review of "Psychological Anthropology" described the psychological concerns of anthropologists. By 1979, two chapters contained research of interest to students of cross-cultural personality development: Jorgensen's on "Cross-cultural Comparisons" and Freedman and DeBoer's on "Biological and Cultural Differences in Early Child Development."

To understand Siegel's exclusion of psychological anthropology in 1969 and his inclusion of Kiefer's chapter in 1977 requires some appreciation of the diversity of anthropological research, the variation in personality conceptualizations and the value assigned to psychological explanations, and the relative marginality of the field of personality and culture in contemporary anthropology. The surveys from 1959 to 1967 in the *Biennial Review of Anthropology* represented the diversity among anthropologists geared to the cross-cultural study of personality. Those reports partially prompted Siegel's action, revealed the continual theoretical and methodological quandary, and fed the emergence of a new culture and personality orientation. Siegel's 1969 editorial decision, the subsequent comparative reviews, the inclusion of the Triandis and associates' analyses, and Kiefer's 1977 accounting again affirmed the shift in leadership in personality and culture study from anthropology to psychology.

*Comparative Child Development*

By the late 1970s there was increasing skepticism about the track record and approach of child development theory and research from anthropologists and psychologists alike (e.g., Bronfenbrenner, 1977; Laboratory, 1979a, 1979b; LeVine, 1979; Werner, 1979). This was the case, despite—or perhaps because of—an increasing availability of published data and an increased level of sophistication about comparative work.

For example, Cole and associates concluded that the overall historical contribution of cross-cultural research to child development research was not noteworthy (Laboratory, 1979a, p. 827). Nevertheless, despite methodological weaknesses in unraveling the interactive social, physical, and cultural variables that affect growth and development, contemporary efforts in cross-cultural psychology seemed simultaneously to be challenging traditional developmental findings and stimulating analysis of common methodological difficulties (e.g., comparing performances of persons from different cultures or ages who are unclear about the investigators' materials, motives, or methods). Particularly critical of child psychology's devotion to experimental laboratory methods, settings, and tasks, Cole and associates felt that such adherence ignored the effects of the culturally embedded context and the individual's specific activities (Laboratory, 1979a, 1979b).

Like Cole and associates, LeVine (1979) criticized the child psychologists, particularly in the United States, for their singleminded adherence to laboratory settings and experiments. He argued that scientific advancement and psychological knowledge in the domains of personality and behavior required naturalistic, descriptive field studies. LeVine also chided psychologists for their preoccupation with cognitive development (cf. Cartwright, 1978; Tapp, 1980). Their choice of culturally confining and ideologically based developmental concepts was faulted as well (e.g., United States concern with mother-infant reciprocal communication patterns). LeVine, who had anticipated the 1960s and early 1970s' upsurge in comparative child development work to yield a pan-cultural psychology of development as well as an integration of cross-cultural evidence into child development theory and research (LeVine, 1970), regretted that neither had occurred by the end of the decade (LeVine, 1979). After surveying developmental, cross-cultural, and anthropological journals from 1974 to 1978, LeVine concluded that mainstream developmental psychology was insular, dominated by the most orthodox traditions of psychology, and undertook few cross-cultural studies. He called for an immediate reshaping of comparative child development research, consistent with his proposals for studying the relationships of personality, culture, and behavior (1973a, 1977). (His approach to the cross-cultural study of personality is examined in greater detail in a subsequent section of this chapter.)

These positions were consistent with other reviews of the nature and direction of personality development research within and across cultures (Helson & Mitchell, 1978; Kiefer, 1977; Thomae, 1979). For example, a non-United States analyst reviewing selected studies on personality development in two cultures stressed that cross-cultural studies generally, and studies of personality development especially, can contribute to developmental psychology in four ways: They can provide information on life-span consistencies and changes, thus clarifying their generality in the life cycle; they can connect personality to cultural variables, thus accepting their interactions in development process; they can offer possible pan-cultural validity to Western-derived theories; and they can call into question Western personality development models, thus encouraging other concepts and orientations (Thomae, 1979, p. 298). Thomae also strongly urged cross-sectional and longitudinal studies on more than one-age group, in order to reduce the confounding effects of method and sample *and* in order to aid in the construction of a strategy to assess the complex patterns of consistency and change. These would help chart the interactions between culture and individual in the development process as well.

## A Review of the Reviews

On balance, although the emphasis among psychologists and anthropologists were not comparable over the past two decades, there was a parallel, enduring chant of dismay, discouragement, and dissatisfaction about personality research and the absence of sustainable constructs for theory and method, definition and procedure. Yet the field of personality and culture continues with unending interest. In the long run, cross-cultural research on personality development may provide a strategy for addressing the substantive, conceptual, and methodological issues basic to understanding personality development both as a product of similarities (universals, psychic unity) and differences (cultural impact, situational phenotype).

## Landmark Literature: Precursors to a Model and a Method

Analyses of historical, landmark personality-culture efforts are basic to the next round of theoretical and methodological synthesis. While others might have chosen differently, the works included here seem appropriate because the materials are available so detailed review is unnecessary. Additionally, more than one disciplinary perspective is considered and, at least, one major representative chosen from each decade, commencing with the 1940s. A description of earlier and additional contributions can be found in Klineberg (1980, see the chapter in Volume 1 of this *Handbook*).

## Kluckhohn and Murray: The Baseline
### (1940s versus 1950s)

Even though the 1920s were heralded as an important era for personality and culture (LeVine, 1973a; Singer, 1961), the Kluckhohn and Murray (1948a) anthology introduced a multidimensional perspective at a time when others' frameworks were "purely biological, or social, or cultural— however much verbal hat-tipping there may be to the other dimensions" (p. xiii). Then, as now, their work provided a baseline for estimating the adequacy of multidimensional conceptions of personality and culture as well as research progress in the area.

Murray and Kluckhohn generally conceptualized personality as a personal ability to organize life. Specifically, they described it as a temporal organization of brain process with the important attributes of all-inclusiveness and organization (1948, p. 7). More than a cluster of traits or a list of adjectives, it encompassed *"the entire sequence of organized governmental processes in the brain from birth to death"* (p. 9). As "the architecture of the whole" (p. 11), it created "a design for living" and, at its highest level of integration, "a philosophy of life" (p. 32).

By 1953, Murray and Kluckhohn revised their conception of personality. The brain was not the personality, but a constitutional determinant. Even though a multidimensional conception of personality integrating the biological, social, and cultural aspects of personality prevailed, their newly extended description shifted from a constitutionally oriented position toward a culturally determined one. This functional characterization of personality formation underscored that the socialization process (with its power to inhibit) had as one goal the "unreluctant emotional identification with the developing ethos of society" (1953, p. 45). Another embedded core goal was moral learning.

In defining personality and describing socialization, Kluckhohn and Murray (1948a, 1948b, 1953b) also touched on the issue of universality (i.e., universal behaviors, values, or hypotheses). Like Homans (1950) also in the 1950s and Spiro later (1978), Kluckhohn and Murray accepted variation in human behavior the world over but believed that relationships between the elements of behavior remained the same. Although they recognized the unique, they stressed the primacy of the universal: "Man is in many respects like no other man" [but] "without the discovery of uniformities there can be no concepts, no classifications, no formulations, no principles, no laws" (1953b, pp. 55–56). Kluckhohn later contended that more anthropologists had stated and tested "universal hypotheses than many psychologists recognize" (1954, p. 952). In short, universality was a domain of mutual relevance to psychologists and anthropologists.

In addition, in both the 1948 and 1953 versions, Kluckhohn and Murray described the interactive impact of external exigencies. In explaining the three universal antecedents of every human, they cited four determinants: constitutional, group membership, role, and situational. At any given point, personality was the product of a long series of complex interactions between biologically inherited potentialities and environmental forces (1953b, p. 56). Most similarities and differences between people were attributed to fairly uniform social and cultural processes (1953b, p. 68). For Kluckhohn and Murray in the 1950s, an interactional model was essential. It was an important effect in the 1960s. It retained its saliency during the 1970s as well (cf. Draguns, 1979; Laboratory, 1979a, 1979b; LeVine, 1973a, 1979; Triandis, 1977a, 1977b, 1977c).

In 1954, Kluckhohn's synoptic review on culture and behavior addressed such variables as internal biological and sexual behavior, perception and cognition, affect and phantasy, abnormal and evaluative behavior, child training and personality, and anthropology and psychology. It was basic to evolving directions in personality and culture research. Kluckhohn reported that few findings provided insight into the relationship between personality and child rearing, despite the area "being so fashionable for the last decade or two" (1954, p. 949; see also Henry & Boggs, 1952). These concerns about the need for research on child development and child rearing were still being expressed in the 1960s and 1970s by anthropologists and psychologists alike (Bronfenbrenner, 1974a, 1974b; Hartup, 1973; Holtzman, 1965; LeVine, 1970, 1979; Werner, 1979). The basic lack of theoretical and methodological progress was and is discouraging. Nevertheless, Kluckhohn and Murray jointly and individually previewed the problems, procedures, and paradigms of the subsequent decades.

## Inkeles and Levinson
### (1950s versus 1960s)

The 1954 and 1969 reviews by Inkeles and Levinson provided an opportunity to chart variables that affected thinking about personality development. For example, in 1954 they reviewed the role of the sociocultural system on personality formation from the perspectives of the infant/child-care disciplines and developmental theory; in 1969, they concentrated on familial, extrafamilial, and sociocultural influences in early childhood and post-childhood personality development. Both versions, however, were guided by "personal and professional predilections" (1954, p. 978) about the relationship between modal personality and the sociocultural order.

Inkeles and Levinson focused on three aspects of modal personalities: the characteristics of such modes, determinants, and their role in their sociocultural systems (1954, p. 979). They argued that modal personality—in this instance, national character—was best studied through large-scale analysis of individuals, not cultural processes or products such as rituals, social structures, or media. Unlike Benedict (1934) or Mead (1951), they did not use the term synonymously with the sum of learned cultural behavior (p. 980). In the Linton tradition (1945), they conceptualized modal personality in statistical terms, arguing that in any society there are many individual personality patterns and any one could be modal within that distribution. Furthermore, to Inkeles and Levinson, national character referred primarily to adult personality.

In both decades, Inkeles and Levinson basically addressed two major issues: (1) the role of sociocultural systems in the formation of modal personality and (2) the role of national character in the functioning of the social system. With regard to the first, they asked about the more or less standard sociocultural *"regularities in the social conditions of development"* that helped *"determine the observed regularities (or modes) in adult personality"* (1954, p. 999). They described the lack of impact of developmental theory and concluded that beyond studying infant and child-care disciplines, "relatively little has been done to explore additional determinants of modal personality structuration" (1954, p. 1001). The basic absence of empirical developmental studies was more conspicuous by 1969. They argued, as had Holtzman (1965), that the "relative paucity of developmental theory concerning later periods" (1969, p. 468) reinforced an almost exclusive focus on early childhood. While Inkeles and Levinson recognized the importance of developmental theory, they did not provide a developmental analysis but described a modal structure by its contemporaneous characteristics.

With regard to Inkeles and Levinson's second concern—the role of national character in the social system—they theorized that sanctions (both rewards and punishments) induced socially appropriate behavior. Even though readiness might vary societally, the effectiveness of any social sanction seemed to depend on the psychological constellations (such as guilt or shame) among members of the social system (1954, p. 1005).

Although Inkeles and Levinson recognized the major contributions of psychoanalytic and learning theory, they described the former's failure to count "environmental forces and the person-environment interaction" (1954, p. 984) and the latter's error in unduly emphasizing childhood training experiences (1954, p. 987). In developing their personality models, they concentrated on a limited number of analytic criteria such as universality; crucial issues such as relationship to authority, modes of cognitive functioning, and styles of expressive behavior; and major psychological dispositions such as aggression, dependency, curiosity, and homosexuality (1954, pp. 989–993).

For the most part then, Inkeles and Levinson's 1954 and 1969 chapters addressed the same problems, sometimes with new studies. For example, they expanded the learning theory discussion to include several critical child-rearing studies, added sections on value-motive-trait theories, and on cognitive effects. The modest changes from 1954 to 1969 must be viewed in the context of Inkeles and Levinson's continuing commitment to the impact of structure—the sociocultural variables—on personality. They pressed for increased attention to the economic, political, and bureaucratic institutional complexes that loom large in modern industrial society (1954, p. 1015 vs. 1969, p. 492). They believed such inquiry would contribute significantly to the development of systematic theory and to an understanding of institutional functioning and change.

Despite the similarities between the two Inkeles and Levinson chapters, the second one did provide a baseline to assess change in culture and personality research over a fifteen-year period. In 1969, Inkeles and Levinson identified two historical periods: Between 1935 and 1955, socially oriented anthropologists intensively explored single societies using ethnographic and clinical methods; between 1955 and 1965, they characteristically used a quantitative, comparative (multisocietal) approach (p. 441). They concluded that since the early 1960s anthropology withdrew from the study of personality and culture generally and from national character specifically (1969, p. 420). Although somewhat premature about the reduced interest of anthropology in culture and personality, Inkeles and Levinson's discussion of the growing influence of academic psychology (versus clinical, psychoanalytic) and sociology was reaffirmed in subsequent reviews (Draguns, 1979; Elder, 1976; Klineberg, 1980; LeVine, 1973a, 1979; Triandis et al., 1972, 1973). In sum, the span from 1954 to 1969 was a crucial time theoretically and methodologically as well as in terms of different disciplinary involvement.

The 1960s

*Hsu versus Kaplan (1961)*

The year 1961 was a critical one for the study of personality development cross-culturally. It marked the publication of two landmark compendia:

one edited by a psychologist (Kaplan, 1961a), the other by an anthropologist (Hsu, 1961a). Even though the composition was interdisciplinary, the contributors in each were primarily anthropologists and psychologists: Six authors—DeVos, Honigmann, Inkeles, Kaplan, Spiro, and Wallace—appeared in both books.

Both Hsu and Kaplan intended to update as well as to indicate future directions for the almost quarter-of-a-century-old field of personality and culture. Neither compendium was comprehensive in its coverage; both focused on the paucity *and* promise of the field with regard to findings, methods, and theories. These two critical commentaries laid the groundwork for analyses in the latter half of the 1960s, as exemplified in reviews by psychologist Child (1968), anthropologists DeVos and Hippler (1969), and the already-described revised Inkeles and Levinson chapter (1969). All, in turn, affected the orientation and renewed interest in personality and culture in the 1970s.

In the Hsu book, Honigmann reported declining enthusiasm for culture and personality research due to "the growing climate of empiricism and operationalism, the high evaluation of objectivity, and the stress put on objective reliability" (1961, p. 126). Spiro declared that culture and personality's original mission had ended and suggested a reorientation (1961a, pp. 468, 470). But Hsu, rather than tolling a death knell, proposed a new approach and a new subdiscipline: "psychological anthropology" (1961b, p. 6). He described the mutually enriching relationship possible between psychological anthropology and social psychology. In part, this turn in anthropology stemmed from difficulties encountered studying personality using such concepts as basic personality structure or modal personality; in part, from a shift in stressing psychoanalytic, statistical, or functional studies to ones exploring biological and cognitive aspects of personality; and in part, from the need felt for a synthesis between the methods of psychology (the collection of individual data) and anthropology (the collection of cultural data).

Kaplan was one of the few psychologists who raised questions about future personality and culture research. He expected his book's authors to recommend empirical techniques that would yield representative expressions about individual personality processes as well as lead to valid statements about typical group processes (1961c, p. 659). An unplanned change occurred: The problem of finding techniques for cross-cultural personality study became overshadowed by the discussion of culture and personality theory. In a shifting theoretical situation, emphasis on methodological issues alone seemed premature (p. 660).

Kaplan's own interests were in the area of social character. He saw as the basic culture and personality issue of the 1960s "not why persons wish to do this or that act, but why they are good citizens" (p. 666). The past symmetry assumed between the social system's role requirements and the individual personalities had been replaced with the notion that social and personality systems need not be isomorphically structured. For Kaplan, not unlike Spiro, this change emancipated motivations from role requirements (1961c, p. 663). The problem, then, was not motivation of specific role behavior, but conformative behavior generally (Spiro, 1961b, p. 122). Even though social character provided a key to conformity motivation and authority relations, the personality and culture approach was "the vital center of a future science of man" (Kaplan, 1961c, p. 669).

*Singer (1961).* In the Kaplan book, Singer (1961) surveyed the culture and personality field through the 1950s. The dominant themes clustered in several areas: the relationships of culture to human nature, culture to typical personality, and culture to individual personality. The culture and human nature dilemma gradually changed from a position of plasticity— "it's not human nature, but only culture" (p. 17)—to a stance on the "psychic unity of man" (p. 18). His concept of universal personality drew on parallel experiences such as helplessness and dependency in infancy, competition for affection, and sibling rivalry. He concurred with Mead and Wolfenstein (1955) that recurrent biological similarities in growth, parent-child relationships, and needs and fears made it possible "to compare childhood in one society with childhood in another" (pp. 6–7). Singer's interest in human nature went beyond the phylogenetic core to a "developed human nature" found in all human societies (p. 21). Accordingly, developed human nature was not explicable entirely on the basis of modal inborn potentialities, but evolved as humans confronted similar realities and environments from birth to death.

The relationship between culture and typical personality, a major concern from 1934 to 1950, was dominated by such constructs as configurational personality, basic personality structure, modal personality, and national character (Bateson, 1936; Benedict, 1934; DuBois, 1944; Fromm, 1941; Gladwin & Sarason, 1953; Gorer, 1949; Kardiner, 1939; Wallace, 1952). These approaches shared a core concept of personality as a product of "learning rather than genetics" (Singer, 1961, p. 22), but they differed regarding the data base for deriving the typical personality. Some inferred it from cultural data; others used psychological data. Singer saw as unworkable the proposal that individual psychological data, largely based on contemporaneous tests, replace cultural data (e.g., ceremonies, songs, war practices). In discussing cultural versus individual data, he argued that the problem was not what data to use, but rather when to use discrepant results.

In his third area, culture and the individual personality, Singer recast the issue as a debate between psychology and anthropology. Like others who had done so earlier (Kroeber, 1948; Sapir, 1938), he also examined the necessary relationship between anthropology and psychology in studying personality. Singer concluded that the culture and personality approach "requires an alternating and almost simultaneous use of two different perspectives—that of culture and that of the individual person" (p. 65). Unlike Inkeles and Levinson, Singer sought a synthesis of cultural and individual data to explain universal personality. Such was the mood of the 1950s as reported in the early 1960s.

## Child (1968)

Anthropologist Singer's discussion of the interdependence of individual and cultural data sharply contrasted with psychologist Child's concentration on hypothesis testing and individual psychological data. Child's review of personality in culture (1968), less integrative in trend, continued the tradition of researching differences to explain personality. His work also exemplified the push toward methodological over conceptual concerns. For example, Child attended to such major problems in cross-cultural data collection as language and conceptual translation, response biases, sampling, and group- or individual-derived data. He argued for using "two or more different *kinds* of tests" (p. 133) to provide more than indifferent or discrepant results and to ferret out the universals in personality formation. Child maintained that much personality and culture research overly emphasized replication of uniformities and insufficiently recognized diversity. He also argued that "if psychologists naturally take for granted the psychic unity of mankind, it by no means follows that their methods are adequate for arriving at an apt characterization of that unity" (p. 85). Child viewed personality as "internally determined consistencies underlying a person's behavior attributable to stable internal characteristics" (p. 83).

In chronicling the relationship between group character and modal personality, Child explored research on traits, states, or characteristics such as aggression, competition and social acceptance, and authoritarianism. In describing the dimensions of personality and differentiations within society, he reported work, for example, on anxiety, on filial aspirations, and on creativity. In assessing group character and historical change, McClelland's research (1961) on achievement motivation was central. In all of the above, as valid as the discrete dimensions of personality were to Child, all important were multiple methods and statistical procedures for testing hypotheses relevant to cross-cultural personality development.

Child further recognized the primacy in United States personality research of cognitive aspects in studies of individual and group differences (p. 105). Examples included Mercado, Diaz, and Gardner's study of cognitive style in Mexican and United States children (1963) and Goodman's report on the conceptualizing styles of Japanese and United States youth (1962). Apparently, psychologists and anthropologists increasingly and independently viewed cognition as a fruitful domain for study. By the 1970s, it became a primary one, sometimes at the price of reduced attention to social effects (cf. Cartwright, 1978; Laboratory, 1979b; LeVine, 1979; Tapp, 1980).

## DeVos and Hippler (1969)

Anthropologists DeVos and Hippler (1969) used the concept of "cultural psychology" to analyze culture and personality. They focused on six major concerns wherein culture was the major variable or effect: physical and motor development; perception and cognition as information processing mechanisms of personality; symbolic thought and expressions; socialization processes such as child-rearing practices, role expectations, and value orientations; social change and innovation on personality systems; and mental health, conformity, and deviancy. Personality was defined as learned patterns dependent on a cultural environment but as "no more reducible to analysis only in cultural terms than cultural patterns are reducible to psychological patterns" (p. 324). Culture was described as "a significant determinant of human behavior" but psychological traits, configurational in nature, were not derived from "an elementalistic or reductionist breakdown into parts" (p. 324).

In relating motor behavior to culture and personality (e.g., aggression), DeVos and Hippler pointed to the need to integrate physiological, individual-psychological, and patterned-cultural explanations. In considering information processing and personality, they stressed the importance of experience and instruction, social origins, and theoretical orientations toward cognition and perception (Frake, 1962/1972, 1971; Hunt, 1961; Segall, Campbell, & Herskovits, 1963). Despite evidence of the Piagetian model's cross-cultural applicability, they provided methodological and administrative criticisms about the approach (DeVos & Hippler, 1969, pp. 339–340; cf. Dasen, 1974; Dasen & Heron, in this volume; Jahoda, 1958; Pick, 1980; Simpson, 1974).

For DeVos and Hippler, the central focus of cross-cultural research on personality was the impact of socialization processes (p. 359). They used social role and psychoanalytic studies to evolve a concept of personality based on the interaction of social environments and individual psychological mechanisms. In tracing how role expectations reflect significant cultural patterns, DeVos and Hippler assumed all people in all places faced "a limited number of fundamental human problems" (p. 366). The relationship of political behavior to personality and culture was also examined using cross-cultural as well as cross-disciplinary studies. In agreement with other analysts, they concluded that future studies should determine the exact manner of transmission of authority patterns by parental and other authority figures (p. 375). The increased attention to personality and political behavior was a phenomenon of the 1960s that paralleled the interest in national character of the 1950s.

On balance, DeVos and Hippler felt that anthropological data severely challenged notions of universality. Illustratively, they reviewed three major areas: traumatic weaning, sleeping patterns, and internalization of moral directives. For example, a survey of cross-cultural personality studies done in Africa showed the generally negative effects of abrupt weaning, but spoke less to ethnocentric effect or rural/urban bias (Geber, 1958, 1961; LeVine, 1961).

DeVos and Hippler's section on culture, mental health, and social deviancy also addressed the issue of the universality of behavior. To them, comparative anthropological data severely challenged (p. 324) the universality conclusions of psychological reports (cf. Butcher & Pancheri, 1976; Dohrenwend & Dohrenwend, 1974; Pedersen, Lonner, & Draguns, 1976). These findings may also reflect disciplinary differences. For example, Western-trained psychologists or psychiatrists, studying disturbed patients in radically different cultures, typically rely on their own cultural background and use Western descriptive psychiatric or psychoanalytic formulations. On the other hand, anthropologists do not define the same overt observed behavior as "illness" in all cultures and, therefore, use "culturally relative yardsticks to measure behavior" (p. 376).

DeVos and Hippler's final section testified to anthropology's adherence to cultural relativity and to the major influences of descriptive psychiatry, psychoanalytic theory, and sociological functionalist theory on culture and personality research. Overall, DeVos and Hippler's effort was another milestone exploring the relevance of psychology, anthropology, and sociology to cross-culture personality study.

*A note on the 1960s.* In comparing the reviews of the late 1960s with the earlier ones, several issues emerged as precursors for the 1970s. For example, Child's strong emphasis on methodology confirmed Kaplan's forecast of a future major concern. The late 1960s generally witnessed Inkeles and Levinson's anticipated influence of academic psychology in the culture and personality field. The importance of conformity and noncongruity on motives and roles, identified earlier by Kaplan, were salient for DeVos and Hippler, too. In discussions of social change and role status, there were more attempts to merge psychological and anthropological perspectives as called for by Singer and Hsu and to reorient personality and culture research as suggested by Spiro. Basically, however, controversies about personality usually involved "internecine squabbling about this or that measure, method, or technique within a specific domain of research" (Adelson, 1969, p. 217).

The late 1960s' chapters exhibited other similarities, despite disciplinary differences. Specifically, increased attention was paid to the role of cognition, the status of developmental theory and method, the socialization process beyond child rearing, the import of cultural and personality differences, and the necessity of interdisciplinary perspectives. The state of the art was again to be critically reviewed in the 1970s, and LeVine's work would be central to such considerations.

## LeVine and the 1970s

LeVine's work may be to the 1970s what Kluckhohn and Murray's had been to the 1940s. It, too, initiated a decade of rethinking about culture and personality (1969, 1970, 1973a, 1973b, 1979). It was as much a marker for psychology as anthropology, arguing as LeVine did that: (1) "there are no serious theoretical disputes among contemporary culture and personality theorists"; (2) "the major difficulties and controversies in culture and personality are methodological"; and that (3) "the demonstration of detailed psychological differences (and similarities) among populations has become a central focus of culture and personality research" (1973a, pp. 11, 98). Despite a psychoanalytic orientation, LeVine well understood the interdisciplinary nature of culture and personality research. Since he maintained that the major controversies in culture and personality were methodological, LeVine easily coupled his psychoanalytic orientation to a Darwinian model of functional interaction between genotype and phenotype. He saw his research strategy as integrating trends from compatible theories (cf. Pervin, 1974; Price-Williams, 1975a).

LeVine characterized personality as "the organization in the individual of those processes that intervene between environmental conditions and behavioral response" (1973a, p. 5). Observed behavioral consistencies are "indicators" of the internal dispositions that influence overt behavior (p. 7). Personality (a tripartite arrangement of indicators, dispositions, and organization) is "internally as well as environmentally adaptive" [and] "has a history of its formation in the life of the organism" (p. 8).

LeVine's omnibus term, *culture,* designated both the distinctive forms of human adaptation and the distinctive organizing ways of different human populations. The culture patterns, an "organized body of rules" (p. 4), facilitate communication and self-awareness, guide behavior toward the environment, and limit the range of variation. Once institutionalized with sanctions and norms, they lead to role expectations that exert normative pressures for correct performance, but also offer opportunities for personal satisfaction.

LeVine's approach to culture and personality implied that whatever the formulations, "cross-cultural differences in personality are the true starting points for culture and personality study" (1973a, p. 39). He further identified questions about human behavior in terms of psychological differences between human populations at individual development and sociocultural levels (pp. 10–12).

The most conspicuous characteristics of LeVine's conceptualization are its eclectic nature and its attention to research strategies (i.e., methodology). He recommended the intensive study of individuals based on a psychoanalytic/ethnographic/ecological/embryological approach to obtain reliable personality indicators. His proposed method included three elements representing the physiological, ecological, and embryological (p. 212). The physiological strategy covered the individual organism; the ecological, the individual in relation to the environment; and the embryological, the growth patterns of the individual within the environmental matrix. Additionally, his research strategy was premised on "an unequivocal mandate from the clinical practitioners of psychoanalysis" (p. 210), but not at the loss of attention to such processes as perception, cognition, memory, and learning. Furthermore, although historically many methods for analyzing personality through cultural material were for "convenience rather than choice" (p. 73), LeVine correctly maintained that the expansion of cross-cultural research by psychologists made "armchair assessment of personality less tolerable than ever" (p. 74).

LeVine's 1970 cross-cultural study of child psychology contained an earlier exposition of his research strategy. LeVine emphasized the centrality of ethnographic and nonethnocentric data collection plus the necessity of etiological (causal) strategies for explaining variations in behavior within and between cultures. Citing the limits of cross-sectional studies, he recommended longitudinal ones to gain needed developmental data. LeVine particularly wanted more data "on young children and in longitudinal measurement" (1970, p. 603). He sought alternative models for studying the antecedent/consequent relations of modernization, educational level, and socioeconomic participation, based on ethnological, ecological, and etiological methods. Cognizant of continuing challenges to statistical and naturalistic observational methods, LeVine concluded that no single study could sufficiently account for the causes of variation across settings: "A multiplicity of experimental, longitudinal, and comparative studies are required to test the variety of alternative hypotheses offered in explanation of the original findings" (p. 566). Such a multimethod and multivariable approach increasingly characterized others in the 1970s (Campbell, 1971, 1974a; Cronbach, 1975; Elms, 1975; Rohner, 1975a, 1975b; Shweder, 1973; Triandis, 1972).

For these reasons, his 1979 presentation to the Society for Research in Child Development (SRCD) is especially significant and provocative. Le-Vine announced that his intent ten years earlier (1970), to bridle the enthusiasm of psychologists to do research in other cultures and to integrate cross-cultural psychology into child development theory and research, was unnecessary. In contrast to the praise bestowed on academic psychology in 1963, LeVine in 1979 took it to task for its ethnocentrism, insularity, and orthodoxy. For example, his survey of articles in child development journals from 1974–1978 revealed only 9.3 percent were cross-cultural in the broadest sense; more than 75 percent of these were from Western industrial societies. LeVine was disturbed by the lack of cross-cultural awareness and noncomparative publications in child development. As noted earlier in this chapter, he felt this "dismal picture" had come about because "child development research is dominated by some of the most orthodox traditions of psychology" (pp. 6–7). In an articulate call to go beyond experimental design and formal hypothesis-testing to include a "tradition of descriptive field studies" (ethnography), LeVine further suggested that much of psychology is a reflection of Western conceptions of the individual and that "all empirical psychology is folk psychology to some degree" (p. 9). He argued avidly for the need to recognize the continuity between folk psychology and concepts of child psychology as a means of understanding personality development more fully. Committed as he has been for almost two decades, LeVine proposed again that cross-cultural evidence (data) can refine understanding about the universals in behavior (e.g., maternal patterns), culture-specific behaviors (e.g., cooperation, moral reasoning), and environmental influences on development.

Overall, LeVine's 1970 review, 1973 book, and 1979 presentation remain important developments for an antecedent-consequent model of inquiry. In all, he singled out the importance of descriptive and developmental data to understanding the origins of cross-cultural differences. In highlighting the variable quality of child development research, LeVine also strongly indicated one cogent form of cross-cultural research and called for a research strategy to provide valid data. That call paralleled other disciplinary and methodological efforts, similarly attempting to revive the area as well as refine definitions of personality, culture, and behavior (Berry & Dasen, 1974a, 1974b; Holtzman, Diaz-Guerrero, & Swartz, 1975; Draguns, 1979; Osgood, May, & Miron, 1975; Spindler, 1978a). Other notable influences, which became apparent in the 1970s, included evidence of the fruitful marriages of social and developmental psychology to culture and personality study (Campbell & Naroll, 1972; Edgerton, 1970/1973, 1974; Hsu, 1972a; Price-Williams, 1974, 1975b). All provided a framework for ordering those issues vital to studying personality development cross-culturally.

*A Note on 1975 Plus*

Although the previous years exhibited a cyclic pattern of enchantment and disenchantment, the late 1970s continued to yield anthropological and psychological researchers who, with decidedly different orientations, tried to seek and refute the "universal" laws governing the human organism, to view cross-cultural research both as a method strategy and data-based theory, and to forsake or extend traditional means of personality investigation. Regardless of orientation, an increasing number tried to dissect the broad but crucial epistemological, experimental, and ethical as well as theoretical and methodological components embedded in cross-cultural personality research. I consider three such efforts briefly.

*Price-Williams.* In an exciting but recondite book, psychologist Price-Williams explored an array of complex, difficult issues in cross-cultural research. Among other topics, his review covered the problems of definitions, categories, and value judgments. Price-Williams variously recommended a consortium of methods from social psychology and cognitive anthropology, an innovative approach distinct from the traditional methods of experimental psychology, and the use of the interpersonal unit rather than the individual trait as a focus in personality and culture studies (Cole, Gay, Glick, & Sharp, 1971; Heider, 1958; Jahoda, 1969; LeVine & Price-Williams, 1974; Triandis, 1972; Tyler, 1969).

*Cattell.* In a 1977 *Handbook*, psychologist Cattell and associates were similarly skeptical of simplistic solutions (Cattell & Dreger, 1977). They preferred an experimentally designed, mathematically bound, and internationally tested approach. Those persuaded by Cattell's statistically inferred approach found many taxonomies lacking in rigor and comprehension. For example, in Madsen's analysis of some twenty personality theorists, most Western theorists were viewed as less than comprehensive (1977). Cattell was convinced that, even though science must be "international and universal" (1977b, p. 473), the problems raised by trait assessment are accentuated in cross-cultural research. Despite Cattell's international concerns, the only chapter in the *Handbook* specifically covering personality and culture was in the section titled, "The Sociological Domain of Personality." Perhaps encouraged by international studies on the structure of personality, Cattell reported with considerable confidence the same number and nature of factors in most cultures, suggesting that "human nature is primarily the same" (p. 475).

*Spiro.* Anthropologist Spiro, in an intensely personal document of his intellectual evolution, recorded some changed conclusions on the relationship of culture and personality based on thirty years of review and research (1978). Increasingly skeptical of the cultural relativism thesis, Spiro asserted that many cultural differences are more apparent than real, representing historically conditioned and, therefore, variable expressions of pan-human structures. His Israeli and Burmese studies suggested the presence of both culturally invariant motivational dispositions and cognitive orientations, potentially indicating some pan-cultural biological and cultural constants.

Spiro discerned both a universal cultural pattern and a universal personality pattern: "For if certain cultural characteristics are pan-cultural, then, *ex hypothesi*, certain personality characteristics are also pan-cultural, and they, at least, comprise man's pan-cultural human nature" (p. 354). In a radical disciplinary departure, Spiro rejected the prevailing thesis (in the United States and England) of cultural relativism to explain the development of personality and human nature. He felt that cultural determinism both lacked explanatory validity and located culture as *the* determinant rather than one determinant.

In his significant restatement, Spiro moved away from culturally determinant or relative definitions of personality and staunchly opted for the biological determinism of Freud to activate the universal variables. He chose the Freudian structural model, stressing that such choices greatly affect the understanding of personality and human nature. Some thirty years of professional and personal exploration (1951, 1954, 1958, 1961a, 1961b, 1967, 1972) moved Spiro to conclude that "the model of a structurally and functionally differentiated personality, which makes no assumptions about social-culture-personality isomorphisms—and which therefore requires that personality be investigated independently of both behavior and culture—supports the hypothesis of pan-cultural human nature" (1978, p. 358).

The contributions of other anthropologists cannot be covered in this limited review despite their importance to cross-cultural research and the issues of universals (Harris, 1968; Levi-Strauss, 1963, 1969; Sahlins, 1976). There is no doubt, however, that by the late 1970s some anthropologists were again interested in similarities and in the problems of psychological anthropology (Kiefer, 1977; Spindler, 1978a).

## Significant Issues for an Emergent
## Model and Method

There is great variation in the terms, topics, and theories of the major Western surveys of personality and culture. The reported studies are further complicated by a problematic reliance on words (i.e., descriptive labels) and complex interactive observer-observed judgments that usually produce only approximately similar results (Bourguignon, 1973; Fiske, 1974, 1975a, 1978; Shweder, 1975). The realization that long ago Allport listed 50 definitions of personality (1937) and that Kroeber and Kluckhohn enumerated 150 definitions of culture (1952) further illustrates the ambiguities. The changing meanings of the two central terms continue to complicate their analysis. Yet, a number of dominant issues have emerged that require the attention of researchers studying personality cross-culturally. For purposes of this chapter, such issues are best explored in the context of the question posed earlier: How could or should cross-cultural researchers ask and answer questions about personality development?

Changes that reflect the continuing debate are seen in several competing definitions of personality, for example, as (1) describable by unitary trait or type, (2) expressed in culture, (3) reflecting social development, (4) resulting from socialization, (5) related to cognition, (6) an outcome of genetics, (7) involving morality, and in some sense (8) all of the above—that is, as incorporating pan-cultural motivational dispositions, cognitive orientations, biosocial interactions. Contemporarily, there is little agreement on the concept of personality. To date, the multiplicity of personality definitions has not yielded a science or any consensus on its content, construction, or measurement. The general evolutionary process of knowledge has yet to provide the basis for a consistent epistemological model and empirical method. At best, we are witnessing a plethora of global theories and a proliferation of mini-theories—some advantageous, some not.

Beyond a picture of personality definitions as evolving phenomena, the persistent issues include: (a) the characterization of the human organism as actor or reactor, (b) the meaning of universal and the condition of comparability, (c) the role of cognition, social and otherwise, and (d) the place of life-span development. These are hardly inclusive, but embedded in them are other theoretical and methodological, experimental and ethical debates. Each incorporates questions, for example, about the search for similarities rather than differences, the impact of mediating psychological processes, the utility of trait assessments, the influence of value judgments, the measurement of biosocial interaction, the domain of socialization, and the designation of personality as social or national, political or moral character. The total assemblage reflects historical attempts to construct a model for understanding personality development and a method for measuring it. A description of changes in perspectives on these four crucial issues can illuminate the heuristic value of cross-cultural, cognitive, developmental, and biosocial constructs for studying personality throughout the life cycle.

The Human Organism
as Active or Passive

The debate about whether the person should be viewed as actor or reactor in the personality-culture equation has been continuous. It has been described as the nature versus nurture, heredity versus environment, innate versus learned, instinct versus culture dilemma. The question of the organism's activity or passivity could be ignored if genetic, individual, or innate factors and environmental, cultural, or learned influences were noninteractive. This is not the case. It is precisely the interactive quality, with its intricate connections between the individual and the total environment, that requires identification and explanation.

Culture and personality have been treated by some as isomorphic, by others as completely independent, and by most as loosely connected. The epistemological and methodological confusions related to the debate are well documented and persistent (Bourguignon, 1973; Campbell, 1970, 1974b; Fiske, 1978; Honigmann, 1968, 1973; Hsu, 1972a; LeVine, 1973a, 1973b; Piaget, 1966/1974; Spindler, 1978a, 1978b). In discussing the isomorphism or independence of personality and culture, some have maintained that individual acts reflect the culture (Bourguignon, 1973). LeVine (1973a), in cataloging culture and personality explanations, found that the prevailing view of the person as a reactor to external *or* to internal contingencies persisted despite the findings of personality theorists that emphasize reactions to both external *and* internal contingencies. The overriding point is that the conventional, convenient, or even capricious division of organism and environment, individual and society, nature and history, personality and culture creates a false dichotomy and a misleading separation of constructs.

As indicated earlier, from the 1940s to 1970s personality variously was conceived as the superordinate governing institution of the human organism, the product of inherited dispositions and environmental experiences, the individual's adaptation to socialization, and/or an organized system of interdependently functioning parts. In the 1950s, Kluckhohn and Murray saw the human organism as a passive, but integrative, receptor responsive to both internal drives and social environment. They rejected the implied dualism of culture and personality, arguing that "culture *in* personality" and "personality *in* culture" suggested conceptual models more in accord with the facts.

Although Child highlighted the interdependency of determinants in the 1960s, the interactive notion succumbed to a cultural emphasis. DeVos and Hippler, limited to "the anthropological concern with culture as a significant determinant of human behavior" (1969, p. 324), saw personality structures as learned patterns dependent on a cultural environment. Even though in the 1970s, culture was conceptualized as the "shared . . . fabric of human minds" (Hsu, 1972b, p. 8) and/or "the psychological process of learning" (Bourguignon, 1973, p. 1077), Hippler described culture as constraining modes such as norms, beliefs, and attitudes that pressure certain ego organizations to develop similarly (1974, p. 451).

None of the definitions of culture can indicate the difficulty in studying personality development nor adequately reveal the interactive influence of the possible determinants. Researchers studying the development of personality cross-culturally have increasingly had to acknowledge the reciprocal and subtle exchanges among the variables of personality, culture, and behavior (Draguns, 1979, p. 181). Current conceptualizations of personality are more likely to see it as the product of biological and cultural factors with certain aspects under the influence of the biological mostly; other aspects, as mostly under the influence of the cultural; and still others, the outcome of biological and cultural interactions. The basic question, however, for the researcher is whether to study personality development as an interactive construct *or* as a separate entity. Since it is the interaction between organism and environment that produces personality, that biosocial interdependency requires attention.

## The Meaning of Universal and the Condition of Comparability

The meaning of *universal* or *pan-cultural* is a continuing issue in explanatory systems of personality and culture. The attempt to identify universality by using a statistical concept of personality remains unresolved. The discovery, however, of individual differences does not disprove universality. The issue is complicated by problems in determining comparable categories, undertaking more than one level of analysis, and drawing inferences from individually and culturally based data (Lambert, 1974; Shweder, 1973; also see Lonner's chapter in Volume 1 of this *Handbook*).

One example illustrates the problem: Shweder (1973) in a reanalysis of the Six Cultures Project data probed the levels of analysis issue. He demonstrated a discrepancy in the cross-cultural and intra-cultural structure of the children's behavior. Shweder reported cross-cultural but not intra-cultural validity on two dimensions (nurturance versus egoism and intimacy versus aggression) (p. 532). Apparently, such indicators as "offers help" or "seeks help" may not necessarily be similarly relevant in cross- and intra-cultural research. This suggests the importance of assessing psychological variables intra- and inter-culturally.

The positions of two notable anthropologists further indicate the ongoing dimensions of the universality debate. Historically, Kluckhohn recommended that cultural anthropologists study the invariant points of reference from the biological, psychological, and sociosituational givens of human life (1954). Kluckhohn (with Murray) described three universals basic to personality development: birth and survival, social interdependence, and gratification and deprivation experiences (1953b). Basically Kluckhohn (1962b) argued for a fundamental uniformity underlying diverse cultural patterns. He cast universality in terms of certain biological and human generalities: pre-cultural limiting conditions, universal psychological and cultural processes, and cultural forms of pan-human values (1954, p. 955; see Linton, 1952; cf. Boas, 1911; Kroeber, 1949). Some twenty-five years later, Spiro (1978) too acknowledged some basic motivational dispositions, cognitive orientations, and a set of common biological, social, and cultural features that interact to produce a universal human nature.

Debates aside, landmark research has identified some pan-cultural personality characteristics and universalities of human life that potentially affect developing personalities. For example, Whiting and Child's (1953) report on pan-cultural behaviors paralleled Kluckhohn and Murray's initial positions and Inkeles and Levinson's later ones. Also studies on the lower stages of Erikson's (1950) epigenetic personality theory (e.g., trust) and Piaget's cognitive hierarchy (1950, 1953) (e.g., sensorimotor intelligence) revealed similarities that suggest developmental universality. All postulated that as the problems of childhood are universal, so are the personality characteristics. Singer (1961, p. 20) reinforced the idea of universality in personality using such common experiences as infant helplessness and dependency, competition for affection, and sibling rivalry. Like Mead and Wolfenstein (1955, pp. 6–7), Singer described the influences of biological growth, parent-child relations, and the comparability of needs or fears. By the 1970s, consistent with earlier positions, Harrington and Whiting maintained that, since personality was an adaptation, socialization events were likely to be universal (1972, p. 472).

Cross-cultural research continues to imply the presence of some noteworthy universals. Rohner reported a systematic set of affective relationships in a study on early childhood care involving a worldwide sample (1975a, 1975b). Using a "triangulation of methodologies" including cross-cultural surveys, intra-cultural studies, and psychological research (cf. Campbell & Fiske, 1959), he found that in one hundred and one societies several species-wide effects of parental acceptance-rejection were supported by the cross-cultural data. For example, societies that were scored as typically rejecting of children contained adults (and some children, too) who displayed low emotional responsiveness and dependence. This finding on affectional ties is supported by other cross-cultural research as well (Barry, Bacon, & Child, 1967; Minturn & Lambert, 1964; Whiting, 1963; Whiting & Whiting, 1975). Werner's (1979) comprehensive, interdisciplinary synthesis of current knowledge about children cross-culturally describes cogent instances of universality in physical, cognitive, and social development (cf. Munroe & Munroe, 1975).

The concern with a statistical conceptualization of personality was another important development in personality and culture research. This approach emphasized individual differences and central tendencies, as measured by psychological tests. Two important efforts during the 1950s used the approach: Wallace in a study of Tuscarora Indians (1952) and Inkeles and Levinson in assessing the development of national character (1954). Despite the general skepticism about scales as measures of individual personality and the specific problem of cross-cultural application, there is sufficient commonality to suggest the utility of this assessment approach as one method (Butcher & Pancheri, 1976; Cattell, 1950, 1957, 1977a; Cattell & Dreger, 1977; Hogan, De Soto, & Solano, 1977).

Discussions frequently focus on whether research should begin with the psychological study of individuals or with cultural ethnographic data. Singer observed that the difference between psychological data and ethnographic data had less to do with their status as primary data and more with the systems of grouping and interpretation (1961, p. 64). LeVine's solution to obtain a universal language for personality psychology was to collaborate in clinical/psychoanalytic relationships with indigenous and foreign behavioral scientists (1973a). Price-Williams recommended that the interpersonal unit replace the individual trait as a focus and basis of personality-culture studies (1975b, pp. 79–80). To recognize the place of culture participation and the methodological problem of comparability, Triandis developed the subjective culture approach (1972, 1975). Indicators of the persistence of this issue include the current debates over etic-emic, calls for *in situ* (naturalistic) approaches as well as triangulation schemas, and clarification not only about the level of analysis but the unit for examining personality, culture, and the interaction. Resolution of the issue has much to do with identifying whether the concepts and categories measured are the same and the scale unit is comparable.

In seeking pan-culturality *or* comparability, researchers must remember that the particular methods used do not necessarily represent a universal paradigm (Przeworski & Teune, 1966–1967; Kaplan & Manners, 1972). Even though there is no lack of obvious universals in human nature, the ethnographic investigations of specific cultures, like the psychological investigations of specific individuals, reveal sufficiently distinct results to indicate the difficulty of drawing universal *or* individual inferences from a singular methodology or with a single set of categories. The assessment of difference or similarity of any sort is probably most effective using cross-cultural samples, multiple interdependent methodologies, and interdisciplinary paradigms. As a result, investigators will have to examine both traditional and newly developed approaches to research, aware of the problems of standardization and equivalence as well as translation and language. Simultaneously, they will have to be unrestricted by their cultural or societal frames (e.g., Eastern or Western), ideological or value orientations (e.g., free-enterprise or collectivist), and/or disciplinary perspectives (e.g., anthropologist versus biologist versus psychologist; clinical versus developmental versus social psychologist).

In sum, many researchers, tackling how scientifically to measure and infer similarities and/or differences, have agreed that the problem is basically a methodological one of creating comparability in the tactics of research. Some have emphasized the influence of theoretical positions and related models of personality development. Growing numbers stress the importance of a multi-method, cross-cultural research strategy as basic to data-derived, species-wide generalizations about behavior, personality, or culture. More will have to accept that "any science must be adequate to explain both the similarities and the differences in the phenomena with which it deals" (Kluckhohn, 1962a, p. 296).

### Cognition and Life-Span Development in Personality Research

The issues of cognition, social or otherwise, and of life-span development are intimately related to the proper study of personality development cross-culturally. Even by the 1960s and clearly by the 1970s, few reviewers exempted cognition as a variable for understanding personality development uni- or cross-culturally *or* as a construction of the personality researcher. Many spoke to the relationship of the cognitive to the affective, the liberation of cross-cultural cognitive psychology from intelligence, and the heuristic value of a multivariate, cross-cultural strategy. Fewer still minimized the importance of developmental studies of a longitudinal or life-span sort to avoid the pitfalls of age cohort data, cross-sectional studies, and single-setting research. Many argued that the most fruitful data on personality formation would come from longitudinal, cross-cultural developmental studies that focused on changing competencies over longer periods of the life than infancy and childhood.

*The Role of Cognition: Psychological and Anthropological Perspectives*

The 1960s ushered in an appreciation of the "unsuspected and extraordinary richness" of cognition, particularly of Piaget's theory of genetic epistemology (Flavell, 1963, p. 411). His hierarchical, invariant sequencing approach to cognitive development was productive cross-culturally on problems from language to legality, mathematics to morality. By the 1970s, research reports from more than one hundred cultures covering Alaska to Argentina, Switzerland to Senegal, and Taiwan to Turkey revealed both striking similarities and marked differences. Such findings raise questions on the meaning of universality. They also showed the impact of Piaget's cognitive-developmental theory on cultural, educational, and social analyses. Pertinent studies include, for example, the effect of cultural environments on cognition, on egocentrism, and on legal or moral development—codes of conduct (Bruner, Olver, & Greenfield, 1966; Feldman, 1974; Jahoda, 1969, 1970; Gorsuch & Barnes, 1973; Greenfield, 1974; Kohlberg, 1969, 1971; Lloyd, 1972; Maccoby & Modiano, 1969; Selman, 1971; Tapp & Kohlberg, 1971; Tapp & Levine, 1974, 1977b; also see Chapter 7, by Dasen & Heron, in this volume of the *Handbook*). Furthermore, Piaget consistently spoke in favor of integrating social, environmental, and emotional factors with the cognitive (1932, 1953, 1968, 1970). Cognition, common to all stages of development, provides continuity amidst structural discontinuity (Flavell, 1963; Piaget, 1968), but affect and intellect are united in the functioning of the personality (Inhelder & Piaget, 1958; Piaget, 1951; Piaget & Inhelder, 1969). Such conceptualization engenders new ways of thinking about continuity and change in personality development (Turner, 1973).

Historical controversy and contemporary skepticism aside, Piaget's evolutionary perspective underlined the importance of cognitive processes on development, social and otherwise (Shantz, 1975). A lack of longitudinal studies, supposed inattention to social or affective influences, and an alleged Western bias have deterred fuller use of the Piagetian framework cross-culturally (Ashton, 1975; Buck-Morss, 1975; Dasen, 1974; Kagan & Klein, 1973; Simpson, 1974; Turner, 1973). However, Piaget continually has discussed the pertinence of cross-cultural research to genetic psychology (1947, 1966, 1968, 1970). Even though his paradigm was used primarily to study development of reasoning and thought, his theory is germane to the cross-cultural study of personality development. This becomes increasingly the case as the connections between personality and cognitive complexity become apparent (LeVine & Price-Williams, 1970; Shantz, 1975; Triandis, 1977a, 1977b; Witkin & Berry, 1975).

During the 1960s and 1970s, others with non-Piagetian perspectives also described the relevance of cognition for understanding social behavior and personality (e.g., Baldwin, 1969; Greenfield & Bruner, 1966; Harrington & Whiting, 1972; Munroe & Munroe, 1975; Werner, 1979; Whiting & Whiting, 1975). Earlier personality theorists had injected cognitive components into their personality and culture conceptualizations (Allport, 1937/1961; 1960; Bateson, 1936; Kluckhohn & Murray, 1948a, 1953a; Murray, 1938; Murphy, 1947). Many of these used limited or specific theories; all addressed the explanatory and interactive quality of cognition. As importantly, they typically rejected the historical and false division between socio-emotional and intellectual (affective and cognitive) life. Several contemporary directions in both psychology and anthropology deserve further comment.

In 1972, Triandis predicted a new vogue of collaboration between anthropology and psychology focusing on human cognition (Triandis et al., p. 3). In part, he reflected the positive reaction to Cole and associates (Cole, Gay, Glick, & Sharp, 1971; Cole & Scribner, 1974; Laboratory, 1979b) who provided an instructive experimental ethnographic model for milieu study; in part, concern with the effect of cognitive complexity on universals in social behavior and personality (Triandis, 1975, 1977a, 1977b). For example, cognition seems tied to many personality characteristics, among them authoritarianism and conformity.

A notable controversy about the relationship of cognition to personality surrounds the social learning theory of Mischel (1969, 1973, 1976). Mischel criticized the trait approach to personality, described the relative absence of consistency and relative presence of change, and assessed the empirical insufficiencies in personality analyses. Mischel urged recognition of the importance of cognitive dimensions, the place of environmental conditions, and the necessity of longitudinal studies. Mischel's critique of phenotypic and genotypic explanations of continuity and change plus the proposition that "discontinuities are part of the genuine phenomena of personality" (1969, p. 1017) characterize his approach; so does an insistence on high consistency in cognitive aspects of personality.

Block, an advocate of the Q-sort technique, queried the adequacy of Mischel's negative evaluation of trait theory and the state of personality assessment (1971, 1977). But he did not counter the cognitive or life-span implications of Mischel's approach. Fiske, equally concerned about personality theory research, maintained that Mischel's reconceptualization of personality gave little explicit guidance on how to assess or observe such variables as construction competencies, encoding strategies, and personal constructs, or self-regulatory systems and plans (1978).

Typically, cognitive concerns have occupied more psychologists interested in personality development than anthropologists over a parallel timespan. Spiro observed that anthropologists devoted more attention to behavioral learning than cognitive variables (1968/1972). He, too, maintained that cognition was a necessary psychological variable to explain personality and performance (DeVos, 1961; Goodenough, 1967; Spradley, 1970, 1972; Wallace, 1961b, 1962). LeVine recommended expanded use of categories of cognition in cross-cultural studies of children with boundaries broad enough to include "intelligence testing, studies addressed to Piaget's developmental formulations, and other research on cognitive processes" (1970, p. 580). LeVine depicted the cognitive structures of adult socializing agents as instrumental in defining prescriptive and prospective guidelines for personality (1973a, p. 105).

A contemporary example, incorporating the cognitive and the developmental, is Tyler's mapping (1969) of the relationship of language to culture. His analysis was done in the context of cognitive sharing (i.e., a uniform cognitive code among members of a society). Another is LeVine and Price-Williams' attempt (1974) to map Hausa kinship categories at different ages. They tried to link them to both environmental factors and Piagetian theory. Shweder's study (1972) on the distinctive cognitive capacities of thirty-three shamans dramatized the importance of using cognition to determine whether such characteristics are best explained in terms of roles, experiences, predisposing personality features, or the product of an interaction.

Even though many anthropological studies have not dealt extensively with cognitive processes, this issue can no longer be ignored in personality research. Whether cognition is the new vogue, in its golden-age, or even the focus of collaborative efforts is the less interesting point.

### Life-Span Development

There is growing consensus that cross-sectional, age-specific, and unicultural research is deficient. It inadequately deals with inter-age networks, long-term ontogenetic linkages, and biosocial interactions. Developmentalists increasingly agree that the goal of life-span research is the identification of key behavior-change processes rather than chronometric age changes. A common concern involves bridging phenotypic and genotypic explanations of continuity and change in personality. The goal is not an age psychology, but a developmental one viewed over time and place.

Traditional personality research has been dominated by an intense focus on infant and child-training studies (Havighurst, 1973; Inkeles & Levinson, 1954, p. 1001; LeVine, 1970, 1979). Yet few would disagree that development occurs at all ages. The psychoanalytic approach so dominated developmental theory that attention beyond child-training studies was long in coming; the trait approach also restricted alternate data and conceptions because of its focus on concurrent data. From a theory construction perspective, both were "short sighted" (Baltes & Schaie, 1973a, p. 367). Gutmann, trying to generate a developmental, species conception for a psychology of aging, argued that the "true" or "best" test for the life-span developmental strategy will be in the cross-cultural arena (1977, p. 302).

The explanatory emphasis in the 1940s and 1950s related child-rearing styles (e.g., swaddling, weaning) to adult personality (e.g. retentive, verbal-oral) (Mead, 1954; Sears, Maccoby, & Levin, 1957; Whiting & Child, 1953). This child-oriented perspective dominated the 1960s also (B. Whiting, 1963; J. Whiting, 1961, 1968). By the 1970s, reviewers were more inclined to look at personality in age stages and through the life cycle (Holzman, 1974), but frequently the phrase "through the life cycle" referred only to the time period bounded by adolescence (e.g., initiation rites, identity conflicts) (Harrington & Whiting, 1972). Typically, the actual state of affairs in the early 1970s revealed large gaps in adolescent, adult, and aging research.

By the late 1970s, the gaps related to the vogues in child-rearing studies and for contemporaneous research strategies were disappearing. For example, the approach of the Munroes to the cross-cultural study of human development stressed the importance of clocking changes over the life span (1975). They focused on the basic issues related to lifespan psychology (such as methodology and research design, cross-cultural and longitudinal studies), the age divisions from infancy through late adulthood, and such developmental areas as cognition and personality. Using interdisciplinary and cross-cultural materials from the traditional societies of the Ainu, Trobriander, and Gusii, the Munroes cast human development in broad perspective. They argued that a cross-cultural perspective extends "both the kinds and range of variables available to investigation" (p. 1). By combining reports on developmental stages (for example, infancy and early childhood) with developmental topics (such as physical growth and cognition), and integrating descriptive and experimentally derived materials, the Munroes provided a theoretical and methodological eclecticism.

Holtzman, Diaz-Guerrero, and Swartz's (1975) fifteen-year study of Mexican and United States children also underscored the validity of using cognitive and comparative, developmental and longitudinal (albeit not life span) approaches to study personality development. This bicultural team determined that developmental plus cognitive, perceptual, and personality variables were more rigorously measured using a longitudinal, cross-cultural approach. To avail themselves of the best features of both cross-sectional and longitudinal methods, they employed an overlapping design. Accordingly, twelve years of development were covered in six calendar years of repeated testing. Their data included performance in testing sessions, ratings of behavior and personality, interviews on family and home environments, and questionnaires of mothers' attitudes and values on parenting. Primary findings revealed that Mexican and United States children differed in coping styles, cognitive structures, and cooperative activities. Beyond representing an intensive effort to utilize a cross-cultural, developmental, and longitudinal research strategy to study personality, this work yielded an abundance of data on the influence of culture on both character and cognition.

Like Neugarten and Bengston (1968), Gutmann (1977) recalled the discomfort that gerontological psychologists have with cross-cultural research. But Gutmann concurred that cross-cultural studies are "a necessary corrective to the cultural blindspots of theory builders" (1977, p. 303). Like Baltes, Reese, and Nesselroade (1977) and other life-span developmentalists, Gutmann anticipated a greater generality of findings and a greater richness of conceptions. Cross-cultural studies particularly establish that any residual, trans-cultural regularities not attributable to social contributions can be referred to developmental forces. Gutmann used cross-cultural, cross-national, cross-ethnic, and rural-urban comparisons to describe persistence and change in adult (gerontological) personality. His review underlines the value of a cross-cultural life-span approach in obtaining new perspectives on personality development *and* in pinpointing psychological universals, characteristic of the latter half of the human life cycle.

From the perspective of a child psychologist with cross-cultural interests (Bronfenbrenner, 1970), Bronfenbrenner presented nine propositions to stimulate new activity in developmental research *and* as a means to move beyond a segmented science that forwards much information about the early years, less through middle childhood and adolescence, virtual silence for decades, some recording of the declining organism, and does any of the above in strange situations for the briefest possible periods of time (1977, pp. 513, 525–526, 529). For him, ecological transitions in the interdependent micro- and macrosystems, meso- and exosystems constitute a framework for understanding developmental changes through the life cycle. Understanding the impact of ecological transitions (e.g., marriage, divorce, death) and ecosystems on the organism is crucial to understanding personality development cross-culturally.

## From Issues to a Heuristic Model

A longitudinal, life span approach should obviate the limitations of cross-sectional studies (Thomae, 1979). For example, a difference between age cohort groups, interpreted as developmental, might be traced to another difference between the age groups. Furthermore, a developmental view usually sees the organism as inherently interactive in environments. As a result, life-span developmental researchers trace sequences of change to ascertain *"which ones* are primarily developmental (in the sense of being tied to maturational change) and *which ones* are primarily situational—if indeed this distinction can be made at all" (Neugarten & Datan, 1973, pp. 68–69; see also Baltes & Schaie, 1973a, 1973b; Goulet & Baltes, 1970; and Nesselroade&Reese,1973).

A cross-cultural, interactive approach should minimize the limitations of unisituational and/or laboratory studies which artificially manipulate both contextual and developmental variables. With proper inter- and intra-cultural controls, a cross-cultural, developmental research strategy should more effectively explain the ontogenetic and biocultural effects. For example, a difference in feminine or masculine qualities might be interepreted not only by gender (sex), but by life period and cultural place.

Despite acknowledged methodological pitfalls, a cross-cultural, cognitive, interactive (biosocial) and life-span developmental strategy is to be valued for mapping the range and universality of personality phenomena. Such a framework potentially provides a pragmatic and powerful paradigm to study personality.

### The Elephant Research Strategy: Approaches to Gain Perspective on the Whole Shape

As the review of landmark literature covering the past four decades revealed, a number of issues moved researchers to study a range of variables related to personality and culture. Coincidentally, there were attempts to integrate the field of personality development intellectually. They were generated by problems, for example, of a single discipline approach (e.g., anthropology versus psychology), a limited theoretical or methodological approach (e.g., the priorities of traditional child, experimental, social, or personality psychology), or attention to noninteractive phenomena of minimal complexity or trivial importance (e.g., limited potential for replicability or generality). Some efforts emphasized theoretical and methodological pushes toward parsimonious cross-cultural research on personality development; others simultaneously clarified the strategies of cross-cultural psychology. Yet, despite the declarations and the research endeavors, confusion and constraint remain in the cross-cultural study of humankind, particularly personality development.

Observations on the need to widen theoretical, methodological, and substantive horizons are not new. Kluckhohn and Murray observed more than thirty years ago that "psychiatrists, psychologists, sociologists, social workers, students of education, biologists and anthropologists have been preoccupied with the relation of the individual to his society" 1948a, p. xi). In 1973, LeVine's list of those preoccupied with the relation of the individual to society included primatologists, developmental psychologists, psychoanalysts, psychiatrists, psycholinguists, sociologists, anthropologists, political scientists, and legal scholars (1973a, p. 61). Human social and mental development is increasingly seen as the confluence of many interrelated, changing systems and subsystems including the biological, social, cultural, and historical (Looft, 1973, p. 51; see also Bronfenbrenner, 1977; Draguns, 1979; Laboratory, 1979b; LeVine, 1979). No single discipline or technique can single-handedly solve the complex problems in the study of personality, albeit in one or more cultures.

Many forces can and do shape the developing personality. As one response to the need for an approach, I present for consideration the Elephant Research Strategy (ERS). It is not mere whimsy that produced the ERS. Rather it was the realization that the study of personality development intra-culturally or inter-culturally requires more than one perspective. The investigator needs multiple frameworks to examine the thick description of life (cf. Cronbach, 1975; Geertz, 1965, 1973; Gergen, 1976). Such a perspective is basic to comprehending the multiple forces that produce personality—and personality theory. Not unlike the parable from which the name of the strategy derived, the person under the elephant—like the one sitting on it, standing in front or in back of it—can describe only one aspect of the total product. Given the size of the problem (i.e., a whole elephant or whole human being), today's cross-cultural personality theory would be remiss and myopic if, for example, either history and nature (biology) *or* history and ecology were viewed as dichotomous or singular, noninteractive forces.

The Elephant Research Strategy (ERS) involves considering the impact of *ecology, ethnography, ethnocentrism, ethology, etiology,* and *ethics* in assessing or planning research on personality development cross-culturally. These six elements provide the researcher with theories and tools for mapping the multiple, interactive forces that affect the development of personality. The ERS proposes criteria for assessing past research or guidelines for designing future research. It furnishes a baseline from which to explore a series of research issues, magnified by the cross-cultural nature of the settings of the answers. It is one reply to the question posed in this chapter: How could or should a cross-cultural researcher ask and answer questions about personality development?

## Ecology

An ecological perspective focuses on systematic descriptions of the complex interaction between the person (organism) and the situation (habitat) in familiar, valid social, and naturally occurring contexts that endure over time. The focus is on the interrelationships and interdependencies within behavior-organism-environment systems (Willems, 1973, p. 199). The approach involves data gathering with analytic categories that permit detailing of individuals, events, and evolving interactions. Investigators map, for example, the immediate settings of home, school, and office describing the embedded networks, roles, and ideologies. Many research models exclude, both conceptually and operationally, examination of properties in enduring environments critical for understanding personality development. As a result, many study "phenomena of behavioral development as if they were simple, single-file, and relatively static" (Willems, 1973, p. 202).

Psychologists from the 1930s to the 1970s stressed the importance of an ecological approach for scientific and social analyses. The ecological perspective is traceable to Kurt Lewin (1935, 1951) and Egon Brunswik (1947). However, only in the mid-1970s was ecological psychology described as beyond the courtship period in its integration of naturalistic (*in situ*) and experimental (laboratory) methods (Willems, 1973) and as generally "coming of age" (Barker, 1975, p. 289). Its "insights" on the socialization of persons in communities with different ecologies created "a newly emerging area for research in personality development and social and developmental psychology" (Kelly, 1975, p. 194). The investigation of enduring experiences and environments seemed to bear implications for social change in various cross-cultural contexts (Bronfenbrenner, 1974a, 1974b, 1977). The generation of naturalistic, unobtrusive methods plus experimental and nonexperimental methods for field and laboratory settings, in the past decade, have added to the viability of psychological ecology and its offspring—environmental psychology (Altman, 1975; Altman & Chemers, 1980; Campbell & Stanley, 1966; Proshansky, Ittelson, & Rivlin, 1970; Webb, Campbell, Schwartz, & Sechrest, 1966; Willems, 1973). Further, the scientific investigation of enduring environments seemed to have implications for policy change.

In their community studies, Barker and Wright (1955/1971) stressed the primacy of the interaction of situational and organismic variables within environmental contexts. The ecology of development approach of the 1970s underscored the importance of understanding how community life styles affect development (Bronfenbrenner, 1977; Kelly, 1975). Ecological psychologists have investigated both molecular and molar behavior in psychological (i.e., subjective, see Lewin's life space) and ecological (i.e., objective, see Bronfenbrenner's valid, enduring) environments. The context of behavior is seen as a phenomenon in and of itself as well as interactive with the organism. The ecological environment has identifiable temporal and physical attributes, characterized by degrees and aspects of interdependence. This interdependence criterion was recognized by Lewin (1951), who described the simultaneous, nonadditive impact of independent variables (forces) interacting in a nonlinear fashion in an integrated system (1935). The task, then, of ecological psychology is to discover "how the properties of the person and the properties of the ecological environment are related, *in situ*" (Barker, 1968, p. 158).

Initially investigating the links between the habitat, behavior, and development of children, Barker and associates developed an ecological psychology of human action of special importance to intra-cultural and inter-cultural comparisons and studies of change. Their first report appeared in *Midwest and Its Children* (1955). The approach was further developed in

*Ecological Psychology* (1968). In *Qualities of Community Life* (1973), it was used to analyze United States and English personality and cultural differences and similarities. As landmark ecological psychologists, Barker and associates used techniques that neither distort nor destroy the natural stream to map everyday behavior in natural habitats. They sought *"methods and concepts for dealing with the ecological environment of molar human behavior"* (Barker, 1968, p. 1). They attended to physical and social milieus—the *behavior settings* of a community—for example, from hospital to library to cemetery. A *behavior episode* described a separate action such as painting the lips or wiping paint off a face. A *specimen record* was a detailed, sequential, and narrative account of an individual's behavior over time. Recently, Barker reiterated the important attributes of the indivisible, physical surroundings of a person (e.g., school classes, hospital wards, business offices). He also underscored the importance of contemporaneous and developmental descriptions of the forces—the real, the observed, and the indivisible physical-social environments—that influence personality development and behavior (Barker, 1975, p. 290). This Barkerian perspective is less consistent with an ecological approach, in which the emphasis is primarily on the physical features of the habitat (Barry, Child, & Bacon, 1959/1965; Berry, 1976; Berry & Annis, 1974a, 1974b) and more consistent with a focus "on the human subjects of the research and their unique milieu" (Bennett & Thaiss, 1967, p. 273).

An important variant of the ecological approach is associated with the work of Berry (1976, 1981; Witkin & Berry, 1975). Berry's study on human ecology and cognitive style included data from eighteen cultural groups with varying patterns in such areas as community size, hunting economy, and family organization. For example, Berry reported a strong relationship between the ecological index (toward autonomous child-rearing practices and away from strict socialization that fosters dependency) and performance on tests of psychological differentiation (1976). Using an ecological emphasis, Berry has attempted to relate behaviors to large spheres of an individual's cultural and physical environment. While some questions have been raised, related to methodological difficulties, about his confirming evidence (Serpell, 1977), Berry (1981) continues to explore the impact of ecology on psychological differentiation cross-culturally and to consider developmental issues basic to comparative studies.

From either vantage point, an ecological orientation permits an appreciation of the interrelationships and interdependencies of organism-environment interactions. In both, the ecologically valid focus is on the enduring, familiar, and social context, not just the contemporaneous interaction.

Finally, there exists little evidence of consensus on the specific characteristics of ecological validity. Willems (1973, pp. 207–209) suggested eleven aspects for obtaining an ecologically valid perspective. They include an emphasis on the mutual and interdependent relations among the organism, its behavior, and its environment; a methodological orientation that is largely naturalistic; an emphasis more on molar than molecular phenomena; a concern with taxonomy, critical in applied problems and mission-oriented research; a strategy for working from more complex to simple and for accepting complicated, intact phenomena; an unmistakable moral concern for prescriptive and proscriptive guidelines; and an allowance for unusually long time periods in research.

## Ethnography

Ethnography, the second strategy of the ERS, speaks to the need for researchers to record and understand the natural histories of the human species. An ethnography is most simply defined as the description of a culture, a catalogue of its customs and contents. The theorizing about such recorded observations is known as ethnology. Both activities are influenced by the ethnographer's tools and taxonomies. Traditionally, they are the domain of the anthropologists.

In 1911, Boas's ethnographic approach of radical empiricism emphasized the inductive collection of masses of data on primitive groups throughout the world. Boas eschewed theory in an effort to avoid the distortion caused by the use of *a priori* ethnocentric classifications. In 1922, Malinowski defined the ethnographer's goal "to grasp the native's point of view, his relation to life, to realise his vision of *his* world" (p. 25). His goal differed little from Kluckhohn's in 1949 who felt the anthropologist's first responsibility was to set down events as seen by the people under study (p. 300). LeVine, in 1970 and again in 1979, reiterated that a detailed ethnography of a community meant more controls in the design to prevent contamination of the independent variables, fewer methodological artifacts, and results of greater permanence. None of these saw an ethnography as an alternative to the systematic psychological study of children or adults, albeit in exotic settings; rather it was a prerequisite to systematic comparison of individual and group differences. Contemporarily, psychologists and anthropologists emphasize the necessity of an ethnographic component in any cross-cultural work designed to "sample" cognitive or personality development (Laboratory, 1979b; LeVine, 1979). Both types of researchers aim to document events and interactions between the habitat (environment) and organism (person) over place and time.

A break with traditional or the "old" ethnography came in the 1960s as cross-cultural researchers increasingly recognized the need to develop classifications (a taxonomy) and further reduce the effect of the ethnographer's personal or cultural bias. One major problem confronting the cross-cultural personality researcher is obtaining ecologically valid data without using false universals. The constructs of etic, emic, and pseudo-etic were advanced in the "new" ethnography to avoid assigning a familiar category to an unfamiliar cultural or personalogical event (Berry, 1969; see Brislin's chapter in Volume 2 of this *Handbook*). Undoubtedly, the utility and validity of such concepts as etic or pseudo-etic will continue to be debated, but psychologist and anthropologist alike—regardless of orientation—stress the importance of obtaining ethnographic reports to provide a detailed, in-field description of the cultural community at study. Such acquaintance should reduce the disciplinary or cultural bias of the ethnographer as well as ease the interpretation of within and between group variations.

In studying personality development, cross-cultural investigators employing an ethnographic strategy should cover the full range of phenomena. For example, they must go beyond simple reports of kinship effects to considerations of ecological impact on role expectations. Ideally, classificatory schema should permit researchers to study behaviors in many cultures (etic or derived etic) and to describe events or elements within a specific culture (emic) as related to personality formation. This involves the difficult, complex task of developing conceptual terminology understood within one culture (i.e., emic), shared across cultures (i.e., etic), and valid across both contexts (i.e., derived etic). A detailed, sophisticated ethnography is a necessary step for the personality researcher in order to avoid missing important intra-cultural emic data, obtaining pseudo-etic intercultural results, applying culturally inappropriate *a priori* etic categories, and/or reporting ecologically invalid information.

Widely divergent researchers agree with LeVine's call for an "ethnography of the daily cycle" (1973a, p. 243). A detailed ethnography of the developmental process would reflect a theoretical *and* methodological concern to investigate fully and over time the biosocial interactions, basic to the emergence of personality. A developmental context gives the study of the daily cycle a reason and a means for monitoring the psychological course of a developmental process. The ethnographic frame of a daily cycle covering the developmental processes permits observation, for example, of physiological and ecological elements. The lack of this kind of naturalistic evidence in comparative personality research has been a major source of skepticism regarding its developmental hypotheses.

A comprehensive personality study then should involve an integration of anthropological and psychological methods, characterized by their two main approaches: the fundamentally descriptive (ethnographic) and the basically experimental. Each exhibits drawbacks necessitating a blending of the two approaches. Munroe and Munroe recommended "taking findings from the cross-cultural method and retesting them in a specially designed field research or by combining experimental designs with long-term, intensive ethnographic work" (1975, p. 6). Despite some methodological problems, there is evidence that original results, when replicated or approached thusly, are relatively robust and reliable. For example, Shweder (1971, 1973) queried the intra-cultural applicability of the apparently valid cross-cultural measures of nurturance and egoism reported in the Six Cultures Project. Even though his reanalysis in no way detracted from the importance of the Whitings' cross-cultural findings, it did raise questions about "the relationship between cross-cultural and intracultural variables and their indicators" (Shweder, 1973, p. 532).

On the other hand, Hsu (1961a, 1972a) commended the interdisciplinary solution of psychological anthropology to study personality development cross-culturally, but did not expect to settle the personality-culture dilemma (1961b, p. 4). Nevertheless, Hsu forecast a mutual enrichment of anthropology and social psychology, especially as psychologists used cross-cultural data to validate their generalizations *and* anthropologists sought to strengthen hypothesis formation and quantitative verification procedures. Bennett and Thaiss (1967) also underscored the necessity of blending approaches. Extensive survey research techniques, using standard stimuli applied to selected samples, seemed "a desirable adjunct to intensive ethnological field work" (Bennett & Thaiss, 1967, p. 274). By 1974, Price-Williams saw some new trends in cross-cultural psychological research illustrative of a sophisticated blending. Triandis and associates' anticipation of greater convergence as the two groups of scientists modified their research strategies seems to be the case (1972, p. 2).


## Ethnocentrism


The phenomenon of ethnocentrism involves evaluating the actions, beliefs, and values of other persons according to the shared prescriptions of one's own group (Swartz & Jordan, 1976). Commonly, the term *ethnocentrism* covers individual attitudes, cultural symbols, and ideologies. At a more complex level, it acknowledges multiple views but discounts them as incorrect, inferior, or immoral (LeVine & Campbell, 1972). It has an important effect on the assignment of meanings and the interpretation of actions. Even though it typically yields a positive evaluation of one's own group and its practices, ethnocentrism often leads to a misconception of others' activities and thus frequently to an unfavorable, negative, or biased evaluation.

Ethnocentrism can affect *both* subject and scientist. In either case, the term refers to a cultural bias or zealous parochialism that potentially distorts perceptions and cognitions *or* restricts observations and judgments. As such, the ethnocentric effect can be academic or disciplinary (e.g., psychological versus anthropological), national or regional (e.g., United States versus U.S.S.R; East versus West). Historically studied as a personality and culture characteristic, ethnocentrism can refer to more than the bias or parochialism that emanates from regarding one's national or cultural group as the only one. It applies as well to a constricted conceptual, disciplinary, or intellectual view that automatically dismisses others as less than valid or reliable. Fishman aptly summarized the problem at both the disciplinary and national levels: "If it is useful and desirable for Americans, Greeks, Indians, and Japanese to know each other better, cannot the same be said for psychologists, sociologists, anthropologists, and linguists?" (1973, p. 558).

The aim of the cross-cultural researcher, then, is to decenter; that is, to unload sufficiently one's own culture—albeit academic or national—so as *not* to be ethnocentric in articulating questions and answers, in developing procedures and policies, in interpreting reactions and results. All methodological and theoretical assumptions probably cannot be decentered, but reducing the ethnocentric effect is a necessary strategy for the cross-cultural researcher. One basic goal of the ERS is to reduce the respective cultural distortions that evoke egocentrism and ethnocentrism in the researcher.

*Ethnocentric and Ethnographic*

Hsu, in distinguishing between British social anthropology and American cultural anthropology, showed the implicit problem in not recognizing the relationship between the ethnocentric and the ethnographic:

> The British way often leads the field worker into a displaced ethnocentrism in which Bongo ethnocentrism takes the place of English ethnocentrism. The American way sometimes leaves the field worker with many factual details but with possibly less sensitivity to the feelings and views of the peoples he has studied. (1961b, p. 5/1972b, p. 6)

Since ethnocentrism can exist in both etic and emic data, the British emphasis highlights the problem of ethnocentrism at the emic level; the American emphasis, the problem of egocentrism at the etic level. Another explanation of the problem follows:

> The pseudo-etic approach is in fact an emic approach developed in a Western culture (usually made in the United States) that is assumed to work as an etic approach. Thus, instruments based on American theories, with items reflecting American conditions, are simply translated and used in other cultures. Only rarely does this approach yield useful results. (Triandis et al., 1972, p. 6)

The assumption that categories developed in one culture are automatically, probably, or unquestioningly shared by another exemplifies the ethnocentric effect. The process of minimizing ethnocentrism by detailed ethnographic analysis of emic categories is complicated because ethnocentrism may influence the perception and inquiry processes (Campbell & LeVine, 1970; LeVine & Campbell, 1972; Segall, Campbell, & Herskovits, 1966; Werner & Campbell, 1970/1973).

The difficulty of the pursuit of objective categories and judgments has produced many techniques for decentering. For some scientists, methodological triangulation (stressing multimeasures and levels of analysis) was the means (Campbell & Fiske, 1959; Rohner, 1975a; Shweder, 1973, 1975). For others, the approach was considerable professional and scientific interaction over the years among psychologists and other behavioral scientists (Holtzman et al., 1975). Still others advocated a field manual, handbook, or cookbook approach (Manaster & Havighurst, 1972; Tapp, 1965–1967; Triandis et al., 1972; Whiting, Child, Lambert et al., 1966; Williams, 1967). A major ingredient of the latter, for example, was decentering from one language to another until there is a set of items not particularly appropriate to one culture but acceptable to all (Triandis et al., 1972, p. 45). Beyond using the procedure of decentering test items, as well as language translations, and to assure equivalency of stimuli, cross-cultural psychologists have increasingly reported unusually satisfactory results when data analysis and interpretation involve local informants (Triandis et al., 1972, pp. 13–14; see also Brislin, 1970, 1976; Brislin et al., 1973; LeVine, 1973a, 1979).

Anthropologist LeVine's report (1966) on outsiders' judgments of group differences in personality is equally instructive on the effect of ethnocentrism. LeVine, mindful of the intuitive attribution of behavior to members of a group, stressed the importance of adequate field experience, the use of a professionally qualified ethnographer, and the necessity of multiple methods to reduce the bias (i.e., loyalistic misperceptions) frequently operative in inter-cultural perception with regard to personality differences. In their instructional handbook on designing and performing cross-national research, Manaster and Havighurst (1972) described specific methodological problems in conducting international cooperative research and means to reduce the ethnocentric effect among investigators. They recommended a joint-development-concurrent approach to abate ethnocentrism. It, for example, was used in a six-nation, socialization study into compliance systems (Hess & Tapp, 1969; Minturn & Tapp, 1970).

Anthropologist LeVine and psychologist Campbell (1972) in their study of intergroup relations, outgroup stereotypes, ingroup self-adulation, and other aspects of ethnocentrism developed an eighty-page field manual to make data collection as comparable as possible from culture to culture. Others also have constructed field manuals with guidelines to reduce further the ethnocentrism of the investigators toward their subjects

as well as toward scientists from other disciplines and from other back-
grounds (Tapp, 1965–1967; Whiting, Child, Lambert et al., 1966; Williams,
1967). LeVine and Campbell studied the efficacy of various social science
theories, for example, to measure the degree of ethnocentrism among
groups and the content of stereotyped images. They found that since the
conceptual territory of ethnocentrism cuts across analytic boundaries, the
phenomenon provided for a "natural" meeting of social science theories.
For a fuller understanding of ethnocentrism, the multidisciplinary team of
Campbell and LeVine had to move beyond their own disciplinary boundaries. In short, they shed the ethnocentric effect of their respective fields
with regard to theory and method in order to study the phenomenon of
ethnocentrism. Cross-cultural personality researchers still may suffer "residual ethnocentrism," a condition experienced even by the ethnographer
conscientiously avoiding ethnocentric provincialisms (Segall et al., 1966,
p. 16).

*Ethnocentrism and Ethics*

The issue of the impact of the researcher on the persons studied ties together the ethical and ethnocentric effects. The potential misuse of inter-
pretative categories or investigative items that reflect subtly the bias of the
scientist's society requires the attention of the cross-cultural researcher at
the data-gathering, data-analysis, and data-reporting points. For example,
an examination between two groups on appositional versus propositional
thinking *or* aggression versus compliance may cause no problem until it is
suggested that one kind of thought or behavior is valued or advantageous
in a particular ecological setting. Furthermore, the past ethnocentric bias
of many Western social scientists has led to a general skepticism by many
being studied *and* many presently inaugurating cross-cultural studies. (An
additional discussion on the topic of ethical research appears later in this
chapter and in Warwick's chapter in Volume 1 of this *Handbook*.)

## Etiology

Etiology, the assignment of causes and the showing of reasons, is a fundamental criterion for a cross-cultural personality researcher. It speaks
to identifying and linking multiple forces and to using multiple measurements as well as common classificatory systems. This epidemiolog-
ical-type orientation, as in studies on disease distribution in human
populations, can help locate undetected factors. For example, in the case
of mental illness, the strategy historically has provided background data
on types and rates of illness within the context of social factors (Hollings-

head & Redlich, 1958; Leighton, 1959). Contemporary cross-cultural efforts reflect the importance of etiological analyses in forecasting the effect of social-culture influences on psychopathology (Dohrenwend & Dohrenwend, 1974, p. 445).

*Etiological Examples*

Because of deficiencies in the theory and method of child psychology, LeVine (1970) advanced the etiological model as an organizing framework to consider antecedent-consequent relations. His was a significant social science effort to adopt the advantageous procedures of an epidemiological orientation. Operationally, his etiological model implied no separation of developmental from cross-cultural studies *or* division of anthropological data from the research process. In addition to cross-group frequencies on disease incidence, information on the impact of such social factors as role or group is basic to proposing methodological guidelines (p. 602). For LeVine, a significant etiology depends on documentation and manipulation of all variations using comparative and longitudinal, quasi-experimental, and experimental studies (pp. 561–566).

Research into causal relations may begin either with a dependent or independent variable. The dependent choice guarantees that the scientist's efforts are directed toward an important phenomenon and a significant search for causes. Theoretically, it reduces the danger of being "trivial, irrelevant, or otherwise uninteresting" judged by external scientific criteria (LeVine, 1970, p. 565), while simultaneously addressing the issue of research goals and methods. As examples, LeVine cited several kibbutzim studies where the impact of collective child-rearing on personality development was "accepted" (assumed) first and "detected" (studied) later. As he observed, the differences in childhood experience between the kibbutz and conventional communities may account for few variations of central concern to students of cross-cultural personality development. Etiological research may well exacerbate an apparent deficiency in cross-cultural psychological research; to wit, a lack of well-documented, comparably explained, or evaluated data that fits into a coherent whole (p. 566). Nevertheless, its inclusion should help the development of more valid, widely accepted measuring instruments and research designs for the cross-cultural study of youth. Also it should aid the accumulation of comparative data on psychological development representing common scientific interests in personality, cognition, and the formation of social dispositions (LeVine, 1970, p. 566).

From a different perspective Werner, Bierman, and French's (1971) cross-cultural and developmental, longitudinal and interdisciplinary study on the children of Kauai was an interesting exercise in deriving an etiology. "Multi" is the key concept and prefix for this ten-year study of offspring from 3735 pregnancies on one Hawaiian island. Multifaceted in concern, multicultural in sample, multisourced in data, and multioriented in prevention/intervention strategies, a multidisciplinary research team (representing maternal and child health, obstetrics, pediatrics, psychology, public health nursing, sociology, and statistics) surveyed many variables to assess the relationship of (1) fetal and postnatal death to perinatal complications, (2) perinatal stress to the physical, social, and cognitive development of pre-and school-age children, and (3) perinatal stress and environmental quality (material being, intellectual stimulation, and emotional support) to children's development at ages 2 and 10. Kauai's Japanese, Hawaiian, Filipino, Portuguese, and Anglo-Caucasian communities provided an unusually stable opportunity (96 percent followed up at 2 years, 90 percent at ten) to consider the impact of environment, education, and ethnicity in selected areas (achievement, intellectual, perceptual, languages, emotional, physical). Basically the researchers considered how in the short and long haul birth trauma, environment, and/or ethnicity influenced the growing child.

Their most important findings involved environmental quality: Ten times more children had problems attributable to a limited early environment than to serious perinatal stress. Environmental quality had significant impact on physical, social, and cognitive development before the second year of life. In addition, the need for supportive, stimulating environments to minimize perinatal damage was evident in the need of almost one third of all Kauai's 10-year-olds for long-term educational and/or mental health services. The study demonstrated the predictive value of combined and early psychological-pediatric diagnostic examinations. It suggested the utility of a multidisciplinary, environmental approach to assess successful adaptation. Despite its singular cultural definition of achievement and ability, the Kauai study illustrated the need and utility of a search for key factors that cumulatively affect children's development.

Essentially, then, the etiological strategy, by expanding the range of observable variations, serves cross-cultural research in personality development as social epidemiology does pathology in medicine. The point of etiology in the ERS is that it links propositions about a particular phenomenon.

*Congruence as an Etiological Aim*

One goal in determining the etiology of a personality phenomenon or process is the establishment of convergent validity for key measures. As illustrated in LeVine's use of outsiders' judgments to describe personality dispositions, methods can vary from personal judgments of individuals to locally agreed-on judgments to standard psychological tests (1966). A multimethod approach stands a better chance of obtaining convergent validation. The paradigm of a multimethod matrix (Campbell, 1970/1973; Campbell & Fiske, 1959; Campbell & LeVine, 1970) is distinctly advantageous theoretically and empirically for cross-culture personality research. For example, typically comparative studies involve only two elements and frequently only two groups. Campbell, Fiske, and LeVine variously have demonstrated that comparisons of a single pair (two entity) are uninterpretable and "hopelessly equivocal for hypothesis testing" (Campbell & Levine, 1970, p. 366; cf. Thomae, 1979). They have concluded that a multiple approach is more likely to tease out the causal effects. Therefore, a multitrait multimethod matrix, a methodological triangulation approach, and/or a convergent operationism orientation should maximize the study of extant variation and heterogeneity *and* optimize the probability of convergent as well as discriminant validation (Campbell, 1970/1973, pp. 63–67).

The successful etiology of a disposition then, like that of a disease, is based on gathering extant and evolving descriptions. It is extended by multifaceted theoretical and methodological designs. Attention to the etiological network is more likely to assure a more complete description, a more diverse methodology, and a more adequate sampling since its aim is a comprehensive, convergent, and congruent explanation. Finally, an etiological focus can help the researcher answer four questions pertinent to studying personality development cross-culturally: (1) whom we may compare; (2) when we could compare; (3) how many we should compare; and (4) how we must compare (apologies to Berry & Dasen, 1974b, p. 14).

## Ethology

Several versions of the nature-nurture (hereditary-environment) debate reappeared in the 1970s. Among the controversial forms were ethology, sociobiology, psychobiology, behavior genetics, and bioanthropology. The ethological framework deserves attention because it provides an avenue to: (a) tease apart the interplay between organism and environment; (b) modulate the tendency to center on human species uniqueness; (c) eschew the dichotomy of instinct and culture, innate and learned, inherited and acquired; (d) examine the time and place factors within developmental and longitudinal perspectives; and (e) map the interplay of biological and social forces affecting personality, culture, and behavior. The strategy builds on Tinbergen's (1963) approach to ethological study, encompassing the four major interrelated problems of cause, function, development, and evolution. It stresses explanations at the levels of causation (proximate and ultimate) and development (ontogenetic and phylogenetic). An ethological approach, then, is an essential ingredient in an effective cross-cultural strategy for personality research.

Ethology emphasizes the evolutionary significance of development and behavior based on over-time (longitudinal) observations in natural habitats. The focus is on evolving functions of the living organism. Ethologists generally make interspecific (e.g., human and nonhuman primate) comparisons at morphological (e.g., eyebrow raising pattern), operational (e.g., pelvic thrusting), functional (e.g., staring and averting gazes), and situational (e.g., patting agitated individuals) levels. They also make intraspecific comparisons using different populations of the same species. By recording behavior directly, ethologists describe functioning in real-life, *in situ*, or habitat situations. In the case of humans, they observe directly and avoid disrupting ongoing behavior.

Human ethology draws on the principles, procedures, and findings of animal ethology to explain human phenomena (McGrew, 1972, p. 222). Decidedly interdisciplinary, it straddles at least psychology, physical and social anthropology, human biology, sociology, and zoology (Smith, 1975, p. 90). The few ethologists who do human research typically work at the descriptive phase formulating an ethogram for the human species, usually based on children's behavior. Most human ethologists regard their findings on the universality of behavior patterns as basic, but primitive and limited.

*Disciplinary Vantage Points*

*Anthropological.* In 1961, anthropologist Singer felt that ethologists made the word *instinct* respectable in the debate relating culture to human nature. In 1971, ethnographic psychologist Cole and associates (in their explanation of experimental anthropology) applauded the utility of the study of animal behavior for human behavior. In 1973, the use of a Darwinian perspective for personality research was elaborately presented by LeVine. An ethological perspective meant emphasizing environmentally stable species characteristics—that is, transcultural, pan-human instinctive, or evolved phylogenetically adaptive behavioral processes in natural settings—rather than the distinctive characteristics of each social group. LeVine's evolutionary perspective encompassed ecology, population genetics, and a variation-selection-retention model in a cross-cultural strategy for studying personality. As described earlier, he recommended three interdependent, but complementary, research strategies drawn from biological research: physiological, ecological, and embryological (1973a; cf. Darwin, 1872/1965).

By the mid-1970s, other anthropologists focused heavily on gene strategies, not on individuals or clusters of animals. Evolutionary biologists had agreed that the potency of natural selection was at the level of the individual (Alexander, 1974); more precisely, at the level of the gene (Dawkins, 1976; Wilson, 1975). Acceptance of the gene principle affected basic anthropological theory, for example, on human sociality (Chagnon & Irons, 1979). Anthropologist DeVore interpreted "all social behavior in terms of one currency, the natural selection of the genes that most promote the individuals' success in reproduction" [and all traits as having] "100 percent genetic causes and 100 percent environmental causes" (De-Vore & Morris, 1977, pp. 45, 86). Therefore, personality is the product of interaction between/of genes and environment; behavioral differences are the adaptive responses to environmental differences. This gene-based focus is compatible to researchers from widely divergent branches of sciences attracted to a biological and a zoological perspective on development. Yet it does not obviate the fact that, among humans, learning can be passed on by culture, thus modulating the genetic contribution. It merely suggests that human culture and personality are more explicable using a gene-based view of life.

*Psychological.* Except for the classic research in ecological psychology, until the 1970s few psychologists seriously entertained ethology. Campbell (1975) proposed that psychology would profit from evolutionary theory, despite the political (ideological) "dangers" of a biological, evolutionary, or ethological approach. Campbell further regretted a possible uncritical, unwarranted suppression of "a legitimate area of biological speculation and research" (1975, p. 111).

In the early 1970s, psychologist Hess reviewed the gains of a genetically determined approach for understanding the human constitution and condition (1970). Decidedly a pacesetter in joining developmental psychology and ethology, Hess maintained that the ethological concern about the complete context (i.e., biological bases and adaptive function) was most valuable for analyzing human behavior (1970, p. 24). Illustratively, Hess noted the limitation of describing aggressive behavior solely in terms of environment (p. 32). He viewed ethological concepts as apropos both in the ontogenetic and phylogenetic senses. Generally, the 1970s witnessed an attempt by developmental psychologists to extend the ethological method of observing animal behavior in natural habitats to the study of child behavior. Some had already pushed for an ecological orientation (see Ecology section); others opted for conducting observational studies in the ethological tradition of naturally occurring events, some in cross-cultural settings (Blurton-Jones, 1967, 1972; Charlesworth, 1973, 1975; Eibl-Eibesfeldt, 1970, 1972; Freedman, 1974, 1976; Freedman & DeBoer, 1979; McGrew, 1972; Smith, 1975).

For example, McGrew linked the rationale and method of ethology to human development in a systematic investigation of preschool children's motor and social plus individual and group behaviors (1972). Formulating an ethogram, he observed facial expressions, gestures, postures, and loco-motions among 3- and 4-year-old nursery school children and related such findings to earlier human and nonhuman primate behavior. In addi-tion to cross-cultural extension of such studies (1972, p. xii), he stressed human ethology's conceptual and procedural advantage to zoologists, bi-ologists, primatologists, psychologists, anthropologists, and sociologists as well as its practical value to pediatricians and teachers.

Another pacesetter was Smith's comprehensive presentation of the comparative ethological approach—interspecific, intraspecific, and cross-cultural (1975). Smith traced the merger of ethology and comparative psy-chology, the growth of primate studies, the ascent of human ethology, and the emergence of social ethology. He presented data on the rough-and-tumble play of children, noting the strategic importance of the few cross-cultural ethologically oriented studies on infant or child behavior. To Smith, there was sufficient data on the culture-invariant aspects of certain characteristics such as nonverbal communication (gestures, facial expres-sions), social development (attachment and aggression, exploration and play), and social organization (incest taboos) to describe certain species-specific personality phenomena. For Smith, then, the evolutionary per-spective of the ethologist affords a profitable perspective for studying cross-culturally the adaptability of human behavior and the resultant per-sonality (e.g., effect of quasi-continuous feeding and carrying of babies).

In 1975 also, developmental psychologist Charlesworth posed the "big unanswered question": "Can ethology be really relevant for the study of humans?" (p. 5). His response was affirmative. Critical of psychology's antihistorical, antinaturalistic, and antipragmatic bent (1973), he hypothe-sized that ethology could ease psychology's social and scientific (episte-mologic and practical) crises—conceptually, methodologically, and attitu-dinally. For example, its methodological contribution could be the classical strategy of studying the spontaneous behavior of free-moving an-imals in natural places over time. Charlesworth's proposed triad of etho-logical contributions was guided by the proposition that "knowledge of behavior in natural habitats contributes first to structuring the questions to be answered by experimentation and secondly to interpreting the answers gained by experimentation" (1973, pp. 39–40).

Freedman's research exemplified the gains possible using an ethologi-cal approach. Studying infants in cross-cultural contexts, he asserted the thesis that "everything that man does, at some level of analysis, is reflec-tive of his biological makeup" [therefore, it is] "a logical fallacy to oppose learning with biology" (Freedman, 1976, pp. 35–36). To demonstrate that similarities between individuals and groups are related to genotype (gene-pools), Freedman studied twenty-four Chinese-American and twenty-four European-American (second through fourth generation) newborns. He used twenty-eight general behavioral items to cover temperament, sensory development, automatic and central nervous system maturity, motor development, and social development aspects. Even though the two ethnic groups decidedly differed on temperament (e.g., excitability/imperturbability), "there was substantial overlap in range on all scales between the Chinese and Caucasian infants" (p. 38). The Chinese-American newborns were less perturbable and more easily consoled, but in all other areas, the two groups were essentially comparable. Freedman reported on an earlier Navajo newborn sample who, like the Chinese-newborn sample, accommodated readily to the testing procedures. The Asiatic origin of the Navajo further explained the heritable component (the gene-pool effect). On the basis of his cross-cultural ethological studies on infants and across sexes, Freedman concluded that human beings were: (1) much more alike than different; (2) like primates in terms of dominance hierarchies; and (3) like any other primate (pp. 42–43). Other research on affective expressions also cogently reveals the significance of the ethological studies to investigating and understanding species-specific behavior (e.g., crying, smiling) (Ainsworth, 1964, 1967, 1978; Bowlby, 1969; Fox & Fleising, 1976; Freedman & DeBoer, 1979; Yarrow & Pedersen, 1972).

## The Evolution of Ethology

For present-day ethologists, singular explanatory categories such as "innate" or "genetically fixed" obscure investigation of interactive developmental processes, confound the meaning of learned and unlearned components of behavior, emphasize a reductionism to instinct and culture (heredity and environment), and perpetuate circular reasoning with respect to evolutionary explanations (Hinde, 1974). Most ethologists, like most behavioral scientists, seek explanations in terms of many influences: some ontogenetic, some experiential, some ecological, some stimulus-related, some genetic loading. In sum, then, ethology is the study of evolving behavior in natural settings. It also emphasizes the developmental perspective as a means of understanding the emergence of behavior and/or personality, while being cross-cultural and cross-species in perspective. Finally, ethological-type research has convincingly demonstrated that there are fairly uniform cross-cultural (i.e., pan-human, universal) outcomes in such areas as affect and language, perception and physical growth (Munroe & Munroe, 1975; Fox & Fleising, 1976; Freedman & De-Boer, 1979; Werner, 1979). As a result, the ethological is a basic aspect of the ERS.

## Ethics and the Experimenting Society

The sixth and final element of the ERS deals with ethics at the individual and institutional levels *and* for the cultures of science and society. Ethics and the experimenting society are inexorably interwoven, not merely for the researcher as "scientist" and the respondent as "subject," but for each as citizen. Both have social and scientific aspects; both bear basic and applied implications; both affect research and reform decisions; and both require education and attention. Therefore, although the politics and ethics of cross-cultural research are comprehensively handled in this *Handbook* by Warwick (1980), the ethical issue is so fundamental to the enterprise of studying personality development cross-culturally that it merits mention here.

Even though the medical sciences may have fueled the current ethics movement in the behavioral and social sciences, the conduct of social research and the protection of human subjects have been of major concern, as marked by the explosion of articles, books, and codes over the past ten years (see for references Reynolds, 1975, 1979; Tapp, Kelman, Triandis, Wrightsman, & Coelho, 1974; Warwick, 1980; cf. resolutions by national and international social science associations). Increasingly, textbooks view the topic as basic to educating the young researcher and sensitizing the older one (Baltes et al., 1977; Selltiz, Wrightsman, & Cook, 1976; Werner, 1979). Further, the issues being confronted vary *from* the right of the subject participant to self-determination *to* the right of the scientist participant to study another's culture. The basic message is that scientists can no longer be oblivious to ethics—their own or others. Regardless of field, the role of scientist involves a dual obligation: to conduct research and to benefit human welfare. At one level, the scientific ethic involves "the honesty implicit in the relationship of theory to fact, the commitment to public report, the basic faith in order" (Price-Williams, 1975b, p. 89; cf. Bronowski, 1956). It also, however, requires a broader set of aspirations and responsibilities—the commitment to study normative values in cultural contexts, to adopt ethical guidelines, to court rational scientific and social laws, and to apply knowledge so gained for humane purposes (Tapp, 1971; Tapp & Levine, 1977a).

It is within this context that cross-cultural researchers generally, and particularly those studying personality development, must address the issues of the rights, roles, and responsibilities of various participants in the settings under study. Research on personality development, with its implications for behavior change, involves some of the most problematic and complex ethical issues. In part, the personality arena is complex because of the selection of populations and problems (e.g., children, emotionally disturbed; authoritarianism, deviance, morality, socialization). Such issues are intensified in the cross-cultural setting, where the findings potentially speak to cultural and individual differences as well as political and ideological ones. In order to insure the welfare of groups and individuals as well as of individuals in groups, cross-cultural personality researchers must aim for both internally and externally valid research using ethically acceptable procedures. In so doing, they potentially furnish an important educational model and serve an essential ethical function.

## An Emergent Ethic

In the 1960s, many were concerned about the ethical implications of theories and methods in social and personality psychology (Adelson, 1969; Kelman, 1967). In the early 1970s, there were serious doubts that rapid reforms in research methodology or educational pedagogy could occur until professors and senior investigators adopted ethical modes in the conduct of inquiry. By the mid-1970s, discussion of ethical considerations pervaded national associations (e.g., American Anthropological Association [AAA]; American Psychological Association [APA], Danish Psychological Association; and so on) and surfaced in a number of international congresses. The problem of cross-cultural research ethics produced a report for the APA (Tapp, 1976; Tapp et al., 1974), evoked international responses (Holtzman, 1976, 1978; Taft, 1976/1977), and stimulated a study by UNESCO on the moral dilemmas associated with the development and application of social science (Reynolds, 1975, 1979).

The Tapp Report, commissioned in 1971 by the APA's Committee on International Relations in Psychology, was the response by a group of United States social psychologists to the need (1) to prepare guidelines for the conduct and training of cross-cultural researchers and (2) to develop "a preliminary set of trans-cultural advisory principles for international consideration" (Tapp et al., 1974, p. 232). The Tapp Report is extensively reviewed by Warwick (1980). The thirteen Advisory Principles advanced under the headings of: (a) responsibilities to the individuals and communities studied; (b) responsibilities to collaborators and colleagues in the host community; and (c) responsibilities to the discipline and the research enterprise are also basic to Reynolds's formulations of a composite code for use of human subjects in research and by investigators for sponsored research (1979).

The most telling finding from the various efforts is the consensus on several issues and procedures that seemed culturally generalizable. On the issue of cultural similarity, for example, Reynolds reported "no significant inconsistency" among twenty-four associations (1975, p. 9). Cross-cultural researchers can no longer rationalize a double standard by hiding behind either the argument of extraordinary cross-cultural differences or the possibilities of behavioral scientists' noncompliance with ethical standards.

The manner in which we define our role as cross-cultural researchers of personality is basic to the way we formulate our methodology: What is the message if we do not ponder the equivalency of the ethical and methodological issue? To the extent that the ethical dimension is overlooked in a research strategy, we may have misinterpreted the cultures of science and society *and* their interactive nature.

*Role and Responsibility in an Experimenting Society*

The ethics of professional role and responsibility for a cross-cultural personality researcher are more than abstract or merely philosophical problems. Choices, for example, as to whether the research is intra- rather than inter-cultural (e.g., United States only), from one disciplinary perspective rather than several (i.e., psychology only), and/or interpreted from only one societal or theoretical vantage (e.g., Western or psychoanalytic) all carry significant pedagogical, political, and psychological implications (Campbell, 1969, 1971, 1974a; Goldberg, 1977; Kelman, 1967; Price-Williams, 1974, 1975b; Reynolds, 1975, 1979; Riegel, 1972, 1973; Tapp, 1976; Tapp et al., 1974: Tapp & Levine, 1977a; Warwick, 1980). Indeed, such ethical concerns are particularly intensified whenever social policy (e.g., educational, economic, familial, legal) is closely connected to scientific studies. A major responsibility of students of personality development, then, is to evaluate the cross-cultural research effort continuously.

By their nature, the phenomena and procedures of cross-cultural personality psychology demand methodologically confident, ethically responsible, and publicly available views of science. For example, descriptions and related decisions on what constitutes "good" or "bad" aggression, "mature" moral judgment, or "educative" cognitive competence involve fundamental questions about the nature of research and the directions for reform. In an open, active, and experimenting society, cross-cultural investigators of basic personality phenomena and users of such findings (the policymakers) must view *both* research *and* reform endeavors as experiments (Campbell, 1969, 1971, 1974a). Such a perspective acknowledges the interdependent and interactive aspects of the scientific and social enterprises.

## An ERS Exercise

Space precludes an exercise herein to test the viability of the proposed ERS perspectives as applied to past research. However, before the researcher uses the ERS in designing a research plan, it would be a constructive, instructive, and validating exercise to examine several representative, landmark cross-cultural personality studies in terms of the ERS. Those recommended for this exercise follow; they are arranged by number of participating cultures:

a. For uni- or single culture, the examples include Ainsworth's *Infancy in Uganda* (1967); Barker and Wright's *Midwest and Its Children* (1955/1971)—U.S.; Fromm and Maccoby's *Social Character in a Mexican Village* (1970); Spiro's *Children of the Kibbutz* (1958/1975); or Werner, Bierman, and French's *The Children of Kauai* (1971).

b. For dual or two cultures, I propose Barker and Schoggen's *Qualities of Community Life* (1973)—England and U.S.; Bronfenbrenner's *Two Worlds of Childhood*—U.S., and U.S.S.R. (1970); Havighurst and Neugarten's *American Indian and White Children* (1955); or Holtzman, Diaz-Guerrero, and Swartz's *Personality Development in Two Cultures* (1975)—Mexico and U.S.

c. For multiculture, I advise Berry's *Human Ecology and Cognitive Style* (1976)—18 societies; Minturn and Lambert's *Mothers of Six Cultures* (1964); Rohner's *They Love Me, They Love Me Not* (1975b)—101 societies; Whiting's *Six Cultures* (1963)—India, Kenya, Mexico, Okinawa, Philippines, U.S.; or Whiting and Whiting's *Children of Six Cultures* (1975).

Even a cursory examination of these benchmark studies suggests some attention to the multimethodological and multidisciplinary demands of the ERS. Nevertheless, even these well-known and important baseline studies may suffer an absence of some ERS perspectives that a current design by the same investigators would address and/or contain.

### Concluding Comment

This chapter recalls the story whose last line is: "The emperor wore no clothes." The discovery that to date the authority—in this case, the behavioral sciences of psychology and anthropology—is limited should be evident, but not discouraging. The authority that evolved from past research, cross- and unicultural, about personality development provides designs and data as to both "dos" and "do nots." Further, prior work offers criteria for developing new strategies for constructing new theories and methods. Whatever the outcome, as earlier reviews and critical analyses have indicated, the problem and the solution remain mutually relevant to the disciplines of psychology and anthropology.

As the 1970s ended, Spindler (1978b), in a fashion similar to this chapter's author, described the dismay and disappointment during previous decades about the study of personality and culture. He drew on the work of founders and current contributors to psychological anthropology. While he emphasized the historical lack of crossovers between cross-cultural psychology and psychological anthropology, Spindler also arrayed increasing evidence of meaningful convergences between psychology's experimentalism and anthropology's naturalism (e.g., experimental method and ethnography). His examples of theoretical and methodological rapprochement suggested the emergence of a more sophisticated interdisciplinary approach to studying personality development cross-culturally. In tracing the past and future directions of psychological anthropology, Spindler (1978b, 1978c) constructed a case for a renewed idealism in the area of personality and culture. Both the conclusions Spindler drew from his review and the methodological strategies he recommended parallel those in the present chapter. His effort affords a reassuringly concurrent analysis of prior trends and future needs.

Several others analyzing the history of cross-cultural personality study found the same pattern of confusion, concern, and, more recently, expectation. For example, Draguns (1979) described the culture-personality state as confused and uncertain, but sees the prospect of integration and a promise of contribution to general psychological knowledge. LeVine (1979), a long-time critic and contributor, maintained that, despite the problematic nature of comparative child studies historically and contemporarily, there was substantial progress in the determination of universals, culture-specifics, and environmental variations. But he warned that factors beyond research quality, such as institutional and attitudinal factors, shape the nature of a scientific contribution.

Basically, then, reviews of the art and science of personality research, whether by anthropologist or psychologist, suggest that, if dismay and disillusionment are to turn to discovery and delight, those studying personality development must become less procedurally parochial and more theoretically expansive. By the end of the decade, there were substantial moves toward such goals in the field of cross-cultural psychology (and in the realms of personality and development as well), judging by the array of handbooks and textbooks (e.g., Bourguignon, 1979; Marsella, Tharp, & Ciborowski, 1979; Munroe, Munroe, & Whiting, 1981; Triandis' *Handbooks;* Warren, in press; Werner, 1979) and the growth of multidisciplinary journals (e.g., *Ethos, International Journal of Psychology, Journal of Cross-Cultural Psychology, Revista Interamericana de Psicologia*). Clearly, also, by the end of the decade, there were sufficiently solid findings to help begin the task of building a viable, if not grand, theory of personality from a cross-cultural perspective with an emphasis on development. This sufficiency also helped formulate the ERS method and so an answer to the question posed in the chapter.

History provided the context for developing an approach to the study of personality; the Elephant Research Strategy (ERS) simply provides one approach to the task. The advantage to the cross-cultural investigator of the ERS lies in its incorporation of strategies from many disciplines. The six elements underscore that a multidisciplinary orientation (e.g., anthropology, biology, law, medicine, philosophy, political science, psychology, psychiatry, sociology, zoology) facilitates reconceptualizing the problem of studying personality development cross-culturally. In addition, such a perspective introduces a pluralism of methods—ecological, ethnographic, ethnocentric, etiological, ethological, and ethical—basic to the elaboration of a model for studying personality. Even though perhaps ideally the researcher should use all six elements of the ERS to insure the greater probability of finding congruence and obtaining convergence, even awareness of each should prove constructive. Further, the ERS is a mechanism that works well for distinctly different theoretical orientations, the cognitively or psychoanalytically oriented as well as the social learning or trait theorist. Finally, the ERS with its six elements helps those involved in the study of personality development to realize that their task is as much to explain how the adult or child came to be as how they can become.

The need for a strategy that considers the elephant—the human organism—from many viewpoints emanates as much from the "overlap and mutual relevance of diverse investigations" (LeVine, 1973a, p. 61) as from a recognition that the complex interaction of person and situation requires pluralistic paradigms and interdependent procedures. Such multiple methods most capably evoke higher order variables and theoretical abstractions, thus helping to lay the groundwork for an heuristic approach to the study of personality. As importantly, the move to multimethods and minitheories is pragmatic. As Cronbach, in reassessing the two disciplines of scientific psychology, recently reminded researchers, "when we step outside the range of our experience, we have to use our heads" (1975, p. 126). It is, therefore, perhaps heartening that by 1979—just twenty years away from anthropologist Honigmann's (1959) and ten years away from psychologist Adelson's (1969) disappointments—that another anthropologist (Spindler, 1978a) and another psychologist (Tapp, herein) believe, on the basis of their respective analyses of the theoretical and empirical literature, that the study of personality development cross-culturally can now be undertaken in a complementary manner.

If there is an analogue to the state of personality and culture study in the human condition, it is that of an enduring, incompatible, involving marriage. Like such a relationship, there are always complaints about the messages, dismay about the methods of communication, reports about its failure, and forecasts about the impossibility of the undertaking. But the participants never give up; they, too, always exhibit a recurrent, resurging, and renewed interest in the problem and process.

## Note

1 John Schneeweis assisted in the early phase of this project. Robert B. Tapp and Felice J. Levine provided helpful comments on earlier versions of the manuscript. Michael Meltzer, Stefanie Miller, Brenda Mann, and Susan Smith-Cunnien helped with the bibliographic activities. Graduate students from my 1979 and 1980 cross-cultural psychology classes (S. Wayne Duncan, Peter LaFreniere, Rose Mae Richardson, & Lauren Robertson) offered cogent comments on the penultimate draft, as did my colleague James Butcher. Lonnie Christensen typed the final version. For all of the above help, I am appreciative. The ideas herein, however, are solely my responsibility.

## References

ADELSON, J. Personality. *Annual Review of Psychology,* 1969, *20,* 217–252.

AINSWORTH, M. D. S. Patterns of attachment behavior shown by the infant in interaction with his mother. *Merrill-Palmer Quarterly of Behavior and Development,* 1964, *10,* 51–58.

————. *Infancy in Uganda: Infant care and the growth of love.* Baltimore, Md.: The Johns Hopkins Press, 1967.

————. Attachment theory and its utility in cross-cultural research. In P. H. Leiderman, S. Tulkin & A. Rosenfeld (Eds.), *Culture and infancy: Variations in the human experience.* New York: Academic Press, 1978.

ALEXANDER, R. D. The evolution of social behavior. *Annual Review of Ecology and Systematics,* 1974, *5,* 325–383.

ALLPORT, G. W. *Pattern and growth in personality.* New York: Holt, Rinehart, & Winston, 1961. (Originally published, 1937.)

————. *Personality and social encounter: Selected essays.* Boston: Beacon Press, 1960.

ALTMAN, I. *The environment and social behavior.* Monterey, Calif.: Brooks/Cole Publishing Co., 1975.

ALTMAN, I., & CHEMERS, M. M. Cultural aspects of environment-behavior relationships. In H. C. Triandis & R. W. Brislin (Eds.), *Handbook of cross-cultural psychology* (Vol. 5): *Social psychology.* Boston: Allyn & Bacon, 1980.

ARENSBERG, C. M. Culture as behavior: Structure and emergence. *Annual Review of Anthropology,* 1972, *1,* 1–26.

ASHTON, P. T. Cross-cultural Piagetian research: An experimental perspective. *Harvard Educational Review,* 1975, *45,* 475–506.

BALDWIN, A. L. A cognitive theory of socialization. In D. A. Goslin (Ed.), *Handbook of socialization theory and research.* Chicago: Rand McNally, 1969.

BALTES, P. B., REESE, H. W., & NESSELROADE, J. R. (Eds.). *Life-span developmental psychology: Introduction to research methods.* Monterey, Calif.: Brooks/Cole Publishing Co., 1977.

BALTES, P. B., & SCHAIE, K. W. (Eds.). *Life-span developmental psychology: Personality and socialization.* New York: Academic Press, 1973. (a)

BALTES, P. B., & SCHAIE, K. W. On life-span developmental research paradigms: Retrospects and prospects. In P. B. Baltes & K. W. Schaie (Eds.), *Life-span developmental psychology: Personality and socialization.* New York: Academic Press, 1973. (b)

BARBER, B. Resistance by scientists to scientific discovery. *Science,* 1961, *134,* 596–602.

BARKER, R. G. *Ecological psychology.* Stanford: Stanford University Press, 1968.

———. A coming of age. (Review of *An introduction to environmental psychology* by W. H. Ittelson, H. M. Proshansky, L. G. Rivlin, & G. H. Winkel.) *Contemporary Psychology,* 1975, *20,* 289–290.

BARKER, R. G., & SCHOGGEN, P. *Qualities of community life.* San Francisco: Jossey-Bass Publishers, 1973.

BARKER, R. G., & WRIGHT, H. F. *Midwest and its children: The psychological ecology of an American town.* Hamden, Connecticut: Anchor Books, 1971. (Originally published, 1955.)

BARRY, H., III, BACON, M. K., & CHILD, I. L. Definitions, ratings, and bibliographic sources for child-training practices of 110 cultures. In C. S. Ford (Ed.), *Cross-cultural approaches.* New Haven: HRAF Press, 1967.

BARRY, H., III, CHILD, I. L., & BACON, M. K. Relation of child training to subsistence economy. In A. D. Ulman (Ed.), *Sociocultural foundations of personality.* Boston: Houghton Mifflin Co., 1965. (Reprinted from *American Anthropologist,* 1959, *61,* 51–63.)

BATESON, G. *Naven: A survey of the problems suggested by a composite picture of the culture of a New Guinea tribe drawn from three points of view.* Stanford: Stanford University Press, 1936. (2d ed., 1958.)

BELL, R. G., & HARPER, L. V. *Child effects on adults.* Hillsdale, N. J.: Erlbaum, 1977.

BENEDICT, R. F. *Patterns of culture.* Boston: Houghton Mifflin Co., 1934.

BENNETT, J. W., & THAISS, G. Survey research and sociocultural anthropology. In C. Y. Glock (Ed.), *Survey research in the social sciences.* New York: Russell Sage Foundation, 1967.

BERRY, J. W. On cross-cultural comparability. *International Journal of Psychology,* 1969, *4,* 119–128.

———. *Human ecology and cognitive style: Comparative studies in cultural and psychological adaptation.* Beverly Hills: Sage/Halsted, 1976.

———. Developmental issues in the comparative study of psychological differentiation. In R. Munroe, R. Munroe, & B. B. Whiting (Eds.), *Handbook of cross-cultural human development.* New York: Garland Publishing Co., 1981.

BERRY, J. W., & ANNIS, R. C. Acculturative stress: The role of ecology, culture and differentiation. *Journal of Cross-Cultural Psychology,* 1974, *5,* 382–406. (a)

———. Ecology, culture and psychological differentiation. *International Journal of Psychology,* 1974, *9,* 173–193. (b)

BERRY, J. W., & DASEN, P. R. (Eds.). *Culture and cognition: Readings in cross-cultural psychology.* London: Methuen & Co. Ltd., 1974. (a)

———. Introduction: History and method in the cross-cultural study of cognition. In J. W. Berry & P. R. Dasen (Eds.), *Culture and cognition: Readings in cross-cultural psychology.* London: Methuen & Co. Ltd., 1974. (b)

BLAKE, R. R., & MOULTON, J. S. Personality. *Annual Review of Psychology,* 1959, *10,* 203–232.

BLOCK, J. *Lives through time.* Berkeley, Calif.: Bancroft Books, 1971.

————. Advancing the science of personality: Paradigmatic shift or improving the quality of research? In D. Magnusson & N. S. Endler (Eds.), *Psychology at the crossroads: Current issues in interactional psychology.* Hillsdale, N.J.: Erlbaum, 1977.

BLURTON-JONES, N. G. An ethological study of some aspects of social behaviour of children in nursery school. In D. Morris (Ed.), *Primate ethology.* London: Werdinfeld & Nicolson, 1967.

————. Characteristics of ethological studies of human behaviour. In N. G. Blurton-Jones (Ed.), *Ethological studies of child behaviour.* Cambridge, England: Cambridge University Press, 1972.

BOAS, F. *The mind of primitive man.* New York: Macmillan Co., 1911. (Rev. ed., 1938.)

BOURGUIGNON, E. Psychological anthropology. In J. J. Honigmann (Ed.), *Handbook of social and cultural anthropology.* Chicago: Rand McNally, 1973.

————. *Psychological anthropology.* New York: Holt, Rinehart, & Winston, 1979.

BOWLBY, J. A. *Attachment and loss* (Vol. 1): *Attachment.* New York: Basic Books, 1969.

BRISLIN, R. W. Back-translation for cross-cultural research. *Journal of Cross-Cultural Psychology,* 1970, *1,* 185–216.

————. Comparative research methodology: Cross-cultural studies. *International Journal of Psychology,* 1976, *11*(3), 215–229.

————. Translation and content analysis of oral and written materials. In H. C. Triandis & J. W. Berry (Eds.), *Handbook of cross-cultural psychology* (Vol. 2): *Methodology.* Boston: Allyn & Bacon, 1980.

BRISLIN, R. W., LONNER, W. J., & THORNDIKE, R. M. *Cross-cultural research methods.* New York: John Wiley & Sons, 1973.

BRONFENBRENNER, U. *Two worlds of childhood: U.S. and U.S.S.R.* New York: Russell Sage Foundation, 1970.

————. Developmental research, public policy, and the ecology of childhood. *Child Development,* 1974, *45,* 1–5. (a)

————. Experimental human ecology: A reorientation to theory and research on socialization. Presidential address to the Division of Personality and Social Psychology at 82nd annual convention of the American Psychological Association, New Orleans, September 1974. (b)

————. Toward an experimental ecology of human development. *American Psychologist,* 1977, *32,* 513–531.

BRONOWSKI, J. *Science and human values.* New York: J. Messner, 1956.

BRUNER, J. S. The course of cognitive growth. *American Psychologist,* 1964, *19,* 1–15.

————. Concluding comments and summary of conference. In J. L. M. Dawson & W. J. Lonner (Eds.), *Readings in cross-cultural psychology.* Hong Kong: University of Hong Kong Press, 1974.

BRUNER, J. S., OLVER, R. R., & GREENFIELD, P. *Studies in cognitive growth.* New York: John Wiley & Sons, 1966.

BRUNSWIK, E. *Systematic and representative design of psychological experiments.* Berkeley: University of California Press, 1947.

BUCK-MORSS, S. Socio-economic bias in Piaget's theory and its implications for cross-cultural studies. *Human Development,* 1975, *18,* 35–49.

BUSS, A. R. The emerging field of the sociology of psychological knowledge. *American Psychologist,* 1975, *30,* 988–1002.

BUTCHER, J. & PANCHERI, P. *A handbook of cross-national MMPI research.* Minneapolis: University of Minnesota Press, 1976.

CAMPBELL, D. T. The mutual relevance of anthropology and psychology. In F. Hsu (Ed.), *Psychological anthropology: Approaches to culture and personality.* Homewood, Ill.: Dorsey Press, 1961.

————. Reforms as experiments. *American Psychologist,* 1969, *24,* 409–429.

————. Natural selection as an epistemological model. In R. Naroll & R. Cohen (Eds.), *A handbook of method in cultural anthropology.* New York: Columbia University Press, 1973. (Originally published, 1970.)

————. Methods for the experimenting society. Paper presented at the annual meeting of the American Psychological Association, Washington, D. C., September 1971.

————. Qualitative knowing in action research. Kurt Lewin Award Address, Society for the Psychological Study of Social Issues, presented at 82nd annual meeting of the American Psychological Association, New Orleans, September 1974. (a)

————. Evolutionary epistemology. In P. A. Schilpp (Ed.), *The philosophy of Karl Popper* (Vol. 14-1): *The library of living philosophers.* LaSalle, Ill.: Open Court Publishing Co., 1974. (b)

————. Reintroducing Konrad Lorenz to psychology. In R. I. Evans (Ed.), *Konrad Lorenz: The man and his ideas.* New York: Harcourt-Brace-Jovanovich, 1975.

CAMPBELL, D. T., & FISKE, D. W. Convergent and discriminant validation by the multitrait-multimethod matrix. *Psychological Bulletin,* 1959, *56,* 81–105.

CAMPBELL, D. T., & LeVINE, R. A. Field-manual anthropology. In R. Naroll & R. Cohen (Eds.), *A handbook of method in cultural anthropology.* New York: Columbia University Press, 1970.

CAMPBELL, D. T., & NAROLL, R. The mutual methodological relevance of anthropology and psychology. In F. L. K. Hsu (Ed.), *Psychological anthropology* (New ed.). Cambridge, Mass.: Schenkman, 1972.

CAMPBELL, D. T., & STANLEY, J. S. *Experimental and quasi-experimental designs for research.* Chicago: Rand McNally, 1966.

CARLSON, R. Personality. *Annual Review of Psychology,* 1975, *26,* 393–414.

CARTWRIGHT, D. Theory and practice. *Journal of Social Issues,* 1978, *34,* (4), 168–180.

CATTELL, R. B. *Personality: A systematic theoretical and factual study.* New York: McGraw-Hill, 1950.

————. *Personality and motivation structure and measurement.* New York: Harcourt-Brace-Jovanovich, 1957.

————. The grammar of science and the evolution of personality theory. In R. B. Cattell & R. M. Dreger (Eds.), *Handbook of modern personality theory.* New York: Halsted Press/John Wiley & Sons, 1977. (a)

————. Personality and culture: General concepts and methodological problems (The Sociological Domain of Personality). In R. B. Cattell & R. M. Dreger (Eds.), *Handbook of modern personality theory.* New York: Halsted Press/John Wiley & Sons, 1977. (b)

CATTELL, R. B., & DREGER, R. M. (Eds.). *Handbook of modern personality theory.* New York: Halsted Press/John Wiley & Sons, 1977.

CHAGNON, N., & IRONS, W. (Eds.). *Evolutionary biology and human social behavior: An anthropological perspective.* North Scituate, Mass.: Duxbury Press, 1979.

CHARLESWORTH, W. R. *Ethology's contribution to a framework for relevant research* (Occasional Paper #24). Project No. 332189, U.S. Office of Education, Bureau of Education to the Handicapped. Minneapolis, Minnesota: University of Minnesota Research, Development and Demonstration Center in Education of Handicapped Children, December 1973.

————. Developmental psychology and human ethology. *Society for Research in Child Development Newsletter,* Winter 1975, pp. 4–6; 11.

CHILD, I. L. Personality in culture. In E. F. Borgatta & W. W. Lambert (Eds.), *Handbook of personality theory and research.* Chicago: Rand McNally, 1968.

COHEN, Y. A. (Ed.). *Social structure and personality: A casebook.* New York: Holt, Rinehart, & Winston, 1961.

COHEN, Y. A. *The transition from childhood to adolescence: Cross-cultural studies of initiation ceremonies, legal systems and incest taboos.* Chicago: Aldine, 1964.

COLE, M., GAY, J., GLICK, J. A., & SHARP, D. W. *The cultural context of learning and thinking: An exploration in experimental anthropology.* New York: Basic Books, 1971.

COLE, M., & SCRIBNER, S. *Culture and thought: A psychological introduction.* New York: John Wiley & Sons, 1974.

CRONBACH, L. J. Beyond the two disciplines of scientific psychology. *American Psychologist,* 1975, *30,* 116–127.

DARWIN, C. *The expression of emotions in man and animals.* Chicago: University of Chicago Press, 1965. (Originally published, London: John Murray, 1872.)

DASEN, P. R. Cross-cultural Piagetian research: A summary. In J. W. Berry & P. R. Dasen (Eds.), *Culture and cognition: Readings in cross-cultural psychology.* London: Methuen & Co. Ltd., 1974. (Reprinted from the *Journal of Cross-Cultural Psychology,* 1972, *3*[1], 23–29.)

DASEN, P. R., & HERON, A. Cross-cultural tests of Piaget's theory. In H. C. Triandis & A. Heron (Eds.), *Handbook of cross-cultural psychology* (Vol. 4): *Developmental psychology.* Boston: Allyn & Bacon, 1981.

DAWKINS, R. *The selfish gene.* Oxford: Oxford University Press, 1976.

DEVORE, I., & MORRIS, S. The new science of genetic self-interest. *Psychology Today,* February 1977, pp. 42–51; 84–88.

DEVOS, G. A. Symbolic analysis in the cross-cultural studies of personality. In B. Kaplan (Ed.), *Studying personality cross-culturally.* Evanston, Ill.: Row, Peterson, 1961.

DEVOS, G. A., & HIPPLER, A. A. Cultural psychology: Comparative studies of human behavior. In G. Lindzey & E. Aronson (Eds.), *The handbook of social psychology* (Vol. 4, 2d ed.). Reading, Mass.: Addison-Wesley, 1969.

DOHRENWEND, B. P., & DOHRENWEND, B. S. Social and cultural influences on psychopathology. *Annual Review of Psychology*, 1974, *25*, 417–452.

DRAGUNS, J. G. Culture and personality. In A. J. Marsella, R. G. Tharp, & T. J. Ciborowski (Eds.), *Perspectives on cross-cultural psychology*. New York: Academic Press, 1979.

DRAPER, P. Comparative studies of socialization. *Annual Review of Anthropology*, 1974, *3*, 263–278.

DUBOIS, C. *The people of Alor*. Minneapolis: University of Minnesota Press, 1944.

EDGERTON, R. B. Method in psychological anthropology. In R. Naroll & R. Cohen (Eds.), *A handbook of method in culural anthropology*. New York: Columbia University Press, 1973. (Originally published, 1970.)

————. Cross-cultural psychology and psychological anthropology: One paradigm or two. (Review of *Cross-cultural research methods* by W. Brislin, W. J. Lonner, & R. M. Thorndike, and *The analysis of subjective culture* by H. C. Triandis in association with V. Vassiliou, G. Vassiliou, Y. Tanaka, & A. V. Shanmugam.) *Reviews in Anthropology*, 1974, *1*, 52–65.

EDWARDS, A. L., & ABBOTT, R. D. Measurement of personality traits: Theory and technique. *Annual Review of Psychology*, 1973, *24*, 241–278.

EIBL-EIBESFELDT, I. *Ethology: The biology of behavior*. New York: Holt, Rinehart, & Winston, 1970.

————. Similarities and differences between cultures in expressive movements. In R. A. Hinde (Ed.), *Nonverbal communication*. Cambridge, England: Cambridge University Press, 1972.

ELDER, J. W. Comparative cross-cultural methodology. *Annual Review of Sociology*, 1976, *2*, 209–230.

ELMS, A. C. The crisis of confidence in social psychology. *American Psychologist*, 1975, *30*, 967–976.

ERIKSON, E. *Childhood and society* (2d ed.). New York: W. W. Norton & Co., 1963. (Originally published, 1950.)

FELDMAN, C. *The development of adaptive intelligence*. San Francisco: Jossey-Bass Publishers, 1974.

FIRTH, R. An appraisal of modern social anthropology. *Annual Review of Anthropology*, 1975, *4*, 1–25.

FISHMAN, J. A. Good work on one side of the ravine. (Review of *The analysis of subjective culture* by H. C. Triandis et al.). *Contemporary Psychology*, 1973, *18*, 557–558.

FISKE, D. W. The limits for the conventional science of personality. *Journal of Personality*, 1974, *42*, 1–11.

————. Personalities, abstractions, and interactions. Paper presented at the Symposium on Interactional Psychology, Saltsjöbaden, June 1975. (a)

————. Cosmopolitan constructs and provincial observations: Some prescriptions for a chronically ill specialty. Paper presented at the Conference on Personality Research, Chicago, August 1975. (b)

————. *Strategies for personality research*. San Francisco: Jossey-Bass Publishers, 1978.

FLAVELL, J. H. *The developmental psychology of Jean Piaget.* New York: D. Van Nostrand Company, 1963.

FOX, R., & FLEISHING, U. Human ethology. *Annual Review of Anthropology,* 1976, 5, 265–288.

FRAKE, C. O. The diagnosis of disease among the Subanun of Mindanao. *American Anthropologist,* 1971, 63,(1), 113–132.

————. The ethnographic study of cognitive systems. In Anthropological Association of Washington D.C. (T. Gladwin & W. C. Sturtevant, Eds.), *Anthropology and human behavior.* Washington D.C.: Smithsonian Inst., 1962. (Also in J. P. Spradley, [Ed.], *Culture and cognition.* San Francisco: Chandler, 1972.)

FREEDMAN, D. G. *Human infancy: An evolutionary perspective.* Hillsdale, N.J.: Erlbaum, 1974.

————. Infancy, biology, and culture. In L. P. Lipsitt (Ed.), *Developmental psychology: The significance of infancy.* New York: Halsted Press, 1976.

FREEDMAN, D. G., & DeBOER, M. M. Biological and cultural differences in early child development. *Annual Review of Anthropology,* 1979, 8, 579–600.

FREUD, S. *Civilization and its discontents.* (J. Strachey, Ed. and Trans.). New York: W. W. Norton, 1961. (Originally published, 1930.)

FROMM, E. *Escape from freedom.* New York: Farrar & Rinehart, 1941.

FROMM, E., & MACCOBY, M. *Social character in a Mexican Village: A sociopsychoanalytic study.* Englewood Cliffs, N.J.: Prentice-Hall, 1970.

GEBER, M. Psychomotor development in African children, the effects of social class and the need for improved tests. *Bulletin of the World Health Organization,* 1958, 18, 471–476.

————. Longitudinal study of psychomotor development among the Boganda children. In *Proceedings of the Fourteenth International Congress of Applied Psychology.* Copenhagen: Munksgaard, 1961.

GEERTZ, C. The impact of the concept of culture on the concept of man. In J. R. Platt (Ed.), *New views of man.* Chicago: University of Chicago Press, 1965.

————. *The interpretation of cultures.* New York: Basic Books, Inc., 1973.

GERGEN, K. J. Social psychology, science, and history. *Personality and Social Psychology Bulletin,* 1976, 2, 373–383.

GINSBURG, H., & KOSLOWSKI, B. Cognitive development. *Annual Review of Psychology,* 1976, 27, 29–62.

GLADWIN, T., & SARASON, S. B. *Truk: Man in paradise* (Viking Fund Publications in Anthropology, No. 20). New York: Wenner-Gren Foundation for Anthropological Research, Inc., 1953.

GOLDBERG, S. Ethics, politics, and multicultural research. In P. H. Leiderman, S. R. Tulkin, & A. Rosenfeld (Eds.), *Culture and infancy.* New York: Academic Press, Inc., 1977.

GOODENOUGH, W. H. Componential analysis. *Science,* 1967, 156 (3779), 1203–1209. (Reprinted in J. P. Spradley [Ed.], *Culture and cognition: Rules, maps, and plans.* San Francisco: Chandler, 1972.)

GOODMAN, M. E. Culture and conceptualization: A study of Japanese and American children. *Ethnology,* 1962, 1, 374–386.

GORER, G. Some aspects of the psychology of the people of great Russia. *American Slavic and East European Review,* 1949, 8, 155–166.

GORSUCH, R. L., & BARNES, M. L. Stages of ethical reasoning and moral norms of Carib youth. *Journal of Cross-Cultural Psychology,* 1973 4, 283–301.

GOULET, L. R., & BALTES, P. B. (Eds.). *Life-span developmental psychology: Research and theory.* New York: Academic Press, 1970.

GREENFIELD, P. M. Comparing dimensional categorization in natural and artificial contexts: A developmental study among the Zinacantecos of Mexico. *Journal of Social Psychology,* 1974, *93,* 157–171.

GREENFIELD, P. M., & BRUNER, J. S. Culture and cognitive growth. *International Journal of Psychology,* 1966, *1,* 89–107.

GUTMANN, D. The cross-cultural perspective: Notes toward a comparative psychology of aging. In J. E. Birren & K. W. Schaie (Eds.), *Handbook of the psychology of aging.* New York: Van Nostrand Reinhold Company, 1977.

HALLOWELL, A. I. Aggression in Saulteaux society. In C. Kluckhohn, H. A. Murray, & D. M. Schneider (Eds.), *Personality in nature, society, and culture* (2d ed.). New York: Alfred A. Knopf, 1953.

———. Personality, culture, and society in behavioral evolution. In S. Koch (Ed.), *Psychology: A study of a science* (Vol. 6). New York: McGraw-Hill, 1963.

———. *Culture and experience.* New York: Schocken Books, 1967. (Originally published, 1955.)

HARING, D. G. (Ed.). *Personal character and cultural milieu.* Syracuse, N.Y.: Syracuse University Press, 1956.

HARRINGTON, C., & WHITING, J. W. M. Socialization process and personality. In F. L. K. Hsu (Ed.), *Psychological anthropology* (New ed.). Cambridge, Mass.: Schenkman, 1972.

HARRIS, M. *The rise of anthropological theory.* New York: Thomas Y. Crowell Co., 1968.

HARTUP, W. W. Social learning, social interaction, and social development. In P. Elich (Ed.), *The fourth western symposium on learning: Social learning.* Bellingham, Washington: Western Washington State College, 1973.

HAVIGHURST, R. J. History and development psychology: Socialization and personality development through the life span. In P. B. Baltes & K. W. Schaie (Eds.), *Life-span developmental psychology: Personality and socialization.* New York: Academic Press, 1973.

HAVIGHURST, R. I., & NEUGARTEN, B. L. *American Indian and white children: A sociopsychological investigation.* Chicago: University of Chicago Press, 1955.

HEIDER, F. *The psychology of interpersonal relations.* New York: John Wiley & Sons, 1958.

HELSON, R., & MITCHELL, V. Personality. *Annual Review of Psychology,* 1978, *29,* 555–585.

HENRY, J., & BOGGS, J. W. Child rearing, culture, and the natural world. *Psychiatry,* 1952, *15,* 261–271.

HESS, E. H. Ethology and developmental psychology. In P. H. Mussen (Ed.), *Carmichael's manual of child psychology* (Vol. 1, 3rd ed.). New York: John Wiley & Sons, 1970.

HESS, R., & TAPP, J. L. *Authority, rules, and aggression: A cross-national study of the socialization of children into compliance systems* (Final report, Part I). Project No.

2947, U.S. Office of Education, Bureau of Research. University of Chicago, March 1969.

HETHERINGTON, E. M., & McINTYRE, C. W. Developmental psychology. *Annual Review of Psychology*, 1975, *26*, 97–136.

HINDE, R. A. *Biological bases of human social behaviour.* New York: McGraw-Hill, 1974.

HIPPLER, A. E. The north Alaska Eskimos: A culture and personality perspective. *American Ethnologist*, 1974, *1*, 449–469.

HOFFMAN, M. L. Personality and social development. *Annual Review of Psychology*, 1977, *28*, 295–321.

HOGAN, R., DeSOTO, C., & SOLANO, C. Traits, tests, and personality research. *American Psychologist*, 1977, *32*, 255–264.

HOLLINGSHEAD, A., & REDLICH, R. *Social class and mental illness.* New York: John Wiley & Sons, 1958.

HOLTZMAN, W. H. Cross-cultural research on personality development. *Human Development*, 1965, *8*, 65–86.

———. Cross-cultural studies in psychology. *International Journal of Psychology*, 1968, *3*, 83–91.

———. (Organizer). *Code of ethics: Problems and processes in ethical decisionmaking by psychologists.* Symposium at 21st meeting of International Congress of Psychology, Paris, July 1976.

———. The IUPS projects on professional ethics and conduct. In W. H. Holtzman (Chair), *International standards of professional ethics and conduct for psychologists.* Symposium presented at the meeting of the International Congress of Applied Psychology, Munich, July 1978.

HOLTZMAN, W. H., DIAZ-GUERRERO, R., & SWARTZ, J. D. *Personality development in two cultures: A cross-cultural longitudinal study of school children in Mexico and the United States.* Austin, Texas: University of Texas Press, 1975.

HOLZMAN, P. S. Personality. *Annual Review of Psychology*, 1974, *25*, 247–276.

HOMANS, G. *The human group.* New York: Harcourt, Brace, 1950.

HONIGMANN, J. J. Psychocultural studies. *Biennial Review of Anthropology 1959*, 1959, *1*, 67–106.

———. North America. In F. L. K. Hsu (Ed.), *Psychological anthropology.* Homewood, Ill.: Dorsey Press, 1961. (Also in Hsu, 1972a.)

———. The study of personality in primitive societies. In E. Norbeck, D. Price-Williams, & W. M. McCord (Eds.), *The study of personality: An interdisciplinary approach.* New York: Holt, Rinehart, & Winston, 1968.

———. (Ed.). *Handbook of social and cultural anthropology.* Chicago: Rand McNally, 1973.

HSU, F. L. K. (Ed.). *Psychological anthropology: Approaches to culture and personality.* Homewood, Ill.: Dorsey Press, 1961. (a) (New edition, Cambridge, Mass.: Schenkman, 1972.[a] )

———. Psychological anthropology in the behavioral sciences. In F. L. K. Hsu (Ed.), *Psychological anthropology: Approaches to culture and personality.* Homewood, Ill.: The Dorsey Press, 1961. (b) (New edition, Cambridge, Mass.: Schenkman, 1972.[b] )

HUNT, J. M. *Intelligence and experience.* New York: Ronald, 1961.

INHELDER, B., & PIAGET, J. *The growth of logical thinking from childhood to adolescence.* New York: Basic Books, 1958.

INKELES, A., & LEVINSON, D. J. National character: The study of modal personality and sociocultural systems. In G. Lindzey (Ed.), *Handbook of social psychology* (Vol. 2). Reading, Mass.: Addison-Wesley, 1954.

————. National character: The study of modal personality and sociocultural systems. In G. Lindzey & E. Aronson (Eds.), *The handbook of social psychology* (Vol. 4). Reading, Mass.: Addison-Wesley, 1969.

JAHODA, G. Child animism: A critical survey of cross-cultural research. *Journal of Social Psychology,* 1958, *47,* 197–212.

————. Understanding the mechanism of bicycles: A cross-cultural study of developmental change after thirteen years. *International Journal of Psychology,* 1969, *4,* 103–108.

————. A cross-cultural perspective in psychology. *The Advancement of Science,* 1970, *27,* 1–14.

JORGENSEN, J. G. Cross-cultural comparisons. *Annual Review of Anthropology,* 1979, *8,* 309–331.

KAGAN, J., & KLEIN, R. E. Cross-cultural perspectives on early development. *American Psychologist,* 1973, *28,* 947–961.

KAPLAN, B. (Ed.). *Studying personality cross-culturally.* Evanston, Ill.: Row, Peterson, & Co., 1961. (a)

————. Personality study and culture. In B. Kaplan (Ed.), *Studying personality cross-culturally.* Evanston, Ill.: Row, Peterson, & Co., 1961. (b)

————. A final word. In B. Kaplan (Ed.), *Studying personality cross-culturally.* Evanston, Ill.: Row, Peterson, & Co., 1961. (c)

————. Personality and social structure. In R. A. Manners & D. Kaplan (Eds.), *Theory in anthropology: A sourcebook.* Chicago: Aldine, 1968.

KAPLAN, D., & MANNERS, R. A. *Culture theory.* Englewood Cliffs, N.J.: Prentice-Hall, Inc., 1972.

KARDINER, A. *The individual and his society.* New York: Columbia University Press, 1939.

KELLY, E. L. Theories and techniques of assessment. *Annual Review of Psychology,* 1954, *5,* 281–310.

KELLY, G. A. *The psychology of personal constructs.* New York: Holt, Rinehart & Winston, 1955.

KELLY, J. G. Two communities through the looking glass. (Review of *Qualities of community life* by R. G. Barker & P. Schoggen.) *Contemporary Psychology,* 1975, *20,* 193–195.

KELMAN, H. C. Psychological research on social change: Some scientific and ethical issues. *International Journal of Psychology,* 1967, *2,* 301–313.

KIEFER, C. W. Psychological anthropology. *Annual Review of Anthropology,* 1977, *6,* 103–119.

KLINEBERG, O. Historical perspectives: Cross-cultural psychology before 1960. In H. C. Triandis & W. W. Lambert (Eds.), *Handbook of cross-cultural psychology* (Vol. 1): *Perspectives.* Boston: Allyn & Bacon, 1980.

KLUCKHOHN, C. The philosophy of the Navajo Indians. In F. S. C. Northrop (Ed.), *Ideological differences and world order.* New Haven: Yale University Press, 1949.

———. Culture and behavior. In G. Lindzey (Ed.), *Handbook of social psychology* (Vol. 2). Reading, Mass.: Addison-Wesley, 1954.

———. Education, values, and anthropological relativity. In R. Kluckhohn (Ed.), *Culture and behavior: Collected essays of Clyde Kluckhohn.* New York: The Free Press, 1962. (a)

———. Ethical relativity: Sic et non. In R. Kluckhohn (Ed.), *Culture and behavior: Collected essays of Clyde Kluckhohn.* New York: The Free Press, 1962. (b)

KLUCKHOHN, C., & MURRAY, H. A. (Eds.). *Personality in nature, society, and culture.* New York: Alfred A. Knopf, 1948. (a)

———. Personality formation: The determinants. In C. Kluckhohn & H. A. Murray (Eds.), *Personality in nature, society, and culture.* New York: Alfred A. Knopf, 1948. (b)

———. Personality formation: The determinants. In C. Kluckhohn, H. A. Murray, & D. M. Schneider (Eds.), *Personality in nature, society, and culture* (2nd ed.). New York: Alfred A. Knopf, 1953. (b)

KLUCKHOHN, C., MURRAY, H. A., & SCHNEIDER, D. M. (Eds.). *Personality in nature, society, and culture* (2nd ed.). New York: Alfred A. Knopf, 1953. (a)

KLUCKHOHN, F. R., & STRODTBECK, F. (Eds.). *Variations in value orientations.* Evanston, Ill.: Row, Peterson, & Co., 1961.

KOHLBERG, L. Stage and sequence: The cognitive-development approach to socialization. In D. A. Goslin (Ed.), *Handbook of socialization theory and research.* Chicago: Rand McNally, 1969.

———. Cognitive-developmental theory and the practice of collective moral education. In M. Wolins & M. Gottesmann (Eds.), *Group care: An Israeli approach.* New York: Gordon & Breach, 1971.

KROEBER, A. L. Totem and taboo: An ethnologic psychoanalysis. *American Anthropologist,* 1920, *22,* 48–55.

———. *Anthropology.* New York: Harcourt, Brace & Co., 1948.

———. The concept of culture in science. *Journal of General Education,* 1949, *3,* 182–188.

KROEBER, A. L., & KLUCKHOHN, C. *Culture: A critical review of concepts and definitions.* New York: Vintage Books, 1952. (Cambridge: Papers of the Peabody Museum of American Archaeology and Ethnology, Harvard University, 47, No. 1.)

KUHN, T. S. *The structure of scientific revolutions.* Chicago: University of Chicago Press, 1962.

LABORATORY OF COMPARATIVE HUMAN COGNITION. Cross-cultural psychology's challenges to our ideas of children and development. *American Psychologist,* 1979, *34,* 827–833.(a)

———. What's cultural about cross-cultural cognitive psychology? *Annual Review of Psychology,* 1979, *30,* 145–172.(b)

LAMBERT, W. W. Promise and problems of cross-cultural exploration of children's aggressive strategies. In J. DeWit & W. W. Hartup (Eds.), *Determinants and origins of aggressive behavior.* The Hague: Mouton, 1974.

LEIGHTON, A. *My name is legion.* New York: Basic Books, 1959.

LEVINE, R. A. Africa. In F. L. K. Hsu (Ed.), *Psychological anthropology.* Homewood, Ill.: Dorsey Press, 1961.

————. Culture and personality. *Biennial Review of Anthropology 1963*, 1963, *3*, 107–146.

————. Outsiders' judgments: An ethnographic approach to group differences in personality. *Southwestern Journal of Anthropology*, 1966, *22*, 101–116.

————. Culture, personality, and socialization: An evolutionary view. In D. A. Goslin (Ed.), *Handbook of socialization theory and research*. Chicago: Rand McNally, 1969.

————. Cross-cultural study in child psychology. In P. H. Mussen (Ed.), *Carmichael's manual of psychology* (Vol. 2, 3rd ed.). New York: John Wiley & Sons, 1970.

————. *Culture, behavior, and personality*. Chicago: Aldine, 1973. (a)

————. Research design in anthropological field work. In R. Naroll & R. Cohen (Eds.), *A handbook of method in cultural anthropology*. New York: Columbia University Press, 1973. (Originally published, 1970.) (b)

————. Child rearing as cultural adaptation. In P. H. Leiderman, S. R. Tulkin, & A. Rosenfeld (Eds.), *Culture and infancy*. New York: Academic Press, 1977.

————. Anthropology and child development. Paper presented at the meeting of the Society for Research in Child Development, San Francisco, March 1979.

LeVine, R. A., & Campbell, D. T. *Ethnocentrism: Theories of conflict, ethnic attitudes and group behavior*. New York: John Wiley & Sons, 1972.

LeVine, R. A., & Price-Williams, D. R. Children's kinship concepts: Preliminary report on a Nigerian study. Paper presented at the annual meeting of the American Anthropological Association, San Diego, 1970.

————. Children's kinship concepts: Cognitive development and early experience among the Hausa. *Ethnology*, 1974, *13*, 25–44.

Levi-Strauss, C. *Structural anthropology*. Garden City, N. Y.: Doubleday, 1963.

————. *The elementary structures of kinship*. Boston: Beacon Press, 1969.

Lewin, K. *Dynamic theory of personality*. (Translated by D. K. Adams & K. E. Zener.) New York & London: McGraw-Hill, 1935.

————. *Field theory in social science*. New York: Harper & Row, 1951.

Linton, R. *The cultural background of personality*. New York: Appleton-Century, 1945.

————. Universal ethical principles: An anthropological view. In R. N. Anshen (Ed.), *Moral principles of action*. New York: Harper & Row, 1952.

Lloyd, B. B. *Perception and cognition: A cross-cultural perspective*. Harmondsworth: Penguin Books, 1972.

Lonner, W. J. The search for psychological universals. In H. C. Triandis & W. W. Lambert (Eds.), *Handbook of cross-cultural psychology* (Vol. 1): *Perspectives*. Boston: Allyn & Bacon, 1980.

Looft, W. R. Socialization and personality throughout the life span: An examination of contemporary psychological approaches. In P. B. Baltes & K. W. Schaie (Eds.), *Life-span developmental psychology: Personality and socialization*. New York: Academic Press, 1973.

Maccoby, M., & Modiano, N. Cognitive style in rural and urban Mexico. *Human Development*, 1969, *12*, 22–23.

MADSEN, K. B. The formal properties of Cattellian personality theory and its relationship to other personality theories. In R. B. Cattell & R. M. Dreger (Eds.), *Handbook of modern personality theory.* New York: Halsted Press/John Wiley & Sons, 1977.

MALINOWSKI, B. *Argonauts of the Western Pacific.* New York: Dutton, 1961. (Originally published, 1922.)

———. *Sex and repression in savage society.* New York: International Library, 1927.

MALPASS, R. S. Theory and method in cross-cultural psychology. *American Psychologist,* 1977, *32,* 1069–1079.

MANASTER, G. J., & HAVIGHURST, R J. *Cross-national research: Socialpsychological methods and problems.* Boston: Houghton Mifflin Co., 1972.

MARSELLA, A. J., THARP, R. G., & CIBOROWSKI, T. J. (Eds.). *Perspectives on cross-cultural psychology.* New York: Academic Press, 1979.

MCCLELLAND, D. C. *The achieving society.* New York: Van Nostrand, 1961.

MCGREW, W. C. *An ethological study of children's behavior.* New York: Academic Press, 1972.

MEAD, M. *Coming of age in Samoa.* New York: William Morrow & Co., 1928.

———. *Soviet attitudes toward authority.* New York: McGraw-Hill, 1951.

———. The swaddling hypothesis: Its reception. *American Anthropologist,* 1954, *56,* 395–409.

———. *New lives for old: Cultural transformation—Manus, 1928–1953.* New York: William Morrow & Co., 1956.

———. *Food habits research: Problems of the 1960's.* Washington, D.C.: National Research Council, 1964.

MEAD, M., & WOLFENSTEIN, M. (Eds.). *Childhood in contemporary cultures.* Chicago: University of Chicago Press, 1955.

MEEHL, P. E. Theory-testing in psychology and physics: A methodological paradox. *Philosophy of Science,* 1967, *34,* 103–115.

MERCADO, S. J., DIAZ, R. D., & GARDNER, R. W. Cognitive control in children of Mexico and the United States. *Journal of Social Psychology,* 1963, *59,* 199–208.

MINTURN, L., & LAMBERT, W. *Mothers of six cultures.* New York: John Wiley & Sons, 1964.

MINTURN, L., & TAPP, J. L. *Authority, rules, and aggression: A cross-national study of children's judgments of the justice of aggressive confrontations* (Final report, Part II). Project No. 2947, U.S. Office of Education, Bureau of Research. University of Chicago, October 1970.

MISCHEL, W. Continuity and change in personality. *American Psychologist,* 1969, *24,* 1012–1018.

———. Towards a cognitive social learning reconceptualization of personality. *Psychological Review,* 1973, *80,* 252–283.

———. The interaction of person and situation. In N. S. Endler & D. Magnusson (Eds.), *Interactional psychology and personality.* New York: Halsted Press, 1976.

MUNROE, R. L., & MUNROE, R. H. *Cross-cultural human development.* Monterey, Calif.: Brooks/Cole Publishing Company, 1975.

MUNROE, R., MUNROE, R., & WHITING, B. B. (Eds.). *Handbook of cross-cultural human development.* New York: Garland Publishing Co., 1981.

MURPHY, G. *Personality: A biosocial approach to origins and structure.* New York: Harper, 1947.

MURRAY, H. A. *Explorations in personality*. New York: Oxford University Press, 1938.

MURRAY, H. A., & KLUCKHOHN, C. Outline of a conception of personality. In C. Kluckhohn & H. A. Murray (Eds.), *Personality in nature, society, and culture*. New York: Alfred A. Knopf, 1948.

————. Outline of a conception of personality. In C. Kluckhohn, H. A. Murray, & D. M. Schneider (Eds.), *Personality in nature, society, and culture* (2d ed.). New York: Alfred A. Knopf, 1953.

MUSSEN, P. H., CONGER, J. J., & KAGAN, J. *Child development and personality* (4th ed.). New York: Harper & Row, 1974.

NESSELROADE, J. R., & REESE, H. W. (Eds.). *Life-span development psychology: Methodological issues*. New York: Academic Press, 1973.

NEUGARTEN, B., & BENGSTON, V. Cross-national studies of adulthood and aging. In E. Shanas & J. Madge (Eds.), *Methodological problems in cross-national studies of aging*. Basel: Karger, 1968.

NEUGARTEN, B. L., & DATAN, N. Sociological perspectives on the life cycle. In P. B. Baltes & K. W. Schaie (Eds.), *Life-span developmental psychology: Personality and socialization*. New York: Academic Press, 1973.

OSGOOD, C., MAY, W. H., & MIRON, M. S. *Cross-cultural universals of affective meaning*. Urbana: University of Illinois Press, 1975.

PEDERSEN, P. Asian personality theories. In R. J. Corsini (Ed.), *Current personality theories*. Itasca, Ill.: F. E. Peacock, 1977.

————. Non-western psychology: The search for alternatives. In A. J. Marsella, R. G. Tharp, & T. J. Ciborowski (Eds.), *Perspectives on cross-cultural psychology*. New York: Academic Press, 1979.

PEDERSEN, P., LONNER, W., & DRAGUNS, J. (Eds.). *Counseling across cultures*. Honolulu: University of Hawaii Press, 1976.

PELTO, P. J. Psychological anthropology. *Biennial Review of Anthropology 1967*, 1967, 5, 140–208.

PERVIN, L. Man and his sociocultural environment. (Review of *Culture, behavior, and personality* by R. A. LeVine.) *Contemporary Psychology*, 1974, 19, 126–127.

PIAGET, J. *The moral judgment of the child*. New York: The Free Press, 1965. (Originally published, 1932.)

————. The moral development of the adolescent in two types of society: Primitive and "modern." Paper presented to the Seminar on Education for International Understanding, United Nations Educational, Scientific, and Cultural Organization, Paris, July 1947.

————. *The psychology of intelligence*. London: Routledge & Kegan Paul, 1950.

————. *Play, dreams and imitation*. London: Heinemann, 1951.

————. *The origins of intelligence in the child*. London: Routledge & Kegan Paul, 1953.

————. Need and significance of cross-cultural studies in genetic psychology. In J. W. Berry & P. R. Dasen (Eds.), *Culture and cognition: Readings in cross-cultural psychology*. London: Methuen & Co., Ltd., 1974. (Reprinted from *International Journal of Psychology*, 1966, *1*[1], 3-13.)

———. *Structuralism*. New York: Harper & Row, 1971. (Originally published, 1968.)

———. *Genetic epistemology*. (E. Duckworth, trans.) New York: Columbia University Press, 1970.

——— & INHELDER, B. *The psychology of the child*. New York: Basic Books, 1969.

PICK, A. D. Cognition: Psychological perspectives. In H. C. Triandis & W. J. Lonner (Eds.), *Handbook of cross-cultural psychology* (Vol. 3): *Basic processes*. Boston: Allyn & Bacon, 1980.

POPPER, K. *Conjectures and refutations: The growth of scientific knowledge*. London: Routledge & Kegan Paul, 1963.

———. *The logic of scientific discovery* (Rev. ed.). London: Hutchinson, 1968.

PRICE-WILLIAMS, D. R. Psychological experiment an anthropology: The problem of categories. *Ethos*, 1974, *2*, 95-114.

———. Culture and personality in the seventies. (Review of *Culture and personality: Contemporary readings* by R. A. LeVine.) *Contemporary Psychology*, 1975, *20*, 429-430. (a)

———. *Explorations in cross-cultural psychology*. San Francisco: Chandler & Sharp Publishers, Inc., 1975. (b)

PROSHANSKY, H. M., ITTELSON, W. H., & RIVLIN, L. G. (Eds.). *Environmental psychology: Man and his physical setting*. New York: Holt, Rinehart, & Winston, 1970.

PRZEWORSKI, A., & TEUNE, H. Equivalence in cross-national research. *Public Opinion Quarterly*, 1966-1967, *30*, 551-568.

REESE, H. W., & OVERTON, W. F. Models of development and theories of development. In L. R. Goulet & P. B. Baltes (Eds.), *Life-span developmental psychology: Research and theory*. New York: Academic Press, 1970.

REYNOLDS, R. D. *Value dilemmas associated with the development and application of social science* (Report, International Social Science Council). Paris: UNESCO, 1975.

REYNOLDS, P. *Ethical dilemmas and social science research: An analysis of moral problems confronting investigators*. San Francisco: Jossey-Bass Publishers, 1979.

RIEGEL, K. F. Influence of economic and political ideologies on the development of developmental psychology. *Psychological Bulletin*, 1972, *78*, 129-141.

———. Developmental psychology and society: Some historical and ethical considerations. In J. R. Nesselroade & H. W. Reese (Eds.), *Life-span developmental psychology: Methodological issues*. New York: Academic Press, 1973.

ROHNER, R. P. Parental acceptance-rejection and personality development: A universalist approach to behavioral science. In R. W. Brislin, S. Bochner, & W. J. Lonner (Eds.), *Cross-cultural perspectives on learning*. Beverly Hills, Calif.: Sage Publications, Inc., 1975. (a)

———. *They love me, they love me not: A worldwide study of the effects of parental acceptance and rejection*. New Haven: HRAF Press, 1975. (b)

SAHLINS, M. *Culture and practical reason*. Chicago: University of Chicago Press, 1976.

SANFORD, N. The field of personality. In D. L. Sills (Ed.), *International encyclopedia of the social sciences* (Vol. 11). New York: Macmillan Co., 1968.

SAPIR, E. The emergence of a concept of personality in a study of culture. *Journal of Social Psychology*, 1934, *5*, 408-415.

————. Why cultural anthropology needs the psychiatrist. *Psychiatry*, 1938, *1*, 7–12.

————. Psychiatric and cultural pitfalls in the business of getting a living. *Mental Health*, 1939, *9*, 237–244.

SARGENT, S. S., & SMITH, M. W. (Eds.). *Culture and personality.* Glen Gardner, N.J.: Viking Fund, 1949.

SCHAIE, K. W., & GRIBBIN, K. Adult development and aging. *Annual Review of Psychology*, 1975, *25*, 65–96.

SEARS, R. R. Transcultural variables and conceptual equivalence. In B. Kaplan (Ed.), *Studying personality cross-culturally.* Evanston, Ill.: Row, Peterson, & Co., 1961.

SEARS, R. R., MACCOBY, E. E., & LEVIN, H. *Patterns of child rearing.* Evanston, Ill.: Row, Peterson, & Co., 1957.

SECHREST, L. Personality. *Annual Review of Psychology*, 1976, *27*, 1–28.

SEGALL, M. H., CAMPBELL, D. T., & HERSKOVITS, M. J. Cultural differences in the perception of geometric illusions. *Science*, 1963, *139*, 769–771.

————. *The influence of culture on visual perception.* Indianapolis: Bobbs-Merrill, 1966.

SELMAN, R. L. Taking another perspective: Role-taking in early childhood. *Child Development*, 1971, *42*(2), 79–92.

SELLTIZ, C., WRIGHTSMAN, L. W., & COOK, S. W. *Research methods in social relations* (3rd ed.). New York: Holt, Rinehart, & Winston, 1976.

SERPELL, R. *Culture's influence on behaviour.* London: Methuen, 1976.

————. Strategies for investigating intelligence in its cultural context. *Quarterly Newsletter of the Institute of Comparative Human Development*, 1977, *3*, 11–14.

SHANTZ, C. U. The development of social cognition. In E. M. Hetherington (Ed.), *Review of child development research* (Vol. 5). Chicago: University of Chicago Press, 1975.

SHWEDER, R. A. Is a culture a situation? Paper prepared for the Stirling Award in Culture and Personality Studies sponsored by the American Anthropological Association, 1971.

————. Aspects of cognition in Zinacanteco shamans: Experimental results. In W. A. Lessa & E. Z. Vogt (Eds.), *Reader in comparative religion* (3rd ed.). New York: Harper & Row, 1972.

————. The between and within of cross-cultural research. *Ethos*, 1973, *1*(4), 531–545.

————. How relevant is an individual difference theory of personality? *Journal of Personality*, 1975, *43*, 455–484.

SIEGEL, B. J. Foreword. *Biennial Review of Anthropology 1969*, 1970, *6*, v–vii.

SIMPSON, E. L. Moral development research: A case study of scientific cultural bias. *Human Development*, 1974, *17*, 81–106.

SINGER, M. A survey of culture and personality theory and research. In B. Kaplan (Ed.), *Studying personality cross-culturally.* Evanston, Ill.: Row, Peterson, & Co., 1961.

SMITH, M. B. Social psychology, science, and history: So what? *Personality and Social Psychology Bulletin*, 1976, *2*, 438–444.

SMITH, P. K. Ethological methods. In B. Foss (Ed.), *New Perspectives in child development*. New York: Penguin, 1975.

SPINDLER, G. D. *The making of psychological anthropology*. Berkeley: University of California Press, 1978. (a)

————. Introduction to Part I. In G. D. Spindler (Ed.), *The making of psychological anthropology*. Berkeley: University of California Press, 1978. (b)

————. Concluding remarks. In G. D. Spindler (Ed.), *The making of psychological anthropology*. Berkeley: University of California Press, 1978. (c)

SPIRO, M. E. Culture and personality: The natural history of a false dichotomy. *Psychiatry*, 1951, *14*, 19–46.

————. Human nature in its psychological dimensions. *American Anthropologist*, 1954, *56*, 19–30.

————. An overview and suggested orientation. In F. L. K. Hsu (Ed.), *Psychological anthropology: Approaches to culture and personality*. Homewood, Ill.: Dorsey Press, 1961. (a) (Also in Hsu, 1972.)

————. Social systems, personality, and functional analysis. In B. Kaplan (Ed.), *Studying personality cross-culturally*. Evanston, Ill.: Row, Peterson, & Co., 1961. (b)

————. *Burmese supernaturalism*. Englewood Cliffs, N.J.: Prentice-Hall, 1967.

————. Cognition in culture-and-personality. In J. P. Spradley (Ed.), *Culture and cognition: Rules, maps, and plans*. San Francisco: Chandler Publishing Co., 1972. (Published originally as Culture and personality. In D. L. Sills [Ed.], *International encyclopedia of the social sciences, 1968* (Vol. 3), 558–563.)

————. Culture and human nature. In G. D. Spindler (Ed.), *The making of psychological anthropology*. Berkeley: University of California Press, 1978.

SPIRO, M. E. with A. Spiro. *Children of the kibbutz: A study in child training and personality*. Cambridge, Mass.: Harvard University Press, 1958. (Rev. ed., 1975.)

SPRADLEY, J. P. *You owe yourself a drunk: An ethnography of urban nomads*. Boston: Little, Brown, 1970.

————. *Culture and cognition: Rules, maps, and plans*. San Francisco: Chandler Publishing Co., 1972.

SWARTZ, M., & JORDAN, D. K. *Anthropology: Perspective on humanity*. New York: John Wiley & Sons, 1976.

TAFT, R. Comments on the 1974 "Tapp" report on the ethics of cross-cultural research. *IACCP Cross-Cultural Psychology Newsletter*, 1977, *11*(4) 2–8. (In R. Taft [Chair], *A symposium on the "Tapp Report": Report of the I.A.C.C.P. Ethics Committee, June 1976*. Symposium presented at the meeting of the International Association for Cross-Cultural Psychology, Tilburg, 1976.)

TAPP, J. L. Field manual for authority, rules, and aggression: *A cross-national study of socialization into compliance systems* (Cooperative Project No. 2947, Working Paper.) Unpublished manuscript, University of Chicago, 1965–67.

————. Reflections. In J. L. Tapp (Ed.), Socialization, the law, and society. *Journal of Social Issues*, 1971, *27*(2). (Whole issue).

————. Ethical issues in cross-cultural research: A U.S. perspective. In O. Klineberg (Chair) & W. H. Holtzman (Organizer), *Code of ethics: Problems and processes in ethical decision-making by psychologists*. Symposium presented at the 21st meeting of the International Congress of Psychology, Paris, July 1976.

————. Psychological and policy perspectives on the law: Reflections on a decade. *Journal of Social Issues*, 1980, *36*(2), 165–192.

TAPP, J. L., KELMAN, H. C., TRIANDIS, H. C., WRIGHTSMAN, L. S., & COELHO, G. V. Continuing concerns in cross-cultural ethics: A report. *International Journal of Psychology*, 1974, *9*(3), 231–249.

TAPP, J. L., & KOHLBERG, L. Developing senses of law and legal justice. *Journal of Social Issues*, 1971, *27*, 65–91.

TAPP, J. L., & LEVINE, F. J. Legal socialization: Strategies for an ethical legality. *Stanford Law Review*, 1974, *27*, 1–72.

————. Reflections and redirections. In J. L. Tapp & F. J. Levine (Eds.), *Law, justice, and the individual in society: Psychological and legal issues*. New York: Holt, Rinehart, & Winston, 1977. (a)

————. The dialectic of legal socialization in community and school. In J. L. Tapp & F. J. Levine (Eds.), *Law, justice, and the individual in society: Psychological and legal issues*. New York: Holt, Rinehart, & Winston, 1977. (b)

THOMAE, H. Personality development in two cultures: A selective review on research aims and issues. *Human Development*, 1979, *22*, 296–319. (In R. Diaz-Guerrero, W. H. Holtzman, & H. Thomae [Issue Eds.], Personality development in two cultures.)

TINBERGEN, N. On the aims and methods of ethology. *Zeitschrift für Tierpsychologie*, 1963, *20*, 410–433.

TRIANDIS, H. C. (in association with Vassiliou, V., Vassiliou, G., Tanaka, Y., & Shanmugam, A. V.). *The analysis of subjective culture*. New York: Wiley-Interscience, 1972.

————. Cultural analysis as a response to the crisis in social psychology. In H. C. Triandis (Chair), *Cross-cultural social psychology*. Symposium presented at the 15th meeting of the Interamerican Society of Psychology, Bogota, December 1974. (a)

————. Major theoretical and methodological issues in cross-cultural psychology. In J. L. M. Dawson & W. J. Lonner (Eds.), *Readings in cross-cultural psychology*. Hong Kong: University of Hong Kong Press, 1974. (b)

————. Culture training, cognitive complexity and interpersonal attitudes. In R. Brislin, S. Bochner, & W. Lonner (Eds.), *Cross-cultural perspectives on learning*. New York: Halsted Press, 1975.

————. Cross-cultural social and personality psychology. *Personality and Social Psychology Bulletin*, 1977, *3*, 143–158. (a)

————. Some universals of social behavior. Paper presented at the meeting of the American Psychological Association, Division of Personality and Social Psychology, San Francisco, August 1977. (b) (Also in *Personality & Social Psychology Bulletin* 1978, *4*, 1–16.)

————. *Interpersonal behavior*. Monterey, Calif.: Brooks/Cole Publishing Co., 1977. (c)

TRIANDIS, H. C., MALPASS, R. S., & DAVIDSON, A. R. Cross-cultural psychology. *Biennial Review of Anthropology 1971*, 1972, *7*, 1–84.

————. Psychology and culture. *Annual Review of Psychology*, 1973, *24*, 355–378.

TURNER, T. Piaget's structuralism. (Review of *Genetic epistemology* by J. Piaget, and *Le structuralisme* by J. Piaget.) *American Anthropologist*, 1973, *75*, 351–373.

TYLER, S. A. (Ed.). *Cognitive anthropology.* New York: Holt, Rinehart, & Winston, 1969.

TYLOR, E. B. *Primitive culture.* London: John Murray & Co., 1871. (Also published in Boston: Estes & Louriat, 1884; reprinted in New York: Harper Torchbooks, 1958.)

UDY, S. H. JR. Cross-cultural analysis: Methods and scope. *Annual Review of Anthropology,* 1973, *2,* 253–270.

VERMEULEN, C. J. J., & DERUIJTER, A. Dominant epistemological presupposition in the use of the cross-cultural survey method. *Current Anthropology,* 1975, *16,* 29–52.

WALLACE, A. F. C. *The modal personality of the Tuscarora Indians as revealed by the Rorschach test.* (Bulletin 150). Washington: Bureau of American Ethnology, 1952.

————. *Culture and personality* (2nd ed., 1970). New York: Random House, 1961. (a)

————. The psychic unity of human groups. In B. Kaplan (Ed.), *Studying personality cross-culturally.* New York: Row Peterson, & Co., 1961. (b)

————. Culture and cognition. *Science,* 1962, *135*(3501), 351–357.

WALLACE, A. F. C., & FOGELSON, R. D. Culture and personality. *Biennial Review of Anthropology 1961,* 1962, *2,* 42–78.

WARREN, N. (Ed.). *Studies in cross-cultural psychology* (Vol. 3). London: Academic Press, in press.

WARWICK, D. P. The politics and ethics of cross-cultural research. In H. C. Triandis & W. W. Lambert (Eds.), *Handbook of cross-cultural psychology* (Vol. 1): *Perspectives.* Boston: Allyn & Bacon, Inc., 1980.

WEBB, E. J., CAMPBELL, D. T., SCHWARTZ, R. D., & SECHREST, L. *Unobtrusive measures: Nonreactive research in the social sciences.* Chicago: Rand-McNally, 1966.

WERNER, E. E. *Cross-cultural child development: A view from the planet Earth.* Monterey, Calif.: Brooks/Cole, 1979.

WERNER, E. E., BIERMAN, J. M., & FRENCH, D. *The children of Kauai: A longitudinal study from the parental period to age ten.* Honolulu: University of Hawaii Press, 1971.

WERNER, O., & CAMPBELL, D. T. Translating, working through interpreters, and the problems of decentering. In R. Naroll & R. Cohen (Eds.), *A handbook of method in cultural anthropology.* New York: Columbia University Press, 1973. (Originally published, 1970).

WHITING, B. B. (Ed.). *Six cultures: Studies of child rearing.* New York: John Wiley & Sons, 1963.

WHITING, B. B., & WHITING, J. W. M. *Children of six cultures: A psychocultural analysis.* Cambridge: Harvard University Press, 1975.

WHITING, J. W. M. Socialization process and personality. In F. L. K. Hsu (Ed.), *Psychological anthropology.* Homewood, Ill.: Dorsey Press, 1961.

————. Methods and problems in cross-cultural research. In G. Lindzey & E. Aronson (Eds.), *The handbook of social psychology* (Vol. 2, 2nd ed.). Reading, Mass.: Addison-Wesley, 1968.

WHITING, J. W. M., & CHILD, I. L. *Child training and personality.* New Haven: Yale University Press, 1953.

WHITING, J. W. M., CHILD, I. L., LAMBERT, W. W., et al. *Field guide for a study of socialization* (Six Cultures Series, Vol. 1). New York: John Wiley & Sons, 1966.

WILLEMS, E. P. Behavioral ecology and experimental analysis: Courtship is not enough. In J. R. Nesselroade & H. W. Reese (Eds.), *Life-span developmental psychology: Methodological issues.* New York: Academic Press, 1973.

WILLIAMS, T. R. *Field methods in the study of culture.* New York: Holt, Rinehart, & Winston, 1967.

WILSON, E. D. *Sociobiology: The new synthesis.* Cambridge, Mass.: Harvard University Press, 1975.

WITKIN, H. A., & BERRY, J. W. Psychological differentiation in cross-cultural perspective. *Journal of Cross-Cultural Psychology,* 1975, *6,* 4–87.

YARROW, L. J., & PEDERSEN, F. A. Attachment: Its origins and course. In W. W. Hartup (Ed.), *The young child* (Vol. 2). Washington, D.C.: National Association for the Education of Young Children, 1972.

# 9

# Play, Games, and Sports

*Brian Sutton-Smith
and John M. Roberts*

~~~~~~~~~~~~~~~~~~~~~~~~~~~~~~~

## Contents

## Abstract

Play research and theorizing is discussed in terms of its antecedents, its structure, and its consequences in relationships to culture. Biological, psychological, and anthropological research is reviewed in order to trace the circumstances that give rise to play. Attention is called to the "flexibility complex" across different species, to the mastery of stimulus conditions, the management of social power, and to the role of customs, complexity and child rearing in the instigations to play. Cognitive, affective, and conative aspects of play structure are dealt with separately. Play phenomena are defined in terms of reversibility, prototypic structure, and vivification. The consequences of play in terms of novelty, flexibility, and autonomy are discussed. It is demonstrated that most socialization theories of play, games, and sports, in turn, deal only with how the play integrates the child into culture. Less, but increasing, attention is given to how these forms permit innovative behavior and prepare the child for cultural change.

## Introduction

*Play* is a subset of voluntary behaviors in which the individual reverses the usual relationships of power (e.g., a child is in charge of a situation), by enacting prototypical behavior patterns in a vivid manner. *Games* are a subset of play, in which a rule-governed system of competitive behavior results in one side winning the competition. *Sports* are a subset of games, in which, in addition to the main participants, other individuals participate vicariously.

The field of play, games, and sports is witnessing an increase in interest, as indicated by the recent establishment of scholarly associations for the study of the anthropology of play (Lancy & Tindall, 1976; Stevens, 1977), the sociology of sport, the psychology of play, and game simulation. Although many areas of inquiry are as yet untapped, active research programs are now examining exploratory behavior, the relationships between play and creativity, the effects of imitation on play, and the sociological and personality characteristics of those involved in sports. The research in these areas, together with the theoretical speculations of Huizinga (1949), Piaget (1962), Berlyne (1960, 1970), Turner (1974), and Csikszentmihalyi (1974), which seriously challenge the nineteenth-century distinctions between work and play, indicate a need for reconceptualization within this field of study. In addition, accumulating cross-cultural research in games and play demonstrates large differences in the kinds of playing to be found among different peoples. Thus, older assumptions about the universality of such phenomena are being questioned.

To clarify the major researchable areas, this chapter is organized around five topics:

1. What are the *antecedents to* play phenomena. That is, what precedes them? What is necessary before they can begin?
2. What *intrinsically* instigates play? What actually triggers off a play response within *extrinsically* suitable circumstances?
3. How is play itself to be defined? What are the *structures* of play, games, and sports when they are viewed from cognitive, conative, and affective perspectives?
4. What are the *consequences* of playing?
5. What are the rules governing the transitions by which the consequences of play have an effect on society?

Although organization into these five categories is made primarily to facilitate a survey of research, a theoretical organization is also intended. It will be argued that play, games, and sports are types of voluntary behavior that are integrative and innovative responses to persistent problems in the lives of the individuals or groups who practice them. It also will be argued that the sphere of cultural reality occupied by these phenomena is from a functional point of view both consolidative and preadaptive. However, because the twentieth century has witnessed a newly accepting attitude to the cultural reality of play, most theoretical interpretations have stressed only their consolidative or socializing contributions to society. The preadaptive or potentiating functions of these phenomena have been overlooked.

It will be argued here that the present condition of society, with its information explosion and its need for novel and highly symbolic methods of control, requires more careful focus on the forms of behavior, such as play, games, and sports (and the arts) that have this innovative potential. Implicit in this more "modern" type of interpretation, however, is the clear message that the functional interpretation of play, games, and sports may vary with the nature and requirements of the type of society within which they are found. Thus, in some societies, games and sports are a compulsory and fairly rigidly prescribed method of maintaining variation within the limits that will support the status quo (Turner, 1974); however, in other societies, such as our own, games are sometimes used as a method of exploring new states of consciousness (Smith, 1975). This view of games is in accord with the approach to mythology taken by Kirk (1970), in which the mythic "structures" are not found to be bound universally to particular cultural functions, but take on different functions in different cultural contexts.

*Historical Overview*

Before proceeding, a brief historical review of comparative source material is in order. Historically, the efforts of late nineteenth-century anthropologists and folklorists were devoted to using play and games to trace patterns of cultural diffusion or to illustrate the origin of games in various forms of ritual. Tylor and Culin in anthropology and Newall and Gomme in folklore are strongly associated with these endeavors. Many others were also involved; their efforts have been reviewed and documented in *The Study of Games* (Avedon & Sutton-Smith, 1971), which includes lengthy bibliographies on the historical, anthropological, folklore, recreative, military, business, educational, therapeutic, and social science study of games.

In recent years, there has been a partial renewal of interest in the ritual contexts in which games occur (Handelman, 1977; Salter, 1972).

Schwartzman and Barbera (1976) have pointed out that among those anthropologists who have thought play worth observing (and many did not), nearly all (including Malinowski, Mead, and Whiting) have assumed that its main function was to socialize the children into adult culture through imitation. This chapter notes throughout that the major part of the thinking on play, games, and sports has been based on this same assumption, that is, that play makes a socializing contribution to the larger culture. The recent attempt to convince the public that "educational toys" exist could be regarded as a part of the same trend.

This attempt at conversion to the values of play probably cannot be understood without taking into account the deep-seated nature of the work ethic with its view that play is merely an inconsequential aspect of human life. In combating the notion that play is trivial, most investigators have found it sufficient merely to show that play is connected with other vital cultural processes. As a result, much of the research in this area, while demonstrating such bonds with other forms of cultural reality, is insufficiently probing for us to understand what the relationship really is.

In fact, very few adequate records of children's play, studied from an anthropological point of view, exist. According to Mead, only those by Kidd (1906) and Grinnell (1923) are satisfactory (1974). For Schwartzman (1976) only that of Centner (1962) approaches the sophistication that modern understanding requires. Most investigators have used play only as an incidental or "projective" demonstration of their other interests (e.g., Henry, 1974). Again, play has usually been ignored in favor of games, which are more formal and codifiable and apparently easier to record. Yet it is doubtful if these more separable pieces of play phenomena, which we call games and sports, are actually as informative as an examination of the spontaneous use of playfulness that we find within the everyday cultural context.

As Csikszentmihalyi has recently demonstrated in his study of surgeons, dancers, rock climbers, and others, some people's work involves more play than do areas that they themselves define as recreation (1974). The reverse is also true that much of what the world calls play (viz., sport) is hard work. As Simri has noted, although the ritual occasion of games was a major concern of nineteenth-century students, and although the facts clearly indicate that games were often to be found in earlier times and in tribal cultures in association with such contexts, this association has been almost completely neglected in twentieth-century scholarship on play and games (1966, 1975).

Unilinear theories about mankind's evolution through games dropped out of currency in the early twentieth century, but the interest transferred into psychology in terms of the play stages, as described by Stanley Hall, through which children were supposed to proceed during their development. These stage theories have been particularly persistent within psychology from Hall's recapitulation theory to Piaget's theory of cognitive development, which still contains some of the "maturational" overtones of its predecessor.

However, an interesting shift in the focus of theories about play has occurred. Earlier theories tended to be of an evolutionary character that dealt with the adaptive nature of play in animal or human evolution and stressed motor and physical play most strongly. With the advent of psychoanalysis and, subsequently, of cognitive developmental theorizing, the major focus has shifted to the fantasies, imaginative powers, and cognitive diversity of the players. That is, what is now regarded as most adaptive about play has shifted from the physical to the mental sphere.

This shift in the theories themselves appears to reflect important twentieth-century economic changes in underlying patterns of work in European-derived cultures. The changes from manual to symbolic work are paralleled by a theoretical shift from an interest in motor facility to an interest in the imagination required for play. One can contrast the apparatus of swings and roundabouts placed in schools in the early twentieth century with the sociodramatic participation advocated by early childhood educators in today's nursery schools. Stanley Hall was concerned to have children live out their atavisms on the swings, just as today Sarah Smilansky (1968) is concerned that children develop their capacity for verbal interaction and fantasy in play that imitates the teacher.

Despite this shift from a focus on the body to a focus on the mind, the two types of theorizing have in common the view that play has *serious* adaptive value. Little effort has been made to deal with the common observation that a lot of activity in play is not serious at all in any sense of the word, but revels in nonsense and facetiousness.

Although good data on cross-cultural aspects of play are relatively scarce, there is no paucity of material on play data as collected by psychologists. In temporal order, some of the more outstanding reviews and data sources are: Lehmann & Witty, 1927; Marshall, 1931; Hurlock, 1934; Erikson, 1972; Beach, 1945; Schlosberg, 1947; Peller, 1952, 1954, 1955; Hartley, Frank, and Goldenson, 1952; Piaget, 1948, 1962, 1970; Bateson, 1956; Levin and Wardwell, 1962; Welker, 1961; Moore and Anderson, 1962; Gilmore, 1971; Hutt, 1971; Millar, 1968; Berlyne, 1970; Klinger, 1971; Singer, 1973; Ellis, 1974. Most of these articles are reviewed in Herron and Sutton-Smiths's *Child's Play* (1971).

As previously mentioned, the cross-cultural data on games are of a higher order than the data on play; this material has provided a base for a series of cross-cultural studies (Roberts, Arth, & Bush, 1959) that will be discussed later. Cross-cultural data on sports has been summarized in *The Cross Cultural Analysis of Sports and Games*, edited by Lüschen (1970). As yet, there is no serious general social science treatise on toys, even intra-culturally, let alone cross-culturally.

It would be desirable to complete this introduction with an indication of sources for a cross-cultural methodology of play, games, sports, and toys, but, with some exceptions, these sources are not well developed. Illustrative of this fact are the difficulties that the teams in the Whiting and Whiting (1975) six-culture study encountered in making comparable observations in the different cultures. A questionnaire for such work has recently been published by Royce (1973); it seems to have considerable value, at least as a starting point. Perhaps the best illustration of what can be done in a systematic way is the large-scale observational studies of Israeli children by Eifermann and her students (1968).

In sum, the domain with which this chapter deals has concerned many scholars. By and large, however, their research has been as ephemeral as their view of the field. As a result, there is a paucity of adequate data and a surplus of descriptive material, which shows only that in some way these expressive phenomena are a vital part of the cultures of which they are a part. Unfortunately, the nature of the relationship is more often assumed than explicated.

## Antecedents

This section focuses on the nature of the necessary preconditions for play to occur. It is assumed that some circumstances may be required to support play, even though these conditions do not actually cause it to occur; they are necessary but not sufficient. Evidence of these antecedent conditions is derived from research in animal psychology, child psychology, and anthropology. The biological and psychological studies refer mainly to play, whereas those in anthropology are more often about games.

### Biological Antecedents

Although this work is concerned primarily with psychological and anthropological issues in the study of play, some mention must be made of the increasing body of work on the biological antecedents of play. Students of animal behavior (comparative psychologists and ethologists) make it clear that diverse species show differences in their amounts of play, and that certain general conditions underlie the amount of playfulness that we find (Aldis, 1975). The Australian anthropologist Peter Reynolds has spoken of these conditions as the "flexibility complex." He says, "There is reason to believe that the history of man consists largely of a progressive phylogenetic elaboration of the flexibility complex" (Reynolds, 1972). He includes in this complex an increased delay in maturation, a condition of semidomestication, and the dependence of the infant on the parents for care-taking. To these he adds the capacity for observational learning, imitation, exploration, and the development of play group subcultures with institutions of their own.

In a number of articles, Jerome Bruner (1972, 1973, 1975) has spoken to the same general set of conditions, but with a greater emphasis on the functional value for skill acquisition of the particular conditions surrounding play. He says, for example,

> There is a well known rule in the psychology of learning, the Yerkes-Dodson Law, that states that the more complex a skill is, the lower the optimum level of motivation required to learn it. That is, too much motivation arousal can interfere with learning. By deemphasizing the importance of the goal, play may serve to reduce excessive drive and thus enable young animals and children to learn more easily the skills they will need when they are older. (1975, p. 82)

Elsewhere, he speaks of play as a program of variation, and points out that even animals, when provided with caretaking, increase innovation.

Therapeutic work with the disabled, disturbed, and deficient child also indicates that only when the child is reassured that he is protected and safe does he attempt to reach out and express himself freely in play behaviors (Reilly, 1974). Safety, protection, security, and trust seem to be as important to animals as they are to human beings. This thesis is supported by Mary Main's (1975) demonstration that secure babies, as compared with insecure ones, explore more intensively and with longer duration; they also smile, laugh, and play more willingly with their playmates.

Obviously, as individuals mature and their playing and gaming capacities strengthen and become internalized, the need for secure external circumstances may be considerably reduced. Studies in humor, for example, indicate that the more secure individual is able to use humor for anxiety reduction in a stressful situation (Goldstein & McGhee, 1972). Reports of soldiers at play on the eve of battle are common. Extremes of motivation (starvation, the midst of battle) may still preclude play, but, for some adults, play is no longer the tentative competence it was in the early years. The conditions of audience behavior under which some modern sports such as soccer are played show the extent to which adults can go in maintaining their play under quite severe circumstances. Only further research will show whether there are culture-specific ratios of security and anxiety in the play of particular games and sports.

*Psychological Antecedents*

Despite the examples just given, it is generally agreed that people do not play when in states of emergency. Usually other psychological drives (hunger or fear) or cultural emergencies (war or revolution) must be dealt with first. The psychological paradox is how such initial states of relaxation or boredom can then lead to the high states of motivation we associate with sports and games. The internal conflict theories of psychoanalysis (Peller, 1952, 1954, 1955; Waelder, 1933; Erikson, 1972) or the child-rearing conflict theory of Roberts and Sutton-Smith (1962) must deal with the fact that such conflicts, if at a high point, interfere with play. Or as a minimum, they do not facilitate it. Only after the play occurs can the conflict be introduced into its content. Apparently, therefore, the conflicts do not explain the game structure, though they may ultimately affect its content.

Recent work in the psychology of play, however, has focused less on the inference of such internal states than on the observations of the antecedent contingencies for play in stimulus conditions, social conditions, and in communication. We discuss these in turn.

*Mastery of stimulus conditions.* There is considerable consensus that the person who plays is at some ease with his environment and his fellows. This state of equanimity is conceptualized as (a) a state of equilibrium; (b) in behaviorist terms, as a state of stimulus-redundancy; (c) in motivational terms, as the absence of drive urgency; (d) in physiological terms, as a below normal level of arousal (boredom); or (e), in affective terms, as a state of relaxation (Berlyne, 1960; Ellis, 1974; Hutt, 1971; Millar, 1968; Nunnally & Lemond, 1973; Piaget, 1962). The problem for play theory is to determine how these preceding states of equanimity (however they may be conceptualized) give way to the high states of alertness and arousal that constitute play. To explain the occasional exceptions when those who play become so involved that they ignore the usual biological indicators of stress (hunger, elimination, pain) is still another problem.

In recent years, increasing research work has clarified certain points. First, it is clear that although play is a voluntary activity (the subject is doing what he or she chooses to do and is not compelled or driven by internal or external need to do this), not all voluntary activity is play. Other voluntary activities, such as exploration, usually precede play (Elkind, 1972). It is argued that despite the voluntariness of exploration, the subject's activity during exploration is still very much dictated by the stimulus conditions in the environment, whereas the essence of play is that it is an activity in which the subject imposes his or her own idea (schema, fantasy, image, response) on the surrounding circumstances (Sutton-Smith, 1967). It has become increasingly clear, from recent research, that we can describe the *phases* in a continuum of voluntary activity that begins with exploration and may end with play. Researchers working with primates, as well as with children, have observed parallel sequences. Thus, Chevalier-Skolnikoff writes:

Primates also react to novel objects first with fear then with careful inspection, which is visual, tactile, and olfactory, and sometimes even includes tast-
ing, and finally with experimentation and play, which will give the animals
maximal information about the object. Note that the exploratory sequence is
similar in the raven and in the primate. (1973, p. 2)

In Hutt's (1971) work with children, the transitions made across four
phases in this continuum of voluntary behavior are the examination of a
novel object, the repetition of an adequate response, the combination of
responses, then finally the transformation into a play response. The point
is that children do not generally play in a novel setting or with novel materials until they have established mastery over that setting and with those
materials.

There is no theoretical difference between saying one must master
the physical setting and master the stimulus conditions in a setting. This is
just a difference in the level of analysis applied. However, we can use this
difference to make a further point: although the player must first be master of the setting, this does not mean that he completely transcends it in
his play. Though he may impose his schema or fantasy on his environment, he nevertheless assimilates that environment into the contents of
the fantasy as he proceeds. By and large, psychologists have gradually reduced their concern with environments or playgrounds from a molar to a
molecular level. They have been far less at home with settings than with
stimuli; an interesting exception is the work of Gump, Schoggen, and Redl
(1963), which shows a variety of interesting relationships between play
and physical setting (Herron & Sutton-Smith, 1971).

One way of clarifying the apparent contradiction in saying both that
the environment influences play and yet that play transcends the environment, is to examine the work of Beatrice and John Whiting (1975), which
involved the study of children in six cultures. They appear to show that
children in more complex cultures play more and with more complexity.
Their findings here parallel those of Roberts and Sutton-Smith (1962) in
finding more types of games in cultures of higher complexity. These findings may be read to mean that the culture makes a direct impact on the
structure of the play and games to be found within it. Technological, social, and economic complexity is paralleled by game complexity.

But the Whiting study also showed that within the complex groups
themselves, there was relatively more play and games in the group in
which the children had the greatest freedom to play. Thus, there was more
play among the Taira of Okinawa than among the Rajputs of India, although both were complex societies. In Taira, the children were much
freer to roam about the community and to play with whomever they
chose, whereas the Rajputs were confined to their backyards and to playmates who were their relatives. This suggests that the "cultural leeway"

that permits play is of greater scope in Taira than Rajput. The idea that there must be leeway for play to develop, so that the child is given scope to react to his cultural circumstances, has been suggested by Erik Erikson (1972), the leading exponent of play analysis. All of this can be summed by saying that culture and ecology make a direct impress on play, but only to the extent that the players are free to use elements available to them from culture or ecology. Just what determines which parts of their culture they use is considered later.

Much of this information fits the type of thinking espoused by Berlyne (1960), in which the activation of the organism is seen as a function of the degrees and kinds of stimulus novelty. In those terms, more complex societies, or more freedom to move around in any society, would bring the subject into contact with more stimuli (more novel, complex, and conflicting stimuli), which would, in turn, lead to more voluntary response on his part. Efforts have been made to interpret most of children's play in these terms (Ellis, 1974; Reilly, 1974) and, more recently, to interpret the activities of sportsmen also in terms of their need for such stimulation (Loy, 1975). Even though there is undoubted truth in these interpretations, they fail to distinguish between exploration and play. Novel stimuli are certainly arousing and effect exploratory activity. Do they also effect playful activity? One suspects a correlation between the two, that is, that the organism aroused to exploratory activity also plays more. But certainly no one-to-one relationship exists between the two, so other critical variables are apparently involved.

An important consequence of the distinction being made between exploratory mastery and play is that mastery may serve to sharpen future observation in cross-cultural work (Finley & Layne, 1971). The two forms of activity appear to have diverse adaptive consequences, as we will argue in the rest of this review.

*The management of social power.* The child must be master of objects and physical setting, as well as of the other players. We use the word *mastery* here for some unspecified degree of sufficient familiarity and freedom from anxiety in the presence of these players. To do this, the child must develop techniques of social influence. Between the ages of 2 and 7 years, children's skill in social tactics increases greatly. In our own observation of playground play, we have noticed that children must solve the management problems before they can begin to play (Sutton-Smith & Savasta, 1972).

Freedman (1974) has asserted that the differences between the sexes in the development and use of power tactics are common both to primates and man. Females are to be found in smaller groups and to be more concerned with affiliation and grooming. Males are to be found in larger groups and to be concerned with dominance and subordination. Whether such sex differences in dominance interests are cross-cultural universals in children's societies has yet to be investigated.

Recent work on primates showing great variations in dominance practices contradicts Freedman's assertions about universality (Kolata, 1976). Tindall (1973) has argued that even at the adult level, unless the underlying matters of power, which he terms "the hidden curriculum of sport," are dealt with, true play cannot proceed. We can be sure that in every society, although in different ratios, the relationship between power outside the game and power modeled within it must be resolved.

*Management as communication.* Knowing how to communicate is one part of knowing one's place in the dominance hierarchy. Following the stimulus of Bateson (1956), an increasing amount of work has been done on the different signal systems (or metacommunications) used within different species to indicate that they intend to play with each other. Thus, Bekoff (1974) has contrasted the play of beagles, wolves, and coyotes and found that these play signals are less critical with the beagles and are most critical with the very hostile coyotes. For the coyotes, all play was preceded by the correct signal.

It is tempting to infer that more hostile humans have to get their signals very much clearer than less hostile ones. Chevalier-Skolnikoff (1973) has contrasted the various types of faces used by macaque, apes, and man to indicate the message: "This is play." Paradoxically, man sometimes signals that he is about to make a joke by looking more serious than usual. A key to play at such higher levels of playfulness is indicated by a subtle manipulation of these signals. Cross-cultural differences most probably exist in these signals for play.

## Cultural Antecedents

Although it is clear in the ethnological data that play usually occurs first in the vicinity of the mother, later with other infants, and then with peers and juveniles, no systematic study has been made of the particular kinds of protections that each of these relationships provides, nor of the implications that each has for the kind and nature of play that ensues. One would assume some setting of boundaries in each case to ensure safety, which would be followed by specific patterns of stimulation. Certainly abundant anecdotal evidence, both on the primate and human level, exists of difference between mother-infant play, toddler play, and the play of peer groups or juveniles (Sutton-Smith, 1972a).

Typically, the investigator has been content to show that some global relationship in fact exists between play and other cultural variables. In significant association with play, we find cultural customs, cultural complexity, cultural differentiation, social class, economic or adaptive strategy, family structure, sex role value, child-rearing practices, and so on. We will deal with some examples of these, keeping in mind that the demonstration of a correlation between the variable and play may justify the view that play is "functional" to the culture in some way, but otherwise tells us very little about the relationship. We may assume either that these variables truly antecede play and are necessary to it, or that these variables and play are implicated in some other pattern of variables that is not determined by this analysis. By and large, the research on cultural antecedents has focused on games and sports.

*Antecedent customs.* Historically, the favorite cultural explanation for games was their occurrence on ritual occasions. It was argued that the game came into being because it fulfilled a religious or magical function. Thus, Simri (1966), after an exhaustive survey of the evidence, concluded that ball games were originated in most cases as a part of fertility cults. The passing of the ball back and forth, he said, signified a tension between man and the powers of nature. Unfortunately for this kind of explanation, too many ball games seem to thrive without this particular set of circumstances. This takes nothing away from the possibility that games of a given sort were used on such ritual occasions, but it does limit the persuasiveness of that type of argument.

In his survey of North American tribes, Salter (1972) found games to be associated with various rituals, such as death, weather, sickness, and fertility. Some games were restricted to one ritual; some served for several. Considerable differences in usage between tribes were also observed. In general, he concluded that the manner of playing the game rather than the outcome was believed by the people themselves to have the greatest "spiritual" effect. Games of physical skill and strategy were more often found in these ritual contexts than were games of chance.

A more illuminating survey, also by Salter (1967), of records of Australian aboriginal games, showed that out of 94 games, the associations with cultural domains were as follows:

| | | | |
|---|---|---|---|
| Economic pursuits | 29 | Cultural identification | 13 |
| Social interaction | 22 | Domestic aspects | 9 |
| Political activity | 13 | Ceremonial rituals | 8 |

Even though there is nothing final about Salter's classifications, there can be little argument with the major outcome: that games as such can be associated with almost any cultural institution or social purpose.

Surveys of the games of Melanesia (Lansley, 1968) and Polynesia (Jones, 1967) have led to similar findings. Even when any particular game or sport is studied, as, for example, Frederickson's (1969) examination of wrestling in various cultures, a similar result follows. In some cultures, she found wrestling used as a legal and judicial mechanism for settling the boundaries of rice fields; elsewhere as a part of puberty rites, a means of selecting a mate, and a demonstration of prestige and power; and, finally, in ritual context, as a means of ensuring a successful harvest. Other general surveys of the function of games in culture also add up to the view that games and sports are multifunctional and may be found in association with a wide variety of antecedent circumstances (Dunlap, 1951; Damm, 1970).

Even though there probably are some limits to the lability of games and sports, the available evidence leaves us uncertain about these limits. All we can say is that they may be found in association with many cultural situations and perform many diverse functions and that, therefore, their explanation cannot be reduced to an account of associated customs.

*Cultural complexity.* To date, the most satisfactory empirical correlations between games and culture have been established with indices of cultural complexity. Thus, Roberts and co-workers in a series of cross-cultural studies involving hundreds of tribal cultures, discovered a relationship between the number of *types* of competitive games in a culture and other measures of complexity in that culture, for example, social stratification or political organization (Roberts, Arth, & Bush, 1959; Roberts & Sutton-Smith, 1962; Roberts, Sutton-Smith, & Kendon, 1963; Roberts & Sutton-Smith, 1966; Barry & Roberts, 1972). In these papers, a game was defined as a "recreational activity characterized by: (a) organized play, (b) competition, (c) two or more sides, (d) criteria for determining the winner, and (e) agreed upon rules" (Roberts, Arth, & Bush, 1959, p. 597).

Three types of games were dealt with: those of physical skill, chance, and strategy. Games of *physical skill* were defined as those in which the outcomes are determined by the player's motor activities (marathon races, darts); game of *chance* were those in which the outcome is determined by a guess or some external artifact such as a die or wheel (bingo, roulette); games of *strategy* were those in which the outcome is determined by rational choices (checkers, chess, go).

In some cultures on record, no such competitive games were reported; but the validity of these records, is questioned seriously: it may have derived from inadequate ethnographic coverage (Murdock, 1967). The few cultures that were reported to have games of strategy or chance or both, but not physical skill, were also regarded as doubtful. Physical skill is so pervasive in world cultures that Roberts believes its absence is suspicious. There are, however, cultures with games of physical skill and strategy, but without games of chance.

The results are quite extensive and cannot all be cited here. In summary, cultures that appeared to lack these competitive games were of very low complexity. Those with physical skill only were of simple technology and subsistence economics. Those with games of chance were of wide-ranging complexity but were noted for various forms of economic and social uncertainty. Those with strategy were noted for their complexity of social organization and severity of child rearing. The most complex of all societies possessed all three types of games. In a subsequent series of studies, Roberts, Sutton-Smith, and others sought to show these cross-cultural correlations could be used to make predictions to game and personality relationships within American society. This validation technique is called *subsystem replication* (Sutton-Smith, Roberts, & Kozelka, 1963; Roberts, Hoffman, & Sutton-Smith, 1965; Sutton-Smith & Roberts, 1964; Sutton-Smith & Roberts, 1967).

In a reconsideration of the Roberts game and cultural complexity data, Ball (1972) argued that the relationships between games and cultural variables could be handled in a statistically more sophisticated manner by weighting the complexity of each form of game and game combination (chance with strategy, physical skill with chance, and so on), rather than simply by comparing the absence or presence of the various basic types. Using this ordinal technique, he discovered higher relationships between game complexity and variables involving social organization (social class, political integration, and size of community), than variables involving economic-technological complexity, although, as he points out, it is not actually easy to differentiate the two. Still, his data are important in the light of the classic controversy between those who interpret games in economic terms and those who find their basis in social behavior (Damm, 1970).

In a subsequent study, Ball (1974) developed a new scale of gaming based not on game complexity, but on the degree of risk involved in the game. In this scale, games of skill and strategy are at the highest end of the scale and games of chance at the lowest end. He calls this a *game control scale;* at the highest end, the players exercise more control over risk and at the lowest they accept the risk. His notion of game control is like that found in the large literature on "locus of control" studies in psychology.

What is interesting is that, although the same units of games are used in both the scales, the results are quite different. Once again the game complexity scale covaries with measures of social complexity. But now, the game control scale covaries with economic measures. Ball (1974, p. 176) argues that the game control scale varies negatively with the more fatalistic activities of hunting, fishing, and gathering, where success depends on climate, nature, luck, and so on, and it varies directly with the more manipulative intervention practices of animal husbandry and agriculture, where efforts are made to conquer and control the vicissitudes of the environment.

Ball also argues that what is important about the relationship of games to economics is not the structure of the organization (fishing, occupational specialization), but the attitude of rationality and control that is associated with it. Not surprisingly, games, as expressive models, are capable of reflecting both this aspect of the social structure and its sheer complexity.

There is much other evidence of a relationship between cultural complexity and the character of games. Most of the evidence is anecdotal or ethnographic, and, although it supports the general proposition that games model society, it does not really explain the relationship in any definitive way (Lüschen, 1967; Allardt, 1970; Eifermann, 1970; Renson, 1976; Lever & Warner, 1975). These works offer various explanations of the relationships. It is said that more complex games go with more complex cultures because of the higher levels of stimulation offered; because there is simply more money and opportunity for play and for the purchase of more complex apparatuses; because higher status groups induce higher achievement motivation; or because complexity in adult social relationships reflects complexity in child social relationships.

The Whitings' (1975) studies contained other clues about the association between cultural complexity and game complexity, which have been discussed by Sutton-Smith (1974).

> The work on the Nyansongo of Kenya, for example, shows that in cultures where the children are an important cog in a fragile economic machine, there is little scope for them to play. The major job for these children is herding the cattle. It is reported that "fantasy play is almost non-existent among these children" (1963, p. 173). All that was observed was some fairly desultory physical play such as blocking streams and swimming, climbing trees, shooting birds with slings, fighting with each other, tussling, chasing and exchanging blows, watching cars on the roads. This is consistent with the studies of Dina Feitelson who reports that in the carpet weaving cultures of the Middle East where children are an economic asset, they also begin early in direct imitation of adult activity and do not indulge greatly in what you or I might call play (1974). The studies of Sarah Smilansky of hierarchical cultural groups in Israel are of similar importance (1967). This does not mean that all relatively simple cultures do not play, because the records of play amongst Australian aboriginal groups are very extensive. What seems to be critical is whether or not the adults have a direct economic need to train the children in highly normalized means of survival. In such cultures the "work ethic" makes real sense. The adults know what must be done to survive and they cannot afford the wasted time of child play. Children are an important cog in the machine. The same position prevailed in England in the early half of the nineteenth century when pauperism was widespread and young children were exploited in mines and factories as a necessary way of helping each family to survive. The Australian aborigines have an open ended environment for their children. There is much they can teach but much also the child must learn through self-reliance, including the fact that he must deal with novel circumstances. Play seems to be most relevant in such "open" societies, and much less relevant in "closed" ones. (Sutton-Smith, 1974, p. 10)

Our point at the moment is that in some cultures and with some segments of complex society, complexity of games cannot develop because the children's labor is needed elsewhere. If we contrast the society studied by the Whitings et al. with the greatest amount of observed play (the Taira of Okinawa) against the society with the least (the Nyansongo of Africa) the following differences also occur:

> The family unit in Taira is nuclear, there are private courtyards (so privacy is possible), children can wander in an open and friendly society of other children, they meet more children who are not their kin, there is a school and there are competitive games at the school, there is more interaction with the father, there are more outsiders in the playgroups, children under five are seldom given chores, they do not have to look after younger children to any extent, there are various specialized buildings such as shops, etc., children are self-assertive. In the Nyansongo by contrast where subsistence agriculture prevails the children must help with the work, they must help with the care of the younger children. Under the mother's control they help with many chores, getting fuel, cooking. They are members of an extended family and they are discouraged from leaving their immediate home environment. There is no school and no organized play (there is some dirt throwing and rough-housing by boys). There is little interaction with the father. They are very much under the mother's control and dominance. These are all interesting contrasts. It is simply not possible yet for us to know which of these variables is intrinsic to the difference in play, and which merely an accidental associate. Intuition suggests that the complexity, the play groups, the privacy, the father stimulation, the lack of chores might all be important contributors. (Sutton-Smith, 1974, p. 11)

*Methods of child rearing.* The record of parallels between forms of cultural or social complexity and game complexity is quite substantial. At a minimal level of explanation, we have suggested that some of the differences cited may reflect only the amount of opportunity available for play by these different groups. Some groups, usually the simpler ones, are needed in the work force and there is less opportunity for complex play. Traditional female socialization requires the girl to be more concerned with family maintenance and restricts her freedom for outdoor play. Still, throughout the studies cited are hints of a more direct connection between the cultural structure and the game structure. The Ball (1972, 1974) game-control measure implies that an attitude of readiness for greater risk taking may be engendered in the family of origin.

This is consistent with Lüschen's (1970) finding of relationships between subcultural value orientations (for example, of achievement) and interest in sports and it is consistent with Glassford's (1970) explanation of Eskimo games in terms of basic types of economic strategies. In comparing three generations of McKenzie Delta Region Eskimoes, he found that the older Eskimoes, following their collaborative economic behavior, showed a greater interest both in cooperative games and in games of individual self-testing, which were of a low order of complexity and involved few step sequences. The younger Eskimoes favored more complex, highly competitive games. Glassford (1976) states the difference in terms of the game theory contrast between "maximin" strategy (security before gain) amd "minimax" strategy (gain before security). Other cultures have also been compared in these cooperative versus competitive game-playing terms (Miller, 1973; Thomas, 1975).

These value systems, as they apply to games, might be carried by the character of the family structure; the more authoritarian that structure, the greater the preference for arbitrary power games. A number of studies of games have pursued that type of parallel (Maccoby, Modiano, & Lander, 1964; Zurcher & Meadow, 1970) by contrasting in particular the more authoritarian Mexican family with the more egalitarian American one. In all these studies, however, we are once again dealing with (a) implied relationships between the parents, (b) parent values, (c) child-rearing practice on the other hand and the children's play at games on the other, when in fact we are usually correlating only two points on the latter continuum, often those at the furthest remove.

In a recent interview and observational study, Watson (1973) attempted to transcend these lacunae by contrasting the different approaches of lower- and middle-class parents to their boys playing Little League baseball. Here the children were playing the same game. What Watson found, however, was that parental values and the nature of the boys' play differed markedly between the social class groups. The lower-class parents showed more involvement in the game, emphasized its value as authority over the boys and the importance of the boys' conformity. The lower-class boys also emphasized belonging to the group and developed a much more highly structured and ritualistic game. By contrast, the middle-class parents emphasized the learning of cooperation. The middle-class boys emphasized the display of their skills in a competitive setting.

One gets a clear contrast between a game used by the middle-class boy as an enhancement of personal status, and a game used by the lower-class boy and parent as a means of collective integration into a community. It is not difficult to believe that games and sports historically have performed the latter role in integrating lower-class and immigrant groups into the larger system of cultural values; in due course these particular "collective" values have given way to the individualistic ones that are more characteristic of the middle-class achiever. The major importance of this study, however, is that it shows a consistency between parent values, child values, and child practices, which is meaningful in terms of the socioeconomic status of the parents. It confirms the expectancies that are implicit in most of the studies already cited, that children are directly *socialized* as they play games.

To date, however, the only direct study of child training and games on a large-scale, cross-cultural basis is that carried out by Roberts and Sutton-Smith (1962) and more recently by Barry and Roberts (1972) and by Roberts and Barry (1976). In these studies, significant relationships were established between patterns of child rearing and distinctive types of games. In general, the more types of games present, the more severe the socialization process. Most illuminating is the paper of Roberts and Barry (1976) showing that cultures with games of strategy and skill present are more likely to require more industry, obedience, and responsibility from their children and yet be low in the inculcation of self-reliance, honesty, and trust. The authors conclude that "if games build character, that character may be less than ideal" (1976, p. 39).

Another reading of the same data could imply that in more complex societies more effort must be spent in assessing the motives of other people. Distrust and dishonesty may be associated with learning how to achieve some distance from, as well as insight into, other people. We must remember that these characteristics are part of a complex that also includes restraint and obedience, as well as industry and responsibility. These characteristics may only imply the importance of avoiding gullibility. Children in Western culture between the ages of 4 and 7 years usually have a critical socialization in not being gullible. In simpler societies, where direct and personal collaboration is often critical for survival, greater emphasis may be given to trust and honesty, and self-reliance is important because survival depends on the physical skills of the individual. In modern society, personal physical skill is often irrelevant to survival in the professions, business, or politics.

On the basis of the data presented, a chain of mediated relationships most probably exists between types of social or economic institutions and games played. Parents, as members of these institutions, convey their own values (obedience, distrust) to their children through the forms of child training that are relevant to their own lives in those institutions. These values are then in turn reflected in the games they teach and approve of in the children's play. Strategy games require deception of the opponent and distrust of his moves. They also require considerable restraint, obedience to rules, and industrious application of an intellectual sort. Still we must confess that the cross-cultural study in which all these variables (institutional, parental, child training, and method of play) are carefully assessed has not yet appeared.

## The Transition to Play

Although it has been popular to interpret play as a "projection" of its preconditions (stimulus conditions, drive states, aggression), such explanations are clearly insufficient. We may suppose that the instigation to play is at least as universal as language, noting that language itself always implies certain sustaining conditions of either a biological or social nature, as the case of deafness and autism indicate. We may suppose that the potentiality for play is universal even though we do not, therefore, have to hold that children everywhere play in the same way or even play the same games. As the Whitings' *Six Culture Study* shows, important cultural differences abound in ways of playing. There is no one language of play or games. There is evidence also of the more obvious fact that, within our own culture, there are social class differences as well as individual patterns of play. Anthropology needs to investigate these different patterns of play and games and the way in which they enter differentially into their appropriate cultural life. Cultures in which self-reliance is very important (Australian aboriginal, Amerindian) stress self-testing though not always contesting. The children spend much time in the rehearsal of physical skills. Again, cultures in which traditional ways of managing the economy are important emphasize strict imitation. In these cultures, children's play appears to be meticulously imitative. In Western society, however, where achievement through symbolic means has become important, children are occupied with creative sociodramas and make-believe constructions, as well as with competitive victories. We would expect the play in each culture to reflect these preferences for certain modes of adaptation over others.

The major implication of these cultural differences is that the greater part of children's play is learned from others; indeed, many experiments on the modeling of children's play would support this argument (Smilansky, 1968; Feitelson & Ross, 1973; Dansky & Silverman, 1973). In a way, such a thesis should be obvious except for the fact that many have assumed for so long that the content of play and games were universally everywhere the same. Many popular books have been written on the theme. Unfortunately, most of the recent experimental studies on play aim to increase children's verbal interactions, their imaginative or fantasizing competences, and so on, as assets in normal schooling. Therefore, they do not tell us of the naturalistic ways in which children *imitate* the play behavior of others. The classic exception is Piaget's (1948) study on marble playing, in which in various steps through which children proceed in their identification with older players are outlined.

In a recent study of the Kpelle, Lancy (1976) outlined some steps that such modeling can take over a period of time:

> Make-believe play seems to be one step in an alternatively collapsing and expanding process. A child of three spends hours observing a blacksmith at work. A child of four brings his stick down on a rock repeatedly and says he is a blacksmith. A child of eight weaves with his friends elaborate reconstruction of the blacksmith's craft, all in make-believe. The child of ten is a blacksmith's helper in reality; he fetches wood for the forge and no more. At twelve he begins learning the actual skills of smithing, adding a new one

every few months or so. At eighteen he is a full fledged blacksmith with his own forge. Parallel patterns can be observed for virtually every class of work. (p. 75)

This account hints at the *timing* of the play modeling. A series of cumulative steps is observed. First, are the years of exploratory observation; then, imitation; next, the play transformation; finally, there is real life behavior. The transition to play modeling seems to have its basis in a regular series of earlier steps in the acquisition of understanding through exploration and imitation. There may be some principle here. Parten's (1931, 1933) classic series of play steps involved first, observation, solitary play, parallel play, and then association and cooperation. More recently, White and Watts (1973) have estimated that approximately 60 percent of a young child's voluntary time is spent in observational behavior.

Some lawfulness probably exists in the relationship between the preceding phases of observation, exploratory activity and the transformation into make-believe play. The immediately prior mastery behavior may be the final stimulus for the play. In the preceding example, beating a stick in imitation of the blacksmith precedes the make-believe expansion into blacksmith life.

It is possible to suggest therefore that what stimulates the play is the attempt to bring the immediately prior accommodation into accord with early forms of response, a process termed "assimilation" by Piaget (1962). The virtue of this explanation is that it can also take into account the classic Freudian conflict theory, insofar as what will persist in play are conflicting responses that have been difficult to assimilate on earlier occasions because they are at variance with the responses usually required of the child and rewarded by others. In these terms, the most persistent content for play would be long-standing conflicts over love, separation, and power. Much of the anecdotal early childhood evidence seems to suggest that this is true (Isaacs, 1933; Piaget, 1962). As cultures vary in their kinds of conflict, so will they vary in play. Further, as we will show, going beyond Piaget (1966), these play behaviors may be sources of innovation.

## The Structures of Play

### Cognitive

To this point, we have attempted to deal with conditions that obtain before the occurrence of play. It has been suggested that the child must first be master of his physical and social conditions before he can play. Second, it has been argued that those prior processes of attempted mastery may themselves be the immediate instigations for the content of the play itelf.

But play, like language or humor, also has its internal organization, and it is to this organization that we now turn. The structures of play and games can be conceptualized in many ways, most of which have already been surveyed (Herron & Sutton-Smith, 1971; Avedon & Sutton-Smith, 1971). In more recent work, the view that play itself is a structuring or rule-engendering process is receiving increasing recognition (Harré and Secord, 1972). Vygotsky (1967) speaks of play as a process of abstraction; Fein (1975) discusses the prototypes formed in play.

These approaches seem to imply that, although the content of play may be derived from past experience (indeed be a projection of it), the organization of play is not. The organization itself is unique and novel in the child's experience, and as such it anticipates the organization the child will use in later problem solving and communication. A number of recent studies indicate that how children play in the second year of life may anticipate the type of pivot grammar that they will use when they begin to speak (Nicolich, 1975). There is other evidence that children are developmentally further ahead (at least in complexity) in play than in other adaptations (Overston & Jackson, 1973; Tucker, 1975; Singer, 1966; Sutton-Smith, 1979b). All of this is additional reason for thinking of play structures as prototypic because they are anticipatory. In these terms, we may suppose that each culture gives rise in the child to an "alphabet" of play anticipations.

Unfortunately, we do not have any very well described accounts of the "play grammar" used by children of different ages as they develop, nor any accounts of the ways in which these grammars change relative to culture. However, there are many descriptions of the general character of the stages through which children proceed in complex societies (Lehmann & Witty, 1927; Eifermann, 1968; Seagoe, 1962), and we do have indications that no universality of these stages exists, even in complex societies (Smilansky, 1968; Eifermann, 1971).

Two free play areas that have come under more systematic study recently have shown their susceptibility to sequential structural analysis. Work on the freely told fantasy stories of children between the ages of 2 and 12 years has shown that they are susceptible to a variety of folkloristic, anthropological, and Piagetian paradigms of structural analysis (Sutton-Smith, Botvin, & Mahony, 1976). For example, a system developed by E. K. and P. Maranda (1971), derived from Lévi-Strauss, involves a series of four steps in which a story is told (a) about a state of threat or deprivation, (b) the threat is first reacted to unsuccessfully, but (c) the threat is then nullified, and finally (d) the total situation is transformed and a hero emerges. The approximate ages at which children tell stories involving these elements in succeeding order are 5, 7, 9, and 11 years. It is possible to argue on these grounds that the story-telling habit in childhood is basic to the development of mythology, a point of view quite consistent with Kirk's (1970) analysis of this subject.

Children's play with riddles has also been analyzed in sequential structural terms (Sutton-Smith, 1976). It has been shown that riddles can be viewed as exercises in classification, reclassification, and multiple classification; and that this approach successfully manages about 70 percent of the riddles, although it is not sufficient for the description of all varieties, for example, riddle parodies. In more recent work, Sutton-Smith and Mahony sought to show that the development of all expressive systems (play, games, toys, sports, graphics, narrative, plastics, humor, music) is susceptible of analysis in terms of a Piagetian structural approach (Mahony, 1977). They seek to discover structural constancies across different media, as, for example, when at the age of about 5, children (a) play games of reversible characters, as in hide and seek, (b) tell stories in which characters reverse their picaresque travels through space, quitting and returning to a home base, (c) sing songs of a similar a–b–a palindromic structure, and (d) carry out cognitive operations, called "concrete operations," involving the same maintenance of identity through reversible phases.

It is pointed out, however, that the use of the Piagetian cognitive system as an analogue for expressive structures in this way involves putting it to quite different functional use, in which the aesthetic issues of tension arousal and resolution, as discussed by Berlyne (1971), become central rather than peripheral modes of functioning. In an aesthetic reversible structure, the focus is on the tension generated by the opposing forces *within* the expressive media. By contrast, in the type of cognitive structure discussed by Piaget the tension is *between* the structure and the external referent. In the latter case, any tension internal to the system is purely an instrumental method of arriving at an appropriate solution. In addition, the resolution that occurs in the aesthetic structure is also internal to the system. Its functional referent is the audience that entertains it rather than a change of adaptation in the external world.

Even though structural analyses of fluid play and expressive behavior are relatively novel, (apart from work on children's drawings), structures in games have been described more often. Since game rule structures are overt, a great deal of game playing is available, even to the players, and can be reported to the investigator.

The current literature on games most often refers to two systems. The first is that of Roberts et al., which was described previously. This group has suggested that these games have a cultural evolutionary order, with physical skill games preceding the combinations of skill and chance, or skill and strategy, and with both these preceding the combinations of all three types. Roberts et al. also believe that this is probably the order of their evolution in child development. Note, however, that this conceptualization of game structure applies only to game outcome determinants. Multiple other aspects of games are not dealt with in this system (Redl, Gump, & Sutton-Smith, 1971), and might be equally fruitful if they could be included.

The other system often referred to is that of Caillois (1961), who classifies games into the categories of competition, chance, simulation, and vertigo. Within each category is an evolutionary and developmental order. Earlier games are characterized more by lack of control and later games by more precise rule behavior. Thus, in competitive games, racing is at the less organized and checkers is at the more organized end; in chance, there is heads or tails versus lotteries; in simulation, there is make-believe versus theater; in vertigo, there is whirling about versus scuba diving. The advantages and limitations of each system as applied to Sudanese children's games have been described by Royce (1972).

Once again, as with the more fluid expressive behaviors of play, a Piagetian type of analysis can be applied to game and sports evolution. As Piaget (1970) has pointed out, structural analysis requires an accounting of the systems of self-regulation and transformation that govern the entity to be described. In these terms, game evolution can be divided into four systems of regulation corresponding to pastimes (farmer in the dell), central person games (tagging), competitive games (marbles), and sports.

Each stage is governed by a different system of coordinations. At the first level, these are prescriptive; at the second, they involve actions only; at the third, they involve signals as well as actions; and at the fourth level, they involve a meta-signal system. Each stage also involves characteristic forms of transformation. Once again, at the first stage, these are prescriptive; at the second, role and action reversals; at the third, group character and success reversals; and at the fourth stage, attack and defense reversals.

This tentative system has been applied to both developmental and cultural data with considerable success, in terms of its ability to order children's play chronologically and cross-cultural data in terms of complexity. The games of pygmies (Mbutu), Australian aborigines, and Amerindian hunters involve dominantly the first two levels, whereas American Villagers, Polynesians, Melanesians, and Africans show a striking increase in the latter two levels. Within this system, sports are defined by the appearance of vicarious groups circumjacent to the game event and are characterized by the marked influence of meta-game activity (rule discussion, referees, judges, audience evocation).

We do not mean to argue that these structural levels imply universality. They imply only that, where games evolve in complexity, these levels provide useful general systems of analysis. We would suggest, however, that a psychologically universal competence *to game* exists, which, like the competence *to speak*, is a part of the human condition. This gaming competence is not used extensively by some tribal groups (pygmies), but it is

**Table 9–1.   Levels of structured interaction in games**

| | Wholeness (type of gestalt) | Self-Regulation (type of coordination) | Transformation (type of reversability) |
|---|---|---|---|
| *I.   Primary Interactions (Actions)* | | | |
| *Game Type A. Prescriptive Games* | | | |
| Level 0 ("Farmer in the Dell") | | Ritual codes | Ritual reversal |
| *Game Type B. Central Person Games* | | | |
| Level 1 ("Tag") | | Uncoordinated roles and actions | Role reversal |
| Level 2 ("Release") | | " | Action reversal |
| *II. Secondary Interactions (Signals)* | | | |
| *Game Type C. Competitive Games (Group and Individual)* | | | |
| Level 3 ("Dodge Ball") | | Coordinated actions roles & signals in one group | Central role reversal |
| Level 4 ("Prisoners Base") | | Coordination between groups | Group reversal in size |
| *III. Tertiary Interactions (Meta Signals)* | | | |
| *Game Type D. Sports (Team and Individual)* | | | |
| Level 5 | | Coordinated external relationships (coaches—audiences) Coordinated team play with specialists | Team reversals in posture |
| Level 6 (Batting Games) | | Differentiated and coordinated defense | Defense reversal |
| Level 7 (Kicking Games) | | Differentiated and coordinated attack and defense | Attack and defense reversals |

From Sutton-Smith, B. "A structural grammar of games and sports," Paper presented at International Society for the Sociology of Sport Meeting, Heidelberg, Oct. 1975.

not absent among them. In these terms, gaming is seen as a generative social procedure whereby oppositions between people, or within a person, are transformed into a set of alternating ludic behaviors. Games in these terms are a cognitive-social device for managing conflict.

As we have seen, the greater the socialization pressure cross-culturally (and implicitly the conflict), the greater the presence of games. The conflicts can be mild, such as an inability to master a set of conditions, as when children play school only for the first several years of schooling, or they can be quite severe, as in the case of adult game addicts who spend most of their life in a driven pursuit of a particular game, such as chess (Kusyszyn, 1972). This, then, is the ultimate source of games: the binary quality of emotional life and the structuring quality of mind that allows it to reconcile these ambivalent pressures by stating them as alternatives within one system of ludic behaviors—the game. In these terms, a game always involves an opposition between forces and proceeds according to rules that allow the oppositions to be resolved in favor of one or another of the parties. A definition at this level can include mother-infant finger play as well as football.

*Conative Reversals*

Two other aspects of play as structure are essential to any adequate conceptualization. These are the conative and affective aspects. In the statement that a state of conflict is translated in play into a set of oppositions, the important thing about those oppositions is that they are reversible. Reversibility is a key to play just as it is to many rituals. It is useful to unite the concept of play with the anthropological concept of ritual. In fact, play may be thought of as a miniature rite. Victor Turner (1974) has discussed ritual in terms of Van Gennep's rites of passage, that is, as transition and reintegration.

Our first section on antecedents may be thought of as dealing with separation. There, we were concerned with getting the play started. The present section deals with the transitional yet circumscribed state that Turner calls liminal. The final section on functions will deal again with the reintegration of play into society. In these terms, the player goes apart from society into a special sphere defined, as Huizinga (1949, p. 28) does, by its limits of time and place, its rules, and its being different. Here, as in all other rituals, the conditions of society may be reversed (Babcock, 1978). Those who are lowly may become high, and those who are high may be debased.

We have discussed the structural sequencing of these reversals in games of increasing complexity. In play, there is at first a reversal of intention (one imposes oneself on external conditions, rather than being subject to them); then, when a group plays together running their own playtime, there is a reversal of social control (they, not their parents, are in charge). Next, at about age 3 when they learn to take turns, there can be a reversal of turn taking (taking turns at being first!). When proper games begin, role reversal is essential as well as the other kinds discussed in the previous section. In competitive games, tactical reversals become pronounced as a way of reaching success. By that age children also become capable of engineering new games, so intentional rule reversal is possible, although it has always been present idiosyncratically in cheating. Cheating is an innovative source of change with players of all ages.

From a cultural point of view, however, perhaps the most interesting form of play reversal occurs when the reversals inherent in the game dictate new adaptations in the culture. Conventional sociological theorizing contends that the culture dominates the game proclivities of the individual. Actual examples show that this is only true sometimes. The game may bolster other social systems or it may reverse them.

If a game is introduced into a culture that is not in a state of uncertainty, the game will tend to be adapted to local norms. Maccoby et al. (1964) illustrate how an egalitarian chasing game from the United States that was introduced into a Mexican village became, over a short period of time, converted into an authoritarian form, similar to other local games with which the players were more comfortable.

On the other hand, there are also examples in which a game introduced from outside is used by one group to express its dissatisfaction with local group norms. Sometimes the game is merely an expressive form of dissatisfaction—a compensation, if you will (Handelman, 1974); sometimes the game becomes a rallying point and is actually the focus for a realistic revolt against the prevailing institutions (Fox, 1969; Lancy, 1976). In these latter cases, where there is some existing cultural conflict, the different or alternative form suggested by the game can become the basis for a change in cultural customs.

We do not need any esoteric examples from the literature to illustrate how games change culture. The history of modern sports and the changes they have brought first to college life and later to the lives of the masses is an indication of vast cultural change. It is reasonable to argue that they brought a message of the rationality of personal and corporate achievement to many people who had not hitherto considered themselves within this domain. In due course, this same ideology became normative and sports became more conservative in import. However, we find that for members of lower social classes sports can still have that life-transforming function, whereas for established members of the culture they do not (Ball & Loy, 1975).

Be cautioned that the present notion that game participation can change the life of an individual, or of a group of individuals within the larger culture, is not meant to imply that it normally will. The relationship between play and life is probabilistic, not irrevocably rehearsive. Play potentiates; it does not itself actualize. Thus, the Olympic Games make a universal world of cooperating nations theoretically possible. Some of their sponsors envisage that possibility. They create a fantasy of unity.

The relationship of that fantasy to what may actually happen is, however, determined, even overwhelmed, by many other variables. But at least the play is a communicative form that can be understood by many people who formerly were completely entrapped within their more parochial boundaries.

We thus argue that play as conative reversal is the seed of alternative attitudes to society. In "Games of Order and Disorder" (1972b), Sutton-Smith has described how even the very youngest children assimilate into their play the first opposition, that of order and anarchy. In games of all circling together then falling down together, or of building blocks and smashing them down, they make fluid and reversible these two fundamental aspects of the children's society. Nursery school teachers frequently find these anarchic aspects quite chaotic because they do not realize the consensual and collaborative achievements that are also involved.

### Affective Qualities

The emotional quality of play usually has been identified as being that of fun (Huizinga, 1949). It is doubtful that this is correct. In a series of studies of players and workers, from rock climbers to surgeons, Csikszentmihalyi (1974) has sought to identify the phenomenology of the player. What stands out is their involvement in what Csikszentmihalyi calls the "flow" of activity. He says that they are very aware but not self-conscious; they are in control of the situation but nevertheless in a state of uncertainty. The stimulus field is limited; the feedback is immediate. From many hours of watching young children at play, we have identified the same affective state as one of *vivification*. The feeling of euphoria seems to be an affective state that arises only after periods of vivid involvement or in between such states. The same notion of vividness is conveyed in Freudian descriptions of primary process; it is even conveyed by linguistic descriptions of play as "light and quick movement." According to Huizinga's (1949) survey of cross-cultural linguistic usages, this is about the most general connotation that the word play receives in different languages.

### Summary

We may summarize these comments on the cognitive, conative, and affective aspects of play by attempting a structural definition appropriate to the materials that have been presented.

It is clear from the discussion of antecedents that we define play only as a subset of voluntary behavior. Much voluntary behavior (for example, exploration) is not play. Essential to play is the reversal of the usual contingencies of power. The player is always in charge. In addition, when play begins the players' integration of their life experiences is unique to them, and that organization is a forecast of their future competences, so we call it a prototypic organization. Again, the players seem to be drawn into these unique autonomous experiences by the vivid and summarized living that is possible within them. Briefly, then, play may be defined as a subset of voluntary behaviors in which individuals reverse the usual contingencies of power by enacting prototypes of experience in a vivifying manner.

In these terms, games themselves are defined as a subset of play in which a rule-governed system of oppositional ludic behaviors, mediated through different phases of activity or playing sides, produces a disequilibrial outcome. Sports are defined as that subset of games in which metagame participation of vicarious groups exercises an influence over the outcome.

These distinctions are meant to be basically structural rather than functional. It is clear, however, from the review of antecedents presented, that we view both play and games as involving a response to either modeled behavior or prior states of conflict. Play arises out of stimulus discrepancy or affective or cognitive conflict. Whether the conflict is of the epistemic stimulus couched variety discussed by Berlyne (1960), the more affective variety discussed in psychoanalysis, or in the cognitive disequilibria of Piaget (1970), we believe that the motivation for play lies at that point. But, as we wish to make clear, motivation does not itself explain the autonomous nature of play as a processing and generative event. Language is not determined by the content of speech, although that content may be its occasion for emergence. Similarly, play structure is not explained by conflict, although such conflict may be the occasion for its emergence.

## The Consequences of Play

When we deal with the consequences of play, we deal essentially with theories of function. There are two broad classes of such theory: integrative and innovative. Integrative or normative theorizing has dominated the discussion of play throughout this century; theories of play as innovation have arisen more recently. We will deal with each in turn.

### Integrative Interpretations

Most explanations of play during the past fifty years are of an integrative nature. That is, they explain how play, games, and sports integrate the members of the society into its larger cultural patterns. Given the neglect and denigration of this area of living in prior centuries, one can see that these "integrative" theories have been a part of the rehabilitation of play into an area of respectable discourse. By showing that play, games, and sports socialize the young, we prove that games are worthwhile (Loy & Ingham, 1973). Unfortunately, even though this approach helps play, games, and sports in the ideological sense by proving their value to society, it may do a disservice to their actual character. If their function is not merely to integrate but also to innovate, their character may be conceptualized from one point of view only. Still, before we consider possible innovative interpretations, some review of integrative interpretations is in order.

*Play.* In describing play as the child's work, as so many have done, an attempt has been made, particularly in the nursery school, to justify its importance. Or, in describing play as the external means by which children organize within themselves the responses they have experienced from others, play is given a fundmental role in social growth (see George H. Mead). Even in suggesting that in play children integrate their feelings through licensed rebellion, the psychoanalysts are arguing that play is mentally healthy. Although play may only "hallucinate" ego strength, it nevertheless contributes to a sense of personal mastery (Erikson, 1972).

But the question that must be raised about all of these explanations, as well as about the more recent ones of Piaget and Bruner along similar lines, is whether we are discussing voluntary activity, which is indeed mastery oriented, or voluntary activity, which is play oriented, as discussed earlier. This distinction is not clearly made in most discussions of the subject, and, as a result, the function of play is not clearly distinguished from the functions of mastery. Even with Piaget, who created this distinction between accommodation (which we call mastery) and assimilation (play), one is often at a loss to know what he ment by playful assimilation. He seemed to treat it as an adjunct to thought but did not clearly delineate the status of that adjunct. In our critique of his theory, we argue that this is because his interpretation of thinking dealt largely with logical operations, rather than with creative and innovative ones (Sutton-Smith, 1966). Play prepares for the latter rather than the former. Piaget would have argued that there is no such distinction in the thought process. All thought is logical. But among those concerned with the arts, much of the relevant thinking is metalogical or metaphorical, and it is here that play seems most relevant.

*Games.* The conflict-enculturation theory of games, offered by Roberts and Sutton-Smith and summarized in the preceding discussion, is a socialization account of games that seeks to explain their role in both individual development and cultural history. It is in the tradition of Malinowskian functionalism. Games play their role in normative enculturation because they symbolize underlying conflicts, arouse people who have these conflicts, involve them in playful representations of the conflicts, and thus induce forms of learning that have cultural relevance. The isomorphism between a conflict induced by child-training conflict and the play representation of that conflict is taken for granted in this theory. The conflict is said to be reflected by the game. Conflict over obedience is seen in a battle between social systems on a chess board; conflict over independence is expressed in chasing and escaping in a game of tag, and so on.

We need to add to this explanation, however, that, even though a game may reflect the poles of a particular conflict, it also allows a flexible access to both poles that is not available in the real life situation. The chess player may be always a subordinate in his life situation, but he may be both superordinate and subordinate in the course of his game. Games exist to render conflict malleable. They do not merely socialize by mirroring. They socialize by mirroring and inverting. They are radical as well as conservative. This element is not really dealt with in the theory of conflict-enculturation, although it can be fitted into a revised version of that paradigm. Such a revised version requires a more careful specification of the types of reversal that a game allows, and the parallel life areas that are thus made more flexible for the players.

In a sense, the whole earlier section on anthropological antecedents represents further documentation of the thesis that play and games parallel culture and, therefore, contribute to it in some way.

*Sports.* The major ideological tradition concerning sports, coming from the nineteenth century, is that they confer the virtues of sportsmanship, courage, and leadership on the participants. They integrate the players into the leading ranks of society. The actual evidence on sports participation and its consequences are much more complex. Sports often do seem to have an upwardly mobile function for those who come to them from a lower social status; whether the sport is itself the escalator or merely the vehicle for the upwardly mobile is not completely clear.

In Watson's work on social status and Little League baseball, described earlier, the middle-class participants used the game as a part of their pursuit of individual ambition, whereas the lower classes emphasized more collectivist and ritualistic usage. The lower-class members and parents both emphasized the good of the larger group, the team, whereas the middle-class boys and parents emphasized the achievement of the individual. Probably, as compared with gang group loyalties, this team ethic on the part of the lower class represents a movement beyond parochial to a more national form of social integration.

In the game, hostilities are structured in larger, more extensive forms than would be the case in the usual kinship urban situation. This behavior fits with the Elias concept of historical change in sports. According to

Elias, the history of sports is a history of socializing aggression into ever larger and more comprehensive forms. In Sutton-Smith's (in press, a) work on the history of the playground in New Zealand from 1840 to 1950, the picture of change in the New Zealand school playgrounds was clearly one in which aggression and violence were gradually domesticated. As far as could be judged, organized sports played a major role in this domestication.

One line of argument across play, game, and sports suggests that a major role in each is the socialization of aggression. This is the major argument of the psychoanalyst Menninger (1942) in his explanations of children's play. It is the major argument of Suomi and Harlow (1971) in their account of what play does for primates. Primates who do not play with their peers cannot control the gradients and appropriateness of aggression. Those who do play know when and where aggression is appropriate, and they know how to turn it off and on. No one has made this argument for children's games, but it has been made for sports. Presumably, games would socialize aggression in the first social groups of the 6- to 12-year-old; sports would do the same in larger groups of that age.

Following a line of argument of this sort implies that socialization through play, games, and sports probably occurs on quite different levels at the same time. Children generally are initiated into games either by their parents or by other children. In each case, the induction involves learning a system of rule-governed behaviors that both control one's own egoistic behavior and permit it expression. This is where the control of aggression is presumably learned and the controls established. By listening to elders and by copying their behavior, the child gradually approximates the approved patterns of play. Often, young children can be seen participating in games with only a vague understanding of their real character. But by copying the other players, taking this role and then that role, they gradually come to penetrate the character of the reciprocation.

Frankly, we do not yet know how young children take the step from copying each role in turn, to the step of having insight into the reciprocity of the roles. The literature on the learning of concrete logical operations in the Piagetian sense is relevant here. Some believe that children learn about the reciprocity of roles by having them made verbally explicit for them, as in rule training. Some believe that simple participation on the different polarities and their contrary relationships, in due course, spontaneously generates new insight into the reciprocity.

At the moment, about all we can contribute to this difficult problem is to suggest that it is in the nature of playfulness to proceed by oppositions, so that play as such is presumably a good arena for the learning of oppositions or negations. This may help to explain why the oppositions of play can be understood several years ahead of the oppositions of concrete logic. Five-year-old children can play hide and seek; but Piaget showed that they do not conserve mass until about 7 years, which is a further example of how play anticipates life. But this in itself does not explain how the opposition of the games themselves are learned. We suspect that the answer lies in a graduated series of such oppositions that have been learned from infancy; each set provides the underpinning of those above it.

The more subtle forms of socialization, other than the control of aggression and the learning of antitheses, have yet to be studied. The conflict-enculturation thesis suggests that an array of reciprocities is to be learned, the meaningful elements of which are provided by the larger cultural system. In analyzing the structure of games, these reciprocities include order-disorder, which we have discussed; types of approach-avoidance, such as chase-escape, attack-defend, accept-reject; and types of success-failure, such as correct-error, deprive-accumulate; and score-outscore (Herron and Sutton-Smith, 1971).

We may assume that games also socialize types of roles (chasers, attackers), agencies (bats, strategies, tactics), actions (running, hitting), spaces (territories), and times. Games provide a successive series of such learnings, each coming in a qualitative gestalt.

In sum, we have put forward a number of explanations of why play, games, and sports might socialize. Different theorists have favored different foci, including the views that games socialize the learning of power tactics, interactional systems, aggression, and reciprocal social interactions. As a final note, we have suggested that many other aspects of games and sports might also be the focus of such socialization inquiries. It seems probable that even though all these aspects may be present in most games, different cultures will tend to emphasize the importance of learning some particular patterns over others.

All these argument might be regarded as intracultural in implication. They focus on how the games or sports contribute to some current institution. There is, however, quite another level at which the play may be thought to conserve society. Thus, we have suggested that the expressive aspects of culture-like games can be regarded as storage systems conserving functions that no longer appear to be relevant, but could, in fact, become relevant in some condition of emergency. Many human activities appear obsolete, but in an emergency they might suffer a reordering:

> Certainly in our culture obsolete artifacts, obsolete that is from the utilitarian point of view, are frequently reordered, as in the case of the bows reordered by modern archers. Archery is so well developed that if nuclear warfare were to destroy the centers of production and if representative groups of expressive archers survived, it might be possible to field armies of bowmen in a very short time. Here the relevant skills are being preserved as part of an expressive complex, but they are being stored surely and reliably. (Roberts, 1971, p. 209)

*Innovative Explanations*

The very notion of playfulness should have warned us long ago that play, games, and sports may not easily fit into our normative interpretations of how society works. After all, with so much nonsense and facetiousness, how can these things really help serious socialization?

In the previous section, we have seen that the orthodox "functional-ism" of this century has supposed that, because societies are structured, "their component institutions and regularized activities are adjusted to each other in such a way that they maintain the system in entirety" (Murphy, 1971, p. 11). In this conceptualization, the task of the game theorist is to rationalize the isomorphism between the game microcosm and the cultural macrocosm. The assumption is that all things are in bal-ance. But, as Murphy argues, chaos and disequilibrium have always been just as much a characteristic of human society as regularity and order. So-ciety is order *and* disorder. Therefore, a functional view of games must in-troduce principles of disorder as well as principles of order. It must deal with the fact that individuals are subject to their culture, and they experi-ence not only the command of norms but also the alienation of their de-sires for autonomy, in relationship to these norms.

In this section, then, we seek some understanding of how play, games, and sports transform both the impulse towards order and the impulse to-wards disorder. Having shown that play expresses the order of the society of which it is a part (the power, the interaction, the economics, the aggres-sion), we must also show how it expresses disorder, or uncertainty, or the desire for change in a society. Our indebtedness to Huizinga (1949) who initiated this way of thinking about play will be apparent.

*Play.* A series of recent studies indicate that play gives rise to *novelty* (Lie-berman, 1978; Wallach and Kogan, 1965; Sutton-Smith, 1968). For exam-ple, Dansky and Silverman (1973) assigned their subjects to three treat-ment conditions: one in which the children were expected to play with a group of objects, another in which they imitated what an adult did with the object, and a third (the control) where they did other things in the same setting. For the play and the imitation groups, the objects included: a pile of ten paper towels; a screwdriver; a wooden board; fifteen blank cards; ten empty kitchen matchboxes; and a tray containing six wet plastic cups. Subjects in all groups were given sketches to do in a first confi-dence-building session. The control group proceeded to do more sketches in a subsequent session.

The play group was told: "You may play with all these things. Do whatever you would like to do with them." The play period lasted ten minutes. If the child ignored any objects, he was reminded that he could use them. Imitation subjects were asked to watch the experimenter as he performed four tasks (turning screws with screwdriver, fastening cards with paperclips; wiping wet cups with a paper towel; putting small sticks in empty matchboxes). This group was asked to repeat the experimenter's actions exactly as they had seen them. The time spent on each task for each imitation subject was matched to the time spent on those objects by the previous play subject.

Immediately after each ten minutes, all subjects were shown four randomly selected objects and told: "You can use this in a lot of different ways. I would like you to tell me all of the things that you could do with it, make with it, or use it for." Responses were scored as standard (a usage for which the object was primarily designed) or nonstandard (all others).

Confirming the earlier study, there was no difference between groups on standard usages, but a very significant difference in favor of the play group on nonstandard usages. Furthermore, the play groups in their nonstandard responses made more use of the surrounding cues. Thus, a child who had played says, "You can use the matchbox to make a lamp (and there is a lamp nearby)." As the imitation and control subjects did not differ significantly, it was clear that it was not mere exposure that afforded the children the opportunity to vary their responses to the objects freely.

Following the present concern with associations between play and novelty, the most impressive piece of recent research is that of Feitelson and Ross (1973) at Harvard. Their study repeated the new play participation techniques initiated by Sara Smilansky (1968). Concerned with raising the level of imagination in children, she did so by playing with them and modeling pretense for them. That is, she joined in the children's imaginative play by pretending to be a mother or a truck driver. Feitelson and Ross play tutored a small group of children twice a week, for half an hour at a time, over a period of five weeks. This play group was compared with children who played alone, without adult imaginative play tutoring, or who had music tutoring. All children received a battery of creativity tests before and after the experimental sessions. The children who had pretense exhibited to them showed significant increases in their levels of combinatory and innovative play and in their scores on the creativity tests.

If we put together the research of Lieberman, Wallach, & Kogan; Dansky & Silverman; Smilansky; Feitelson & Ross and some others of a parallel character not mentioned here (e.g., Singer, 1973), we have at least tentative evidence to confirm the view that play is associated with the emergence of novel responses, responses that may be employed to good effect on creativity tests in which uniqueness is the major criterion for success.

Let us now take a further, quite speculative step and see if this evidence on novelty can be included in some larger adaptive definition of play. It is useful to note that in the relevant animal studies, various species have been recorded as using objects optionally in an extraordinary variety of ways when they have been free from the obligatory pressures of need or reward. This finding remarkably parallels the human studies just introduced. We know that higher animals play more than do lower animals. In addition, we know that there is more play in more complex cultures and in more "open" societies. Bruner speculates that the dividing line in animals is between species that have to specialize and species that are opportunistic with respect to environmental resources and also have more challenging environments. Aldis (1975) argues simply that more play is found where more training in skill and strength is necessary because the species has more difficult life tasks ahead, such as when they must kill prey larger than themselves. When their life tasks are simpler, such as feeding on small prey, there is less play.

There may be a parallel for this on the human scene. In cultures in which cultural roles are prescribed for survival purposes and children are inducted early into the world of adult work (such as carpet weaving in the Middle East or silk weaving in India), there is little encouragement for or time to play. By contrast, modern society demands adaptation to novel requirements, so more children create model worlds, indulge in imaginary companions, and act out flexible sociodramas than were ever envisioned for children throughout the bulk of recorded human history. Play may prepare the child to deal with novel contingencies by creating novel responses in areas that are not firmly under normative control in the culture and yet are still important to the adult group.

Thus, in modern society we cannot predict what the child's economic role as an adult will be, and children play at a great variety of adult roles. They must build a repertoire of potential adult roles if they are to be ready when the appropriate time arrives. Responses are brought into being that *might* have some future value. For this reason, we can say that such responses are potentiated, and we can speak of play's cultural role (perhaps of its biological role) as that of *adaptive potentiation* (Sutton-Smith, 1975).

To make such a statement is, of course, to take an Olympian view. No player thinks of such things. It may be true that those who potentiate through play are those who survive in changing circumstances, but such an argument deals, like evolutionary theories, with the general drift of things across large populations. On a more mundane level, however, we might argue that those who played extensively would be those who as a consequence build repertoires of novel responses. They would have been experiencing an unprogrammed form of innovation training.

*Games.* Unfortunately, the work on games and sports as forms of innovation is not as well developed as it is on play. Games are forms of socialization that are more clearly understood by adults and, therefore, are more systematically a part of the normative educational apparatus. Still, a great deal of anecdotal data from the widespread use of games in *game simulation* indicates that children who participate in those activities become more skillful at game construction. Children who participate in courses in which the object is to have insight into games and to make games, not merely to play them, appear to acquire a considerable ability to govern their own voluntary activities and also to bring other children into their orbit.

Here, of course, we are doing for them, within education, what they used to do for themselves by folk tradition. Groups that had such game-playing folk traditions always had a considerable amount of game variation, particularly by children in early adolescence. In most present circumstances, however, these children are organized into adult sports during their free activity and lose the opportunity for free variation on traditional themes. On the other hand, one should not underemphasize the extent to which this still occurs in sand-lot games.

We have seen evidence exists that, cognitively speaking, play leads to novelty. However, hardly any thought exists on the topic of what the conative reversibilities in play and games imply. Our favorite candidate for this conative outcome is *flexibility.* As we move along a continuum from more sober play to more excited playfulness, the reversals seem to increase in number and quality. Humor or comedy or wit, which are species of conversational play, are characterized by lightning shifts in set. One would expect that those who indulge in such play must, of necessity, be more flexible with respect to the conventions of language and behavior, which they upset in order to produce these results.

Here, again, little direct evidence exists, although for many years play therapists and psychodramatic therapists have been claiming that, as a result of the role playing in which their subjects participate, they do become more flexible in the management of life decisions. As a tentative proposition, then, we would advance the view that just as play structures provide novel repertoires, the reversibilities of games provide for a more flexible adjustment to social roles.

*Sports.* Innovation in sports seems to be even rarer than in play and games. In recent years, however, groups such as the Esalen Sports Institute have explored the possibility of creating new sports and have staged sports days for all members of the family. These happenings have emphasized a more collaborative approach to game playing than we usually associate with sport (De Koven, 1978).

Various investigations of the changing nature of sports in different countries have shown a more heterogeneous dispersion of interest than was formerly the case. This might lead us to assume that more and more people are using sports in a "smorgasbord" fashion as a symbol of their own freedom to choose their own form of play. Here the innovation may not be so much in the sport form itself, but rather in the possibility of making varied choices among many sport forms.

Early in this century, many people were absorbed in only one or two forms of sport. With increased prosperity, more people have been able to imitate the varied sporting activities and interests that were once the preserve of the wealthy. Once the masses were lucky to be able to attend these sports of kings. Now the masses, as consumers, are king, and the games cannot hold their attention unless they continue to be suitably modified to suit the consumer taste.

The various ways in which modern games, even football and baseball, are changed every few years in order to retain audience interest provides a new model of what can be done to innovate sports. Here the pursuit of vivification in the audience (and of the consequent commercial pay-off) becomes the criterion rather than any historical necessity for retaining the traditional form of the game. Abbreviated versions of cricket, always an endless and tedious game that could last for several days, are a good example of this recently innovative aspect of modern sports; team tennis is another such example. Professional hockey is an example in which the trend of violence in the game conflicts with other mores in the larger community but is exploited because of consumer interest.

Despite these examples, however, one is not overly impressed with the novelty or flexibility that derives from sports, although these variables do seem potential candidates for socialization. Perhaps the more striking outcome from sports involvement may be the increased autonomy that it gives to the players and the audience.

Even though most modern critics tend to think of attendance at sports as a passive concern, the anecdotal evidence from Third World and Eastern European countries indicates that the introduction of sports has contributed to a change in the audience from passive other-directed expectancies to a greater degree of inner direction and active participation in community affairs. At least so it is asserted is the case in Eastern European accounts of the impact of sports on various rural economies (Wohl, 1969). The village without a sports team is said to be a dispirited affair with low economic output. The village with a team is a spirited group with higher output. The finding of Nerlove, Roberts, Klein, and Yarbrough (1974) that play autonomy in Guatamalan children is associated with other measures of independence might perhaps be taken as a support for this hypothesis.

## Play as Enculturation

Even if play, games, and sports produce novelty, flexibility, and autonomy, as well as a working understanding or socialization into prevailing cultural models, what evidence is there that any of these transfer back to society at large? After all, we have emphasized that this function is only a potentiating one.

Whether or not there is any transfer would seem to be a function of the larger ideologies of play within which the child actually plays. In a Puritan ideology, the novelty and flexibility might be treated as facetiousness and impudence and therefore be discouraged. We have seen that in tribal cultures, where bows and arrows and dolls are provided for the children by the adults, the adults themselves clearly make the linkage between such provision and adult sex role requirements. In today's world, where many children have hundreds of toys in their bedrooms (Rheingold & Cook, 1975), the connection between the play and the society is not always so easily assessed, but there is probably a relationship between the technology of toys and the technology of ovens, autos, dishwashers, or toasters.

In their conflict enculturation theory, Sutton-Smith and Roberts (1964) conjectured that the major form of learning engendered by the game was learning various power tactics (of force, fortunism, and strategy). Others have demonstrated that types of interaction, such as competition, as compared with collaboration, appear to be learned by cultures in transition towards Westernization, for example, Blackfoot Indians (Miller & Thomas, 1972; Miller, 1973); sometimes it is the newer form of strategy (checkers) versus the older Kpelle traditional form (mancala) (Lancy, 1976), or the newer white man's role models versus the traditional Eskimo role models (Ager, 1974) that are learned.

Cultures in transition are a particularly suitable site for the study of games, because the conflict of values is often an open one, so that it is possible, as in these examples, to see the direct contribution that a novel game culture is having on social change. There is evidence that in such transitional situations rituals can function in the same innovative manner (Manning, 1974) as can music (McCleod, 1974).

Although the permissiveness or conflict in the surrounding culture is one way in which the play or game exercises a novel influence, we would insist that the potential is always there. Roberts's archers are always potential hunters or potential soldiers. Their moment may never arrive, although they will seek, as most recreationists do, to make their avocation as important in the larger culture as they can. The playful humorist does not keep his radical wit to himself any more than does the coin collector work in secret. Reynolds has suggested that the whole adolescent culture, whether of primates or humans, plays at the active investigation of alternative cultures. Adolescents effectively play at culture, whatever it may be called by them or their parents.

In this latter sense, the play, games, and sports themselves with their imitation and novelty intrude on the larger society, and interact with the prevailing ideologies or conflicts in ideology to introduce new forms into the social scene. Just what the probabilities are of such enculturation and the relevant variables to account for it are not well established at this point.

## Summary

We have presented a five-phase theory of play, games, and sports, in which, first, play phenomena have been distinguished from other voluntary behavior. It has been argued that the greater part of children's voluntary behavior concerns exploration and power struggles and need not be called play.

Second, play arises from two sources. It is an imitation of others, and it is a response to internal sources of epistemic and affective conflict. Third, play has been defined structurally as a voluntary behavior in which the usual power contingencies are reversed and thus permit the subject to enact a prototype of experience in a vivifying manner.

Fourth, it has been argued that these novel organizations of individual or group experience could either integrate the individual into general group experience by providing a socializing model of that experience, or they could provide the opportunity for an innovative management of the contraries to be found in prior experience. Even though both are always present, it has been suggested that different cultures tend to emphasize one or other alternative. Most twentieth-century theorizing has tended to emphasize the socialization or integrative impact of play, apparently in order to rehabilitate play as a subject matter for serious scholarly discourse. The present state of culture as well as research, however, would argue a greater need for a better understanding of the innovative impact of these phenomena.

Fifth, it has been pointed out that even if play gives rise to useful or novel responses, these are only potentially adaptive. They still must be reintegrated with culture, and this only occurs if the conditions in the larger culture are propitious for such adaptation.

## References

AGER, L. P. Play among Alaskan Eskimoes. *Theory into practice,* Ohio State University, 1974, *12*, 252–256.

ALDIS, O. *Play fighting.* New York: Academic Press, 1975.

ALLARDT, E. Basic approaches in comparative sociological research and the study of sport. In G. Lüschen (Ed.), *The cross-cultural analysis of sport and games.* Champaign, Ill.: Stipes, 1970.

AVEDON, E., & SUTTON-SMITH, B. *The study of games.* New York: John Wiley & Sons, 1971.

BABCOCK, B. *The reversible world: Essays on symbolic inversion.* Ithaca: Cornell Univ., 1978.

BACH, G. R. Young children's play fantasies. *Psychological Monographs,* 1945, *59* (2), 3–69.

BALL, D. The scaling of gaming. *Pacific Sociological Review,* 1972, *15,* 277–294.

———. Control versus complexity—continuities in the scaling of gaming. *Pacific Sociological Review,* 1974, *17,* 167–184.

BALL, D. W., & LOY, J. W. *Sport and social order: Contribution to the sociology of sport.* Reading, Mass.: Addison-Wesley, 1975.

BARKER, R. G., DEMBO, L., & LEWIN, K. Frustration and regression: an experiment with young children. *University of Iowa Studies in Child Welfare,* 1941, *18,* No. 386.

BARRY, H., III, & ROBERTS, J. M. Infant socialization and games of chance. *Ethnology,* 1972, *11,* 296–308.

BATESON, G. The message, 'This is play.' In B. Schaffner (Ed.), *Group processes: Transactions of the second conference.* Josiah Macy Foundation, 1956, 145–246.

BEACH, F. A. Current concepts of play in animals. *American Naturalist,* 1945, *79* (785), 523–541.

BEKOFF, M. Social play and play soliciting in infant candids. *Bioscience,* 1974, *24,* 225–230.

BERLYNE, D. E. *Conflict, arousal and curiosity.* New York: McGraw-Hill, 1960.

———. Laughter, humor and play. In G. Lindzey & E. Aronson (Eds.), *Handbook of social psychology* (2nd ed.). Reading, Mass.: Addison-Wesley, 1970, 795–852.

———. *Aesthetics and psychobiology.* New York: Appleton-Century Crofts, 1971.

BRUNER, J. Nature and uses of immaturity. *American Psychologist,* 1972, *27,* 1–22.

———. Organization of early skilled action. *Child Development,* 1973, *44,* 1–11.

———. Play is serious business. *Psychology Today,* 1975, *8,* 81–83.

CAILLOIS, R. *Man, play and games.* New York: Free Press of Glencoe, 1961.

CENTNER, T. H. *L'enfant Africain et ses jeux.* Elisabethville: CEPSI, 1962.

CHEVALIER-SKOLNIKOFF. S. The primate play face: A possible key to the determinants and evolution of play. Paper presented to Annual Meeting of The American Anthropological Association, New Orleans, 1973. (Author's address, Department of Anthropology, Stanford University)

CSIKSZENTMIHALYI, M. *Flow: Studies of enjoyment.* P. H. S. Report, University of Chicago, 1974.

DAMM, H. The so-called sport activities of primitive people. A contribution towards the genesis of sport. In G. Lüschen (Ed.), *The cross-cultural analysis of sport and games.* Champaign, Ill.: Stipes, 1970.

DANSKY, J. L., & SILVERMAN, I. W. Effects of play on associative fluency in preschool children. *Developmental Psychology,* 1973, *9,* 38–43.

DE KOVEN, B. *The well-played game.* New York: Dell, 1978.

Dunlap, H. Games, sports, dancing and other vigorous recreational activities and their function in Samoan culture. *The Research Quarterly*, 1951, 22, 298–331.

Ehrmann, J. (Ed.). *Game, play and literature*. Boston: Beacon Press, 1971.

Eifermann, R. R. *School children's games*. Final Report, Contract #OE-6-21-010, U.S. HEW, 1968.

———. Level of children's play as expressed in group size. *British Journal of Educational Psychology*, 1970, 40, 161–170.

———. Social play in childhood. In R. Herron & B. Sutton-Smith (Eds.), *Child's play*. New York: John Wiley & Sons, 1971.

———. *Determinants of children's game styles*. Jerusalem: Israel Academy of Sciences and Humanities, 1971.

———. Cooperativeness and egalitarianism in kibbutz children's games. *Human Relations*, 1972, 23, 579–587.

Elkind, D. Cognitive growth cycles in mental development. *Nebraska Symposium in Motivation*, 1972, Vol. 20.

Ellis, M. J. *Why people play*. Englewood Cliffs, N.J.: Prentice-Hall, 1974.

Erikson, E. H. *Childhood and society*. New York: Norton Books, 1972.

Fein, G. A transformational analysis of pretending. *Developmental Psychology*, 1975, 11, 297–303.

Feitelson, D., & Ross, G. S. The neglected factor: Play. *Human Development*, 1973, 16, 202–223.

Finley, G. E., & Layne, C. Play behavior in young children: A cross-cultural study. *Journal of Genetic Psychology*, 1971, 119, 203–210.

Fox, J. R. Pueblo baseball: A new use for old witchcraft. In J. W. Loy & G. S. Kenyon, *Sport, culture and society*. New York: Macmillan, 1969.

Frederickson, F. S. Sport and the cultures of man. In J. W. Loy & G. S. Kenyon, *Sport, culture and society*. New York: Macmillan, 1969.

Freedman, D. G. *Human infancy, an evolutionary perspective*. New York: John Wiley & Sons, 1974.

Gilmore, J. B. Play: A special behavior. In R. E. Heron & B. Sutton-Smith (Eds.), *Child's play*. New York: John Wiley & Sons, 1971, 311–325.

Goldstein, J. H., & McGhee, P. E. *The psychology of humor*. New York: Academic Press, 1972.

Glassford, R. G. Organization of games and adaptive strategies of the Canadian Eskimo. In Lüschen (Ed.), *A cross-cultural analysis of sports and games*. Champaign, Ill.: Stipes, 1970, 70–81.

———. *Application of a theory of games to the transitional Eskimo culture*. New York: Arno Press, 1976.

Griffiths, R. *A study of imagination in early childhood*. London: Kegan Paul, 1935.

Grinnell, G. B. *The Cheyenne Indians*. 2 vols. New Haven: Yale University Press, 1923.

Grupe, O. (Ed.). Play as the mediation of novelty (557–561) & Games as the socialization of conflict (70–75). In *Sport in the modern world: Chances and problems*. Berlin: Springer-Verlag, 1973.

Gump, P. V., & Sutton-Smith, B. The 'It' role in children's games. *The Group*, 1955, 17, 3–8.

GUMP, P. V., SCHOGGEN, P., & REDL, F. The behavior of the same child in different milieus. In R. G. Barker. *The stream of behavior.* New York: Appleton-Century Crofts, 1963, pp. 169–202.

HANDELMAN, D. A note on play. *American Anthropologist,* 1974, 76, 66–69.

————. Play and ritual: Complementary frames of Meta communication. In H. J. Chapman & H. Foot (Eds.), *It's a funny thing, humor.* London: Pergamon, 1977.

HARRÉ, R., & SECORD, P. F. *The explanation of social behavior.* Totowa, N.J.: Rowman & Littlefield, 1972.

HARTLEY, R. E., FRANK, L. K., & GOLDENSON, R. *Understanding children's play.* New York: Columbia University Press, 1952.

HENRY, J. *Doll play of Pilaga Indian children.* New York: Vintage Books, 1974 edition.

HERRON, R., & SUTTON-SMITH, B. *Child's play.* New York: John Wiley & Sons, Inc., 1971.

HOPKINS, J. B. *Amish children's games.* M. S. thesis, University of Illinois, 1969.

HUIZINGA, J. *Homo ludens: A study of the play element in culture.* London: Routledge and Kegan Paul, 1949.

HURLOCK, E. B. Experimental investigations of childhood play. *Psychological Bulletin,* 1934, 31, 47–66.

HUTT, C. Exploration and play in children. In R. E. Herron & B. Sutton-Smith (Eds.), *Child's play.* New York: John Wiley & Sons, 1971.

ISAACS, S. *Social development in young children.* New York: Harcourt, Brace, 1933.

JONES, K. G. *Games and physical activities of the ancient Polynesians and relationships to culture.* M. A. thesis, University of Alberta, 1967.

KIDD, D. *Savage childhood: A study of Kafir children.* London: Black, 1906.

KIRK, G. S. *Myth: Its meanings and functions in ancient and other cultures.* Cambridge, England: Cambridge University Press, 1970.

KLINGER, E. *Structure and functions of fantasy.* New York: John Wiley & Sons, 1971.

KOLATA, G. B. Primate behavior: Sex and the dominant male. *Science,* 1976, 191, 55–56.

KUSYSZYN, I. *Studies in the psychology of gambling.* New York: Simon and Schuster, 1972.

LANCY, D. F. The play behavior of Kpelle children during rapid cultural change. In D. F. Lancy & B. A. Tindall (Eds.), *The anthropological study of play problems and prospects.* Cornwall, N.Y.: Leisure Press, 1976.

LANCY, D. F., & TINDALL, B. A. (Eds.). *The anthropological study of play problems and prospects.* Cornwall, N.Y.: Leisure Press, 1976.

LANSLEY, K. *A collection and classification of the traditional Melanesian play activities with a supplementary bibliography.* M. A. Thesis, University of Alberta, 1968.

LAURENCE, B., & SUTTON-SMITH, B. Novel responses to toys: A replication. *Merrill-Palmer Quarterly,* 1968, 14, 159–160.

LEHMANN, H. C. & WITTY, P. A. *The psychology of play activities.* New York: A. S. Barnes & Co., 1927.

LEVER, J., & WARNER, R. S. Sex role socialization and social structure. The place of complexity in children's games. *Pacific Sociological Association,* Victoria, B.C., April 1975.

LEVIN, H., & WARDWELL, E. The research uses of doll play. *Psychological Bulletin,* 1962, *59* (1), 27–56.

LIEBERMAN, J. N. Playfulness. New York Academic Press, 1978.

LOWENFELD, M. *Play in childhood.* London: Gollancz, 1935.

LOY, J. Sport involvement in terms of motives, values and attitudes. Paper presented to the American Medical Association: The mental health aspects of sports, exercise and recreation. Atlantic City, June, 1975.

LOY, J. W., & INGHAM, A. G. Play, games and sports in the psycho-social development of children and youth. In *Physical activity,* New York: Academic Press, 1973.

LOY, J. W., & KENYON, G. S. *Sport, culture and society.* New York: Macmillan, 1969.

LÜSCHEN, G. The interdependence of sport and culture. *International Review of Sport Sociology,* 1967, *2,* 127–141

————. *The cross-cultural analysis of sport and games.* Champaign, Ill.: Stipes, 1970.

MACCOBY, E. E., & JACKLIN, C. N. *The psychology of sex differences.* Palo Alto: Stanford University Press, 1975.

MACCOBY, M., MODIANO, N., & LANDER, P. Games and social character in a Mexican village. *Psychiatry,* 1964, *27,* 150–162.

MAHONY, D. H. The society and geography of the story world. In P. Stevens (Ed.) *Studies in the anthropology of play.* West Point, N.Y.: Leisure Press, 1977.

MAIN, M. Exploration, play, cognitive functions and the mother-child relationship. Paper presented in *Society for the Research in Child Development,* Denver, Colorado, April 1975, (Author's address, Psychology Dept., University of California, Berkeley.)

MANNING, F. E. Secular rituals considered: Prolegomenon toward a theory of ritual, ceremony and formality. *Burg Wartenstein Symposium,* 1974, *64,* 1–31.

MARANDA, E. K. & P. *Structural models in folklore and transformational essays.* The Hague: Mouton, 1971.

MARSHALL, H. Children's play, games and amusements. In C. Murchison (Ed.), *A handbook of child psychology.* Worcester, Mass.: Clark University Press, 1931, 515–526.

McCLEOD, N. Ethnomusicological research and anthropology. In B. J. Siegel et al. (Eds.), *Annual Review of Anthropology.* Palo Alto, Calif.: Annual Reviews, Inc., 1974.

McGHEE, P. E. Cognitive mastery and children's humor. *Psychological Bulletin,* 1974, *81,* 10, 721–730.

MEAD, M. "Discussion." Symposium on play. Annual meeting of American Anthropological Association, New Orleans, November, 1974.

————. The primitive child. In C. Murchison, (Ed.), *A handbook of child psychology.* Worcester, Mass.: Clark University Press, 1931, 669–686.

————. Research on primitive children. In L. Carmichael (Ed.), *Manual of child psychology.* New York: John Wiley & Sons, 1954, 735–780.

MENNINGER, K. *Love against hate.* New York: Harcourt, 1942.

MILLAR, S. *The psychology of play.* London: Pelican, 1968.

MILLER, A. G., & THOMAS, R. Cooperation and competition among Blackfoot Indian and urban Canadian children. *Child Development,* 1972, *43,* 1104–1110.

———. Integration and acculturation of cooperative behavior among Blackfoot Indian and non-Indian Canadian children. *Journal of Cross-Cultural Psychology,* 1973, *4,* 374–380.

MILLER, S. Ends, means and galumphings: Some leitmotifs of play. *American Anthropologist,* 1973, *75,* 87–98.

MOORE, C. K., & ANDERSON, A. R. Some puzzling aspects of social interaction. *Review of Metaphysics,* 1962, *XV,* 409–433.

MOORE, T. Realism and fantasy in children's play. *Journal of Child Psychology and Psychiatry,* 1964, *5,* 15–36.

MOYER, K. E., & GILMER, B. VON H. Attention spans of children for experimentally designed toys. *Journal of Genetic Psychology,* 1955, *87,* 187–201.

MURDOCK, G. P. *Ethnographic Atlas.* Pittsburgh, Pa.: University of Pittsburgh, 1967.

MURDOCK, G. P. & PROVOST, C. Measurement of cultural complexity. *Ethnology,* 1973, *12,* 379–392.

MURPHY, R. E. *The dialectics of social life.* New York: Basic Books, 1971.

NERLOVE, S. B., ROBERTS, J. M., KLEIN, R. E., YARBROUGH, C., & HABICHT, J. P. Natural indicators of cognitive development: An observational study of rural Guatemalan children. *Ethos,* 1974, *2,* 265–295.

NICOLICH, L. M. A longitudinal study of representational play in relation to spontaneous imitation and development of multiword utterances. Final Report, National Institute of Education, Rutgers, N.J., 1975.

NORBECK, E. (Ed.). The anthropological study of human play. *Rice University Studies,* 1974, *60,* 1–94.

NUNNALLY, J. C., & LEMOND, L. C. Exploratory behavior and human development. In L. P. Lipsett & L. W. Reese (Eds.), *Advances in child development and behavior.* New York: Academic Press, 1973.

OVERTON, W. F., & JACKSON, J. P. The representation of imagined objects in action sequences: A developmental study. *Child Development,* 1973, *44,* 309–314.

PARTEN, M. B. Social participation among pre-school children. *Journal of Abnormal and Social Psychology,* 1931, *27,* 243–269.

———. Social play among pre-school children. *Journal of Abnormal and Social Psychology,* 1933, *28,* 136–147.

PELLER, L. E. Models of children's play. *Mental Hygiene,* 1952, *36,* 66–83.

———. Libidinal phases, ego development and play. *Psychoanalytical Study of the Child,* 1954, *9,* 178–198.

———. Libidinal development as reflected in play. *Psychoanalysis,* 1955, *3,* (3), 3–12.

PIAGET, J. *The moral judgment of the child.* Glencoe, Ill.: Free Press, 1948.

———. *Play, dreams and imitation in childhood.* New York: W. W. Norton and Company, 1962.

———. *Structuralism.* New York: Basic Books, 1970.

REDL, F., GUMP, P., & SUTTON-SMITH, B. The dimensions of games. In E. Avedon

& B. Sutton-Smith (Eds.), *The study of games.* New York: John Wiley & Sons, 1971, 408–418.

REILLY, M. *Play as exploratory learning.* Los Angeles: Sage, 1974.

RENSON, R. Social status symbolism of sport stratification. Paper presented to Olympic Sports Congress on Physical Activity, Quebec, July 1976.

REYNOLDS, P. Play, language and human evolution. Paper presented to A. A. A. S., Washington, D.C., December 1972. (Author's address, Australian National University, Canberra )

RHEINGOLD, H. L., & COOK, K. V. The contents of boys' and girls' rooms as an index of parent behavior. *Child Development,* 1975, *46,* 459–463.

ROBERTS, J. M. Expressive aspects of technological development. *Philosophy and Social Science,* 1971, *1,* 207–220.

ROBERTS, J. M., ARTH, M. J., & BUSH, R. R. Games in culture. *American Anthropologist,* 1959, *61,* 597–605.

ROBERTS, J. M., & BARRY, H., III. Inculcated traits and games type combinations: A cross-cultural view. In T. T. Craig (Ed.), *The humanistic and mental health aspects of sports, exercise and recreation.* Chicago: American Medical Association, 1976.

ROBERTS, J. M., HOFFMAN, H., & SUTTON-SMITH, B. Pattern and competence: A consideration of tick tack toe. *El Palacio,* 1965, *72,* 17–30.

ROBERTS, J. M., & SUTTON-SMITH, B. Child training and game involvement. *Ethnology,* 1962, *1,* 166–185.

———. Cross-cultural correlates of games of chance. *Behavior Science Notes,* 1966, *3,* 131–144.

ROBERTS, J. M. & SUTTON-SMITH, B., & KENDON, A. Strategy in folktales and games. *Journal of Social Psychology,* 1963, *61,* 185–199.

ROBERTS, J. M., THOMPSON, W. E., & SUTTON-SMITH, B. Expressive self-testing and driving. *Human Organization,* 1966, *25,* 54–63.

ROYCE, J. "Validation" of game classification models against Sudanese children's games. *Anthropos,* 1972, *67,* 138–151.

———. Guide to notation of games observation. *Anthropos,* 1973, *68,* 604–610.

SALTER, A. *Games and pastimes of the Australian aboriginal.* Masters thesis, University of Alberta, 1967.

SALTER, M. A. *Games in ritual: A study of selected North American Indian tribes.* Ph. D. dissertation, University of Alberta. Alberta, 1972.

SCHLOSBERG, H. The concept of play. *Psychological Review,* 1947, *54,* 229–231.

SCHWARTZMAN, H. B., The anthropological study of children's play. *Annual Review of Anthropology,* 1976, *5:* 289–328.

———. *Transformations: the anthropology of children's play.* New York: Plenum, 1978.

SCHWARTZMAN, H. B. & BARBERA, L. Children's play in Africa and South America: A review of the ethnographic literature. In D. F. Lancy & B. A. Tindall (Eds.), *The anthropological study of play.* Cornwall, N.Y.: Leisure Press, 1976.

SEAGOE, M. V. Children's play as an indicator of cross-cultural and intra-cultural difference. *Journal of Educational Sociology,* 1962, *35,* 278–283.

SIMRI, U. *The religious and magical functions of ball games in various cultures.* Unpublished dissertation, West Virginia University, 1966.

————. The religious and magical dimensions of play involving physical activities. Paper presented to the International Seminar on Play in Physical Education and Sport, Wingate Institute, March 1975.

SINGER, J. L. *Daydreaming: An introduction to the experimental study of inner experience.* New York: Random House, 1966.

————. *The child's world of make believe.* New York: Academic Press, 1973.

SMILANSKY, S. *The effects of socio-dramatic play on disadvantaged children.* New York: John Wiley & Sons, 1968.

SMITH, A. Sport is a Western Yoga. *Psychology Today,* 1975, *9,* 48–51.

SNYDER, E. E., & SPREITZER, E. Involvement in sports and psychological well-being. *International Journal of Sport Psychology,* 1974, *5,* 28–39.

STEVENS, P. *Studies in anthropology of play.* West Point, N.Y.: Leisure Press, 1977.

SUOMI, S. J., & HARLOW, H. F. Monkeys at play. In 'Play,' *Natural History Magazine Supplement,* December 1971, 72–75.

SUTTON-SMITH, B. Piaget, on play: A critique. *Psychological Review,* 1966, *73,* 111–112.

————. The role of play in cognitive development. *Young Children,* 1967, *6,* 361–370.

————. Novel responses to toys. *Merrill-Palmer Quarterly,* 1968, *14,* 151–158.

————. Play, games and controls. In J. P. Scott (Ed.), *Social Control.* Chicago: University of Chicago Press, 1971, 73–102. (a)

————. The expressive profile. *Journal of American Folklore,* 1971, *84,* 80–92. (b)

————. *The folkgames of children.* Austin: University of Texas Press, 1972. (a)

————. Games of order and disorder. Annual Meeting of The American Anthropological Association, Toronto, November 1972. (b)

————. The anthropology of play. *Association for the Anthropological Study of Play,* 1974, *2,* 8–12.

————. Play as adaptive potentiation. *Sportwissenschaft,* 1975, *5,* 103–118.

————. A history of the playground in New Zealand from 1840–1950. Philadelphia: University of Pennsylvania Press, in press.

————. A developmental structural account of riddles. In B. Kirschenblatt-Gimblatt (Ed.), *Speech play research and resources for studying linguistic creativity.* Philadelphia: University of Pennsylvania Press, 1976.

————. *Dialektik des Spiels.* Schorndorf: Verlag Karl Hoffman, 1979. (a)

————. (Ed.). *Play and learning.* New York: Gardner, 1979. (b)

SUTTON-SMITH. B., BOTVIN, G., & MAHONY, D. Developmental structures in fantasy narratives. *Human Development,* 1976, *19,* 1–13.

SUTTON-SMITH, B., & ROBERTS, J. M. Rubrics of competitive behavior. *Journal of Genetic Psychology,* 1964, 13–37, 105.

————. Studies in elementary strategic competence. (A monograph in collaboration with Vaughn Crandall and Don Broverman.) *Genetic Psychological Monograph,* 1967, *75,* 3–42.

————. The cross-cultural and psychological study of games. In Sutton-Smith, B. *The folkgames of children.* Austin: University of Texas Press, 1972.

SUTTON-SMITH, B., ROBERTS, J. M., & KOZELKA, R. M. Game involvement in adults. *Journal of Social Psychology,* 1963, *60,* 15–30.

SUTTON-SMITH, B., & SAVASTA, M. Sex differences in play and power. Paper presented at the Annual Meeting of the Eastern Psychological Association, Boston, April 1972.

TEXTOR, R. B. *A cross-cultural summary.* New Haven: Yale University Press, 1967.

THOMAS, D. R., Co-operation and competition among Polynesian and European children. *Child Development,* 1975, *46,* 948–953.

TINDALL, A. The hidden curriculum in sport. Paper presented to symposium in Sports, Games and Culture. North Eastern Anthropological Meeting, Vermont, 1973. (Author's address S. U. N.Y., Buffalo, New York.)

TUCKER, J. *The role of fantasy in cognitive-affective functioning,* Ph.D. Thesis, Teachers College, Columbia University, 1975.

TURNER, V. W. Liminal to liminoid, in play, flow, and ritual: An essay in comparative symbology. *Rice University Studies,* 1974, *60,* 53–92.

VYGOTSKY, L. S. Play and its role in the mental development of the child. *Soviet Psychology,* 1967, *5,* 6–18.

WAELDER, R. The psychoanalytic theory of play. *Psychoanal Quarterly,* 1933, *2,* 208–224.

WALLACH, M. A., & KOGAN, N. *Modes of thinking in young children.* New York: Holt, Rinehart & Winston, 1965.

WATSON, G. *Game interaction in Little League Baseball and family organization.* Unpublished Doctoral Dissertation, University of Illinois, 1973.

WELKER, W. I. An analysis of exploratory and play behavior in animals. In D. W. Fiske, & S. R. Maddi (Eds.), *Functions of varied experience.* Homewood, Ill.: Dorsey Press, 1961.

WHITE, B. L., & WATTS, J. C. *Experience and environment: Major influences on the development of the young child* (Vol. 1). Englewood Cliffs, N.J.: Prentice-Hall, 1973.

WHITING, B. B., & WHITING, J. *Children of six cultures, a psycho-cultural analysis.* Cambridge, Mass.: Harvard University Press, 1975.

WOHL, A. Sociology of sports: Poland. Paper delivered to International Workshop, Sociology of Sport, Macolin, Switzerland, September 1969.

ZURCHER, L. A., & MEADOW, A. On bullfights and baseball: An example of interaction of social institutions. In G. Lüschen (Ed.), *The cross-cultural analysis of sports and games.* Champaign, Ill: Stipes, 1970.

# Name Index

# Subject Index